ASIAN JOURNALS

The Collected Works of Joseph Campbell

Thou Art That:
Transforming Religious Metaphor

The Inner Reaches of Outer Space:
Metaphor as Myth and as Religion

The Flight of the Wild Gander: Selected Essays 1944–1968

The Hero's Journey:
Joseph Campbell on His Life and Work

Myths of Light:
Eastern Metaphors of the Eternal

Mythic Worlds, Modern Words:
Joseph Campbell on the Art of James Joyce

Pathways to Bliss:
Mythology and Personal Transformation

A Skeleton Key to Finnegans Wake:
Unlocking James Joyce's Masterwork

The Mythic Dimension: Selected Essays 1959–1987

The Hero with a Thousand Faces

Mythic Imagination: Collected Short Fiction

Goddesses: Mysteries of the Feminine Divine

Romance of the Grail: The Magic and Mystery of Arthurian Myth

Asian Journals: India and Japan

The Ecstasy of Being: Mythology and Dance

More titles forthcoming

JOSEPH CAMPBELL

ASIAN JOURNALS

INDIA AND JAPAN

JOSEPH CAMPBELL FOUNDATION

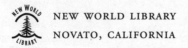

NEW WORLD LIBRARY
NOVATO, CALIFORNIA

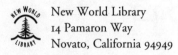

New World Library
14 Pamaron Way
Novato, California 94949

Grateful acknowledgment is made for the permission to reprint from *The Art of Indian Asia: Its Mythology and Transformations* and *Philosophies of India* by Heinrich Zimmer, edited and completed by Joseph Campbell. Copyright © 1955, 1960 by Princeton University Press. Used by permission of Princeton University Press.

Text design and typography by Tona Pearce Myers
Illustrations and maps by Carol Pentleton

Library of Congress Cataloging-in-Publication data is available.

First paperback printing, August 2017
ISBN 978-1-60868-504-2

Printed in Canada on 100% postconsumer-waste recycled paper

New World Library is proud to be a Gold Certified Environmentally Responsible Publisher. Publisher certification awarded by Green Press Initiative. www.greenpressinitiative.org

10 9 8 7 6 5 4 3 2 1

CONTENTS

⟩⟨⟩⟨⟩

BOOK II. SAKE & SATORI: JAPAN

ABOUT THE COLLECTED WORKS OF JOSEPH CAMPBELL

At his death in 1987, Joseph Campbell left a significant body of published work that explored his lifelong passion, the complex of universal myths and symbols that he called "Mankind's one great story." He also left, however, a large volume of unreleased work: uncollected articles, notes, letters, and diaries, as well as audio- and videotape recorded lectures.

The Joseph Campbell Foundation was founded in 1991 to preserve, protect, and perpetuate Campbell's work. The Foundation has undertaken to archive his papers and recordings in digital format, and to publish previously unavailable material and out-of-print works as *The Collected Works of Joseph Campbell*.

THE COLLECTED WORKS OF JOSEPH CAMPBELL
Robert Walter, Executive Editor
David Kudler, Managing Editor

NOTES ON THE TEXT

Campbell's Asian journals were originally published in two separate volumes, *Baksheesh & Brahman* and *Sake & Satori*, each of which is now a section of the current volume. Book I: Baksheesh & Brahman covers the first six months of Campbell's journey through Asia, mostly in Hindu India. Book II: Sake & Satori covers the final six months of his trip, which moved into largely Buddhist territory, including Sri Lanka, Southeast Asia, and, in particular, Japan. The journals should be readily accessible to the general reader and require no prior reading of Campbell. Readers familiar with Campbell's work will find them especially fascinating for the glimpse they offer into the central period of his life and his intellectual development.

The journal entries were not made daily, although Campbell organized them so. Often they were composed at the end of a trip, and sometimes he would spend an entire day catching up on the previous week. He wrote some of it, at least, with an eye to eventual publication, although certainly not in the form presented here. The book is therefore at some points closely written, at others wide-ranging and informal. There is much philosophical meat in these pages, and each reader will chew and digest it according to his or her own constitution. The extensive endnotes should help; they offer pointers also to Campbell's later work, where ideas that appear here briefly bear full fruit.

The text has been edited to preserve the flow and interest of Campbell's narrative. Cut from the text are tentative itineraries, times of missed appointments, names of people met in passing and never seen again, long quotes from contemporary newspapers, and other details. Also removed are several political meditations that are later repeated in more cogent forms. Punctuation has been altered where necessary for ease of reading, and the occasionally awkward sentence has been recast. Many of Campbell's frequent lists are now run on in narrative text. Nowhere has the meaning been altered.

Sanskrit and Japanese words have been transliterated with full diacritical marks. Place-names, where usage dictates, are spelled without diacriticals. Campbell was inconsistent in the way in which he presented Japanese and other Asian names in these journals. We have chosen to present East Asian names in the conventional Western manner, with the family name after the personal name. The only exceptions are names such as Chiang Kai-shek and Ho Chi Minh and those of other historic figures that are best known to Western readers in their traditional order.

Campbell himself footnoted his work. These parenthetical notes, quotations, and citations can be found at the bottom of the page within the text proper. Endnotes, on the other hand, were added by the editors and their contributors, and mark historical, linguistic, and bibliographic references.

Campbell from time to time included rough drawings to illustrate his text. These have been redrawn and placed without captions in the text where they occurred. The photographs included were all taken with Campbell's camera, either by his own hand or by a traveling companion. The maps were commissioned by the editors to help the reader follow the geography of Campbell's travels.

BOOK I

BAKSHEESH & BRAHMAN: INDIA

EDITORS' FOREWORD:
BAKSHEESH & BRAHMAN

The journal from which this book was fashioned comprised over a thousand pages in its original handwritten form. It was kept from 1954 to 1955, as Joseph Campbell traveled throughout India, Southeast Asia, and Japan. Later he would flirt with the idea of publishing it, though he never attempted it. Now, eight years after his death, this work will hold a central place in the *Collected Works of Joseph Campbell*, helping us to form a more complete evaluation of both the man and his work.

The journal appears at times to be a personal diary—as close as Campbell ever came to autobiography. In other places he seems to be keeping an intellectual notebook, grappling with the scholarly details of an Indian cave temple, or getting indigestion over the rampant anti-Americanism in the Indian tabloids. At times he wrestles with the difficulties of arranging a dance tour for his wife, Jean Erdman, throughout India; at others he notes his ambivalent reactions to meeting with a guru. In general, he records entries several times a week, with characteristic thoroughness, perhaps in part for documentation of the details of his trip for the Bollingen Foundation, from whom he was continuing to receive grant support during this time; sometimes, obviously, as formulations related to future writing projects.

As editors we faced many choices; for example, of retaining or omitting what to some might seem obsessive rumination, and to others a fascinating scholarly detail. Our objective throughout has been to keep the reader moving right along with Campbell's own explorations, encounters, and revelations. Wherever possible we have tried to add reference material to help identify people, places, events, and ideas that are significant elsewhere in Campbell's life and work.

In the first half of his life, Joseph Campbell had not yet identified himself as a comparative mythologist. In 1954 he had just turned fifty: time, perhaps, for a reevaluation of his life purpose, or a midlife crisis. In fact, it was to be a little of each. Often it is apparent from the outside that Campbell was the last one to see how his own experience was at work upon him. Some of the most painful conflicts he experienced led to the very insights and personal breakthroughs he sought. Today, with his biography completed and much of his work in print, we can see how Joseph Campbell's approach to mythology emerged from this one seminal geographical and psychological journey.

In order to understand the significance of this expedition more fully, we need to consider the evolution of Joseph Campbell's romance with the East, which certainly constitutes one of the major foci of his scholarship. At the time of his trip to India, he was best known in many circles as the editor of Heinrich Zimmer's works on Indian art and civilization. But much earlier biographical and intellectual events paved the way to Campbell's midlife encounter with the Orient, which is the subject of this book.

In 1924 the twenty-year-old Joseph Campbell, a student at Columbia College, traveled to Europe. On the ocean liner were some young people with whom he felt a ready affiliation: an aristocratic-looking Indian man with a philosophical penchant, whom Campbell, in his diary of the time, and without a clue as to his real identity, called "Krishna." There were a couple of other Indian men, and two American women spending time with them.[1] The Indian was Jiddu Krishnamurti, the messiah-elect of the world Theosophical movement. An electrical atmosphere of spiritual and intellectual excitement seemed to crackle around the conversations of this little group, and when one of the two women gave Campbell *The Light of Asia,* Edwin Arnold's moving life of the Buddha, his own life, as he later declared, was changed forever.[2]

In 1927 Campbell went to Europe again, this time on a Proudfit Fellowship to study Arthurian romance and Provençal literature at the Sorbonne. Campbell encountered Krishnamurti again. (They had corresponded in the intervening years, and Campbell now knew his identity.) At one of Krishnamurti's public lectures, Campbell had, by his own report, an important personal realization. It was right after this time that he ceased to practice Catholicism, the religion of his upbringing, in any formal way, though he continued an intense kind of metaphysical self-questioning that persisted the rest of his life. Perhaps the transformation was triggered by Krishnamurti's ideas on spiritual self-determination.[3]

After a year in Paris, during which time he also discovered the writings of James Joyce, Campbell's enthusiasm for Old French and Provençal waned, and Oriental and German philosophy began to beckon. When the Proudfit committee agreed to extend Campbell's fellowship for another year, he horrified his Francophile friends by deciding to study German, and to attend the University of Munich. Soon he was reading Freud and Jung, and taking courses in Sanskrit at the University. Simultaneously, then, Campbell discovered German Romantic philosophy, Depth Psychology, and the Sanskrit spiritual literature. His fascination with India had been deepened by many of the Theosophists he met at Krishnamurti's estate at Eerde, the Netherlands, and he began to plan his own trip to India at the end of the year. But news of the onset of the Depression, and his family's precarious financial situation, brought Campbell back to the United States in 1929. The plan would not be fulfilled until twenty-five years later, as the trip which is the subject of this journal.

Campbell now tried to weather the Great Depression through a career in writing fiction, but his personal journals of this time abound with metaphysical speculations and insights triggered by his association with Krishnamurti. In 1934 Campbell was hired to the faculty of Comparative Literature at Sarah Lawrence College in Bronxville, N.Y. His preferred sources, kindled by his readings in Germany, were Kant and Schopenhauer, Thomas Mann, historical visionary Oswald Spengler, whose writings he had encountered in Carmel, California,[4] ethnologist Leo Frobenius, Sir James Frazer of the Golden Bough, Freud and Jung, and James Joyce. His Oriental interests seem to have became more or less dormant through his early years of teaching—except of course for the references to the Sanskrit literature he kept finding throughout Schopenhauer and Joyce.

That interest was abruptly reawakened, however, in 1940. Through the family of one of his Sarah Lawrence students, Peggy Davidson, Campbell had met their spiritual teacher, Swami Nikhilananda. (Both Elizabeth Davidson, Peggy's mother, and the Swami appear prominently in this book.) The Swami was very impressed by Campbell's knowledge of Sanskrit literature as well as his literary abilities. Nikhilananda asked Campbell to help him complete the book on which he was working—the life of the nineteenth-century Hindu saint, Ramakrishna. Ramakrishna had had an overwhelming experience of divine bliss—*nirvikalpa samādhi*—and thereafter was "God-intoxicated." Ramakrishna said, speaking of his own illumination, "Like a madman I began to shower flowers in every direction. Whatever I saw, I worshipped!"

Having rejected formal religion, Campbell was nonetheless impressed by the profundity revealed in the thought and life of Ramakrishna and the idea that neither a religious organization nor elaborate rituals were necessary to encounter the sacred—a humble, uneducated man of relatively modern times could enter the realm of divine intoxication at will. References to Ramakrishna are found throughout Campbell's later lectures and writings.

Through Nikhilananda and the Davidsons, Campbell met in 1941 the man whom he later named as the most important intellectual influence of his life, Heinrich Zimmer, the German professor of Oriental studies. Older than Campbell by fourteen years, a man of immense erudition and great personal charm, Zimmer arrived penniless in New York with his wife and three boys, as refugees from the Nazis. As a well-known university professor, he had spoken out publicly against Nazism; and his wife Christiane von Hofmannsthal, daughter of the famous poet Hugo, was half-Jewish. They fled, first to England, then to America.

Zimmer had been invited to lecture at Columbia University. Zimmer's lectures soon required a larger room—then one still larger. Joseph Campbell became numbered among the most loyal students of the Orientalist.

In 1943, however, a shocking event occurred that drastically altered the course of Campbell's life and work. The seemingly robust Zimmer caught walking pneumonia, but kept working and teaching. The illness finally brought him down and on March 20, Heinrich Zimmer suddenly died.

Zimmer's widow, Christiane, asked Campbell to take on the job of editing Zimmer's papers, which existed in the form of copious and somewhat disordered notes, jottings, and marginalia. The Bollingen Foundation, publisher of Jung's writings and other classics in the creative arts, religion, and mythology, agreed to support the project. Campbell put aside his other work and began an intellectual labor that saw into print *Myths and Symbols in Indian Art and Civilization* (1946), *The King and the Corpse* (1948), and *Philosophies of India* (1951), published under Zimmer's name, but with himself as editor. The work culminated in the year of the Indian journey that is the subject of this book, with the publication of the illustrated two-volume *The Art of Indian Asia* (1954). Campbell was still correcting the proofs as he traveled through India, and the published work would reach him the following year, in Japan.

These experiences set the stage, then, for Campbell's journey to India. If it seems a journal of disillusionment, we must remember that neither Campbell nor his esteemed mentor, Zimmer, had ever encountered the realities of India. The learning that had so inspired them was from the sacred texts, mostly from ancient times. The social, political, and economic actualities of India would provide a rude awakening for Campbell.

If Swami Nikhilananda had been less of an enthusiast, perhaps Campbell would have encountered India differently. "In a queer way," Campbell wrote in his journal a few weeks after arrival, "I am beginning to be afraid that Swami Nikhilananda and Mrs. D. are ruining my experience of India. Everything that we see evokes some unpleasant comparison with its American counterpart and a patriotic waving of the new Indian flag."

Campbell had, up to this point in his life (and later as well), tried to identify himself as "apolitical." He would rather talk philosophy or literature, feeling, probably correctly, that politics was not one of his strengths. But here, somehow, spirituality and politics were getting all mixed up, and it triggered something in him. "I came to India to hear of Brahman" (transcendent wisdom), Campbell wrote, "and all I have heard so far is politics and patriotism."

Moreover the spirituality he was encountering in India seemed not to be transcendent (*brahman*), but devotional (*bhakti*). As Swami Nikhilananda and his devoted ladies marked their foreheads with *tilaka,* prostrating themselves before every temple and shrine, Campbell recoiled somewhat from the odor of sanctity. After all, he had always identified himself with *jñāna,* gnosis, the intellectual path.

Nationalistic or religious chauvinism with a spiritual rationale, whether Indian or American, Hindu or Christian or Jewish, often provoked an angry response from Campbell. "Zimmer's formula appears to be correct," he wrote in his journal a few weeks later in India, "devotion to the Mother has become a devotion to Mother India. We are witnessing the birth of a new, patriotically oriented religiosity; or perhaps, only religiously flavored patriotism, somewhat comparable to the American Protestant idea that Christianity and American Democracy are the same thing."

When he stayed for any length of time in India's major cities, Campbell moved in rarefied circles. During his half-year stay he met many of India's more prominent citizens, including President Nehru and his sisters; the Vice President and scholar Sarvepalli Radhakrishnan; the wealthy Sarabhai family of Ahmedabad; the Yuvaraj Karan Singh of Kashmir; Pupul Jayakar, the biographer of Krishnamurti, and many others. But in these circles and in the daily papers the atmosphere was the same. America was generally disparaged, and the Soviet Union and Communist China glorified.

"I am definitely on the other side of the Iron Curtain," he lamented to his journal. "I have a strong feeling that the U.S.A. has lost the world, will be used by everybody as a 'fall guy,' and is the Dragon to be tricked and plundered: old Fafnir with his gold-horde and grandfatherly willingness to be of help to his own destroyer. My sympathy, this time, is with the Dragon."

Two decades earlier Campbell had idealistically espoused the cause of Communism, but after the horrors of Stalinism he did an about-face and considered it a mind-enslaving and authoritarian system. His reaction to Communism was exacerbated by encounters with leftward-leaning faculty at Sarah Lawrence who emphasized the social and political dimensions of most issues, while Campbell preferred to dwell on the philosophical and transcendental aspects. Now here it was again, only mixed with spiritual chauvinism—which he had himself engaged in, often vaunting the deep and luminous insights of Eastern spirituality over Western religion's

Biblical literalism and sense of historical mission. Now it was being turned around on him and he didn't like it very much.

His resolutions began to betray an acknowledgment of his earlier romanticism about India: "I, personally, shall do nothing more to advertise, blurb, and explicate India, for India and Asia are obviously at the beginning of a prodigious boom and can be counted on to take care of themselves."

Campbell's greatest annoyance during this trip was what he came to call "the Baksheesh Complex." Other Westerners traveling in India have experienced its more public manifestation: insouciant beggars in the streets, plucking the heartstrings of pity and guilt. Campbell learned to his disgust that many were professionals, some even maimed by their families to suit them for their unhappy role. At another level Campbell found the unsolicited, unctuous con men, selling something, anything—including psychic and spiritual advice. Campbell found himself susceptible to one of them, and then, falling into shame and anger at his own vulnerability, began to compare his experience to being drafted to working on the Ramakrishna project—without compensation—by Nikhilananda.

Probably the event that upset Campbell the most was an instance of public plagiarism. He found his own prose, from one of the Zimmer books, in the daily paper—without any attribution whatsoever. In a fury, he wrote: "Mr. Pyarelal Nayar steals my paragraphs; an urchin tries to rob my pocket; an Indian movie firm steals an American film; Mr. Nehru accepts American aid and abuses America in every public pronouncement." Campbell did not like ingratitude. Perhaps in an unconscious way, he felt identified with the image of the generous, ugly American with which he kept being presented; it rankled him that the fiercest critics were, at the same time, asking for a handout. Everyone, he swore, was trying to get something from him—and putting down his culture. Again and again he heard the Americans described as inept do-gooders—their programs and initiatives as self-serving. He rankled, half agreeing, half offended.

Culture shock was evident in Campbell throughout this journey, but it seemed to work in two directions. Hearing the ugly American so described, Campbell began to notice that Westerners in India knew nothing of its languages and cultures, and seemed to care less. He often found himself identifying with his hosts' caustic assessment of individual visitors from America, and beholding, with a certain horror, their cultural gaucherie.

"Americans who are not vulgar always hear the remark (which is regarded as a compliment), 'But you aren't like an American!'" which Campbell resented for its patronizing tone. A resolve began to crystallize in Campbell to do something about this situation. It would mature on his return—through the sixties and into the seventies—as years of service with very little compensation for the Foreign Service Institute, a branch of the U.S. State Department. His unremitting goal was to help to prepare American diplomats more adequately for service abroad.[5]

It took months for Campbell to realize that he himself was the victim of archetypal factors: his socialization as a Westerner, and his own self-inflicted idealization of the Orient. Oriental cultures, he wrote, were ruled by archetypes, individuality drowning in the collective patterns. He began to see his own (archetypal) romanticization: "For a Westerner, Oriental literature, which is a rendition of archetypes, has the quality of fairy tale."

At his most insightful, Campbell seemed to realize his own defensiveness, and became determined to let the trip open his mind and his feelings. On encountering the Dīpāvalī, the festival of lights, he wrote,

> It is a festival of the New Moon, representing re-creation and rebirth—and I have actually a feeling that I can make it a rebirth festival of my own, if I go at it correctly. This morning, in that horrible train compartment, I was sitting up at the hour of sunrise, looking out the window. And there appeared in the sky, about an hour before the sun, a lovely object, the dark moon, lightly revealed by the coming sun, and with its lower surface brightly illuminated—like a silver platter holding the darker disk. . . . And I had a pleasant feeling about my India journey. . . .

On another occasion, watching a film, we see him setting his own subjective confusions aside. The sublimity of his own journey breaks upon him:

> Seeing again in the movies what I had already seen with my own eyes, I had a very pleasant sense of the magnitude of the experience that I have been having this year. In the course of my tour I have been seeing India only piece by piece, little by little. Seeing it all again—as it were all at once—I felt how big this whole thing is. The Orient is a vast natural phenomenon, like a continent of trees, mountains, animals and peoples.

At times he seemed to grow by virtue of the very contradictions—little enlightenments triggered by a succession of irresolvable koans: "When you look at India from the outside it is a squalid mess and a haven of fakers; but when you look at it from the inside...it is an epiphany of the spirit...the eye sees a river of mud and the inner eye sees a river of grace."

Campbell had admitted to himself in one of his earlier journals that the reason that he taught at a women's college (Sarah Lawrence) was that he loved to be surrounded by beautiful and intelligent women. To the best of posterity's knowledge, Campbell never engaged in improprieties of any kind—he just seemed to admire and enjoy the company of women. He began to admit to himself in the Indian portion of his journal just how much he missed the mingling, the little flirtations that one experienced in Western high society.

"India is without romance," he wrote, "the sun dries the juices out of the body." At the social clubs the men sat on one side, the women on the other. "Indian wives cannot talk of anything except the three K's: *Kirche, Küche, Kinder,*" he complained. And again, "Women in the Orient represent archetypes and do not have to depend upon the radiance of their individual personalities. Furthermore, since marriages are arranged by families, they do not have to pull themselves together to 'win' someone. As a result, they seem comparatively secure and uninteresting."

It takes some discernment to locate the emotional heart of this journal, his relationship to his wife, the dancer Jean Erdman. While Joseph traveled throughout India, Jean was teaching at Bard College in New York state. She only joined him for a month in India, at midwinter.

Campbell's vexation and emotionality may have been fueled by an enforced monasticism. He didn't acknowledge his loneliness much, but his entries became almost breathless as Jean was about to arrive, and after she left, he immediately got quite sick.

Jean Erdman was the first modern dancer from America to do a solo tour of India. (Martha Graham's more publicized tour would take place several years later.) But all of the Campbells' efforts ahead of time to seek government and institutional support for the project were futile. It was only Joseph's individual efforts that brought the tour into being. In each major city he had to identify key people and arrange venues and advance publicity. Not infrequently much more was promised than fulfilled, and often and again he found he had to persevere in the arrangements.

With Jean's arrival, not unexpectedly, the journal, companion of his solitude, was neglected—the entries almost disappear. Thus we are deprived of much detail about the love affair that was probably the central event of Joseph Campbell's emotional life. He never wavered in the care and concern that he showed toward his partner as she moved around the globe toward him. What was more important for him was obviously what was more important for her—her artistic fulfillment. Though they moved in different orbits, it was characteristic of these two highly creative people to be totally devoted to each other. Joseph's perseverance as advance agent paid off. With several successful concerts and demonstrations in the three major cities of New Delhi, Bombay, and Madras, and highly favorable reviews, the U.S.I.S. and embassy cultural services—too late to be of any use, as Campbell lamented to his journal—began to take notice of the presence of a major American artist in India.

Not infrequently Westerners go to India to find a guru. Campbell acknowledged himself to be in search of *brahman*—but, as he wrote, "I doubt that I shall find a guru here." When he had an actual encounter with a living God-intoxicated saint, Ānanda Mayī Ma, Campbell retreated to his *jñāna* position and asked her a doctrinal question based on the Vedas. Though he liked her answer, it is clear that he was not thrown into *samādhi*, or rapture, by the *darśana*. But he appreciated the feisty individuality of a 116-year-old guru, whom he heard about but missed seeing: "'Anxiety doesn't eat me,' says the old chap, I eat anxiety.' Heavens and hells, past and future, are all figments of the mind. 'God is not the creator of man; man is the creator of God.' This sounds to me like the type of holy man I came to India to see," he wrote.

The spiritual high point of Campbell's trip, nonetheless, was to be his meeting with a guru: Sri Krishna Menon of Trivandrum, a living saint who had earlier had a career as a postal employee. The guru was surrounded by Westerners, who generally filled Campbell with disdain—"mostly psychological cases!" he thought. Campbell found two things remarkable in his meeting with the guru. First that Krishna Menon was able to encounter him lucidly on his own intellectual level, and in fact gave a discourse on states of consciousness from the *Māṇḍūkya Upaniṣad* that was one of Campbell's favorite summations of spiritual wisdom. Second, the guru told him that the question Campbell first asked him was the very one that Menon had first asked his own guru many years before.

"And I feel (I think properly) that my India journey has been perfectly fulfilled," Campbell wrote of this meeting. Though he was invited by the guru to stay for an additional five days of instruction—in part because he himself was, as the guru put it, "so close to realization"—he declined, being unwilling to impose upon the elderly teacher who had been advised by his doctor not to tax himself. "I think what he (already) gave me today will be enough for me," Campbell decided. "The chief value of my conversation with Krishna Menon is that it assures me that my own reading of the teaching coincides with the authority of at least one Indian sage. I know, furthermore, that the conversation and image of the teacher in his room of teaching will remain very clearly in my mind." Thus Campbell felt he had been given the signal to go on to the next stage of his journey, toward Japan, just six months after he had first landed in India.

A kind of core realization can be found in Campbell's confession of the paradoxical nature of his thought—matching the contradictions he found in India—"In the Orient I am for the West; in the West for the Orient. In Honolulu I am for the 'liberals,' in New York for big business. In the temple I am for the university, in the university for the temple. The blood, apparently, is Irish."

PRELUDE

Wednesday, August 25, 1954   **New York–Beirut**

Pan American Airlines tourist class to Beirut via Shannon; Paris, with a four-hour delay for repairs and two breakfasts; Rome and an Italian lunch; and finally the Bristol Hotel in Beirut, two days plus four hours from New York. Air-conditioned room with shower, and nice Arabs—great, but dog-tired. Nikhilananda[1] is supposed to arrive tonight.

Friday, August 27   **Beirut–Jerusalem**

Up at nine or so. Breakfast in the hotel dining room and a walk to town. Gradual recognition of the Orient: *Arabian Nights* associations at every hand.[2] But what a city! New buildings going up everywhere: concrete, modern style, and good. The first part of my walk was through a residential section. A young woman, approaching alone, pulled her black veil down over her face like a hangman's hood, and I had my first experience of *purdah*. Lots of it, here and there, in the town thereafter. An old man with a long stick, in the long white gown and red-fez white-turban head-gear of the *Arabian Nights* went by. Craftsmen in their shops, various characters on various asses, porters, girls with loads on their heads: the whole picture built up gradually, and when I came, finally, to the heavy traffic of the city and the vivid markets, then the wharfs and various busy squares, the whole thing was around me and I was in it.

I finally realized that I did not know how to find a taxi. Then I saw a man who looked like a doorman, before a theater. *"Parlez-vous français?"* I asked. He took me in to the verandah where there was a girl at a table. She asked whether I wanted to ride alone (that would be expensive: five *livres*), or with others (one *livre*). I said with others and she pointed down the street. I went off and knew that I still did not know how to find a taxi; but more of the shops attracted me and I moved on, vaguely, until a man called "Taxi?" and I got in. Price: two *livres;* about sixty-five cents.

After lunch I went up to my room, and I was sitting pleasantly on the toilet when there was a knock at my door; another; and another. I was finally able to open it, and there was Swami Nikhilananda, looking healthy and happy, with his camera over his shoulder. Two ladies, Mrs. Davidson[3] and "the Countess,"[4] were down the hall. "Come! Come!" said Swami. "Come to lunch!" "I've already had my lunch. I was just going to lie down." So they went to lunch, and I lay down. Then we packed off to the airport; in another hour and a half, we would be in Jerusalem.

The hostess on the plane was a very handsome Armenian girl, and when she returned to take my empty ice cream plate, I asked where she had learned her English, which was very good. She looked a little embarrassed and said, "Beirut." I thought I had offended her, but shortly later, she returned and asked if I would like to go up forward, into the captain's cabin. She took me through the door, forward, and introduced me to the captain and co-pilot. The Dead Sea could be seen to the left; Jericho, other places, and then Jerusalem. The captain let me stay up there for the landing; then my pretty girl called me and we disembarked.

A Franciscan, Father Eugene, was at the little airport in Jerusalem to meet us. Irish, he was very strong in his feeling of what the Jews had done: three-quarters of Jerusalem had been taken by Israel; only the Old City remained to "us"; "they" had the cenacle of the Last Supper, but everything else (except decent lodging) was on "our side." To cut the city in two, a great wall had been built, with holes in it here and there, through which to shoot. And there was a barrier across the road through which the car had to wind. "We're at war," said Father Eugene. "Six years of it."

Joseph Campbell's passport photo

We were driven to a little hotel, the Orient House, where we left our things. Then Father Eugene's secretary, a refugee from the other Jerusalem and a very competent guide, took us to the gate of the Old City. The Jewish wall was just to the right, and there were sandbags and stacks of tar-barrels, behind which the citizens could duck when the Jews began to shoot. We entered the gate—and suddenly we were back several centuries: the covered alleys, lined with little shops; the women, many of them veiled; the donkeys, amazing old men, running kids; smells of fries and spices; lots of stepped streets, climbing up and down, criss-crossing. And then suddenly our guide said: "This is the Via Dolorosa, and this is the place of the seventh station." I was struck pretty hard. And from there on the visit was a weird experience.

We saw the Church of the Holy Sepulchre, within which are Calvary, the so-called tombs of Joseph of Arimathea and Nicodemus, and the Mosque of Omar. After dinner, I sat in the garden, listening to the dance music, under a lovely sky, and wrote cards and letters home.

Saturday, August 28   Jerusalem–Bethlehem–Beirut

Visit to the great Mosque of Suleiman, then to a convent (Sisters of Zion, French) built over the court of Peter's denial of Christ. Plenary indulgence for an Our Father, Hail Mary, and Gloria. After visiting the Mount of Olives, spot of the Ascension, and so on, we drove to Bethlehem.

After lunch, plane back to Beirut and dinner with the Pan American agent, Mr. Cornwall, and his wife. Finale with Cornwall and wife in the Bristol Bar after the retirement of the angels.[5]

Sunday, August 29   Baalbek–Damascus

A long, twelve-hour, fatiguing, but very interesting drive: camel herds, camel caravans, wild driving, Bedouins, gypsies, refugees from the Jews. Damascus is a wonderful city—a vast oasis in a Western-type desert, a boom town like Beirut: buildings going up everywhere in a strong, modern, Los Angeles style; wonderful market streets; and a charming, *Arabian Nights* garden.

CHAPTER I

TRAVELS WITH SWAMI

NEW DELHI

Monday, August 30   **Basra–Karachi–New Delhi**

After stops at Basra (amazing scenery: desert and date palm gardens—incredible from the air) and Karachi (dreary desert set-up), we arrive in New Delhi at 8:30 P.M.

Tuesday, August 31   **New Delhi**

Upon arrival last night at the Palam Airport on the Pan American Clipper Ponce de León, we were met at the gangplank by a *sadhu* in a saffron robe,[6] holding a lei for Nikhilananda. Assorted press photographers (gentle, soft-spoken) stopped photographing Senator So-and-so, who had arrived on the same Clipper, to make the four of us line up: Nikhilananda with his lei, handbag and several cameras; Mrs. Davidson, mild and hardly touching the world, holding satchels; the Countess, whining tentative complaints through her long nose; and myself, pouring beads of perspiration from every pore, my blue Dacron suit as heavy as an Eskimo parka, my second-hand Leica slipping from my shoulder, my thirty-year-old English raincoat over my sweating arm, my equally old Zeiss field glasses in that hand, and in my other hand a leather bag that Jean and I had bought in a Madison Avenue luggage shop seven days before. More *sadhus* appeared, all standing, quietly smiling with luminous eyes, regarding principally their returned brother, Nikhilananda. Then a great deal of "this way please," "passports please," luggage examination, filling out of forms, forgetting of this and going back to get it, misplacing of that, and general search.

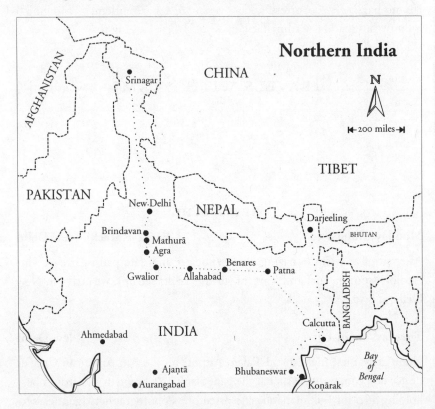

I was pleased to see, at every hand, examples of the modern Indian masculine types: one tall, good looking, young officer of some kind with a black beard and well-set turban was particularly conspicuous in the last stage of the processing of our company, and as we left bade us "a sweet night and a sweet trip." One helpful official in civilian gear loaned me a pen at one point, and then disappeared; no one then knew who was the owner, and a young assistant, with a smile, after holding it up to ask whose it was, tucked it into his own pocket. *Sadhus* were everywhere, helping, two carrying in their fists their closed umbrellas. Nikhilananda was losing and then finding everything, searching his pockets, and receiving help. Some kind of government person appeared and said a few words to the customs man who was to examine my bags; the customs official told me not to open them, asked me a couple of questions, and then gave his rubber stamp.

In the waiting room of the airport a thousand people were attending to our bags: *sadhus,* porters, and a number of other gentlemen. Clinging to all my things and sweating like a cheese, I was beginning to become a spectacle. Smiling cameramen and newspaper reporters were still looking for something to do. Leis had by now gotten around the necks of us all, and the fellow with the beard asked if he could take our picture again. He said he had done something wrong and had not gotten us right before. And so it took another fifteen minutes or so before Nikhilananda, Mrs. Davidson, the Countess, and I were again lined up properly and shot. Then we entered automobiles and started for the Hotel Cecil in Old Delhi.

The drive, through the dark, revealed brief glimpses of practically everything I had expected to see in India: wandering cows, multitudes of wildly assorted people, people sleeping in beds out along the sidewalks, a holy man with a little circle of people around him, bullock carts, water buffaloes, turban varieties, saris, etc. The same general Oriental effect of Beirut, but definitely of another racial cast: a different swing, a different set of details or motifs. We turned in first to the mission—and there was a live *nandi* reclining, by chance, near the gate. The Ramakrishna Mission was adorned with the East 94th Street motifs.7 Then we drove to the hotel. Nice room suites with ceiling fans (salvation). I showered, and then went down to the Honolulu-style porch for two sodas and salt, and listened to the middle-class British talk of cricket.

This morning (Wednesday), to the Ramakrishna Mission. *Pūjā* in the chapel, Swami now in his yellow robe. Plans for our visit to New Delhi, Swami Ranganathananda presiding (a fine, clean-cut, intelligent, efficient man: the one who first met us at the plane). Visits to the Jama Masjid and the site of Gandhi's cremation, which is now a great park of well-kept lawns, with a sort of cenotaph in the center. We placed leis on the cenotaph.

In the evening we drove to the university, where the swamis began talking with a gentleman about some lectures that were to be given. I gathered that they were speaking of me—and became a little peeved. I got the idea that Swami was trying to use me as an advertisement of the sort of American he is winning to his work in the U.S.A. This has made me a little sore. I managed to kick the thing off—but I'm in for a lecture at the Ramakrishna Mission itself.

Wednesday, September 1

Visit to the Red Fort:[8] a wonderful suggestion of the harem world of the Mughals: "The Land of Paradise." An inscription on one of the walls, from some Persian poem: "If there is a paradise, it is here, it is here," an echo of a Tantric theme.[9] Various baths and dressing rooms of queens and concubines: The Mughal had four legitimate wives and 175 concubines. As we moved about the green lawns, I saw a woman speak to one of the guards; he pointed to a water faucet on a standing pipe, and without ceremony she opened her sari and crouched under it for a bath.

We next went to the Indian Tourist Office, and I to the American Express to collect my mail: a lovely letter from Jean and a few lost bits of proof from Pantheon with a couple of notes from Bill McGuire.[10] I decided not to go with my party tomorrow to Kurukshatra, but to stay home and do a bit of work. It took us from ten till about one to finish our plan-making at the Tourist Office and to get our permits for Kashmir. Then I cashed a fifty-dollar travelers check at the American Express office and returned to the hotel for lunch.

After lunch: a nap, tea, then a lively bit of sight-seeing. First to the Tomb of Humayun[11]; then the Qutb Minār Enclosure, Guwwat ul Islam Mosque, and Iron Pillar—elements of earlier Hindu and Jain temples, with stone handled as wood, and the most interesting affair so far. After that, now nearly dark, a visit to the new Birla temple, Hinduism modern style, and visits to all the shrines: Viṣṇu and Lakṣmī, Śiva, Durgā. Finally on to the Buddha temple, and then the Durgā temple, where we had a taste of holy water and sweets; and then home.

Thursday, September 2

Up at seven to the knock of the man with the tea. After breakfast, I attended to my proofs, and then I took a taxi to the National Museum to see what items had been brought there from the other Indian museums.

Filled with priceless pieces, the National Museum is an old, domed, government building lit by a vast, old-fashioned chandelier hanging from the ceiling. So I had the experience of viewing sculpture in semi-darkness—an absolutely crazy situation. As I was looking closely at a case of Indus Valley seals, I was addressed by a Sikh police officer: "Who are you? Where do you come from? How long will you

be in Delhi?" I told him that I was on a tour of India. "Well," he said, "I am a free man. I will go with you. Where are you staying? What is your room number?" He wanted to visit me at the hotel. I was having a hard time shaking him off, so I asked him to help me get to see the director of the museum, and he turned me over to one of the guards. We shook hands, and then I shook hands with his sidekick, and finally I was led into a room, where one man sat at a desk and several others stood around. "My name," I said, "is Joseph Campbell." "Joseph Campbell?" said a young man dressed in white, who was standing at the director's left hand. "The editor of Heinrich Zimmer's books?"[12] I nodded, and I was "in": a delegation was assembled to help me get the measurements that I needed, and the young man, Pramod Chandra—whose father, now the curator of the museum in Bombay, was formerly at the National Museum, but quit because of government red tape—invited me to have lunch with him tomorrow.

After lunch at the hotel, we had a series of contrasting visits to make: first, Swami Ranganathananda showed us the new tuberculosis hospital being erected by the Ramakrishna Mission; then, we proceeded to a new, low rental, housing development (quite vast), where a devotee of Swami Nikhilananda's writings entertained us in a very touching—and utterly embarrassing—style; for the tenement was without plumbing yet, and none of us dared to take more than a token nibble of the bounteous fare that was set, almost as an offering, before us: drinking water (from a well or pipe line of some kind) with a lemon infusion, and then trays of sliced apples, pears, curds with grapes, grapes, and so on and so forth. It was a heartbreaking event: We sat on the floor and gingerly sipped, while the denizens of the tenement, crowded at the doors and windows, watched. They were people from the Punjab and Kashmir; refugees. One young woman, a teacher, talking strongly with Swami Ranganathananda, told him of her work: a school of eight hundred. One got a sense of serious and important social work being carried forward bravely and in good style.

Our next tea was with Radhakrishnan, Vice President of India. He greeted us cordially and talked for an hour and ten minutes in his living room about how America, hurt by the defection of China after the years of help and so on, could not be expected to know how to take it and was going to be hurt next by Germany and Japan (Adenauer had told him that the Germans would let the U.S.A. help them back to their feet and would then know how to handle us); about America's aid to Pakistan being the real thorn in India's side,[13] but there being a basic good will toward India on the part of the American people, and so on and so forth; and about how India, in seven years, had gained the respect of the world for integrity, was acceptable to both the U.S.A. and Russia as a "middle man," was mastering its economic problems, and was looking forward to peaceful coexistence, as a "block," with China and Southeast Asia.

Friday, September 3

A morning visit to Parliament: Upper House, Lower House, and then a talk with Mr. Mavlankar, Speaker of the House. Swami asks why congress doesn't open with a prayer and is brushed off with smiles. Then I had them leave me at the door of Gaylord's restaurant, where I was to meet my young friend Chandra. I had an hour and a half to spare. After wandering in the hot streets for a while, I went into a movie house and took a seat in a box. The film—*Chālīs Bābā Ek Chor* (my Hindi dictionary is in New York, so I don't know what this means: forty somethings and one something)[14] was horrible: a young woman taxi driver and a horde of kids—corn *à l'indienne;* but the newsreel was interesting: Indian water and river projects on the grand scale; an Indian cultural delegation (dancers, musicians, and such) to Russia.

Then my lunch with Pramod Chandra. A graceful lad of twenty-four, he studied at Harvard for government service, but then met the Coomaraswamys and learned of art.[15] Now, disappointed in government work, he wants to return to Harvard to study museology. I told him that would be an important work for India. We ordered cocktails: they didn't know what a daiquiri was, so we settled, he for a martini, and I for a gin and tonic. (Later, the poor kid spilled most of his cocktail over his pretty dhoti). Then we had a light curry and rice, ice cream, and a fine chat in that air-conditioned restaurant.

Tea this afternoon was *chez* Madam Pandit.[16] She talked of her recent visit to Indonesia: how India should be sending cultural delegations there and not only to China and Russia. (I thought of the film I had just seen.) Swami asked, "Would Americans be ill-treated in Indonesia?" Answer: America was not liked there, but Americans individually were welcome and should go to help good will. Swami asked, "How did India know that China would not continue to try to expand into Indo-China?" Answer: India didn't know, but believed that China had enough to do now at home to keep busy.

My own feeling, now, about Asia, world anti-Americanism, and so on, is that our do-goodism should now be definitely and absolutely stopped, since it is succeeding only in fostering a malevolence that may be our ruin, and any giving or helping should be precisely and firmly of the sort that it is everywhere said and thought to be—namely, carefully selfish; and also that I, personally, shall do nothing more to advertise, blurb, and explicate India, for India and Asia are obviously at the beginning of a prodigious boom and can be counted on to take care of themselves. Moreover, why should it be Americans who are always trying to create an understanding of others, when no one seems to feel the least impulse to seek to understand America? In fact, to hell with this whole "service-to-this-or-that-section-of-the-world" idea.

Which returns me to the basic and original purpose of my visit to the Orient: to study, not India primarily, but mythology in operation.

In this context, my most interesting observations so far are: the modern, self-sufficient, progressive Orient, secular style; then, the Birla Temple: a typical bourgeois transformation of an ancient religion, comparable to American church-life. Also, the relationship of the Ramakrishna Mission to, first of all, the Birla Temple devotees, who everywhere get down on their knees to take the dust from the Swami's feet; then to the ministers of the state—who all know and accept them familiarly into their homes and confidences; and finally to the TB clinic: comparable to St. Vincent's Hospital, but, of course, as yet much smaller. The Mission, with ten hospitals and seventy open-air clinics, treated two million patients last year.

There has been a bit of religious agitation of an amusing sort since our arrival: anti–cow-slaughter demonstrations by old-style *sadhus* are being quelled by the police. Yesterday morning I saw a group of them parading toward Parliament with yellow pennants on their staffs. They were a wild-looking lot: one was practically naked, with only a minute black apron before his second *cakra*.[17] Their stratagem was described in *The Statesman*[18] with pictures as follows:

> Small groups organized by the Ram Rajya Parishad have been demonstrating outside Parliament almost every day this session demanding a ban on cow slaughter. The sadhus carry a saffron flag inscribed with a swastika.[19] On arrival they meet in an orderly manner behind the fencing and try to convince the Sub-Inspector of Police on duty of the rightness of their cause. Then suddenly they rush and try to break the police cordon outside Parliament House and are brought back to the original enclosure when one of the oldest among them gives a religious discourse.

> Swami Ranganathananda declares that such oldsters represent a rapidly dwindling and unimportant religious force.

Saturday, September 4

Saturday, after breakfast, a reading of the papers, and a bit of brooding. I came to India to hear of *brahman*,[20] and all I have heard so far is politics and patriotism. Zimmer's formula appears to be correct: devotion to the Mother has become a devotion to Mother India. We are witnessing the birth of a new, patriotically oriented religiosity; or, perhaps, only religiously flavored patriotism, somewhat comparable to the American Protestant idea of Christianity and American Democracy being the same thing.

I am now definitely on the other side of the Iron Curtain. The main links of sympathy are with China, Southeast Asia, Russia, and, perhaps, even East Germany—this morning's paper features pictures of an East

German trade delegation. Britain, moreover, is flirting with China; and France, with Russia. I have a strong feeling that the U.S.A. has lost the world, will be used by everybody as a "fall guy," and is the Dragon to be tricked and plundered: old Fafnir with his gold-horde and grandfatherly willingness to be of help to his own destroyer.[21] My sympathy, this time, is with the Dragon.

What I thus far have witnessed and heard of the *sadhus* is not particularly impressive. They appear to be associated with the misery of the "old India" that is being sloughed off, and—like all clergymen everywhere—they manifest themselves in the role of reaction: for example, their anti–cow-slaughter demonstrations.

The Ramakrishna Mission, Birla Temple kind of Hinduism is comparable to the Christianity of the bourgeois church and Catholic hospital—and the people representing this movement, moreover, have their precise counterparts in the church circles of the United States.

The present leaders of the Government are of a distinctly secular mentality: witness, particularly, Speaker of the House Mavlankar, who parried all of Swami's requests that religious forms of some kind—opening prayers and so on—should be introduced into the conduct of the Indian Parliament. Again I see a parallel to the two traditional strains in the U.S.A.: that of the Puritan tradition ("In God We Trust") and that of the 18th-century Enlightenment ("*Novus Ordo Seclorum*").[22] Said Mavlankar, with a knowing smile, "But are we really following, or has anyone really followed, Gandhiji?"

Today with one of the swamis' little lady patronesses to help, and under instructions from Swami, I bought two dhotis, two Indian shirts, and a shoulder cloth. Then I went for a stroll and was accosted by a sly fortune-teller swami who managed to seduce me out of thirty rupees by telling me nothing. I felt—and am still feeling—greatly the fool. As soon as I left him, another approached me with the same voice and line; and when I reached the hotel, there was a phone call from a young man who has been pestering me for an interview—and again the same voice and line. By chain-reaction, I have now associated the principle of my fortune teller with Swami, who seduced me into editing his books for him—always keeping me, in a very subtle way, pitched forward toward a vacuum, where, finally, I would discover that I had been used. And again by association, I now think of India-Russia-China and the U.S.A. I am going to keep, as a sign of my shame, the little token that the guy left with me.

KASHMIR

Monday, September 6   **Kashmir: Pathānkot to Srinagar**

Two swamis saw us off on the night train to Pathānkot—and the night and subsequent day are not to be forgotten. We had a second class compartment, designed for "six persons sitting, four sleeping." The two seats were converted into four bleak bunks, onto which we opened our four bed-rolls: I above, Swami below me; Mrs. D. above, the Countess below her. Two electric fans did not suffice to keep the heat down. It was actually a furnace of a night. I fell asleep slightly, well after midnight, though we turned our light out about 8:30.

At 7 A.M. we were in Pathānkot, where a gentle couple met us and supplied us with breakfast in the waiting room. Swami took a shower and was looking spry. The rest of us were a bit shaken. What impressed me most here was the vitality and virtuosity of the porters. They piled the luggage on their heads, hooked more to their arms, and, when they had delivered their burdens, trotted back to the train for more.

The Kashmir problem is at present rather hot, and so there was a conspicuously military character to the event of getting us across the border. The kind gentleman who had met us supervised the packing of our luggage into a large Chevrolet station-wagon; he then preceded us in a military jeep to the checking post, where two extremely polite officers made notations from our passes, after which we returned to the station wagon for the wildest mountain drive that I can remember.

The driver was a Sikh. The road went from Lakhanpur, the place of the Customs barrier, 56 miles to Jammu (1,000 ft.), then 41 miles to Udhampur (2,248 ft.), where the ladies paused for refreshment at a Dak bungalow, and I sat in the car watching our stuff. The driver drove me to a spot in the market, where he simply left the car and went off to attend to some business of his own. At this point—having seen a good many Oriental markets—I began to feel that I had gotten the idea and that it was no longer very interesting. The driver returned, we drove back to the bungalow, all the others got in, and we were off. After another twenty-four miles, we were in Kud (5,700 ft.), where again we descended before a Dak bungalow—this time for lunch. It was already about 2 P.M., and there was some question as to whether we would make Srinagar that night. Ants had somehow gotten into the best part of our provisions, so we had to content ourselves with

tea, hard-boiled eggs, and bananas. From Kud, we drove four miles to Patni Top (6,447 ft.), and from there, eight miles to Bator (5,170 ft.).

By now it was evident that our driver was a phenomenon: over a pretty rugged and occasionally heavily populated road, he kept a pace of 35 to 40 miles per hour, negotiating the turns with an apparently reckless precision and with unwavering alertness: people, chickens, water buffaloes, trucks, goat herds, cows—nothing stopped him.

From Bator, we careened seventeen miles to Ramban (2,250 ft.) and then began the climb to Banihal (5,650 ft.). All along the way, we passed trucks—perhaps over a hundred—coming in a steady stream in the opposite direction, and since we were on the outside ("keep to the left") of a precipitous mountain highway, some of the moments were pretty spectacular. Swami became distinctly nervous and, at one moment, actually scared: that was when we backed up a little—without any wall between us and the precipitous drop—to let a van wriggle by. At about 6 P.M. we arrived before the Dak bungalow at Banihal, where the driver stopped. He very much wanted us to spend the night there, but the ladies and Swami, after examining the premises, decided to press on.

During this pause I had another remarkable glimpse into the character of our driver. Before him, propped against the windshield, he had a little picture of the Sikh prophet Nānak. At Banihal, while the bungalow was being examined by his passengers, he got out of his seat, went to a hedge of flowers, and plucked a big red blossom of some kind, which he then tucked above the picture. When Swami returned, the driver argued strongly for going no further, but acquiesced without any intentional display of impatience—though I noted that, while preparing for the hard run ahead, he was a bit more grim and firm in his manner than he had been before.

To quote from the tourist pamphlet:

> From Banihal the road ascends at an easy grade in a wonderful series of zig-zags on which one can look down from above. As the automobile climbs, the spectacle of the thin white road winding around the hills at various levels and disappearing into the hazy valley below presents a magnificent view. Banihal pass road is the highest highway in the world and is at a height of 8,985 ft. above sea level. [They apparently don't know about Pikes Peak, Independence Pass and Monarch Pass, Mt. Wilson, Long's Peak, and so on.] From the summit one gets a most thrilling view of the Banihal Valley, stretching in pensive quietness below. White clouds float around you. There is a sudden change in the landscape as the automobile passes through a tunnel and crosses straight through to the other side of the mountain. From the tunnel, the road descends in sweeping hair-pin bends for twenty-nine miles.

During the course of the descent, night came upon us, and we entered the Vale of Kashmir in darkness. Upper Munda, the first village after Banihal, is at a height of 7,227 ft. Lower Munda is five miles further on; Qazigund, four miles further, is at a height of 5,667 ft. Then come Khanabal, after eleven miles; Avantipur (where the ruins of the temples of King Avanti Varman[23] have been excavated), Pampur, and finally Srinagar (5,214 ft.). We pulled in at about 9 P.M. and were soon settled into Nedon's Hotel, which reminds me a good deal of Mokuleia[24]. The lights are the dimmest, however, that I have ever encountered in a public building. The bar was teeming with Englishmen. The atmosphere is that of a wealthy family resort. Dead tired, we ate, and, as soon as possible, went to bed.

During the night and morning, rain, even thunder—the first since my departure from New York. And then I realized that my raincoat, which I had bought in London in 1928 and had brought with me to be left in India, had indeed been left—I had left it hanging in the waiting room at Pathānkot, where we'd had our breakfast.

After breakfast at Nedon's, Swami and the ladies joined a swami who had arrived from the Ramakrishna Mission—lately established here, it's interpreted by the Pakistanis as an effort to convert to Hinduism the 90-percent–Muslim population—while I, on the pretext of preparing my talk for Sunday night, strolled off alone. I viewed a series of bad watercolors by some Hindu lady, which included a piece labeled "McCarthyism" that depicted a sort of green-eyed, wild-haired monster. Then, as I moved out for a stroll to town, I was approached by taxi men, guides, merchants: "Please let me alone; I don't need you," was my formula, and it finally worked. But the rain began again, and, trotting, I took refuge in a couple of shops that shared a verandah. The proprietors, of course, tried to sell me something. I was shown bolts of fine Kashmir tweeds and rich furs: a pair of slacks would cost about seventy rupees, a fur coat about five hundred rupees (one hundred dollars)! But I was firm—perhaps too firm—being somewhat desperate about my money, which is rolling out these days at about three times the rate anticipated.

Returning to the hotel when the rain cleared, I settled to the present piece of writing. With respect to my general impression of the Orient and India, a couple of matters are to be recorded:

The gentleness and politeness of everyone is most remarkable. This struck me first, and immediately, when I stepped from the plane at Beirut; and it has remained the rule (without exception), from the approaches of the beggars, to the reception by Radhakrishnan and the attitude toward Swami of our remarkable Sikh driver.

The religious atmosphere and attitude are ubiquitous and strong. I was hit by it myself in Jerusalem. In New Delhi, wherever Swami goes he is greeted by men and women who stoop to touch his feet. Our taxi driver had his picture of Nānak on the windshield. Our tourist questionnaires for Kashmir, India, and Nepal had the query "Religion," and it is expected to be answered. Swami Ranganathananda tells me that more than 95 percent of the Indians practice, outwardly at least, the forms of some religion. Some of the Western-educated intellectuals have rejected religion, but they are rare exceptions to the general rule.

The principal lack that I feel in India—and, I dare say, should have felt in the Near East also, had I remained there—is the lack of beauty, and of any feeling for beauty, in the contemporary life. In Beirut I saw, at least, some beautiful women; but in India, I have not yet seen even a beautiful young girl. The city of New Delhi is, from an aesthetic point of view, simply an un-thing. The circumstances of the masses are simply squalid. The housing projects and the new buildings are, from a practical point of view, good and sound, but hardly beautiful. The bourgeois homes that we have visited are decorated in a trite, sort of Grand Rapids, manner. The British contribution to the city is a horror. And the Muslim remains—apparently the last creations of taste (and a rather flamboyant, though elegant, taste it was) in all of India—are mostly ruins. I am curious to know at what point in my travels an experience of aesthetic form will occur.

In a queer way, I am beginning to believe that I have already experienced, in New York, the best of what India is going to offer me. In my visit to the National Museum, I actually saw some of the objects that I had learned to know through my photographs; but the Museum's lighting was so bad that the effects of the actual objects were slighter, in every case, than those of the photos.

But in a queer way, also, I am beginning to be afraid that Swami Nikhilananda and Mrs. D. are ruining my experience of India. Everything that we see evokes some unpleasant comparison with its American counterpart and a patriotic waving of the new Indian flag. I cannot permit myself to admire anything any more; for even a word will call forth the question: "Is it not better than your American so-and-so?" This situation, coupled with Swami's anti-Americanism in the matter of the U.S.-Pakistan *vs.* U.S.S.R.-China tie-up, makes for a very unpleasant atmosphere.

Swami himself has begun to sense my disappointment, and he has suggested that, given my interest in museums, I should perhaps plan for a slightly looser relationship to his tour. This I am going to do. For the most part, Swami is dashing about a little more than I like, and the money is pouring out like water. I've got to find my own feet now, and pinpoint my searches according to my own set of problems. Today, for instance, I am letting them worship the Mother, while I sit here writing. I believe I shall stay in New Delhi for a few days after their departure and perhaps meet them again in Benares; go on with them to Calcutta, and decide then whether I want to join them in their visit to the south.

The two ladies returned from their worship of the Mother with red dots on their foreheads, which they wore until bedtime—like Catholics, on Ash Wednesday, bearing on their foreheads the dust of time's ruin. I find it a little difficult to walk with composure beside all this.

Swami has learned, to his considerable discomposure, that the Muslims of Kashmir (56 per cent of the population), who, he had thought, were solidly for India, actually are inclining to Pakistan. Furthermore, Kashmiri rice, which here sells for seven rupees per mound, in India sells for twenty; hence, there is a lively smuggling commerce going on. As we saw on our drive, Kashmir is occupied by the Indian army, which is a deli-cate situation for Nehru, who has been crowing about alien armies supporting puppet governments in Korea and Indo-China.

At the time of Partition, in 1948, there was a great raid of Muslim "tribesmen" (as they are called here) into Kashmir. And the story goes that Kashmir was saved by its women. The raiders were so busy raping them that the Indian army had time to arrive and drive them off.

Tuesday, September 7   **Srinagar**

Worked on the outline for the talk I'm to give until 10:15, when I had my interview with Mr. Pandit. Upon returning, I changed into my blue Dacron suit and went with Swami and the ladies to lunch with Yuvaraj Karan Singh, the twenty-four-year-old son of the former Maharaja of Kashmir, who is now the first president of the province. A very handsome and gracious young man with a game right leg (from tuberculosis—it was operated on in a New York hospital), he received us in the most gentle fashion, with his two bodyguards always in the room, conducted us to an elegant lunch, and then sat with us on his lawn, overlooking the two vales of Kashmir. The conversation ranged considerably over a variety of subjects—the Ramakrishna Mission, education in India and America, the scenery of Kashmir, and so on—with certain points of importance being:

The U.S.A.'s support to Pakistan has definitely queered us with India, and our support to the French in Indo-China has queered us with Asia. This young man confessed that his sympathies and those of all of India had been with the Viet Minh.[25]

Communism is not the least bit frightening to Asia. The people see what it has done for Russia in forty years, and the benefits seem to warrant whatever sufferings, injustices, and so on may have been entailed. "What good is freedom, if it is only freedom to starve?" This attitude—the true sign, by the way, of the Fellaheen—is something very different from Spengler's "Better dead than a slave."[26] Perhaps we can say that to the Asiatic world—which, for centuries at least, has not known the taste and feel of freedom—our American experience and consequent ideals can have no meaning whatsoever. The Sikh Sub-Inspector of Police at the National Museum told me that he was dissatisfied because there was no higher position for him to achieve. He had killed a man and been cited for bravery; the job was a dangerous one, and he wanted out: however, there was no out. Such a chap, I should think, might have an idea that freedom of opportunity would be a good thing, but he certainly could never have *experienced*—that is, actually known the feel of— freedom.

In the late afternoon, we took a boat ride through the canals to Dal Lake: a lovely, lotus-bordered, mountain-girded lake with many large houseboats, many cruising boats like our own, and many work boats. Indeed, everybody lives in boats, and kids hardly big enough to walk can paddle. The people look vigorous, courageous, and filthy dirty. Hundreds live in a squalid series of houseboats along the willow banks. Floating gardens abound, and the water—near the houseboats, at any rate—is quite foul. We had four paddlers: one, probably the father; the others, young boys, one of them blind—and they chugged away at a sharp clip, without letup, for three-and-a-half hours.

At the dinner table I had a conversation with Swami: Indian scholars and historians are now taking an anti-European position, which is the counterpart of the earlier European neglectfulness of Asia. It's a kind of revenge situation, ill-becoming the scholar. Resolution: no patriotism, no partisanship, in my further writings and, again, no more blurbs for India. They're doing it, and let them do it, themselves. In fact, this whole patriotic atmosphere is extremely disappointing. Yet, I should have expected it. It is certainly timely; but it is far, indeed, from the sort of equipoise that is supposed to be the particular gift and lesson of India to the world.

Early to bed tonight. A big day tomorrow: some kind of great trip through the valley, and then, in the evening, the Yuvaraj's movies of his trip to Amarnāth. As we left, he gave us copies of his account of his trip and, when he learned that I was the editor of Heinrich Zimmer, said that he had just read *Myths and Symbols* with great delight—a pleasant bit of news—and that he also owned and knew *Philosophies of India.*[27]

Wednesday, September 8   **Amarnāth**

At 8:10 A.M. we got into a car for a drive to neighboring towns, and particularly to pause at Pahalgam, which is the traditional starting point for the annual pilgrimage, about the middle of August, to the Śiva Sanctuary, a natural cave with an ice-covered stalagmite, at Amarnāth. There we had a picnic lunch in a setting very like a Rocky Mountain valley; and we returned to the hotel about 5 P.M.

The drive gave me a rather solid impression of the people of this valley, as well as of the valley itself: a great flat plain, about seventy miles long by twenty wide, surrounded by Himalayan foothills about ten thousand feet high. The valley is fertile, planted with rice (of which we saw a great deal), saffron (of which we saw several fields), and wheat. The people: in the fields, peasants with short hand-adzes and sickles; handsome, very dark, dark-eyed, sturdy people, bearing burdens on their backs or tending flocks of cows, goats, or sheep; mostly Muslim, with little skull caps or caps of fur; the women, the handsomest I have seen so far, but almost all in dirty rags. More people: in the towns, the shopkeepers, cobblers, fruitsellers, and so on; the river-people in their houseboats and long skiffs; a wild tribe of nomads, who came trudging with their cute kids and stocky pack-ponies to a bit of grassland beside a stream and pitched their tents—the women, somewhat like Navaho, only not so big and handsome; the priests at the little folk temples.

We visited two temple compounds, each with several such temples. In the temple ponds were multitudes of fish. At one of the ponds, a few bas-relief fragments (showing deities that I could not identify from my distance) were set up against a wall, and people would stoop to splash a few handfuls of water at them, then sip a bit of water from their cupped hands. In this compound, a holy man, smeared with ashes and quite black, was squatting among brass vessels filled with water and, a few, with flowers. At another of the temples was a great crowd of Hindu visitors, who had arrived in a van; the priests of the temple had great long visitors' books, in which all were asked to sign. The chief guardian of the place recognized Swami as a Ramakrishna monk and even knew his name. Swami and the ladies visited the Sūrya Temple that was there, and we all signed the book.

We also found and photographed two Hindu temple ruins from about

A.D. 1050: one, a neat little *garbhagṛha* set in a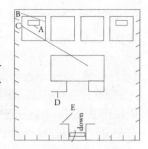
square pond; the other, a large compound with
a high shrine (destroyed) in the center and a run
of four shrines behind it. I took photos of the *yonī*
(at A); of the shrine with the *yonī* (from B); of
the central shrine (from C); of a damaged panel
of Śiva, Devī, and an attendant (at D); and of another damaged panel of a *maithuna* (at E).

During the drive I had time to brood a bit more on the Indian problem. It was interesting to be in a landscape so close to that of the Rockies
and certain parts of Switzerland, and yet in a world of such different feeling. In contrast with Switzerland: there were no flowers, there was no
charm, there was no *intentional* decoration or beautification of anything
except of the temples, and the beautification there, of course, was simply
vulgar and gaudy. A comparison with America might be possible if one
thought of the America of the Indians. That tribe of gypsy-like campers
made me think of the Navahos a bit. They were the same kind of rugged
race. But the tilling of the soil belonged to the 6000 B.C. category—and
the work of the peasants, some of the images that I saw, rang echoes for me
from Europe as well as from Japan.

Here, then, is a great base of the agricultural stratum—with its religiosity; which has jumped the Atlantic to shape the Bible Belt. The world
of religion that I entered at Jerusalem was there represented to me by the
French nun who showed us through the Convent of the Sisters of Zion and
reminded me of Aunt Clara, and the Irish Franciscan, Father Eugene (recall that Grandma belonged to the lay order of St. Francis). Let it be the
Bible Belt or the Koran Belt, a temple of Kālī or of Notre Dame, the fundamental context, today, is the same: that of a folk piety rooted ultimately
in the sphere of agriculture and the petty shop. Ancillary to this sphere is
that of the nomads and their flocks: many of the men that I saw today
could well have been Abraham, Isaac, or Jacob. The most vivid symbol of
this religious sphere is the solitary Muslim, on a rug somewhere (in a grove,
in a field, beside a pond), bowing in prayer. Last evening, during our boat
ride, I saw a woman standing alone, in one of those canal-vistas, and she
seemed to me to be linked to nature in the way of these people, that is to
say, linked to nature by being linked to a principle beyond nature, through
a ritual attitude: something very different from the romantic return to nature and intuition of God through nature.

Against the ground base of this primary population and religious attitude (as capable of fanatical fury as of gentleness), the bourgeois Hindu girls in their saris or pajamas look distinctly like something else. For these, the religion of the Birla Temple.

And then, one remembers, above these, the well-Westernized Nehrus and Mavlankars: of a secular cast of mind, for whom religion, surely, is either a pose or a slight problem.

But the source of ideology of this directive group is Europe and America, and it is they who are building, through the vehicle of education, the contemporary sari and pajama girls. And so we arrive at a formula:

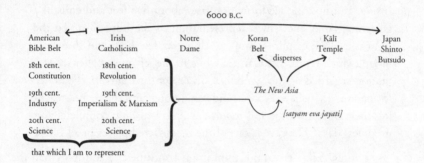

6000 B.C.

American Bible Belt — Irish Catholicism — Notre Dame — Koran Belt — Kālī Temple — Japan Shinto Butsudo

18th cent. Constitution — 18th cent. Revolution

19th cent. Industry — 19th cent. Imperialism & Marxism

20th cent. Science — 20th cent. Science

disperses

The New Asia

[satyam eva jayati]

that which I am to represent

The lead is definitely with the West. The new world that I thought might be found in the Orient is certainly not here yet—and will not be here in my lifetime. They are learning from *us*. Europe is the *present* home of *my* mind—and of Asia's too.

But, on the other hand, what I am to study is definitely here: folk religion, with its roots in the deep past; aristocratic religion, represented in the ruins of the temple art of India; the phenomenon of the *sadhu*—past, present, future; the bourgeois religion of the Birla Temple (and compare that with St. Patrick's Cathedral) and Swami's idea that the priests of India (as distinguished from the *sadhus*) should have degrees in Hindu theology; then, finally, the operation of science in this context. Moreover, it is just possible that there may be someone in all of this from whom I may wish to learn something fundamental.

After dinner, we drove up to the palace of Yuvaraj Karan Singh to view his color movies of his pilgrimage to Amarnāth and his visit to Ladakh. In his little booklet on "The Glory of Amarnāth," he has stated the principle of pilgrimage in the following way:

A pilgrimage symbolizes, as it were, the long pilgrimage of the soul towards its ultimate, sublime goal. Almost all the most important pilgrimages in India take the devotee along dangerous and hazardous paths, testing his devotion at every step. It is seldom possible for the pilgrim, if he is deterred, to reach the goal. If he pushes on bravely with courage and confidence, and with faith in God, he is bound to triumph.[28]

The goal of pilgrimage at Amarnāth is a cave of

truly colossal dimensions. Its outer mouth must measure almost forty yards across, and it is about seventy-five feet high and at least eighty feet deep along its downward slope into the heart of the mountain. Inside, an imposing ice formation rises about five feet and ends in a glistening cone, the famed representation of the Lord Śiva. To the right is a block of pure white ice, about six feet high and three feet broad, which represents Ganeśa, while to the left is a smaller ice formation regarded as the symbol of Śiva's consort, Pārvatī. These ice formations are believed to wax and wane along with the moon, reaching their climax on the full-moon day and vanishing completely on moonless days. The cave is one of the most sacred places in all India.

"As I entered it," Yuvaraj Karan Singh continues, "I suddenly had the curious feeling that I had been there before, and, certainly, the unusual atmosphere of the cave affects many people powerfully. I was overawed as I entered its hallowed precincts."[29]

Swami Vivekananda visited this cave in 1898, after his return from America. Sister Nivedita records in her "Notes on Some Wanderings with the Swami Vivekananda," that the swami was so overwhelmed when he entered the cave that his whole frame shook and he almost swooned with emotion. "I thought the ice-*liṅga* was Śiva himself," the Swami said later. "And there were no thievish brahmins, no trade, nothing wrong. It was all worship. I never enjoyed any religious place so much." Vivekananda imagined at this time that Śiva himself appeared before him and granted him the Boon of Amarnāth, the Lord of Immortality—not to die until he himself should choose to throw off his mortal bonds.[30]

This illustrates very well the radical difference between the modern Orient and modern Occident, which I am feeling, one way or another, all the time. I think again of Tenzing Norgay and Hillary on Mt. Everest:[31]

the expedition as pilgrimage, and the expedition as conquest.[32] On the pilgrimage to Amarnāth the pilgrims sing *kīrtanas,* meditate on Śiva, etc.—as we used to meditate on Jesus at Canterbury School retreats.[33] The conquest idea, on the other hand, belongs to the romanticism of Rousseau, and before him, of Petrarch. The impact of the cave and *liṅga* ("I suddenly had the curious feeling," as the Yuvaraj wrote, "that I had been there before") is probably adequately explained by the rather obvious psychoanalytic interpretation: that is to say, the legendary interpretations of the force of the experience as being a revelation of the god are merely rationalizations—as are also the Western explanations given by our mountain conquerors for the fascination of the peak that is to be climbed. What is the lure of Mt. Everest? What is the lure of Śiva? Coomaraswamy has written respectfully of *le symbolisme qui sait* and disrespectfully of *le symbolisme qui cherche,* identifying the first with traditional and the second with modern art and thinking. Let us now say, rather, *le symbolisme qui pense qu'il sait,* and we are in better perspective.[34]

Following the film of Amarnāth came that of Ladakh—and here was something great. The Yellow Cap Lamas—"Devil" dancers—great horns—people greeting their Yuvaraj. On the wall of Karan Singh's thoroughly Occidental living room there hangs a lovely *tanka* of the Buddha in the *bhūmi-sparśa-mudrā,* framed handsomely and simply, as a picture, with a sort of tan silk matting and not a gilt but a golden-toned simple wooden frame, lightly decorated at the four corners.

A final film was a glimpse of the Indian folk-dance festival that is held in Delhi every January 25. (A *must* for Jean.) Among the glimpses there were three greats: the Santāls of Bengal, the Nāgas of Assam, and another group from Hyderabad—the latter pure Africa-Haiti: shoulder dances and precisely the rhythms.

Thursday, September 9

The sky is a bit overcast and Swami seems disinclined to adventure, so we are not doing anything until this afternoon. At breakfast he sounded off about how horrible he thought Indian girls looked in Western dress. There was such passion in his tone that it actually spoiled my breakfast. I find him an extraordinarily mixed-up person: he really hates the West but thinks he has some love for it. The whole Ramakrishna-Vivekananda movement has been heavily supported by Americans—India is being helped more than it will admit by America—and these fake non-dualists, who have transcended the sphere of the senses, so hate to think of their debt, that everything flashes and cracks. The disciple is supposed to take the dust from the feet of his guru voluntarily. America is the guru, India the disciple in all that matters today. But in order to stand erect, the Indian saintly one brings the great message of India (non-dualism and the harmony of religions) as a gift superior to that which he is receiving, and those mildly mixed-up souls who find consolation in the words become the symbols of America's discipleship. Meanwhile, the actual religiosity of India is dualistic *bhakti*—the *iṣṭadevatā* of this particular swami being, not God, but India—as that of the Jews is not God, but Jewry. This, I think, is perhaps the inevitable formula for the tribal-local as contrasted with the world religious.[35] That little glimpse of Ladakh, last evening, in Yuvaraj's film gave me a feeling of participation that I am unable to bring to these Hindu forms—though, God knows, if I actually visited Ladakh (which I can't, apparently, for political reasons: too close to Pakistan) I might well find that it too is not quite what it seems.

As for Hinduism and its future: I am convinced that in India it is secure. The Yuvaraj was at his evening *pūjā* when we arrived. He is a thoroughly religious young man—and Swami, by the way, has made a conquest. (My guess: when Nikhilananda leaves 94th St. he comes into the palaces of Yuvaraj Karan Singh of Kashmir, if the Yuvaraj is still in a fortunate position.) The closeness of these swamis to everybody in the government is amazing. The pandits, for patriotic reasons, are going to line our modern learning up with Indian, rather than European, history and philosophy—which should actually be even easier than the alignment of Christianity with science which our theologians think they have achieved.

In the main, I should say, popular Hinduism is much like popular Catholicism: a little dirtier and less well-organized, but with much that I find woefully familiar. The two additional features that I see are the ash-smeared *sadhus,* and the doctrine of non-dualism and the harmony of religions, which has no visible effect. Even the swamis are really dualistic patriots and worshippers.

Swami let drop a good observation, on the difference between the

American and the Indian social attitude: the American cherishes and expresses fellowship and equality, but the Hindu, reverence. That is the explanation, I believe, of the impact that I felt of the gentleness of the Orient.

Friday, September 10

Yesterday afternoon we drove out to see some of the nearby sights: the reservoir—with no water in it; the trout hatchery—with almost no trout in it; the Mughal gardens—with a lot of big chinar trees that in the past two or three hundred years have grown to such a height that the proportions of the garden design are completely lost—and again the water, which must have been the jewel in the setting of the garden, was completely lacking; and finally, another garden—a great affair in raised stages, which, if the central flow of water and fountains had been there, would have been a considerable spectacle. As we walked about the garden grounds we heard two or three guys hooting and shouting up at the trees, and then we saw that they were trying to kill the pretty green parrots with an old fashioned slingshot—the David and Goliath kind.

Mrs. D. and the Countess

Following this event we proceeded to the Srinagar Ramakrishna Mission where Swami delivered an excellent talk to a little outdoor gathering. Here he did what could be done to stress the contribution of America and Americans to the work of the Mission and to India. Only two questions were put to him; the first, by a somewhat aggressive youth of a type that I remembered having seen before: "You have said that Americans are idealistic; but we know also that they are pragmatists: how do you reconcile these two positions?" Reply: "The Americans are idealists; they are generous; they love freedom, they believe in equality, and they *help* people to these. And they are pragmatists because they believe that ideals that do not show themselves in life are worthless." The second question had to do simply with the actual work of Swami's mission in New York. What did he do there? He answered and the meeting closed.

A number of young students came up to talk with us. One of them said that the Ramakrishna Mission was the one institution that could bridge the way between America and India. He had formerly been impressed by Communist writings and despised America; but then he had read Vivekananda and had seen that Americans were good people.

The Indian press and government seem actually to be suppressing all news of America's contributions to India's fight for a decent level of life. Russia has not yet contributed a thing—and is India's hero. In yesterday's *Statesman* I read an article on the problem of the Outcastes in India. The case is much like that of the Negros in the south: legally there is no recognition of caste, but actually there is discrimination—job discrimination and educational discrimination, with no practical means of redress.

It is now time for me to pack and prepare myself for our return (by air, thank God) to Delhi.

From New Delhi to Calcutta

Saturday, September 11   **New Delhi**

The flight back was very pleasant. We saw, from the sky, the Golden Temple in Amritsar. The plane paused at Jummu, and Amritsar, and arrived in New Delhi last night at 7:10. *Sadhus*. The Mission. The Hotel Cecil, same room. After dinner I had a soda and salt with the young man who is manager, and talked with him of Kashmir, of poverty in a rich land, because the people were drained by the father and grandfather, he said, of the gentle young man Yuvaraj, who, with his wife, was performing *pūjā* when we arrived. My host showed me the swimming pool in this place, and I thought, a nice place to be with Jean when we come for the Dance Festival, January 26.

With Swami, at the Mission, I met a nice young man named Jnanendra Jain—who turned out to be the editor and publisher of *Seva Gram,* the little paper in Hindi with which I learned to read. His wife, apparently, knows one of the celebrated Indian dancers—and so, another lead for Jean. Today we are to meet Rajendra Prasad, the President of the Republic.

I went this morning to see Mr. William B. King, Isadora Bennett's friend, at the American Embassy. We talked of Jean's plans for a concert, and I was invited to luncheon tomorrow at the Kings' home. My thoughts are, now, that I should return to New Delhi in January to get things moving for Jean's concert. Jean could arrive here, give her concert, see the Dance Festival, proceed to Bombay, dance there, and then go on to the south.

Swami delivered his lecture tonight at the Mission before an audience of about 1,500, introduced by Madam Pandit. A young Mr. and Mrs. Anderson were present—here on the American Technical Aid to India program.

Monday, September 13

Yesterday morning I worked on the talk that I was to deliver in the evening at the Ramakrishna Mission.

At noon I went for lunch with the Kings, who are now dwelling in the stately, air-conditioned mansion of Mr. George Allen, the U.S. Ambassador to India. Also present were a Mr. and Mrs. Flanagan, Roman Catholics, just back from Holy Mass, who are in charge of U.S. Information and Cultural Accord (or something such) in India. It was evident after the first two minutes that neither the Flanagans nor the Kings knew anything whatsoever about Hinduism, though they had had a great number of glimpses of its operation; e.g. the sacrificial beheading of a water buffalo in Jaipur; the reaction of an Indian crowd to the death of a cow in an automobile collision, the obscurity of Radhakrishnan's book on Indian philosophy.[36]

Mrs. King had been to a Hindu concert the evening before, where she had discussed the possibility of a concert by Jean with various people, and the prospects seem favorable. A certain Mrs. Menon said, "Jean Erdman? Well, indeed!" Mrs. King wants information about Jean's recent work, and this should come from Isadora Bennett.

Following lunch I went with Mrs. King to an exhibition of Indian Home Industries, and saw a lot of pretty cloths and bowls, some Jagannātha Purī pictures, etc. Then I returned to the Cecil, to prepare myself for my talk.

The crowd was about the size of Swami's last evening and the talk went off rather well. The chairman introducing me was a Mr. Kamarkar, President of the New Delhi mission and a former cabinet officer, who, by chance had visited Sarah Lawrence in 1949. Following the talk a horde of young students flocked up to hear further words. I have the impression that the young crowd is considerably less anti-American than the Nehru contingent; that is to say, when they are not young Communists.

At luncheon this afternoon it was claimed that the Hindus who lose Hinduism become Marxists. This may be so. But if it is, then America's best bet here are the Hindus: not, perhaps, the old-guard *sadhus,* but certainly the Ramakrishna following.

After the talk I was both greatly relieved and greatly fatigued. I came back to the hotel for dinner, and went early to bed.

This morning, before I was up, Mrs. Davidson and the Countess took off with Swami for Haridvār. My day began with a conversation here at the hotel with a young man named K. Narasimhan, who has been pestering me for a meeting. The young man, rather nervous but charming, talked for an hour. He wants me to do something for him but can't bring himself to tell me what it is. The history: age twenty; five years ago evacuated from Pakistan to India, when he lost his father, mother, brother, and sister; taken in by the Ramakrishna Mission. Works as stenographer at Parliament for 250 rupees a month; is studying the *vīnā* with a master who charges forty rupees a month for lessons. There is no future in the Parliament job: enormous competition here for even the most menial posts (same story, approximately, as that of the Sikh Police Inspector who picked me up in the museum). The boy hopes that some day he may be playing the *vīnā* for cash of some kind—though, as he said, "I hate to sell my art."

He talked of the dance here. Bala Saraswati is the great one: rather old now. Kamala is the young hope: about eighteen or twenty. Rukmani Devi is a next: also rather old. Many Indian artists are going to Russia on cultural missions—and the U.S. refuses visas to those who have done so; so, it seems, the Indian boys and girls have to decide which state they would prefer to visit. (Situation comparable to that of the Arabs and Israel.) After an hour the youth departed, hoping to see me again when I return to New Delhi from my Indian tour.

September 14   **Mathurā**

Got off to a good start, and was sitting in the train, in my second-class (no first class in India now) compartment, when two Americans came—Mr. and Mrs. Cummings, a husband and wife of the Bible Belt variety—with nine pieces of luggage, including a violin. The man spoke Hindi to the coolies, very easily, and the lady too. They were definitely missionaries. The man was John Cage,[37] at the age of about sixty. A young Indian joined us, and for the better part of the trip he and the lady conversed; but she had her prayer book in her hand and presently went to that, whereupon the youth fell asleep. Meanwhile, Mr. Cummings told me of his visions (literally) of Christ, with a charming, boyish, forthright confidence that he was now fit to be a witness unto..., etc. His exposition of his experience was liberally ornamented with Biblical quotations and there was no question in his mind but that his way was *it*. He was a Pentecostalist. He had been a missionary largely among the Muslims, who had argued back hard, asking how he could bear witness, etc., if he hadn't witnessed. And so he had called upon Christ, arguing with his deity that if he was to bear witness to Christ among these people, Christ should allow him at least as much of an experience as that which the twelve—who had already witnessed him in the flesh—received on Pentecost, when the Spirit descended in tongues of flame and they spoke in tongues. Well, the long and the short of it is, that Christ came through, and he had a wonderful experience, and spoke in an unknown tongue, and then later his wife had a wonderful experience too (she was now reading her prayer book) and they were very happy missionaries (obviously they were).

When, later, he began on Hinduism, and the importance of the Christian concept of personality, I said that I thought their experience was of the transcendent aspect of divinity, the unutterable. "Yes," he said, "they always retreat to that position." "It isn't a retreat," I said, "it is the positive content of their experience: it is affirmed in all of their writings. Moreover," I went on, "for me, who have had no experience, it is not to judge between such an experience as yours and such an experience as that of the Indian tradition. I simply compare them—and if I have a faith in such things, it is that what the Indians have experienced *this way,* Christians experience *your way:* the two are glimpses of a mystery of the spirit." But the dear man had nothing in his head but his Christ and his Christian work. He asked if the college in which I taught comparative religion was sectarian. Mathurā came, and I got out with their good wishes. They would be seeing the Taj Mahal tonight by moonlight and I should probably meet them there.

The Mathurā adventure was something!

My porter brought my things to the second-class waiting room, and I gave the Sikh attendant one rupee to keep them under his surveillance. Then I took a tonga to the museum. Arrival at 10:00; museum not yet open. An attendant pointed around to the side, so my driver conducted me around there and a gate was open. Simultaneously, an English lady who had arrived in a car was hoping to get in and she followed. I had the experience of going through the Curzon Museum of Archaeology, Mathurā, attended, and sometimes closely followed, by my tonga driver, half a dozen kids, and three museum guards.

My impression of the sculpture was less strong than I had expected it to be. I think the exhibition of these important pieces is simply no exhibition at all. Too many things in too little space. Also, the actual carving on the early *yakṣas* was, from some of the less photographed angles, rather sketchy. Perhaps the light was not quite right. In any case, I went through the museum carefully, pleased to see a number of fine things that I recognized from the Coomaraswamy photos. Even the celebrated Gupta Buddha[38] was hard to experience, however, and I concluded with a distinct sense of disappointment. If the better pieces had been isolated and the others either stored or placed as they are, but in a separate room, the effect would have been much better.

The curator, Mr. K. B. Bajpai, was not in; but I had a look into his office, and could see that he knew very well how to arrange things for himself. It was a very nice, spacious office, with the desk in the center, on a rug that left a handsome margin around the edges: bookcases around the walls, and well placed pictures—including, high on the right, that photo of Coomaraswamy that appears on the dust jacket of *Time and Eternity*. The office and photograph made me feel at home in this spot, in a way, somehow, that the art did not!

Following my somewhat disappointing visit to the museum, I said to my driver, "Hotel," hoping that I might find someone who could speak English and from whom I might procure a bit of help—for my Hindi was a complete blank: I was unable even to formulate the simplest problem (I have not had time even to look into my Hindi books since my last lesson, a week before my departure from New York.) I was driven through a pretty cluttered series of streets to a hotel; but I entered a shop across from it—a kind of accounting office—and found a very gracious gentleman who told me that Brindavan (which I wanted to see) was only five miles away, and that it would be quite possible to go in a tonga. The fee was arranged for ten rupees, and I started away.

Five plus five miles in a tonga on a hot day, from 10:45 A.M. until about 3:00 P.M.—too much.

The country is perfectly flat—whatever forest may once have been here is completely gone. After about a mile we paused at a large new temple of precisely the Birla Temple type—same stone, same art and architecture. The main image was of Kṛṣṇa holding a *cakra,* like a saucer, on the tip of his right forefinger: black image dressed in red cloth, with a garland. There was a stone sign, inlaid in both Hindi and English, that appeared at several points around the outside and at the doors of the temple, welcoming all Indians of all sects, but warning: "Spitting, deciphering and disfiguring strictly forbidden."

Here we picked up a chap who offered to be my guide to the temples of Brindavan, and spoke an almost intelligible English. He followed my tonga on a bicycle, occasionally shouting out the names of the places we were passing. I felt quite romantic about Kṛṣṇa's boyhood. The peasants were in the fields and along the roads. We passed a couple of camels and a little baboon sat by the roadside like a very small man.

Then we came to Brindavan and a wildly rushing visit to the temples began. I thought of Jerusalem: same idea only a little shoddier. A great number of hideous temples. We climbed around the outside of one that had a number of southern-style *gopuras,* the Rangji Temple, biggest in the city, built between 1845–1851, and had a good view of the whole city from one of its towers. The Govind Dev Temple ruin, c. A.D. 1590, I saw from the road: a considerably better style. Next, I was conducted through a run of narrow streets, and entered a place with votive stones all over the floor. Leaving my shoes, I was conducted into a small room with a number of priests sitting around before a shrine, which was lighted for me. Within were five images—father and mother in the rear and rather large, three children before—Kṛṣṇa, Bālarāma, Subhadrā—all crude and tawdry, dressed and completely unalive. I was told that this was one of the oldest temples in Brindavan and these very old images, and I was to make a donation of three-quarters of a rupee. When I offered three-quarters I was told that that was the minimum. Having seen a good deal of misery on the streets and believing for a moment what I had been told, namely, that the money was for the poor, I gave six rupees and annas (about two dollars) and was given *prasāda,* asked to write my name and that of my father in the big book, and pleasantly dismissed.

At the place of departure, there was a scattering of annas on a tablet. I was told that four annas had to be given here. And then there was the shoe boy: two annas. "No more temples," I said to my guide. "Back to the tonga." He conducted me around a few corners and before I knew it I was in a second "very old" temple, where I was given almost exactly the same story—and I was now sore. "I told you," I said to my guide who was sitting beside me, "no more. I will not give six rupees or three rupees." But to save the situation I gave two: refused however to sign my name in the book—took the *prasāda* angrily, and left. We returned to the tonga. I was shown the place (tree and pond) "where Kṛṣṇa dove from the tree to kill Kāliya"!39 The guide demanded ten rupees (like a fool, I had failed to ask his fee at the start), and I sat in the tonga while my driver finished eating.

The drive back to Mathurā was distinguished, pleasantly, by two events. When we passed the little baboon the driver tossed him some food, and a whole tribe of his kind came down from all the trees; little mothers with their babies hanging to their necks, underneath; and they were still coming the last we saw them. Then, suddenly, I heard in loud duet: "Baksheesh Sahib!..." on and on, and turning to look back found two youngsters, a boy and a girl, hanging on to my tonga, running magnificently, and shouting into my face. When they had run about one hundred and fifty yards, I handed each two annas and they let me go.

Passing the museum again, I thought for a moment that it might be worth stopping to see if the curator had come in, but decided against it. I was dead tired, disgruntled, and had a bit of a headache. So I returned to the station. My train to Agra was to leave at 7:00 P.M., which meant that I had four hours to spend. But when I entered the waiting room the Sikh attendant drew a large easy chair up to a table for me, and a little boy brought me tea and cake. I drank all the ice water out of my thermos, I had a little doze, and I woke up about four, feeling fine. Then—chastened by the adventures of the day—I got out my Berlitz Hindi book and reviewed the first forty pages before it began to get dark.

Life in the waiting room and on the station platform was something wonderful. People sleeping, changing their clothes, monks, soldiers, whatnots. When the trains arrive, they get in and out from both sides—the platform side and the other. They hop down onto the tracks and run across. Guys are urinating everywhere. Vendors are shouting everywhere, with stoves smoking on their heads, trays of cakes etc.—and wicker stands in their hands upon which they set their trays, taking them down from their heads. Two earlier trains for Agra passed, but they were only third-class and I let them go. I was having a fine time at the station. Then at seven my train came and I was off for Agra.

Another good hotel, Laurie's: same management as the Cecil in Delhi. The taxi driver who took me from the train offered to drive me to the Taj for seven rupees, after dinner. I got cleaned up, had dinner, and went to the Taj. Full moon. Really lovely. Like a fool I had left my camera at the hotel—could easily have taken a picture. At the gate, I met the Cunninghams, who helped me get past a little guide named Jimmy, so that I might see the Taj alone. And I remained about an hour. Went down into the crypt. Heard all the stories, paid all the little tolls, and returned to the hotel for a good night's sleep.

September 15   Agra

Mother's birthday: last year Jean and I were in Paris.

Agra, definitely, is for tourists, and the hotel reveals, even at this early, pre-tourist season, a number of the standard American types: the fat ladies with their husbands, from Ohio or New York, the drinks before dinner crowd, etc. At the entrance to the hotel sits a man with a snake—once it was two men, one with a cobra in a basket, the other with a mongoose on a string. For a sum, one could see the mongoose and cobra fight.

My driver took me to the Fort, where I had an excellent guide, then to the Taj—where Jimmy got hold of me, and finally to the tomb of I'timad-ud-daula across the river. In the afternoon I decided to go to Fatehpur Sikri by bus. I received my information from the Tourist Bureau, and took a bicycle-rickshaw to the bus terminal. I was about an hour ahead of time, and so, went for a walk through town.

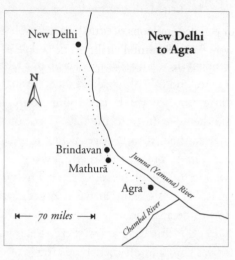

Quite a town! Camels here and there. One naked old man blandly walking around. One young woman with a rather stupid look and her head shaved, wearing a dirty sari without bodice, and the end of the sari simply flung over one shoulder. Cows and water buffalo everywhere, of course. Streets and streets of shops. A great emphasis on shoe shops and shoe manufacture. Horrible food displays. Kids, half or totally naked, everywhere. I took another rickshaw back to the stinking bus terminal. Men's urinals and women's urinals: the air was thick.

The bus was full of noisy and pleasant males on their way back to their villages. Beside me, however, in the "upper class" seat was a surly Indian gentleman, who was totally out of the picture. It took an hour and a quarter, with very long stops at two or three villages, for us to reach Fatehpur Sikri, so that I had very little time in which to see the buildings. A tall youth showed me the old walled city of Akbar in excellent style, and I returned to the road just in time to catch the bus home.

These two days have given me a rather close look at the village life of this part of India. The level of dirt and well-being is about that of the Pueblos of New Mexico, I should say. This, apparently, is the basic level of India. The peasant life, in fact, might be said to have determined the character, also, of the cities: cows, water buffalo herds, goat, donkey, and sheep droves even on the main streets. But in the cities one finds a heavily populated level even lower than this: that of the beggars and the utterly destitute. These two levels are met by that of the tiny shopkeeps in the towns and cities. Millions of people—millions of little jobs well done—and the total is a curiously un-systematized cultural vitality. The people in their misery and absolutely gentle and strong. And yet the whole thing has something crazy about it, which is epitomized in this nutty business of the cows. India will never become a modern nation as long as these cows are here—even the trains have to watch out for them. It is the cows that slow down the whole pace and make for a kind of general Bohemia. With them, naked old men and everything else is possible. Without them, India will be out of her troubles!

My train left at ten-something, and at Gwalior, 12:20 A.M., I took a tonga to the hotel—an Indian-run hotel this time. The porter was sound asleep at the entrance. The door was open for me. I was conducted to my suite of rooms (glorious, but with practically all of the mechanical elements somewhat out of order), and went right off to sleep.

Thursday, September 16 — Gwalior

I woke up to rain—a strong pouring. The man who brought my bed tea said it was going to rain all day, and for several days. I thought of giving up my Khajurāho plans; but decided to wait before making my decision. I wrote all morning in my diary. But by lunchtime it was clear and I went with a guide to the fine tomb of Muhammad Guus—with a squad of soldiers sleeping in its verandah; then up to the Fort. On the way up to the Fort, the gigantic Jain statues of Gwalior. On the plateau of the Fort, a perfectly charming series of Hindu palaces and little temples including a frightening subterranean chamber where Prince Murad was hanged from what formerly had been the rings of a swing, by his younger brother Aurangzeb. Yesterday I saw where this same Aurangzeb imprisoned and then blinded his father Akbar.[40]

Also the tomb of the musician Tansen. (The tree that is supposed to give one a singer's voice is no longer there.) By far the most interesting adventure so far.

The Archaeological Museum has a fine lot of Śuṅga, Gupta, and later pieces—not too well displayed, however, in the rooms of what was once a palace. Many pieces of sculpture with which I was familiar turned up. The bronzes are exceptionally interesting: many Hindu and Buddhist Tantric pieces—crudely labeled, and exhibited in glass cases (some with rippled glass) that make it very difficult to see.

The Gwalior palaces give a somewhat richer and more charming effect than the Muslim palaces that I have seen. It is clear, also, that the basic architectural principles of the Muslim works in India are not very different— if different at all—from the Hindu. The Muslims had a much more grandiose eye than the Hindus for geometrical spatial arrangements of buildings over and against each other; also, apparently, for all their abhorrence of sensuous pictures and images, a much stronger emphasis on actual erotic enjoyment: checker boards with girls for pieces—hide-and-seek buildings—ponds where girls would sit playing lutes while Akbar bathed, etc. etc. The Hindu princes may have had all this too—but it doesn't show in the buildings: or rather, perhaps yes; for what went on in these curious little swing rooms?

The palace was a new experience for me; and the little temples that I saw were charming. The day gave me a pleasant feeling of having broken through the Muslim crust, at last, into the Hindu world.

Friday, September 17   Gwalior–Allahabad

A railroad record: Gwalior to Allahabad in fifteen hours and forty minutes—a distance of about 250 miles—average rate of travel, about fifteen miles an hour. But I saw the countryside and the villages.

I got up at 5:30 A.M., had tea and toast, walked to the station beside a man who was carrying my luggage on his head, and boarded my train. Two sleepers in the lower berths. I opened my bed roll on an upper, and lay down. At 6:00 A.M. change trains at Jhansi, in the pouring rain. We arrived at Harpalpur, the place from which I was supposed to take a bus to Khajurāho at about 9:00 A.M. But the station master refused to take charge of my baggage (it was a minute and dirty county station, about as big as Mast Hope,[41] in which there would not be any place for me to sleep—and, besides, it was raining a little), so I decided to pass up Khajurāho and go

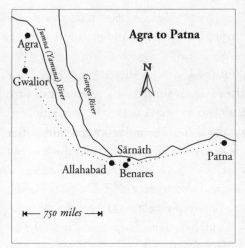

Agra to Patna

N

Agra

Jumna (Yamuna) River

Gwalior

Ganges River

Sārnāth

Patna

Allahabad   Benares

|◄── 750 miles ──►|

on to Allahabad. At Manikpur I had tea and a cake of chocolate (my only bite since 3:45 A.M.) and a little chat with a gent at the station. He said that the richest part of India agriculturally was that between the Ganges and the Jumna. The area that I was in, however, was rocky and poor. The people looked poor, all right, but they have looked poor everywhere I have been.

The rain now was coming down hard, and the rivers that the train crossed were flowing, full of muddy water, between sprawling banks. Made me think of the Kansas-Nebraska area. And the people looked like figures from eighteenth-century travelers' engravings of India—the men with moustaches and shaved heads, save for the orthodox hair tuft at the place of the cowlick; wearing dhotis, either with or without a shirt; and the women, of course, simply bundled in their usually rather drab and dirty saris. (I find that though the sari may look fine as a sort of surprise in a New York drawing room, as a regular thing it is a dismal flop.) Particularly notable following the rains was the vivid bird life all along the way: the most beautiful herons and cranes in every field and puddle.

At one of the stations before Manikpur, a young couple with their baby got into the compartment and conversed a bit in English together. The baby slept soundly; the girl paid close attention to her needlework; the husband looked out the window. At Manikpur they waited, not far from me, in the "Refreshments" building—the girl again strictly devoted to her needlework. I have the impression that men and women do not have much in common in this country, except their children, whom they treat very sweetly. I notice few couples. Usually it's men together and bunches of women together. (At the Mission talks, the men and women sat separately.)

When I finally boarded my train I was placed in a compartment with three large gents—a Sikh and two others. One of the others invited me to sit on the bench with him, and recognized me as American (in fact every-one does). We conversed in a strong yet friendly fashion, and I got the whole Indian picture, I think, of the U.S.A:

(1) Not Russia and China, but the U.S.A., is the power itching for a fight. The concept of Asia for the Asians is simply an *a priori* in this part of the world, so that China's claim to Formosa is simply unquestioned. Chiang Kai Shek is despised, and the U.S. support of him is regarded as a belligerent act. (2) The U.N. is not really a union of all nations, but a clique, representing a limited set of interests. (3) American aid to India is a device to create military allies, and also to get rid of American goods, so that the wheels of our industry can keep turning. (4) The war criminal trials were a farce: Roosevelt and Churchill should have been tried. (5) The two atom bombs on two cities in Japan were dropped *after* peace negotia-tions had been opened, as a military test of the force of this weapon. (6) War is on the way right now, and will probably break in two or three years. (7) This war will finish both Russia and the U.S.A. (8) The hot spots are Formosa and Pakistan.

This gentleman, Mr. Ghosh of Calcutta, is an engineer, and has no love for the British. He has a cousin who was in a British jail during the troubles, and is now an invalid—from what they did to him: they made him sleep naked between two cakes of ice, one above, one below; and they hung him from the ceiling by the wrists, with weights on his ankles, so that now all his joints are ruptured. Mr. Ghosh, also, was born in Dacca, and tells the old tale of what Warren Hastings did to the weavers of Dacca.[42] He invited me to visit him in Calcutta, and we exchanged addresses.

Saturday, September 18   **Allahabad**

After breakfast I took a cycle-rickshaw to the museum, which is full of both good and bad: the bad is modern—and includes the Roerich Collection that used to hang in New York. The good is a fine lot of sculpture, from Bhārhut to Khajurāho; and a wonderful collection of Mughal and Rajput paintings. Practically everything is displayed against the light or in glass cabinets, so that it is impossible to see.

Following my visit to the museum, I asked my boy to peddle me to the Fort, where there is an Aśoka pillar: but we found that the Fort was now

Restricted Military Property—and so I asked to go to the junction of the Ganges and the Jumna. Presently and suddenly four shouting men were hooked to my rickshaw, running beside me. They wanted me to ride in their boat. Finally I gave in and was whisked up an embankment and into one of the large skiffs that lined the shore.

Four men rowed, one steered, and we soon were out in the vast stretch of muddy water where the two rivers (waters of different colors) joined—just off a little island formed of the silt, where a colony of little hut-shrines, with staffs and banners, could be seen, filled with people attending to various religious tasks. I was told to take a sip of the water and place a paper rupee on the water as an offering. I obeyed, and one of the boatmen, with a laugh, took up the rupee.

We went around behind the island and put to shore, at a point below the wall of the Fort, where there was an entrance. A childish figure of Kālī, with her tongue out, was on the shore—a kind of doll, which an old woman had set up and was guarding—before which money might be dropped. Also there was a man there with a cow that had a curious loose growth coming out of its neck with an extra set of horns at the end. The man was exhibiting his animal and collecting coins. And there were the usual saintly beggars—as at Brindavan and Jerusalem.

I followed a guide who took me through the portal along a narrow walk between high walls, to an open area, where a lot of voices could be heard coming up through air vents, out of the ground. "Underground Temple," I was told; and so it was. I removed my shoes and went down with a swarm of pilgrims. I was conducted through the underground vestibules, where there were dozens of assorted images: a few old pieces in a style of c. A.D. 1000–1200 (dancing Gaṇeśa, Śiva, Pārvatī, Viṣṇu, etc.) but also many curious folk-pieces of gods whose names I had never heard. The full list of gods: Dharmrājā, Annapūrṇā, Viṣṇu, Lakṣmī, Gaṇeśa, Bālamukunda, Durvāsa, Prayāgrājā, Satyanarāyaṇa, Kāla Bhairava, Dattatreya, Narasiṁha, Śaṅkarajī, Surya Narāyaṇa, Hanumān, Yamunā, Siddha Nātha (a *liṅga*), Gaṅgā, Kubera, Veda Vyāsa, Pārvatī (with the child Gaṇeśa), Gorakha Nātha, Agni Deva, Venimādhava, Sarasvatī, Ram and Sītā with Lakṣmana, Śeṣanāga, Yamarājā, Jagannātha and two or three more *liṅgas*.

I returned to my boat, purchasing on the way a picture of the temple with its gods, and was rowed ashore. A quibble over the fees, and then a rickshaw ride back to my hotel.

The name of the underground temple is Akṣaya Vṛkṣa, and it is the temple (I now read in *Murray's Guide*) of the "Undying Banyan."[43] The tree was described by Hsüen-tsang (A.D. 605–664): "In the midst of the city," he states, "stood a Brahmanical temple to which the presentation of a single piece of money procured as much merit as that of a thousand pieces elsewhere. Before the principal room of the temple was a tree surrounded by the bones of pilgrims who had sacrificed their lives there." All seems to be associated with some sacred banyan Akṣaya Vṛkṣa. The pilgrims, like myself, went from image to image as their guide, like mine, rapidly named the deities. Many placed little coins at the feet of the figures, touched the feet and then touched their heads.

The Ganges at this place is one-and-a-half miles broad, and the Jumna half a mile broad. "The shallower and more rapid Ganges [on which my trip commenced] is of a muddy color, the Jumna is bluer with a deeper bed. The Māgha Melā, a religious fair of great antiquity, is held at Triveṇī every year, between 15th January and 15th February...and every twelfth year the festival is known as the Kumbha Melā." Here, then, was that great calamity of this year when hundreds were killed in a great crush. Off these shores, also, is the place where Gandhi's ashes were consigned to the waters. Well, it was a considerable spot to which I was conducted by my lunatic boatmen: and now I do not begrudge them their fee of—twenty rupees! Very tired, I simply remained in my room, sleeping and writing, all afternoon.

Allahabad, I find, is a comparatively clean and orderly city—quite modern, really (at least, what I have seen of it), except, of course, for the ubiquitous cows. I have a feeling that there must have been an American military post here during the war, because everything has a rather American tone. My hotel is an Indian hotel—with the radio playing American jazz and the girl at the desk (daughter of the manager) wearing a Western dress.

And I should record that when my train pulled, last night, into the big station, I felt—after my week of little whistle stops, quaint villages, and rural scenery—definitely at home and greatly relieved. The city, I guess, is the normal place for man, because shaped by man to the needs of man;

whereas the country is simply a transitional zone, which man inhabits between his state as animal and his full estate as man. (A bit of heresy, to contradict the Romantic "back to Nature.")

Sunday, September 19   Allahabad–Benares

I begin to think that the main division between the past and the future of civilization is that of *literacy*—made possible by the machine (the press), and representing the viewpoint of the scientific method.[44] In India, Jerusalem, and Lourdes, we see the survival of the past. The dark side of literacy is Yellow Journalism and Demagoguery. Meeting the minds of the not-yet-quite literate. I do not know how far the crude proletariat atheism of the Russians and the late nineteenth century counts in all this, but perhaps it should be reckoned to the dark side of literacy.

The chief spiritual problem of literacy is to retain the positive values of the ancient mythological mode of pedagogy without falling back into superstition. This problem is being faced by the Zimmer-Jung-Eranos team.[45]

The educated preachers of religion today are the protectors of the Western soul, for which an effective new pedagogy has not yet been devised. In the past, the creative, vitalizing principle in religion was the intelligent thinking and self-discipline of the élite. Today this élite is not religious. The religious, consequently, have declined to the level of popular superstition, and on two levels: that of bourgeois religiosity, and that of folk or peasant religiosity.[46]

And so now to Benares.

No second-class car on the train, so I rode third class: not uncomfortable, though a hard seat; and not as smelly as second class, because the toilet was down the other end of the car instead of immediately next door. Nice people, as always; mostly of the farmer type, with a couple of something else: fine old gentlemen (one spoke English very well) with Śiva marks on their foreheads. One had his white beard knotted curiously underneath.

Arrival in Mughal Sarai about 3:20. Another case of very slow travel: three hours for about seventy-five miles. Then a *tonga,* some eight miles, to Clark's Hotel, Benares. Tired, I showered, had dinner, and went early to bed.

A few thoughts on the road and in the hotel. I am now realizing that much of what I at first thought was great poverty is only the norm of peasant life in a pre-industrial society—that, let us say, is the norm of India. Below that, however, there is real poverty in abundance. There is no bottom here to the distance one can drop.

Everywhere, one meets with the same gentleness and general good humor, also an easy friendliness with life's dirt, reminding me, I think, more of Italy than of any place else I've ever seen. Again a fundamental peasant quality? On the other hand, a certain very hard attitude toward each other in the matter of money. The tipping of porters, etc., is on a cruel level. I watched a tea-vendor wait for the last *paisa* from a blind beggar boy before he would hand out his cup of tea.

At the hotel a radio was playing American jazz music, with advertisements, etc., in an English accent, broadcast from somewhere in India. A curious shock: but not unwelcome either. Someone sang *Mammy* (can you believe it?)—and I thought, not a bad song at all in Annapūrṇa's city! "I'd go a million miles for one of your smiles, my Ma...ammy." And the town is full of pilgrims; full also of Indian holy pictures no less awful, as art, than Jolson's *Mammy*.

At the hotel, also, a number of American guests: one male with an appallingly coarse-looking, leather-tanned, heavily developed face. A very different type than the noble Indian faces I had been seeing on the peasants. But then, also, a few non-peasant Indians are in the hotel also—and they are nothing better than the Americans. On the other hand, when I think of Vermont farmers, etc., it seems to me that we may have a touch of the peasant type also: just a touch, however, since our peasantry is not of the primary stock, for the most part, but rather a deterioration from originally bourgeois immigrants.

Monday, September 20   Benares

I went in the morning, by cycle-rickshaw, to the Ramakrishna Mission, where I found Swami and the ladies. Mrs. D. was laid up with a broken toe, fractured in a slip at that temple-dock at Allahabad. I was conducted through the premises. Impressive: a considerable hospital and old-folks home with an ashram attached; many monks, doing hospital work: about a thousand patients treated a day—I went through some of the wards. The Ramakrishna Mission is definitely a strong and respectable organization; and it now is enjoying the support of the Indian government. It seems likely that this kind of work will continue to grow, and will represent a valid and effective adjustment of Hinduism to the modern world. Compare the work of the Franciscans, Little Sisters of the Poor, St. Vincent's Hospital, etc.

Stayed for lunch at the ashram (sattvic food and edible); then had my cycle-rickshaw take me to the river, where I visited a couple of the ghats. And here again, I was properly impressed—by the faces and quietness of the people at the Ganges. Strange little streets leading right to the water; little shrines close to the river; a young cow standing on a platform; people sitting; a few dipping into the water; many with forehead markings. Boatmen approached me, but my reply was "not today," and they didn't overdo their pressing (for a pleasant change).

I returned to the hotel and rested. Worked a little on proofs and Hindi and went to bed. The weather is fearfully humid and hot, and I seem to get tired very fast.

Tonight I feel that in Benares I have found something closer to the India I came to see than anything I saw in New Delhi. A great inconvenience, however, is the distance of the hotel from everything. One can

Benares along the Ganges

understand it, though—one can also understand the British dinner-jacket formula. The whole pattern of Indian life is so alien—and dirty—and so many of the people are sick—that, unless one is bent on "losing oneself" it is not possible to move right into the native cities. These English "cantonments," furthermore, show what India would be if the Indians would pay a bit of attention to space: and I note that they are supplying the model for much of the building of the new India.

A few little notes: I perceive that my table cloth is slightly dirty, from the people who were at the table before me. In no hotel that I have visited have the fixtures been in perfect repair—except, perhaps, the Hotel Cecil in New Delhi, where the only trouble was the archaic character of the fixtures. The meals, in general, are to be graded "poor to fair." Too bad it was the English kitchen (the worst in the Occident) that was introduced to India. I am sure that there is not a really decent place to eat in the whole subcontinent—and that the Indians don't even know it. My formula for touring in India now is: *the most interesting and least enjoyable country in the world.*

Tuesday, September 21

This afternoon immediately after lunch, I set off for Benares Hindu University with my same cycle-rickshaw to meet a Professor Das Gupta[47] who was going to show me around. It took over an hour to complete the trip, however, and the campus was huge, so I failed to find him.

I paused first at the Museum, and asked my way; then went to the Arts Building and goofed around. Went finally into a room marked "Philosophy," where I had seen a huge, light-colored monk (plump and about 6 ft. 9 in. tall), and this man met me at the door.

"*Guten tag,*" he said. "*Sind Sie Deutscher?*"

"*Nein,*" I answered, "*Ich bin Amerikaner.*"

"*Aber Sie sprechen sehr gutes Deutsch,*" he said.

He was Viennese—now a Śaṅkara monk—and knew Swami Nikhilananda; his name: Swami Agehananda.[48]

And so my first encounter with India's pandits was in German.

On the wall of the office were photos of Jung, Freud, Charles Moore of the University of Hawai'i, Radhakrishnan, and some others. The Viennese swami is teaching philosophy at the college and attended to a few students while I sat and recovered a bit from my rickshaw ride. He failed to help me find Das Gupta, and presently, after cruising a bit more around the campus, I returned home.

My sins must be dropping from me, because I begin to feel that I am recovering something of a repose that I remember from long, long ago: I don't know when. Part of it, of course, is that I am taking things very easily. Part of it is that no more jobs-to-do are piling in on me. But there is something more than that to it, and I think it's very nice.

Wednesday, September 22

I spent the morning preparing the talk for this afternoon, then took my rickshaw to Vasant College at Raj Ghat, at the northern terminus of Benares, where the Varuna River enters the Ganges. A Miss Telang met me and introduced me to her brother and another gentleman—all teachers at the college. Then we had a nice Indian lunch—on the mild side as to heat. I was shown about the establishment: the little ones were at lunch; sitting in a large circle on the floor of their kindergartens—very cute. I saw the art class, a dance class, a music class, and glimpsed several lecture rooms at work. The whole effect, quite idyllic and pleasant. The youngsters learn history and geography of India, mathematics, music, Hindi, a bit of Sanskrit, science, and a few other items. I noticed some emphasis on crafts (leatherwork).

I had been told that my lecture would be for faculty and a few upper classmen. Actually, a large auditorium was full of students sitting on the floor: three quarters girls, in front; one quarter boys. My first lecture without shoes. The questions were cute: What is done in America about the health and recreation of the students? What about military training? Have you been to Red China? What do American students think of Indian students? What about sport? Do you teach gardening? Are students interested in music? What do you think of Indian students? I had tea with some members of the faculty and took my rickshaw home.

Thursday, September 23   Sārnāth

Took my rickshaw at 9 A.M. to Sārnāth, about five miles: a beautiful museum, and a beautiful visit, with my scrawny rickshaw man as guide. Returned to the hotel by 1 P.M, and at 5 P.M. I took my rickshaw to the

Durgā (Monkey) Temple. The priests sort of fastened onto me, and I was sitting with one of them in the rickshaw, when a car stopped: Swami and his party! Pleasant greetings, and our separate cruises continued.

The whole political level of the visit, has, I hope, been passed. My last observation on the subject: Nehru told Swami, when Swami visited him, that it might well be that China and India would grow geographically. "Strong nations always grow." And so what has this to do with the Peaceful Coexistence formula? Answer: Peaceful Coexistence is the *Artha Śāstra's sāman*—singing a soothing song, till strength is available for *daṇḍa*, hitting.

As I look at this country and think of America, I see two very different worlds. The two cultures have stemmed from the conditions of two very different sets of historical circumstances. As I stated in my Delhi lecture— Indian philosophy, inasmuch as it has influenced the American mind, has done so only to the extent of giving fresh stimulus to ideas that were present in the American philosophy in the first place, e.g. a metaphysical tone to the "all men are equal" idea. Comparably, the American machines, democratic principles, etc. are going to be taken by India in her own way.

At Sārnāth, the lovely spirituality of the Buddhist images was immensely impressive. I visited the museum, where I was addressed by a Hindu gentleman who was there with his wife and family. When he learned I was from New York his wife couldn't drag him away. And I soon was wishing that she would succeed. He was full of advice for me, as to how to see India. Really a charming gent, but enough was enough. He was tall, lean, with shining eyes, a prodigious voice, and a heroic flourish. A kind of Bengali Don Quixote. When his wife finally walked out and later sent the guard in to get him, he left, but soon was back; then at last left for keeps. "If I were alone," he said, "we could talk; but, you see: I am with my wife!"and then a Jain temple: quite modern: the guard showed me the main image: obviously Ṛṣabhanātha (with the bull symbol on the pedestal) but the guard declared it was Pārśvanātha.

Then on to a modern Buddhist temple built with money from Ceylon, Japan, and Honolulu: pictures of the Buddha's life by a Japanese artist. The Chinese Buddhist temple I saw next was somewhat different in spirit: the pictures around the walls, however, were trite English prints of the Buddha's life in a semi-Indian style.

Finally I came to the Monkey Temple mentioned above. The same impression overcame me here as in Brindavan: the main interest of the priest was that I should put some money down on the altars. He had a couple of worn heads, from perhaps the Gupta period, and a coarse statue of Hanumān. He wanted rupees for each. I gave him one rupee for all—and seeing that I knew what he was doing, he finally had to smile.

I noticed that the place where a goat is sacrificed every morning (and a buffalo on feast days) is situated about where the *nandi* is placed in a Śiva temple compound. So: *nandi,* the sacrifice, has become the vehicle of the god (a general law here for *vāhana?*). Is the buffalo sacrifice (beheaded with one stroke of the priest's sword) related to the theme of Durgā, slayer of the buffalo demon? Here is a great sacrifice, as in voodoo. Mediterranean goddess associated with goats (see Ras Shamra bas relief); goat sacrifice belongs to same culture context as pig sacrifice, in the Melanesian context, cf. Sebseb of Malekula. It is said that earlier than the goat sacrifice in this temple was a human sacrifice (Polynesian context).[49]

Next to the Monkey Temple, across the pond, is a white marble tomb, to Swami Bhāskarānanda—the only object of beauty that I have seen in Benares.

Friday, September 24

Submitted this morning, before breakfast, to the quiet barber who has been pestering me every day: and he gave me a very good haircut. I felt like an eighteenth-century gentleman with the barber visiting me in my own rooms.

After breakfast my rickshaw man carried me off toward the river. Near the Daśāśvamedha Ghat he stopped, got off his cycle, and fetched me a man with yellow and white lines on his forehead, who was to be my guide for the trip. This gentleman saw me into a skiff, climbed in beside me, and named the buildings and ghats as we passed them: first, upstream close to shore, then downstream, out in the river, then back upstream again (with great difficulty) to the Daśāśvamedha Ghat, or rather something close to it, where we disembarked. I paid the boatman and followed my guide through a labyrinth of narrow alleys, populated as heavily with cows as with Hindus. We saw the Nepalese temple of Paśupati Nātha (the so-called Temple of Love) with its mildly obscene little carvings, the Golden Temple, the Jñāna Vāpī (Well of Knowledge), Temple of Annapūrṇa and

Temple of Sākhī Vināyaka—all crowded among narrow cow-filled alleys. Cows were in the temples. Beggars lined the walls of the alleys. There was one spectacular row of some thirty widows, sitting in silence with their empty rice bowls. A fantastic place. I was again pursued by priests for baksheesh, and was finally glad to get out. We then passed through alleys of shops and finally sat down for a nice warm Coca-Cola.

My rickshaw next brought me to the Ramakrishna Mission, where I found Swami down with a slight fever and sore throat, Mrs. D. with her foot still in a cast, and the Countess with some kind of stomach ailment. I had lunch with the ladies—a slightly palatable monk's meal (no wonder they all feel ill!)—and decided that I had just about finished my visit to Benares. So I told them I'd see them all in Calcutta and pushed off.

I spent the afternoon asleep and writing to Jean. They had a letter from her over at the Mission. Nice news about Bard.[50]

Benares traffic: cows, goats, a few dogs, stray chickens, occasional camels, millions of bicycles and cycle-rickshaws; occasional cars, bullock carts, donkeys, guys everywhere taking leaks, kids shitting in the gutter, hundreds of little shops full of people, other shops, larger, nicely rugged, with gentleman-shopkeepers peacefully lounging, often reading books.

The temple traffic: a great business of tossing flowers at gods, touching their feet, sipping water, and passing along. I now want to see Lourdes.

Saturday, September 25   · Benares–Patna

I think what strikes me most about Benares is the combination of ancient Indian religiosity with the new institutions of learning. The city is full of schools and colleges: Vasant College, Hindu University, Anglo-Bengali College, and others; also, Theosophical Society, and the Ramakrishna Mission. It is definitely a focus of a typically Indian spiritual ferment.

One month ago today, my departure from New York. I have come to some thoughts on Sārnāth-Benares.

The spirituality of the Gupta Buddhas and bodhisattvas was dramatically evident in contrast to the coarse quality of the contemporary Hindu cults. The Hindu gods represent those very powers of *māyā* from the grip of which the bodhisattvas bring release.[51] Consider the Monkey Temple, the coarse images of Ganeśa, Hanumān, etc., and the religious traffic of the ghats and temples. Durgā leads us back to Melanesia.

The Buddhas and bodhisattvas have absorbed many elements from Hinduism, but an essentially psychological orientation remains fundamental to their character.

The Jain attempt to break free from the clutches of the gods is less sophisticated than the Buddhist; Śaṅkara's way seems to carry more of the Jain world-negation than of the Buddhist world-assimilation via psychology.[52]

Zimmer's suggestion was that Hinduism spiritualized through the influence of Buddhism, and with the disappearance of Buddhism, the Hindu image returned to the level of the folk fetish. The problem here is: Buddhism is a continuation of the Upanishadic direction. What is the relationship of the Upanishadic tradition to folk-Hinduism?

Here is a project for a second visit to Benares: to study, one by one, the several cults of the several ghats—their histories and disciplines—also, to study the functioning and influence of the modern institutions: the colleges, Ramakrishna Mission, Theosophical Society, philanthropic institutions, etc.

Finally, a question for Ceylon, Burma, Siam, and Japan: what is the degree of Buddhism's decline in the realms of the folk?

At noon I leave for my train to Patna, which is due to arrive about 8 P.M. Another of these Indian locals. The guide, Mr. Alley, accompanied me to the station, bought my ticket, and, while waiting for the train, talked about religion. He is a Mohammedan. Most of the boys and men I saw this morning were Mohammedans. He said that the Hindus in Benares are trying to pass a ruling forbidding Mohammedans to serve as guides in that city. (One sees how the Hindus can make it difficult, here and there.)

Then he gave me his statement on religion. All religions teach love, peace, and the road to heaven. Also, it is like a circle with a central point: some stress the central point, some the radii to the center, others, with many gods, the circumference; but all recognize the central point. And so all religions agree. But the priests of the religions teach prejudice and the supremacy of their own religion—and this is to their personal interest. Religion is all right, it is only what we make of it that is wrong.

Not bad, from a tourist guide: it can be used as a basic formula.

Sunday, September 26   **Patna–Gaya–Patna**

I'm at the Grand Hotel in Patna. Very conspicuous plumbing: no water, except in a bucket.

My day in Patna began with the discovery that to get to Nālandā, I should have gotten up for a 6:25 train. I would have to save that for to-morrow. Gaya, however, could be reached by a 10:50 train. I had a cycle-rickshaw take me for a look at the nearer parts of the town and a pause at the museum. Along with several *satī* stones, lots of terracottas from Maurya and later times, and the Chowry-bearer from Didarganj; all rather clut-tered but not too badly arranged.

On the train to Gaya I shared the compartment with two Mohammedan gentlemen, one, a supervisor of schools in the Bihar area, about to retire; the other a district government supervisor of some kind. The latter, particularly, was eager to talk. I should visit Pakistan he said; they were very grateful there for American aid. "That is surprising," I said, "that anyone should be grateful there for American aid." "No," said my friend; "in Pakistan they are really grateful. They are different from the Hindus. Give to Hindu, they say, and he will insult you." I got the feeling that the Mohammedans in India do not share the Hindu resentment for American aid to Pakistan. They said that what America has given India in the way of aid is actually more than what is being given to Pakistan.

In Gaya I had a Sikh driver take me by taxi to Bodhgayā, where I viewed the temple and adjacent lotus tank, with bathers, for about an hour. My Bengali friend from Sārnāth came shouting up the stairs to greet me. And I took a lot of photos. There was not time enough to visit the Viṣṇupada Temple, where there is an imprint of Viṣṇu's foot; but did visit an Akṣaya Vṛkṣa (another "deathless banyan"—cf. Allahabad[53]), where I found a rather nice ancient temple (perhaps A.D. 1100) beside the affair now in use. Two of the priests approached me, smiling, and, now as tired of priests as of beggars, I made my escape by pleading train time.

On the return train, which left Gaya at 4 P.M., I shared the compart-ment with a doctor, supervisor of the work being done in these districts. I asked whether his work had been helped at all by the World Health Organization. "Yes," he said, "but..." And the buts were that the WHO does not employ enough Hindu doctors—they could make more use of the good men already in India; and that the people they send out are not par-ticularly great: they sent one Dane who was no good, and a woman from somewhere else, who was better. He spoke also of the American technical aid to the farmers as though it meant something positive.

And then, of course, we droned off onto the problems of India's reconstruction and the differences between India and America. As for the slowness of the trains: India had had two terrible accidents some years ago, and now the trains (those, that is to say, that are not the great Mail trains) have to keep below 30 miles per hour—the tracks, for the most part, won't stand anything faster. And he advised me, furthermore, to go to Nālandā and Rajgir by a 6:00 A.M. bus.

When our train pulled into the station at 7 P.M. (again a three-hour ride) a multitude of students swarmed out of it, shouting, and gaily hopped all the barriers past the guard.

Monday, September 27   **Patna–Nālandā–Patna**

Up at 4:45 A.M. for breakfast and a get-away to the bus station. My hotel proprietor had his two men-of-all-work give me a package of sandwiches for the day, and I took also a thermos of cold water. The bus actually left at 6:30 A.M., and at 11 A.M. it set me down at a crossroad marked Nālandā, sixty-three miles from Patna. A boy with a cart and a poor, miserable horse offered to drive me to the University ruins[54] for two rupees, so I boarded his contraption. He kept striking his nag on the tip of its prominent spine, which was such a torture for the poor animal that it continually kicked; I was dead tired, besides, and the sun was like fire. When I was set down at the path to the University, I walked slowly and was gradually revived by the sight of the red brick walls. One could already feel the campus atmosphere! The size of the compound is impressive, and the orderliness very pleasant. The guard had me sign in his book, and I was so shaken I spilt the bottle of ink over the page. In silence we blotted it up. I toured the grounds and took a few photos, then went to visit the museum; Moitessier's Buddha, Naga King, and the rest.

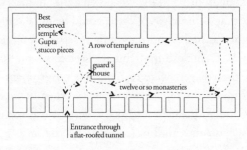

On the drive back the horse was made to kick more than ever, and I was really irritated, but my Hindi was not up to telling the kid to quit, since I was in no hurry. Getting back to the crossroad about noon, I managed, however, to learn that the next bus to Patna would not come until 3:00 P.M. I would have time to drive the four miles to Rajgir, but I would have to go with that kid and horse, and besides, the sun was getting worse; I decided instead to go and lie down under a tree and eat my lunch. At the crossroad there were a few little huts with people consuming food, and so I moved down the road a few yards. At the huts were a number of students who had been to visit the ruins, and a few of the peasants of the neighborhood with their kids.

I am getting quite a view of the peasant life of India on these trips, so the hours spent are not a total loss. This time, as I opened my package, a tall man approached and quietly stood watching me. I found that I had a bunch of little bananas in my bag. Taking one of them I gave him the rest and he went away. When I had finished eating I lay down for a rest, and another nice man came and stood by smiling. I had left about two bread-and-butter sandwiches in the bag. So I gave him these and he went away. A chipmunk halfway up the tree presently discovered me and made a lot of amusing noise.

At about 1:15 P.M. there was a lot of noise over toward the crossroad and along came a little narrow-gauge train, heading Patna way. I got up, ran for it, and caught it. The students caught it also. They boarded the first car, I the other. The inhabitants were peasants, and one young fellow in the usual white started a conversation; he proved to be an inspector of the villages in connection with the government's rehabilitation project. The conductor of the train, who could hardly catch our English, sat and listened. I was told of the work being done and of some of the problems. One problem was that of arousing in the villagers a desire to help themselves; another, of course, that of money: very little could be done, but a few selected villages were being assisted—and these might serve as examples for others. The main plan was to furnish implements, seeds, etc. on long- and short-term payments, the villagers were to repay the government from the proceeds of their produce; the repaid money would then be invested for other villages. One of India's great problems of the past was the absentee land-lord (*zamindar*), who did nothing to improve the farm's condition but simply received his money (contrast the American big farmer and rancher, e.g. Ronald von Holt[55]). India now has to breed its stock, crops, and everything else. (I have noticed that the native plows and method of plowing is precisely that shown on Egyptian reliefs!)

Presently the conversation shifted toward America and I was back in my act. The kibitzer-conductor asked the standard Communist-line question—"Why does America want war?"—but walked away before I could reply.

The night ended at 6:00 A.M. with a great banging at my door. I opened, and an Indian gentleman got in; but his wife called that she had found an absolutely empty compartment, so with a brief apology he got out again. I ordered tea and started the day. At 7:00 A.M. we stopped again. A sweeper came in and dusted out the sooty compartment, and two gentlemen entered. The one who sat on my side of the car was an engineer, and his conversation was another of those fine things that make one realize how much of old India is living still in these unlikely circumstances. We rehearsed what are by now the trite themes of India's improvement, the contrast with America, Nehru's importance ("we don't know what will happen when he goes"—my own guess: "peaceful coexistence" boys will move in from points north), and so on. Then we began talking about India's philosophy, and this engineer had the whole thing: he was a Hindu, and looked forward to the spread of education and elimination of superstition among the masses. He saw yoga as "achieving while alive what is achieved in death," and named an important sage, somewhere, whose name I have mislaid.

CALCUTTA

Tuesday, September 28

Calcutta is a great and very welcome change. I like the feel of a big city after all the rural life. One feels England here, more than any place so far. A considerable port. A sort of Chinatown with a great new city growing all around it. Cows are fewer than elsewhere. The rickshaws are hand-drawn. The traffic is heavy.

When I had rested and cleaned up, shaved and bathed in cold water at the Grand Eastern (vast hotel, cold water: India!), and felt a bit refreshed (the amount of soot that came off was incredible), I found my way to the American Express, collected my mail, and then began arranging for a visit to Darjeeling by air. The rest of the day was sleep. Good god I was tired. After dinner I went out for a stroll and was approached by about eight pimps advertising whore houses: "beautiful French girls." Even if they *had* been beautiful I would have been too sleepy even to look! I went back to my room and again hit the sheets.

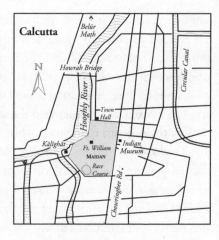

Wednesday, September 29

I woke up, greatly refreshed, at about 6:00 A.M. and began writing. At 7:00 A.M. my morning tea arrived with the newspaper. Headline: *Seventy-three killed in rail crash near Hyderabad* (later news: more than 126). Train plunges into flooded river as bridge collapses. It gave me a chill. Every river in India is in flood. Srinagar, since our departure, has been nearly lost: villages are being dumped into rivers everywhere.

A meditation: this has been going on here for 8,000 years. Only the Occidental contribution of dams and river control, which the Indians are now installing, will relieve the situation—and create simultaneously the electric power and adequate irrigation.

After breakfast I went to the Indian Museum and viewed the rich but horribly exhibited collection. The Bhārhut railing and *toraṇa*[56] in the pitch dark! Then I went upstairs to a highly advertised exhibit, visited by thousands, of "World History in Pictures"—a puerile series of Communist-type posters illustrating the epochs of world history. The point: Imperialism, Capitalism, Fascism *vs.* Democracy, Socialism, Communism. Where have I heard that one before? But what hit me, seeing it all so simply set forth at this late date, was the curious spottiness of the whole historical panorama of these people, as well as the curious suggestion that, although everything has somehow been progressing, it has somehow been all wrong. Two or three amusing curiosities: Mesopotamia was placed in Turkey; A.D. was consistently written A.C.; Russia's absorption of Lithuania, Latvia, and Estonia was represented as a recovery of lands rightfully Russian. The last word on the Machine was that it had made the rich richer but had done nothing for the poor—a view that *may* have been correct in 1890, but certainly has no application to the only land where the Machine has really been made to work: capitalistic U.S.A., where every worker drives to work in his own car.

After lunch I went out to Belūr Maṭh, in time to greet Swami and his two angels. It was a lovely change: suburban quiet, on the Ganges shore. One can see Dakṣineśvara from the *matha*. Many, many monks. Tea among them. Visits to the principals. A frightful Church-Temple designed by Vivekananda (reminds me of the Mahayana Buddhist Cathedral in Honolulu), where an incredible image of Durgā was being fashioned by a couple of artist craftsmen. During the evening worship of the Ramakrishna image I sat forward among the monks, and let me say that the gestures and posture of the young monk offering the fire, water, flowers, etc., and swinging the chowry were the first evidences of real elegance that I have seen, to date, in India. At this service I got the feel of India's monastic life—and talking with the monks in their yellow robes, I required only a slight jog to find myself at Elūrā and Ajaṇṭā. Hurray for the monks.

The drive home, with two of the order, was wonderful: at the Howrah Bridge, a two-hour traffic jam, the like of which I have never seen and would never have thought possible. Rickshaws, hand trucks, busses, herds of cows and goats, porters with loads on their heads, beggars, yogis, trolley cars, pedestrians infiltrating everywhere, shouting, honking, taxis, motor-cycles, bikes, more cows, a peasant girl with a filled basket on her head shouting "Mama," trying to cross through ten lanes of traffic; five plus five lanes of traffic trying to converge into two; every tenth truck unable to start again after stopping; one truck with a flat tire trying to cut across the side; guys jumping out every two minutes to crank their cars; more cows; po-licemen here and there; people sleeping along the sidewalks of the great bridge; boat traffic below; a crescent moon in the dark by the time we ar-rived. It was simply great, that's all.

Thursday, September 30

One month in India, and beginning to feel that I know how to handle a few of the problems. Perhaps time, too, for a few more reflections.

As to who broke India: Islam. The humanistic glow given by Akbar and Shah Jahan, at the last minute, to a period of some nine hundred al-most unrecorded years of war and iconoclasm, should not be allowed to distort the picture. Moreover, these good men were followed by Aurangzeb.[57]

Or blame the Caste System: for it is said that India was betrayed from within, the chief converts to Islam being members of the *śūdra* and scheduled classes. It is also said, on the other hand, that the caste system became petrified only *after* the coming of Islam, which cannot be true if the other theory is true. And a reading of the pre-Mohammedan Laws of Manu and Institutes of Viṣṇu makes the first theory seem the more likely.

As to what I have found of real power and value in India: certainly, the character and quality of the peasants and the poor (something, however, perhaps not peculiar to the peasants and poor of India—compare Italy, France, perhaps even Mexico); also, a comparable graciousness and hospitality right up to the top (for instance, *chez* Radhakrishnan, and the people we met in Delhi—again, perhaps, to be matched elsewhere, but I still think there is something special about the quality or tone); then the work of the Ramakrishna monks, their social work, their *pūjā*. Also of value: the Five Year Plan; the spiritual span, in Benares, between the Durgā Temple and the Hindu University; and the conversations I have had in the trains.

But, heavily on the debit side: the poverty, which has conduced to a certain miserliness on the part of the wealthy (or perhaps it was vice-versa). They do not let their well-being shine out into the city, but close it away behind walls. Corollary: instead of turning for investment money to its own rich, India turns to the World Bank. Exceptional men have endowed and built temples—for which they gain heavy credits in heaven. There is also among all literate Indians a fantastic spiritual pride which gives rise to a pose of spiritual superiority; and there is also a class of grossly Westernized persons, quite conspicuous in a way, which I cannot yet judge, since I have not conversed: they are rude in trains and seem to represent the antithesis of my "good Indians."

As to Islam: I find the Mohammedans that I have met entirely praiseworthy—forthright and intelligent; also, I should say, somewhat more Occidental in character than the Hindus.

I note also a couple of themes for research: the cults of the temples of Benares; and the symbolism of the *satī* stones.[58]

I spent most of this day in my room, writing, and dealing with New York problems: Zimmer proofs and the Irma Brandeis-Bollingen project.[59]

At 6:30 P.M. I went to the Calcutta Club to meet the pleasant man whom I encountered on the train: and here was a view indeed of another of India's million faces. The club is Calcutta's second, the top club is the Bengal Club, where Indians are excluded. But in the Calcutta Club the organization is such that the Board of Directors is half Indian, half European, and the presidency alternates. At present the membership is mostly Indian, but they are holding to the 50-50 organizational principles.

I entered, in my blue Dacron suit, and my friend met me at the door, in open shirt. I noted both types of dress in the Club, and so felt at home. He ordered drinks (he later told me he did not drink ordinarily, and I noticed that he dallied long), showed me around and introduced me to friends, but every friend to whom he introduced me ordered drinks immediately—apparently they've taken on drinks as the primary symbol of British good fellowship. Anyhow, before the evening was over I had had a lot of whiskey and soda.

The atmosphere was entirely that of a club in London or New York, and I was filled all evening with a kind of admiration for the power of certain British ideas to make a world statement. We sat for a while in the pool room and watched a number of the members put on a standard American or British pool-room performance. I recalled every sound, every phrase, every gesture from those old pool games, long ago, at the Forest Lake Club.[60] We watched the poker and bridge games, and talked of stud poker. After about seven whiskey-and-sodas and a good deal of wandering around we sat down to an excellent chicken dinner—and I had to revise some of my thoughts about the Indian handling of Western food.

The members of the Club are, of course, business, industrial, and professional gentlemen; mostly Indians, but I also met a couple of second-class Europeans—or rather, Britishers. One of the members, putting on a fairly good performance at the pool table, was said to be India's most successful industrialist—owner of all kinds of things. Another, with whom I had a pleasant chat about Darjeeling, had the name of Birla. He was more interested in his racing fillies than in Hinduism, and was, apparently, the black sheep of the pious Birla family (donor of the big New Delhi temple). A sane gentleman, a Mr. Sen Gupta, claimed to be an atheist, but his wife was a pious devotee of everything.

Certain meditations, following my conversations of last evening, have absorbed me and I sent part of them off in a letter to Jean. They have to do with my feelings about India and India's women.

Ever since my arrival I have felt an obscure sense of disappointment in my perambulation of India. I have been trying to put my finger on it: blaming the railroad service, poverty, drabness of the buildings, lack of civic pride, etc. I now realize that there are practically no women visible—and that, consequently, what the hell? The streets and buildings, coffee houses, and so on are swarming with men—but the only women (save for an occasional exception) are the poor drab beggar women with their naked kids and almost equally drab vendors. It is to be noted that these miserables often wear their dirty saris without bodices, and that frequently the right breast is either almost or completely uncovered—and that it doesn't matter. The worst I ever saw was this afternoon: a blind beggar woman with a naked, scrofulous kid on her arm, the other hand holding out a begging bowl. The kid had pus of some kind dripping from its nose, and the woman, like all of these poor things, simply walked ahead slowly, in her darkness, calling "Babu," rather softly. At this point my beggar resistance broke.

The very few women above the beggar-vendor level that one does see (in the cities, that is to say; for in the villages and fields the women—drab, however, as beggars—were much more in evidence) fall into two classes: matrons—with the look, very often, of Durgā; and childlike, nice-looking, little girls and young wives. I have noted also, for example in the case of the couple who entered my railway carriage on the way from Gwalior to Allahabad, that the wives are absolutely of the domestic sort—and I have heard that Indian wives cannot talk of anything but the orthodox three K's (*Kirche, Küche, Kinder*). The concept of a spiritual companionship of the sexes seems not to exist. And this whole thing about India was impressed upon me dramatically at lunch today, when I saw an elegant modern Japanese wife with her husband and two youngsters at a nearby table. She had a real style—decent, wifely, but interestingly sophisticated. I thought, "My god, these Indians have a long way to go!"

I would say that in India the French *jeune fille de famille* idea prevails, without, however, the French correction of the marital triangle. As a result of all this the cities have the air of a men's club: the step to the Calcutta Club is not a great one: nor is the step to the Monastery. *Purdah* and the Mohammedan *burqa'* (covering veil) represent, therefore, only a vivid presentation of a formula that is ubiquitous in the Orient that I have seen.

What is the relationship of all this to the lovely *maithunas* (the tender and gentle ones) of Bādāmi and others? What is the relationship of all this to the heroic spirit of the epics? Can it be that we here have something that came into India with the Mohammedans? I think not. I think it was here before, but that there was some kind of shift of emphasis at that time, which screened the other out.

At this point, another series of meditations not unrelated to the above: India has turned its poverty into a kind of *sādhanā;* Gandhi stressed this. There is consequently a quality of spirituality about this Indian poverty, which is impressive. Other *sādhanās,* however, were possible in the past: the kingly *sādhanā* of Arjuna, for example.[61]

Involuntary poverty is not the same thing as the voluntary poverty of the monk; it may lead to and represent a quite different spiritual state. Outwardly, however, the two poverties tend to complement each other, and the monk easily becomes the elder brother of the poor man—himself, perhaps, even tending to identify wealth with sin.

Involuntary poverty—unless spiritually transcended—keeps its victim in a subject, servile, dependent position: this position is that of the dependent child to its mother. Entirely appropriate to India's poverty, therefore, is the Mother-*bhakti* recommended by Ramakrishna to his devotees and represented in the Durgā Pūjā (which is to be celebrated in Calcutta next week).

The way of *bhakti,* the *kīrtana,* the Mother, etc. became stressed in India following the Mohammedan conquest and the liquidation of the medieval aristocratic tradition (Caitanya, Tul Sidas, Ramakrishna).

Here, then, is a possible formula:

Hinduism, post A.D. 1200 \ Medieval India
sādhana of Poverty \ Aristocratic *sādhana*
Śakti as Mother *(paśu)* \ *maithuna (vīra)*

As for the formula of the city as a men's club and the *purdah* of the *jeune fille* and matron—I ran into the inevitable corollary in the course of my after-dinner stroll. I went along Chowrunghee Road, slowly, looking for a possible movie theater—accosted, of course, by pimps (another touch of France), rickshaw boys, taxi drivers, and vendors of all kinds; then turned to the left following the lights, and was amazed at the vitality of the business life at this hour: all the shops open, as ever—though I never see anyone buying—and the streets simply crowded. At one point I passed a huge, covered fruit and vegetable market. At this point a rickshaw boy started following me, jangling his bell, to my great annoyance, and I determined to walk him off. I don't know how long he followed, but in the course of my stroll, and while he was still with me, I suddenly realized that I was deep in a red-light district.

I haven't seen anything on this level outside of Panama City:[62] on either side of the street, little stalls, each with its filthy girl, and occasional larger doorways in which a number of women would be standing and where a team of pimps, like Indian shopkeepers, would be loudly calling and beckoning you. The doors of these larger establishments were open and one had vistas of very dirty rooms and patios, with a few dreary whores in their saris, sitting quietly on chairs. The girls, for the most part, looked just like any other Indian women you might see—childlike, as unsexy as any women I've ever seen; but a few of them were dolled up with slightly colorful saris (nothing gaudy) and powdered faces (the sort of purple powder used by the girls in Harlem). Four or five were dressed in short skirts and brazen sweaters, like Western picture-book whores. But on the whole, it was an amazingly subdued bunch of sirens—extremely easy to pass. And my rickshaw boy kept right at my heels.

I knew that I was past the whorehouses when I got the reek of a brace of urinals. After that, the business was hardware, vegetables, candy, magazines, and the general whatnots of India. The rickshaw boy dropped me and I hailed a taxi (taxis have meters, so you know what to pay: the rickshaw boys always ask for more—and having watched them run for a couple of miles at their amazing dog-trot, I always feel like paying them more than the ride was worth). At the door of my taxi a pimp kept telling me to come with him and see the beautiful girls. "Just look," he said, like every storekeeper, "I have one very nice girl for you. Just look. Sahib, Sahib. No?" I let my Sikh taxi-driver drive me home to the Great Eastern Hotel.

Saturday, October 2

Something very interesting in the morning paper (*The Statesman*, p. 8, continued on p. 6!): an article by a certain Pyarelal Nayar on Gandhi. A statement is given here on Gandhi's two fundamental propositions:

I recognize no other God except the God that is to be found in the heart of the dumb millions... and I worship the God that is Truth or Truth which is God, through the service of these millions. [i.e. Vivekananda's formula after his visit to America.]

I believe in the absolute oneness of God and therefore of humanity. What though we have many bodies? We have but one soul. The rays of the sun are many through refraction. But they have the same source. I cannot, therefore, detach myself from the wickedest soul, nor may I identify myself with the most virtuous. [This is not so clear: but it rings a bit like Ramakrishna.]

Further on in this article we come to a discussion of *satyagrāha*—and what do you think?—lifted (without credit) from Zimmer-Campbell, *Philosophies of India*. As follows:

There is an ancient philosophical belief in India that one who has been true to the law of his essential being without a single fault throughout his life, can cause anything to happen by the simple act of calling that fact to witness. He becomes a "living conduit" of cosmic power, the power of Truth (*satya*) "the highest expression of the soul." This is known as making "an act of Truth." The truth must be firmly rooted in the heart so that it manifests itself in human relations as infinite compassion or identification with everything that feels.... [63]

After lunch I went to the racetrack, hoping to see a crowd, but the fields and stands were empty (actually, I learned later, I was three-quarters of an hour early), and so I took another walk. I went to the great market that I had seen last night: it was a lovely spot. I was amused to see a number of precisely such porters with their baskets, as they appear in "The Porter and the Three Ladies of Baghdad" in the *Arabian Nights*. I also sought and found again the street of whores: four or five blocks of them, just off Surendranath Banerji Road, on a street called Mistree Lane (!) which intersects with Umā Dās Road—and at the intersection, standing with a bored look at her stall, was an actually beautiful, tall, dark, girl. The whole area was almost as busy as the night before—in fact, perhaps more so; for, to my surprise, there were a number of shops and craft workshops scattered among the whores, kids were flying kites in the streets, and the whole thing was just like any other shopping neighborhood. The time was about 3 P.M.

At 6:30 P.M. I was joined by my Hindu friend
Dhar, who took me, this time, to the Calcutta
Punjab Club—a smaller, more intimate club than
the other, and one where the husbands are allowed
to bring their wives. The idea was to let me see a bit
of Calcutta's mixed society. When we arrived, two
poker games were in progress on the lawn—and a

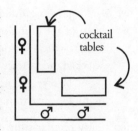

few of Dhar's friends were at the bar. Everything was male. The game of
drinks began. Presently four couples arrived. I was introduced and sat among
them in a corner on a couple of wall-benches; the women were all on one
with the men on the other. Result: the women talked together; the men
talked together. More couples arrived and divided. Presently the men were
all standing at the bar and only the women were seated. And finally the
women were somewhere else (I don't know where), and I was having dinner
with three men. A mixed party in the Orient. Dhar said: "Well, you see, the
women don't drink whiskey, and they like to talk of their own affairs."

Sunday, October 3

This morning I decided to go to the Kālīghāt Temple, took a taxi, and was
met, as I descended, by a brahmin priest who showed me the whole job.
Obviously a very busy resort: beggars, pilgrims, vendors, priests, in multitudes.
Had some of the air of the Benares temple labyrinth—only here it was all a
great open area with lots of buildings: the temple itself (from A.D. 1601) a hostel for pilgrims, and many other buildings. It had been my hope that I might
see the sacrifice of a goat or buffalo, but I lost interest when I saw the two
stocks: big, for the buffalo; little, for the goat, the latter fresh with brilliant
blood, with the severed bodies and heads of four little animals laid out in state
at one side. Presently, a pilgrim and priest began preparing a cute little black
fellow for his immolation, and I was glad to follow my priest-guide as he bore
me along to other sights: the riverside, where the pilgrims were descending to
bathe; the areas where the brahmins of the temple sat in great number, reading the *Gītā;* the numerous booths where the little packets of offerings were for
sale; puddle of water from the goddess's feet, which the pilgrims stooped
to take up in their hands and even to sip; a great line of pilgrims going into the
temple. The priest then took me to the burning ghat, and I could see and smell
(and found myself in the smoke of) three cremations.

My brahmin had the usual priestly talent of extracting money, but I didn't mind this time: it was quite a show; and as he showed me around he gave explanations that were clear and concise. The allegorical reading of the goat and buffalo sacrifices was interesting: the goat is the symbol of lust, the buffalo of anger; these passions are sacrificed with the sacrifice of the animals.[64] They are placed in the stock, and are slain with a single stroke: not at any regular time of day, but whenever a pilgrim makes the offering.

Following this event I returned to my street of whores to see whether it was at work also in the morning—and it was, though I didn't see any male actually go into any of the stalls or reception halls. As in all of the Oriental shopping areas I've seen, the noise and circumstance were all out of proportion to the business done. (The stall at the corner of Umā Dās and Mistree, however, was closed and locked from the outside.) Oh yes, and by the way, when I mentioned this street to Dhar last night, he was amazed: prostitution, he said, is against the law!

I spent the afternoon sleeping and writing in my room, and after dinner went for a long walk through all kinds of streets, finding Durgā Pūjā shrines set up everywhere in little sheds, often of sheet metal, decorated with colorful paper and brightly lit. These shrines have as the central figure a representation of the Goddess slaying the Buffalo Demon. The demon has emerged from the buffalo completely and is receiving the blow of the Goddess's lance full in the chest. He is moustached and the Goddess, in some of the shrines, has lassoed his neck with a cobra. The rendition of this formula varies slightly from shrine to shrine. The scene is flanked by four standing figures: two represent the goddesses Lakṣmī and Sarasvatī; two are Ganeśa (pink!—origin here of the pink elephant idea?) and Kārttikeya—Ganeśa may be accompanied by his rat, and Kārttikeya rides the peacock. The shrines had just been completed, and many of the neighborhood's old ladies and their families—often nicely and freshly dressed—were coming out to view the local version.

Before one of the shrines a large crowd of men and boys was gathered, and there was the beating of a drum and clank of cymbals. I went to see what was going on and found two fellows, one with a moustache, engaged in the sort of stick-duel that I had witnessed in Benares. The fellow with the moustache put one adversary out and another got up to engage him. The new contestant was a lively chap in a green dhoti and blue shirt.

The contestants moved about quickly, keeping time with the music, and most of the time at some distance from each other; then they would come in for a couple of cracks and slashes and quickly duck out.

When I had seen enough I took a rickshaw home—and again, the boy didn't know where he was going and dragged me about three miles.

Monday, October 4

I was roused this morning at about 5:30 by a sound of quick drums and cymbals going past the hotel. Then again, some ten minutes later, this motif was repeated. Finally getting up, I saw the procession: a chap with a plant of some kind held aloft, followed by a man with a drum and a boy with a metal clank-instrument, who were followed in turn by a man bearing an offering on his head. This little procession simply passed along the street, and a beggar woman made a gesture of reverence. Other processions were a little larger. In one, there were two men in bright red robes and another holding a bright red umbrella over the head of a man with a small image on his head. Still other processions were smaller: a man bearing something and a kid following beating a gong.

I learned from the morning paper that the little shrines are called *pandals;* also, that last evening at about 10:30 (just after my return home) ceremonials invoking the Goddess into her image were performed throughout the city.

This morning right after breakfast I went to Belūr Maṭh for their morning *pūjā,* which lasted from 9 until 12. It was conducted before their temporary image (same type as those of the *pandals* in town), which is placed halfway down the aisle of their temple, on the Ganges side. Before it, on the floor, there is a large lotus mandala in the paving: above, in the temporary cloth decorations of the ceiling, there was another mandala. Since the ceremonial of the Durgā Pūjā is one for laymen and not properly for monks, the celebrant was a young *brahmacārin* (but of brahmin caste), who has learned this whole four-day series of ceremonials by heart and must fast each day until evening.

According to Swami, there are several layers of allegorical reference implicated in the Durgā Pūjā:[65]

The Vegetational: this is the period of the harvest. The plant that I saw this morning was a plantain bough and leaf, with a few sprigs of paddy.[66] This is the goddess: it is also the first fruits. (We are here on the trail of Demeter and Kore: but definitely!)[67]

The Domestic: at the time of her marriage, the Bengali girl, shortly after the wedding ceremonies, returns to her family for three days: Umā returned to King Himālaya for three days after her marriage to Śiva: the three days of the Durgā Pūjā are comparable to those three days[68]—at the end, the immersion of the image is the departure of the bride from her family: the Bengali mothers cry at this time. (Here again we must keep Demeter and Kore in mind.)

The Moral: the Goddess's slaying of the Demon Buffalo is the conquest of evil by good.

The Spiritual: during the hot and rainy seasons one's spiritual life is sluggish, but with the clearing of the skies the spirit is to be cleared and renewed. (Consider the Anthesteria.)[69]

A still deeper mystery is indicated, however, in the ceremonial enacted this morning; for not only the Goddess and her entourage, but also the Buffalo is invoked and garlanded as a god. (Here is Zimmer's great theme.)[70]

At the ceremonial this morning I was impressed very strongly by a number of elements in the liturgy suggesting the Roman Catholic Mass; and when I tried to think of the possible background of these correspondences, I could not get Ephesus out of my mind. The great cult and temple of Artemis, source of so much in the Catholic cult and worship of the Virgin,[71] is *certainly* a Near Eastern counterpart of this Bengali Durgā. Theme for research: the history and sources of the Christian Liturgy; the history and sources of the Tantric Liturgy.

When I entered the temple the sound was precisely that of a Catholic service: someone was reading in a liturgical monotone, and the Sanskrit, for a moment, sounded like Latin, and the ornamental inflections were like those of certain parts of a Gregorian Mass. This continuous reading went on throughout two of the three hours of the service: part of the text was from the *Devī Mahātmya,* where the account is given of Durgā's slaying of the Buffalo Demon. Over the ground bass of this chant the rite was performed.[72]

The *brahmacārin* celebrant, seated before the panel of images, among the vessels and offerings of the service, chanted for three hours the prayers of offering. A monk sat at his right with the text of the liturgy before him—as prompter; and another monk, very tall, stood behind the celebrant and supervised the actions of the piece. A youth in a fine white dhoti and shawl served as altar boy, lighting the incense sticks, placing the blessed flowers on the images, and so on. The celebrant *brahmacārin* was in white, and his head, save for the brāhman tuft, had been freshly shaved.

The area of the ceremonial action was marked off from the rest of the temple floor by a low barrier of wood, and within this area sat the monks of the *maṭha* (Nikhilananda, of course, among them). To the left of the celebrant (right of the image) were the women (on the side of Ganeśa and Lakṣmī) and the men were opposite (side of Sarasvatī and Kārttikeya). The service consisted in blessing flower and food offerings, the latter brought in on lovely trays (somewhat like those carried on the heads of the Balinese in all the movies!), and the former, after each blessing, placed in the hands or around the neck of the intended image. The blessing rite involved sprinkling water and tossing flowers over the fruits etc., then waving a stick of incense, while ringing the service bell with the left hand. At one great moment, about one hour after the commencement of the service, drums, gongs, and other machines of noise began going outside, and everyone who was standing (myself included) went down in a long salaam: as though the Goddess, at this moment, were accepting the sacrifice.

(Before I forget: the Goddess slays the Buffalo, and so Mithra slays the World Bull.[73] In Africa, the Goddess is shown standing between the horns of the bull[74]—compare the Pallava image of Durgā in the Boston Museum,[75] and see also Frobenius's account of the founding of a Syrian city (clay houses—of India!).[76] Also to be seen here: the bullfight,[77] the Assamese bull ring, the Cretan bull ring, the Kālīghāt buffalo sacrifice.)[78]

After this great moment in the service there was nothing new in the way of motifs. Presently the chant of the *Devī Mahātmya* ceased and the service went on, in comparative silence for another hour or so. The old monk who is the President of the *maṭha* came in, sat a special mat for a while, performed his *pūjā,* and went out. The youngsters in the temple began to be a bit restless, and there was a good deal of incidental noise. The length of the service was determined by the number of offerings that had to be blessed and presented. A team of boys was busy throughout, bringing in sets of trays and then taking them away (this food was distributed after the service to the poor). Food and garlands went first to the Goddess herself, then to Ganeśa, Lakṣmī, Sarasvatī, Kārttikeya, and the Snake and Buffalo.

The celebrant then tossed a great handful of flowers at the whole affair. Flowers next were distributed to the monks: they all tossed, salaamed, and withdrew. A lively, sturdy monk then sprinkled holy water over the women and men. Flowers were passed to the women. They were led in a brief prayer by the monk, and all tossed their flowers. Same for the men. Finis.

I had lunch with Swami and the two ladies and returned to the hotel.

Elements immediately suggestive of the Catholic liturgy: the chant, the choir area for the monks, separation of the sexes (Russian Orthodox—the mixing in Europe has something to do with my major discovery about the Orient-Occident sexual crisis!), holy water, flowers before images (all, however, here blessed), ringing of the bell at the moment of the offering, concept of the divine presence, motif of the sacrifice (here the buffalo; there the Savior himself), prayers for the faithful after the main service, celebrant and assistants, some of the *mudrās* of the celebrant, all the demonstrations of piety on the part of the faithful (ladies bowing, making the prayer sign with their hands), and finally, the look of the whole congregation coming out of the church.

This afternoon I started work, seriously, on the Sarah Lawrence chapter that I have to write, and this evening went for another walk along Surendranath Banerji Road. There was an immense crowd, a great noise of *pūjā* gongs and drums, flashing neon lights and illuminated archways—mostly concentrated, however, in the neighborhood of wonderful Mistree Lane. The population of the streets tonight had a larger proportion of women than usual—all (or rather, many) prettily dressed and on their way to do *pūjā*.

The little side streets leading to the shrines have illuminated archways before them (there were five or six, not very far from each other, just beyond the "Elite" movie theater), and there comes out, from far down a little street, a great din of gongs and drums. A dividing rope runs down the middle of the street: ladies right; men left; and this division goes right up to the shrine. The men's side is jammed; there are very few women. The crowd moves slowly down the little street, its storekeepers and inhabitants lining the way, and then comes to the bedlam of the shrine, where a priest sits waving a lamp before the panel of images and a cluster of boys bang drums and gongs. There is a policeman in a white suit and tall red hat to keep order. People stand a while, press up to the shrine, receive some smear on their forehead, make the usual pious gestures, and move away, going back the way they came—the two crowds in the crowded men's aisle, slowly passing each other.

The fun, of course, was the shrine that carries its crowd directly down one of the streets of the Quarter. Here the girls, like the other shopkeepers, stood at their doors, lining the way, and plucked off their customers. There was no lack of business in this little system of streets tonight! There was no shouting of pimps: it was unnecessary. Some of the girls quietly tossed little *pūjā* firecrackers, to call attention to themselves; but in general they were busy enough. I noticed that in many cases, men simply walked past the girl door guardian into her stall and she remained: these were simply doors, apparently, to larger establishments in the rear. I noticed also, tonight, one rather cute little room, open to the street, as though perhaps prepared for an exhibition of some kind; so when the procuress sitting before it beckoned to me I went over. She was fat and middle aged. "Young girl," she said. "Very nice, very good." I looked toward what she was showing me. A kid about thirteen years old in a kid's red-figured wash dress. "That?" I said. "No thanks." "Very nice," she said. "Very good." "No thanks," I repeated; and moved away. Many of the stalls that were open were simply that: stalls—dirty and small, with a bed (also small—one, amazingly small, about three feet square) in a corner. No sanitary facilities anywhere to be seen. One of the houses had a batch of lively Chinese girls before it.

On Surendranath Banerji Road I came across a great crowd gathered around a bundle of noise, and when I approached saw a group of five musicians—one with a musette, two with drums hung from their necks, two with cymbals—capering a little while they played. I paused a while to watch. Rupees were being handed to them occasionally. But they were not much good, and I moved along. Another batch of chaps was trying to get a bull to mount a cow. Everywhere, scattered along the sidewalks, were the usual sleepers, beggars, and vendors. At every other step I would be set upon by kids, rickshaw boys, vendors, and pimps. I must say, walking in Calcutta is an aggravation, particularly for a "Sahib" with a high degree of social visibility. The worst tonight was a kid who followed me for six blocks, saying, continuously, "I very poor, no matha, no fatha, no seesta, no bratha, no khana, you rich, you Sahib, I very poor, no matha..." etc. *de cape, ad nauseam.* He finally dropped me, but when I was returning to my hotel hooked on again, soon to be followed by another, then one with a still smaller kid in his arms: a rickshaw boy, meanwhile, had begun to follow me along the gutter, clanking his bell to attract my attention. I told him no, but he continued. The kids began touching my hands, then I felt the hand of the original fellow try to slip into my pocket and I wheeled with a slap. "Say!" I said: and before you could say Henry Morton Robinson[79] all the kids had vanished.

I must say, the whole thing gives me a sick feeling at this moment: Sri Pyarelal Nayar, in yesterday's paper, lifts two paragraphs, without credit, from my book; a youngster, tonight, tries to lift from my pocket; Dhar told me of an Indian movie company that had copied an American film *in toto*—and when the Americans sent a group to investigate, they found such an incredibly squalid studio that they knew there was no point in suing; the papers are full of articles by Indian pandits on Indian philosophy, religion, etc. all quoting—and simultaneously abusing—the Western scholars: India has a so-much-higher spiritual threshold.

Well, in a way, India has: in its rituals and in its mythological and philosophical traditions there is a more successful rendition of the nondualistic principle than in the liturgies and traditions (orthodox, that is to say) of the West. This comes down, like a thin thread of gold, from ages past: but what the ages present have added to the inheritance is largely pretentiousness and poor taste. I am, today, in a strongly negative mood.

Tuesday, October 5

I have now seen everything. Actually, an ash-smeared yogi lying in a bed, not of nails, but of tangled barbed wire—on one of the walks of the Howrah Bridge. He was a big fellow, of handsome physique, perfectly smeared, and with the proper hair and whisker do.

I drove out to Belūr Maṭh to see a charming *kumārī pūjā* (worship of a little girl), which Swami had told me was to commence at 11 A.M. I arrived at 10:30—and there was a prodigious crowd of people at the grounds and swarming into and out of the temple. Swami saw me. "Have you just come?" he said. "Yes," I answered. "Well," he said, "you have missed everything." I was a bit sore, but, I think, concealed it. He introduced me to some gentlemen on the monastery porch, and I sat down, to make the best of it. He himself went into the temple, in a little while, for whatever was going on in there; and I conversed about India with a couple of the gentlemen on the porch, while watching the lovely crowd move about the grounds and temple. India's middle class: professional men and their families, small business people, clerks. All were very nicely dressed; the women —at last—looked charming, and the atmosphere was that of a gentle, sort of Easter Sunday, social-religious event. People, men and women, were everywhere touching the various swamis' feet. This group, or stratum, constituted, I was told, about forty percent of Calcutta.

Piety, *bhakti*, was evident everywhere, and can be said—certainly—to be a distinguishing trait of India. One of my gentlemen discoursed to me on the permeation of the Indian spirit by the principles of Indian philosophy and religion: in the Vedic age the principles were the possession of a few; in the Puranic age they were allowed to suffuse and revitalize the popular cults and became the possession of all; and in the period of the *bhakti* poets ("*Bhakti* originated in the south, came north with Rāmānanda, and was disseminated by Kabīr and Nānak"), the folk languages were infused with the quality of piety that has distinguished Indian thought ever since. It is this spirit, this piety, which is the sustaining force of Indian life.

The transcendental emphasis of Indian metaphysics makes all cults acceptable as approaches. The masses (this gentleman admitted) know nothing of the experience of *brahman;* those that I had seen swarming to the *pandals* and these now at Belūr Math represent, for the most part, simply an experience of *bhakti,* not of transcendent realization—but they are on the path. The important thing about Indian religion is that from this step of simple *bhakti* to the ultimate realization there is an open way, without barrier.

As far as I can see, this is the great point about India: and (I am sorry to say) as far as I have seen, this is the only point about India today.[80]

I spoke to the gentlemen about the yogi in the barbed wire bed. "Such fellows," he said, "know nothing but how to lie on nails."

One of the swamis spoke of his attempts to get in touch with and learn the *sādhanā* of a group in the south, called *siddhas,* said to be the followers of old Agastya. He himself was from the south; he heard a good deal about these men and their wonders, but he never came close enough to any of them (if any actually existed) to find out what it was all about.

Another of the swamis spoke of a group called *nāgas* (L. *nag,* naked), who are an extremely aggressive lot and seem to have as their philosophy "We come first." When they come to bathing places, in force, they make all stand aside, etc. They flourish in Uttar Pradesh and put on demonstrations. They are the descendants of a military group that was formed, originally, to protect *sadhus*. They have evolved, however, into a sort of *sadhu*-sport themselves: militant *sadhus!*

After the temple service, literally thousands of people were served *prasāda* on the temple grounds. I went around to the guest house where Mrs. D. and the Countess are staying, and found there a handsome Hindu girl from Trinidad: an M.D. here working in a hospital. Swami arrived, and we had lunch. In the conversation after lunch I rose to the defense of the modern world against Swami and the Hindu girl who were talking the usual line about the deterioration of the spirit in the modern age. This conversation has led me to another formula. It came to me when I forced Swami back to his second line of defenses. "Well," he said, "there is no progress, only change." "I used to think that too, Swamiji," I said, "but since coming to India I have changed my mind. I think there is progress, and I think India will begin to experience progress too, pretty soon." Swami was shocked. He ended with the grandiose declaration that he would rather see India remain as it is than become what America is: there would be no Buddhas, no Ramakrishnas, any more.

And so *there* is a problem.

But my formula touches something else: Swami's "change" theory, and the often heard Indian line of "no progress," which has been my own line too, is based, I now think, on India's unquenchable *pride.* It is obvious (I should think) to anyone who has actually beheld the two culture worlds, that not only mechanically, but also in the matters of physical health, social well-being, intellectual vitality and originality, philanthropic sympathy, general knowledge, science, scholarship, ability to help others, etc., there has been an actual and even measurable advance. But since Indians cannot admit inferiority, they counter all this with a spiritual claim, which is supposed to settle everything.

My review of the spiritual claim is set forth [see p. 72]: I not only admit it; I celebrate it. But in its actual effect on Indian life, I wonder how far it goes beyond the rendition of a spectacle of piety. Besides this spectacle of piety, I can record also—and have recorded—my delight at the manner in which Indian philosophy pours forth from the mouths of the people whom I meet in trains. There is no question: it is functioning here and now. One hears from contemporary mouths ideas announced in the texts of the eighth century B.C. Moreover, with Gandhi these ideas were given social expression (we shall come back to this in a minute).

But: a learned Mr. Pyarelal Nayar steals my paragraphs; an urchin tries to rob my pocket; an Indian movie firm steals an American film; Mr. Nehru accepts American aid and abuses America in every public pronouncement; everyone I meet is trying to get something from me, plans to come to America some day, wants a handout right now, or something; the rich in India hang on to their cash and let the whole place starve. I don't know; it is an odd thing: when you look at India from the outside it is a squalid mess and a haven of fakers; but when you look at it from the inside (perspective Belūr Maṭh), it is an epiphany of the spirit: Buddhas and Ramakrishnas and pious men and ladies. The eye sees a river of mud and the inner eye sees a river of grace.

Gandhi, sitting on the ghat at Belūr Maṭh, was heard to say that his whole life was an effort to bring into action the ideas of Vivekananda. Vivekananda learned a lot about social service in the U.S.A. A lot of the money for Belūr Maṭh came from the U.S.A.—and more is coming, if I may judge from words let drop today by Mrs. D. and the Countess. Talk about spiritual influence! I think that a good deal of what today looks like an application to life of the Indian spirit is actually an Indianization of the American spirit.

I drove back from Belūr Maṭh with the Indian M.D. girl and some other people, in a large Packard, to have a bit of a nap and to write these pages. Tonight I am going out there again for the *great* service of the Durgā Pūjā: that of the *sandhi,* the juncture—marriage—of the second and third days of the festival, at midnight.

When coming to India one is told: "Don't see the dirt only; see the spirit." I think it is proper to reply: "When looking at America, don't see the chromium only, see the spirit." The spirit is everywhere—as far as my own experience of people goes; and I must say, I don't think the actual Indian inflection is anymore impressive than what I know of the French, German, or American. People are nice everywhere. People are pious, sympathetic, and intelligent everywhere. But people aren't everywhere quite as poor as they are in India—and if one has a particular reverence for poverty, one may be fooled into thinking that the poverty itself is a sign of the spirit—whereas it is a sign only of a sociological or technological failure.

The spiritual principles that India expresses with a metaphysical inflection (all is *brahman*), the Christian expresses theologically (love thy neighbor as thyself for the love of God), and the secular democrat rationally (all are equal before the law). India's destiny may be to keep the metaphysical drone bass sounding while the rest of the world works out the actualization of man's equality on a level somewhat higher than that of the dust bin and the village cottage. The great traditions of India's past have been channeled now into the piety represented by *bhakti*. But the new age is also approaching India.

My present personal problem is that of assimilating a large-scale disappointment in India. The problem is not the dirt and poverty—those I expected. Nor is it finally that of the armed camp or lumbercamp atmosphere, which I did not expect. It is not the nature of the religion—that is even more interesting and easy to study than I expected. So then what is it?

The arrogant anti-Americanism, when they are doing everything they can to take over American ideas, is point one. This I did not expect; I do not like; and I cannot feel sweet about it. It is coupled with a frequently expressed disdain for American "rush," "materialism," and "money," expressed to your face while you are looking at a mess of beggars sleeping in an open drain. And these feats of the spirit are not rare, but normal. This, I believe, is what has gotten my goat. And I am trying, meanwhile, "not to see the dirt only, but the spirit." When I sit talking with the representatives of the spirit, they talk like sociological idiots. I think perhaps Swami's foolishness has aggravated the situation for me; but he is only an acute case of something that is chronic. Mr. Nehru is the keynoter of this refrain.

The anti-Americanism is the negative side of an Asia-for-the-Asians' patriotism, which is actually anti–white-man. This has resulted in a sentimental line-up with China that has thrown India into the Communist camp as a fellow-traveler. Nehru's great talk of Neutralism—which was an attempt to play, on a world scale, Britain's balance of power game, with the metaphysical air, however, of being beyond the pairs of opposites—has ended simply in the sort of thing that distinguishes the Sarah Lawrence Social Science Department. This is a fine lesson to have come all the way to India to learn.

The economic plight of India is of disaster proportions, and although much is being done to help the situation, there is so much to be done that India will certainly not be out of trouble (that is to say, will not have overcome its inferiority complex) before the end of this century.

The economic plight is matched by a cultural plight. The pandits are a shoddy lot, showing all the traits of the mind of small learning. They seem to be more interested in glorifying and whitewashing India than in objective scholarship, and their principal sources seem to be the Occidental scholars. I see little possibility of profit from a large-scale study of their works at this time. In contemporary literature and art also, there is going to be little to devour. Perhaps two or three individuals will be met, but are not likely to be of the stature of, say, Tagore—not to mention Joyce, Mann, Proust, or even Gide or Sartre.

In other words:

A. *India as a modern nation does not interest me at all.* It would be of great interest, however, to a sociologist, engineer, or industrialist.

But, on the other hand:

B. *As an archaeological museum, India is even more interesting than I had expected it to be.* Most valuable, I think, is the survival here (as in the Orient in general) of a religious atmosphere that has simply vanished from the West. This is a prodigious force—and I doubt very much whether science and technology are going to do much to dispel it within the next hundred years. I can no longer think of this as something of the past. Valuable also is my experience here of the character of the Fellaheen (in Spengler's sense).[81]

Finally:

C. *As to whether anyone whom I am likely to encounter here would be one to serve, in any sense, as a guru—I very much doubt.* So far, the people I have spoken to keep repeating things I already know—what may be called the clichés of India's opinion of herself.

Countering the negatives of points one and three, on the other hand, are my numerous and continuous experiences of the personal charm of Indian individuals. This positive personal factor (call it D) and the archaeological (B), are henceforth to hold my eye. The various disappointments and irritations of the A category can be disregarded—or at least endured. And, of course, there is always the possibility of an interesting vista into the realm suggested by C.

The visit this evening to Belūr Maṭh was very interesting. The crowd in the temple was not large and it was easy to see what was going on. The service was conducted with great dignity by the same functionaries as yesterday's. Commencing at about 11 P.M., it lasted about an hour.

I was particularly interested in watching the opening phase, when the chief celebrant performed the rite of dedicating his body. This was followed by a blessing of the food and garland offerings. Then three pans of lights were lighted and the main part of the service began. It consisted of a waving of lights, etc., like the service I had observed on my first visit to the *matha*. First is waved a great stand of lights, then a smaller, then a conch containing water, then a cloth, then a flower, and finally a chowry—the celebrant ringing, all the time, a bell with his left hand. When this was finished there came an event of even higher tension. The assisting monk arose and picked up a small sickle-like knife, touched the buffalo of the image, and then, with a sharp little cry, came down on—what should have been a goat, but was in this case a substitute: a banana! Meanwhile, from the beginning of the light-waving, a noise of drums, gongs, and cymbals. This event was followed by the *pūjā* of the President of the Order, the monks, and the congregation. I returned home by taxi.

Wednesday, October 6

Having admitted to myself that India is a large disappointment, I today had a very pleasant day. In the morning I went to a very nice dance concert, a "Manipur Dance Festival," presented by the Manipur Sangeet Natak Sammelan. The event had received a very unfavorable review in *The Statesman* by "Our Art Critic," but was, on the contrary, very good indeed. An excellent company presented twelve numbers to an audience of about two hundred, who seemed not to know how to applaud. I found that after sixteen or twenty claps I was going it alone. If it hadn't been for myself and an American couple down in the orchestra, there wouldn't even have been a second bow after the final number. It was a nice theater and I tried to see the General Manager, but his office was closed for the holiday.

This afternoon I took a bus out to Dakṣineśvara to see the temple in which Ramakrishna served as priest. There was a great crowd of visitors, very much like the crowd yesterday at Belūr Maṭh. I strolled around for about three quarters of an hour, saw the banyan, the Kālī image, and the secondary shrines. It was a pretty evening. Then I took a bus home, sat up front with the driver, and had a really wild and amazing drive. The city, the suburbs, in fact every inch of the way from Dakṣineśvara, was swarming with people in holiday gear. The bus—every bus—was jammed. The noise was incredible. *Paṇḍal* gongs the whole length of the way, shouting people, horns, rickshaw bells, and our driver with a voice like a tiger. I had a headache when I got to the hotel—but the drive had been well worth it. India seemed, for a moment, a different place: the crowd was gay and lovely and full of pretty women! I don't understand this place at all.

Thursday, October 7

Let me, this morning, try to start a summary of the positive values that I can discover in India for the modern world. I am taking for granted India's value as an ethnological museum. At present I can think of the following points:

1. *Brahman-ātman:* stress on the transcendent—this breaks the claim of every orthodoxy to exclusive validity, supplies a metaphysical background to the tolerance of the secular state, supports a democratic world affirmation, and points up the secondary character of all moral (mores) systems.
2. *Śakti:* mythology and psychology of the experience of the world as energy.
3. *Yoga:* techniques and psychology of the transformation of the personality.

These, briefly (*ātman–śakti–yoga*), are the sum total of what I can draw from the main line of Indian thought as pertinent to the modern West (that is to say, the future world); and I can add one or two more:

4. *Rasa:* Indian aesthetic theory, Oriental aesthetic theory.
5. *Purāṇa:* Indian mythology, an elucidated mythos.

Perhaps I should also add:

6. *Pūjā:* the principles of effective rite.

Most valuable for an understanding of these is the history of Indian philosophy and art from the Vedic period to circa A.D. 1250 (Koṇārak).

The patterns of *bhakti* belong essentially, I now think, to folk religion. It may be that in the West this will grow in force with the coming of

Spengler's "Second Religiousness";[82] however, it is also possible that with the critical transformation of the personality, which literacy, science, and technology are effecting, *bhakti* is to disappear. My present decision is to regard it as a phenomenon of the past, belonging to what may be called the medieval structure of consciousness. I do not see how it can be brought into accord with modern spirit, since wherever it prevails (in the West, for example, in the Catholic Church), there is an actual resentment of modernity (Nikhilananda shows this conspicuously).

Archaism number one, then, is *bhakti*. It is to be studied as an ethnological phenomenon. On the other hand, as general reverence for life, it is to be fostered. I would not know where precisely to draw the line between *bhakti* and reverence—particularly if one adds to reverence the concept of "all is *brahman*." Perhaps the line is between worship and reverence.

There have been rains during Durgā Pūjā, and these have left the air cooler and lighter. It is pleasanter than it was to move around. Also, the memory of yesterday's crowds (*la vie en fleuve*) has given me a better feeling than I'd had about India. One thinks of Disney's *The Living Desert:* at certain moments it shows its hidden life, and after one has seen it, one looks at the desert in a somewhat different way. And finally, my thoughts this morning about *ātman–śakti–yoga–rasa–purāṇa–pūjā* have given me a positive attitude toward the tradition. The little concert yesterday helped a lot too.

Spent the morning at the American Express making arrangements for my Bhubaneshwar-Puri-Koṇārak and Bhubaneshwar to Madras stages. In the middle afternoon took a taxi up to Belūr Maṭh, to see the last event of the Durgā Pūjā, the Immersion, which would take place after dark. There was a moderate crowd. I sat around among them, here and there, took a couple of pictures, and then had tea with the ladies and Swami.

At tea, Swami noted my improved mood about India, and this loosened his tongue pleasantly; but then, as always in his conversation, a good feeling about India implied, and gave an occasion for his communicating a disdain for the West, and particularly for America. This pattern, which is not peculiar to Swami (see, for example, A. K. Coomaraswamy, Danielou, Guénon[83]), I shall have to accept as normal before I can begin to look at India properly. Swami told of conversations he has had here with swamis and pandits, all of whom have a positive hatred for America. One had said, "A nation of upstarts, they will have their day and disappear." You get this every day in the papers too. I felt the attitude most strongly, and almost fiercely, in New Delhi, in Mme. Pandit, particularly in a look that she gave me as she introduced Swami and told her audience that the Westerners whom they saw in India were examples of the confusion and emptiness of the foreigners, who had to come to India to find something of value.[84] After tea I wandered around some more, watched a bit of the *pūjā* before the Ramakrishna image from outside the temple, and noticed that the women were watching it from outside too (apparently, in certain monk rites, woman's place is *not* in the temple). The crowd was gathering along the river wall and at the ghat, so I moved in that direction.

Then a young man in white, a Ramakrishna *brahmacārin,* approached me and very cautiously opened conversation. I was from America? Came with Swami? A devotee? (No.) What religion? (None.) What was my interest in religion? What religion flourished in the U.S.A? What did Americans think of Ramakrishna? (When I told him that not many more than one in a hundred thousand had ever heard of Ramakrishna, he was a little shocked and saddened.) What did they think of Vivekananda? Gandhi? (I gave him a nice blurb for Gandhi.) Nehru? (They are not so sure, I told him, about Nehru.) Did Americans drink? Why? Did it not destroy character? What about divorce? What about purity? (I gave him some real surprises here.) Did Americans believe in God? Why did I not let the monks initiate me into Hinduism? What did I think happened after death? What about spirit? Then I was a materialist? ("Yes," I said, "in this context I am a materialist.") Were there beggars in America? What are the buildings like? What salaries do professors get? How much did my shoes cost? Did I have a car? Did all Americans have cars? What was the situation about the Negroes?

Presently the image was brought out of the temple. Empty brass jars were carried before it down to the Ganges. The image was set on the top step of the ghat with its back to the river. The drums and gongs were going great guns and a little hopping dance of boys and swamis took place before the figure. "It is only an image now," my *brahmacārin* told me. "Everything has been withdrawn." After the dance (simply hopping and clapping the hands above the head) the image was carried down to the river, set on the lowest step, and one by one the goddess's weapons then were taken from her: trident, sickle, sword, etc. Then, to a cry, she was tipped back and into the water. Four or five men pushed her out into the Ganges, and she sank.

The brass jars then were filled with Ganges water and carried into the temple to be splashed about onto people's heads. Some people went into the temple, the rest dispersed.

I returned to Howrah by bus, walked across the bridge, and saw a number of the *paṇḍal* images going into the river. The images are made of clay, painted and dressed. The different neighborhoods, I have learned, take up collections and build their *paṇḍals;* but this is a relatively new custom. Formerly, the images were in private homes, where, however, caste rules made for a kind of exclusiveness that is no longer favored. All castes can participate in the ceremonies of the neighborhood *paṇḍals.* The first night the Goddess is invoked, then, in the morning of the first full day (October 4), is the ceremony that I observed at length, *saptamī pūjā.* On the second day, *mahāṣṭamī,* the biggest day of the *pūjā,* comes the *kumārī* ceremony, and that evening, toward midnight, the *sandhi.* Day number three, *mahā-navamī,* was a day of throngs, and was for me the brightest day, so far, in India. Then, at the conclusion of the fourth day (today), we had the Immersions. The goddess had come and gone—and was rather cute.

Friday, October 8

The general social atmosphere of India is that of a co-ed boarding school with segregated sexes and depleted finances.

Surprise: I went at four to pay a small sum at the American Express, and sitting on the sidewalk, flat against the office-building, was an absolutely naked little black woman with buck teeth and a grimace of disgust, right leg out straight before her and left knee up against her left shoulder, leaving her *yonī* exposed and blazing red at the world. Over her left shoulder was a filthy piece of cloth, about the size of a face towel. Otherwise, as far as I could see, there wasn't another woman in the city. The streets were full of men, as usual, pissing in the gutters, etc., and nobody but myself even turned to look at this incarnation of Kālī. Well: in India it's either too little or too much. And both leave you cold. In this case, however, I think the woman's vagina was perhaps inflamed and that she was exhibiting her disability intentionally, just as the leper, some thirty yards further along the wall, was exhibiting his disabled hands. The first time I saw the woman—when I went into the American Express office—she was sitting with her right side to the wall and her left knee up against her chin; as though, having taken off her shred of cloth, she were now waiting to get up the nerve to proceed to the next stage of her exposure. When I came out of the office, some fifteen minutes later, the exposure was complete.

Inside the office were, by chance, Swami Nikhilananda, the Countess, and two other swamis. One, who is leaving next week to take charge of the New York Center until Nikhilananda returns, asked how I had liked the Durgā Pūjā; he said that most of the images in the town *paṇḍals* were sort of new-fangled: neither traditional nor graced by any significant innovation—"like a modern Indian girl." And so there it was again: the monks representing a resentment of the modern movement. He next asked me if I knew Professor Spiegelberg in California. I said I had met him. "He was in India to see if Indian religion was still functioning, or something," said the swami, "and I believe he wrote a little book about it; but I don't think he met the right people." "The right people," I said, "are hard to meet in India. The Indians hide their jewels." But what I had in mind, was that in India, one authority's "right person," is every other authority's "wrong person."

Saturday, October 9   Darjeeling

Things have begun to happen so fast that I shall just note events for the next few days, and perhaps develop my thoughts when I get to Madras. Up this morning at 5 A.M. to catch 6:15 airplane-bus. A boorish Indian family had copped all the window-seats in the plane. I sat beside one of the sons, who was a fidget. Plane landed at Baghdagra airport at about 10 A.M. Controversy about seats in the automobile. Mountain drive to Darjeeling: two Californian ladies in the car on a world tour, Miss Ronni Leitner and Miss Pam Tylor, about forty and fifty-eight respectively, gave me a lot of dope on travel in Japan, and became my pals for the Darjeeling day.

On the first part of the drive I noticed a lot of interesting black people wearing colorful

Darjeeling and Vicinity

TIBET
BHUTAN
Darjeeling
INDIA
NEPAL   Baghdagra
BANGLADESH
N
←— 25 miles —→

reds and greens: Santāls? They inhabited very neat palm-thatch huts, quite un-Hindu in appearance. As we got up into the mountains Nepalese and Tibetan types began to appear, and by the time we reached Darjeeling we were practically in Tibet. Beautiful view of Mt. Kanchenjunga (28,156 feet) from the Mt. Everest Hotel. Good lunch, with a superb treacle tart, the best pastry since New York.

After lunch we took a car to see a nearby pair of lakes and a Red-cap Lamasery, which was almost (if not actually) abandoned. When we descended from the car an obliging little monk met us at the entrance and conducted us into the temple; we were not required to remove our shoes. There was a great, ceiling-high image of the Buddha wearing the crown and teaching (golden face and hands), and at either side, in cases, two shelves of smaller figures: Mañjuśrī, Avalokiteśvara, the founder of the order, the local abbot, and others. A number of votive lights, two slowly revolving prayer wheels turned by the hot air rising from burning wicks, and several images filled the little room. The walls were lined with pigeon holes containing prayer-book packets, and there were also Buddha murals, in a style suggesting that of twelfth-century Nepalese palm-leaf manuscripts. We left our offerings, were shown a palm leaf manuscript, and went out, only to be beckoned into another building by another little man, who had a sort of machine shop of prayer wheels: one was turned by pulling a rope, others were turned by hot air. The little man showed us his beads, Buddha images, prayer book, and paraphernalia—and when we left our offerings presented his son, who was to receive something too. Our chauffeur told us that the first man was a monk and could not marry, but that the second was a priest and married.

We returned to town in time to watch the breaking up of the Saturday market—and what an assortment of faces! Tibetans, Nepalese, Bengalis, Lepchas, and whatnots! Simply wonderful!

We then returned to the hotel, had a couple of drinks, chatted with some of the tourist gentry, and afterwards retired early, since we are to be called at 3:30 A.M. to see the sunrise from Tiger Hill. There is some question as to whether there may be too many clouds: but if it will be impossible to see anything, we shall not be called.

The rather general and carefree talk about travel and touring with these nice, simple people gave me a strong feeling of the wonderful privilege that my year of sheer sightseeing really is, and I began to feel silly about my heavy-headed East-West agony. Darjeeling, I believe, is somewhat clearing my mind.

Sunday, October 10

Up at 3:30 A.M.; morning tea; and a drive with my two friends to Tiger Hill to see the sunrise strike Mt. Kanchenjunga. Tiger Hill itself is 8,514 feet high and has a little observatory on its summit, which was thronged with Hindus from Calcutta when we arrived. There were heavy clouds in the valleys below us, and the eastern horizon, as well as much of the vast mountain panorama, was obscured; but Kanchenjunga was there and when the clouds shifted we caught views of the other peaks. At the moment of the sunrise Kanchenjunga became wonderfully luminous; one could only imagine what the whole mountain scene would have been had the clouds not been there. On the way down, our driver paused to show us the peak of Mt. Everest peeping over a mountain ridge far away.

After breakfast we strolled slowly down to the town, where I arranged to leave on the afternoon plane from Baghdagra. A telegram arrived last night from the American Express to tell me that it would be impossible to visit Koṇārak on the twelfth, since the pilot of the plane would then be in Calcutta, so I am trying to advance my schedule by one day. We next paid a visit to the new home of Tenzing Norgay, conqueror of Mt. Everest, where we found a huge crowd of visitors, but no Tenzing Norgay. He was away for the day. His wife, however, played hostess, while the swarm of Bengalis and ourselves examined all the trophies, wrote in the guest book, and took pictures.

The ride back to Baghdagra seemed very long. We hit a dog on the way and had to pause in the town while the driver talked it off with a man whose hand the dog then bit. I felt very strongly the transition from the mountain world, with its atmosphere of Tibet, to the land of the plains—Santāls and Bengalis.

An easy flight to Calcutta; beside me, a very nice young Hindu, Ram Sharma, who had spent a year at some college in America. We talked of the American-Indian contrast, and, when we arrived at the air field, had a drink. In Calcutta, I got a pleasant reception from all the waiters, doormen, etc. at the Hotel Great Eastern. Found Pam and Ronni at a table in one of the lounges penning an irate letter of some kind to the American Express office, had dinner with a little couple I'd met in Darjeeling, and, leaving an order for tea at 4 A.M., went to bed.

ORISSA

Monday, October 11   **Bhubaneshwar**

Woke with a threatening throat-cold, caught, I dare say, on Tiger Hill. Got the 5:15 A.M. bus to the airport. Early morning in Calcutta: all the people who sleep on the sidewalks in various stages of getting up, cleaning their teeth at muddy hydrants, and so on. At one point the bus had to go around a young man doing his sitting-up exercises in the middle of the road—stark naked.

At the airport: Nikhilananda, two or three Ramakrishna monks, and the two ladies. Greetings! I took breakfast in the airport restaurant, and our plane took off at about seven. At 8:45 A.M. we began coming down, and I could see to the left the great Liṅgarāja Temple compound, and to the right the new city, laid out in blocks, with its new, California-type buildings—in one case facing a block of palm-thatch homes.

Orissa I find really fine: the best thing so far in India: lovely air, beautiful skies, fertile flatland by the sea, and, after Calcutta, clean and orderly looking people. Orissa, I am told, has a population that is between twenty and fifty percent tribal. I notice many very black people, and garb has a lot of color in it, like that of the Baghdagra area.

Our comical party are the State Guests of Orissa, and so we were met at the plane by a pleasant delegation of young men and their superiors, packed into cars, and driven to the State Guest House—a nice, clean, well-serviced sort of small hotel—one-storied, with the rooms along a long verandah, and patriotically Indian-type toilets. After a brief wash-up, we were ready to go visit temples, but Swami said that if I wished to go *into* the temples I would have to wear Indian dress. One of the young men helped me into the

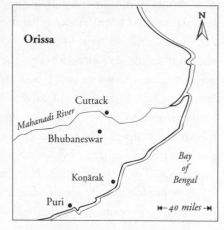

yards of khaki I had bought, on Swami's suggestion, in New Delhi; then Swami took my picture, and we were off.

The temples that we visited—the Rājarāṇī, Paraśurāmeśvara, Mukteśvara, and Vaitāl Deul—were all old and abandoned and required no such rigging at all; I was surprised at the charming smallness of them all: some of the figures were no larger than my little finger. I also began to realize what a job of photographing Eliot Elisofon[85] had done. I took a few pitiful photos myself, and then was driven to the railroad station to cancel my ticket to Madras (since I must now go at a later date). The station master took one hour and a half to fill out half a sheet of form. I sat in the station feeling like a perfect fool: the only white man in the place, and the only man in the place wearing full Indian regalia.

When I got back to the Guest House I changed back into slacks and a shirt and joined my friends for lunch. We all then had our naps and at about 4:00 P.M. began to get ready for our visit to the great Liṅgarāja compound. I remained in my Western gear and Swami said it would be all right, that I could take photos from the outside while they went in. We drove up to the small space before the temple, and two of our young men were there. They had arranged everything for us and had a priest who would be our guide. So we took off our shoes and socks, left our leather camera-cases and wristwatches with leather straps, and went in.

I stuck close to B. B. Nath, the Museum Curator, and he showed me the details of the sculptural decor. I made appreciative sounds and remarks. Priests, meanwhile, were shouting at us from every direction to come visit *their* shrines—just like the shopkeepers of Calcutta. Nath took me up to a Gaṇeśa shrine. The priest was at hand. Semi-reverently I laid a rupee at the deity's feet, and we went off. Next we visited Kārttikeya—another priest and another rupee. I bowed before the image and we went away. Pārvatī was next: one more rupee. I bowed, took the dust off the goddess's feet, was given a garland, and gave another rupee. Next came a shrine of Viṣṇu (surprise!). A rupee—but by now a swarm of priests, shouting like fishwives for rupees. I had no more one-rupee notes. "Five rupees for all!" they shouted. "Yes! Yes!" I dallied a while, and finally produced the five-rupee note. Twenty hands were before me. Everybody was shouting.

I looked quizzically about, and then they all got together on it and pointed to one young hand that was held out with a dramatic readiness.

"That one?" I said. "Yes! Yes!" the priest-swarm shouted. "O.K." and I placed the five-rupee note in the hand. They all ran off like urchins: all except one. "One rupee, one rupee!" he said, with his hand held out, and he followed me until, on the point of leaving the temple, I gave him ten annas; whereupon he turned away in glee. But at the other side of the gate I was met by a swarm of beggars; and then Swami came, followed by the whole horde of priests. The car, pulling away, had to begin very slowly, or we should have been held for mass homicide.

Tuesday, October 12   **Puri**

Up early and off to Puri, for a complicated day. First we paused at the Liṅgarāja Temple again, so that Swami and the ladies could go into the main sanctuary, which, last night, was closed. I was glad to remain outside and take a few photos—one from the platform erected outside the wall for *mlecchas* like myself. But when the holy ones came out again (followed, of course, by the brahmins, every one of whom I recognized) I was told that they had asked where the man was who had accompanied them the day before: namely, the man with all the rupees.

Next we paused at a little town of thatched huts around a temple called Sakhī Gopāl, where I drank some coconut milk while the others went inside.

After that, we headed straight for Puri and arrived about 10:15 A.M. I and one of the young men went in for a swim. The sand of the broad beach was so hot I could hardly bear it, and I ran for the water. Then two lifeguards came trotting up the beach to help us (they had already been sent for), and each of us went in then, like girls, to breast the waves. There was great talk of a heavy undertow, but I didn't feel it. Still, I didn't feel like making a scene either, so I submitted to this silly affair. The little lifeguards wore curious, tall white cones on their heads, each with a number. After our swim, we tipped them one rupee each.

After lunch, Swami wanted to sleep, and his two ladies, who had already been sent up to sleep for the morning, were overtly annoyed. B. B. Nath and I drove with them to town so that they might buy some cards and writing paper and cigarettes, after which they returned willingly to the seraglio. Nath took me to visit a few craft shops and when we returned, Nath went to sleep while I sat and looked out the door at the sea.

At 3:30 P.M. all were again astir and our viewing of Puri commenced.

First, the great square before the temple with its three wagons (Jagannātha's with sixteen wheels, Subhadrā's with twelve, and Balabhadra's with fourteen). They were in the (slow) process of being dismantled. We went up into the Ramakrishna library for a magnificent view of the temple and city. Three elephants were in the square, mildly entertaining people; beggars, *sadhus,* pilgrims, were everywhere; the shops were full, and the commerce of the god was great. We next drove around the city a bit, visiting places of interest to Swami, where he and the ladies could bow before various deceased people's shoes, cots, and photographs. Traveling along the main Jagannātha road I had the real feeling of being in India: it was rich and delightful. We came at one point to a ghat by a pond inhabited by great tortoises, and a priest made a calling sound that brought one blinking to the surface. The people tossed food of some kind, at which he snapped.

Before a monastery said to have been founded by Śaṅkara, one of our two cars ran its back left spring up onto an iron spike, and it took us some time, in the gathering twilight, to get it down. Meanwhile, the other car went off to deliver Swami to the temple, and from this point onward the mix-up was great. Following his visit to the temple (which lasted two hours), Swami wanted to visit some old Ramakrishna monk; and so it was about 9:00 P.M. before we started the long drive home. The Countess, meanwhile, lost a purse containing a thousand rupees; and for a moment I thought I had lost my camera.

But the main thing was that in Puri—a city devoted to a celebration that takes place once a year, and to its temple—I felt for the first time the real throb of India. A fully medieval combination of religion and life, with people doing crazy things (way better than the Surrealist effort) because of the God—a great clatter everywhere, and all with a transcendental reference.

At one moment a little cluster of late middle-aged and oldish men went past, clanking cymbals, beating a drum, bearing staffs, and with religious markings on their foreheads, singing a *kīrtana* of Caitanya; I thought their physiques looked very much like those with which I was familiar from the New York Athletic Club baths. Then I asked myself what the counterparts of these oldsters would be in New York: the members, perhaps, of some poetry society with an aesthetic-rational orientation; humanists perhaps. And then it came over me that:

The great difference between our two civilizations is the humanist versus transcendental orientation; the humanist now having broken through to a subliminal and even transcendental level, but the reference-emphasis remaining, even so, phenomenal man.

The second great difference (which is perhaps a function of the other) is a consequence of the partition of the sexes. The chance of a personal adventure, determined by the personality of a representative of the opposite world and energized by an unpredicted interplay of the two fundamental human attitudes, is simply not permitted to occur. The results are numerous, among them being a sort of proto-homosexuality, a lack of life-inventiveness, and a satisfaction with clichés.

A third difference (perhaps a function of the second) is the caste principle: no one is an individual—everyone is but a fraction—which accounts, I believe, for the absence of anything resembling civic consciousness.

In my chats with one of the young men who are watching over us in Orissa, I have gotten a bit of the feeling of the young Indian marriage. He is a handsome, very gentle and affectionate young brahmin—about twenty-eight, I should say. He is married and has two children, never saw his wife until the day of their marriage, and now lives in the same house with his elder brother, who is also married. These two days have been his holidays—and instead of having planned some sort of holiday with his wife and kids, he has been free (and glad) to spend them with us. Puri, anyplace but in India, I should think, would be a booming beach resort, but here four meager little hotels and the big house of some maharaja constitute the beach front. The young man and I went swimming this morning, and there was no one else in sight. This evening, while waiting for Swami, we walked on the beach in the light of the full moon. It was

Dryad beneath a palm, Bhubaneshwar

lovely. There were perhaps two hundred people sitting along the high-wave mark—all in their saris and dhotis and shirts, all in absolute silence: a very mild affair indeed. I remarked on this, and my young man said that Indians don't have any idea of what to do on holidays. To go to the beach would be an enormous operation: children, servants, problems of cooking, procuring food; and then who would be there? Etc., etc. My god! What a joyless lot!

After dinner, I sat out on the lawn of the Bhubaneshwar State Guest House, chatting with a character with a pipe, about fifty-four, who has been pestering me for a talk ever since I arrived. South Indian brahmin family; proud of his service with the British Navy, now writing a book on contemporary Orissa. He wished to talk to me about Koṇārak, which I am to visit tomorrow, and had two ideas about the erotica, and then a third which he simply rejected as unlikely:

1. They had something to do with the idea of heat, the sun's heat, and generation.
2. They were to be transcended by the one seeking *mokṣa*.
3. They were there to protect the temple from lightning.

I suggested that 1 and 2 might be readily combined, since the sun (sun-door) was both the generator and sustainer of this world and the symbol of the way to the transcendent.

The solar symbolism of the temple, the gentleman said, was an intricate representation of the diurnal, planetary, annual, etc. rhythms and cycles; and there was some sort of order to the sequence of symbols on the twenty-four wheels that had not yet been deciphered. I was to look out for it tomorrow.

He spoke also of the great gurus and sages, who are the life of India, though hardly to be seen; told how it is in the blood of all Hindus to begin hankering for a guru at the age of about forty-five: spoke of Sri Shivananda Saraswati, and Aurobindo (whom I brought up). He spoke also of the two contemporary Vaiṣṇava attitudes: that of the baby monkey (∪ on forehead) and that of the kitten (with a ∨)—see Ramakrishna's discussions of these two attitudes—clinging to the mother, and crying for the mother.[86]

Wednesday, October 13   Koṇārak

Woke at 5:30, got up and shaved. At about 5:50 my morning tea arrived, and by six I was ready for the car that was to take me to the Flying Club, my date with the airplane being for 6:30. By 6:10 I began to be impatient and started walking down the road. No car. I saw a squad of about sixteen lusties in khaki trunks and white shirts trotting in unison, on some kind of early morning drill. They were followed by a man who was trotting also, but with a bicycle by the handlebars. I asked the latter which way to the airdrome, and he pointed ahead, then mounted his bicycle and caught up with his crowd. Chaps were beginning to drop out and walk back to what I now saw was their fire-house. I began to trot myself, holding my camera with my left hand and field glasses with my right. At the next crossroad I asked a kid: "airplane?" He pointed and I trotted some more. I began to get tired after fifteen minutes, but could see the airdrome just ahead, and so pressed on. At 6:35 I arrived. A young man with a beard was up in the tower. Dog tired, I got up to him, only to be told that the Flying Club was down the other end of the runway—about half a mile more. It was the longest half mile I ever ran in my life—longest and slowest.[87] I came wobbling toward my little biplane two-seater at about 6:50. The flyer, Mr. K. S. Krishnan, piled me into his plane and flew me to my goal.

A great thrill! Eighty-one miles per hour, 1,100 feet in the air, in an open cockpit—over the Liṅgarāja Temple compound and then, twenty minutes later, over Koṇārak. We landed in an open field between the temple and the sea. Mr. Krishnan asked a boy to get me a coconut for refreshment and I drank the milk while we walked to the temple. I spent a lovely hour and a half there, and the return home was even more delightful, somehow, than the trip out.

Mr. Krishnan then invited me to his house, right by the airport, for a cup of tea. I met his wife and saw the photos from a trip that he had taken with her and his children: got the feeling that life here was a bit more modern than the Indian norm. Then my State Car drove me to the airport, where I found Swami and the girls, as well as the Director General of Archaeology and his friends, who were to be flown to Koṇārak next. In fact it was their date with Mr. Krishnan that had thrown my plans, as well as Swami's, into a cocked hat. Swami and the ladies, finally, couldn't get to Koṇārak at all.

We visited the caves of Udayagiri, but were too fatigued to climb; then the Khandagiri hill to the Ananta cave.

I got home, at last, took a shower, and went to sleep, while the others went back to Cuttack where Swami was to deliver a lecture. I woke at about

6:00 and took another shower; but this time felt a chill and knew that I had a fever. After dressing, I had tea with the man with the pipe, who talked now about his drinking adventures in the navy. Swami & Co. arrived: we dined and went to bed. I first, however, took two full doses of aspirin.

I feel at this point that I know a great deal more about India than I did five days ago. At Darjeeling I acquired a fresh taste for my year of travel, and in Orissa I got a sense, at last, of touching the India I had come to find. A few meditations:

1. India's enormous tolerance of apparently irreconcilable elements.
2. India's strength: her transcendental orientation; the guru idea.
3. India's homosexual atmosphere: sex separation, momism (Durgā), phallic interest (*liṅga*), woman for reproduction (Platonism); no individual experience of unpredicted relationships with individuals of opposite sex—lack of life invention, satisfaction with clichés; no real life verve.
4. Caste system—failure of civic interest and adventure.
5. India's contemporary problem:
   a. Spiritual aspect: Can an Oriental state be a secular state? Can a non-secular state be a democratic state?
   b. Political aspect: A common border of several thousand miles with Communist powers; a great need for U.S. aid and advice; a greater need for time (perhaps a hundred years).
   c. Emotional aspect: A feeling of common cause with Asia; a feeling of common cause with British democracy; a feeling that India should somehow be the world axis.
   d. Mechanical aspect: Can India make the machine serve Indian ends? The machines that she is buying and copying were invented by Westerners to serve Western ends: they tend to bring their entelechies with them[88] and so create in the Orient a pathological anxiety about machines and what they are doing to the world. For machines to serve Indian ends Indian inventors must arise. What is the likelihood of such an event?
6. The line of contrast between Oriental and Occidental ideals:[89]
   a. Western humanism: The total man, not the caste man. This ideal may be Greek, but in Greece the sex partition was probably as strong as it is here. This ideal belongs, I think, to a much later Europe: the Europe of the Germanic north. It is an aristocratic idea, I think, and *may* have played a brief role in the Orient of the Epic period. But Koṇārak represents a more idyllic eroticism, less personal than that here involved.
   b. Western eroticism: The sense of life's adventure and play, and of personal growth through these.

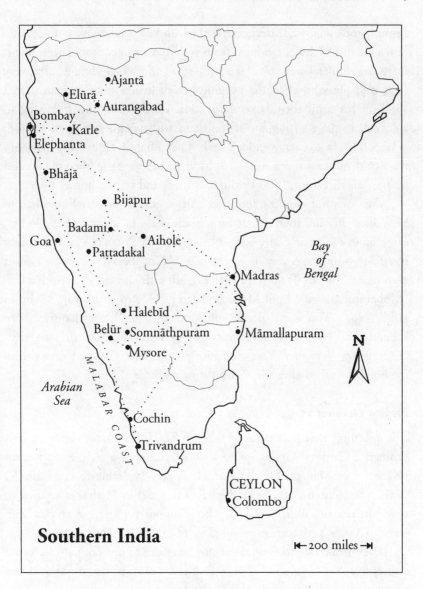

Southern India

↦ 200 miles ↤

MADRAS

Thursday, October 14   **Madras**

Flight from Bhubaneshwar to Madras, 9 A.M. to 1:30 P.M. A huge delegation of monks showed up to meet the plane. Lunch at the Connemara Hotel, and a nap. My temperature has gone and the cold is about gone too.

I simply took it easy all afternoon, bathed, and enjoyed my very nice room. Still a bit stiff (Achilles tendons) from yesterday's three- or four-mile jaunt.

After dinner I went out for a little stroll and was finding Madras very clean and pleasant when the begging began: first, a dirty woman with a child on her arm, then a couple of kids. I came with this following to a crowded square with a lot of stalls and with people sitting all around: "Ha! Sahib!" from every vendor's stall; "OOO Babu!" from every beggar in the world. When I saw a man with bandaged legs see me, then get up and walk in my direction, I was through, turned, and started home.

Two kids hung on for about six blocks. Several rickshaw boys had to be walked off, and then a neat little black chap, in white Indian clothes, came up to me. "Girls?" he said. "Nice girls?" "No thanks." "Boys? Young boys? My young boys very nice; very nice." "No," I said, "not boys. I don't even like the idea." "You want nice English girl?" he asked. "No thanks." "Mohammedan girl? I got Mohammedan girl." "No thank you." "Hindu girl?" "No." "You want nice hospital nurse? I got hospital nurse. Nice Indian girl." "Well," I said, "you got everything!" "Yes sir," he said, "Everything. Very nice. You want nice young boys?" When I turned into the hotel, he called after me, "Tomorrow night? Yes! Very nice!"

Friday, October 15

The morning newspapers carry the story of India's new Cardinal, His Eminence Cardinal Gracias, who is to be accorded a civic reception on his arrival in Madras. The long article is very favorable to the Catholic spirit. The Roman Catholic Cathedral (A.D. 1504) in Madras is reputed to cover the remains of St. Thomas, who is supposed to have been martyred on St. Thomas's Mount (mentioned by Marco Polo) while praying.

After breakfast I took a taxi to the American Express office and found a letter from the Hindu kid in New Delhi who came to visit me at the hotel after my talk. After lunch I rented a car and toured the town.

Madras is by far the cleanest and pleasantest Indian city so far, with many modern buildings and more going up; a large, wealthy looking section of new American estates, and another of new Indian estates (copying the American exactly in design): also new office buildings. The city is growing rapidly.

There is something neater about palm thatch than about mud for the poor. Madras, consequently, though apparently as full of the very poor as New Delhi, seems very much tidier. More women are visible in the streets here than elsewhere, and many look very nice. And the hand-cart men, nearly naked, have strong, handsome physiques. (The more I live here, the better I understand Monroe Wheeler's joy in the place!)

The main language, after Tamil, is not Hindi but English. In contrast to the north, all signs are in English. Most people speak it. Many Europeans and Americans are visible. The Catholic Church is very strong. One sees also YMCA and YWCA set-ups.

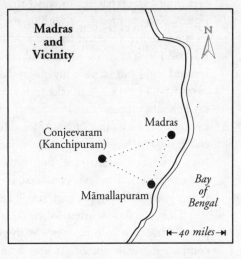

And, I must say, after what I have seen of Hindu *bhakti,* Roman Catholicism doesn't look too bad for the Indians. Mrs. D. tells me that it is very strong in the south because here the very conservative brahminism was extremely hard on the *śūdras,* Untouchables and Tribes. Well, O.K. It has all worked out very nicely.

During my tour I visited St. Mary's Church (built 1678–1680), the first English church in India (rebuilt 1759), and paused a while to read the epitaphs on the grave slabs in the churchyard: mostly young and young middle-aged men, c. 1652–1759. Made me think of the Honolulu Christians a century later. Strange, bold, and fateful old days! I visited also the great Śiva Temple: my first view of one of these gaudy southern things: freshly painted: my oh my!

And so now, the gem for today: my letter from New Delhi.

My dear Professor,
Received your kind letter of today. Extremely glad to go thro' the contents. when. I was completely disappointed, for, I never received a reply for a long time. [He wrote to me in Calcutta and I sent him an answer after some delay.] But I understand the situation for the delay. I have seen [?] your acquising [sic] me in your letter "your expression

of feelings...indeed is bad..." [He must have misread something.] How can you say that. It is not a brief one or for the time being till I forget you. It has come naturally in my heart when I saw you on the very first day. So whether I am in your company or not that will be the same. Since it became so deep, even your photo, why so much as even your letter is enough to satisfy that hunger. When the love is too intense physical meeting is nothing to do with that. That is only till we are together. One can enjoy ever if it is from the heart. If you say it is bad I won't agree. and that will not disappoint me. Always I look forward and I will sacrifice myself for that when I feel it is normal and correct. Still I am ready to take your advice. Do then do you mean to say I should suppress that love and affection towards you because we cannot meet each other often. At least in our mythology there are several instances, where two met only once in this lifetime, they were friends through out their life. But if you say this is modern age I want to know that. Can we not be united, even without seeing each other? Don't you think it is true [*sic*], it will be so sincere also.

Then you have written "when one travels this kind of thing happens." Here also I do not agree with you. How can you judge and compare me with others? At least why don't you test my sincerity after coming across though several such instances(?) Have some patience to find out whether I am sincere or not. Why you see me like a passerby. Test my sincerity. I can repeat only this.

Only so much I can say whether you show your affection towards me or not. I do not mind. Still I love you. Hereafter also it will be the same and I sacrifice myself for that.

From your letter I understand you are extremely happy in my place of India. Why don't you write in details where—[?] you had been to show you enjoyed, so that I too will share the happiness. At least when you go to Madras and when you see temples in south and those beautiful Belūr, Halebīd, and Somnāthpuram in Mysore you please write a detailed letter about how you have enjoyed and how you are interested. As you are a professor in literature I have no doubt that you will give me a fine description about what you have seen.

Expecting eagerly the month of December I hope we will meet in Delhi.

All are doing well here.

with love from K. Narasimhan

N. B. Nobody can go against God's will. He created this in you in my mind. At the same time if he wish that we should not meet each other and we should be far, I can't help. I have to suffer for that.

K. N.

Excuse me for writing in pencil.

Saturday, October 16

Started the day with an answer to young K. N.

My dear Narasimhan:

I am sorry that my last letter disappointed you and am afraid that the present one is going to disappoint you too. For it appears that you are expecting much more from me than I am going to give. Please remember when you write to me that I am a rather busy person, of late middle age, happily married, with many many friends to whom I am writing; I simply cannot begin writing long letters to you descriptive of my travels, feelings, thoughts, or anything else. Moreover, the whole prospect of a love union is to me, at my age, utterly uninteresting. A quarter of a century ago I had a number of such eternal unions—all, however, with members of the female sex. And my present eternal union is with my wife. I am not going to test your sincerity, ask you to sacrifice yourself, or engage in any of the great gestures of love. You asked me to be your friend and to reply to your letters; I shall be pleased to do so. But I must tell you now—simply and coldly—that I am extremely busy; already well taken care of, as far as love is concerned; disinclined to love affairs with males; and too old for romance of an idealizing nature.

If you wish to write to me again, please do not do so right away. Read this letter of mine several times. Let ten days pass and read it again. Realize in your ardent heart that you are writing to a person who has not fallen in love with you, of whose life you know absolutely nothing, whom you have no right to command, and who does not want to hear any more about sincerity, sacrifice, or eternity. You may regard me as a friend, if you wish, but not as a lover.

What you are in love with is a projection of your own imagination. You cannot be in love with me because you do not know me. Break up this figment of *māyā* that has caught you and please do not begin to write to me again until you begin to feel (sincerely) that your attitude has changed. This is the only sacrifice that I shall ask of you.

And so, with sincere good wishes, and the suggestion that you begin this difficult work of spiritual discipline right away, I am, Yours very sincerely, &c.

After breakfast, walked to the Madras Government Museum, which is, by far, the best museum I have visited in India. The bronze collection is elegant; also, of course, the Amarāvatī panels and fragments. Among the bronzes are a number of Buddhas with the flame rising from the *uṣṇiṣa*. There are a couple of Rāma and Sītā pairs, a handsome sitting Mahiṣāsura-mardinī, three fine Śiva Naṭarājas, and an interesting collection of carved wooden beams and jambs. Also rooms of tribal and folk exhibits, including a couple of figures of the village deity Aiyanār, with his wives Puranai and Pudkalai; some wooden, painted deities of the fishermen of Orissa; a cute set of the avatars of Viṣṇu; and some photos of the dancing dress of Indian shamans that suggested, on the one hand, the Kathakali costumes and, on the other, some of the dancing gear of Melanesia. There was a carved figure from Malabar used in sorcery which suggested Africa. I noticed also that an exhibited zither was called a *swara maṇḍala* and wondered whether the word mandolin might be related. Certainly sitar, zither, and guitar go together.

At 3:30 this afternoon I joined Mrs. D. and the Countess for a visit to the Ramakrishna Maṭh. A particularly fine set of buildings. We then went with Nikhilananda and another swami to the home of a Dr. Ramakrishnan (M.D.), where we had a delightful "tea": tasty Indian sweets, prepared and served by the gentleman's daughter and granddaughter, and then a won-derful café au lait (tasting like a mocha). The people showed us through their house, which was one of the new buildings that I saw from outside while on my sightseeing tour: two stories, upstairs verandah, lots of air, handsome Burma-teak woodwork (doors, windows, stairs), and dull-red, shinily waxed, tile-like, composition floors; living and bedrooms in Western style; kitchen and pantry store-room, however, rather Indian. The first room that they showed us was a little family chapel, with a figure of Ramakrishna and about ten of those holy pictures of the Hindu gods. Dr. Ramakrishnan himself had his sleeping quarters in a little pseudo-simple, neatly housekept "hut" in a slightly removed corner of the lot.

From this pleasant household we drove to the Vivekananda College, where Swami lectured on the Upaniṣads to a large gathering sponsored by the Philosophical Society of Madras. The lecture was a pell-mell of all those themes introduced to me during that year in New York when I was editing *The Gospel of Sri Ramakrishna*. I don't know what the "philosophers" really thought of it, but the words of praise that I heard seemed sincere enough. There were as many as three introductory speeches and two envois. The Indians certainly like to sit and listen!

We next toured the building and then went to a Ramakrishna orphanage, where Swami was asked to say a few words to a very well-behaved and attentive lot of nice-looking young boys. He told them to enshrine Mother India in their hearts. I then was asked to speak, and I told them that everybody in the world was telling Americans that their American patriotism was out of date, that we were trying hard to put it behind us and become true citizens of the world, and that I hoped that they too would try to make their patriotism harmonize with a feeling of world brotherhood and love. (I think I won the day.)

From the orphanage we were driven to a large mansion inhabited by a charming family from Calcutta: father, mother, two sisters, and a boy who wants to go into the navy (but his father is for Oxford). Western style with Indian effects. We were greeted with leis (jasmine) and treated to the supreme dinner of the Indian tour. The younger daughter was really worth looking at, and the elder (Indian chubby type) sang two *kīrtanas* very simply and well to the accompaniment of her harmonium. I was impressed to see—again— a family chapel (in this case rather elaborate) with figures and pictures of Ramakrishna, Vivekananda, and the Holy Mother. The family had two photo volumes, which they showed us: one full of Vivekananda photos and the other with pictures of the other early members of the Order. Swami allowed himself to be praised considerably and at 10:45 we left for home.

Today I have the feeling that I have caught a glimpse of the point of view of the well-off group in India: I can see, how, for them, the spectacle of the poverty of the poorer classes would be comparable to that of the Pittsburgh slums for the well-off people of Pittsburgh. In America, being of the well-off class oneself, one sees the poverty as an evil that is counterbalanced by the happiness of the majority. In India, when one comes as a visitor, all that one sees are the poor. Dr. Ramakrishnan spoke of the rising demands and pay of workers in precisely the terms that I have heard in

Honolulu and Mount Kisco; yet here a bricklayer gets five rupees (one dollar) a day, whereas in America (last I heard) the pay was twenty-seven times that sum. The people on top, whether in India or the U.S.A., regard the life needs of the worker as greatly less than their own.

Let me develop a theme that came to my mind while Swami was lecturing. There are two blocks of people in India: the "Folk" and the "Leaders."

The Folk, whom I would identify with the "working class" of Priestley's remarks, can be divided into the Non-literate (India's majority), and the Literate (not numerous in India). The Folk *receive* ideas, are filled with *bhakti,* and desire simply to look (*darśana*). In a non-literate state they are moved by the traditional ideas of a steady, slowly changed, ancient inheritance, which is religious in tone. In a modern, literate society, they are moved also by the press, radio, and political parties.

The Leaders are, in all modern societies, literate; and it is they who render the ideas to which the Folk respond. The Leaders may be divided into two main groups: the Traditional (*le symbolisme qui pense qu'il sait*), and the Creative (*le symbolisme qui cherche*).[90]

The Traditional, whether proper to the culture (in India, Jainism, Hinduism, etc.), or Intrusive (in India, Zoroastrianism, Islam, Christianity), tends everywhere to be religious in style. In India the Traditional—represented by monks, priests, and Catholic clergy—is predominant.

The Creative, which predominates in the West, is secular and of two types: the Ephemeral (journalistic, sensationalist) and the Epochal (scientific-scholarly, fundamental). In the popular view of America, the Ephemeral type is conspicuous; actually, however, the Epochal type is perhaps even more effective in America today than in Europe.

Representatives of the Creative in India are my friends the Well-Offs, but they are only *secondarily* creative. Their function is to apply to India the findings of the West; and in this function they face a sensitive problem: to let the principles of Indian civilization transform the intrusive heritage, rather than allow the reception of the Western forms to Westernize the Indian mind.

The machines, for example, have been shaped by Western minds to serve the ends of a Western—that is to say, a fundamentally humanistic—life orientation. If it is true, as Gandhi has said, that "India has a greater destiny than merely to copy the West," then some sort of Indian mind has to begin thinking about creating machines to facilitate the rendition of Indian life-aims, which, I believe, are trans-humanistic. If Western humanism is accepted, there is no problem—we shall have, simply, a Western province with Oriental effects. But if Western humanism is rejected, then the machines will have to be creatively transformed. A machine tends to impose upon its master the teleology of its own form—and this explains, I think, some of the impulsive anti-Westernism in the Westernized Indian of the Nehru type. The machine and aid that you know you require, yet haven't yourself created, tend to press you toward the alien life-style that brought it forth, and you react by biting the hand that's feeding you.

In terms of my division above, what strikes the eye of the voyager in India is the poverty and *bhakti* of the Non-literate Folk. What seems to strike the eye of everyone looking at America is the hurly-burly of the Literate Folk/Creative Leaders combination. To judge either community by this surface flash is to be superficial. The substance of India is in the Traditional Leaders, but also of the Intrusive types; and that of the West is in the Creative Leaders of the Ephemeral type, with an icing of the Epochal.

The Well-Offs of India are of two types: the Tradition-oriented and the Creative-oriented. The Tradition-oriented have altars in their homes; the Creative-oriented drink.

Sunday, October 17

Decided this morning that it would be interesting to see a group of Indian Catholics at mass, and so, asked a taxi driver to take me to San Thome's Cathedral. He took me, instead, to St. Thomas's Mount, where a guide immediately took me to the summit—up the 135 steps to the little chapel. There was sound of singing in the chapel. My guide made a sign to someone inside, and out came a nice little Irish nun who invited me inside for Benediction. I found a little company of about five nuns (mostly Indian) who sang the hymns (which I remembered from Canterbury School), and some twenty very tiny Indian girls in white veils, who said their prayers aloud and in unison. The celebrant was a young Indian priest whose Latin was clear and nicely pronounced. The children, I had been told, were "unwanted children": and this little rescue party seemed to me to epitomize the whole pattern of the Christian mission in India: "the stones rejected by the builders"; "the excluded factor." Islam had built from the same root in India.

Moreover, while listening to the Catholic hymns and prayers, after having heard for some weeks only the Hindu, I found myself not caring much which system prevailed. *Bhakti* is *bhakti*.

After Benediction the nice little nun showed me the so-called Bleeding Cross, a stone with engraved cross, supposedly carved and revered by St. Thomas himself, and said to have sweated water on December 18 very frequently between the years 1551 and 1704; and the "Picture of Our Lady," supposedly painted by St. Luke and brought to India by Thomas, but looking rather like a 14th-century Siennese job. Then I went down the hill again, boarded a bus, and returned, hot and tired, to the Connemara Hotel.

At 6 P.M. I went to the inauguration of the new Madras Roman Catholic Cultural Center, where a crowd of about three thousand saw a dance concert given in honor of India's first cardinal, Cardinal Gracias—a tall, good looking Indian with grace and elegance in his language and presence. After the surprise of this morning and my afternoon of reading about St. Thomas in India, this evening's event gave me a considerable sense of the force of Catholicism in India.

Cardinal Gracias spoke with sympathy of the new nationalist interests of India. Formerly, he said, parents used to tell him that their daughters were studying French and the piano; now they told him they were studying Hindi and Indian dance. One of the numbers this evening, performed by the students of Stella Maris College, was a semi-Indian dance interpretation of St. Francis's "The Canticle of the Sun." I was reminded of much that is going on in New York, and particularly of Haddasah's performances. Apparently the whole female world has become dance conscious. In India, however, the dance is now on a strictly amateur level—when the girls marry, I am told, it is finished.

Monday, October 18

Up early in the morning for an expedition to Māmallapuram[91] and Conjeevaram.[92] By taxi with Mrs. D. and the Countess to the Ramakrishna Maṭh, where we learned that Swami had a fever and would not be able to come; in fact, he would probably not be able to leave for our tour of the south tomorrow. Besides, it was raining cats and dogs. Nevertheless, the party would proceed—and indeed it did, after a delay of about an hour.

The party consisted of myself and the two ladies, two swamis, a young Indian lady, and seven gentlemen in white, with various types of tonsure and beard. All very gay and pleased to be starting off on a semi-religious *bāt*.

We started at about 8:15 and arrived about an hour later at a crossroad where we were met by four additional gentlemen and a car. Their car soon had a flat, however, so they sifted into ours and left someone to fix their flat. We drove to the Dak bungalow at Māmallapuram, where we were met by a young man in khaki, a "sub-inspector," who would be our guide to the monuments—and here we made the first pause of the day. All drank coconut milk and chatted pleasantly, while an old black man silently pulled rhythmically on a rope that set in motion a large fan-contraption hanging from the ceiling.

After the coconut milk we stepped into the cars and drove to the five *rathas*,[93] next walked to the Descent of the Ganges complex,[94] and to the Shore Temple,[95] then returned to the cars, which had come to meet us. I was impressed particularly by the cave containing the Viṣṇu Anantaśāyī[96]

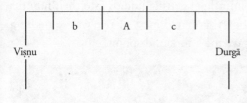

and Mahiṣāsura-mardinī[97] panels. In the central shrine (A) was a panel of Śiva-Pārvatī with a male figure at the lower left sacrificing his head. I couldn't photograph the panel because the light was very bad. I realized when we were in Conjeevaram that we had missed the Ādi Varāha Cave,[98] but we had been shown everything else that I wanted to see, and I was delighted with the place. The visit was marred a bit by a couple of beggars who concentrated on me, but otherwise was fine.

We drove next to Chingleput to visit the Ramakrishna Mission and school, which involved standing reverently before a number of Ramakrishna-Vivekananda-Holy Mother shrines and inspecting, first, the boys' school, then the girls'. In the latter, a darling moment when, in the auditorium, which contained the shrine and was chock full of standing students, the whole group sang in unison a rather complex hymn. I was particularly fascinated by a cluster of sixteen little eight- or nine-year-olds who sang with their big eyes and funny little faces covertly inspecting every inch of the clothing of Mrs. D. and the Countess. After the hymn these little things spun around two or three times quickly patting their own cheeks. I don't know what this means; but I saw it again, later in the day, in one of the temples of Conjeevaram.

On our visit to the schools we were joined by a couple of gentlemen with odd tonsures and were driven to somebody's home for the most fantastic lunch that I've ever shared. Later we learned that these people had never entertained Westerners in their home before. The lunch, presently, was served on the living room floor. Sixteen or twenty cushions were placed around the walls, and before each was half of a banana leaf, which was to serve as plate and table for the occupant of the cushion. All took their places. Rice, dal, various thick liquids, odds and ends and whatnot were dumped in various quantities directly onto the banana leaves; grace was sung; and the company, including the ladies, set to work with their right hands. Water was drunk from brass cups, but poured into the mouth, so that the cup should not touch the lips. For this feat of acrobatics the left hand was used. It was a wild half-hour: all I could think of was a Hawai'ian luau. To see them perform the miracle of getting liquids into their mouths from the banana leaves by way of a saturated mess of rice was something of a marvel. Thank God they gave me a fork and spoon.

Descent of the Ganges

Following the meal, we sat around for about an hour and a half and then began our drive to Conjeevaram—but again we stopped at the Ramakrishna Maṭh and again we found ourselves doing reverence to one of those shrines. I was pretty tired of *bhakti* by now; and since Conjeevaram is full of important temples I was becoming a bit impatient. This particular shrine was up on the roof, under a corrugated iron canopy; and since there were a number of cameras present a great many pictures had to be taken of various groupings. We then descended to the main room, where there was a big round table and lots of floor space: many sat on the floor, a few joined the ladies and me at the table, whereupon tea was served: that is to say, a considerable meal. I thought we'd never move. However, we presently did—about an hour before dusk.

We drove first to the Kailāśanātha Temple, which for me was a disappointment.[99] The seventh-century sculpture had been covered, at some date, with a plaster coating, into which eyes, noses, mouths, etc. had been incised. The effect was crude and worthless. But here and there the plaster was gone, and a lovely seventh-century face or two peeked through.

We next went to the great Viṣṇu Temple and when we came out it was dark. But I had seen enough of the carved *maṇḍapas,* colonnades, and so on, to get the feel of it. In the dark we visited the temple of Śiva (the great temple of the *bhūmi liṅga*)[100] and the temple of the Goddess Kāmākṣī. At both, our numerous friends led us around gaily through the magical labyrinths of the corridors and shrines. We circumambulated a great mango tree; stood before Śiva's *liṅga* while the priest recited *mantras* and finally gave us each a handful of ashes to rub on our foreheads; and again stood before the *yonī* of the Goddess while the priest recited her 108 names—at each name tossing a pinch of vermillion into the *yonī;* we then received some of the vermillion back from the *yonī,* carried it to a little side shrine, deposited it there and then took a fingertip amount for our foreheads. The whole thing was wild and great. And, of course, at the exit of each temple the beggars were terrific. The priests though—I must say—were decently behaved.

The drive home was interrupted by a pause for lemon pop at the town where Rāmānuja was born.[101] We arrived in Madras about 9:15. I went up to see Swami, who was in bed still, and said he would not be leaving tomorrow and for me to decide what I wanted to do. I got home by rickshaw, and, after a bit of tea and bread and butter, went to bed.

Tuesday, October 19

Decided to postpone my tour of the deeper south until Jean arrives, and to go tomorrow to Bangalore. Went to the American Express to make arrangements, and finally returned to the hotel for lunch with the two ladies, who had been to see Swami. Apparently he is feeling better, but is going to remain another week in Madras. He thought my plan a good one, and so tomorrow I start the second stage of my India visit—definitely alone.

After lunch I went to the Museum (second trip) to measure a few of the Amarāvatī pieces, and the remainder of the day was spent writing in this book and writing letters.

Three nice letters arrived two days ago from Jean and one from Helen McMaster: all giving a wonderful account of Jean at Bard and of her great lecture demonstration at Cooper Union. It sounds as though everything was going really beautifully.

There was an article in yesterday's newspaper about Vinoba Bhave[102] which I liked. He spoke out against Nehru's "welfare state," and declared that what was required was local initiative and spirit on the part of the villagers. He also spoke out a bit against *bhakti* and caste: *pūjā* before images and then caste avoidances before men he found untimely. Reading his words, I thought it would be men like Vinoba who would rescue Hinduism from its own past. Ram Mohan Roy, Ramakrishna, Vivekananda, Gandhi, Vinoba: that would seem to be the line.

Meanwhile, something can also be said for the images, the pilgrimage centers, the *bhakti* and all. They are focal points of communal concentration, representing syndromes of ideas and ideals. The problem is to release the ideas and ideals into contemporary life: the Redemption to the Redeemer theme. That is the problem of my course and study.

An amusing set of exchanges while driving to and from Māmallapuram: through an idyllic rural countryside of paddy fields, thatched villages, coconut palms, goats and cattle. On the way out, a gentleman sitting beside me spoke of the landowners to whom all the property belonged, told of how these people starved when the rains failed, as they had recently for a run of some five to seven years, and lamented their ignorant misery, which, he thought, better agricultural methods were already beginning to improve. On the way back, one of the monks was beside me, and he spoke of the wonderful timelessness of it all, and of how happy these people were in their simple lives.

India seems right now to be in a state, as it were, of nonentity: drawing its future from Europe while at the same time searching into its own past to try to find out what it once was. The question is: Will the past (India's proper dynamism) have the power to convert the Western gift into a vehicle for *Indian* life? Or will India become simply a sort of Western nation with Oriental effects (saris in their movies instead of low-cut gowns)? In other words: will Vinoba win or will Nehru?

CHAPTER 2

TEMPLES AND MONUMENTS

BANGALORE AND MYSORE

Wednesday, October 20   **Bangalore**

Packing finished, I joined the ladies for a brief visit and farewell to Swami, then returned to the hotel for lunch, after which I caught my plane.

Arrived about 3:30 in Bangalore, found the West End Hotel, where they gave me a whole cottage (too bad Jean isn't here!), and I went then to arrange for my visits, tomorrow and the next day, to Mysore, Somnāthpuram, Belūr, Halebīd and the great Gommaṭa statue.

Bangalore is cool, high, and pleasant. A clean, attractive city—but hardly Indian. The atmosphere is that of a pleasant Anglo-Saxon resort. I even put on my blue suit for dinner. Then I repacked for the great expedition and went to bed.

I think that my earlier edginess has worn off. It was partly Swami and the ladies; they could never see anything in India without running down its counterpart in the U.S.A. Yet I'm glad for our time together; it helped me to see the absurdity in this India *über alles* attitude: it also helped me to appreciate the U.S.A. Anyhow, that one's over—and I seem to be enjoying India very much.

Thursday to Saturday, October 21–23   **Mysore**

The great Mysore adventure! Rain, rain, rain—but no rain check. I went through with it nobly: visited the charming little temple of Somnāthpuram on Thursday afternoon, toured the larger and even more marvelous temples of Belūr and Halebīd Friday morning and early afternoon, and on the way back to Mysore ascended barefoot the 650 rock-cut steps to the great Gommaṭa statue at Śravana Belgoḷā—only to find the image completely covered with bamboo scaffolding for the workmen who are trying to do something about some cracks that have begun to appear. Furthermore, with roads comparable to those of the Navaho reservation (we actually got stuck once fording a stream) and the car hire eight annas per mile, I lost all desire to go on with this rough game of visiting the great Hindu monuments. I abandoned the Hyderabad-Aurangabad idea and came back to Bangalore by bus (eighty-eight miles in five hours), and will leave tomorrow by train to reach Bombay at noon on Monday. And, by God, if Bombay doesn't register you can have Mother India anyway you like her, for all of me.

It is strange but important that all of the temples of the great pre-Mohammedan days are in spots that once were great capitals, but now are practically abandoned, and can be reached only by private or hired car, or by airplane (too expensive), or by train or bus, which is more than the body can stand—practically all day going and coming, with a brief moment at the monument. Perhaps I shall find some other way to manage when I get to Bombay, but if I don't, I think I'll settle for Elephanta, Ajaṇṭā, and Elūrā, which I can reach from Bombay.

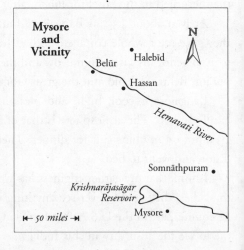

In other words, there is a geographical as well as a temporal and a spiritual break between the classic periods of Hindu art and the modern so-called Indian (actually Islamic-Hindu-Occidental) world.

The influence of the ancient art has simply withdrawn from the modern field; or rather, the capitals of modern India have grown in new sites (mostly ports: Calcutta, Madras, Bombay), with Delhi on a site where all the Hindu monuments have been razed, except that ruined and re-used temple by the iron column. Modern India, reaching back to make contact with the earlier styles, isn't going to manage it.

A fantastic example of the contemporary effort is the new palace of the Maharaja of Mysore, which I saw this morning, before leaving for Bangalore. The palace stands in a great, grandly landscaped enclosure. In fact, the landscape situation in Mysore is by far the best that I have seen in India: the Maharajas have actually designed their city: they have also provided a handsome holiday resort with gardens and lovely fountains at the great reservoir of Krishnarājasāgar. But—my Lord!—when you enter the palace! (My guide said that I should take my time in the palace, because in the whole world there was no palace so beautiful: a combination of Madison Square Garden and Coney Island would be elegant in contrast). Green, yellow, and maroon are the predominant colors: bulbous columns with maroon base, green and yellow shafts and capitals support (with a curiously chunky effect) huge domes of green-, yellow-, and maroon-stained glass.

There is a great ballroom or audience hall, then another, then something that looked like a magnification of the old Hippodrome. The door frames are carved of ivory (cracking) and silver, elaborately figured with imitations of ancient motifs; there are rooms with carved sandalwood panels, and one with a waxwork image of the present Maharaja's father, with a life-sized, cut-out color photograph of a palace officer standing beside him. And along the walls! In one room, ten or twelve large paintings, English-Indian olios, of gods and goddesses; in another room, wall after wall of an absolutely naturalistic portrait-panorama of the Mysore state processions (painted 1938 or 1939), showing every soldier of the band, horse guards-man, the Maharaja on his elephant, and so on; and finally in another room, a lot of bric-à-brac connected with images of the gods, including (believe it or not) Ganeśa flanked by two mirrors—one concave, the other convex—so that when you stood before the god you see yourself transformed to right and to left.

In the nearby *citraśāla* (painting gallery), I saw rooms of recent Indian art labeled "Gujarati School," "Āndhra School," "Malabar School," "Santineketan School," etc. And what were they? Maxfield Parrish, Aubrey Beardsley, pre-Raphaelite, and (more commonly) fairy-tale illustrations—*à l'indienne*—nearly all, of course, of *Mahābhārata* and *Rāmāyaṇa* themes. (They'll wear these out some day.) There were a couple of attempts at more modern watercolor styles, and a room or two with works imitating the standard British Academy brand of naturalism.

Slightly more interesting than those upper-caste efforts were the lower-caste achievements: cabinets of sandalwood, ivory, or ivory-inlay, intricate carving, and such impossible stunts as images of the basic Hindu pantheon carved from rice-grains. So what! Whereas in the Hoyśala temples of Somnāthpuram, Belūr, and Halebīd one marvels at the art as well as the craftsman's patience, now one marvels only at the patience and the craft. The vision has withdrawn.

Amen to the past.

The Maharaja has sixteen Rolls Royces; but he has done so well by his people that Mysore is far and away the comeliest, least squalid province of India that I have seen. The villages have comparatively sturdy houses, most of them with tile roofs (there is a tile factory in Mysore). Most of the villages have electricity: the only electric power lines I've seen in India crossed the rich paddy fields of Mysore. Both Mysore and Bangalore are very pleasant, clean, and well-off cities. Besides, the climate is nice, and the little mountains add a touch of scenic interest. So Mysore illustrates for me what the new India may be, if it's lucky: a great rural area rendered prosperous by a well-calculated application of modern—i.e., Western—improvement (dams, electricity, fertilizer, etc.), with pleasant provincial cities full of bicycles, and with a few great metropolises of a completely Western character, but with Indian effects: movies in Hindi, Bengali, and Kannada; photos of Indian babies; little shops with people sitting on the floor.

On the other hand, a little episode that I spied in the train may point to something further. In Bangalore, a gentleman in European clothes, a professional man of some sort in his middle or late fifties, entered the compartment, sat at one end of the seat across from me, took a booklet from his satchel, and began quietly reading. He was hardly seated when some coolies brought in a great number of pieces of luggage and began stowing them under the seats and on various shelves. Then three people entered, two young men and a young woman who wore an ugly dark greenish sari and spoke Indian English. She and one of the men sat on my side of the car, the other sat across from me. They ordered three breakfasts and talked a good deal, somewhat cryptically, among themselves. One of the young men had a small book, V. Gordon Childe's *History,* from which he occasionally read excerpts to the young woman: their rather effortful, unseasoned intellectualism made me think of New School of Social Research people.

The breakfast I had ordered was brought to me, and when the bells and whistles of departure sounded, I had already finished it. The breakfasts of the trio, however, had not yet appeared. They looked from the window; one of them got up and went to the door. The train moved, and then a couple of waiters came running down the platform, one of them with a heavily loaded tray, which he passed to the man at the door. There was a questionable moment—but the tray was safe. We all laughed, and one of the waiters climbed aboard.

He was a very dark little man, with fine features, dressed in the dirty white of the station waiters and wearing the turban. He helped the trio with their plates and then sat inconspicuously on the floor near the entrance while they ate. I sat watching the scenery go past beneath a heavily clouded and rainy sky. The gentleman who had entered alone continued to read his book; the trio, eating, carried on their unconvincing conversation. When they had finished, the waiter got up and began collecting the plates. He took my tray first and set it on the floor. Then, coming up to take the trio's tray, he briefly, quickly, and very lightly touched the shoes of the gentleman who was still quietly reading and then brushed his hands swiftly over his own forehead and chest. I don't think the gentleman himself knew that anything had happened, and certainly the chattering trio saw nothing. The waiter caught my eye and saw that I had seen but made no sign and went on with his work. When the dishes and two trays were stowed on the floor, he resumed his self-effacing position, silently squatting on the floor by the door, and when the train reached its next stop, about an hour later, he picked up his trays and left.

Having seen the act of reverence to the gentleman's feet—precisely the kind of reverence that is brought to the feet of the swamis—I tried to think what might have been the cause. Was there any sign on the man to indicate what he was? I could discover nothing. But then I saw that the book that he was reading was the Ramakrishna Maṭh edition of the *Taittirīya Upaniṣad*—and I was amazed: the waiter must have seen the word *"Upaniṣad."* If he did, and if his reverence was to the spiritual moment of a man reading the Upaniṣads—then I think there is something here that can hardly be matched by anything known to me in the West. No effort was made to touch the feet of the chap reading V. Gordon Childe.

In the Hotel Metropole in Mysore, where there were bats in my bathroom, a number of Americans of a sort of "expert" type were talking seriously about something with a company of Indians, which included—lo!—my trio of the train. My guide told me that this was a conference on tax collection; and later, when I climbed the 650 steps to the scaffolded image at Śravana Belgoḷā, I learned that American experts had been called to analyze the stone and make suggestions about how best to fix the cracks. Furthermore, I read in the newspapers that a review of the Indian educational system has been undertaken by a committee of experts, on a grant from the Ford Foundation.

American aid, American advice, American money and brains: but in the newspapers and out of Nehru's mouth, no good word for America, but only for the "peace-loving" Communists and Russia's offer to install one steel mill. India's collision with America is based partly on the fact that, for us, the China issue is a problem of Democracy *vs.* Communism, whereas Nehru (the great liberal!) sees only Occident (Colonialism) *vs.* Orient. Such willy-nilly identification with the Orient is related to the present Indian effort to recover its own Asian roots. It may also be related, however, to England's anti-American operations, rendered in this case by way of Lady Mountbatten.

Modern India's disconnection from its own past is vividly symbolized, it seems to me, by the geographical remoteness of *all* of the great Indian monuments of the classical periods, by the almost impassable roads that lead to them, and by the lack of accommodations in the neighboring towns. In the modern northern cities there are only modern buildings and Mohammedan monuments, while in the south, the large Hindu temples that rise in the cities are of the late southern style—which even in the twelfth century represented a decline in India's religious art.

Since the classical art of India is so geographically and spiritually remote from the modern Hindu world, the modern Hindu, not really appreciative of its beauty, says, "How beautiful!" with equal rapture before a modern Durgā Pūjā shrine. Nor can he interpret one of its most conspicuous elements—namely, the erotica.

In the decor of the temples of Somnāthpuram, Belūr, and Halebīd, I found erotic scenes quite as obscene as anything at Koṇārak, only not quite so conspicuous. The temples are of precisely the same period. One motif, repeated at Belūr and Halebīd, was that of a woman taking one man's penis in her mouth and another's in her tail. Figures of this sort cannot be explained in terms of Coomaraswamy's "each is both" idea;[103] neither can some of those complicated arrangements at Khajurāho. The problem of India's temple erotica, therefore, would seem to require discussion under two headings:

1.) I don't know when the earliest examples of the Loving Couple theme occurs: perhaps the royal donor couples on the Bhārhut pillars can be regarded as announcements of the motif; the *gandharva* couples at Aihoḷe and Māmallapuram perhaps come next; and then the overtly loving couples on the balcony railings in the Laṅkeśvara Cave[104] at Elūrā, where "each is both."

2.) I think there may be some connection between the Multiple Lover motifs at Khajurāho, Koṇārak,[105] Belūr and Halebīd, and the Black Mass which appeared in Europe at about this time.[106] The Khajurāho fragments suggest some sort of erotic yoga. At Koṇārak there is another effect to be noted, a type of visage that suggests the Greek satyr—this whole thing has to be worked out, somehow, for my *Basic Mythologies*[107] book.

Indian religious history falls into three main periods: the Vedic Upanishadic–Early Buddhistic; the Puranic Tantric (Mahāyāna and Hindu)–Vedantic; and the Popular (*bhakti* cults, *kīrtanas*, etc.)–Monastic. Indian art of the classic periods illustrates the Puranic Tantric. Its tone is aristocratic, and though many of the religious motifs survive (e.g. *pūjā;* Durgā; Mahiṣāsura-mardinī), the spirit has changed, so it is very difficult to connect it with the Popular period.

And now we may add a fourth period: the Modern, which at present I interpret as being almost completely a translation of Western, humanistic, progressive, spiritual ideals into Indian, metaphysically toned terms. The primary Moden sequence: Ram Mohan Roy, Vivekananda, Gandhi, Vinoba. Ramakrishna comes in as a focal center of Popular period ideals, rendering them as a foil to the Occidental side of Vivekananda.

It is important to note in this connection that both Vinoba and Aurobindo[108] have found ways of transforming the Indian idea of declining history (the four *yugas*) into a kind of apocalyptic progressive view. According to Vinoba, the Kālī Yuga is almost at its end and will be followed immediately by the Kṛta Yuga (no period of dissolution between).[109] Aurobindo's idea is a bit more complicated.

As far as western ideals of social improvement and optimism for the future are concerned, I think India will be able to integrate these without too great a case of indigestion—though I should not like to try to predict what will happen to the current sort of *bhakti* when literacy, science, and scholarship become general (if they ever do). A great, almost immediate problem, will be the total psychological transformation that may supervene when Indian boys and girls begin to become interested in each other as individual personalities, not merely as functionaries in a bio-mythological mystery. When that happens, the present almost absolute segregation of the sexes outside of the home will begin to break down, people will begin to make their own decisions about whom they shall marry, the sexes will begin to act upon each other psychologically and pedagogically, and the present pattern of willed infantilism will dissolve. What precedent in Indian life will the young people then be able to find? My suggestion would be to search the annals and art of the Tantric Puranic period.

There is a subtle problem here, however. I have a feeling that in the Orient there *never* was the kind of humanistic intellectual intercourse between the sexes that is characteristic of the modern West. (It did not exist in ancient Greece either.) The *sahaja* ideal is still bio-mythological—and so, our spontaneously humanistic reading of the *maithunas* is probably a misinterpretation. Certainly, here there is a pattern suggesting the corybantic orgy and the yogic crisis rather than the humanistically toned heterosexual relationship.

All of this makes me see much more clearly the point of Jung's warning that Westerners cannot safely take over the symbolism of the East.[110] The reference of the symbols is to a psychological structure very different from ours. It is a structure such as was the West's, perhaps, in the Middle Ages; but for the modern man, who has had too much of the rational and humanistic and is searching for a fruitful contact with *his own* unconscious, these symbols from a world that has not yet developed an effective humanistic view can serve only as hints of what is to be found. In the conscious life of the Indian there are all these Divine Mother images to which the actual women are held subordinate, in the conscious life of the modern Westerner are a number of actual women, each quite different from the other, whom he hardly associates with the Great Mother archetype— though in his unconscious he is certainly doing so.

Sunday, October 24   **En route to Bombay**

Off on the 9:45 A.M. for Bombay. At about 5:45 P.M. arrived at a junction where I had to change trains. I had gone all day without food, but had a rather good dinner at the junction railroad station. My train for Bombay pulled in a little over an hour late, and I was assigned to a compartment with two utterly horrible Indian gents. One, a dark-visaged, sturdy, middle-class thug, shouted at the waiter who brought him his three-rupee dinner because salt and butter had been omitted from the tray, raised his hand as if to strike him, and then shouted some more at the obsequious restaurant manager who came rushing to see what was the matter. I thought, My God, to have to cater to men like this! Then I had a new illumination about the gentleness of servants in India: gentleness to those above, brutality to those below.

The other gent in the car was a paunchy, somewhat older man, who wheezed, coughed, cleared his throat hideously and spat out the window, and kept going into the stinking Indian-style toilet room, all night. Every time he would come out of the toilet room, he would fail to lock the door, so that it soon would swing open, letting the reek fill our compartment. Neither of the Indians seemed to mind; so it was I who got up every time, walked the length of the compartment, and fixed the latch.

BOMBAY AND AURANGABAD

Monday, October 25   **Bombay**

At 6 A.M. I got tea and toast at a station, while my gentlemen companions cleared their throats, got up, spit out the window, and prepared to face the day. At another station, at 9 A.M., I ate another breakfast with an omelette. We arrived in Bombay at about 1:30 P.M. (775 miles in 28 hrs., or about 28 miles an hour). The weather in Bombay was clear and cool: very nice for a change.

The Grand Hotel is pleasant and reasonable: eighteen rupees a day, with good meals. I bathed, shaved, had lunch, and took a taxi to American Express, to find no mail. After tea I took a long walk past Victoria Station and along Mohammed Ali Road, viewing the markets and the wonderfully busy and crowded streets, to Sandhurst Road, where I took a taxi home. After a good dinner I returned to my room and wrote to Jean.

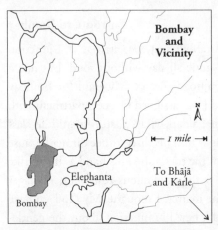

I have arrived at a festival moment, namely that of the Dīvalī or Dīpāvalī, the Festival of Lights, a festival of the New Moon, representing re-creation and rebirth—and I have a feeling that I can make it a rebirth festival of my own, if I go at it correctly. This morning, about an hour before sunrise, I was sitting up in that horrible train compartment, looking out the window, when a lovely object, lightly revealed by the coming sun, appeared in the sky: the *dark* moon, and with its lower surface brightly illuminated—like a silver platter holding the darker disk. We were passing through pleasant country when from a little farmhouse, decorated with the colorful lanterns and strings of paper pennants characteristic of the festival, there came the sound of firecrackers greeting the festival, and I had a pleasant feeling that with Bombay my India journey commences. I have been voyaging for two months, have circumambulated the country in the sunwise direction, have assimilated the unpleasant aspect of the Indian picture, and now I can begin to take things at my own pace and in my own way.

Tuesday, October 26

In this morning's *Times of India* there were a couple of feature articles about the Dīvalī festival, from which I glean the following:

The name *dīpāvalī* is derived from the Sanskrit *dīpa* (lamp) and *valī* (line): a line of lamps. Another name is *dīpa-mālikā* or *dīpa-mālā;* a string or garland of lamps. It is a festival of lights.

It is compared, in one of the articles, to the fire festivals of the Celts: the Halloween Fires (with a quote from Frazer[III]), which come at about the same time of year. On the primitive level, such a feast is regarded as a dispeller of baneful influences; among the cultured of India it is celebrated as symbolizing the triumph of light over darkness (the same interpretation was given to the Durgā Pūjā in Bengal).

"In many parts of India the night of the Divālī is known as the Kāla-Rātrī, the most dreaded of all nights, when the goddess Mahā-Kālī with her attendant deities and Devils, known respectively as *bhairavas* and *pisācas,* is to be propitiated by the performance of secret rites and orgies at dead of night [a clue here to the multiple-partner class of erotica?]. On this night, it is believed that evil spirits, both disembodied and natural [sic], hover about, and that they must be kept away from the homes of the living by the lighting of lamps and fires, the performance of ceremonies for the propitiation of the deity whose will they obey. These illuminations came to form an integral part of the Divālī festival."

Gambling is permitted during the Divālī. The feast is associated with the myths of Kṛṣṇa's slaying of Narakāsura, Rāma's return from exile to be King of Ayodhya, and Viṣṇu's marriage to Lakṣmī.

After breakfast I went for a long walk, all the way from my hotel, which is in the Ballard Road area, to Malabar Hill, where I took a bus all the way back again and around to Colaba, where I had another walk. I returned again by bus, in time for a little nap and then lunch.

It was a lovely walk and put me in a good mood for Bombay. A few people were fishing along the sea-wall by the gymkhanas,[112] and others quietly praying, a touch that one would hardly encounter in the West. On the bus ride I saw a Jain monk and then a couple of nuns, with their mouths covered—but no brooms! All afternoon I worked to bring this diary up to date, and after supper I went again to Malabar Hill, by bus, and returned.

The city was full of lights and gaiety and noise. I could see parties going on in many homes and in shops. The feast is a kind of combination of Christmas, New Year, and the Fourth of July. Firecrackers, sparklers, and simple rockets everywhere, set off in the teeming streets. Kids everywhere.

Lights everywhere. People nicely dressed, going to parties everywhere. During the morning, I passed many little groups of women and girls with food presents which they were bringing to someone. Many cars and taxis were decorated with garlands of mango-leaves and yellow flowers. During the course of my evening walk a large firecracker went off right under my feet and a squirt of beetle-nut juice from some window just missed my head. Quite a night for a hike!

Wednesday, October 27

I find I like Bombay best of anything I've found in India, but I'm glad I saw the other places first, because the typically Hindu motifs are comparatively subdued, and I might have missed them had I come here first. Bombay reminds me a bit of San Francisco: they are about the same size—and you feel the port, the water, in the same way. It is not as handsome—but its crowds make up for that. In the markets and streets are many more types of people—more urban, livelier, more fantastic—than in other Indian cities, and the buildings are stranger, more Oriental: comparatively, every other city I've seen is rural, much less mixed and cosmopolitan. Being out on this peninsula, the city is cut off from the farmers, and you don't have herds of cattle and wandering cows, or peasants. More women, better dressed and better looking women, are visible in the streets: but males still outnumber females about a thousand to one. Bombay, perhaps, represents best the focus of new industrial and Occidental influences in India. The city is full of American movies. Also, I note, there are more Europeans and Americans here than elsewhere.

In this morning's *The Indian Express* I read what seems to me to be about the ultimate in the anti-American campaign: "The most disturbing phenomenon of our times is the horde of international spies—too often really national spies—operating under the temporary halo of Point Four Aid or the sanctity of the U.N. welfare organization. Even if we brush aside the American attempts to dictate to the U.N. Secretary-General on the treatment of staff, this is not a negligible affair for us."

I went out for a walk and, when I reached the Prince of Wales Museum, entered. Whom do I see, almost immediately? Alfred Salmony, with two gents, one American, one Indian (their bearer).[113] Great greetings, and a museum cruise together. Salmony spoke almost immediately of the anti-American atmosphere. Monday night he gave a lecture, and the Indian who introduced him spent twenty minutes abusing America, the Ford Foundation, Fulbright grantees, etc. Salmony also spoke of the unloading of some ships that had arrived in India with wheat: American ships bringing free wheat, and one Russian ship bringing wheat that India had paid for. The former were unloaded normally, in silence; but for the latter there was a great ceremony with speeches.

I think that the arrogant anti-Americanism is what sticks in my craw the hardest here. The poverty, the people trying to sell something, the beggars, the bad railroads, and the dreary hotels: these I can now swallow; but not the arrogant insults.

I guess it can be said that India is undergoing a sort of psychological enantiodromia of self-rediscovery,[114] and consequently cannot be expected to behave in a civilized manner. Psychological crises always make for a sort of compulsive boorishness.

But I renew my resolve never to speak or write again *for* India. *About* India, perhaps; but not *for*. I shall return in my work, as rapidly as possible, to my main line of comparative mythology, and then press on to the problem of the present crisis in our *Western* consciousness—a very different consciousness, as I now realize, from that of the East. Or perhaps India's situation is an acute parody of our own, brought on by its forced Westernization under the British. As we are seeking contact with our own unconscious, so are they with theirs, and their problem is stranger than our own, because the archetypes in *their* past are not related to the Occidental rational principles that are even now shaping their world. The very machines that they are buying, their psyches reject as alien. They're in a mess—and I shall try now to regard them with more charity. And, incidentally, it is possible to regard the whole contemporary moment as one in which the various peoples of the world are undergoing—each in its own way—an acute psychological crisis. Here is a theme for the conclusion of *Basic Mythologies.*

Spent the afternoon catching up with this diary, and, after dinner, went around to the Taj Mahal Hotel for a chat on the fine second-floor balcony with Alfred Salmony, his friend Jason Grossman (who has a car!), and an English collector of bronzes, a Mr. Dane. Our principal topic was plans for a visit at the end of this week to Elūrā and Ajaṇṭā—in Grossman's car. We drank lime juice, and disbanded about 10:30 P.M.

Thursday, October 28

Met Salmony at the Taj Mahal Hotel at 10 A.M. and went with him to see Father H. Heras, S.J., a wonderful old man with a white beard and white cassock. One of the big experiences of the trip: the meeting of three scholars with a common range of interests: Father Heras, plump, humorous, and very learned, knew Salmony's name, and Salmony asked him for contributions to his periodical. Then it began: first, a view of Father Heras's publications (just out: *Studies in Proto-Indo-Mediterranean Culture*—a must), then a view of his college library, one of the best Orientalist libraries in the country, and finally, his collection of bronzes. "Fabulous! Fabulous!" was all Salmony could say. Our visit lasted two hours, and was great.

In the afternoon I went to American Express and found a lovely letter from Jean; also a repentant and chastened letter from my Narasimhan.

All the clouds in my heart has vanished. With clear mind I am writing that there is not the least of selfishness in my heart. I fully realized my mistake. I request you kindly excuse me taking me as your own child. This is a sort of experience for me to go to a better life. . . .

I tried to catch up with my mail. A quiet afternoon and evening alone.

Friday, October 29

Taj Mahal at 10 A.M. to plan trip to Aurangabad and caves. Nasli's mother and brother at hotel.[115] Salmony told me that Rudy and Nena von Leyden (friends of Mme. Moitessier) would like to see me for dinner.[116] Afternoon packing and writing. Evening at the von Leydens'; a very nice couple. Rudy showed me his collection of Indian playing cards.

Saturday, October 30   Aurangabad (Elūrā)

Off in the dark at 5:45 to meet Salmony and Grossman at Grossman's West End Hotel. Fine drive to Aurangabad. Made two stops on the way to look at country markets, one for lunch. Arrival, about 5 P.M. Tea, dinner, bed.

Sunday, October 31

Elūrā, Caves I–XII (Buddhist) and XIII (Hindu).[117] Great experience. At lunch we ate at Cave XIII, then had a chat with a Swedish scholar named Lamm, with whom Salmony picked an argument. He was the type of European who tries to make surprising yet precisely pertinent observations—this time about Elūrā: but they were not surprising and almost inevitably missed the mark. A bit hard to drop him but we finally got away. Then, toward dusk, a first quick view of Kailāśanātha.[118]

Monday, November 1

Elūrā again, from Cave XIV to the end; skipping Kailāśanātha, then returning to it for the grand finale. Of the Buddhist caves seen yesterday, the most impressive were Caves II, X (Viśvakarman), and XII (Tīn Thal). Of the Hindu: XV (Das Avatāra), which offers a series of magnificent sculptural panels, XVI (Kailāśanātha), XXI (Rāmeśvara), and XXIX (Dhumar Lena), where we discovered an obscene crude engraving scratched on the face of a pillar, perhaps by the workmen. The little Jain cluster of caves at the end was surprisingly charming.

Returning from the caves this afternoon, we paused for a chat with the young director of the Archaeological Survey office and his wife, the Hapars; then we stayed for tea and invited them to the hotel for dinner. They are vegetarians of brahmin family and represent what is beginning to seem to me to be the best type of young person in India: the intelligent, modern yet orthodox, upper-class Hindu.

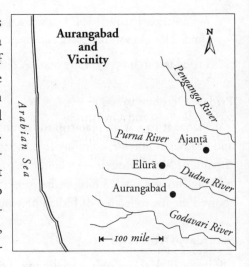

Tuesday, November 2

To Ajaṇṭā, a rather longer drive. I have been doing all the driving: a Hillman station wagon with four gear shifts forward and one reverse. We spent the morning in the caves with wall paintings, where a light was required; the afternoon in the remainder. A lovely day. Ajaṇṭā is not as great an experience as Elūrā, but it is somehow more charming. The valley is glorious, and the caves, all Buddhist, constitute a wonderful unit.[119]

Wednesday, November 3

This morning we visited a small series of caves in Aurangabad. Cluster I–V was in rather bad shape and seemed to me to be not too exciting, but among the cluster VI to IX there was one, Cave VII, that is certainly a match for much that we have seen. It is a Buddhist cave with elegant *dvarāpālas,* then at either side of the entrance to the cellar two panels showing female deities and attendants of a glorious, late Gupta elegance. Within the cella itself is a magnificent Buddha; on the left wall there is an extraordinary panel of a female dancer with six musicians, three musicians arranged symmetrically on each side, in a powerfully rhythmical composition; on the right wall is a standing male and female. Query: Does the dancer represent a *devadāsī?* If so, is this not exceptional for the Buddhist cult?

In the afternoon we visited two Muslim monuments: first, the tomb of the wife of Aurangzeb—built by her son, in imitation of the Taj Mahal—smaller, made in cheaper materials, and less magnificently proportioned, a good example of a poor second; then the so-called *pañcika*—a garden, pond, library, mosque, and tomb, pleasantly arranged in a typically Muslim style. Salmony and Grossman, at this point, seemed to lose their minds, making believe they couldn't imagine why we were looking at these things; but I found the jump from the Gupta-Cālukya days to the Muslims rather exciting and illuminating. The power of the Muslim garden to cast a spell is to me amazing—and whether the garden is large or small, in Damascus or Aurangabad, the spell is always the same.

Thursday, November 4

Off to an early start for a good day's drive back to Bombay. This whole visit to Aurangabad and its caves has been delightful. The weather was lovely, the hotel one of the best in India, and the monuments easy to reach. The road quite good, and we arrived in time for a bath and dinner—Grossman this time coming to my hotel, while Salmony returned to the Taj.

Friday, November 5

Ten A.M. meeting with Salmony at the Taj to make plans for our trip to Bādāmi–Aiholẹ–Paṭṭadakal. Visit to the Indian Tourist Bureau for advice, and then with Grossman to the Indian Automobile Association. Letter writing in the afternoon, after which a visit to the American Express to cash some money, when, behold!—Swami and his two ladies. Pleasant greetings, and my promise to look them up. After dinner, a stroll with Grossman through the lively streets in the neighborhood of the hotel.

Saturday, November 6

Morning: to automobile license bureau to get an Indian driving license; very polite and pleasant treatment from the officers, but the slowest kind of office work I've ever seen. After two hours and seven rupees, I had my license.

Afternoon: with the von Leydens and Salmony, in a motor boat to

Elephanta. Lovely, lovely, lovely—the top experience of the trip. The great central figure is simply something.[120] "Walk right in, slowly, and let it come," said Rudy: and it did. We spent a long while in the cave, and then went in again to see it in terms of Rudy's idea that the original entrance was the one at the left. Makes very good sense. We visited the caves around at the side of the hill. Then Nena and I went back into Cave I. On the ride back we had a pleasant snack from a picnic basket; later, at the von Leydens', we had a lovely dinner. An excellent day.

Sunday, November 7

Sent off some proofs and corrections to Pantheon[121] at 10 A.M. and joined the von Leydens for a visit to their swimming-pool club, where Westerners and Indians (the latter, mostly Parsees) were sitting around under parasols. At the table next to the one at which we settled there was a company of Hindus, including one young woman who turned out to be the sister of Rama Mehta.[122] When she heard my name she said, "You are a friend of my sister. I am reading your book. It is inscribed, 'To Rama, with love...'!" Apparently Rama and her husband will be coming to Bombay next week.

I had met at the pool some of the people from the von Leydens' two Sundays ago, and the sense of pleasant social fooling around was very soothing. For lunch we had a sort of second breakfast and left at about 3:00 P.M.

I returned by bus to my hotel, and then tried to get to Swami Nikhilananda's talk at the Ramakrishna Mission; but when I reached Malabar Hill, I learned that the Mission is some twelve miles out of town, and so I abandoned the try. Took a pleasant walk in the lofty garden on Malabar Hill then returned for dinner and early bed.

Bombay to Bangalore and Back

Monday, November 8   Poona

Up at 5:30 A.M. to prepare for an early start to Bādāmi. Packed, sent my bags downstairs, and sat down for breakfast at 6:45. Meanwhile, Salmony and Grossman were outside by the car with Kashi (Grossman's charming bearer) and a flock of porters, discovering that the combined bulk of their two vast sets of luggage was too much for the car to hold. It took until eight o'clock or so for the realization to sink in.

A series of discussions, phone calls, and conferences was initiated, involving all kinds of surprising people, including taxi drivers and passersby on the street. Presently we all got into a taxi behind a driver whom Kashi had consulted, and were driven to the office of a man who earlier in the morning had suggested over the phone that a light car like the Hillman would not be able to make the trip at all. Both Salmony and I were by this time ready to drop the whole thing, but Grossman seemed willing to risk anything. The man came out of his office, which opened like a stage (as do all Oriental shops) right onto the street, and, with his wife protesting, stepped into our taxi. He directed our driver to the State Transport Office, where he very kindly conducted us to the desk of a young man, Mr. T. V. S. Iyengar, for a consultation on the problem of getting our luggage and ourselves to Bādāmi.

The roads, Iyengar said, would be all right for the car as far as to Bādāmi; Aiholẹ, also, would probably be all right; Paṭṭadakal, on the other hand, would be out of the question. This agreed with most of the other advice we had received, and so we accepted it as a working hypothesis. Next, as to the luggage: it would be dangerous to ship it without an attendant. A man could be sent, however, to Bādāmi *with* the luggage. He could go by train, leaving tonight, and would be there when we arrived. The cost would be about two hundred rupees (a jolt for me, but the others seemed to think it great). O.K. The young man himself would come to our hotel this afternoon at two, to be introduced to the luggage, and then, at seven, would return with the fellow who would see it through to Bādāmi. We could depart with carefree hearts after the two o'clock look. Splendid!

Return to the hotel. Further sitting around. Three for lunch. Further sitting around. It was 3:30 before we got away—but at last we were off and heading for Poona.

What a lovely countryside inland from Bombay!—and I do like the way the peasant women in this part of India wear their saris—hiked up like pants. The saris are of many colors, in contrast to the monotonous dirty white of the Gangetic area. And the countryside is wonderfully mountainous, in contrast to that utterly flat land of paddy fields. At one of the higher points of our mountain driving we came to a sort of resort area, with nice-looking city Hindus strolling along the roads—in direct contrast with the peasants who were likewise on the roads, but with loads on their heads. I could not but think of the Woodstock area—the city vacationers and the natives.

Poona, which we pulled into shortly after dusk, proved to be a rather large and pleasant city. The hotel was about on the order of that in Gwalior. Kashi took over and settled us in our rooms. We lay down for a brief rest, and after dinner took a short stroll before retiring.

Tuesday, November 9   Bījāpur

The cooks in the kitchen began clattering dishes and shouting (in India, "talking") to each other at about 4 A.M. and I got the full benefit of it all through my window. We got up at six, had breakfast, and set off for Bījāpur.

Again a lovely drive, along adequate roads. Toward 4 P.M. we approached the city across a great plain and began to notice that the bullock-carts that we were passing were exceptionally colorful. Most of them crowded with men and women in bright attire—the men with clean turbans of yellow, blue or green, and the women with lots of trinkets. Moreover the horns of the bullocks (beautiful, long-horned zebus) had been freshly painted—green, or red, or, most often, a brilliant magenta. Some of the animals wore gay shoulder capes. And all had jingling bells about their necks. The bullock-carts were trotting at a lively clip and were exceptionally numerous: also, the animals were exceptionally difficult for their drivers when our car went past.

We entered Bījāpur and found that the two Dak bungalows were occupied. Jason Grossman and Kashi did most of the talking, and neither seemed to be able to make very fortunate connections. The language here is Kannada, so that Kashi was hardly better off than his boss. We were sent from place to place, looking first for the Dak bungalows, then for the "Collector"—the officer in charge of their occupancy—and finally, with no success of any kind to our credit, back to one of the Dak bungalows, where we picked up a sort of porter in a dirty white turban who scratched himself a bit too much. This chap guided us first to a large area surrounded by buildings, where it was learned, through a brief conversation, that there were no rooms, and then to a crowded street where he told us to stop before a Hindu hotel.

This was going to be good.

Grossman and Kashi went into the hotel where, it appeared, there were a couple of empty rooms; Salmony went across the street to an apothecary shop, where he thought he would probably discover someone who spoke English; and I remained in the car, which almost immediately attracted a multitude of kids and adults, who simply stood around, peering in at me and examining the contents of the car through all the windows. One cute little girl stood in front of the car and I flashed the lights. Her eyes grew wide and she laughed. Then I made them dim, and she was delighted. I made the "left turn" wink and then the "right turn"; flashed the high, the dim, and the parking lights, etc., made the windshield wipers work, and again flashed the lights. It was a great entertainment. Presently Salmony came out of the apothecary shop and joined me at the car, standing outside and playing with the kids, until Kashi came out of the hotel and we all moved in. I drove the car into the small yard of the hotel, and the game was over.

The proprietor was a tall, very nice gentleman, in the usual dhoti and long white shirt, whose desk was at the left of the veran-dah. Upstairs there was a little balcony, where two Hindu gentlemen were sitting, and a number of small, stone-floored rooms. Kashi super-vised the porters and we were soon installed—Salmony and I in a room at the back, which had a little balcony of its own, and Grossman with Kashi in a larger room (no private balcony) at the front.

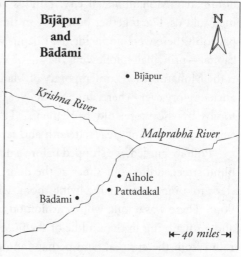

Both rooms had just been washed down for us, under Kashi's supervision, so that the effect was one of sanitation. The smell elsewhere in the hotel, however, was a bit heavy, and we were told that it would be all right for us to urinate on our balcony: there was a drain that would carry the water to the eaves, whence it would fall harmlessly into a back yard.

Buckets of water were brought to us and we all bathed on the little back porch; Salmony first, then Grossman and I. And I was later engaged in helping Kashi open our bed-rolls onto the two beds in our room, when

Salmony came up to invite me downstairs to meet his friends: the friends being the fruit of his trip to the apothecary—a darling cluster of young men, all interested in art, who, when he had presented his card to the proprietor of the shop, declaring that he was an art historian in quest of a bed, had gradually accumulated around him. They were now downstairs, in the main sort of dining room of our hotel, inviting us to have some tea. Kashi and Grossman joined us. And the youths then invited us to have dinner with them at their home: they were the sons of a large brahmin family—brothers and cousins—and their chief father was a banker, one of the big men of the city. Now, since we had been about to retire on practically empty stomachs, this invitation was a valuable surprise—quickly accepted.

The youths returned for us at nine and we drove to their home, through the crowded streets of Bījāpur in a holiday mood. The festival is a Mohammedan one—the birthday of the Prophet—and Bījāpur is a predominately Mohammedan city. Hindus and Mohammedans, the young men told us, live together peacefully in this area: during the period of the partition there were no incidents. Bījāpur was once a great Mohammedan capital—principally, following the fall of Vijayanagar in 1565: thus the city is the Mohammedan contemporary of Madura. One sees the remains of its ancient glory everywhere, and far out over the flat plain: old Mohammedan tombs by the score; old battlements. The modern city is considerably smaller than that of great sixteenth and seventeenth centuries.

Politely guided, we stopped before a decent house at the end of a short blind street, doffed our shoes at the door, and ascended a stone flight of steps to a moderately large living room, without windows, on the second floor. There was a long white cushion on the floor along one of the walls, and a square rug in the middle of the floor; a row of stiff chairs across the room from the cushion, and perhaps another chair or two: but we all sat on the floor. We also viewed with interest and cordial remarks the pictures hung about the walls, which proved to be the needlework of the young men's aunt. The lady herself appeared, briefly, for congratulations, and we were shown some newspaper articles celebrating her work. Three of the pictures were copies of Mughal paintings, one was the portrait of a horse, others were of birds and flowers. Salmony was particularly unctuous and utterly noncommittal in his polite remarks; for, as an authority, he had to protect his honor while honoring his role as guest. The youths brought out their poems, pictures, and thoughts, and we had a sort of spiritual repast before our trip downstairs to the Hindu meal.

It was an acrobatic, orthodox Hindu affair, in which a company of gentlemen sit on slightly raised wooden platforms placed in mathematical order around the room, and convey rice, dhal, liquids and chopped-up surprises to their mouths with their unaided hands. Jason Grossman studiously tried to do it and dropped only very little on his clothes. Salmony sat sideways, with his legs out to the west, and tried to look happy while eating in a radical position of twist. I simply asked for a spoon. Salmony then got a spoon too. The ladies served, like furtive servants, and when they arrived, severally, with their bowls and serving spoons, they were introduced as Mother, Wife, Auntie, etc. We men presently finished and returned to the upper room for a continuation of our elevated conversation.

The question of Hinduism and caste arose, and when our Hindu hosts looked a little amused at the thought that Westerners should think caste intrinsic to Hinduism, I quoted Śaṅkara to the effect that one was lucky who was born a brahmin and a male, because only he was capable of *mokṣa.* The youths concurred, with accurate quotations, and it appeared that a problem was indeed present. The talk moved to Communism in American colleges—and Jason was sounding off, in what I was displeased to recognize as the regular Communist direction, when one of the young men signaled me to his room for a talk about how to get into an American college.

It was a typical student's room: bed, desk, a few chairs, and significant pictures on the walls. The pictures, however, were of Krishnamurti (looking much as he looked when I knew him, 1924–29, only with graying hair),[123] Sri Ramana Maharishi,[124] and T. S. Eliot, with a tiny figure of Christ crucified hanging on one of the walls, suspended from the molding—with the cross missing. Written on the wall under each of these icons was a quotation from the savior in question. The typical problem of an earnest modern youth religiously oriented, of coordinating in terms of modern life the wisdoms of the past and present!

We all descended, finally, to the ground floor, where, I believe, we committed our only real faux pas of the evening. For we entered a room in which the ladies were assembled, one of them with a little baby in her arms, and imagining that we had stumbled into the seraglio, we quickly withdrew. I realized later that they must have been assembled there to hear us marvel at the baby.

Before we left, we were treated to the culminating marvel of this actually quite marvelous adventure, namely, an interview with the mighty father of this clan. He sat in his special room, on the floor, clothed in his white dhoti and brahminical thread—greatly paunched, cordial and smiling. Around him, in a convenient semi-circle, was a low book-stand supporting six identical closed volumes, which I thought for a moment might be the *Mahābhārata* but which, more probably, were his account books. Behind him, against the walls, was an array of safes. And he spoke to us in Kannada, with his eldest son serving as interpreter. The great brahmin's thesis: that the philosophy of the West is materialistic, that of India spiritual (an old Indian cliché: shades of Nikhilananda); that the condition (the poverty and squalor) of India is a consequence of its philosophy; and that therefore the philosophy of India is inferior to the philosophy of the West (surprise!).

We thanked our hosts, returned to our Indian hotel, and went to bed.

Wednesday, November 10

On the quiet morning air, the muezzin from a nearby mosque—my first since Constantinople in 1929. A wondrous sound. After a chary breakfast of tea, bread and butter, and bananas, we were taken by one of the young men of last evening to see the sights of the city—these included the ancient fortress, with a great bronze cannon, a large Muslim tomb, and another tomb, the largest (or perhaps second largest) dome in the world. This young man also brought us in touch with the clerk of the Collector, who arranged for us to occupy the Dak bungalow at Bādāmi, but failed to give us a slip as certificate. The Collector himself, a Mohammedan, had been supervising worship the night before and consequently had been inaccessible. We were assured, however, that everything would be O.K., unless some department head appeared in Bādāmi. The protocol now gives top rights to the Government Heads, next rights to tourists, and then come the lesser officials. The Forest Officer of Poona had been scheduled for this bungalow, but we had precedence, and he would simply have to get out.

We invited the young man to have a Hindu lunch with us as our hotel. He was a large, rather sleek young man, and ate like a bear. I took very little. Salmony and Grossman seemed to like the rice. And then we set off, with eager hearts, for Bādāmi, arrived at five, drove to the bungalow and found— guess who—Iyengar himself with Salmony's and Grossman's bags and gear.

Among the objects to have been transported there was a heavy box containing a dozen bottles of Vichy and Evian water; which the officials at the Bombay railroad station had challenged as possibly containing wine or champagne. Bombay has prohibition. The chap who was to have accompanied the luggage took fright at this point and refused to go, lest he be challenged again; so Iyengar took over.

We thanked him profusely. After the Bījāpur adventure, we were now completely overwhelmed by the evidences of the kindness and hospitality of the people of India.

The Dak bungalow, however, contained but one grim bed and the only water was in a large washtub in one of the three washrooms. The groundplan of the sturdy building was about like this:

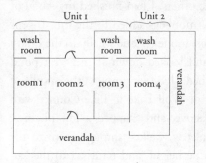

Unit I contained three rooms and two washrooms; Unit II one room and washroom. The portable toilet was placed in the washroom at the far left; the luggage was in Unit II, and the bed in the sleeping room at the far left. We decided that Iyengar, who had no bed-roll, should sleep on the bed and the rest of us on the hard stone floor, Salmony and I in Room 2, Grossman and Kashi in Room 4. We uncanned a bit of supper: tuna, asparagus, cheese and crackers, sweet limes and Vichy—and using the Vichy as champagne, toasted Salmony, whose 64th birthday was this day. My God, I never knew that any water could taste so good. It was, in fact, the first thing with a really interesting taste that I had had since the treacle tart in Darjeeling. After dinner I took a little, final cup of the water and drank it as a liqueur.

Thursday, November 11   Bādāmi–Paṭṭadakal

In a building behind the Dak bungalow there lives the caretaker with his wife and son—a pitiful wisp of a little man, with a high, thin voice, thin black arms and shanks, a prodigious white turban, from beneath which his gaunt little face looks out like a sort of joke, and a simply horrifying, long, and loosely rattling cough. The wife is like every other poor Indian woman with a short broom. And the son is a polite little, helpful boy of about 12.

These poor people and Kashi prepared our hot water, tea, and boiled eggs. After breakfast, we locked all our affairs into Room 4, and drove off to Bādāmi to visit the four caves:[125] Salmony, Grossman, Iyengar, Kashi, and myself. It is a charming town—like a vast pueblo—in a beautiful setting, with high rocks around it crowned by battlements, and with a lovely pond or tank, where the noise of the washers beating clothes filled the quiet air. We spent an excessively long time waiting for Iyengar to give instructions to some old restaurant owner who was to prepare our lunch. We wanted a roast chicken, plain rice, and bit of dhal. The discussion of how to prepare these things went on for about an hour.

Then we set off for the caves. I turned off, alone, to wander a bit through the village—at every turn reminded of the New Mexican Pueblos— and I came to the caves long before the others. I had finished my study of Cave I before they arrived. A couple of monkeys added to the fun. I went up to Cave II,[126] then to Cave III (the great one)[127] and finally to the pretty little Jain cave, Cave IV. Then I sat and looked down at the great pond below, with its thumping washers, watched a kid swimming in the middle of the pond plop the water, and thought of Wolf Lake in Pike County with nostalgia. I climbed next to the fort above, and snapped a few pictures, and then, having lost my friends completely, walked through town to the Malegiṭṭi Shivalaya Temple[128] on its little height, and returned to the car. The group presently arrived, having arranged with a taximan to drive us that afternoon to Paṭṭadakal. We fetched our lunch from the restaurant and returned to the Dak bungalow to eat it: mutton curry, rice with sand, and a spicy dhal. I quit very soon, but the others went on a little longer. And then we lay down to wait for the taximan, who was to call for us at 1:30.

At 2:15 we decided to go and see whether he was still in town and encountered him on the road with his taxi (a Dodge station wagon) full of Hindus. We all returned to the bungalow and learned that all but two of the passengers were policemen, come to look at our passports and papers. They were somewhat illiterate; so Iyengar took over, filled out the forms for them; and at 2:45 we took off for Paṭṭadakal.

The road was no road. The twenty-five yards along the bottom of a broadly flowing stream were the best. At three quarters of a mile from Paṭṭadakal we had to get out and walk. But the visit was great. We visited first the Mallikārjuna Temple (c. A.D. 740), the Virupākṣa (c. A.D. 740), Jambhuliṅga, and finally Pāpanātha, with hasty glimpses of several others.[129]

We had pitifully little time. And the village, furthermore, in which this beautiful cluster of temples stood, was worth a long study too. Grossman was audible in his protests against viewing such things in a hurry and thought we should promise to return. Salmony and I, however, hurried on, knowing that it was now or never. Toward dark we started our return, and if the drive out was difficult, the drive back was worse; for at "the hour of cowdust" one is faced, in India, by homing droves of cattle—flocks of goats and sheep, herds of water buffalo and other kine, not to mention the peasants themselves, bearing hay, baskets, or whatnot, on their poised heads.

We arrived at our Dak bungalow after dark, only to find that Unit I—that is to say, three quarters of our establishment—had been padlocked by some servant of the Forest Inspector of Poona, who, coming to prepare the way for his superior, had found the bungalow occupied, scolded the wearer of the turban, and claimed his master's portion. The master, that night, did not arrive; we all slept, however, on the floor of Unit II. Before retiring, Grossman decided that he would remain in Bādāmi and let Salmony go on to Bangalore alone. He wished to live as an artist—not as an art historian: he would relax into this idyll of rural India—as, formerly, he had relaxed into that of rural Mexico, rural Italy, rural Spain. He is a rather heavy-headed type and I think has become pretty well tired of the dates and periods of ancient Indian art.

Friday, November 12   Bādāmi–Aihoḷe–Bādāmi

Salmony announced this morning that he had been unable to sleep because of the tumult of Jason's snoring. "You are a monumental snorer," he declared. It was all with a laugh; but the atmosphere was not altogether good. The first thing I did was to go out and look at the padlock that had been put on the door. I saw that the staple could be pried open—so I opened it, removed the lock, and flung open the doors of Unit I. We bathed, breakfasted, and prepared for a visit to Aihoḷe.

I drove Iyengar to the station and sat and talked with him for a while. He was returning to Bombay—with my watch, which had stopped two days ago. We would get in touch with each other when I returned. Then I drove Salmony, Grossman, and Kashi to town, where we wired Bījāpur for a confirmation of our occupancy and I pretended, before some local officers, to be very angry because of the impudent padlock. The idea of jungle

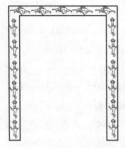

law being very powerful, apparently, in the circles of Indian officialdom, I decided to be a sort of lion.

Then we set off for the temples of Aiho!e,[130] with a package lunch, which we ate on the verandah of the lovely Durgā Temple. It was an excellent visit. I was impressed particularly by the figures in the shallow cave temple, which have a brilliancy of form that is quite unique. I realized that the way the women wear their saris, hitched up between the legs, is the fashion of the peasant women around Bombay to this day. We cruised around to the Huchimalliguḍi, Lāḍ Khān, and numerous other temples—including one small Jain unit, and a Śiva temple with an interior door-frame (to the sanctuary) of obscene, cunnilingus arrangements; the earliest, as far as I know, in the history of Indian art.

Returning, somewhat fatigued, to Bādāmi, we plodded up the hill to the Malegiṭṭi Temple, which Salmony and Grossman had not yet seen, and then returned to our Dak—holding, in triumph, a telegram from Bījāpur.

The Forest Inspector of Poona, a young man of considerable self-assurance, had complacently installed himself during our absence in the great three room section of our house, and it was pleasant to make him realize that he had to go. It had been our intention to invite him to share the building; but when we saw his style of taking over, we let him have it on the nose. The exit was graceful enough. A tonga came, about 11 P.M., and took him to the home of a friend in town! Nice guy! Nice ad for the Indian Tourist Office!

Saturday, November 13

Salmony, two evenings ago, on learning that he was going to have to go to Bangalore by train, had invited me to accompany him and declared that, in return, he pay my air passage from Bangalore back to Bombay. Both of us wanted to visit Hampi (Vijayanagar) on the way. And we had managed, by psychological pressure, to get Grossman to consent to drive with us to Hampi and let us take the train, then, from there.

Sunday, November 14   Bangalore

Our train pulled into Bangalore at 5:50 A.M. We found that the West End Hotel was full, and went to the Central. Nice room. Hot baths, etc. Finis to the Bādāmi adventure: hello again to Bangalore.

It is a charming city and we were in a mood for repose. After baths and a pleasant breakfast we took a short stroll to the museum. Nicely arranged exhibit of paleolithic, neolithic, and later materials. We visited the young curator: another of these enthusiastic young Indian scholars.

Shortly after our return to the hotel we were visited by a distinguished retired officer of the state, Rājamantrapravīṇa (that is his title) A. V. Ramanathan, and his son Subrakhmanya. Salmony chatted with the father and I with the son, who, when he learned that my wife is a dancer, waxed eloquent and enthusiastic about the life of art. He told me, too, that the great dance festival of the year is held at Madras, December 20 to January 20 every year. (A great change of plans for Jean's visit is indicated.) After a cordial visit the two gentlemen left, with an invitation for us to visit them at five tomorrow afternoon.

Shortly after lunch we received the visit of another distinguished citizen, Dharmaprakāśa Rao Bahādur (his title) K. Kuppuswamy! After tea, he offered to introduce us to the city, and so we joined him in his little car.

I could not make out whether he was pleased to be showing us the city or just doing it out of a sense of duty, but he did an excellent job. He showed us the great gardens and the botanical exhibition hall, two interesting temples (where Salmony had his first experience of *pūjā*), and his own home, with its garden (his pet) and family chapel.

The first of the two temples was to the bull Nandi—a big stone animal, like that on the hill at Mysore and those before the temple of Halebīd. Precisely the same form. The interesting point was that here Nandi was not the mere vehicle of the god but the worshipped deity. It is the only Nandi temple in India, we were told.

The second temple was a cave temple—a natural cave, but with a circumambulatory tunnel carved around the central shrine. Particularly interesting were four large stone standards set up in the court before the

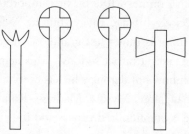

temple entrance. The first two were, respectively, a *trisūla* and an hour-glass drum—the latter looking very much like a double ax. The second two were identical wheels with crosses—and their total effect was that of the Christian cross with a halo.

Interesting in the very rich gentleman's own chapel was a large picture just above the main Kṛṣṇa shrine, showing a brahmin talking to an earnestly listening young Kṛṣṇa. Our host told the story—of a poor brahmin who performed some pious act in honor of Kṛṣṇa and immediately found his poor home turned into a palace of wealth. (The wonderful complacency of the rich. Like that of the so-called Boston brahmins!)

Mr. Kuppuswamy invited us in for a cup of hot milk (can you believe it?), introduced us to his nice son and daughter, and then told us that he was making arrangements to "give" his daughter (age 18) to a young man who for the past five years has been working for an engineering degree at the University of California. The girl had never seen the boy, nor the boy the girl. But he was earning considerable money in California, and would probably make an excellent husband. (I could not but wonder what the boy had been learning about American erotic ideals in California... and the girl is lovely.)

We next were driven to the really palatial home of a somewhat chubby Indian tycoon, who had a handsome German Police Dog: the first nicely bred dog I have seen in Indian hands—and whose whole manner and attitude reminded me of my friend Dhar in Calcutta. Whiskey and soda for the Westerners. A pleasant talk about Belūr and Halebīd, which at Kuppuswamy's invitation we are to visit Tuesday.

Monday, November 15

A quiet day—and welcome. I am enjoying my sojourn with Salmony. He is the scholar for whom Zimmer wrote his first important article: Zimmer would have been precisely his age today: but he is not the spirit that Zimmer was. His learning is much less grandiose, much more restricted and pedantic—and he takes it rather seriously, this being a scholar. It has been amusing to watch how ponderously he lets everyone know of the lectures he is to give in Bangalore, Mysore, Madras—Rome, and Paris. Then one learns that the fee is one hundred rupees and the audience a group of about forty. He has with him a batch of the brief offprints of an article on a Gandhāra Buddha that he published in his *Artibus Asiae,* and he passes these out to people with enormous solemnity—his head thrust a little too far forward. Also, his new book, *Antler and Tongue,* is here. I am reading it today with interest; reading, also, the articles in the new *Artibus Asiae.* After my months among the swamis the breath of the harvest (even though stuffy) air of scholarship is great joy.

In the morning we set off on a gentle stroll—went to a bank, paused at the library of the U.S. Information Service, visited the Mysore information office to procure a pamphlet on the monuments of Talkad, stopped again at the Museum (where Alfred presented his offprint to the young Curator), and then went to the Indian Airlines office, where he bought and paid for my ticket to Bombay.

After lunch, we visited a second-hand bookshop on Mahatma Gandhi Road, where we met a bookish Englishman who, with the bookseller, declared he would be present at "Alfred's" lecture tomorrow evening at the Mythic Society. We returned to the hotel to plan our visit to Belūr and Halebīd. And then Subrakhamanya arrived to drive us to his home for tea.

Apparently this family is of an older vintage than that of the newly rich Kuppuswamy. The father, Ramanathan, dresses, like Kuppuswamy, in a business suit, but wears a white turban with bands of red and gold. Kuppuswamy showed us with pride when we visited his house, a gold medal with jewels, given him by the Maharaja for some philanthropic deed, and a copper medal on a broad red ribbon awarded by the English king. No such display of honors in the modest, Victorianly cluttered home of Ramanathan. The "old" gentleman—now sixty-six—had retired at the age of fifty-five. When I told him that I had edited Nikhilananda's *Gospel of Sri Ramakrishna,* he said, "Then you understand the nature of my present life." Apparently he regarded himself as in the life-stage of *vānaprastha,* retirement from the world for contemplation. The son brought in tea and sweets; and the father was gently solicitous that we should taste of everything—a little awkward in passing the plates—clearly a much older gentleman than Salmony, who was sixty-four!

The son then showed us his works of amateur sculpture and painting (Śivas, Pārvatīs, Venuses, and *apsarases*): remarkably good. And on the way home he talked with touching earnestness and feeling of his art. "When I work in clay," he said, "Mother tells me to be careful: I will catch cold from the wet clay. And when I work in stone, Father tells me to be careful, the dust will get in my lungs and I will catch cold." His hope—his ideal—is to get to France, to experience the world of art. But he is a good *fils de famille* in provincial Bangalore.

After dinner the bookseller of yesterday evening's guest arrived to take us to his shop—and Salmony bought a number of rare books.

Tuesday, November 16   Belūr–Halebīd

6 A.M. departure by taxi (paid by Kuppuswamy) for Hassan, Belūr and Halebīd.[131] It was a delight to see these temples again, in the sunshine. I took a lot of photos. At Belūr we had the guide who had shown me the temple before. I was impressed particularly, this time, by the bracket figures of Belūr, and the gods as well as the epic scenes of Halebīd. Salmony pointed out that the figures at Halebīd were less vital than those of Belūr. He was immensely impressed by both.

On the way home our car ran out of gas two miles from Hassan, and we waited an hour while our two boys walked to town and came back with a can.

Home after dark (about 7:30 P.M.)—a pleasant dinner, and early to bed.

Wednesday, November 17   Bangalore

Two booksellers arrived at 8 A.M. and at 8:30 the secretary and curator of the Mythic Society came to show us the hall in which Salmony is to lecture this evening. During the course of our genteel visit, it gradually dawned on my good friend that he was not going to be paid for this lecture. He took it manfully, and we continued to give fulsome praise to the library that we were being shown.

After we returned to the hotel, I began reading a booklet that Salmony had found on the problems of Indian archaeology, and suddenly the main pattern of the scholarly work before me on this trip, and after my return to New York, fell neatly into form—as outlined on the following page. We spent a quiet afternoon, at a quarter to six went to the society for Alfred's talk (the curator, at the slide machine, got all fouled up), went with Kuppuswamy to his club for a drink, and went early to bed.

Orientation Plan, Bangalore, November 17, 1954

I. Coordination of India Studies with Mythology Studies

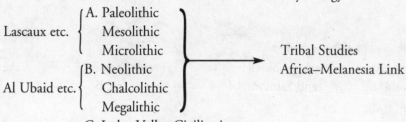

Lascaux etc. { A. Paleolithic / Mesolithic / Microlithic }

Al Ubaid etc. { B. Neolithic / Chalcolithic / Megalithic }

→ Tribal Studies
Africa–Melanesia Link

    C. Indus Valley Civilization
    D. Aryan Problem
    E. Vedic–Upanishadic Age
    F. Buddhism and Jainism
    G. Early History (Maurya through Gupta)
    H. Medieval History (Cālukya–Vijayanagar)
    I. Late History
      1. Islam and *bhakti*
      2. Arrival of the Europeans
    J. India Today

II. Similar schedules for
    1. Ceylon
    2. Burma
    3. S.E. Asia and Indonesia
    4. Philippines
    5. Japan

III. Eranos–Basic Mythologies coordination

IV. SLC course revision

V. Writing program:
    1. Viking Book—Introduction to Mythology
    2. Bollingen Book—Basic Mythologies
    3. Related articles (for *Artibus Asiae*)
    4. Related stories (King & Corpse type?)
    5. The New World of Bartolomé de las Casas

Go to work immediately on III, IV, and V.1 (Viking). When III is finished, begin work on V.2 notes (Bollingen). Keep V.1 writing going, watching leads for the commencement and chapters of V.2.

CHAPTER 3

THE SPACE-PLATFORM

BOMBAY

Thursday, November 18   **Bombay**

Up at 4:45 A.M. for goodbye and good wishes to Alfred. Plane off at seven, arrival at Bombay Airport at 12:05, then by bus to the Grand Hotel. To the American Express for my mail, then the rest of the day in my room, reading letters and *Time Magazine,* to catch up on the U.S.A.

Jean's affairs are taking handsome shape: a warm review of her Cooper Union demonstration in the *Dance Observer,* by Louis Horst himself;[132] dates settled for concerts in California and Hawai'i. Then a concert at Bard and one at Sarah Lawrence in April—and a return in June to Colorado.

Friday, November 19

Letters to Jean and Helen McMaster and an attempt to catch up on my diary. Mild walks through town, bebrooding a few ideas. Saw von Leyden in the hotel after lunch, and gave him the story of our Bādāmi adventure.

Saturday, November 20

I spent the day catching up on my diary, and now (6:15 P.M.) have arrived here. As for the new ideas:

They take off from a "letter to the editor" in the *Times of India* for November 18, in which the author, an Indian, takes precisely the position of brahmin-banker host of Bījāpur, namely, that everything worthy of the name of civilization has come to India from the West—while her own philosophers have been priding themselves on their Sanskrit. With technology, new social ideals, anti-toxins, and money pouring into destitute India from the Occident, how can any Indian dare to vaunt the "spirituality" of his Oriental culture with the dictum "Happiness lies within"?

With this letter in my mind I have been strolling through the squalid bazaars of Bombay—and I find here much the same general mood and style of life that I have just seen in the Indian villages—only with no trees about, and consequently no sense of the idyll. What I see is that these people are amazingly composed and yield an air (in spite of their obvious misery) of well-being.

I think of Boethius's title *The Consolation of Philosophy,* and recall his saying that if philosophy cannot support us in the time of our misfortune it is little good. India's time of misfortune, apparently, is forever: and India's philosophy in this circumstance, one might say, has stood her in good stead.

The Orient	*The Occident*
Terminus of the Neolithic	Growing point of the New World
Tradition (Guru)	Revolution (Hero)
Faithful obedience	Intelligent striving
The Archetypes	The personal factor
Immutable law	Volition
Caste	Equality
Transformation of Consciousness	Transformation of the world

And now a slightly different train of thought; once again, with a take-off from *The Times of India:* this time, November 19, editorial page, a review-essay based on Stella Kramrisch's new book on Indian art,[133] by a gent named Adib. He queries the Coomaraswamy idea that Indian art is throughout a religious intuition of reality and identity—and now that I have had my view of India I suddenly see a certain point; to wit: that, from the U.S.A., a student of Vedanta is likely to see India as a function of Vedanta, but from the vantage ground of India itself one sees Vedanta as a function of a certain aspect of India.

A. India, as viewed from the U.S.A

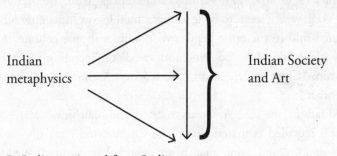

Indian metaphysics — Indian Society and Art

B. India, as viewed from India

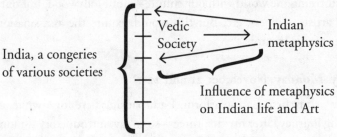

India, a congeries of various societies — Vedic Society — Indian metaphysics — Influence of metaphysics on Indian life and Art

Somehow, this idea means a great deal to me just now. It seems to summarize the whole import of my reaction to this Indian experience during the past three months. Moreover, it is an idea that can be applied to any viewing of any society. The idea has given me a great feeling of release from something—Coomaraswamy, perhaps, and all my other gurus.[134]

In relation to Indian art, for example, one may think of the gent who scratched the obscene engraving on the pillar in the Dhumar Lena cave at Elūrā. Was he unique? Or has something of his inspiring spirit perhaps contributed to the obscenities of Konārak and Belūr? May it be that these are not primarily religious intuitions of reality and identity, but more nearly what they seem to be?

Yesterday's *Times of India* contained a second section, of twenty full pages, celebrating the "Formal Opening of Stauvac Bombay Refinery" and describing the progress, projects, contributions to civilization, etc. of

Standard Oil. In today's edition we read of the opening ceremonies and learn that this was the "First Industrial Project With Foreign Capital." Suddenly (dope!) a little light goes up for J. C.! Standard Oil deeply involved in India. Standard Oil—the Rockefellers—the Rockefeller Foundation—curious interest of the Rockefeller Foundation in the business-philosophy of India: my various conferences with the fellowship people. Well, well! I seem to be learning something in India after all.

Then I find in the same paper two headlines in one column. At the top: "World-Wide U.S. Aid Programme: Major Spending in Asia." At the bottom: "Chinese Delegation expected from Canton in the first week of December."

Meditation: the U.S.A. sends money and machines, and, consequently, is regarded as materialistic. The Chinese and Russians send cultural delegations, and, consequently are regarded as cultured. We should begin storming the world with our culture—not Hollywood, but our composers, artists, dancers, etc. But this would require the assassination of a number of our senators.

Sunday–Monday, November 21 and 22

Bombay is my first space-platform. I am pausing here for a while, on the outgoing journey, after my first three—so to say, introductory—months in the Orient, to finish off all unfinished business, all of those last tag-ends still dragging from New York, and to refurbish my light equipment, straighten out my thoughts, and prepare for the real experience—whatever it is to be.

My first Indian visa expires this week and I am making application for a second three-months touring permission. That one will expire about the time Jean leaves, and I should be ready by then to push off for Japan.[135] So I have ahead of me three more months in India, then two months of travel to reach Japan and perhaps one month (May) of touring in Japan, after which I shall arrive at my second space-platform, that of the return threshold, where I shall pause again, again collect my thoughts, and prepare—for New York. Kyoto, I think will be that platform.

And so, from here to there is the far curve of the adventure, with something—I don't know what—that is to happen as a climax.

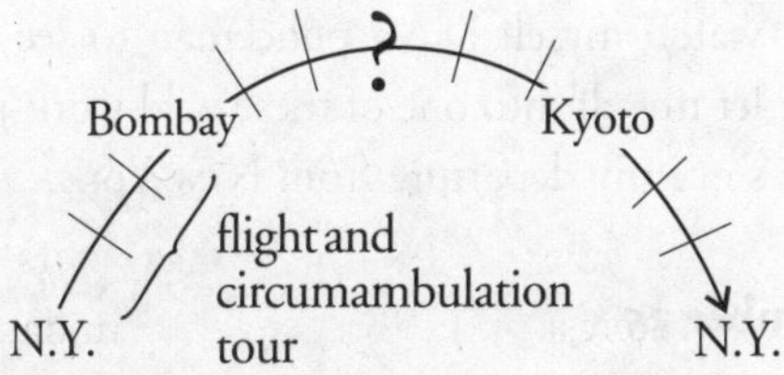

Diagram: arc showing "Bombay" and "Kyoto" with "?" at top; "N.Y." at lower left and "N.Y." at lower right; labeled "flight and circumambulation tour"

Tuesday, November 23

Continued work on the Sarah Lawrence chapter.[136] Yesterday I began operations to have my three-month visa, which expires November 29, extended for another period of three months; today I paid a visit to a third office. Someone has to guarantee my financial condition, and I think Rudy von Leyden is the one to do it.

While at work this morning I received from Rudy an invitation to a vernissage—of a painter named K. H. Ara, to whom Rudy has been a patron. A large and handsome exhibition room full of people and with a great splash of colorful paintings all around the room. They were imitations of the various masters of the Paris school, but with a cheerful brightness of their own that was frank and charming. A number of the still-lifes and two or three of the stylish nudes were particularly good. A slightly stilted young man of the world, however, opined that the exhibition looked like something collected from the ash-cans of Paris. I broke the question to Rudy about guaranteeing my visa. He consented to help.

From the exhibition I went to the home of Rama Mehta's father and sister—for a delightful dinner and evening's talk. Mr. Mehta's collection of Rajput paintings, bronzes, and other figures, is quite wonderful, and the gentleman himself I fell for right away.

A younger man named Roy Hawkins, from the Oxford Book Shop, was at dinner. Ferenc Berko had told him to watch for me—and had written to me to watch for him. So a number of things are coming together in Bombay. Hawkins drove me home and invited me to drive with him on Sunday to Kanheri. O.K. Very nice indeed.

Wednesday, November 24

Finished the Sarah Lawrence chapter about 4:00 P.M. Feeling great, feeling free: that darned Sarah Lawrence chapter is the last of the great commitments.

I must henceforth watch myself like a policeman to see that I never never never get myself or let myself into one of these wild work-jams again. It is exactly three months since my departure from New York.

Thursday, November 25

Wrote letters, mailed them, then went to the Oxford Book Store to discuss with Roy Hawkins plans for Sunday's trip to Kanheri, then by taxi to the Sarabhai[137] office. It turned out that Gautam and Gira were in town (arrived yesterday—leave tonight).

After lunch I went to von Leyden's office, and obtained his signature on the financial guarantee for my visa; delivered the visa papers to the C.I.D. office, and returned home for tea, nap, reading, bath, etc. At 5:45 P.M. Gautam phoned. I am to have dinner with him.

It was an exceedingly deluxe, New York–style apartment with Oriental effects. Gautam and Gira looked as sweet and fine as ever. We drove then to Gautam's father's apartment, which was equally deluxe, with great views of the panorama of the city. Dinner commenced at 8:00 P.M., and their train would leave at 9:05. Gautam gave me a lot of names to help me arrange for Jean's concert in Bombay. His father asked me about my relationship to Indian philosophy and phoned to make an appointment for me with Sophia Wadia. After dinner, a great dash to the station. A very pleasant atmosphere and event.

Friday, November 26

Mail and shopping tour in the morning. More letters written. Still finishing off the last tag-ends of my Pantheon affairs.[138]

While I was at lunch old Mr. Sarabhai walked into the hotel dining room and joined me for the meal. He had a little trouble getting the vegetarian meal that he wanted; but finally won. Later I went around to the Sarabhai office to meet Mr. Ezekiel, director of the Bombay Theatre Unit. He seemed to be interested in presenting Jean's concert, and I felt sure that the way was beginning to open.

At 8:30 P.M. at the hotel I played host to the von Leydens. Rudy thought the Bombay Theatre Unit was correct for Jean's concert; Nena thought the bigger possibility should be tried by way of Pipsi Wadia, who would be arriving in town next week. Rudy contended, however, that Pipsi's set were interested in the Menuhin type of thing because of highly advertised names, but that the theater set were interested in the modern movement. Nena suggested that I should send for Jean's publicity, etc.: that would help her to judge.

Saturday, November 27

Post Office and American Express route in the morning. Letters, wires, and diary the rest of the day, until 6:00 P.M., when I visited Mr. Mehta again. He took me to the Willingdon Sports Club for fruit juice and a pleasant chat. Good jazz band and a very Honoluluish sort of club atmosphere. People (Indians) actually dancing Sambas. Then—in a vast limousine—Mr. Mehta saw me back to my hotel. It looks very much as though Jean and I should lean a bit on this Bombay group: sweet people, delighted to introduce us to *their* India, and with promising connections all over the map.

I telephoned Mrs. Sophia Wadia: I am to go to a dance concert at her house Tuesday evening. See? It works as quickly as that!

Sunday, November 28

Up at 5:30 A.M. to meet Roy Hawkins at his place and drive in his little Fiat to the Kanheri caves. A lovely morning. There were literally thousands of people—schools and families—walking from the nearest railroad depot the several miles to the caves, and as we passed through them in our tiny car they cheered and laughed. When they arrived at the caves they set up their picnics in the various old monastic cells and were a lively and colorful addition to the delightful height: a volcanic-rock dome into which over a hundred Buddhist caves—a few large, most of them fairly small—were carved during the centuries between 100 B.C. and A.D. 900. Hawkins led me through underbrush and woods over the brow of a hill to a cave that is still occupied—but the *sadhu* was out. His yellow pennant, on a long bamboo staff, was flying, and his cave was locked with a padlock! (Not *much* of a *sadhu*, I'm afraid.) He had converted the front part into a nice little verandah, with a high wall of clay, and before him was the bed of a steep mountain stream. I could not but think of Hervey White at Woodstock: precisely his ideal![139] Except that within the cave, behind the locked gate, there was a little shrine.

We next drove, over a lovely wood road and along the shore of a beautiful lake, to a large, model dairy farm, where we stopped to have ice-cream at the farm restaurant—much as at the dairy farm near Bennington, Vermont. Once again, there were crowds of prettily dressed people, lively and full of color: a set of young chaps playing a crazy ball game on the lawn, and many families sitting about.

We got back to Hawkins's rooms at about 1:30 P.M. and were served a pleasant luncheon by his two manservants. Then he drove me home.

The contrast of what I am seeing and hearing these days in Bombay with the world and point of view of Swami and his monks is considerable. My India visit is falling neatly into three divisions: Religion–Archaeology–Dance.

I. My period with the monks—from New Delhi to Madras; devoted to an experience of the contemporary religious situation;
II. My period alone and with Alfred Salmony—in Bombay, Aurangabad, Bādāmi, and Bangalore; devoted to a recovery of my proper, scholarly position and an experience of the great works of the great middle period of Indian religious art;
III. My period, beginning now, with the Mehtas and Sarabhais, which will include the months with Jean; devoted to an experience of the contemporary acculturation through the influence of the West, in the worlds of modern social life and art: the central theme will be the dance.

I am greatly interested in the conversation and point of view of Mr. Mehta, who is no worshipper (his wife has a shrine, he tells me; but *his* point of view is not that of the *bhakta*), and yet is a Hindu. He has thought of the dark side of Indian mythology: the crime of Kṛṣṇa's parents in their swapping of the children at the time of Kṛṣṇa's birth; the crime of Rāma in his dropping of Sītā.... He recognizes the profound psychological interest of the implications: *these crimes represent, as it were, the dark side of the Indian dharma: bringing them out into the open is an act of importance for the modern Indian mind.*

Here is a formula for the literary treatment of the ancient mythological material that would be of considerable psychological and sociological interest.

I find it interesting, also, that the schoolchildren of Bombay are being brought in great number to the ancient sites—in a manner that makes me think of New York's kids at Bear Mountain Park. Here we have a Western influence that is being referred, however, to Indian themes and experiences. The holiday crowd at Kanheri is comparable to the holiday droves leaving New York by car—only here the travel is by train and foot.

Monday, November 29

I took the usual walk to the Post Office and the American Express mail desk; then to Oxford Book Shop to give Hawkins a copy of *Philosophies of India* and finally to the police office for the extension of my residence permit. Pleasant chap in the office gave me my permanent "number" for India: 42931, which will be my number if I ever return. I have also to keep reporting my movements to the police, and I have to get an exit permit to leave. I'm glad I'm not *quite* behind the Iron Curtain.

When I returned to the hotel I found a phone call from Mr. Ezekiel, whom I presently went to see at the Sarabhai office, and learned that his Bombay Theatre Unit will present Jean: first in a concert, then in a lecture demonstration, and finally at a dinner. They will handle all publicity, radio interviews, etc. Simply great. Came home and wrote Jean all about it and sent a wire.

Spent the afternoon and evening reading and taking notes on the strata of Indian archaeology and history.

   I. Paleolithic, Mesolithic, Microlithic
  II. Neolithic, Chalcolithic, Megalithic
 III. Indus Valley
 IV. The Aryans
  V. Pre-Maurya Period (Vedas—Buddhism and Jainism)
 VI. The Great Dynasties
VII. Islamic Period
    1. Conquest (1175–1400)
    2. Early *bhakti* poets (1400–1550)
    3. Mughal Period (1550–1800)
VIII. British Period
 IX. Svarāj[140]

It appeared to me—and I think that I have here found something— that the great division that one now feels between the religious and social patterns of India and the West derives from the period of A.D. 1400–1550. Whereas that is the period in Europe of the Italian Renaissance, with its breakthrough into psychological adulthood from the religious formulae of the Middle Ages, India at that time, overwhelmed by Islam, stressed the folk-religion of *bhakti.* This was the period of Rāmānanda, Kabīr, Nānak—the founders of modern Hinduism: anti-Sanskrit, anti-brahmin, in a sense. There was a stress on *the childlike attitude of refuge in a personal God* (kitten-monkey differentiation;[141] yet both remain childlike). Contrast to this the attitude of the *vīra,* rendered in the medieval temples. The stress now is on the Mother and Father images, as found in the approach to Catholicism in its *paśu* formulae.[142] Whereas in the period of the dynasties India's religion was heroic and that of Europe largely childlike, after A.D. 1400–1550 the contrast was reversed.

This explains to me why all the patterns of Indian life and religion now seem to me to be precisely what I left behind when I broke with the Church, whereas the philosophies of India suggested a bold adulthood even surpassing that of the European-American ideal.

Tuesday, November 30

It might be noted that the *dialogue with Islam* was the prelude to both the Indian and the European transformation. India collapsed before Islam and assumed the attitude of the child; Europe overcame Islam and became the master of the world. It is perhaps significant also that Europe's democratic movement immediately followed, as did also the anti-caste inflection of the Indian *bhaktas.* To this day the democracy of Islam is a model unsurpassed.

Rudy thought that the Indian loss of power had commenced already when Islam broke through. The flowering and culmination of the temple architecture in the seventh to thirteenth centuries (compare the parallel in Europe) had been accompanied by a scholastic crystallization of the religion. Formula and reference to the books of the past instead of creative attention to the symbolizations demanded for the present, is a prelude to collapse.[143]

In Europe the conquest of Islam led to a vigorous, humanistic movement, adult, and breaking the shell of scholastic *bhakti.* In India the conquest by Islam led to a loss of nerve and an infantile attitude of submission.

Another idea here: whether in Europe or in India, the religious attitude has lost its style. Where style is lost, the spirit has withdrawn. Religion, both in India and the West, is fundamentally folk religion today. The condition of the folk dictates the character of the cult: American Methodism, Italian Catholicism, Irish Catholicism, Indian Vaiṣṇavism.

History-making man has passed into a new stage. The date of this passage: 1492.[144]

After dinner I taxied to the Mehtas' to pick up Lila. I found the family at their dessert course: Lila, her father, and her mother—the latter, who has been ill for some time, looking quite haggard and full of self-pity, but gracious—for brief moments—nevertheless. Lila and I departed, then, in the Mehtas' sumptuous limousine, for the palatial (that's the only word for it) residence, "Āryasangha," of Mrs. Sophia Wadia. I met the hostess at the steps, and we entered a large, airy hall with tile flooring, set with chairs, and with a stage area marked out with flowers.

The occasion was a performance of Indian dance in honor of Mr. Novokof, general secretary of the Council for Cultural Freedom, who is on a brief visit to Bombay and New Delhi. The first dance, "Peacock Dance," by a spry young woman in a blue "sleeper" with peacock's tail attached— was simply bad. The second dance, however, by a pretty little girl dressed as a *devadāsī,* was excellent. I was reminded of the young Balinese dancers. After that came the queen of the evening—the wife of a gentleman of some importance who, as secretary or something of the Council for Cultural Freedom in Bombay, was largely responsible for this event: and she was not good. A folk dance in the second part of the program, by eight men with sticks; a brilliant Manipuri drum dance, then, toward the close, a gypsy dance by the pretty little girl, were very good. Finally the queen returned while I was watching the musicians.

I was satisfied, when the evening was over, that I had done the right thing in arranging for Jean to be presented by the Theatre Unit instead of the society crowd. Behind me, at this event, sat the inspiring spirit of Bombay's socially patronized events, Pipsi Wadia—and if she had been dressed in a low-cut evening gown instead of in a sari, she could easily have appeared *chez* Mrs. Murray Crane. I was amused to see a face, furthermore, dimly remembered from somewhere else, which turned out to be that of a self-concerned young poet, Arthur Gregor, from New York; just arrived in

Bombay today, en route to Trivandrum, where he will seek his soul under the pilotage of Sri Krishna Menon.

An elegant evening, in the high social atmosphere—and I was driven back to my hotel, again in the sumptuous car, with Lila. Nice finale for my first three months in India.

Wednesday, December 1

In the morning, after my walk to the American Express office, I left my passport at the Ceylonese Consulate for a visa, and went to the Prince of Wales Museum to meet Dr. Moti Chandra,[145] father of the young man, Pramod, who greeted me in the New Delhi museum. A surprisingly boyish and sweet gentleman, of about my own age: a very pleasant conversation. I left with a lot of museum bulletins in hand and an invitation to lunch on Friday.

At 5:30 P.M. I went around to the Sarabhai office to go with Ezekiel to the workshop of his Theatre Unit. At the office I met his nice little wife, who will be too busy with their child to come to dinner this evening at the home of the inspiring genius of the group, Mr. Alkazi. A long, slow bus-ride to the workshop—a lovely, fresh, well-planned building with the workshop on the roof and studios (sculpture and music) below: a sort of foundation, in memory of an Indian patriot, Desai.[146] The atmosphere was familiar and pleasant—that of a seriously working New Theater group—with the additional touch of being the *only* serious theater unit in the metropolis of a prodigious country. I watched their rehearsal of *Oedipus,* which I enjoyed immensely. I was then taken to the home of Alkazi. It was up five flights, and there was his pregnant young wife—it could have been in Greenwich Village. There was a lovely crowd, and a nice evening of talk, in which I took over on the history of the American Dance: they want me to talk of this to their group next Wednesday evening.

Fortunately, in their workshop library, I put my hand on the *Borzoi Book of the Modern Dance* and opened to the pictures of Jean.

Thursday, December 2

At 11:15 A.M. I went to Mrs. Sophia Wadia's place, and found that the palatial house of two evenings ago is very busy during the day, with a children's class in something or other being conducted on the seaside verandah, and young editors of P.E.N. and Theosophical journals busy in various rooms of the house. A tiny tot conducted me to an editor, who showed me upstairs, where another editor pointed the way to a large sitting room (just above the salon of the dance recital), and as I entered Mrs. Wadia came to meet me. We sat down for an hour's talk on India, my journey, and her works here, the Bollingen Foundation, the Ramakrishna Mission, and Jiddu Krishnamurti. I left with an invitation to a P.E.N. lecture next Tuesday on "The Humanities and Literary Criticism"—to be given by Richard McKean![147]

During the course of our talk I told of my arrival and voyage with Swami Nikhilananda: and Mrs. Wadia told of being on the platform with Swami at the Bombay mission in honor of the Holy Mother. She had not liked Swami's stress on the idea that Ramakrishna and his "wife" had lived without sexual relations—and I agreed. She thought also that the dressing, feeding, and putting to bed of images at the *maṭha* is a pretty shameful business—and again I agreed. The whole pattern of the thinking of the monks is backward-looking, even in spite of their very good social work.

She told of an organization with which she worked that was trying to help Indian wives to solve their problems when they come up against blank walls of suppression and misunderstanding in their marriages. The number of suicides, apparently, is very high. Among many of the orthodox members of the community, though, there is a great resentment of this work. This came out in connection with my discussion of the impression I had of a pretty harsh marriage situation. The organization was founded by an Indian gentleman who remains anonymous: it is called, simply, "Father's House," and is run entirely (necessarily in India) by women. She told me also of the difficulties encountered when she tries to mix boys and girls in classes. They are soon sitting again in segregated groups.

It was a lovely talk, and confirmed me in many of my thoughts about the *archetypal* vs. *personal* principles in Indian life: also about the unpalatability of Swami's "spiritual" fare: his notion that the West has "material" and the Orient "spiritual" goods to offer.

I wonder if it might not be said that *the Orient is essentially archetypal in its thought and life and the West personal*—and that what the Orient has to offer the West is an image of the archetypal, whereas the spiritual contribution of the West to the Orient is an awakening of the personal. The response of each should not be to parody the other, but rather, to bring his own newly activated function into a significant balance with the excessively dominant function in his own personal way.

On the way to take a taxi to the von Leydens' for dinner, I was accosted by a young man who has frequently hailed me in the neighborhood of Ballard Pier. His usual call is "Want any beer, whiskey, gin, rum? Dope? I got anything you want!" This time he hooked on to me and began telling me that he hadn't chosen this kind of business because he liked it. He required food: and when the police brought him to jail he always told them to tell him how to earn a decent living in India and he would quit this line. He was talking at a great clip and I let him delay me some twenty minutes.

"India doesn't need America's money," he told me. "India has lots of money—in the wrong places—in private hands and in the temple coffers. A contractor gets money from America for a job. Where does the money go? Lakhs of rupees into the pockets of the contractor: annas to the workers.[148]

"What about Goa? Goa's a nice city: the people of Goa were perfectly happy as they were. Now Salazar in Lisbon and Nehru in Delhi begin to make things hot for all. India's blockade of food to Goa has raised all prices way above the reach of the people. Looks like they're trying to get a war going. Who will suffer? Not Salazar in Lisbon or Nehru in Delhi.

"The anti-cow-slaughter people want to stop the killing of cattle for beef. They tell you, 'Eat vegetables.' They prevent the killing of cows: the price of vegetables goes up: who wins? I don't know: these people are crazy. They got millions of gods and they want more.

"The preachers of religion: they come and they tell you to believe in God. What good is that? Everyone believes in God already: the poor man, the rich man, they all believe in God. I say to them: you don't have to tell me about God, you have to tell me how to lead a decent life in this rotten country. What does it matter if I call God Jesus, Śiva, God or Allah?

"My father was a fool to spend all he had on my education. I graduate and I get two rupees a day. During the war I was in the navy—Indian Navy under the British. After the war I work in the merchant marine. The work and life were hard and the pay no good. I gave it up. I worked for contractors: they paid with annas. Now I sell only monkey business—nothing honest. Dope, liquor: the city's full of it. Black market. Anything. These kids in the street that you see: lots of them are full of dope."

Earlier in the day I had bumped into a young waiter from my hotel who had been serving me at table, but then had been dropped from the staff. He told me that eight had been dropped, because business in the hotel was not good this year. Formerly they had had a Swiss manager and business had been fine. Now the manager was not very good. And prohibition had made things bad. They had dropped him after a month's notice and now he was looking for a job. It was hard to get a job. The state was favoring Hindus (he, I took it, was a Christian).

At von Leydens' I met a Swiss gentleman, here on business for a pharmaceutical firm. I told him of the complaints I had heard from my recent conversationalist, and he generally supported them. Indian businessmen will not invest unless they can foresee a large rake-off for themselves almost immediately—within a year. Long-term investments involving patience and foresight don't interest them. The moneylenders get as high as 80%. When they say 4% they mean 4% a month. So Indian money is not going toward the development of Indian business.

The policy of the government in business, furthermore, is a bit crazy. They want everything all at once. They want to manufacture in India what is already manufactured better abroad instead of developing ideas and products of their own. And their imitated articles are inferior.

I spoke of my impression of a rich land, as I traveled through India: a rich land with poor people. They complain of drought, but they get three or four crops a year. Where in Europe or the United States do you get three or four crops a year? The people, we agreed, had been exploited to the marrow of their bones. And exploited, I should say, since God knows when? Certainly the Mughal "pleasure gardens" that I have seen ("If there is a paradise anywhere, it is here, it is here!"[149]) represent an application of monies to dynastic luxury instead of to the development of the well-being of the state, and the same pattern of absolutely selfish exploitation—though on a scale, comparatively, of peanuts—can be said to underlie the *zamindar* system.

An additional item to this theme: an article in the *Illustrated Weekly of India* points out that most of the beggars are the agents of a manager who takes a large percentage of their receipts. (I recall the flower-seller of Greenwich Village whom Jean and I saw stepping, with her tray, into an elegant Chrysler.) They are trained and given their props (children to carry in their arms, for example) and then sent out. I noticed, long ago, that the beggars everywhere in India use identical formulae of approach, identical tones of voice, etc.

Perhaps it can now be concluded that, for a number of reasons, the spectacle of dire poverty that India presents to the eye of the visitor is misleading. It is true that the huge majority of the people in India are poor; but it does not follow that *India* is poor. The rich in India tend to be miserly to a criminal degree, and the poor in India do not exert themselves even to clean the dirt out of the alleys of their own neighborhoods. Whereas one day of mildly energetic activity on the part of the people sitting around by the score in any given street would suffice to clean at least the surface filth away, the people add to the filth that day by defecating and urinating in every corner and gutter. Moreover, the beggars are in the employ of hidden managers, so that the spectacle which they are presenting (and which is one of the horrors that the visitor has to learn to assimilate) is partly a fraud. And Swami tells me that many of the people seen sleeping in the streets are not destitute. ("It is the most superficial way to judge India!" he said with proud indignation.)

Friday, December 3

I went at one to the Prince of Wales Museum to meet Dr. Moti Chandra for a very pleasant lunch, then I went at four for tea at the Mehtas' to see Rama.

The conversations at tea, the Club, and dinner, ranged widely, and finally, under a couple of questions put to me by Rama, got to pretty touchy ground. At the Club, Mr. Mehta offered an interesting idea to account for India's failure to advance into the scientific age before the West. In the traditional Indian family, he said, where everyone lives in very close association, closely observed all the time, and in an atmosphere established by the concerns of a group ranging through all ages, from childhood to old age, there is no place or time for privacy, and no period in life when the individual, thrown onto the world, is forced to experiment with life. Moreover, this circumstance accounts also for the erotic idealism of India's poetry and art. The individual has no opportunity for actual adventure and so, in his imagination, compensates with images of delight, and these lead to no disillusionment in reality.

Rama's questions were: "Do you find India very spiritual?" To which I had to answer, "No. No more than other places." "What do you think of East-West relationships?" To which I had to answer that I thought the West was giving India not only machines and money, but also ideas and ideals—and that these would have to be given in great quantity so that a world balance might be established. The influence of the East upon the West, however, was at present only very slight—in the form of an intellectual contribution to the intellectual élite.

I added (perhaps ineptly) that I thought it was still a little early for India to begin seeking to build its tourist trade because, first of all, the hotel and food accommodations were spectacularly inadequate; and the beggar-menace was not only fiercely troublesome to the tourist but also a bad advertisement for India—an impression of squalor, disease (lepers), and of especial aggression (since the tourist can readily see that Indians on the street are not being assaulted by the beggars as he is: I have never seen a beggar, vendor, or rickshaw boy hang on to an Indian for six blocks, whereas for me it has been, outside of Bombay, a daily—almost hourly—experience). Worst of all, it is impossible to discover the true art and life of contemporary India: no music or dance performances, unless expertly sought out and found; all social life hidden within the family walls; e.g. no restaurant or theater life. Rama took issue, but Lila supported me, and Mr. Mehta maintained a balance—but I think the whole subject was a little too close to the quick. The conversation has left me feeling a bit shaken.

The conversation of the day, in other phases, touched on the question of India's contemporary teachers and sages:

Krishnamurti emerged as an important figure (as a break with the guru tradition, and the idea of people thinking their problems out for themselves). *Aurobindo's* ashram was described as a nicely organized American institution, but *Dilip Kumar Roy* (the great quack-quack of last winter's New York season), who is Aurobindo's chief disciple, seemed to receive a bit of carefully phrased respect (I had already said something about the unsteady impression he had made on me last year).[150]

Sri Krishna Menon of Trivandrum came off best. A number of instances were cited of people who had found "ineffable peace" in his sphere of influence. He is a *jñāna* yogi, who talks things through.

Mr. Mehta's opinion of the Ramakrishna monks is very high, and he spoke at length of their work in India. I praised the influence of their writings in America, but had to confess that I thought that most of the people who frequent the Centers were psychological cases.

Mr. Mehta has taken on the task of introducing Jean and me to the Indian dance, and so has planned a number of valuable meetings. I am to come to his house tomorrow afternoon to meet a number of artists and Sunday evening shall attend a dance concert by special invitation. I was driven home in the great limousine, with Rama and Lila as companions.

Saturday, December 4

Spent part of the day reading a little book about Vinoba Bhave that I bought on my morning walk, and part writing to Jean and making plans for our month together. She will come via Colombo and will arrive about January 12. I suppose she will have to leave about February 20. The concert is to be about February 3 in Bombay.

Sunday, December 5

With my plans for the next five months fairly well straightened out, I begin to feel that my space-platform days in Bombay are drawing to a close.[151] My business now is to finish off my affairs here and push off. The most pressing affairs, I should say, are those connected with the two talks I am to give next week (one to the Theatre Unit, and one over the Radio), and the matter of a text either about or by Jean for the *Theatre Unit Bulletin,* set for December 20. The talks are going to require me to settle a few ideas in my unsettled mind, and this, perhaps, might be termed the final task of the platform. Two aspects of this task are to be distinguished:

A) What are my fundamental ideas about my place in the world of scholarship? i.e. What is my central subject, and what is its relationship to the numerous wisps and strays of my wandering interest?

B) What is the status of my present field-trip study of the Orient? What have I learned? What are the outstanding problems? What plans should I make for specific research?

The need for a bit of basic thinking of this kind struck me rather forcefully this morning when I opened the morning paper. For the past day and a half I have been feeling rather badly and uneasy about the dinner conversation Friday night at the Mehtas' where I seemed to be taking an essentially negative, largely frustrated attitude toward my Indian experience. A couple of particularly unpleasant beggars had revived in me, earlier in the day, a number of my earlier attitudes toward India and my growing feeling of pleasure and interest in the country had been momentarily subdued. My negative reply to the question as to whether I found life in India very spiritual was the one that troubled me most; for I realized that it must have been unnecessarily harsh and rude. Had I possessed the wit to elaborate a bit on my negation, the situation would have been greatly improved. But I had found myself unable to develop the point—and this, I now realize, was the consequence of a lack of clarity, in my own mind.

Then, this morning, in the paper, I found a number of challenging items. Firstly, a front page spread, featuring the Opening of the Marian Congress in Bombay. Cardinal Gracias presiding. Swami Radhakrishnan the guest speaker. A great assemblage on the Azad Maidan (I had seen the crowd, on my way last evening to the Mehtas'). Then, a large gobbet from Radhakrishnan's speech: "Mankind Must Be Guided by Spirit of Religion: Vice-President's Call." And next on the inner pages, pictures of Richard McKean, with whom I studied at Columbia, and Professor L. Venturi, whom I met the other evening at von Leydens', with a couple of good quotations from their firm and self-confident remarks. The contrast with my own, present state of philosophical fluidity hit me hard—and I determined to pull myself together. After my decade of work along the lines of Zimmer, which I have brought to an end right here on my space-platform, it is time for me to begin—right here on the platform—a straightening out of my own basic ideas. And what more appropriate place for such a task than India, which is itself trying to locate its own mind? So then:

What are my fundamental ideas about my place in the world of scholarship?

The name that best suits my field of study is *Comparative Mythology:* it is a study of symbols, in relation, primarily, to the fields of art, literature, philosophy and religion. M. René Guénon has distinguished two great categories of symbol. The one he calls *le symbolisme qui sait* and the other *le symbolisme qui cherche.* Guénon's (and Coomaraswamy's) fixed preference was for the former, the symbolism that *knows;* my own, on the other hand, is for the latter, the symbolism that *seeks*—and here, I believe, I am in accord with Zimmer.[152] This interest in the active, questioning attitude toward symbols has led me to give considerable stress, in my studies and writings, to the work of the psychoanalysts, Freud, Jung, Roheim and the rest, since there one can see the process of symbol formation and interpretation from within. Guénon and Coomaraswamy, on the other hand, have given their whole attention to a comparative study of the symbolical vocabularies of the past. I am interested also in modern art and literature, as controlled renditions of the symbolic themes of contemporary significance, and my chief masters in this field have been Joyce and Mann, Klee and Picasso, with Jean and her associates as my immediate guides and examples.

In Sanskrit two words appear, which designate two categories of the inherited Indian tradition, namely *śruti* ("what is heard") and *smṛti* ("what is remembered"). The Vedic hymns belong to the former and the brahminical theological writings to the latter.[153] Essentially, the priestly attitude represented in *smṛti*, preserving the past, looking back and interpreting what has already been found, represents the attitude of *le symbolisme qui sait*—the analysis of "the fixed and the set fast"—whereas the poetical attitude that yielded *śruti*, harkening to the voice of the living God, the Muse, represents *le symbolisme qui cherche*—"striving toward the divine through the becoming and the changing." Compare Goethe's (and Spengler's) *Vernunft* and *Verstand*.[154] I tend, therefore, to associate the work of the creative genius in art, literature, science and mathematics with the living, creative aspect of my subject, and the work of the scholiast, priest, and academician (preserving, judging, and formulating rules on the basis of the created works of the past) with the dead and the anatomical or schematic. As in all fields of the spirit, so here: the footsteps or traces (*mārga*) of the spirit, which may guide us to the spirit, derive from the past, and are to be studied by all candidates for illumination, but the living, immediate presence of the spirit is one step in front of the last footstep—out in the air over the bottomless abyss.[155]

In *The Hero with a Thousand Faces* I distinguished between the spheres of the village compound and the realm of adventure. In the former the "religious" people remain, whose spiritual needs can be satisfied by the fixed patterns of the already found, while into the latter go the heroes who meet and become the vehicles of the living spirit. In *The Basic Mythologies of Mankind* I shall review the history of the symbolisms of the past (the village compound, *le symbolisme qui sait, smṛti*), from the standpoint, however, of the living realizations through which they were brought into being; and the work will conclude with a stance taken in the immediate present.

Briefly, the historical circumstance determining the field of pertinence of any one of the various "village" religions is a function of the economic-political scene. The course of history shows a gradual enlargement of the "compounds," from a village size to tribal, from tribal to regional, from regional to sectarian (the so-called "world religions"), and now to global. The immediate problem is to formulate an effective symbolism for the "global compound," through which, on the one hand, simple people will be held in form, and on the other, creative geniuses will be led to seek their destiny.

What is the status of my present field-trip study of the Orient? What have I learned? What are the outstanding problems? What plans should I make for further research?

The genesis of my interest in the Orient and specifically in India is twofold:

The first is *personal:* the help that I received in solving my adolescent philosophical and religious problems through my meetings with Krishnamurti and his friends (1924–29), the help that I received in resolving my Schopenhauer-Nietzsche dilemma[156] through a reading of Nikhilananda's translation of the *Māṇḍūkya Upaniṣad,* Coomaraswamy's *Dance of Śiva,* and my subsequent study of the Upaniṣads, with a bit of Ramakrishna (1939–41); and the impact of Zimmer (1940–54).

The second is *scholarly:* the recognition that in the field of folklore and myth India constitutes a kind of axial tradition, with a continuity dating from the Chalcolithic and surviving, still alive, to this day (this dating from about 1934); a period of heavy concentration on Indian materials following the death of Zimmer (1943–54); and the need now to find a point of view of my own with respect to the relationship of my India studies to the whole field of my science.

My reactions to my experience of India have been somewhat emotional because of the implication of my personal interests in matters that I should have liked to have handled in a purely scholarly way.

So, with reference to my *personal reactions* I have made some important kindergarten discoveries, as follows.

Indian society is not a function of Indian philosophy, but on the contrary, Indian philosophy is a function of *one* section of Indian society.

Consequently, Indian society as a whole does not illustrate (as Coomaraswamy suggests it should) the ideals of Indian philosophy.

The *poverty* of India is not a result of English exploitation alone, but also of the Muslim conquest, the caste system, the dishonesty of contemporary Indian officials, and the Indian love for a restful life.

The *squalor* of India is not a result of Indian *poverty* alone, but also of an indifference to dirt, the inefficiency of city officials, and an intentional spectacle of poverty presented by professional beggars: moreover, the assault that the visitor endures from the beggars gives him an exaggerated view of the seedier aspects of the Indian scene. This whole matter of Indian poverty and squalor may be summed up as a function of the *Baksheesh Complex*, which has two major forms of manifestation: that of the beggar, that of the retired pensioner. The formula for both is *Something for Nothing*.

India's pretext of spiritual superiority is another consequence of the Baksheesh Complex and does not accord with the actualities of the modern international scene. India is in fact receiving all of her progressive ideals (spiritual principles) as well as machines (technological principles) from the West. The clue to the Indian psychology of "spiritual superiority" is supplied by Nikhilananda's statement that Vivekananda was a proud man and did not wish to receive something for nothing: he saw that India required the machinery and organizations of the West. He therefore determined to give the West the spiritual goods of India in return. The fact was, however, that the West did not need these "spiritual" goods as badly as the Orient needed the West's "material" goods; also, that the Oriental spiritual gift was not quite as great as Vivekananda had to pretend to himself, to bolster his pride. The pattern has been to pretend that the West is without native spiritual fare, so that the exchange will seem to the Indians themselves to be a fair one.

What India has received from England is its whole character as a modern state. If England asked and took a lot for the teaching of this indispensable modern lesson: such a toll has a precedent in the Indian concept of the rights of the guru. Moreover, India was left with the difficult, yet not impossible task, of finding her own feet—which is good pedagogy. All of my earlier opinions of English imperialism have had to be revised.

The Oriental psyche is structured so differently from that of the West (symptom: the absolute separation of the sexes in public life; consequent limitation of heterosexual experiences to the archetypal realm of marriage and prostitution; no development of intersexual personality influences) that the guidance of an Oriental guru cannot but mislead the Westerner. Each psyche must develop along its own lines (at least for the present) in a world that is receiving all of its creative life and inspiration from the West. We cannot yet speak, therefore, of the Orient having something very important to teach us, which we should learn. What is important for us in the Eastern tradition has already been found and presented to us by Occidental scholars—Jones, Wilson, Muller, Rhys-Davids, Oldenburg, Zimmer, etc., with a couple of Easterners working in the Occidental frame—Coomaraswamy and Suzuki. I am sure that more work remains to be done, but it does not have the importance of a historically necessary task for us. It will be a joy for us and an amplification of what we know of a great and beautiful world age, which is now in its twilight, and the descendants of which will certainly, one day (but hardly in this century), have a creative contribution to make to our global civilization.[157]

The hope, the immediate future, and the teacher of the modern world is the West. The main problems of the modern world are functions of the Western style of life and thought. The most significant approach to the modern problems, therefore, must be via the modern Western psyche— and most emphatically, via the modern American psyche, since America, at the present moment, is the ideal-giver even to Europe. This realization has moved me to dissolve my earlier thoughts of a series of works on Oriental religion and legend—for example, my *Life and Lives of the Buddha, Questions of King Milinda*—and to plan to concentrate on the legendary and mythological themes of the West—for example, *The Life of Judas, The New World of Bartholomé de las Casas*,[158] *The Death of Captain Cook*.[159] I think also of the comparative themes of my *Twelfth Century*[160] idea, as still good, because here a panorama might be presented of the whole global context of our variously inflected world culture without suggesting that one or another had the answer for all. This line of thought has led me to abandon the intention that I brought with me to India to make a big thing of my Hindi and Sanskrit; better now, develop my European languages: French, German, Spanish, and Italian; also, perhaps, a bit of Greek and Latin. Become a Westerner again. And finally, the *Eranos Tagung*,[161] with its Occidental emphasis, now seems to me an excellent field. What my own special *Fach*[162] would be in this vortex, I do not quite see. So much, then, for the personal aspect of the lessons that I am learning on this journey.

What now of the *scholarly?*

Like a damn fool, I left in New York the papers in which I had stated for the Bollingen Foundation the headings and purposes of my India project; however, I believe I can recall the best part of the plan—and perhaps it is just as well that my dear mind should be called upon to formulate the whole thing in the terms that I can conjure up here today.

My primary project was, to study the functioning today of the traditional Indian philosophies of *artha, kāma, dharma,* and *mokṣa,* and I listed under the last named heading, the patterns of the Vedic-Upanishadic tradition, those of Buddhism and Jainism, the *Purāṇic* and *Tantric, Vaiṣṇava* and *Śaiva,* the philosophies of Śaṅkara and Rāmānuja; and then the *alien* philosophies and religions of India; Zoroastrianism, Islam, Christianity, Western Science and Scholarship, Democratic Constitutionalism and Totalitarian Despotism. Also to be considered were the fates of the 19th-century movements: Theosophy, Brahmo-Samaj, Ramakrishna Mission—and of the 20th-century personalities: Tagore, Vivekananda, Ramana Maharishi, Krishnamurti, Gandhi—to which now I should add Vinoba Bhave and Sri Krishna Menon. I believe that I have learned a great deal about all of these things, but I shall postpone my discussion until I have covered first the minor projects of my journey.

My second project was, to visit, if possible, some of the tribal villages of India. This I have not even attempted, nor am I likely to make any attempt. I have had a few glimpses, however, of tribal peoples: those horse people in Kashmir, the Lambanis that we saw in Gadag, and the Santāls on the way to Darjeeling. One thing that is perfectly clear is that they are not Hindus, and that they have hung on hard to their non-Aryan, tribal ways. Actually, now, I don't think it would make much point to go and try to study them for a day or two. It would require weeks to gain more than a surface view of their lives. Better simply to be satisfied with the works of Verrier Elwin.[163]

A third project, which emerged during the course of my spring and summer work on the Zimmer material, was to visit as many as possible of the important monuments of Hindu art—and this I have accomplished pretty well. I can say, I think, that I know the feeling of the cave temples and *vihāras,* the great medieval temples, and the temples of the southern style; also of some of the smaller gems. There remains the experience of the *stūpa,* which I shall get when I visit Sāñcī. There remain also a number of specific monuments that I wish to see, and these I shall try to include in the itinerary of the remaining weeks of my stay in India.

Project number four (three, I believe, in my original statement) was, to acquire experiences that should assist me in the organization of my *Basic Mythologies.* These I have had in abundance: the majority, where they do not coincide precisely with the findings for my primary project, might be said to be those points discussed above as affecting my personal interests and beliefs.

A fifth project has emerged in connection with the planning of Jean's visit to India, namely, the experience of the contemporary state of the arts of dance and music, which in turn is but part of a possible study of the problem of the contemporary Indian artist. It might be said that I have just begun this study (if it can be given such a ponderous name) with my meeting of the Theatre Unit, visit to Ara's exhibition, chat yesterday with Mr. Mehta's artist guests, and proposed continuation of this line of action. In the light of what I have just written about the *smṛti* and *śruti* aspects of my subject,[164] this art project might be said to be a necessary complement of my primary study of the functioning today of Indian philosophy and religion.

And finally, project number six is a comparative study of the religious areas of the Oriental world (this links in with project number four). This plan emerged after my first few weeks in India, to continue the comparative experience that I had already had through pausing in Beirut, Jerusalem, and Damascus. The reduction of my stay in India to six months was a radical transformation of my plan, brought about directly by my disappointment in India, but now justified, I think, by my realization that my main subject is rather comparative than Indian mythology, and my conviction that the sort of deeply driving teaching that would justify a long stay, or even a two-month period of concentrated language study, is no longer demanded in my revised view of the role that India is to play in my scholarly life.

So now to the *review of the present status of my primary project,* the study of the functioning today of the traditional Indian philosophies.

My first realization was that throughout the Orient religion is in a much stronger position than it is in the West. The visit to Jerusalem and then that to Brindavan let me know that Catholicism and Hinduism are not radically different and that in the Orient Catholicism is definitely an Oriental faith. My friend Mr. Cage, the Pentecostalist, was equally at home in this religiously oriented world. My view of Cardinal Gracias in Madras and the talk with Father Heras here in Bombay have reinforced this picture of a fundamental religious continuum in which all faiths operate in the Orient—a continuum, which, in our civilization, was radically shattered *circa* 1492 and has been falling to bits ever since.

In the Orient, then—or at least in as much of it as I have experienced—religion is as strong as it was in Europe in the Middle Ages. A man's religion determines his character, position in society, and everything else. The concept of the Free Thinker is almost totally lacking. A few Westernized gentlemen may claim to be atheists, but their wives will be religious. And those who grow past the elementary patterns of their religious practice still think of themselves as members of the religious community of the birth (or conversion). (This I have from Mr. Mehta.)

My second realization was that the predominant atmosphere of contemporary Hinduism is that of *bhakti*—the *bhakti* of the post-Mohammedan period; that of Rāmānanda, Kabīr, and Nānak, where the reference to a personal God is as good as final. (This, of course, increases the resemblance to Catholicism.) Even the Ramakrishna monks, who are supposed to be the followers of Śaṅkara, not only behave publicly, but also talk, as though a God were the final term. In the *maṭhas* the worship of the Ramakrishna image is quite orthodox Hindu in style. I am told that in the ashrams there is a Vedantic emphasis; but when I said one day, before Swami Nikhilananda, "there is no Vedanta in India, there is only *bhakti*," he said: "We think of the two as the same." One can say that in Catholicism too there is a realization among the clergy that "God is far superior to anything that man can think or say of God"; but the emphasis in both cases is equally on God and his worship through rite and meditation.

My third realization was that a radical division exists between the largely illiterate lower castes and the upper, so that the whole problem of religion in India breaks in two. We have to consider first the religions and religious life of the lower and vastly larger section of the population (perhaps 80%, i.e. about 320,000,000 if the total population is 400,000,000) and then, separately, as a smaller yet more active force, the religions and religious life of the upper fraction (perhaps 20%, i.e. about 80,000,000).

A. Lower Castes:

    1. Hindu — about 150,000,000
    2. Mohammedan — about 30,000,000
    3. Sikh — about 6,000,000
    4. Tribal — about 1,700,000
    5. Catholic — about 5,000,000
    6. Protestant — about 2,500,000
    7. Buddhist — about 200,000

B. Upper Castes:

    1. Hindu — 150,000,000   8. Brahma Samāj
    2. Mohammedan — 5,500,000   9. Ārya Samāj
    3. Jain — 1,600,000   10. Theosophist
    4. Sikh — 200,000   11. "Atheist"
    5. Parsee — 100,000
    6. Catholic — 500,000   The "Gurus" (int'l
    7. Protestant — 200,000   following)
                               Tagore (Sautiniketan)
    The "Leaders"   Ramana Maharishi
         Gandhi   Aurobindo
         Nehru   Krishnamurti
         Vinoba Bhave   Krishna Menon

The report of the opening of the Marian Congress on the Azad Maidan states that there were 50,000 Catholics present, "representative of the entire five million Catholic population of India," with seventy archbishops and bishops from all over India as well as from Rangoon, Singapore, Syria and Lebanon. S. Radhakrishnan made the following statement: "The great need of our age is revival of spiritual values.... The need of the world today is human unity, and religions are proving to be great obstacles in its way.... Love of God is not a mere phrase, not an intellectual proposition to which we consent with our minds. It is a transforming experience, a burning conviction. The destiny of man is not natural perfection, but it is life in God. Human nature finds its fulfillment in God. Religion in all its forms declares that the human being should be made into a new man.... He has to reach inner completion through *meta-noia,* which is not adequately translated as repentance.... Religion is the force which can bring about this inward renewal.... The followers of the different religions are partners in one spiritual quest, pursuing alternative approaches to the goal of a spiritual life, the vision of God. It is this view that has been adopted by this country from ancient times...."

Nehru, on the other hand, sent the following words: "I am not concerned with the religious aspect of this Congress, but I am interested in the civic aspect. I understand that this civic aspect will receive much attention at the Congress. I welcome this attention to the cultural and civic aspects of our national life. We want our people to maintain and develop their rich culture in all its variety, at the same time always remembering the essential unity of our nation. Therefore, every community should help in this development of unity in diversity...."

A nice contrast of the spiritual and the patriotic points of view—the two that in Swami Nikhilananda have become inextricably confused. And I am afraid that Swami and the Nehrus have helped to pitch me into a patriotic mood too, so that my view of India is being somewhat distorted by antagonistic reactions. Let me try to forget that I am an American, even though every beggar in the street is reminding me that I *am* one. Let me try to see India as it *is*—not comparatively. Let me try to be the one who asks the questions from now on, rather than the one who answers: this will bring out news instead of mere reactions.

I spent the whole day writing the diary entries for Saturday and Sunday—except for an hour and a half in the late afternoon (6:15 to 7:45) when I went to the meeting room of the United Lodge of Theosophists to hear Mrs. Sophia Wadia deliver a lecture on "This Is an Honest Universe." She lectured well, to an audience of about 175, in a large, neatly kept hall-and-library. I spoke to one of the members afterward, and learned that the United Lodge is a sort of fundamentalist Theosophical group, which reacted to the innovations of the Annie Besant faction back in the 1890s and owes allegiance to Blavatsky-Judge, not Blavatsky-Besant-Leadbeater. The Besant group is centered in Adyar, and has more lodges in India than the United; also, Krishnamurti talks largely under their auspices. The United Lodge has its headquarters in New York, and has (as I recall) about seven lodges in India—in Bombay, Bangalore, Baroda, and some four or five other cities. My impression of the attendance was very good: almost completely Indian, intelligent and nice looking people—rather different in tone, I should say, from what I have seen of Theosophy in America. And the talk of *karma* and reincarnation seemed more natural here than it does in the West. Finally, I should say that although the number of Theosophists in India may be small, when one considers the force of the intellectual élite in this country, their importance may be great.

And so, today I have gathered a bit of news on Catholicism and Theosophy in India. I have also been reading, lately, about Vinoba, and here I have run into a number of important bits of information, which I shall bring together later on. With respect to the religious statistics, I must learn what the geographical and economic distributions are of the various groups.

Monday, December 6

An item in this morning's paper places the number of Jains in India at about 20 lakhs, i.e. 2,000,000. A sacred *cādar* has been presented to the spiritual leader of the Jains, Maharaj Atmaram. The *cādar* is from the All-India Vardhaman Asthanik Vasi Jain Shramak Sangh. On receiving it the leader said that love, justice, truth and non-violence are the pillars of peace, and that truth and non-violence are interlinked. Here, certainly, is traditional Jain doctrine—and one sees the link with Gandhi's *satyagrāha*.

Mr. Mehta has spoken to me a bit about the Jains. Largely a wealthy group (bankers), now concentrated in Gujarat and the Bombay areas. Their *sadhus* are still serious: "no hanky-panky yogis." The laymen do not like to see their own children become monks and nuns, but are glad to support the religious institutions. There is almost no creed in Jainism, but a great deal of emphasis on rules. He regards it as a very curious, unspirited religion.

After lunch a young man named Ralph Mendonça, from one of the newspapers, came for an interview (Ezekiel-Alkazi context),[165] and remained until about 4:30 P.M., and had lots to say about India and the West. He liked Radhakrishnan's talk at the Marian Congress, but thought Nehru's greeting inept. He said that Joyce was no longer read in India, and seemed to accept my suggestion that the Western psychological problem, which Joyce typifies (humanistic personality discovering play of the archetypes in the field of experience), is the opposite to India's (archetypal life awakening to the humanistic values and seeking to incorporate them).

I developed the idea, which has been growing in my mind, of the East

West contrast: in the Western unconscious, the forgotten, security-yielding archetypes; in the Oriental, the disregarded personal values. *Every instant of traditional Oriental life is one of* satī, *wherein the claims of the individual personality are immolated.*

That was *one* of my bright remarks. Another had to do with the corresponding focal point of the West: that of the tragic decision. *Every moment of a Western life is one of personal decision, wherein a consciously considered choice is made: the individual takes upon himself the responsibility and does not assign it simply to his* dharma. The result is a psychological tension and complexity of character, which has been wrongly interpreted as a function of the "speed" of Western life. The tragic tension will be found in the country as well as in the city. Moreover the "speed" of our life is much less apparent to one living in America than to one looking at us. Going eighty miles an hour on an American road is more restful than going forty on an Indian road. Life on an American campus is quieter than life in Bombay or Calcutta. It is not speed, but our psychological focus, that supports our tension.

The typical Indian (perhaps Oriental) tension, on the other hand (and now I am developing a point that did not come out in our talk) is that between the archetypal patterns of life and the experience of eternal rest—as symbolized in the Dancing Śiva, repose in action. To the modern Western mind, caught in the vortex of time's dilemmas and decisions, this spectacle and symbol of balance has a great appeal: it is rendered in the whole range of India's great art (from Sāñcī to Koṇārak and Belūr). However, the balance there rendered, between eternity and the great archetypes of the cosmic and collective round-of-existence (*nirvāṇa* and *saṁsāra*), does not quite resolve our problem. Our experience of history and life is not that of the round (*yugas* and rebirth: a changeless society since the millenniums of the Neolithic), but that of the destiny-shaping decision, and that of conflict of values implicated in every decision—the rejected continuing to assert their claim, if not in our consciousness, at least in our unconscious.[166]

In Indian life (and here I am back in the conversation of this afternoon), where each caste, each life-way, is insulated from all the rest, the individual has only to enact his *dharma,* immolating his personal resistances indeed, but never doubting the rightness of his "right action." On the other hand, as soon as a modern Occidental child enters school, he finds himself in a room with children whose backgrounds, whose system of inherited ideals, are different from his own. The result is an immediate crisis of decision: and from there on, his spiritual life will be one of decisions made and then experienced as either right or wrong, apt or inept, just or unjust. In this sense, every man is a king on the judgment seat: the jury system is a consequence and symbol of this experience.[167]

For a Westerner, Oriental literature, which is a rendition of archetypes, has the quality of fairy tale. The problem of the modern Indian poet and artist might be said to be that of recognizing and bringing to consciousness the traditional "sins" of his tradition, e.g. that of Rāma *vis-à-vis* Sītā. Contrast the historic decision of Edward VIII in giving up his throne.[168] Edward's decision, from the point of view of the royal *dharma,* was a shameful sin (the old Queen Mother felt that); but from the point of view of the individual Rāma's act (not decision, since he never for a moment doubted the claim of his *dharma*) was a brutal sin.[169] We cannot say that either position is right or wrong absolutely. Each, however, involves a repression of the claims of the other, and these claims live in the unconscious in the form of character-making pressures or insensibilities.

Women, in the Orient, represent archetypes and do not have to depend upon the radiance of their individual personalities. Furthermore, since marriages are arranged, they do not have to pull themselves together to "win" someone. As a result, they seem comparatively secure and uninteresting.

The problem of the Westerner "dropping back" into an Oriental way of "resting on the *guṇas*" is not convincingly solved. We are committed, so to say, to the symbol of the Crucifixion—the Tragedy.

Problem: what about the *Greek* tragedy? Sophocles' *Philoctetes* would seem to be a prelude to the modern experience. *Oedipus,* on the other hand, treats the problem of conflict on the unconscious level: it is a tragedy of "irony." In the mythological sphere there is no sense of irony or of tragedy: the archetypal act takes place in perfect innocence of its own darker implications. A study of this whole problem is indicated.[170]

Orientals tend to dress according to their group commitments. This defends them against personal criticism and explains their acts. The modern Western dress is largely non-committal: the individual is responsible, from moment to moment, for his irrevocable history-making decisions!

During the course of our conversation, Ralph Mendonça told me of a Jain *sadhu* now in Bombay, whom I may be able to visit. He travels with a great entourage. They all have to walk (no use of machines); they go to the seashore (four miles) to defecate (no use of machines), they carry their manuscript library of thousands of volumes wherever they go. Their hair is pulled out by hand, etc. This *sadhu* has been publicly revered by Nehru. He cannot eat food cooked for him, but may eat cooked food that has been prepared for others; if, however, the others who have given him of their food then prepare more food for themselves, to supplement the lack, they sin.

He told of a guru (perhaps this one: I didn't get it quite clearly) who had a very devoted devotee, a businessman, who kept clinging to his leg. The guru asked for a drink. Cocoa was prepared. He left a little in the cup, spit into the cup, and passed it to his devotee as *prasāda*. It was taken with joy.

The whole pattern of *mokṣa* and guru now appears to me as a perfect counterpart of the Indian experience of the social archetypes. The way is given—not found. Something of the quality and character of Theosophy seemed rather clear to me yesterday as I heard Mrs. Wadia talking of *karma* and honesty: the honesty of the universe and the honesty in life that puts one into tune or accord with the universe. Theosophy takes certain themes from Indian thought and stresses them, giving them an application meanwhile to certain Western problems of ethical life. It is consequently, a rather good bridge—but it tends to misrepresent, meanwhile, both shores.

I dashed home to be picked up by Adi Heeremaneck for dinner at his sister's apartment. Two sisters, one very beautiful and with four equally handsome children and a rather interesting yet ominous, dark husband; the other sister, very nice and warm, with a tight, sort of jockey-boy of a husband. Old Mrs. Heeremaneck was lovely.

They served me drinks—and when there was a knock on the door were a little afraid. In Bombay, the police can enter a home and nab people for drinking. (I think our scheme, horrible as it was, was better than this!) The knock, however, was simply that of the arriving second husband.

This was a family of Parsees.[171] More emancipated I should say, than a Hindu family: yet perfectly Indian. I asked about the Parsee temples. I have seen that they are closed to non-Parsees. They are flanked by Assyrian sphinxes, have the symbol of Assur in his sun ring over the door, and on the verandah have a little box containing neat sticks of kindling. My guess was that the devotees purchase their stick at the door and place it on the fire—correct! The sticks are of sandalwood and cost about a rupee. They are handed to the priest who places them on the fire. "But don't say," said the lesser husband with a laugh, "that we are fire worshippers!" "No," I replied, "I think I know better than that."[172]

One feels, actually, that there is little difference between this and *pūjā:* sticks on a fire, flowers before the god. The general attitude is the same. However, here, fire, the symbol of light (*Agni,* Mazda) visibly consumes the stick (the offering, the body of this death). It is a very vivid and simple event. I must ask, next time, whether hymns are sung, what sort of prayers are recited.

Tuesday, December 7

At the American Express this morning I found a lively letter from Jean and a packet of publicity materials. It begins to feel as though our trip together had actually commenced. I am going to see the theater people tomorrow and get things started.

While on my walk, to and from Flora Fountain, I kept thinking of this new, and I believe very keen idea, about the Orient and its time-eternity archetypes and the West with its tragic-ironic decision tension. Everything seemed to fit into it very neatly. I felt as though I had found, at last, the best answer to one of my most puzzling problems.

At 5:20 P.M. Mendonça called for me and we went to the home of Farouk Mulla, whom I had met last week at von Leyden's, to view a small exhibition of the young modern painters in Bombay. Professor Venturi was present, and after he had carefully studied the offerings he sat down and was closely questioned by the artists and newspaper people present. He spoke of the modern movement in Italy: the comeback of the painters who had been disregarded by the Fascist group, and the present status of their work.

Asked whether he thought Indian art could be presented in Europe, he answered yes—an exhibition should be arranged of 150 to 200 paintings—with *no* examples of the restoration movement, copying Ajaṇṭā, etc. The international movement that began with the post-Impressionists in Paris is modern art, and to be in the game one must participate in this move-ment—speak with this vocabulary but say what you will. Indian artists, as evinced by the present showing, were making their own statements and would inevitably be "Indian" no matter how consciously so.

Represented in the showing were Ara, Hussein, and Samant, whom I had met Saturday at Mr. Mehta's, both quite interesting, Hussein doing thin two-dimensional compositions and Samant working with a strong and heavy quality of rich paint. Pals Seker was another like Samant. One— or rather I—could not find anything particularly Indian about either of these. They could easily have hung in Betty Parsons's gallery. A painter named Raval, to whom Mulla, our host, was special patron, had a number of canvasses—rather Gauguinish and lyrically charming. To these Venturi paid little attention. Samant and Pals Seker seemed to be his choices. Another painter, Bendre, had done an interesting fresco-like little piece, showing a well fused composition of a ceramic horse, elephant, and bird-like form.

I had to leave while Venturi still was talking, to keep an appointment with Mrs. Puri (also met at Mr. Mehta's party) to see her film of Amarnāth, Kashmir. She was ill however, and so her very gracious husband treated me to a drink and a chat about India. His main point: in India one finds the sublime and the ridiculous side by side—which certainly is true enough. One finds also, I should say, the squalid and the luxurious.

Mr. Ezekiel came to Mulla's and gave me a copy of the new *Theatre Unit Bulletin.* I am to talk to the group tomorrow on "The Development of the Modern American Dance."[173]

Wednesday, December 8

The mail today brings news from Helen McMaster that my chapter MS. has arrived. Great relief. *Strich darunter.*[174] Bill McGuire writes that the title of the Indian book is to be *The Art of Indian Asia.* Sounds fine to me. I am arranging to leave here next Tuesday night—two days before Jean's departure from New York—spend Wednesday in Baroda, and land in Ahmedabad Wednesday night, December 15. This will give me time to attend to everything pertaining to Jean's concert before my departure from Bombay.

A letter from Lisa Coomaraswamy contains the following:

"You can see, now, it is 'we' and our way that is different, the old-world-wide mode of living (before the industrial era) was really one and the same from one end of the world to the other...it took so very little to upset the applecart, but that is so only because it (the cart) was already somewhat tipsy.... I love your description of the two 'cops' being friends, it's like a picture out of Plato! And, of course, the same goes for the women in the *zanāna,* they are so close..."

Thinking over all my great brain waves, I think that three are the best.

1. The sex separation theme.
2. The archetypal *dharma* vs. individual decision theme; *and*
3. That of Indian civilization not being a function of Indian philosophy but Indian philosophy a function of one section of Indian society.

Number 3 above has to be weighed against 1 and 2, which represent a general background for an Oriental and archaic philosophy. The specifically Indian patterns, however, have to be bounded carefully according to history, geography, and social stratum. How much of Indian philosophy belongs to layers 1 and 2 of this formula, and how much to layer 3? Very important.

But the new age—new India and new everything else—belongs definitely to what knocked the applecart over. In the arts, this is represented, as Venturi stated yesterday, to the post-Impressionist movement that originated in Paris. All the nationalist, Fascist, and Communist politically and regionally oriented "restorations" are sentimental, romantic exoticisms. Likewise, it can be said that all sectarian religions are out of date. The problem is to find the "grave and constant"[175] in the world tradition and see it rendered in the vocabulary of the International Age of modern art, poetry, music, and prose. It occurred to me today, however, as I was walking along the street, that in contemporary India Western dress actually functions as a caste mark, setting its wearers apart and indicating their spiritual commitment.

This evening, at the Theatre Unit's place, I gave my talk to a gathering of about thirty people, then came home, had dinner, and went early to bed.

Thursday, December 9   Karle–Bhājā

Up at 6 A.M. to catch the 7:15 train from Victoria Station to Lonāvale: arrival about 10:15 (three hours to go 75 miles). Tonga to Karle Caves, arriving about 11:30. Stayed about an hour and a half and then went in the tonga to Bhājā—two wonderful sites. My tonga got me back to Lonāvale just in time to catch the 3:15 for Bombay: arrival at 6 P.M. Walk to hotel. Tea. Bath. Sleep. Dinner. Diary. And so on to bed, dead tired. But now I've seen everything I came to Bombay to see.

A couple of thoughts about Indian philosophy:

Mokṣa: when it means the attainment of the standpoint of eternity (*nirvāṇa*) is one thing; when it means renunciation of the world of time, however (as it does with the monks), that is something very very different indeed.

The step from the normal Indian social situation of sex separation to the state of monkhood is a very small one. The turn from our modern Occidental life context to monkhood is a very different crisis.

Since the chief problem of Indian youth is not whom to marry, but "am I going to pass the exams and get a high-paying job?" it is no wonder that the Indian layman's libido is all tied up in money. (In no other country have I ever been asked how much I earn. In India, every gentleman who has conversed with me has asked that question—without exception.)

Since "peace of mind" seems to be the inheritance of everybody in India, from the lepers on up to Radhakrishnan, I suppose it is natural that Indian philosophy should be one yielding "peace of mind," but in India such a boon would seem to be supererogatory.

But now I am taking a vow: henceforth I shall try to seek out and announce, not the disillusionments of my trip, but the positive aspect of what I am finding in India.

Friday, December 10

A word about duties, rights, and spirituality: the Neolithic-Oriental stress on duties seems, at first, to be more spiritual than the Western-modern stress on rights—and when considered from the point of view of the individual in bondage it may indeed be the less selfish view: however, when considered from the point of view of the individual in the commanding position, it is definitely not so. The whole Afro-Asian movement now for freedom and equal rights finds support not in native ideologies but in the European-American doctrine of rights. And the remarkable (spiritual) fact is, that the claims are being recognized by the West; just as, in the U.S.A., the claims of the Negro slaves were recognized in the 1860s. A theme for my Bartholomé de las Casas work. The "new world" is that of recognized and conceded rights.

Try to imagine what the case would be of India today if England's mode of conduct had been that of the Aryans to the subjugated Dravidians—forbidding them, on pain of torture and death, even to read or hear the Vedas[176] (in the case of the English, the works of Burke, Locke, etc., and the doctrine of freedom and rights). Not a single idea now inspiring Asia's fight against the West has been drawn from an Oriental text.

A question to be asked when Orientals speak of "spirituality" (which they love to do), is, "What do you understand by this term?"

And so I find that I have already broken my vow of yesterday evening. In the Orient I am for the West; in the West for the Orient. In Honolulu I am for the "liberals," in New York for big business. In the temple I am for the University, in the University for the temple. The blood, apparently, is Irish.[177]

One more new thought, however: this time, touching the matter of the relationship of religion to philosophy. I have been regarding it as unquestionably good that the two should be kept in close relationship, as they have been in the Orient. However, I now wonder whether it is exactly edifying to see philosophers taking the dust off the feet of monks, and so-called Vedantist monks dressing and undressing the images of Sri Ramakrishna? Does this not place too much weight where weight already resides, namely on the side of superstition, leaving the cooler, cleaner side without its proper champions? May it not be that the Western break with religion and the consequent attempt on the part of the clergy to come over to the obviously winning side without reversing their collars has served to clarify our religious and our whole spiritual atmosphere in a manner that would have been impossible had the Darwins and Nietzsches fallen flat in front of the Cross? An important point to keep in mind.

During the course of my trip to Karle and Bhājā, I considered, though vaguely, the status of my present plans for my studies and work after returning to New York. My former idea of stressing the Orient-Occident interplay, with works on the Buddha etc., is definitely out. I am regarding my present visit to India as a kind of Graduation Tour, not Commencement Tour.

I believe that my next two books, *An Introduction to Mythology*, and

The Basic Mythologies of Mankind,[178] in that order, coupled with my work on the Eranos Series,[179] the Coomaraswamy volumes,[180] and my Mythology Course at Sarah Lawrence College, should serve to put me back onto my own rails—and my effort should be, while working on these vast, *general* projects, to bring my work to focus on some pertinent, *specific* aspect of the mythology–modern man problem. Perhaps a definition of the transformation of symbolic thinking in the Western sphere. I have thought of some themes that might be helpful, working around *The New World of Bartholomé de Las Casas* (Rights *vs.* Duties);[181] *Apollonius of Tyana* (Alexandrian period);[182] and *The Life of Judas* (Orthodox-Heterodox Symbology).

And in my scholarly papers, special studies of the Eastern and Western development of common symbols.[183]

Now let us turn to the possible contribution that India (the Orient) may make to the West. First, in the fields of philosophy and religion:

1. *Ātman-brahman idea—śunyatā idea.* Stress on the transcendent aspect of the divine (an idea present, but not stressed, in Western religion). This idea tends to be lost, however, in the modern *bhakti* religions of India, where, as far as the eye can see, sectarian gods and the attitude of sheer worship prevail.

2. *Ātman-jīva idea.* Stress on the immanence of the divine (hardly felt at all in the Western cults).

3. *Avidyā-māyā idea.* Instead of "the Fall." No "original sin." Stress on the problem of knowledge, rather than on that of guilt: "righteousness" a matter of wisdom, not simply of ethics.[184]

4. *Bodhi-mokṣa idea.* Instead of "repentance." (The idea is lost, however, when it becomes linked with "*escape* from the world of temporal sorrow.")

5. *Iti iti idea*—the eternal *Now.* Release from Heaven-Hell and afterlife thinking. (Lost entirely, however, in the transmigration image when the latter is read concretely.)[185]

6. *Cosmic śakti idea*—The world as power: eternal Creation.

7. *Erotic mysticism*—Anti-Platonic (anti-homosexual) orientation. Body-Spirit polarity undone. Theme of mutual instruction. (Plays no role whatsoever, however, in Indian life. Actually better represented in the Occidental post-Troubador approach to sex.)

8. *Kuṇḍalinī yoga*—to be studied via C. G. Jung.[186]

9. *The harmony of religions*—to be studied via Comparative

Mythology. In practical Hinduism the idea does not really operate—except in such fine moments as Radhakrishnan's Marian
Congress speech, where it is for world consumption. (The true
Indian attitude is that of Nikhilananda: Harmony of Religions, yes;
but Hinduism, having recognized this, is the supreme religion.)

Second, in the fields of aesthetics and art:

1. *Theory of the rasas*—a vast amplification of the Aristotelian Tragic
   and Comic principle.[187]
2. *Stillness in movement, movement in stillness*—Elūrā (Das Avatāra:
   Tīn Thal), Elephanta, etc.
3. *Art as yoga*—the invocation of inspiration. (Amplification of the
   Muse-inspiration principle.)
4. *Theory of the rāgas*—static-cumulative (instead of progressive)
   music: music as the coming into manifestation of permanent strata
   of accord, consonant with certain spiritual states. I do not know
   whether any counterpart to this view exists in the West.[188]
5. *Rāga-mālā principle*—harmony of the arts: all the arts as manifestations of the one spirit.

Third, in the sociological field:

1. *Society as an icon*—

Bing!

Life has begun to speed up. At 11:15 Alkazi arrived to drive me to the
Bhulabhai Institute to see some photographs of Indian temple art; then to
a new Bombay building, to see some more, used as wall decorations; then
to the offices of *Marg*,[189] to talk about pictures with one of the editors.
Next he came to the hotel to have lunch with me. Ezekiel joined us, and
we had a conference on Jean's Bombay concert. We drove to the proposed
theater, Jai Hind Auditorium, and settled the date. I measured the stage.

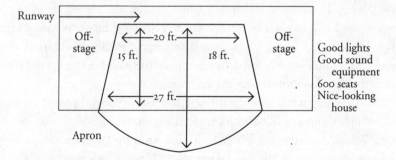

Certain writings are required, and I am to furnish them: an article (1,250 words) about Jean, for the *Theatre Unit Bulletin* and program notes, including two pages on modern American dance; two pages on Jean; and a page or half a page on each dance.

Alkazi dropped me at the American Express office and I went in to get my mail: a letter from Jean. She will arrive in New Delhi (not Colombo) January 15 (not January 12). This involves a total shift of plan both for her visit and for my remaining weeks alone. I decided also that unless things develop surprisingly in New Delhi, one concert in India will be about all that can be handled—that is to say, if Jean is also to see any Indian dance. How are we to do it?

I wrote a letter to Jean—realizing that it will be too late for her to receive it in New York. I must wire her the concert-date news. The letter I addressed c/o Watts in San Francisco.[190]

When I returned to the hotel from the American Express, I had to sit for a newspaper photographer in my room. One hour later he phoned to ask if he could shoot me again—there had been no photographic plates in his camera.

As I was preparing to go to bed, the phone rang. Rama Mehta, rebuking me for failing to phone her this week and inviting me to lunch at the Willingdon Sports Club, tomorrow at 1 P.M.

Saturday, December 11   **Bombay**

According to the morning paper, a Digambar Jain yogi, Śri Nemisāgar (chief disciple of His Holiness, Śri Śānti Sāgar, head of the *digambara* community) has come to town. He is on his way to Girnār in Saurashtra and will spend a month in Bombay, giving religious discourses in a temple at Bhuleśvar. "The 66-year old muni, who does not use any mode of transport, visited Jain temples in Bhuleśvar and Kalbadevi before reaching Hira Bag. He will stay at the Digambar Jain Temple in Bhuleśvar from next week. His Holiness Śri Nemisāgar renounced the world at the age of 33 and since then has been preaching the message of *ahimsā*."

Last evening while strolling through my part of town, I passed an open hall all lighted up and filled with people. Two rooms: one of women, one of men. When I passed again, a little later, all were in the larger room (formerly the men's) and a wedding was taking place. A nice gentleman came to my side and explained what was happening. The ceremonial area was marked out by four little towers of diminishing-sized pots with bamboo teepee uprights tied above them. The "four legs"—whole—totality—my informer told me.

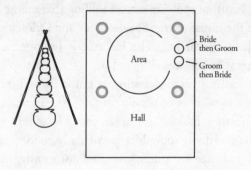

The two youngsters walked clockwise, bride following groom, with a tied white cloth connecting them, then sat down. Again. Again. Again. Last time sitting with groom at bride's right.

There were lots of kids and stray watchers who finally so blocked my view that I left.

New worry: a dangerous sensation in upper right first molar, which supports a bridge. Today, for some reason, I feel that this whole trip may be falling apart at the seams.

An appropriate word, culled from a London magazine: *Always behave like a duck—keep calm and unruffled on the surface but paddle like the Devil underneath*—Lord Brabagon.

At 1 P.M., I arrived at the Willingdon Sports Club to have lunch with Mrs. Pupul Jayakar and the Mehta girls and Rama's husband.[191] Very pleasant affair. Mrs. Jayakar had a lot of photos of late Gupta sculpture and temples in Rajasthan and invited me to visit a few such monuments with her and her husband in New Delhi.

After the luncheon, which ended about 4 P.M., Mrs. Jayakar drove me to the Bhulabhai Memorial Institute, where I watched the Theatre Unit people rehearse their *Oedipus*. The rehearsal went on till 8:30, at which time I was told that in half an hour a music concert would begin downstairs. I decided to skip dinner and let Mrs. Desai take me to the concert.

This Institute's building, I was told, was the home of her father-in-law, Bhulabhai Desai, who was one of the great companions of Gandhi at the time of the national struggle. Gandhi, Nehru, Bhulabhai had all lived and worked here, and if Bhulabhai had not died, it would have been he, not Nehru, who would now be leading the nation. With the passing away, first of Bhulabhai and then of her husband, Mrs. Desai decided to convert this building into an institute of living art; a building that young artists could use. So it is now the home of the Theatre Unit and of a sculpture school, dance school, music school, etc. The Institute is responsible also for the map of Indian Art that one sees all over India.[192]

The concert was not very interesting as music. When the young sitar player got through two hours of tuning up the first part was over. He was accompanied by a strong-looking drummer, whose head movements always indicated when he was doing something particularly good. A large and very nicely mannered audience sat quietly, on the floor mostly, in obvious appreciation. I thought the whole affair comparable to an American jam-session, where jazz and bebop appreciators will sit for hours listening to the ad lib virtuoso stunts of a team of artists. The present team, however, never really got going: I'm quite sure of that.

If the performance was any indication of what Indian live music is like, it can be compared, roughly, to a six day bicycle race, where the riders pedal along uneventfully for long stretches and then suddenly burst into important sprints. The concert was scheduled for 9; got going at 9:45, and at 10:45 or so, the first *rāga* was suddenly terminated.

Then a girl child of about nine came out and performed Bharata Natyam[193] movements for three-quarters of an hour. She was astonishingly firm, clipped, and sophisticated in style, when she was actually dancing, and charmingly simple in her moments of non-performance.

I bade Mrs. Desai good night at 11:30 and drove in a taxi to my hotel. Having no dinner, I asked for tea and sandwiches at the desk, and they ushered me into the hotel's air conditioned "Rainbow Room" for a hand-out. There I found a band playing Hawai'ian tunes with an electric-steel guitar: a jammed dance floor with the usual types; tea and cheese sandwiches for Joe, and at 12:15 to bed.

Sunday, December 12

I spent the first part of the day trying to write the article on Jean for the *Theatre Unit Bulletin*. No luck. At about 10:30 Salmony's friend Lance

Dane phoned and drove me out to a lovely residence at Juhu to see Mr. Fielden's bronzes and remain for lunch. Lunch went on till four; Dane drove me home and I got dressed to attend the "initiation" ceremony of the seven-year-old son of a Parsee gentleman, Mr. Farouk Mulla.

What a party! 350 guests for dinner—mostly Parsees; the men in their little hats (once the cores, I have been told, of turbans) and the women in a spectacular display of saris. Lights on the trees in the front yard, and hundreds of chairs, lining the driveways and scattered among the trees. "*Es ist wie ein Oper!*" said the little Hungarian mother of Mrs. von Leyden.

I arrived at 5:20 and got a second row seat for the ceremony. The little boy was darling, sitting cross-legged in the center of a white rectangle, with two candles burning at either side and the Parsee fire of sandalwood sticks burning at his right, behind him, on a silver salver placed on a large silver urn. Nine priests appeared—looking precisely like surgeons in their white gear and little round white hats. Five sat before the boy, with their backs to the company, and four behind him.

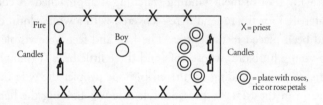

The ceremony began with the priests beginning to mumble in unison. Then the main priest took over and said a prayer in Old Persian, which the little boy repeated. He put a big lei around the little boy's neck, dusted him with rose petals, then rice (if I remember correctly), then handed him a rose. He handed a rose to each of the priests. Next he and the other priests stood around the boy, removed the red shawl that was covering his shoulders and put on a little white shirt. The priest then took the sacred thread, and standing behind the boy (who looked like a little angel) held the thread in front of him, took his hands in his own, looped the thread around the boy's waist and around itself in a special way, while reciting a prayer, which the boy followed in unison. It was extremely gentle and sweet. The high pitch of the priest's voice was something special to hear. The priest then sat down. Mr. Mulla came and placed a pay envelope in each priestly hand and the clergy withdrew. The boy's mother and aunts then came forward, stood before the little chap, kissed him, and dressed him in his new suit—long-trousers, Western style; a cute little white suit. Daddy knotted the red necktie, put a little red cap on the boy, where formerly there had been a white one—and, immediately, the orchestra on the front porch struck up a rhumba! After that, congratulations all round. "How sweet! Wie süss!" and it had actually been darling.

I stayed for dinner—an endless mess of Indian stuff flopped onto banana leaves before you—but, thank god, on a table, and with a fork and spoon close at hand.

Mrs. Jayakar was there and I had dinner with her, talking: about India, etc. At about 9:30 I left for home.

Monday, December 13

Slightly sick last night after all the cockeyed food! No mail at the American Express this morning. On the way home, heard some drumming and singing, with a lot of men standing watching. I approached. A corpse was being prepared for the funeral pyre—covered with a white cloth, on a bier that had been placed in the gutter. The face and feet were visible: a good looking young husband, whose wife and three little boys (I thought of the Zimmers)[194] were standing on the curb, poor people: the wife in a green sari, put on in the Marathi peasant style: she was holding the hem to her eyes and simply standing and weeping. The oldest boy was wiping his tears. The two little fellows were simply standing. They stood on the curb while the priests put flowers all over the white shroud, and then a lot of vermillion. They cracked a coconut and let the family, in turn, splash a handful of its sweet water over the dead father. The band meanwhile, squatting at the foot of the bier, was chanting, clanking symbols and beating a drum. They got up. The bier was lifted and, feet first, carried away behind them while the mother and her three boys remained standing on the curb. The crowd withdrew. They remained about two minutes, weeping and dazed. Then the mother turned and took her three boys into the house.

This afternoon I went to four o'clock tea at the Mehtas': talked of plans. At 6:45 I went to the von Leydens', who took me to a lovely apartment where we saw some movies of Darjeeling, Kashmir, and Orissa. Seeing again in the movies what I had already seen with my own eyes, I had a very pleasant sense of the magnitude of the experience that I have been having this year. In the course of my tour I have been seeing India only piece by piece, little by little. Seeing it all again—as it were all at once—I felt how big this whole thing is. The Orient as a vast natural phenomenon, like a continent of trees, mountains, animals, and peoples.

We had a late dinner at the von Leydens' and I returned home at about midnight.

Today my article on Jean got going, and I began to feel that I might be able to complete it on time.

Tuesday, December 14

A day of getting ready to leave. A nice letter from Jean in this morning's mail. She leaves Thursday (December 16) for San Francisco, where she will give a dance concert there December 18. I am to write her now to Honolulu. Did a bit of shopping, got a haircut and tried my hand again at that essay on Jean for the *Bulletin*.

I got a taxi to Central Station to catch the 9:05 P.M. Gujarati Mail. Ezekiel and his little wife came trotting down the platform to see me off about two minutes before the departure of the train.

AHMEDABAD AND NEW DELHI

Wednesday, December 15   Ahmedabad

Three of us filled the compartment. Myself, a Hindu gentleman, and a young Mohammedan. The night was rather cold and I was awake a good deal of the time. At about 5:30 A.M. I got up and dressed. Then the Hindu got up, then the Mohammedan, who was in an upper berth. When he was dressed, he returned to his berth, put a scarf over his head in a certain way, and sat absolutely still for about twenty minutes, saying his prayers.

The train pulled into the station about half an hour late. Geeta Sarabhai was there to meet me. She brought me to a large limousine and we drove to the great gate of the estate—and in. After all I had heard about the squalor of Ahmedabad, the city seemed to me less squalid than, say, Calcutta or Benares. It was interesting to see and feel oneself in an Indian industrial town. Compared with what I have seen in England and Pennsylvania, it seemed to me quite O.K. Nor did the Sarabhai estate seem to me to be exorbitantly large. After all—five or six families are dwelling here, and the Sarabhais *are* rich. Moreover, they are doing a great deal to improve the community. Kamalini is running a nursery school on the estate for 150 kids—only eight of whom pay full tuition. Gautam is building museums to help teach the people about such things as town planning, house building, and machine weaving. Mrs. Sarabhai is involved very deeply in the work of the village-rehabilitation groups. Bharati is involved in some kind of little theater group. Gira works with Gautam in the factory. And Geeta has her darling little family of three.

I had breakfast with Geeta on the verandah outside of my suite. (Corbusier is in the suite next door to me.)[195] Then she showed me about the estate. What a collection of bronzes! Second only to the Madras museum, but better displayed. Then Gautam and Kamalini paid me a brief visit and I went off with Geeta and her youngsters to visit some of the sights of the town.

Our first visit was to the Temple of Swami Narāyaṇa—a large Hindu establishment with a temple in which there are many shrines with rather garish, doll-like images and innumerable pictures on the walls which visitors went around touching and worshipping. Men went around close in to the shrines, women remained further out, beyond a high rail fence. I was taken on by a nice old man who grabbed my hand and showed me all the shrines. When he had done so I offered him a tip—which he declined and I apologized with a *namaskāra* gesture to which he responded deeply. He took me by the hand again, and led me to the ashram—part of the temple compound. Here a lot of saffron-clad monks were sitting around on a vast verandah. I went above and saw some more chapels, then came down and went to the center of the compound, where I found Geeta again, who had visited the women's section: a building for widows who have decided to quit the world. No male—even a male child—can enter their building.

From this temple we proceeded to the Jain Nagar Sethis Temple. The atmosphere was distinctly different from that of the other, and yet the *pūjā* seemed about the same. Little ladies were moving rapidly from shrine to shrine, reciting their prayers. The temple compound was trim and clean, and the sculpture on the buildings suggested Mt. Abu. In the main shrine and sanctuary, a number of people were sitting on the floor in quiet worship—a man reading to himself from a prayer book. And one old lady with a large chowry in her hand waved it before the image while doing a dance (cute as could be!). I noticed after that that a number of the women visiting the temple were carrying chowries.[196]

We returned after this to the beautiful Sarabhai compound, and had lunch with Mrs. Sarabhai and Kamalini. On the floor in the corner was an old gentleman—Geeta's drum and music teacher—eating his lunch Indian style. During the afternoon I worked at my attempt to write a paper about Jean for the Theatre Unit. Tea was served to me on the verandah outside my rooms; then at six I was driven to Gira and Gautam's Calico Museum; I visited the offices at the Sarabhai factory—Modern Art Museum style. Very nice indeed. Dinner was at Gautam's "farm house," where I stayed after the others had left, to talk with Gautam and Kamalini. Lots of changes of balance in my orientation to India are already beginning to take place.

Thursday, December 16

I had asked for morning tea at seven. The light was turned on in the living room at that hour and I got up to find the tea in place. After dressing in the wonderful bathroom, I attempted to do something about Jean's article. A table was being set up on the verandah for breakfast. Geeta arrived at nine and about half way through breakfast the nurse arrived with her children. I worked some more on Jean's paper—beginning now to feel a bit of panic, because I can't seem to find any angle from which to begin. At about eleven I went in quest of Gautam, with whom I was to have an early lunch and found him, finally, in his modern little house in the compound. Gautam and Kamalini drove me in their new, zippy roadster to a point where I was transferred into another car and then driven to the home of a learned gentleman, Sarabhai Nawab, who for two hours showed me his illuminated Jain manuscripts, early (pre–12th-century) Jain bronzes, and several of his own learned publications. Big news here. The man knows a lot—and has been plundered somewhat (according to his own account) by W. Norman Brown, who visits him but manages not to mention his name when he publishes. (Stella Kramrisch has resided with this man's family also.) Nawab showed me the room in which Brown stayed. He has written to Brown for the names of institutions in America that might be interested in his publications but has received no help. I promised to send him a full list when I got home.

During the afternoon I worked some more on that stubborn paper, and began to feel that I had found a line that I could follow to some sort of end. Gautam wants me to give a talk of some kind in Ahmedabad—and this now creates a double pressure. I hope I can get through this thing!

Gautam and Kamalini took me to the movies at the "Club." Horrible. Betty Hutton in some silly thing about the career of a cabaret singer. I suddenly realized that in thinking about America I tend to be ignorant of what foreigners see, just as Indians, in thinking about India, tend to ignore what I have been seeing. We left at the intermission and I tried my hand again at the article on Jean.

Friday, December 17

This morning I transferred the scene of my writing efforts to the bathroom, where I feel a bit more closed in and in control of the situation. Had a nice breakfast again with Geeta and then was taken next door, to the Khasturbhais' to see a magnificent collection of Mughal, Rajput, Lucknow, and Śāntiniketan-style paintings. Simply wonderful. The paintings were stored in racks and a couple of servants took them out and handed them to me while I sat royally in a chair, for about an hour and a half. One amusing number was of Kṛṣṇa riding on an elephant composed of *gopīs*.

After lunch I retired to the bathroom to work on Jean's paper. The situation is approaching the critical stage. I begin to feel that I am going to produce a mess!

I went down to Papa Sarabhai's, where I chatted with him for about an hour, waiting for guests to arrive from Baroda: a young American couple named English, she badly bent in the middle (crippled), he a psychiatrist over here on a Fulbright. They know zero about Indian thought and are a bit touchy on the point, when their psychoanalytic judgments of the phenomena that they observe are challenged.

Saturday, December 18

Mr. English and wife were at breakfast with Geeta and myself on the verandah. While the set table and I were waiting for them to arrive a crow flew to the verandah, hopped onto the table, picked up a napkin and winged away to a neighboring balcony. When I went to the railing to watch, I heard the flutter of another bird and behold! there descended onto one of the high cornices of the building a male peacock. He walked along the cornice and disappeared behind a wall. I felt then that I was living in a Rajput painting—which I believe I am. This whole thing of living here is simply dreamily delightful.

The morning was spent once again in the bathroom at work on Jean's article. It is really going now, and I think it may not be too bad. The only problem is time. The due date is December 20, which is Monday.

Sunday, December 19

I took breakfast on Papa's piazza with Geeta and the Englishes. Then another morning in the bathroom devoted to Jean's article (almost finished), and to preparing a talk that I am to give this afternoon to an invited audience. At 11 A.M. I went with Geeta to the library of the Vidya Sabha, where I was shown a few late Rajput manuscripts and some 13th-century paper. Nice visit.

At five the people began to arrive for the talk. It was an impressive gathering: the vice-chancellor of the University, the head of the psychiatric profession here, head of the nursery school, head of some sort of psychological institute, scholars of various sorts, their wives, etc. I was really on the spot. All settled in one of the large living rooms and I talked for about an hour; then a fine discussion developed, which went on till after seven. After that came dinner and a quiet evening of sitting around while Gautam exhibited the various manners of wearing a dhoti.

My talk had as title *A Comparison of Indian Thought and Psychoanalytic Theory*.[197] I introduced the talk by pointing to the East-West contrast of gods soaring on rapture with gods soaring on wings: the Oriental experience of vision-rapture and the Occidental interest in mechanics. We have turned to the dream world from the sphere of waking consciousness and see dream as a fact for science to consider; the Orient turns to life from the realm of rapture and sees life as a dream. In the whole range of Western science it would seem that the field of psychology approaches the closest to the Orient in its findings.

Part I of the talk was concerned with a brief review of the main themes of psychoanalysis:

A. Conscious - unconscious
  1. Charcot - Breuer (hypnosis)
  2. Freud: Free association

  conscious   { resistance
  unconscious { censor ⟶
  "repressions"

  3. Jung: Conscious   { personal ←
           Unconscious   { collective ⟶
  4. Myths and Deep Dreams ←
  Heavens (expanding consciousness) – Hells (constricting)
  5. "World" a function of psyche
  yoga/māyā – Image/Analysis

B. Libido
  1. As sex
  2. As *eros* - *thanatos*
  3. Compare Kāma-Māra in the legend of the Buddha

C. The Two Aims
  1. Curing the patient back to society (Freud) } Rank
  2. Curing the patient beyond society (Jung) } theses

Lead of unconscious

Part II (very brief) was a review of the *Māṇḍūkya Upaniṣad* formula: Waking Consciousness, Dream Consciousness, Deep Sleep, *turīya*.

And in conclusion I presented my idea that in the Orient the Personal Unconscious is very strong (*satī* of the personality at every moment: conscious acceptance of the collective patterns), while in the Occident the collective is in the Unconscious. Orient resists individualism, Occident resists the relaxation to the collective—"oceanic" feeling, etc. My finale was the myth of the Churning of the Milky Ocean: *asuras* (Occident) and gods (Orient) combine to produce, first the poison (which our generation must hold in its throat) and then the ambrosia of immortal life.[198]

The discussion commenced immediately with a Mohammedan gentleman holding the floor at length. His best point: *karma* serves to help the individual submit to the collective, to his fate, etc. and blocks the development of an individualistic effort.

A Dr. Maiti then held forth very well indeed on the relationship of

Indian thought to psychoanalysis. Main points: Kṛṣṇa in the *Gītā* is like an analyst: Arjuna's confusion healed by a synthesizing formula (cf. Jung-uniting symbol[199]): he is then returned to life, fit to act.

India is more permissive than the West of *psychological deviations*. In the West, heterodox behavior runs into trouble sooner than it does in India: anxiety is increased thereby and neurosis rendered the more likely. It is more difficult to push through to a transcending realization. (Later query in my mind: This applies, I believe, only to the male. In the Orient the deviant female is absolutely blocked.)

Mr. English made the good point that the aim of psychiatry is to set people at ease with themselves and their world—and this involves taking their religion into account when they have a religion: but psychiatry does not teach religion.

The vice-chancellor was asking whether people could be cured without religion. Dr. Maiti cited some cases where they had, others where they hadn't, and still others where, with religion, they had *not* been cured. It was a fine afternoon.

At dinner Papa Sarabhai asked about the problem of Catholics in the West: were they not as strictly held to the archetypes as Orientals?

At dinner, also, Mrs. English challenged the term "Collective Unconscious," and finally decided that what it meant was "Capacities."[200]

And after dinner, in a conversation with Gira, I realized that in the Orient individuals are no less individual than they are in the West: the difference is really that in the West the individual is *attached* to his individuality, whereas in the Orient the chief attachment is to some group: family, caste, tribe.

With respect to the problem of women. Some days ago I said that Indians were not much interested in sex, and Geeta said, later, that she was surprised that I had already noticed this. Then she said that she thought the reason was that people marry without love affairs and think immediately of having children. Sex is simply a means to children. It is not experienced in its own right as something pleasurable. Moreover, for many women it is experienced too soon.

Monday, December 20

I finished my piece on Jean before breakfast this morning, had breakfast with Geeta (the Englishes have gone), and then went over to Gira's to talk with her about some of the problems of the Museum that Gautam and she are interested in. I made a few suggestions for possible exhibitions and came home, to begin catching up on my diary. Later we conversed about the problem of taste in India—destroyed, according to Mrs. Sarabhai, by the British. (That tale of the cutting off of the fingers of the weavers is one of the major legends of modern India.)[201] Mrs. Sarabhai also explained to me why it is that the saris in eastern India (Bihar, Bengal, etc.) are not colored. It is the result of a boycott that was instituted against British dyes at one time during the course of the nationalist struggle. Mrs. Sarabhai has a very strong Gandhian inclination. She is busy now arranging for a large meeting of the village workers, which is to take place in a couple of weeks. Last evening at dinner I spoke with her about Vinoba Bhave. His direction, she thinks (as I do), is the proper one for India and she believes that Nehru is coming around to that view too. I glimpsed an article in yesterday's paper that seemed to be saying that neither the West's way nor Russia's way is right for India—and if that reflects the thinking of Nehru, it is a good sign.

After lunch I returned to my diary and at 3:15 P.M. was called for by a gentleman named Dr. Trivedi, who had attended yesterday's event. He drove me to his home, some distance away, to meet and talk with his father, an old gentleman of eighty-one, who is a Vedantist. The old man—a lovely old gentleman—entered the room wearing his black cap and jacket and we sat down. His first question was, did we in America take an interest in spiritualism? (Not much *here* of Vedanta!) Then he asked me if I had seen any spiritualistic phenomena. I replied in the negative and asked if he had. He too replied in the negative and so did the other gentlemen in the room—Dr. Trivedi and a Mr. Shah who had entered with the old man.

There was a shout from outside and an old friend, Mr. Vyasa, about seventy-five years old, came in and joined us—a rather taller man, genial and amusing. We now turned to Vedanta. What did I think of Śaṅkara's Vedanta?[202] I said I preferred the *Bhagavad Gītā's karma yoga* to the monastic rejection of the world. I said (and this is a nice idea) that the main problem is, what is *mokṣa?* Is it release from the world? or is it release from ignorance? If it is the latter and if *ātman* is *in* the world, release from the world is superfluous and may even represent a wrong notion about the nature of *mokṣa.* Old Mr. Shah said that when acting we always acted with desire for the fruits: there would be no action without desire. Drinking tea (and we were drinking tea) would not take place without desire for the tea. It was getting late and so I let the argument stay at this pleasant point, suggesting, however, that if one had found or even heard about the still point in the center of Śiva's dance, involvement in the fury of the world was different from what it would be without that knowledge.

On the way home, with Dr. Trivedi, I did somewhat better. If one knows of the immanence of *ātman-brahman* in all things, then what if one responds to desire? I should gladly go crazy with desire, knowing of its divinity—and perhaps this very point is the one illustrated in the sculpture of such temples as Koṇārak. O.K. Bull's-eye.

Returning home at about 4:30 and settling down on my verandah, I started work again at my diary, and have finally brought it, now, to here. So at this point I can begin to relax a bit and discuss some of my new impressions and recent conversations.

Yesterday's talk: I think that here, in the field of psychoanalysis, India can be said to stand ahead, even though they may not have such good psychoanalysts as we have; because the easy transition from psychoanalysis to the doctrine of the *Gītā*, etc., is not only possible but is actually taken for granted by such a man as Maiti. My whole argument was completely supported by him—and apparently as something that he already takes for granted.

The yogi problem is prettily illustrated here in Ahmedabad by the case of a little man who planted himself under a tree three years ago and is still there. Mani told me of him first and showed him to me as we drove home from Vikram's. The tree is not far from the entrance to a factory—so the place selected was far from quiet. The advantage, however, is that people clear away the little man's filth for him, give him water and food, and even a piece of cloth to protect him in the winter—which is now. I have seen him five or six times. At night, he was sitting up asleep, covered by his cloth. Once he was smoking a big cigar. Twice he was lying down beneath his cloth. Once he seemed to be sitting in meditation.

Jung's image of the stage of becoming a tree is well illustrated here.[203] The little man is stuck. In the West he would be taken away, perhaps, to an institution and cured back (shock treatment, etc.) to society. Here, he is permitted to sit it out and perhaps go through to Buddhahood—perhaps, on the other hand, simply to remain stuck, as a living symbol of spiritual effort.

There are no hospitals, there are no asylums. The lepers sit out on the streets and so do the madmen. But some of the madmen can break through, and these breakthroughs are giving India *something that the West really lacks.*

Gira, the other evening, spoke of the dismal impression she had had of the American small towns and small cities. This is something that we all recognize. But we live, as far as possible, in places and with people who are not dismal, and *our* America is the one we like. Similarly in India—what the tourist sees is not what the inhabitant sees.

Here, in the Sarabhai household, I am having an experience of Indian life that is the best and strongest I have had so far. The mansion itself, as I already remarked, is something out of a Rajput painting. And the other homes that I have seen are comparably beautiful. Gautam, of course, has elegant taste; and his influence—in the splendid bronzes that are everywhere for instance—gives a tone of grandeur that may be particular to *this* establishment. But one can see that India, with many people of this kind, would have its own way of being perfectly modern.

The Sarabhais are interested in modernizing Ahmedabad. Other rich men here, they tell me, are interested in patronizing holy men. (The latter, of course, would be more to Nikhilananda's taste.) And so, one feels that both ends of the line are meeting here—as they must be in many Indian cities.

My principal term of comparison for the Sarabhai family is the Eugene and Agnes Meyer family in America.[204] The same pattern of a large family (here eight), great wealth, and an active (exceptionally active) interest in the community.

My new image of India is that of an old mansion full of bats and dust (people sleeping on the pavements, etc.). On first beholding, one sees mostly the dust: afterwards the handsome lines and strong structure of the house begin to be apparent. Then, finally, one doesn't see the dust anymore. Visiting India is like visiting an antique shop: one has to develop an eye. I think that my eye, at last, is developing. I find myself with a new feeling for this whole adventure.

One remarkable thing that I have observed in the course of my visit with the Sarabhais is the absolute freedom of the numerous servants to come and go at all times anywhere, to break in on conversations, and to be generally present all the time. Also, there is a close and gently familiar relationship between master and servant, mistress and servant, that is much more "democratic," it seems to me, than anything I have ever observed in the West. A corollary of the ever-present servants is that one is almost completely without privacy. No wonder the yogis retreated to the Himalayas. My own bathroom retreat for the writing of Jean's article was the only possible answer.

Mani called for me, to take me to dinner with a very interesting fellow—Yashoda Mehta—whom the Indians regard as a sort of bad boy. He is a lawyer, and some time ago wrote a book that has been banned under section 292 of the legal code: against obscenity. He is a lively chap, in the middle forties I should say. He and his wife greeted us at the door of their home, and he immediately served the only alcoholic drink permitted in Bombay, a "medicinated" port known as Hall's. This he and I drank while he began a few lively opening gambits to test me out: early dating of the Vedas, etc. I steadied down his wild Indian style of flinging little chunks of information around, and we finally came to some of his chief interests:

India's present negative philosophy, he rejected. For him, the one way to enlightenment is sex. (His wife said nothing to this point.) We agreed that the Ramakrishna attitude of the child was not appropriate to India's present state of freedom, where the attitude of the hero is called for (this point was mine), and that the present puritanism of India was English not Indian (this point was his). Then he told me of an old man, 116 years old, who will be arriving in Ahmedabad Wednesday and whom I must stay to see. He is a holy man with a positive orientation to the world. "Anxiety doesn't eat me," says the old chap, "I eat anxiety." Heavens and hells, past and future, are all figments of the mind. "God is not the creator of man; man is the creator of God." This sounds to me like the type of holy man I came to India to see.

They told me also that there is a holy woman in town whom I should see. Mani will take me to see her.

And then, of course, there is the little old chap under the tree. Yashoda Mehta declared that he has been known to speak, and he says that he is in such rapture sitting there that there is no point in going anywhere else. That is to say, the little man has already gotten over the bump and is a symbol of the joy of the world!

I am beginning to hear about all kinds of holy people wandering about India. Apparently the country is full of them. There are, for instance, the two Jain holy men who are in Bombay right now—one Svetambar and one Digambar. And then there are people like these in Ahmedabad. Also, there are the ash-covered yogis that I have seen. Furthermore, there are the well-known teachers, such as Aurobindo, Ramana Maharishi, and Sri Krishna Menon. Their influence is actual and perhaps very strong. One must add also Vinoba, and the Gandhian tradition.

Yashoda Mehta told of two encounters, one at Nasih and one at Haridvār, where he approached holy men in a critical mood and was astounded to have them speak to him his very thoughts.

Tuesday, December 21

At about 10:30 A.M. I began to be worried about a car to take me to my date with Dr. Maiti at the Child Study Institute. I went downstairs and found Kamalini, who was to take me, taking care of one of the little children of her school who had just fallen and cut its face. Presently I got off in a large car and, after driving quite a way, arrived at a large building near the University. Here I was met by the young people working with Dr. Maiti. They told me something about the history of the Institute and then took me into a room with charts along both walls illustrating their plans and work methods. I was greatly thrilled and impressed: a beautifully planned campaign for the study of the problems of Culture and Personality Development in India today. As I was looking at the charts, Dr. Maiti came in, and when I had finished studying them, we all sat down in a room—Kamalini had meanwhile arrived—and talked till about 1 P.M. about mythology and culture. I learned many things pertinent to my own interests, of which the most important are perhaps the following:

The young expectant mother goes to her own mother's house to bear her child and returns to the husband only after forty days (I think it's forty). Compare the legend of the Buddha's mother on her way to her own family when she bore the Buddha. Child and mother are taboo and are gradually inducted into society by means of a series of rites—here is the Hero-journey motif. The mother brings her earlier children with her on the journey.

The mild, permissive treatment that I have observed in India in relation to children lasts until about the tenth to twelfth years, when, suddenly, the child is expected to be an adult. Here is the maturity in action that I have noticed among youngsters working in shops, in the fields, etc. This amounts to a traumatic change, leaving childhood behind as a Golden Age. Here, perhaps, *a clue to the religious crises of Ramakrishna and others at the age of twelve or so.* Ecstacy is as a return to childhood, taken care of henceforth by the community, and is fed, etc., as an image is fed. Note the little yogi outside the factory: most often when I pass him he is lying down under his cloth. Note, also, Ramakrishna's statement, to the effect that the one who, instead of going out into the world (and becoming adult), cries for the mother to take him back will surely be taken back by the mother.

There is no tradition of conduct for the successful individual who makes a lot of money and gets ahead: hence the rawness of certain Indian money men. They are out on their own (rugged individuals more blatantly than our American variety of the pre-Depression era).

I was impressed by the exhaustive approach of Dr. Maiti and his people to every scrap of evidence they can gather. At my meeting Sunday, they were taking notes not only of my talk but also of the audience reactions. They were interested, for instance, in the attitude of the vice-chancellor: his anti-science, anti-West pattern. He represents a certain large group of the Indian intelligentsia.

Several Indians have remarked, by the way, the contrast at our Sunday talk between the objectivity of the approach of the Westerners (English and myself) and the tendency to vast abstraction and loose terminology of the Indians. This criticism, however, would not apply at all to Dr. Maiti.

This Child Study Institute was set up in plan by Lois and Gardiner Murphy[205] when they were over here two or three years ago. Their first director died, and the Institute remained dormant then until Dr. Maiti arrived. It has been functioning in its present style for less than a year.

I had lunch with Kamalini at Gautam's (he is in Bombay) and we had an excellent talk, from which the following ideas emerged: Gautam, at the Sunday talk, had been a little upset by the use of such terms as *ātman,* which have no meaning: why did I let such terms get into the discussion and what role did they play? Answers: the term *ātman* has a transcendent reference and so cannot be defined; and the fact that India recognizes such a term is important for Indian psychology and psychoanalysis because it enlarges infinitely the field into which the libido is permitted to flow;[206] i.e., *the Hero Adventure into the abyss is facilitated,* since the society itself recognizes by a nondefining term the area in which a total dissolution and restoration is effected. This in turn reduces the likelihood of neurotic developments in the individual who feels himself moving out of the social cadre: *he* is not afraid and neither is the society.

At the Institute, I asked Dr. Maiti whether he agreed that India's permissive attitude applied more to men than to women, since women are compelled by very strict formulae to fit into the patterns designed for them in the matter most important to them, namely sex; and he—reluctantly, it seemed to me—agreed.

America's innocence of the fear that it is creating everywhere in the world is partly the result of America's failure to realize the magnitude of its own strength. Others see it, and feel its impact in every sphere, spiritual as well as material, and are afraid that it will destroy their own heritage, one way or another.

When I remarked that it was unfortunate that the most vulgar aspect of America was what was presented first to the world in such films as the one we saw the other night, Kamalini said that it was precisely the vulgarity that India wanted and, in its own films, imitated. This was a release of much that the Indian norms failed to free.

After leaving Kamalini, I went to give a talk to the faculty of Mani's school. Theme: My Impressions of the Contrast of America and India. It was simply a restatement of my present ideas: India's reception of America's ideas as well as machines, in flat imitation. India's own religious heritage and repose in the archetypes. What will the process of assimilation be?

The questions afterward were good, and brought out one suggestion, namely, that the blatant interest of the Indians in money might be the result, partly at least, of the fact that it was a merchant nation that conquered India. I noticed here as everywhere in India a tendency to blame as much as possible on the British while taking for granted the boons bestowed by the modernization of the country.

When the talk was over we drove to a home that, for the moment, was sheltering a holy woman, Ānanda Mayī.[207] In the car, accompanying us, was a French chap, who is teaching in Mani's school, and he challenged my whole talk on the score that it had misrepresented the West by not mentioning Marx (these tiresome people!). I said that I was not pretending to talk about Poland, Yugoslavia, Estonia, Latvia, Lithuania, Czechoslovakia, and the other Communized countries of Europe, but the West—Western Europe and America—which may shelter a number of Communists but in the visible aspects of its life is democratic and individualistic. Perhaps Communism would help India to find the way to a non-individualistic assimilation of the machine; but India would have to decide whether mass liquidations were quite what she wanted to pay as a price. In my lecture I had favored the way of Vinoba Bhave, but I did not press it at this juncture.

The *darśana* of Ānanda Mayī was *something!* Ramakrishna all over again. Apparently, she experienced her first *samādhi* at the age of twelve, and has been treated as a kind of incarnation ever since. She does not use her hands to eat, but is fed.

We entered a large tent full of people, with a platform in the upstage left corner, where a woman in white was sitting in the crosslegged posture, with a mild smile on her lightly tan features and her hair done up in a bun on top in the manner of a yogi. Music was playing and someone singing a *kīrtana,* but almost as soon as we arrived the music stopped and the session was over. We remained as the crowd cleared. Ānanda Mayī left the tent and we waited. Then it was possible to follow into a room of the host's house, where Ānanda Mayī was to be seen seated (or half-reclining) on a wide bed, with standards at the four corners to which strings of flowers were attached.

People were sitting on the floor, all around the walls, simply watching her, and she too, was simply sitting quietly, with her mild smile, and her eyes only half-looking: and yet she was taking everything in. Her nose came down straight from her high forehead, like the classical Greek nose, but there was something of a slightly bent or crumpled look about it. The woman was in her forties, I should say, and pleasant to see. Young girls were numerous in her environment, some of them, with cropped hair and wearing coarse saris, were her nuns, so to say. A few women and girls bowed deeply before her when they entered or left the room.

Mani asked me if I would like to ask any questions. She explained that I was a college teacher and student of comparative religions. I asked whether the four *yogas* of the *Gītā* were of equal value or were to be regarded as representing progressive stages. She looked a bit puzzled for a moment, then turned a quick question to a monk in yellow robe who was standing at the foot of her bed-couch, and he replied, "*karma, bhakti, jñāna, rāja*,"[208] after which Ānanda Mayī replied to me twice. First she said they represented a series, a road, and then she said that each was a way. Mani asked if I would like to ask another question. I asked whether *mokṣa* meant renunciation of the world or release from ignorance *in* the world. She replied that when *mokṣa* is experienced there is no question of renunciation or acceptance. I bowed my appreciation and for another few minutes the room sat in silence.

Presently there came a question from the host: Was the Kṛṣṇa of the *Bhāgavata* historical or merely a legend? Her reply: the Kṛṣṇa of the *Bhāgavata* is the *līlā* of god, and so, a mystery, not to be understood in such human terms. (True enough, as Kamalini whispered to me, but the question is left unanswered: No, I said, that was the proper answer. It centered the mind in the transcendent, from which point of view the historical query is irrelevant, and the function of this *darśana* is to point the mind to the transcendent.)

The host next asked: "Why am I attracted to you?" The attitude in the room was gently humorous yet sincere and there was a pleasant laugh. The reply was that he was attracted to the Spirit which is present in all, and in all things, but in some more apparently than in others. A few more questions were asked, but for the most part the situation was simply that of a lot of people sitting peacefully in a room. There were more people outside, at the windows, and the windows were presently thrown open, so that they should see.

Presently there was a stir at the door, and a young man tried to enter with a harmonium. Something was said to suggest that all should go back into the tent for a *pūjā* session. Out went the young man with the harmonium and finally everybody was back in the tent. The young Frenchman and I, sticking to Mani and Kamalini, realized presently that we were sitting on the female side of the tent. I, of course, was the one who began to feel uncomfortable. I got up and walked over to the back of the tent, on the men's side, and sat down; then he followed. We talked French for a while, about the gentleness and non-Western tone of ease in this fantastic religious affair.

Ānanda Mayī came into the tent and resumed her position on the platform. The harmonium was playing and a young woman with a good voice was singing a *bhajana*. Ānanda Mayī simply sat there, swaying a little, and halfway inward turned. The music changed a couple of times and then Ānanda Mayī herself began to sing in a slightly rusty voice. The whole tent repeated the phrase. There were several sessions of this, then the lights for the *pūjā* were lighted, a garland was placed around Ānanda Mayī's neck and the waving of lights began. This went on for a long time. The crowd now was standing. (They had stood also when Ānanda Mayī entered the tent.) And while she was being worshipped, she sat there in her half abstracted way, gently swaying and with her gentle smile.

I was full of thoughts of Ramakrishna. This certainly was a close reproduction of the scenes at Dakṣiṇeśvara.[209] I thought also of the conversation this morning, and my idea of this kind of ecstasy as a refusal of the adult threshold. The worship of the young girl at Belūr Maṭh and this worship ran together for me, and I could see how image worship and saint worship were all pretty much the same thing. The worship of Ramakrishna's image is a continuation of the worship of Ramakrishna himself. And the rites of image worship—feeding, clothing the image—are all duplicated in the worship of such a figure as Ānanda Mayī. No doubt, also, the rites of defecation require outside assistance. The life is exactly that of an admired baby.

Directly from Ānanda Mayī we drove to the home of a relative of Mani to have dinner with the children and a grand nephew of Tagore. A beautiful tall man in white dhoti and with a coquettish purse to his lips. And that's all there is to say about this beautiful man. His hair was pageboy bobbed at the back in the style that means in India "I am a poet." He had absolutely nothing to say all evening, but simply sat and would be looked upon. Dinner was on the floor and like all Indian dinners of this kind simply an attack on food—no conversation.

We got home about ten and I went directly to bed—after perhaps the fullest day of my visit to India: certainly one of the richest.

Wednesday, December 22—Winter Solstice

At breakfast this morning and yesterday morning with Geeta we discussed Aldous Huxley, Krishnamurti, and Danielou. Geeta matched Huxley's interest in mescaline by telling me that many of the Indian *sadhus* smoked bhang (perhaps this is what our yogi under the tree was smoking), which produced visions comparable to those of mescaline.[210] The point about

Krishnamurti was that though he would not say whether he was an incarnation or not, he would not have allowed such *pūjā* as I saw last evening. About Danielou: he presses his zeal for Indian music too far, pretending that the notes known as the peacock note, elephant note, etc. are called such because of the overtone intervals actually to be heard in the cries of the animals. Geeta said that when she heard Western fifths they always sounded to her a bit flat: Lou Harrison then explained to her the "corrected" scale of the well-tempered clavichord.[211]

We talked about the lack of romance in India. One does not feel any interest whatsoever in the erotic here—and so, why? Geeta's guess: early marriage, and routine of children. No mystery, and somewhat of a surfeit besides. My additions:

Family-planned marriage relieves young women of the necessity to spruce themselves up for competition; the women do not concentrate on sex allure, the men are therefore left without the heightened stimulation, and nobody wins!

The heat burns all the juices out of the body. One way or another, it is certainly true that there is no romance here, no call to romance, and not even a feeling that there ought to be romance. Europe and America represent a totally different erotic climate—and, ironically, think of the Orient as a realm of Romance. But their Orient, I guess, is largely that of the Arabs—*Arabian Nights*—which *may* be different, though I doubt it.

During the morning Kamalini showed me her nursery school: a wonderful affair. The nine-year-olds, today, were preparing the lunch for the school, rolling out chapatis, etc. The kids who didn't want to do that were doing something else: two were sitting up on top of a jungle-gym and one was lying on a window seat reading a little book.

Mani drove me to the chief monuments and mosques of Ahmedabad. We saw, among other things, Shah Alam's Mosque, from c. A.D. 1420 which has, as Murray's Guide says "inner details are as rich as Hindu art could make them"—i.e. given the Mohammedan restrictions. On this morning's trip I had a very strong sense of India's Mohammedan art as a transformation of the Hindu art. The columns have the same feeling as the Hindu. The stone is wonderfully carved.

We went on to the Rani-No-Hajero: another mosque, closely surrounded by exceptionally interesting shops. Indeed, the market streets of

Ahmedabad are thrillingly crowded with everything India has to offer—yogis, camels, donkey caravans, people, people, and people.

I had lunch again with Kamalini and spent the afternoon catching up on my diary. Mani just phoned to say that the 116-year-old holy man whom I was to meet tomorrow will not arrive till Sunday—the day I was hoping to get to Delhi to catch the Theatre Unit crowd. He will remain in Ahmedabad a week or ten days, however, and so I might come back. My feeling is that I had better let this one go.

During the course of our drive through Ahmedabad, Mani, discussing various things, told me that there was a great difference in cultural attitude between the Hindus and Mohammedans in Ahmedabad. The Mohammedans are excellent craftsmen. One always prefers Mohammedan-made to Hindu-made objects: they work better. The Mohammedans also have an elegant sense of decorum and grace in their speech. They put Hindus to shame in this matter. Moreover, they have a talent for the enjoyment of life, which the Hindus lack. The remarkable thing is that both the Hindus and the Mohammedans are Indians: add to this the words of my two Mohammedan companions in the train to Gaya: Mohammedans are grateful for U.S. aid, but give to a Hindu and he will insult you at the next turn. Mani spoke of the great loyalty and sense of honor of the Mohammedans (a virtue celebrated in the *Arabian Nights*).

An interesting thing about the streets of Ahmedabad is the arrangement of doors opening onto the street, which are doors not to houses but to little neighborhoods or quarters of dwellings. Mani says that the social unit is the neighborhood, and the neighborhood loyalty very great. The Sarabhai family at weddings, etc. invites the neighborhood from which the family sprang—if they did not, at the time of a funeral there would be no one to lift the coffin.

One of Dr. Maiti's patients brought him a dream today that supports my statement that dreams can reproduce myth sequences. A violent, paranoid, and homosexually-inclined fellow of a height of about 6 ft. 5 in. After a long history of troubles, his dream last week: a lion, swallowing all kinds of dark objects. Association: Śiva Nīlakaṇṭha swallowing the poison—I am that lion—must hold the poison in my throat and not be killed by it. His dream today: a lovely Goddess with a lotus. Associations: the giving—the will to give—the capacity to give: I have that and would like to give myself.

Dr. Maiti's remark: a recognition of the feminine aspect of his own nature. The myth: Churning of the Milky Ocean mentioned in my Sunday lecture.

. Kamalini's younger girl, Sharma, at the age of two-and-a-half, suddenly declared that she would never wear girl's clothes, only boy's. She tries to behave like a boy, and I recall that I thought she was a boy until Kamalini told me she was a girl. Kamalini gives this as an example of Freud's penis envy actually proven. The little girl, as it were, took a vow at the age of two-and-a-half! I noticed this evening that whenever Dr. Maiti thanked the little girl (now about five) for passing the beans, etc. to him, he said, "Thank you madam," or something similar, to remind her that she is a girl.

Thursday, December 23

Thinking some more about this *ātman* concept, I think perhaps that just as the individual feels free to slip into its sphere of emptiness so does the culture—hence the failure to be disturbed by the general formlessness of Indian life today. The whole culture, so to say, is permitting itself the luxury of a period of disintegration. The general attitude of India seems to be one of permitting and even favoring chaos.

A couple of themes: *India without Romance*—based on the talk yesterday morning with Geeta: why this lack of erotic zeal? how much of Indian life reflects it?

Also, the traditional West (Europe's Middle Ages) contrasted with the traditional East: tradition minus *ātman*-concept and plus Romantic Love. Is there a connection? Lack of reincarnation idea perhaps important: *stress in the West on the poignancy of the irrevocable moment* (compare Nietzsche, *The Birth of Tragedy*).[212] No tragedy in India. This may be a very bright idea. (Read de Rougemont's *Love in the Western World*.)

This West-East contrast is adding up to quite a number of points:[213]

West	East
God	*Ātman*
Image of God	*Śakti*
Transcendence	Immanence
Outward Effort	Inward Plunge
Formation	Disintegration
Dogma	*Sādhanā-samādhi*

Neurosis	Transformation
Purgatory	Reincarnation
Straight line	Cycle
Unique Moment	No Death
Birth of Tragedy	No Tragedy
Love in the Western World	No Romance
(*Post Renaissance*)	
Value Collisions	*Dharma*
Choice of mate	Family Marriage / Separation of Sexes
Sex competition	Early marriage: surfeit
Sex mystery and research	No mystery: all out in the open
A room of one's own	No privacy
"The Life Bud"	"The Completely Open Flower"— Petals falling!

A new turn to Nietzsche's warning: "Be careful lest in casting out your Devil you cast out the best that is in you." No Devil in India—all is *brahman*. Situation of the completely filletted analysand. Spengler's Fellaheen—the neurosis of the Culture Period quite gone.[214] All is out on the surface—"like a fruit on the palm of the hand." Problem: How much of the difference is West-East? How much is Culture-Civilization?[215]

When this was done I piled into a tiny car with Geeta, Mani, Geeta's two children, a chauffeur and a man to watch the kids. Geeta went shopping and Mani took me and the children to a very interesting sort of yogi farm: a temple compound that dispenses free food to all that come. They have a large herd of cattle. I saw the kitchens where dal, etc. was being prepared by priests and *sadhus* in immense cauldrons. The images in the outer shrines resemble those at Puri and the foundation supporting this amazing institution is connected somehow with Jagannātha. Mani brought us to one of the verandahs, where a very old man, called simply Maharaj, who is regarded as a holy man, sat amid food and cloths. He is the head of this sanctuary, and doles out food, as *prasāda,* all day. We paid our respects and for about four minutes sat in a row along the wall beside him. He gave *prasāda* to the children and prepared a large packet for Mani and me. I noticed that annas and *paisa* had been left with him by devotees, but when I moved to leave something too, he stopped me. Then, with *namaskāras,* we left him, and wandered slowly among the devotees and shrines. All around and out in front of the temple were *sadhus,* many covered with ash, all looking quite authentic—and their principal preoccupation seemed to be with themselves: combing their hair, praying and touching themselves in the sacred places, sitting, snoozing, or waiting for the food that would be served at twelve. A beggar approached as we left: in a place of free food and lodging, still begging. And near the temple were many poor hovels.

We drove back into town and I watched Geeta bargain for a bit of cloth, and then we drove home. I went next, again with Mani, to the police, to report on my presence in Ahmedabad, and as we drove we saw a *sadhu.* "They are very dangerous," she said. "Many smoke opium and are homosexuals; they kidnap boys." She told me also that one class of poor people living hereabouts were Chharas—a caste of thieves. Gautam, when he drives to his farmhouse, has a man with a rifle and bullet belts in the back of the car, for protection against these.

Tea this afternoon with the lovely old couple next door, the Sarabhais' aunt and uncle. The old gentleman had heard my talk Sunday and Geeta had given him Zimmer's *Myths and Symbols* to read. When we spoke about the influence of Indian thought on my students and I told him that the renunciation motif did not appeal, he came through with the formula that I have been wanting to hear, namely, that detachment not renunciation is the goal, and that this detachment has its counterpart in aesthetic detachment. He also declared that he thought the chief religious difference between East and West was in the stress on God's immanence in the East and on God's transcendence in the West. However, people of both worlds held both positions so that the difference is not in kind but in emphasis.

At about seven I went down for an hour's chat with Mr. Sarabhai. He spoke of the Maharaj of the yogi farm as a real holy man, now thinking of ceasing to eat. The farm has a couple of elephants and every year there is a great procession in Ahmedabad. He said also that he regarded Ānanda Mayī as genuine; however, some of the people who were devoted to her were scoundrels. "Some people are generally good and kind but have specific mean points: people whom they ill-treat; conversely, some people are ruthless and mean, but have special points of kindness. Perhaps these in Ānanda Mayī's company feel that they are making up for their guilt in this way." He said also that people like Ramakrishna and Ānanda Mayī may be interpreting their experiences falsely. One can admit that the phenomena of their lives are mysterious without conceding the theological interpretation. Smallpox, for example, used to be interpreted as the wrath of God. Ānanda Mayī, it is said, was three days old when her paternal grandfather visited her and she spoke to him in clear words, asking why he had come.

Friday, December 24   **Mt. Abu, en route to New Delhi**

A single compartment mate: a silent but gracious gentleman with one peg leg. I had lunch in the dining car and arrived at Abu Road about 2:15 P.M., then took a taxi up the wonderful Mt. Abu, and afterwards drove to Dilwārā and the Jain temples. The temples are being repaired by a large team of craftsmen-workmen, and I watched them for some time. They file down the marble with metal files and chip at it with pointed chisels. They make plaster models of the parts to be replaced and then translate the plaster into marble.

The temples are both worse and better than I expected: the overall effect is greatly cluttered, but each little chapel is simply ravishing. The great marvel is the work on the ceilings—they are delicious, delicate and luminous.

Returning to my hotel, I had tea and then was taken afoot by the hotel runner to Sunset Point: a fabulous view from 3,800 ft. of a great plain and remote hills. The sunset was witnessed by a multitude of amusing Hindu families. Then I walked back with an Indian gentleman who wants to hike with me tomorrow to Achal Garh—five or six miles each way, and my bus leaves at eleven! Can it be done?

After the sunset the weather became quite chilly, but in an invigorating, dry way. Abu, I find, is an abandoned Hill Station—palaces here of all the maharajas, but since the State of Bombay is now dry, the place has been abandoned. I think it could easily be turned into a good tourist halt. My hotel-keeper declares that the government is promising to build up the tourist trade but will actually do nothing. "It is a paper government," he declared.

On the train, a couple of new thoughts occurred to me with respect to my West-East problem.

In relation to the above, I have two writing tasks: Biographies, legends, etc. with alchemist-gnosis orientation; *The Life of Judas* could open this series. Second, *Bartolomé de las Casas*. The first is psychological-metaphysical, the second ethical-historical. Perhaps later the two themes could be combined.

I.

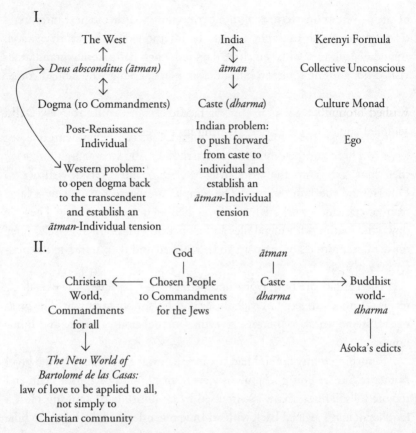

The West   India   Kerenyi Formula

↑   ↕

Deus absconditus (ātman)   *ātman*   Collective Unconscious

↕   ↓

Dogma (10 Commandments)   Caste (*dharma*)   Culture Monad

Post-Renaissance   Indian problem:
Individual   to push forward   Ego
   from caste to
Western problem: individual and
to open dogma back   establish an
to the transcendent   *ātman*-Individual
and establish an   tension
ātman-Individual tension

II.

God   *ātman*

| |

Christian ← Chosen People   Caste ——→ Buddhist
World,   10 Commandments   *dharma*   world-
Commandments   for the Jews   *dharma*
for all

↓ |

The New World of   Aśoka's edicts
Bartolomé de las Casas:
law of love to be applied to all,
not simply to
Christian community

A couple of items from my conversations with Geeta: the Indian woman, repressed, looks forward to the day when she is a mother-in-law. The repressed sadistic impulses, when they break out, let loose the horror of the massacres.

Saturday, December 25—Christmas Day

Up at 7:15 to get ready to meet my Indian gentleman at 7:45. Shaved, while shivering, over a mug of warm water. At 7:45 I went out into the sunshine, after two cups of tea, toast, and a banana; but the gentleman had not shown up by 8:00; so I started on a stroll of my own. After yesterday's catastrophe with the film I vowed to steady down and take only good shots very carefully: too much money pouring out in blank films. Presently, I found myself back on the path to Sunset Point—followed it and admired the view for a while. A world of utter silence—with the bark of a dog some-where off to the right. Then I walked back and found myself at the cele-brated Nail Lake (Nahki Talaō). I walked around it and was amused to see the little cave temples carved into the rocks around it—two or three—the entrances, small squares about three feet high and with the rocks white-washed around them, as a kind of façade. From within the Hanumān temple I could hear someone chanting his prayers.

I got back to the hotel at 10:15; the table was set for my breakfast. The host and hostess were extremely solicitous for my happiness and Merry Christmas. The porter put my bags on the head of a woman who walked ahead to the bus—about half a mile down hill, then I went with the porter, and for the rest of the day had the usual experiences of Indian travel.

Sunday, December 26   New Delhi

Taxi to the Swiss Hotel, which I had wired for a room because it had ad-vertised Room and Bath for fifteen rupees. When I had inscribed, they told me my room would be thirty-five rupees. I decided to remain for the day and night, bathe, freshen up, and recover my poise, then go back to the Cecil, which is almost next door and very much pleasanter, English-run in-stead of Indian. I drove to town to buy my Theatre Unit ticket for tonight;[216] the event that I have rushed to catch, so that I may get in touch with some of the folk who might help me settle for a concert.

Took a taxi later to the place of the great event: a brand new audito-rium, where the National Drama Festival has just concluded a month or so of highly advertised productions. I wandered around the building to see what it was like and then went into the auditorium. Presently P. D. Shenoy discovered me—the Theatre Unit's stage manager, and he introduced me to a nice chap named S. A. Krishnan, one of the directors of the National Academy of Art (Lalit Kala Akademi). I made a date with this fellow for to-morrow morning. Then the play took place—*Oedipus Rex*—surprisingly well played and certainly a gripper. I went backstage to congratulate the cast and saw a rather conspicuous blond European.

"Who is that?" I asked Krishnan.

"That is Mr. Fabri, the art critic."

"Fabri?" I said—remembering a lot that I had heard about this man from Salmony. "I want to meet him." So I was introduced.

"Campbell?" said Fabri. "Why, I've just been hearing all about you from Alfred Salmony!"

"Salmony's in town?" I said.

"At the Imperial. My wife's having lunch with him tomorrow."

Fabri asked how long I was going to be in Delhi, and I said until I have arranged for my wife's concert. There was a blurb for Jean's Bombay concert in the program, so it was easy to be convincing. Fabri then introduced me to the head of the Little Theatre Group, urging him to take Jean on, and even talking as though the whole thing were already taken for granted. I began to feel fine. Next I met Y. C. Rai, who seems to be one of the probably helpful people, and finally, with Alkazi, planned a meeting with him and Krishnan tomorrow.

Fabri joined me in my taxi and we went to his home, where I met his Indian wife. The Fabris' cute little four-year-old boy—blond as Fabri— was playing with a train on the floor and there were Christmas decorations. So we drank a bit of wine, in honor of Christmas, and they gave me a bit of mince pie. It was all very warm and pleasant, and friendly. I think this thing has gotten off to a good start.

Monday, December 27

At about nine, my laundry was returned, I packed, had breakfast, and removed to the Cecil Hotel. Felt fine on the old premises, my India circuit now quite completed.

When I had settled my things in my pleasant rooms, I took a taxi to the Lalit Kala Akademi, where I was greeted by the chap that I met last evening, S. A. Krishnan. He introduced me to the Secretary of the Academy, Mr. Barada Ukil, who discussed with me the work of the newly founded organization. Its function: to foster the revival of the craftsmen, the work of artists in India, and the arrangement of inter-cultural exhibitions. Krishnan then showed me an exhibition of painting and sculpture, much of which was quite good, and mostly Paris-inspired. The paintings of a young woman, Amrita Sher Gil, who had died circa 1940, were particularly revealing: at first, standard Paris studio student work, which suddenly, in India, crystalized into an interesting style—Cézanne base but Indian feeling, or atmosphere. There was a roomful of revivalist stuff—like fairy-tale illustrations, with an erotic atmosphere that is altogether out of keeping with the asexual life of modern India. Krishnan agreed that these were of no interest whatsoever as art, but declared that Ukil greatly favored it. Finis. Officials and art: the same stupid story as in the U.S.A.

It was about noon when I left the Academy. I left a note for Salmony at the Imperial Hotel, then went for a long slow stroll along Queens Way and around Connaught Circle, stopping on the way at the American Express to see if there was any mail for me, and to cash the last two $20 Travelers Checks of my original $1,500 packet. Four months, average $375 per month.

I went to the restaurant Volga and sat down to wait for Krishnan and Alkazi. Across the room I saw Mrs. Jayakar at a table with a gentleman. She greeted me and I went over to say hello, whereupon she invited me to dinner tonight, at the Delhi Gymkhana Club. Krishnan arrived, then Alkazi. We talked of the performance last night and of the newspaper reviews and then of the plans for Jean's concert. All agreed that the Little Theatre Group, under Mr. Inder Das, was the best organization to present the performance. They would handle the theater problems all right, but would have to be watched on their advertising and printing of programs, which they might do badly. Krishnan promised to help me. Then we left (I paid the check) and while Alkazi went to hunt for a hotel room, I proceeded to hunt for Inder Das.

Strolling about New Delhi, on the same streets that I found four months ago, I am amused by the transformation of my level of experience. Whereas then I was coming in touch for the first time with the more prominent surprises and surface phenomena of Indian cities, those are now rather well known to me and I find that I can bump them off and get through to the city itself—which I am finding rather pleasant. I notice that many more Americans are here now and that the police have cleared the streets of the most hideous of the beggars—the lepers; also, they shoo the others away from their victims. It is still, however, something of a trial to walk about: I was approached at least eight or ten times per block, and once or twice rather crudely and forcefully. Finally, I discovered the offices of Inder Das, who will meet with his Theatre Group tomorrow and by Wednesday morning will let me know how things stand.

At about 4:30 P.M. I went to the U.S. Information Office to see Mr. King, and while I was waiting for him to appear, who should come into the office but Salmony. Greetings and cheers. He is planning to go to Kabul, has had a wonderful trip, is chilled to the bone and trying to find an overcoat. Presently King arrived and we had a talk. Then I left Salmony, who will have tea with me tomorrow. I had told Mr. King that I would report to him Wednesday or Thursday on the outcome of the Inder Das conversation.

I arrived at the Gymkhana Club that evening and was conducted by a page to the cottage of Mr. and Mrs. Jayakar, where I found Neogy, whom I had met about seven years ago in New York and who is now director of some branch of the Village Industries organization. We had a wonderful talk and a fine dinner—Neogy turning out to be quite learned and objective, as well as eloquent, in his discussions of Indian history and art. A number of extremely interesting and suggestive ideas emerged.

In general, the materials for a social and philosophical history of India are extremely scanty. The picture that we now have is largely a creation of the imagination of Occidental scholars, augmented by Indians trying to beat them at their own game. As a corollary, it is probable that the main interest of Indian thinkers was not spiritual, as the Europeans and Anglicised Indians suppose, but highly materialistic (this coincides with Zimmer's formula). *The concept of the spiritual that has been applied to Indian thought is not Indian but European.* (O.K.—Bull's-eye.)

In regard to art, there is no word in Sanskrit for "obscene": the Koṇārak sculpture cannot, therefore, have seemed "obscene" to the people of pre-English India. In a conversation with an old man of the village near the temple, Neogy had said that the sculpture was "obscene" and had asked why it was there—to which the old man had replied that anyone who thought that way was unfit to look at a temple: this sculpture was good, and perfectly natural, and exactly what should be on a temple.

The Koṇārak temple has a much stronger architectural interest than those of Khajurāho. One sees first the great overall form; closer, one perceives the main blocks of the secondary elements; still closer the fine lacework and details emerge; and finally, the details of each piece are seen in their formal organization. (I indicated Zimmer's point, however, that at Khajurāho the horizontal bands of the friezes are balanced and absorbed by the verticals of the *śikāra* composition.)[217]

The figures at Khajurāho have a definitely human quality while those at Koṇārak are rather satyrs and nymphs (my point). Neogy mentioned the attempt that was made at Khajurāho to achieve a surface effect of actual skin, whereas at Koṇārak the figures are definitely of stone.

At Koṇārak are six figures of Śiva dancing not on a bull vehicle but on a ship of a kind used not for river but for sea traffic, such as the coastal people manufacture to this day. Just as the bull is the animal form of the god (Nandi) and the god the human form of the bull, so here with the ship. There is an important connection between Koṇārak and the sea trade of the 12th and 13th centuries. The Sun God at Koṇārak shows several interesting forms and traits: riding on a single horse (an archaic form); combined with Śiva elements; and combined with Viṣṇu elements. There are Sun God associations with the west coast forms—sea trade connections again?[218]

The disintegration that I noted at Mt. Abu—where the sense of the whole is lost and the charm is in the intricacy and perfection of the details—is matched in the late periods of Indian literature and music. In literature, the device of the frame story becomes so elaborately developed that one simply cannot follow any main thread whatsoever. And in music the present beginningless and endless run of impromptu passages on a timeless *rāga* becomes the rule—we don't know quite when; but there is evidence that in earlier periods Indian musical compositions had a beginning, middle and end. In music the change may have taken place after the Gupta period or toward its close. In architecture, the change is later; in literature it was perhaps earlier.[219]

Related to this, perhaps, is a remark of this afternoon, that for anyone who has learned about the neat structure of the early idea of the caste system, what is actually found in India today comes as a baffling surprise. Here again we have a congeries of discrete interests and systems, with almost no overall structure to hold them in formal relationship to each other.

The female ideal represented by the sari is in radical contrast to that of the ancient queens, who are represented as clad only in jewels. One should observe that in some works (e.g. at Ajaṇṭā), whereas the queen is almost naked, her serving maid may be covered from neck to ankle. There is some relationship, apparently, of the ideal of jewel-clad body to the aristocratic principle.

At this point I can add an idea that occurred to me in Ahmedabad, as I was sitting, looking at the Pārvatī on my verandah. Namely, that the

arrangement of the garb at the level of
the genitals tends to exaggerate the general theme of the organs in such a way
as to suggest a trans-human reference:
the female as the cavern from which life
pours; the male as an axial, cosmic *liṅga*.

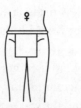

This *reduces* the erotic element by converting personal into archetypal references! In daily life, where the cosmic aspect of woman is continually
stressed, this reduction is maintained.

A new aspect of this problem occurs to me now; namely, that where
women are beautiful (in the aristocratic élite) the cosmic theme can be suggested by their nudity bejeweled, but where women are simply lumpish
(folk, bourgeoisie) the archetype is best suggested by covering in a certain
standard way. Hence, the naked ladies of the past and veiled of the present
achieve, respectively by positive and by negative means, the same end of archetypalization. The first, however, yields a heroic atmosphere and the second a sentimental.

Well, it was a good evening's talk.

Tuesday, December 28

I am rather amused at my present attitude toward the British atmosphere
at the Cecil: after four months of India, with all of my spiritual transformations, I find it thoroughly agreeable. Item from the morning paper, the
Statesman.

> Dr. Radhakrishnan today called for a "revivalism" in which the reli-
> gion of caste and dogmas will give place to the religion of unity and
> oneness.
>
> The challenge today, Dr. Radhakrishnan said, was world unity.
>
> Religion is an obstacle to achieving this unity. Just as there is rivalry
> between nation and nation, the religious rivalries stand in the way of
> international unity.... We want a religion which is of socialist nature:
> which gives us freedom to think, freedom to act, and which main-
> tains our privacy.... The Socialism that we should acquire should be
> that which maintains the fundamental dignity of men. It should
> be built on the basis of deep ethical and moral values: it should not
> violate the independence and privacy of man....

Truth and love were the basis of all religions, Dr. Radhakrishnan said. This country had made a great contribution to the world in carrying these principles all over...

If only we can discard hate, jealousy and rivalry, then we need not fear the atom bomb or anything even worse than that.

Perhaps it can be said that whereas the negative task of the West is that of transcending nationalism, that of the Orient is the transcendence of sectarianism; and that the positive task of the West is that of continually advancing in its freeing both of the individual and of each moment of life for free expressivity, while the positive task of India is that of insisting on its primordial experience of *ātman-brahman* as a dogma-transcending truth. One may well ask: *how can religions be said to favor truth when they insist upon fictions as real?*

I found a pack of mail for me at American Express. Bollingen is still operating on the Zimmer book: they sent proofs to Bachhofer for careful reading and he thought the renderings of OM should be changed. His remark: "I have no idea where these characters come from; they are certainly very unusual; they refer to two different spellings, OM and AUM. There is a possibility that the first character can be identified as OM, though the horizontal bar at the top, so typical of *devanāgarī,* is missing; but the second one, supposed to stand for AUM, looks utterly strange. If you want to be absolutely sure use the characters I gave you. For the others I can take no responsibility..." Lovely. How to sound learned while displaying ignorance! One can learn a lot from some of those old boys.[220]

Later, I had dinner with Salmony at the Imperial. Fabri arrived for a brief chat and listened to Alfred's recital of his plans. Says Salmony: "Everybody says the worst things possible about everybody else. I have heard Stella Kramrisch accused of everything but murder." This is important. I have noted it too. I think perhaps that the social disapproval of overt violence leaves all of the aggressive instincts rankling for expression. They come out in petty malice—and in mass explosions.

About the art of Koṇārak: Salmony says he noticed not only heterosexual, but also homosexual groups, male and female; also human and animal. Coomaraswamy's metaphysical explanation just doesn't apply here, he agrees.

He has learned from his directors of archaeology here and there, that the temples to which childless women came for children from the god kept a crew of lusties on hand who did the work of the god. The women entering the temple would leave their bodices at the door. The lusties would choose bodices, and then take care of the women to whom the bodices belonged: an impersonal, blind date arrangement—and the work indeed of the god Śiva or Viṣṇu.

There are parallels here to the Phoenician, Cyprean, and Armenian temples of Venus. Also, I should now re-examine the legends of the Indian saints.

Wednesday, December 29

Visited Inder Das to learn that Delhi is jammed with plays and concerts for the period of Jean's visit, but that the Little Theatre Group is going to try to help arrange something for Jean between the time of the Bombay concert and the date of her departure two weeks later. At American Express, I picked up a wire from her "No Japan Concert Arriving Delhi January 11. Leaving for Tokyo January 3rd Love Jean."

I am now trying to plan Jean's visit and a possible trip of my own, before her arrival, to Khajurāho, Sāñcī, and Jaipur. Went to the Indian Tourist Bureau this morning to try to make plans for the Khajurāho-Sāñcī trip, and found things about as difficult as ever.

I strolled down to Fabri's in the afternoon and found the master in his bathrobe, shushing me to be quiet because his blond little son had just been put to sleep. He sat down and talked, and I let him beat around the bush for a while, then I said that Inder Das and his group were unwilling to back the concert and so I thought I might go to Madras and try to arrange for something down there. He was immediately very firm in insisting that there *had* to be a concert by Jean in New Delhi. He asked if I would be willing to put up a thousand rupees for the hall and advertising and I answered yes. Then we were off on plans: to get the American Women's Club to sponsor it and help arrange for a hall, and to begin enlisting other interests. I felt when he was through that this thing might be a lot of fun for all concerned. He wanted me to bring Krishnan down to his place after dinner for a chat.

Krishnan arrived at my hotel a bit after eight, full of eagerness to push

Jean's concert through, and we talked over plans all evening, beginning with brandy for him and whiskey for me, then through dinner, and finally, up in my room until 11 P.M.

This is a very interesting and lively young man—twenty-eight years old, of a Mysore brahmin family; left his family to be an artist (which they regarded as *infra dig*[221]) and has ended as a newspaper critic—helped (according to Fabri) very much by the advice and instruction of Fabri, of whom he is overtly critical. His pride is in his honesty and critical integrity. When I went out of the room to fetch him a tin of cigarettes, I returned to find him jotting the following observation on the corner of a newspaper:

> This is an age of individualism. I do not mean by individualism an excessive representation of one's eccentricities, but the reaction of a man or woman as an individual in the form of any human activity. This reaction may be different from what we know or what we think we know...

The inspiration for this jotting was our conversation about the modern creative as contrasted with the various traditional dance forms—and the jotting itself represents pretty well, I think, the problem of the modern young Indian, whose culture has no tradition of search and freedom. Alkazi, Ezekiel, and Krishnan are pretty good representatives of the young intellectuals in India—Hussein, Samant, Ara, and the other young painters can be added to the list—and on the wealthier level are the Sarabhais, whose father was already a free spirit.

Krishnan asked me, with some emotion, how long I thought he and Alkazi had known each other. Having noted that they were very close friends, I said well, perhaps, since boyhood. "Two days!" said Krishnan intensely, and with a smile. "When we met, we embraced, and he picked me up in the air!" They had read each other's works and had been in correspondence. "When he left this morning, I know that he would have stayed if I had asked him to, but I knew that he was disturbed and I didn't feel that I had the right." (Alkazi's wife is on the point of having a child.) And so here it is again—the same highly passionate relationship between males that I have already met with in young Narasimhan. "When he left," said Krishnan, "we kissed each other; we just couldn't help it."

Thursday, December 30

To William King's office for the next move. He suggested Mrs. J. Wesley Adams, wife of one of the embassy secretary generals and chairman of the American Women's Club. I paused to make a date for tomorrow with Jack Macy, and proceeded to Mrs. Adams—a nice young mother, very much like a Sarah Lawrence alumna, who showed great interest in the idea, said that she would break it to her club at their meeting on Monday.

Invited to lunch by Salmony, I spent the afternoon with him at the main offices of the Archaeological Survey of India, watching films of Sāñcī, Agra, Khajurāho, and the newly found frescoes of the great temple at Tanjore done c. A.D. 980, between Ajaṇṭā and the Gujarat illuminations: a beautiful series.

Our host for this occasion was Ramachandran, one of the two chief directors of the Survey. He was deaf, tall, and impetuous. He bossed his menials around like a petty king, but he gave us a wonderful view of the work that his survey is doing.

Ramachandran talked almost without stopping during the course of our visit and let fall a good many ideas, some good, some no good. One

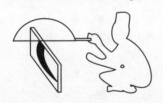

that was no good was that he could place Kālidāsa in the Śuṅga or Āndhra period, or perhaps earlier, by showing on the Sāñcī *stūpas* motifs comparable to those in Kālidāsa's poems.[222] Two interesting items were the following: the king who built Koṇārak was a leper; and the artisans restoring the inlay arabesques of the Taj Mahal first make a mica tracing, then, from this, a thin sheet-metal stencil which is fixed to the bit of precious stone that is to be cut, and then cut the stone with a metal-wire bowstring and abrasives.

Salmony and I walked from the Survey offices to the Imperial, where we had tea together on the verandah. I bade him goodbye (he is off to Agra, Mathurā, and Gwalior), and returned to the Cecil for dinner and an evening of diary and letters.

Friday, December 31

End of the year 1954, and therewith of the Zimmer project.[223] This morning I found that the hotel situation in Delhi for the months of January and

February is quite jammed. Another score for India: When the tourist season finally arrives, they have no room. I made reservations at the Cecil for the following dates: January 1, 5, 8, 15, and February 5, 7, 12, 18.

Spent most of the day writing letters, and then went to meet Jack Macy for lunch. He brought me to his flat, and we talked in lively fashion about India and the U.S.A. Why is America viewed so unfavorably in India?

The American technique of disposing of its money creates an unfavorable impression. The money then *has* to be spent, and the officers in charge of getting rid of it practically shove it down the receiver's throat—not caring much *how* it is spent.

Diplomats are people interested in cocktail parties. The best cocktail parties are in Paris, London, Rome, Copenhagen, etc., and the Orient is therefore a sort of probation area to which diplomats are assigned for a period of two years before they can become eligible for the better life. Result: no interest in the Orient or understanding of the Orient in the Oriental staffs.

American tourists leave a bad impression. The irony of the situation is that it is precisely the people who most love America and are most complacent about themselves as fine citizens who leave the appalling impression behind.

Our cultural exhibits misrepresent our cultural life by stressing the dull, traditionally archaic art works, which can be of no interest to anybody anywhere, and rejecting the avant gardistes, whom the young artists abroad would like to see and who might exert an influence.

The performing artists sent over here have been *very* few. The Americans appearing in India have been: Yehudi Menuhin, at the invitation of the Government of India; Helen Traubel, who was passing through; Isaac Stern, the only one brought over by the U.S.; and (soon to be) Jean Erdman, who was passing through and had to arrange her own concerts. (Her bid for help—after A.N.T.A. had approached her to learn how she had fashioned her tour—was rejected by A.N.T.A.'s dance committee: Martin, Terry, Martha Hill.)[224]

The Voice of America is not heard. It plays for one hour a day on a clouded beam. On the other hand, Hollywood, Tin Pan Alley, and paperbound detective stories are everywhere: no wonder we are thought of as a vulgar lot. Americans who are not vulgar always hear the remark (which is regarded as a compliment): "But *you* aren't like an American!"

In any case, contemporary India is totally devoid of an aesthetic sense. An exception is in Indian music. The new Punjab capital built by Corbusier is a case in point: it is already falling apart, electric wires dangling, etc. One gentleman hung on his great clean Corbusier wall, a little print of Gandhi in a tawdry frame, hung awry. India's tolerance, however (or, perhaps, consequently), is enormous: the real land of laissez-faire. It is a land where one is forever surprised by things previously unseen.

After a very nice lunch, Macy played me a beautiful record (which he then gave to me), which he had made from a tape recording of a duet played by Ali Akbar Khan (on the sarod) and Ravi Shankar[225] (on the sitar—Uday Shankar's brother). It is based on the Bhairavī *rāga,* which is to be played at 11 P.M. He then took me to the Indian Radio Broadcasting building, to meet Narayan Menon.

I returned home at and wrote letters (still a huge stack to go!). Then I set off for the Jayakars' for New Year's Eve.

There were three stages to the evening. The first was at Mr. Jayakar's, where I met some of the guests of the evening: a pleasant little, white moustached Belgian count, who did not like to be called Monsieur le Conte; his haughty daughter, who, I am glad to say, soon departed; and Nehru's younger sister Mrs. Hutheesingh, who greeted me very pleasantly, as though she had met me before (quite in contrast to Mme. Pandit, who always makes believe she has never seen me before).[226] We proceeded, after a brief drink, to Mr. and Mrs. K. V. K. Sunduram's, where there was another count—a tall one this time, and French. A lot of pictures by Amrita Sher Gil were on the wall, and Mrs. Sunduram told me that she was her sister.[227] Mr. Sunduram was a sweet but slightly rigid man in white trousers and black Indian full-dress jacket. All the other gentlemen were in tuxedos—and I was in my usual Dacron blue. On to a lovely dinner, then off to the Gymkhana Club for twelve o'clock.

Behold—a roomful of Indians behaving like Europeans at a New Year's Eve Party: the Sikhs had their paper hats up on top of their turbans. A large ballroom jammed full of dancers, some in costumes, and all but a couple of dozen, Indian. At midnight I was standing and talking when Mrs. Hutheesingh approached and suggested that we should dance— which we did—and I felt that to start off the year dancing with the sister of the Prime Minister of India wasn't too bad.

Sunday, January 2

During the course of the afternoon I read an offprint that Agnes Meyer[228] had sent me some time ago of her article on *Democracy and Clericalism*. Very good. A fine attack on the American counterparts of Nikhilananda who speak disparagingly of "materialism," "scientism," and "secularism," as evils that have thwarted the development of America's "spirituality." Agnes's article first outlines the history of the development of our secular morality and then shows why the claims of the right-wing clergy that morality is *exclusively* grounded on a theological dogma would endanger our nation, secular institutions, and freedoms, both civil and religious, as well as our peaceful relations with the other free nations.

Monday, January 3

An idea that must not be lost: "My sins dropped away from me not at the Ganges, but at Koṇārak."

One more idea: mythology as the second womb—it must be constructed of the stuff of modern life. The tendency of the clergy is to hold to the past and therefore reject, not redeem, the contemporary world.[229] A variant of this is the romantic exoticism of the American devotees of the swamis. In my visit to India I have found myself more interested in the relationship of the West to the East than in the East itself.

A vow for the New Year: *Finis* to all exoticism—whether into the past, or into the East, or into the occult! Back to Nietzsche.

An interesting item in the morning paper:

Mr. A. S. Sthalekar, Principal of Children's Academy, Bombay, said that if education was neglected the spirit of democracy would become stale and dead. "A nation which educates her millions only to be wage-earners, has certainly failed in her duties towards arousing the higher abilities of the human spirit. The wages of such neglect will be a highly materialistic society which recognizes no other values but the immediate ones.... Character building is the final test of all education.... The student must find an answer other than a mere utilitarian one to the question: 'Why am I at school.'"

All of this, in combination with Agnes Meyer's observations suggests certain common themes and problems of education for democracy throughout the world.

The fundamental energy of democracy is the illuminated public mind, and the generator of this energy is public education. Modern education must cover the following:

1. Science: physical, biological, anthropological
2. Morality: social science and citizenship
3. Psychology: i.e. self-management (including psychoanalysis)—the task of social reference (training to society); the task of the hero adventure (training to the transcendent)
4. Art: i.e. the generation of vision—the history and principles of art and literature; the crafts of the arts (creative art and writing); the aesthetic experience (static rapture)
5. Illumination—"Redemption"—*mokṣa* (meditation): the *Gītā* religion and Buddhism; the Chinese sages; Sufism; the Christian mystics; miscellaneous examples of the mystical experience; the great poets and philosophers of the modern world
6. Vocation: specialized technical training
7. How to enter a room.

The archaic inheritance (of the various local culture traditions, Oriental as well as Occidental) must be gradually transformed. Reactionary hard cores (e.g. the Roman Catholic Church, the Maha Sabha[230]) have to be carefully held in check. Liberal clergymen can be cautiously favored as transformers of the archaic vocabularies (e.g. the Protestant liberal clergy in America, and the Ramakrishna movement and Vinoba Bhave in India). Artists, poets, creative writers, and philosophers should be helped to function, not as Bohemian outcasts, but as respected agents of the society. Academic councils, foundations, etc. should be assisted, and avant gardistes given space in which to function.

In all of this, India's problem, everywhere except under heading 5, is more acute than ours.

Tuesday, January 4

This morning I woke up with the firm idea that Swami Nikhilananda is a crazyman. His patriotic monasticism is a form of lunacy—and his wild ambition is on the Savonarola side. He is Agnes Meyer's archetypal "cleric."

Yesterday at Fabri's H. Goetz, discussing Stella Kramrisch's new book,[231] rejected her idea (and Coomaraswamy's) about Indian art being religious. I asked him to be specific. I said that most of the Indian art that we knew was religious at least to the extent of being in temples. He replied that there is plenty of evidence that there was also non-religious art in India; moreover, the actual artisans introduced motifs and attitudes that were not religious at all. Much of their work was simply mass-production craft work. The idea of Indian art as religious is simply a projection onto the Orient of the old romantic idea about the Middle Ages. We are going to have to talk about this (Goetz and I) at some later date. Fabri, last evening, also lit into Stella. Her theory that the Aryan altar and the temple were related as cause and effect, he declared, was quite wrong. The altar is a place where sacrifices are burned for the gods above: the temple is a *garbha-gṛha*—womb cell—*within which* the divinity resides (one could object, however, that *Agni* resides in the altar).

Out of the cogitations of the past few pages the idea may be derived that the great spiritual conflict of today is not merely (as so often phrased) between religion and science, but between religion and the whole context of modern morality, science, and art—i.e., modern life—insofar as the religious mind insists on holding to the archaic moral and scientific contexts through which its basic principles have been transmitted. The basic principles themselves, however, when they are abstracted from their temporal context, do not controvert but readily supplement and vitalize the modern forms—just as they vitalized those of the past.[232] These basic principles are those of the relativity of all knowledge to the knowing subject, the transcendency of the transcendent, and the yogas through which the mind and feelings are brought into accord with these primary conditions of its being. The yogas are as follows: *karma* (work without fear or desire); *bhakti* (devotion to an image-god-thing-person-symbol); *jñāna* (philosophy); *rājā* and *kuṇḍalini* (psychological athletics); and art and poetry (*karma* and *bhakti* and *jñāna* and craft).[233]

The art and poetry of the last is art and poetry in what Goetz calls the Romantic sense. In a sense, however, I think that all art and poetry tends in this direction inasmuch as its effect is to establish a harmony, inspire pleasure (charm-rapture), and represent perfection (perfection, if nowhere else, in the skill of the craftsman who made it).

India's vast problem, in this sphere, would seem to be that of effecting . a rapid and total transformation of its science and morality without losing the foundations of its meditation.

Fabri told me the other day that vast numbers of the youth of India believe in nothing: his wife Ratna believes in nothing.

"Well," said I, "I too believe in nothing."

All one has to do to make this a profoundly mystical statement is to stress the word "believe." We have come, thus, very fast to the *śunyatāvāda* of the Mahāyāna.[234]

The main danger of Indian philosophy, as I now see it, is not in its ultimate doctrine of *mokṣa* as *vidyā,* but in the incorrigible tendency of the Indian mind to interpret *mokṣa* in the Jain and Sāṅkhya sense of isolation-integration. The more sophisticated psychological reading of the Mahāyāna is perhaps finally uncongenial to the Indian mind. For I notice that even when Indians state that the meaning of *mokṣa* is release, not from the world but from illusion, they tend to add: and so, from the world. Ānanda Mayī's statement that when *mokṣa* is experienced there is no question anymore of either affirmation or negation is somewhat dampened by the spectacle that she herself presents—sitting in a state of semi-rapturous semi-abstraction, being worshipped like an image and fed like a baby. This certainly suggests an attitude of life-negation. (See above, my discussion of the crises at the age of twelve.)[235]

The great deed of Zarathustra, apparently, was directed *against* the Indian yoga of world-withdrawal. The individual was summoned to act—to increase the field of the good. Zarathustra's ethical dualism (good and evil) was as absolute as the Jain metaphysical (*karma* and *jīva*), but life-oriented instead of death-oriented. Perhaps we can say that in the history of the Western world this oversimplified ethical dualism underwent a development and sophistication (culminating perhaps in Nietzsche), somewhat comparable to the development and sophistication of the metaphysical dualism in India, China, and Japan that I shall have to study when I get to Kyoto.

When *mokṣa* is realized, one is beyond not only affirmation and negation, but also good and evil, and the mythologies associated with *karma,* on the one hand, and judgment, on the other, are transcended.

The Indian penchant for renunciation is manifested in many ways:

retirement at fifty-five, to meditate (or loaf); stress on the negative aspect of *mokṣa* (the *jīvan-mukti* idea seems not to have made much of a dent); stress on the negative aspect of *karma* (submission, rather than active creation of good new *karma*—the point usually stressed by Occidental Theosophists like Sophia Wadia). *Actually, the fundamental principles of Indian philosophy can be read either way:* it is evident to me now, however, that the principal tendency of the Indians themselves is to give them the negative stress.

Perhaps what seems so odd about Theosophy is the positive active reading (ethical and Western) that it gives to all the Indian ideas. Which would suggest that it may be doing violence to Indian thought, after all, to read it that way.

Thursday, January 6

With respect to the character and work of the Communists *within* India, Nehru and Vinoba (whom I take to represent pretty well the thinking of the Indian leaders who are interested fundamentally in *India*) are in essential agreement. I read in Vinoba's words:

> Communism with the Communists is not a living thought. They have turned it into a dogma based on a book. Like the Ārya Samājists[236] they pin their faith in that book and take leave of both the existing conditions in a given place and their intelligence. Actually there should be a proper synthesis between the book, the conditions, and one's own reasoning. But they regard the book as their *Veda*. Had Marx been living today in India, he would have certainly changed his ideas. I tell the Communists that you may be Marxists, but Marx was not a Marxist. He was simply Marx and therefore he could change. The Communists have no knowledge of the ten thousand years of the development of Indian thought. Even assuming that this ancient Indian thought is defective in certain respects, its knowledge would still be necessary if only to know those defects. I therefore find that the Communists have two very serious defects: One, they are book-worshippers, and two, they are ignorant of the development of Indian thought.[237]

And now the words of Nehru, in this morning's *Statesman*.

The Prime Minister criticized the Communist and Marxist Parties in India and said that without understanding the problems of their own country they were trying to foster an ideology which was outdated and could not fit in here. They should first understand the problems of their country and try to find out a solution internally.[238]

Vinoba's ideals for society can be said to resemble in many ways those of the Communists: e.g. no private possession of land, no disdain for the laborer, or for the work of the hands, no more money for work than the worker requires for living, etc. etc.—but his fundamental belief that the *mind* must change first is diametrically opposite to theirs, that by a vigorous *daṇḍa-śakti* the true *loka-śakti* will be ushered in.

Had a visit this morning from Fabri, inviting me to dinner tonight. He introduced me to a young couple on a Ford Foundation grant, to study "India's Reactions to Federalism"—sounds a little obscure, but I think those are the correct words. "I suppose your husband has been studying India for some time?" I said to the young man's wife, and not without malice. "Well," she said, a little bit off balance, "we have been interested in India."

A happy letter from Jean at the American Express office today and a happier telegram from Tokyo, sent this morning: "Tokyo Lecture Recital, American Embassy, Monday; See you Tuesday; Love—Jean." How nice! How wonderful! That gives her a complete tour: San Francisco, Honolulu, Tokyo, and India (Ahmedabad, Baroda, Bombay lecture demonstration and Recital, New Delhi—and whatever else we may decide to arrange after she arrives). *The First Modern Dance Tour in the Modern Orient.* We've got to find some way to make this thing stick.

I went next to the Old Secretariat (only a few blocks, I find, from the Cecil) to look for Pramod Chandra, but found Y. C. Rai instead. Had tea with him and another gentleman, and talked about the dance. I found, to my pleasure, that Pramod and Krishnan are friends. I think this concert is going to catch the whole young crowd of New Delhi. I keep stressing the point that it will be the first example of a free dance form to be seen in India. Rai thought that we ought to publish and sell Jean's *What Is Modern Dance?* I think so too.

A wonderful thing about today! Jean's good break in Tokyo, and mine here: I've actually finished every single task hanging over from New York and today finished (completely) my list of left-over letters to write. I feel, for the first time since I can remember, completely released from dead *karma*—and the luncheon tomorrow with Nehru will sort of celebrate the occasion. I walked around all afternoon on air. India, in fact, seemed quite fine to me. In fact, I notice that when I travel India becomes bad, and when I stay in one place, it's O.K.

Friday, January 7

As I now look back over the ranges of my interest during the four months of my India journey, I find that during the first two months of my stay, I was largely among temples and swamis: the whole *religious* phase of the problem was the principal concern. The second stage of my trip was largely in the company of Salmony, and my chief interests were the *aesthetic and scholarly*. From now until Jean's departure, it will be the young and Westernized intellectuals and artists who will be our chief associates—whom I regard as the effective antipole to the world represented by the temple priests, *sadhus,* and swamis: what I may call, the *educational* aspect of modern Indian life is the chief focus here. In short, the problem of my concern has been, in these different spheres: *The impact of the modern (i.e. Western) age on the traditional forms of Indian thought and life.*

My original formulation was turned the other way round, namely: the operation of the traditional religious and philosophical forms in modern Indian life. The operation, I should say, in all parts of India is all-pervasive. The pattern, primarily is *bhakti,* which, in its outward form and probable emotional appeal is practically the same, whether the details of the cult are Vaiṣṇava, Śaiva, Jain, or even Parsee: one can say even that the Roman Catholic pattern of *bhakti* has here been somewhat Indianized. Islam stands apart: but again, the attitude is *bhakti.* As in the West, so here: the great question is whether the religious mode represented by *all* of these sects can survive (or should be encouraged to survive) the impact of the modern age. In so far as they stand for archaic scientific, moral, or psychological dogmas (superstitions) they will certainly be eradicated—not immediately, but gradually and naturally, as a result of the inevitable swing away from them of the educated. However, as supports of meditation—references out of the sphere of time and space to the "ground" of eternity, and consequently as supports of the individual battered by the waves of time—they deserve to be maintained—at least until in the modern pedagogical context an effective representation of the "Enlightenment-Redemption-*mokṣa*" experience can be rendered. The most important means of developing the modern vehicle of this experience, I believe, is that of creative writing and art: poetry, vision, metaphor, held in relation to the researches of psychology—and perhaps, also, physics.

In a way, when seen in this large context of the modern *vs.* the archaic, the problem is essentially the same as that of the West—except that our institutions of modern education are far in advance, both in their development and in their effect—than those of India. There is a special problem to be met in India, however, since the modern scientific world has not grown, by slow stages (as in the West) from the mother soil of the native religious tradition: it comes from without, as a quite alien graft. However, in compensation for this disadvantage, India has the distinct advantage of a transcendentally-based philosophical system, for which all temporal forms are equally secondary. Within the context of Indian thought itself the transition of the individual from *bhakti* to *jñāna* can be readily achieved, from theistic to non-theistic thinking: I should think it likely, therefore, that without too much of a jolt, the young modern Indian could be assisted from his grandmother's *bhakti* to his grandson's science; holding all the while to the stand in the transcendent. Possible indeed!—but honestly speaking, not likely. What is most probable is that the youth of India are going to have to work this thing out themselves—just about as the youth of the West have done and are doing—without much real help from their teachers.

For the old swamis, I find, hang pretty vigorously to what I am calling an archaic religion: a kind of melange of Victorianism and Hindu *bhakti*. An important attempt is being made to convert the archaic world-renouncing patterns into progressive, socially oriented ones; e.g. in the formulae of Vivekananda and Vinoba. But Ramakrishna and Vivekananda were Victorians, and their Victorianism remains imprinted on the Order for which they are the ideals; while Gandhi and Vinoba are primitivists, and their alienation from the inevitables of modern life makes for a kind of romantic escapism.

Let me take as examples of the young men trying to work things out for themselves, the young man in Bījāpur who had hanging on his walls, the figures of Jesus, T. S. Eliot, Krishnamurti, and Ramana Maharishi; also young Subrakhmanya in Bangalore, trying to carry on his art, with his soul in Paris; then the young people of the Bombay Theatre Unit; the young people I have met here in New Delhi (Pramod Chandra, Rai, Krishnan), and Fabri's wife, Ratna, who "does not believe in anything," and "can't take blows" (whereas, obviously, every peasant can).

What has the West to offer here, and what has India to offer the West?

I think the best lead to an answer to this point will be found in my discussions with Maiti in Ahmedabad: psychology (especially, I should say, of the Jungian school) and *ātman* (as an operative supplement to the hypothesis of the unconscious).

Certainly the social danger of India's orientation, however, is what Thomas Mann has called "the sympathy with death." The appearance of the meditating yogi in India as early as the period of Mohenjo-daro[239] points to a long experience here of the bliss (*ānanda*) of *samādhi*. And this has tended to support a romantical interest in renunciation as well as a lazy (heat-inspired) interest in doing nothing (retirement at the age of 55). The holocaust (one might say) of India's best minds—all in quest of *ānanda*— is something quite unique in the history of the world. In the periods of the great dynasties it was counterbalanced by a forcefully heroic attitude; but in modern India this counterforce does not exist.

Within the Indian philosophic systems there is ground enough for an affirmative attitude. It is questionable, however, whether it will ever actually take over. Zarathustra's reform, pitching the mind in the direction of an ethical as opposed to metaphysical dualism, was perhaps the first sign of the world affirmative penchant of the Occident (which finds its manifestation even in the monastic life of the Catholic Church, where a balance is insisted upon between works and meditation). Whether India is going to be able to develop an *ethos of hard work* (which is what Nehru asked for in a speech that he made the other day) without some kind of radical philosophical transformation, it is very hard to say. The Ramakrishna monks represent a sort of transitional form—but their *bhakti* is extremely reactionary, it seems to me. Whether anyone is working really intelligently and fundamentally on the problem I do not know: perhaps Radhakrishnan— but he is now in politics.

A series of phone calls this morning settled the matter of Jean's New Delhi recital. She will perform under the auspices of the American Women's Club and the New Delhi Unity Theatre with the Little Theatre Group assisting on the lights and staging. (At least, that's the way it all sounds. One must always remember that India has that other, hidden face.)

A little after noon I took a taxi to the Prime Minister's mansion—but since it appeared that I was arriving fifteen minutes ahead of schedule, I had my taxi driver let me off outside the gate and took a ten minute stroll. At the gate—click, click!—the guard; and a young man sitting at a table got up to approach me. Producing my invitation-card (which had arrived in this morning's mail), I was turned over to a military man in olive drab and a fine turban, who walked with me along the spacious, curving driveway, to the *porte cochère,* and there I was immediately greeted by Mrs. Krishna Hutheesingh, who conducted me up spacious stairways. The whole building is filled with mediocre examples of Indian art—mostly Tibetan bronzes—and large photographs of the chief temples—perhaps by the Bhulabhai Institute people. We arrived in Mrs. Hutheesingh's sitting-room and bedroom and were presently joined by others. Gimlets were served, all round: twice for some. We then were summoned, and, after gulping the last inch, went below.

The great English lawns and gardens at the back of the prodigious estate were to be our setting. Two tables were set—for fourteen.

The Prime Minister,[240] in his usual costume (white cap, brown jacket about to the knees, and tight trousers) came along the lawn with the Indian members of the party and shook hands graciously with us all, then led us to a cage containing a pair of pet Himalayan pandas, who turned out to be the principal ice-breakers of the occasion. Their cute, long, low hung bodies and long, long-furred tails, were a lovely russet, while their woolly legs and paws were black. They were delightful little animals, and when the Prime Minister, putting on a pair of heavy white gloves to protect his hands from their heavy claws, went into their cage and fed them, first bamboo leaves and then peas, the company was enchanted and the scene was that of the simplicity of the great. Actually, it would have made a sweet little picture.

Leaving the door open, so that the animals might roam at will, the Prime Minister next turned to a set of chairs around which we stood while some sort of fruit juice was brought to us for a cocktail; and then we all sat down. If I do say so myself, I was the only one who was willing to broach a conversation, and so the Prime Minister and I talked about *sadhus,* Buddhism, and the influence of metaphysics on Indian life, while the others sat, largely mum. I was particularly impressed by the three deaf-mutes representing the Ford Foundation, who, as soon as possible after the meal, shook hands all round and took their departure.

Mrs. Hutheesingh told me later that the Prime Minister had been in a particularly pleasant mood today. To me he seemed pleasant and courteous enough, but without very much life—way over on the weary side—and why not, with such a nondescript set of brushed-together companions.

But for me, it was a kind of great climax to my visit to India. The opportunity to meet and talk with the man whose anti-American attitude has been one of the strong experiences of my visit somewhat softened the sense of sheer animosity; and the opportunity to place on the level of human judgment a figure whose importance in the present world scene is perhaps paramount, gave me a new sense of the forces that operate in a world scene. Besides—it was a delightful afternoon.

I left the great mansion, again on foot, and strolled down one of the avenues to a taxi that I saw standing, and drove off to tell Mr. King that Jean's recital in Delhi now was definitely going to take place. "If it goes well," he said, "perhaps we could arrange a tour for her in India. How much longer would she be staying?"

This one almost did me in. Isadora Bennett had written to the Kings four months ago for a bit of help in building up a recital.

"Well," I said, very graciously; for Mr. King, while doing absolutely nothing, has been a very friendly and gracious man, "she will be leaving India for her job in New York within a couple of days." Then I recited the list of the recitals that I had arranged for her on my own, and he said he thought that that would be a very good showing.

I was to call for Mrs. Hutheesingh to go with her to the recital of Shanta Rao at Sapru House, and at the proper time I taxied to the Prime Minister's house, and after passing the challenge at the gate, drove to the *porte cochère,* feeling like an old friend of the family by now.

The performance of Shanta Rao seemed to me magnificent, and yet without magic. She is a powerful and splendid dancer, and, unlike all of the other Indian performers I have seen, made no attempt whatsoever to pretty up either the stage or herself.[241] The dances, as far as I could see, were not composed as carefully structured units, but were more like strings of beads, which could have gone on forever, had the audience the endurance: Shanta Rao certainly had the endurance; a couple of her dances went on for nearly forty-five minutes. Nor were the dances composed with any sense or need for a floor pattern. The dancer came in from the wings to upstage center, and then slowly worked forward to the edge of the footboard; whereupon that passage (or bead) would end, and in a slow, backward walk of rest, she would return to the commencing position of upstage center for another sequence. Neogy's words about the lack of beginning, middle, and end in Indian music would seem to apply to this dance art too. Moreover, as far as my experience went, neither the movements nor the facial expressions had very much feeling-value. They came and went, somewhat as tap-dance steps: and the principal comment of the Indian audience seemed to be one of sheer marvel at the woman's physical endurance.

The dancer had two costumes, one for the Bharata Natyam of part I of the program, and one for the Mohini Attam of part II. The latter, according to the program notes, is a dance form from Kerala that has become extinct, except for the bit preserved by Shanta Rao, who "happens to be the only pupil to whom this art form is passed on along with its special kind of music.... Mohini Attam means the dance of the Enchantress, and as such this is one of the most lyrical and subtle of the dance forms belonging to Malabar. The form is danced by women alone and is always danced solo." As far as I could see, it was not *very* different from the Bharata Natyam.

I was sorry that Jean could not be here, because it seemed to me that we were seeing something pretty sheer and straight. In the intermission, Pramod Chandra came up to me, where I was standing, in front of my super-duper seat—front row center—and expressed his delight in the performance: "This is *Vijayanagar*," he said; and I felt so too. But my two friends, the critics, Fabri and Krishnan, were of a negative opinion. (What are little critics made of?) They said that Shanta Rao's art lacked beauty and gentleness—was too athletic. Well, as one who had never seen Bharata Natyam decently danced before, I could have no opinion. It is, of course, one of the limitations of an academic art that will not allow much scope to the individual talent that has special qualities of its own; but it is my guess that in the lost days of long ago the *devadāsīs* must have been of the stuff of Shanta Rao.

Sunday, January 9

I have begun to feel a bit heavy-headed and I sat around sort of vaguely, till about five, when I went to the Ramakrishna Mission to hear Swami Ranganathananda give his Sunday talk on the *Gītā*. People from last evening's party arrived, reverently—and I felt that my India trip had now come full circle. The talk was good and clear, and was very well attended—Swami sitting cross-legged upon the platform and the audience cross-legged before him. I have heard all these ideas so often, however, that I now feel that it's surely time for me to be getting on to something else. Following the talk, I exchanged a few words with Swami (Nikhilananda and the ladies are sailing today from Bombay). Full circle indeed, except that now I felt that I was definitely on the *outside* of the monastery. Swami Nikhilananda, undoubtedly, had told them something of the secular turn of my interests during the course of the trip.

CHAPTER 4

Dance Tour with Jean Erdman

New Delhi

Tuesday, January 11

The day of Jean's arrival. I went in the morning to pick up a letter from Mrs. Hutheesingh, requesting the Customs Officers to let Jean through with her dancing gear; had a gimlet with the lady in her room in the Prime Minister's house and returned to the hotel for lunch. Next went to the Chandi Chauk[242] to look for flowers for Jean, but though I wandered about in the markets for over an hour, could find nothing but rather dead garlands. I went home, dressed for Jean's arrival, drove to the Hanumān Temple for flowers (Fabri's suggestion), and met Krishnan at the bus. We drove to the airport where I had arrived months ago: cool now. Jean appeared...customs...bus ride to the Imperial...taxi with Krishnan to Gaylords for a supper...Krishnan delivered at his home...and then home with Jean. A magical, strange and lovely, half-stunned, completely unreal world.

Wednesday, January 12

Fabri arrived in the morning and we went with him to Sapru House to settle the date for Jean's recital. We went with him next to Mr. Inder Das to arrange for the Little Theatre Group to take care of all the stage and lighting problems.

We had the Fabris, Krishnan, and the dancer Indrani Rahman and her husband to dinner with us at the hotel. A very pleasant party, with some rather interesting talk about the problem of composing music to dance and dance to music. Fabri began to sound like a European romantic rather fixed in his ideas.

Thursday, January 13

In the morning we went to the Cottage Industries Emporium, where Jean fell in love with everything she saw and we realized that we had a large operation ahead of us in the choice of objects for our friends back home.

Young Pramod Chandra and his colleague Rai came for lunch with us at the Cecil, and Pramod again was charming and certainly one of the most intelligent young men I have met in India. When they left, we spent an easy afternoon talking and planning before the fire in our room. In the evening we went to a dinner party given by Mrs. Adams, which had been described as an opener for Jean's recital propaganda; however, the majority of the people invited were simply Americans who would hardly have any interest in the matter or be of any use.

The others present at the dinner were Mrs. Hutheesingh, Fabri, Krishnan, and a Miss Sheilu, who will represent the Unity Theatre group in our joint project. I was greatly discouraged by what I heard this evening; for it appeared that Mrs. Adams and Miss Sheilu expected Krishnan, Fabri and myself to carry the whole responsibility of the concert—all that the American Women's Club and Unity Theatre were prepared to do was to supply their names at the head of the billing and accept the profits for their various purposes.

Friday, January 14

During the morning Jean and I drove about in a taxi, searching for the office that would give us tax exemption, only to learn, finally, that no exemption would be granted unless *all* the receipts (i.e. the gross) were devoted to charity.

Saturday, January 15

A letter from Mrs. Adams arrived this morning, suggesting that the Unity Theatre and American Women's Club should take over more of the work on the recital than originally planned by them: their names would appear as sponsors, and they were afraid that Krishnan was not competent to do a good job. Also, they wondered whether Jean would like a reception for the press, before the program. Actually, they had read the copy of the *Theatre Unit Bulletin* from Bombay, where the plans for Jean's Bombay recital are outlined, and they finally got the idea of what it means to be sponsoring a recital. Jean and I went over to see Mrs. Adams and discussed the matter. She presented us with a typed-out plan and everything seemed fine.

We went home for lunch and a rest, then, at four, we continued on to an open-air tea and reception given by Mr. Inder Das for Dame Sybil Thorndike and her husband. A very nice affair, where the fine old couple were presented with a hideous plaque of some kind, and made speeches. Her theme: that actors learn to sympathize with and to understand all sorts of people and that the theater is a dispenser of good will to men of many kinds (the Irish are more alien to the English than the Indians are, and yet the Abbey Theatre had succeeded in communicating to the English!). His theme: that India, before building a national theater, should wait to see what form of theater best suited the national consciousness (the old Shakespearean theater was a folk theater, with spectators on the stage; the Restoration, however, had brought an aristocratic theater, with a proscenium separating the audience from the stage: probably for India a folk theater in the round would be more appropriate than a proscenium).

We picked up Krishnan and drove to the Cecil, where Jean, Krishnan, Fabri and I had a meeting, preparing plans for the recital. Krishnan stayed for dinner with us. We packed in a great hurry and rushed to the train that was to take us to Jaipur, with Krishnan in attendance.

To my great displeasure, there were two gents already installed in the upper berths in the compartment that I thought had been reserved for Jean and me. I made a great noise. The conductor arrived and sold us an air-conditioned–class compartment for thirty more rupees. We transferred at the last minute and were safe for the night.

Sunday, January 16   Jaipur

An amusing day in Jaipur. The conductor rapped on our compartment door at about 5 A.M. and we hurried to dress and disentrain. It was still a bit dark. At the station a thin man held out a card that said Hotel Kaiser-i-Hind, and I let him pile us into a station wagon that took us to a nice little place, where an extremely cordial, burly fellow got up from his sleeping-shroud before the door, and showed us to a suite of rooms, then told us what our day was to be. Did we want to ride on the elephant at Amber, price thirty rupees? No? Well then, in the morning we should go to Amber and in the afternoon see the sights of Jaipur; we should have a guide; we should have the station wagon. Meanwhile, we should go to sleep till about 7:30 and then have morning tea and breakfast. And so it went. We seemed to be the only guests at the hotel, except at meal time, when a single, somewhat melancholy chap sat at another table in silence. Shortly after tea, we paid our bill, took our package dinner into our luggage, and piled again into the station wagon, to board the train for Ahmedabad.

Monday, January 17   Ahmedabad

It was quite a night. Again we had a compartment for four, and I was determined that we should have it alone; so, as soon as we entered, I pulled up the blinds and bolted the doors. We ate our package dinner and retired early; but at intervals during the night there would be a banging at the door. Once I opened, and a conductor asked for the numbers of our tickets, then left us alone. The bangings went on, but I did not open again.

   We arrived in Ahmedabad at 11 A.M. and were met at the station by the household manager of the Sarabhais. It was a fine feeling I had, being back

Jean Erdman and Alexander Calder

again in this lovely place—and Jean was enjoying it too. We were installed in the room next to the one that I had occupied before, and for lunch we went around to Gautam's house, where we found Kamalini and the Calders (Alexander Calder, the mobile man, and his wife).[243] A charming lunch out under the trees; after which Kamalini drove us to the Gymkhana Club, where Jean is to perform tomorrow.

My own chief problem now is to get that darned program written for the Bombay recital. Once again, I have had to shut myself into the Ahmedabad bathroom to write. We went out to a neighboring mansion to see a large wedding dance and show held in a great tent: dull dancing of *jeunes filles de famille,* but a colorful company—outshone, however, by the color of Calder's shirt.

Tuesday, January 18

The day of Jean's first recital in India. I worked all morning on the Bombay program notes, while Jean had her work-out at the Gymkhana Club, where she is to dance. The recital commenced at six, with Jean giving a lecture on the modern dance that went on till seven; then the recital began:

Upon Enchanted Ground
Ophelia
Creature on a Journey
Passage
The Transformations of Medusa
INTERVAL

Lecture on modern dance, repeating *Creature* as an example; then:

Changing-Woman
Bagatelle

The recital ended at about nine, and we went to Gautam's place for dinner. Finis at about midnight. A lovely day. A warm reception for Jean, and, now, a feeling of relaxation all round.

Wednesday, January 19

In the morning Kamalini drove us and the Calders over to Mrinalini's home for a wonderful day of Bharata Natyam and Kathakali. During the forenoon we watched a rehearsal of Mrinalini's group. I found a good deal more here than I had found in Shanta Rao's performance. Mrinalini has a better sense of stage than Shanta Rao, and so has made her works considerably less stark than those that I saw in the Sapru Hall recital.[244] On the other hand, the vigor of the Bharata Natyam was still here: the choreography and the well-rendered facial expressions made it all seem less harsh than the vigor of Shanta Rao. The first two dances were Bharata Natyam, and then, came the thrill of the day: Chatunni Panniker's Kathakali. He danced in his dhoti and shirt, not in costume; and this gave us an opportunity to experience directly the character of his work as dance. The first piece was a hunter's account of his having seen an elephant seized by a serpent and slain by a lion; the second was a group work, including Mrinalini and her three girls, telling the tale of Nala and Damayantī.[245] As Mrinalini pointed out, in Kathakali the male roles are very strong and the female very gentle, whereas in Bharata Natyam the female dance is almost masculine in its strength.

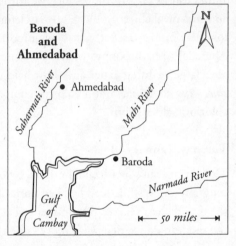

Panniker showed us in detail the posture of the Kathakali—which is danced on the outside edges of the feet, not on the soles, and involves an extraordinary hyperextension of the back. The facial movements are tremendously effective, and the pantomime hits a new level of significant stylization. It is a perfect art for the rendition of myth and fairy tale—and perhaps also for *any* narrative. All that is required, it seems to me, is a creative imagination to carry the style across the modern field of observed experience as it has already been carried across that of the south-Indian peasant world.

A problem that we discussed a little was that of the possible development of the traditional Indian dance in a modern world. It seems to me that as long as the Indian mythology supplies the foundations of an important part of Indian life, this art will be relevant. To be modern, however, an aspect of, or point of view toward, the great motifs will have to be revealed that will be relevant to the problems of the contemporary in his attempts to hold himself in balance between the archetypological stress of the past and the individualistic stress of the present. For example, the attitude of Rāma to Sītā can be rendered questionable through a stress on the personal relationship of the mythological pair. Certainly the Kathakali (which now seems to me to be a much more important and wonderful art than the Bharata Natyam) is well fitted to move in such a direction. To begin with, the mythological costumes could be removed immediately, the personal, human factor would be unshelled.

A more general problem that seemed to me to be greatly illuminated by my experience today of the Kathakali is that of the function and power of *style*. The style itself is the function of a standpoint, and it functions as a "mirror held up to nature," from that particular standpoint or position. Everything that can be brought into its frame is freshly seen from that position—freshly experienced and newly understood. The problem of an artist who is striving to create within the frame of—or rather, on the plane of—a certain given style, is to expand its range without breaking or spoiling the surface. The problem, on the other hand, of the artist creating in the spirit of a completely modern mind, is to find styles that will define new positions: Nietzsche's "perspectivism," in contrast to the single-stance position of an academy or dogmatic canon.

Following the rehearsal, we had lunch with Mrinalini and her husband, Vikram, then went home for

Member of Mrinalini Sarabhai's dance company

a brief rest, and returning at four, found the company on the roof, in full costume, for pictures.

Following our day at Mrinalini's we were taken to a large wedding reception—for which I donned my white-jacketed tuxedo (dating from my first visit with Jean to Hawai'i and carried with me on my present trip to no great purpose). The reception was at the home of a wealthy brahmin family whose daughter is marrying a young man of inferior caste who is a great cricket player. They are both university graduates and they met at college. The crowd was immense, and we stood around for a while meeting people—among whom were a few from my earlier visit to Ahmedabad: and then we watched part of the ceremony from close range.

Jean and I had dinner this evening with Bharati Sarabhai in her rooms. The conversation—which gradually subsided as Jean began to fall asleep— touched, among other matters, that of the problem of the contemporary

Member of Mrinalini Sarabhai's dance company on the roof of the Sarabhais' Ahmedabad house

Indian theater. Bharati is associated with a theater group in Ahmedabad, and holds it against Alkazi's Theatre Unit that all of their plays so far have been European and in English. She finds that though she has been brought up speaking English, the language does not carry the full meaning of her thoughts and feeling: it is not fully appropriate to Indian life: therefore, a theater in the native language must be developed. She is writing in Gujarati.

And so here we have another aspect of this complex problem of modern Indian art and thought. In the dance it is ancient *vs.* modern; in literature it is also English *vs.* regional languages *vs.* Hindi—a perplex indeed.

Thursday, January 20

I spent the whole day at work on Jean's program notes. In the early evening, a charming party at Kamalini and Gautam's, where a large company of invited guests were shown two films about Calder's work (one with music by John Cage) and then were invited to have fruit juice and snacks in a garden where Calder mobiles were hanging from the trees.

Gira Sarabhai, who seems to be the chief patroness and protagonist of Calder, Bauhaus and *l'art moderne* in Ahmedabad, challenged Jean on the position Jean had taken with respect to the future of the Kathakali style. According to Gira, every attempt to develop the Kathakali into a modern art was only destructive of its proper character. The art survives and can survive only in the villages of the south, where it exists as a popular form. It and its world are completely apart from the modern. Modern man must seek his art in modern art. The only possible relationship of a modern mind to the mythological art of the Kathakali is that of modern man to a museum piece. Gira, apparently, is completely at odds with Mrinalini on this point.

Following the Calder event, we all went back to the wedding party of last evening for the great dinner of the day following the rite of the marriage. The bride and groom, who last evening were seated in a little central pagoda, while everybody else sat in chairs to watch the long rite but actually sat only briefly, to indicate that they had accepted the invitation, now were seated before their dinner on little platforms before the pagoda, and the whole company of about four hundred sat likewise on little platforms all around the walls of the garden. Calder couldn't cross his legs and so devised a position for himself with his dinner tray on the ground before him and his legs at either side. "I feel," he said, "as though I were driving a sulky." We had to eat with our fingers and, for the most part, made out pretty well. The host and hostess were generous to our peculiar plight, and on the whole, the adventure came off pretty well.

A curious day—of traditional India and the modern U.S.A. As far as I was concerned, the Calder films and John's musical accompaniment were something of a bore: a *merely* aesthetic game of effects—like the twinkle of light on a pond, I did not feel that there was much to be said for it, and certainly Calder himself had nothing to say for it except that he enjoyed making mobiles. He has told people, also, that he did not find Elephanta interesting: but, I dare say, if one were to declare that his mobiles were utterly uninteresting he would feel that his critic was somewhat less than bright. I think it's wonderful to know that Alexander Calder, America's mobile master, did not find Elephanta interesting. In diametric contrast, one can take the position of Alfred Salmony, who found anything created after A.D. 1400 of no interest. Gira, so to say, is in both positions; or rather, represents the negative of both positions: the past is interesting for museums, modern art (including Sandy Calder) for modern life. My impression of the Indian reaction to Calder's art was that it was not enthusiastic. "Our vendors," said one lady, "do similar work."

Friday, January 21

I'm still at work on the notes for Jean's program. Geeta took a copy of the first portion with her to Baroda for Jean's concert there. Jean and I had breakfast together on our own verandah, then set off with Gira, Kamalini, Gautam, and the Calders, to the great Friday morning cattle market. A wonderful sight—and we, a wonderful sight for the shepherds and herders who followed us in droves everywhere we moved.

Gautam then drove us to his factory and Gira took us to the Calico Museum. Later in the afternoon, Jean went shopping with Kamalini and the Calders and I was called for by Dr. Trivedi (of my last visit),[246] to be driven in his disintegrating Citroën to the home of another gentleman. While I drank tea, the gentleman splurged his Sanskrit, asked what I knew about the Vedas, and read to me a speech that he had once given, wherein he bemoaned the crass materialism of the modern West and celebrated the saints and spiritual traditions of India as the coming salvation of a crumbling world. When he stopped, I said, "Well, you have been pretty severe on the modern world!" He laughed, and we had a pleasant conversation. Then he assigned his son to me—an intelligent youth with a little fuzz of beard—to show me his house in the town, "a typical Gujarati home." I admired the cow-dung floor of one of the rooms, the fine court, the pots and pans, and a carved wooden table, supported by a carved wooden camel, "all of one piece."

The young man asked me whether I thought the history of the next one hundred years would be determined by the East or by the West—a theme, he said, which had been debated in a Cambridge *vs.* India debating contest. I said I thought the West—since the principal need and determining factor in the world today was the development of the machine, of industry, of dams, irrigation projects, etc., in which development the West is the leader, beyond question. This he conceded, but, he said, the raw materials are largely in Asia and if Asia wishes.... The car pulled up before the house that we were to visit and the subject was lost.

But I felt again, beneath all of the sincere cordiality and personal friendliness of my host and his son, the profound run of hatred against the West, brought to focus specifically on the United States as the primary representative of the new world that is coming—willy-nilly—to transform the timeless, ageless repose of this otherwise fairly stagnant world. The main themes of reproach are: The atom bomb; divorce; spiritual restlessness (greed for gadgets); materialism (greed for money); support of the European imperialists (who, ironically, are now better loved than we); support of Chiang Kai Shek (a desire for war); a desire to impose our will on the domestic policies of nations (Formosa-China problem again). Not a word of reproach have I heard against Russia throughout the five months of my visit.

Dinner, tonight, was at Gautam's "farm": our final dinner in Ahmedabad. Mr. and Mrs. Sarabhai were present, and on the drive out Mr. Sarabhai asked me what I thought of India's political position; did I think, as *Time Magazine* did, that the Prime Minister was a Communist. "Nehru is not a Communist," I said, "but in the International field he supports the Communist position against the Democracies every time." "He believes," said Mr. Sarabhai, "that one nation should not try to impose its ideals of government upon another." "On that point," I answered, "I believe we all would agree." Then I changed the subject.

Mrs. Sarabhai was particularly fond of this older, more Indian house of Gautam's. "This," she said, "is Gautam *before* he went to America." It is a lovely house, full of Indian carved woodwork, and with cow-dung floors. We had a handsome dinner, and then returned to Gautam's post-America house (Bauhaus, Museum of Modern Art), where we played some of Jean's records, coaxed Jean to dance her *Portrait of a Lady,* helped her decide what sari to buy for Ramona in Colorado, and finally said good night to all.

Finis Ahmedabad, and I finally got the program notes into the mail.

Saturday, January 22   Baroda

We had breakfast on the verandah before our room. Mani and Gautam arrived to say good-bye; we got into the station wagon and were driven to the station. The train arrived in Baroda at about eleven, where we were met by Geeta at the train and driven to her home: a nice big house with pleasant rooms. Immediately we were taken to see the hall and stage where Jean is to perform at the Maharaja Sayaji Rao University. It's a fantastic little stage with a concrete wall dividing it from its own proper walls.

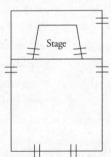

Jean looked over the situation, and we met Anjali Mehr, dancer, who is in charge of Jean's event; also the sculptor Shankho Chawdhury, who took us to his home to meet his father and his wife, and then tried to scout out a tape recorder for Jean's music. The town is very busy today with an important cricket match, and so we had to drive around a lot to find people. Everything moving very slowly. Chawdhury was very cordial and helpful. During the afternoon, Jean took a workout in Geeta's living room, and before dinner Geeta and her drummer gave Jean a lesson in the principles of Indian drum-beats.

Sunday, January 23

Breakfast, then Jean's lecture at ten. She did an excellent job. We then worked at the theater, and, before lunch, I fixed her recorder tapes so that there should be no need to swap reels around during the recital. We got to

the theater and had to wait till almost too late for the tape recorder to arrive with its operator. Then we had a brief run-through for cues and lights
and at 6 P.M. the recital began.

Salutatio
·   *Ophelia*
Creature on a Journey
Passage
The Transformation of Medusa

INTERVAL

Changing-Woman

INTERVAL

Upon Enchanted Ground
Pierrot, the Moon
Bagatelle

The recital lasted two hours and five minutes, and Jean was terribly
tired after the second interval. We decided that for the next recital she
should omit *Upon Enchanted Ground*.

The hall was filled and the response excellent, with lots of autograph-
seekers on the stage. The people who had been at last night's party came
up and from their remarks it was apparent that Jean's lecture of the morning had helped considerably toward their understanding of what they saw.

We got packed and returned to Geeta's place for dinner—and were interrupted by a gentleman who arrived with his twenty-two or -three-year-
old daughter, the latter wishing to learn from Jean how to fall, and the
former coming to tell us about his son who has been in America for seven
years. The son's universal religion, we heard, goes beyond Theosophy: it is
kind to all things, and not only all beings: one is kind, for example, to furniture. The man was very silly and sweet, and invited us to tea tomorrow.
Shortly after his departure, we turned in for the night.

Monday, January 24

We went to the Baroda Museum in the morning. Fine collections: wonderful bronzes (a Ṛṣabhanātha from c. A.D. 450 in particular) and a fine series of late Gupta stone pieces from Idar. We stayed for about an hour and
a half, then went out and sat under the trees until the car arrived.

After lunch we went to a dwelling in the town to see Anjali Mehr rehearse her program of Bharata Natyam for a recital Wednesday night. She did one of the dances that Shanta Rao performed— less magnificently, but with her own charm. Her *gopī* dances were particularly charming. But I have begun to feel a bit bored with the same old themes returning in the same old way, again and again. Before her dance she saluted the earth and the room, with a quick little ritual gesture. The rhythms of her feet were particularly good, and her facial expressions the best I have seen so far.

Joseph Campbell with a prop from *Pierrot the Moon*

We next went to tea at Mrs. English's place and met a curious American, a social scientist from Columbia, here on some kind of exchange arrangement; has lectured all over India under the auspices of the U.S.I.S. on American and Indian Education on such subjects as "What is an American?" When I asked him about the first theme, he said that in Indian education there was an almost complete lack of criticism: the students simply accepted what the professors told them and the professors were overly soft on the students.

He next went on to tell of other ideas that he had for the Indians—all implying a criticism of India. He complained, for instance, that in India he was never accepted or befriended as he would like to be, but always in terms of a category of some kind; he never felt that people liked him for himself. Well, actually, he was not a particularly likeable chap: friendly as could be, but his voice was harsh and his speech aggressive. Can the U.S.I.S. not find more attractive Americans to send around in advertisement of the American man?

This whole problem of the official picture of America presented to the Orient is one that ought to be carefully reviewed. Businessmen, politicians, industrialists, and experts (educationalists included), are not always the most agreeable human beings. The U.S.I.S. office in Delhi had stacks of pictures of the U.S.A.—farmers with ears of corn, etc.; factories, and what-not. What not?—not anything having to do with American art and music and literature. We tend to export machines and machine men; our U.S.I.S. should present the other side of the picture.

Geeta had another company for dinner: the American-trained Indians this time. All are in the Social Work College: they do not mix well with the English-trained group, and they had not much appreciated Jean's recital. But they were a very nice lot, and we had a pleasant evening. Geeta feels that America is not good for young Indians. They come back with all the superficial wildness, she says; and they are thrown off balance by the wide difference in morals. English ideals are closer than American to the Indians: besides, they are used to England, and in England the donning system keeps them under surveillance—they do not run wild.

Jean Erdman Campbell with a prop from her dance *Pierrot the Moon*

Among the guests was an older gentleman, a medical doctor, who caught my ear and talked it off, but let fall a number of good ideas.

Though the final insights of Indian philosophy are not life-negating, the general tenor of Indian moral ideals is negative, and these ideals have tended to keep the main run of Indian thought going in a negative direction. (This idea supplements my observation of the negative disposition of Indian thought, even in spite of its positive possibilities.) The man who seeks release is actually following a desire, and so is not really negating his desires. He is only subordinating his many lesser desires to his one major desire.

Dharma is not really a negation of individual desires either; for *dharma* is an expression of man's desire for social approval. *Artha, dharma, kāmā, mokṣa,* thus, are all manifestations of the human will to life.

The doctrine of the *Gītā* is a positive doctrine; the negative reading is the consequence of a misreading.

Hinduism's affirmation of the divinity of life is what lies behind the obscene images in the temples.

The party ended at about eleven. Our train was to leave for Delhi at 2 A.M. The remainder of the evening, therefore, went into packings and departures.

Tuesday, January 25   **Baroda to New Delhi**

The Frontier Mail, Baroda to New Delhi, six hours. We had a second-class set-up again (no air-conditioned class available), and there were two gents in the upper berths. But everything was managed decently, and one of the two left the train at 6 A.M. The other was a strange chap with a very high, thin voice, who spent most of his time neatening out his things. He was on his way from Ahmedabad to New Delhi just to see the Republic Day celebrations.

In New Delhi, there was no letter from Mrs. Hutheesingh: no tickets for the Parade Stand and Reception tomorrow. Great disappointment, so we tried to phone Pupul Jayakar, but there was no answer.

Wednesday, January 26—Republic Day   **New Delhi**

There was lots of early-morning noise outside from hundreds of tongas, full of families, trotting to the parade areas. I phoned the Prime Minister's house to ask about our tickets: no help. So we went off at 9:00 A.M. to stand on Curzon Road and wait for the parade to come.

Jean was not feeling very well: something about her stomach: result, perhaps, of yesterday's lunch. So the whole parade thing was a bit uncomfortable. The best events were the camel corps and the elephants. Almost all of the bands played Scotch bagpipes. One brass band was on horses. The parade lasted for about an hour. We returned to the hotel and I got in touch with Mrs. Adams.

A little problem has developed in the matter of Jean's recital. While in

Ahmedabad I received a letter from Mrs. Adams complaining of Fabri's high-handed assumption of authority: she offered to withdraw. Krishnan has managed to appease her, and at six we went around (Krishnan and I, while Jean continued to sleep) for a meeting. Sheilu (the Unity Theatre woman) was there, and several others. The Adamses arrived in full dress from the reception (which Jean and I should have attended too) and we got down to work: straightened everything out, and went off with Sheilu, whom I invited to dine with Jean, Krishnan, and me at the Volga. Pleasant evening at the Volga and in Sheilu's Greenwich-Village–like apartment.

She teaches English literature at Indrarastha College, and has never studied in Europe or America; yet her attitude and style of intelligence is quite Western. In her room hang two pictures in a modern style—and they did not seem more out of place here than their counterparts in a Midwestern or New York apartment. It seemed to me that young college and university people throughout the non-Communist world must be facing just about comparable problems. At dinner she spoke about the problems of literature in India.

As a consequence of the introduction of Hindi, English is deteriorating; Hindi also is deteriorating (since it is being spoken now by multitudes who have just learned it); and the regional languages are deteriorating. India is becoming a nation without a well-formed language.

French, German, Spanish, and other European literatures are studied only in special language classes. American literature, too, is hardly known. There is nothing like our comparative literature courses in India. The link with the West is primarily via England.

Sheilu's own library resembled that of almost any young student of literature in America. We saw lots of Modern Library Giants and similar editions, which used to be cheap here, but now are hard to buy.

Thursday, January 27

Krishnan arrived at breakfast time, and up we went to Fabri's, to settle his side of this recital affair. All went very well. Finally, at four, I managed to get in touch with Mr. Jayakar at his office, only to learn that he had gotten us tickets for tomorrow's folkdance, not tonight's, and that the Prime Minister's house had been trying for two days to get in touch with me and deliver the Parade tickets. Everything, for a moment, seemed a mess. I drove to the National Stadium and bought two tickets for tonight, and when I returned Jean told me that Jayakar had phoned again and we were set for tonight.

We got to the crowded stadium in good time. A rich and beautiful evening of folkdances, after which we went to the Gymkhana Club for dinner. The dances gave one a fine sense of the wealth and variety of India's cultural life. The groups were from:

Sikkim—Tibetan-like

Assam—*Nāgas:* like American Plains Indians

Rajasthan—Dandia Dance

Vindhya Pradesh—Tribal Karma Dance

Bombay—Goan Dakni Dance

Travancore-Cochin—a circle dance of girls (*Thiruvathirakali*)

Bihar—Tribal Oraons of Chhota Nagpur: girls in a row.

North East Frontier Agency

Madhya Bharat

Rajasthan—Drum dance—Large drums—(quite wonderful)

INTERVAL

Pondicherry—French Indian Ballet (to a Viennese Waltz!)

Punjab—Great cries from the Punjabi gallery

Saurashtra—Pole with strings—wind up, wind back

Madras—Harvest dance: scenes of harvest

Orissa—Jadur, to Barubonga, god of the Bhunrijas

Bombay—Lion Dance; from *Yakṣa Gaṇa* dance drama

Uttar Pradesh—Divali dance of the Ahīrs of Bundelkhand

P.E.P.S.U.—Punjab rainy-season dance

Himachal Pradesh—a Cossack-like group

Madhya Pradesh—Marias with their bison horns

Manipur—folk style

Hyderabad—Sidis (African style)

BOMBAY

Friday, January 28   **Bombay**

We are met at airport by Alkazi. Bombay is much hotter than New Delhi. I feel greatly at home, and enjoy bringing Jean to *my* hotel. Back again in

the Grand—my space-platform.²⁴⁷ And again I am to try to bring everything up to date. Jean's concert problems are now largely solved, but I have
let my diary and mail and other plan-making lag. I am going to try to bring
everything up even again while in Bombay, and press on, if possible, to
something new.

No sooner in our room than Ezekiel arrived with a copy of the January
30 edition of the *Times of India Illustrated Weekly*—one full page devoted
to Jean: great joy. Jean was really thrilled. Ezekiel went back to work, Jean
and I rested, and at 6:00 P.M. Ezekiel returned for tea and a drive to the
Bhulabhai Memorial Institute, where the Theatre Unit gave their final performance of *Oedipus*.

Monday, January 31

In the morning to American Express, to buy our air tickets for Madras, and
then to Laffans, where I ordered a suit made: I had a great sense of being
the leopard changing his spots. We shopped a bit in the Cottage Industries
Emporium and Jean went off for her work-out. After lunch we returned to
Laffans and I ordered a second suit. Tremendous day! Further work on my
diary until 5:15, when we had to begin preparing for Jean's first Bombay
event, her reception and lecture-demonstration at the Bhulabhai Institute.

A fine crowd of about one hundred and fifty was at the little place on
the roof, and Jean's talk was superb. Mr. Mehta was sitting beside me and
leaned over to say: "Lucky there aren't many of these talking dancers going
around; for we bookmen would be completely discredited. Why, she's
wonderful!"

Tuesday, February 1

All morning arranging matters for Jean's recital: recorder, practice time on
the stage, slide projector, U.S.I.S. pictures; and, at 1 P.M., back for lunch.
The whole U.S.I.S. set-up is really pretty funny: a large building, lots
of people, but no clear program for cultural (as distinguished from political) propaganda. In fact, no-one in the office knows very much about
American culture. Alkazi is trying to set up a photographic exhibit of
the American modern dance in the lobby of Jean's recital, and so he went
around to the U.S.I.S. a few days ago to ask if they had any photos. They

offered ballet shots, and he had to explain to them that a new dance form has developed in America. He now has found some photos in the *Borzoi Book of American Dance,* and they are going to reproduce them for him.

After lunch I returned to work on my diary and at 2 P.M. (now) have arrived, at last, at the point of now. Thank god! I feel that I can go ahead now on my future instead of simply trying to catch up with my past. The Bombay space-platform is about to have served its full purpose.

Jean's discoveries about Indian music make clearer than ever the homology in Indian arts. Two prime matters are involved, the *tāla* and the *rāga.* Each is stated, and the work then continues in the manner of a *theme and variations,* the variations consisting of increasingly intricate, layer-over-layer developments of rhythmical and melodic intricacies. Compare the chapels of the temples of Mt. Abu.

We had an engagement to go visit a Manipuri dance school under the direction of the Jhaveri sisters (whom I had seen perform in the Indian National Theatre production in Ahmedabad). But before we left, a note arrived from a gentleman named Dinshah Malegamvala, who had read my *Hero,* had met Gregor[248] in Trivandrum with Sri Krishna Menon, and wanted to meet me. Mr. Malegamvala himself arrived right after the note, and we sat down for a chat.

Promptly at 5:45 the young men arrived who were to take us to the Manipuri *nartanālaya.* The special performance for Jean's benefit was cute and instructive: first the first year class went through its paces, then the second, then the third, then two prize students, then the Jhaveri sisters themselves, and finally the drummers (actually from Manipuri) in a sequence of about five dances, which came to a climax in the drum dance that I had seen these same fellows perform at Mrs. Sophia Wadia's. It was obvious after what we had already seen of the Indian dance, that Bharata Natyam is a *tāṇḍava* and Manipuri a *lāsya* form of the same art. Jean, apparently, has learned something important for the dance from the idea of the *tālas,* which are long enough (as our four-beat units are not) to permit a dance phrase to develop.

Wednesday, February 2

At five Dinshah Malegamvala arrived to continue the conversation of yesterday: he is an engineer, who began his spiritual quest in Sweden:

Krishnamurti and Krishna Menon are chief on his guru list. Krishnamurti, he thinks, lacks love; has an intellectual orientation; takes everything away from his disciples, gives them nothing to cling to, and then castigates them for clinging to him and not understanding. The Ramakrishna monks, he feels, did not have a sound guru, have run off the rails, and have no Vedanta in them. I slightly shocked the gentleman by telling him that I did not feel that I was searching any more, but was quite satisfied with the richness of the materials and life that I had found: that I was not seeking a guru, but that I should look for Krishna Menon when I go to Trivandrum.

At eight to the Mehtas' for a very pleasant evening. Much talk of art, Jean's talk, and Indian religion. Rama told of seeing Krishna Menon go into *samādhi* while watching Ram Gopal dance before an image. Rama also said that she thought I should see Krishnamurti: Mr. Mehta distinguished between Krishnamurti's intellectual and Krishna Menon's *samādhi* approach to truth.

We talked of Ānanda Mayī, and Mr. Mehta pointed out that she had given me the essence of India's teaching when she declared that in *mokṣa* there is no question of affirmation or negation (this is the counterpart of *saṁsāra-nirvāṇa* transcendence). Krishna Menon has pointed out, apparently, that peace of mind and *mokṣa* are not the same—that is, in the *guṇas* we do not have *ātman* experience. The calm mirror, however, reflects *ātman* more clearly, or rather, more obviously for the candidate. The problem of affirmation-negation, passion-dispassion, is one of the path, not of the realization.

Jean and I returned home at about eleven.

Thursday, February 3

Great tension these days over Formosa. Even Mr. Mehta, last evening, took the position against the U.S.A. Nehru in London is supporting the Communist claims. India, from top to bottom, seems to be for China in this thing.

Friday, February 4

Jean's Bombay Recital. Alkazi and the girl who was to be Jean's dresser arrived at breakfast time and drove us to the Jai Hind College Auditorium.

Everybody preparing gels for the borders; great work all day. There was a lull from eleven to three, however, while various people did various outside jobs. Late start for rehearsal, hence a couple of slips with the lights during the program. Just before the commencement of the show the Pierrot moon fell from its thin strings, adding a fine motif of strain to the whole affair. Full house, fine response. Gautam was present, to our surprise. There were farewells, and dinner in the Rainbow Room.

Saturday, February 5

Our last day in Bombay: busy and full of surprises. At ten Mr. Malegamvala arrived and took us to the studio of an excellent photographer, R. R. Bharadwaj, who had hundreds of beautiful shots of Indian temple art. After visiting Bharadwaj, we dropped in on Ezekiel for a brief good-bye and a cup of tea—and discussed a bit the position and work of the U.S.I.S. in India. He told of receiving scads of pamphlets full of speeches by Dulles and various senators. He told also of a handicrafts exhibit in November: third-rate items (no match for India's handicrafts) but a luxurious display, suggesting money, money, money. It made a very bad impression. Actually, the best propaganda for America among the intellectuals were the poetry readings of the Theatre Unit itself—first, of Marianne Moore, then of e.e. cummings. I went to the Bhulabhai Institute to pick up Jean's Pierrot moon, then off to the Gateway of India, to take a boat to Elephanta.

I managed to arrange for a fare of 35 rupees, plus a 5-rupee tip, and off we started. Lovely voyage. At the cave I attempted a few photographs and Jean went around looking at the sculpture. The Maheśvara, she said, scared her a little this time: it was like looking at God. I felt the same thing when I really stood and looked at it.

The sea was choppy, and on the trip home the motor conked out and we were left to drift; but, fortunately, a large launch came along and took us in tow. It went around to the other side of Elephanta, where a lot of engineering equipment was at work. The main occupant of the launch asked us to come in; then he got out, a lot more people got in, and I paid our stupid boatman twenty rupees and they acted as though they'd been shot. The launch started, and we were off for Bombay.

There was a vigorous Englishman aboard with a rich tan, who has been in India as soldier and as engineer since 1938. "Glad to be helping to build the new India." India had gotten into his blood. I thought of the many others of his type, unsung in India's official annals, who have been, and still are, teaching the Orientals how to work like modern man. They will never be appreciated.

MADRAS

Sunday, February 6   **Madras**

Yesterday the Swedish liner *Kungsholm* docked in Bombay with a load of millionaires and a number of them were at the airport—simple looking, oldish folks, flying today to various parts of India.²⁴⁹

At 12:15 we landed in Madras and were met by Mrinalini's sisters-in-law. We took a car to their compound, and found that we had a whole house to ourselves. We lunched, then continued on to a very colorful sort of National Fair, where we visited a number of the exhibits and watched the wonderful crowds. Madras is very different from Bombay and it's pleasant to be here again—darker people, tropical atmosphere, houses with lots of ground around them, palms and huts of thatch.

Mrinalini's brother we met at dinner time; they took us for a drive around town and at the big temple tank we saw the barge of the Goddess, shining with lights, being poled around the central shrine, where a statue of Śiva was placed in state. It was a lovely, crazy event, with a huge crowd to enjoy it. Tonight the barge goes five times around; tomorrow seven; and the next night nine (in honor of the full moon).

Monday, February 7

After breakfast we were off to see if the U.S.I.S. can arrange for Jean to give a recital in Madras. We met a Mr. Paul Sherbert (much like William King) who took a long time to tell us that nothing could be arranged.

At four we drove to the University to see Dr. Raghavan, who wanted me to give a talk; but I suggested that it would be more interesting if Jean should talk; so, immediately, what had been impossible this morning was settled. Tomorrow we shall go to the Kalakshatra School at Adyar and tomorrow evening to Bala Saraswati's school. Wednesday evening we shall see Bala Saraswati perform.²⁵⁰ Thursday evening Jean will lecture about

American creative dance at the Madras Academy of Music. Friday morning we fly to Delhi—the schedule is full.

At 4:30 we arrived at the Institute of Fine Arts, which is the dance school where the old master Chockalingam Pillai teaches. A delightful two hours and I think I have finally caught onto something about Bharata Natyam.

The dances are hymns in gesture and action—wooing the God, as Christian hymns do, but overtly. Each passage is one verse. The dances are those that were danced by the *devadāsīs* on the dance platform of the temples. Bharata Natyam ·is thus, emphatically, a religious dance—of a piece with the whole Hindu religious tradition. Performance for a public on the stage is comparable to the singing of Bach's hymns, or medieval hymns, on the concert stage—a major shift of values.

The student learning dance is simultaneously studying and practicing her religion. The strong erotic accent, referred however to the deity, amounts to a sublimation, and in marriage this accent is continued: the husband is worshipped as the god who was wooed. Indeed, he is experienced as the agent or earthly manifestation of the god. The whole sexual theme is thus archetypal—not personal. The effectiveness of this dance, when performed even by children, is constant in character.

There were at least four very good little dancers in the school. The secretary spoke English and explained in detail the meanings of the dances. We had a wonderful afternoon.

Late dinner with Mrinalini's brother's family, the Swaminathans— and to bed.

Tuesday, February 8

In the morning, to the Museum, for a look at the Amarāvatī panels and the bronzes: climax, the great Naṭarāja.[251] Then to the University again for a chat with Dr. Raghavan. Three themes: Indian Dance; Sanskrit, Hindi, and English; and traditional *vs.* modern values.

In the dance of India we have an art descending from the period of Mohenjo-daro.[252] Bharata Natyam was performed in the temples (it still is in some places); but was also a court dance, with different themes; the same dancers were masters of both arts, and were masters also of the art of the dance-theater.

In the first decades of the present century there was an anti-dance campaign; but this has been counteracted recently by an anti–anti-dance movement. Indian dance is greatly popular today, and consequently the forms have been debased, as we see in amateur dancers and movie dancers. The Madras Academy of Music represents the traditional standard, and seeks to maintain them, in spite of the contemporary tide, although many of the dance postures employed in the past are not used today: high kicks, etc. (These are considered unladylike: Dr. Raghavan seemed to approve of the omission.) Dance is an emanation of the spirit of music: dance, poetry and music are three facets of a single manifold. Jean added later: the sculptured *naṭarājas* that we had seen this morning were also related in beauty to the art of the dance.

Sanskrit poetry and drama are still being written, devoted to religious themes. Sanskrit is the core language of India's religious culture. In South India, there is resistance to Hindi; nevertheless, Hindi is more closely related than English to the spirit and character of South Indian thought and language. The resistance will probably break down.

English, however, is a vehicle of scientific thought; consequently, of great importance. But learning English as the major language does violence to the Indian thought-style, divorces the individual from his culture, and places him in a perpetually inferior position to the Englishman, who does not admire his English and represents to him a strongly critical factor. (I thought of the Irish and Americans outdoing the English in their own tongue and not caring a damn for the criticism—but held my peace.)

Raghavan's resentment of the West came out in his statement that our scholars, interested only in India's *ancient* philosophy and art, were trying to represent India as of no contemporary moment. He felt that Nehru's turning away from the past was a reaction against this archaization of India. (I did not mention my own feeling that modern India had nothing to teach the West.) Raghavan's resentment came out further in his contrast of the ancient Indian ideal of womanhood with the modern American. The ancient woman was the mistress of sixty-four arts: not only music and dance, but also cooking, household medicine, etc. His aunt was much better than his wife, who had to keep referring to doctors to cure the children. (I did not point out that in recent years the infant mortality in India had greatly decreased.) Maladjustment in marriage was in ancient

India exceptional, whereas in America it is the rule. And what, after all, does the modern, educated woman really know?

Rāma and Sītā decided to share equally the suffering of their separation in the name of their *dharma:* this ideal is in radical contrast to that of the contemporary world. I believe that this is a rather sophisticated rereading of the legend. Sītā was publicly spurned and there is no evidence of any such preliminary consideration and mutual decision as Raghavan's statement implies. I was amused to come across the Rāma and Sītā problem again. Apparently it is one that the Indians are having a hard time resolving.

Raghavan then pointed out, however (and here my own thoughts were echoed) that it was the work of the European scholars that awakened the Indians to the dignity of their own tradition. He believed that India's gift to the world would be the Vedantic *advaita* philosophy, which would transcend, yet at the same time support, all religions.[253] He declared, furthermore, that the great majority of Indian intellectuals were *advaitists.* The sectarian Vaiṣṇava pandits, etc., were a minority. He agreed with Coomaraswamy's position essentially to the effect that all Indian art and music and dance is essentially religious: he differed with the professors (Neogy, for example) who reject this view.

I felt again, beneath the wonderful cordiality of Raghavan, the anti-Western resentment. I feel it equally in the household that we are at present inhabiting, where it is curiously out of place; for these are extremely Westernized people. They speak of the very bad impression that the American army made; of the futility of modern medicine (whereas all are at present in the hands of doctors); of the futility of speed and modern methods (in their own bathroom, quaintly enough, in spite of the fairly modern plumbing, one has to bathe from buckets, as though at a village well).

Mrs. Swaminathan spoke with great disfavor of Aubrey Menen's *Life of Rama,* which she had not read, but about which there is, apparently, much talk in these parts. Raghavan's reference to Rāma may have been a reaction to Menen's book. Sacred things, she felt, should not be held up to mockery. No Voltaire for India. Apparently, Menen's book is about the first of its kind.

One can say, perhaps, that the crux of the West-East problem is in the mutual fascination and repugnance of India and America. As Zimmer pointed out, India came to a crossroad in the sixth century B.C. that we in

the West are just approaching: that of the step from dualism to *advaita*.[254]
But equally (and even more obviously) we in the West passed a crossroad
five hundred years ago, that India is now approaching—that of the ration-
alization of human life, which leads to the machine world of science and
the sense of a social conscience.

Raghavan spoke with fervor of the virtues of the great group family,
where a sort of social security was supplied to the ne'er-do-well. The great
fault of this system, however, was that the social conscience operated only
within the horizon of the family. The poor family was left to be poor.

At five we drove to the Music Academy to see Bala Saraswati teach a
dance class. We had been told that she was old and fat—actually, we found
a woman of about the age and plumpness of the people who had been
telling us she was old and fat: in her forties, and moderately sleek; very
likely what would have been found dancing in the temples in the older
days. The Music Academy, where she teaches, is housed in an old mansion.
Some of the officers were present; and before the classes started we heard a
good deal about the bad state of the dance in modern India: lots of people
who want to learn quickly, no-one willing to take the necessary time.

Bala Saraswati demanded three years of her student for the learning of
the fundamentals, seven years were required for the making of a perfect
dancer. She taught her little class of four with careful attention—and, immediately, both Jean and I could see that her approach to the task was much
more serious than that of the school that we visited yesterday. Attention was
directed exclusively to the feet and arms (no neck yet or *abhināya*). Steps
were executed in three speeds (six, on one occasion) and on all sides, in various rhythms. When the class was half over a tiny thing appeared for her special, introductory lesson in the movement of the feet. Bala Saraswati drew a
little rectangle on the floor in chalk, and the child tried to remain within it.
For about ten minutes she followed the counts, in the turned-out plié of the
Bharata Natyam. Then her lesson was over and she scooted from the room,
returned to say thank you to teacher, and scooted again.

Dr. Raghavan's daughter of seven years, who was the best in the class,
was a lovely little thing to see. She reminded me perfectly of one of those
apsarases in photographed frieze of Angkor Thom.

When the dance class was ended we drove to a large tent-covered area
where a great male singer was performing, in honor of the thousandth

anniversary of Avicenna.[255] The man's voice was considerably better than that of the chap who sang in Bombay, but his chief accompanying instrument was a harmonium—so that, finally, the musical tones were not particularly agreeable. On the way home, Mrs. Swaminathan talked of the music: how the singer had been sent a note requesting more popular, less classical themes, and so, had sung a series of *ghazals* in Urdu: the best language in the world for love poetry; and how, since the restrictions on action are so strong in the Orient, the whole weight of love gets into words.

Wednesday, February 9

We went in the morning to Adyar to the Theosophical Library, to meet Radha (dancer in *The River*) Bournier[256] and Danielou.[257] We had a pleasant talk in the main entrance hall around a little wicker table. Radha was a pupil of Chockalingam Pillai, and declared that he too could teach seriously, like Bala Saraswati; but most of his pupils want to learn in a year, and so he makes concessions.

We spent the afternoon napping and writing letters, then, at about 5:00 P.M., had tea on the lawn with Mrs. Swaminathan's sister, who accompanied us back to the Music Academy for an evening of dance by Bala Saraswati. A supreme event. Bala Saraswati had sent for her best drummer and musicians; her dance class and the members of the Academy were present; Jean was the chief member of the audience and Dr. Raghavan interpreted all of the performances for her. The recital lasted from 6:15 to 9:00. I could have sat for another three hours.

We learned, that, when performing *abhināya,* the dancer improvises verse after verse upon a theme (e.g. "she was beautiful") that is repeated *ad infinitum* by the singer. Another example of the Indian "Variations on a Theme" pattern of composition. Cumulative pantomime.

Thursday, February 10

Spent the morning shopping and writing letters. Jean practiced dancing a bit on the porch of the house we are inhabiting, and, at four, with the dance equipment in a bag, we went out to Adyar again to visit Radha and Bournier. Danielou came as company. They have a perfectly beautiful house on a beach, handsomely furnished. And I felt, for the first time since I've been in India (Ahmedabad, of course, excluded) that I had found a house in which it would be a delight to dwell. We had a very pleasant tea, during the course of which Bournier exhibited a beautiful camera that he had recently purchased, and then he drove Jean and me to the Music Academy, where Jean delivered her lecture demonstration before a company—seated on three sides of her—which commenced as a company of a dozen or so and ended with about fifty. Most odd was a bearded gentleman of seventy-two, who tried to tell us, when the talk was over, about some dance that he'd seen, where the dancer stood on a needle with the needle piercing his eyeball—or something of the sort.

Jean had been a bit scared about this lecture all day, feeling that Madras is the conservative center of the classical Indian dance; but she found a warmly sympathetic audience before her—including Bala Saraswati and her mother. She lectured for about an hour and then performed *Creature on a Journey* and *Ophelia*.

Mrs. Swaminathan then drove us to dinner at the home of a gentleman who had been in a Japanese prison camp in Burma during the war, had had one whole side of his face shot away and plastically restored, and now was married to an extremely Protestant lady with white hair. I found that I was in a veritable nest of Protestant zeal. When a queer gent named Alexandrovitch asked me what my subject was and I replied "Mythology, which for me means religion," a hot argument opened—mainly to the effect that Christian theology had nothing to do with mythology. "The creation and fall in the Garden of Eden is mythology," I replied. "But that is not Christianity!" the hostess said. "Theology is based on Aristotle: it is a science," said Mr. Alexandrovitch. Apparently, I had run into something really queer here: some Protestant notion of Christianity minus the motif of Fall-and-Redemption. These people seemed never to have heard of the Christianity of the Middle Ages.

Before going to bed we packed, in preparation for an early departure by plane in the morning.

NEW DELHI

Friday, February 11   **New Delhi**

At 2:45 A.M. there was a knock at the door: our bearer and his wife, who thought the time was 5:00 A.M. At 5:00 A.M. they knocked again and we got up. It has been a bit weird living in this house: two watchmen sleep right outside our windows and greet us like spooks every time we move in or out. Our hostesses were present to see us off. Mrs. Swaminathan even drove with us to the airport—all dressed up in her early-morning riding-breeches.

With pauses at Hyderabad and Nagpur, our flight arrived at New Delhi at 3:15. Bus to the Imperial Hotel, tea on the lawn. Letters and a rest. Then to Mrs. Adams's, for news of the plans that have been made for the recital. Apparently Fabri and Mrs. Adams have not been able to get along together at all—but the plans have nevertheless developed; as follows: tomorrow a lecture at the University, next day a reception and lecture at Lady Irwin College, and on Tuesday the great recital. Sheilu came to see us at the hotel just before dinner, and Jean—who had just discovered that she had left her black leotard, which is worn in the first dance on her program, somewhere in Madras—made a date with her for tomorrow morning, to hunt for material. The trouble is that in India they have no stretchy jersey: all of their clothes are made to be draped.

Saturday, February 12

We met Sheilu at the store at ten. I left them and went around to the U.S.I.S. office to have a chat with William King. He took me to the Alps for coffee and discussed the problem of the U.S.I.S. and A.N.T.A.²⁵⁸ Briefly, A.N.T.A. seems to be taking the lead from the Show Biz people in New York and is trying to use the U.S.I.S. as ticket agents for large companies that would be utterly useless in the Orient, for instance the Jubilee Singers or the N.B.C. Symphony Orchestra of ninety pieces—there is no place for them. Much better would be ninety separate artists like Jean. He wants me to send him a report of *our* findings in India. Also, he is interested in knowing more about the Bollingen Series for the U.S.I.S. libraries.

While Jean and I were having lunch in the Imperial Krishnan arrived in a highly emotional state and stayed with us while we packed and drove out to the Cecil. We hurried then to the University, where Jean gave a superb lecture demonstration to a group of about five hundred students at the University of Delhi. One of the lady teachers held a tea party for Jean right after the lecture, and we hurried then to the Kings' for a drink (Krishnan still at hand). The Kings drove us home, dropping Krishnan at Connaught Circle, and soon after dinner we went to bed.

Sunday, February 13

We managed to soothe the greatly ruffled feathers of our difficult friend Fabri when we arrived at his house at ten. Then we all moved on to Lady Irwin College, where Jean gave another superb lecture demonstration on the lawn. Among those present was our exchange student from Sarah Lawrence. "How do you like it?" I asked her. She shook her head. The restrictions are those of a girls' boarding school and the courses about on the high school level. Sarah Lawrence College has made a bad bargain here, I believe.

Tuesday, February 15

The great day of the recital. Jean and I got to the theater at about eleven and Jean had a good morning of dance. The rehearsal was supposed to begin at one but practically no one arrived. By two the man working the recorder wanted to go out for lunch. Jean and I went out with Fay King to have a good meal and Fay helped Jean with her sewing—donating a black zipper to the good work. We returned to the theater at four and I conducted a light and music run-through till 6:15, when we had to let the crowd into the theater. The house has been sold out for two days. About three hundred people were turned away at the door. Great pleas for a second recital were reluctantly ignored (no time). Jean danced greatly and had a good time doing it. Dinner, after the recital, was at the Adamses'. Finally we got home, delighted.

Wednesday, February 16

Narayan Menon in *The Times of India* gave Jean an excellent review. Fabri's, in the *Statesman,* was all messed up with a poor attempt to make connections between the Modern Dance and the Ballet. We went around to Fabri's after breakfast and he was all apologies, yet stated clearly the critic's credo: "Some day, Jean," he said, "I will write a good review of you, showing all that's good in your work and all that's wrong, and making suggestions." He complained that there was not enough mugging in *Ophelia* and spoke of various ballets where the facial expressions were as important as in the Indian dance. "My expression," said Jean, "is in my whole body."

Thursday, February 17

"Shall I stay?" said Jean. It was very sad, as though a hole had opened through the floor of our busily programmed life together to show the possibility of another level of relationship.

At nine Krishnan arrived with the bed roll we had left with him at the time of the Republic Day visit. Narasimhan arrived with a friend to present Jean with a carved box and take a photo of us. We had breakfast, finished packing, drove with Krishnan to Fabri's to pick up Ratna, who then spent the morning helping Jean shop. We left Krishnan at Jaipur House and bought tons of beautiful stuff. Then we had to buy a suitcase for Jean to carry it all home. Fabri arrived at the Cecil for lunch and at 2:15, breathless, we got into our taxi and drove to the B.O.A.C. office, where Krishnan met us, and saw us off on the bus. Long drive to the airport. Long wait in the airport. Plane departure at 5:10.

Jean was in her nice red Honolulu dress and we snapped pictures of each other while we waited. I accompanied her to the stairs to the plane. After she got aboard I could see her through the door until the stewardess closed it. Then the big thing taxied around and down the long track, turned, warmed up, and started. I watched it leave the ground, make a long U turn, and cruised away into the blue, until it became only a flashing dot and disappeared.

I went back to New Delhi in the bus. I went to the Volga for a farewell dinner with Krishnan, who was excessively emotional at the moment of parting. I drove Krishnan to his home and proceeded to the Fabris' for a farewell moment. Then home to pack, and to bed at two. I leave in the morning for Cochin, via Bombay.

Friday, February 18   **Bombay**

When I woke this morning my chief adjunct was a very heavy head cold. I arrived in Bombay at about two and I went directly to the Airlines office to buy my tickets to Cochin and through to Trivandrum—I am not sure yet to which one I should go first. Later in the afternoon I went to the Bhulabhai Institute for a farewell to the Theatre Unit crowd. They handed me three hundred rupees—Jean's share of the net (their share, 195). Ezekiel told me, also, of an attempt that John Cage is making to get himself, Merce Cunningham, and five others to India on an A.N.T.A. junket: promised support by Virgil Thompson. News for Jean!

CHAPTER 5

A Guru and His Devotees

Cochin and Trivandrum

Saturday, February 19   **Cochin–Trivandrum**

I caught the plane to Cochin at 6:30 A.M. At Cochin I asked to continue to
Trivandrum, where I arrived at about 11:30. I am definitely in the tropics.
At first I felt a slight spell of elation at commencing the next stage of my
journey. After lunch, however, I
took a rickshaw to the Post
Office, to mail my letter to Jean,
send her a wire, and post some
books to New York. I got tired
waiting to register the books—
everyone pushing in ahead of
me. I suddenly lost all my eu-
phoria, and felt sort of at the
bottom of the well: a fierce din
of loudspeakers all over town,
Indian music till I thought my
head would split.

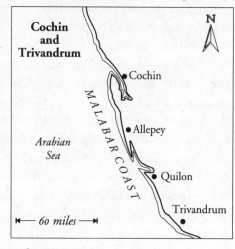

I took a nap and went to work on my diary. Later I took a walk to town to see what was making all the noise, and found an All-India Exposition in progress and several other events besides. I returned at 9:30 to bring my diary up to date, and now, at last, at 10:00 P.M. I am here. Jean right now (11:30 New York time) must be in the Customs at Idlewild Airport. Adventure finis.

Sunday, February 20—Jean's birthday   Trivandrum

What I had in mind, coming down here yesterday, was that I should meet Sri Krishna Menon. As soon as I arrived, however, I realized that I did not know where or how to get in touch with him. I realized, also, that if I am going to see Cochin, I should have stopped there on the way down. All of these mistakes gave me the feeling that I had begun to make mistakes— that is to say, had run off the rails. Furthermore, way down here, all of my pleasant Indian connections are broken. I have only the name of Nissim Ezekiel's brother in Cochin and a friend of Jason Grossman here in Trivandrum. I don't know what I expected to find when I set out on this southern spree, but certainly, if I had thought twice I should have proceeded more carefully and written ahead.

However, this morning, in spite of the heavy cold in my head, I feel that it may be possible to make something out of this wrong move, after all. Today I shall simply do the regular tourist act: visit the town and take a drive to Cape Comorin. I have dropped a note to Grossman's friend, who will receive the note tomorrow. And meanwhile, tomorrow morning I can pay a visit to the U.S.I.S. office, to see if they can help me discover the wise man, Sri Krishna Menon.

The hotel in which I am staying takes me back in feeling to the first stages of my India journey—though it is definitely more tropical in atmosphere than anything that I have encountered so far. Yesterday, while flying, after our plane had come down for a brief pause in Belgaum, I had a strong sense of the change in the world below. The predominant tone became green, instead of dust, and there were acres of neatly squared off rice fields—but no villages. Instead, the houses were scattered among the fields—more as in America than as in Europe. Wooden houses, wooden temple compounds, became prominent, and palms, palms, palms, were everywhere.

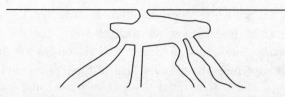

Over Mangalore, I could see the harbor that St. Thomas is supposed to have entered; the harbor that the Romans must have known: a break in the endless beach at a point where four or five streams converge to enter the sea. And over Cochin I beheld a most remarkable landscape: thousands of acres of palm gardens, geometrically marked out in rectangles, and flooded, it seemed, with great sheets of water: the closest thing I have seen to the air view above Basra. There the palms were date; here coconut.

Trivandrum is a rather large, pleasantly clean city, and the Mascot a neat, orderly hotel, with its two floors of rooms strung along a long, two-storeyed verandah. The populace of the hotel is of two kinds: one, very silent, solitary business people from Europe, America, and India; the other, very silent, spiritually shocked Americans, here, undoubtedly, to be cured by the sage of Trivandrum. All have elaborate food taboos, which are driving the hotel proprietor to distraction. The male and female at the table facing mine were seen to eat only raw vegetables and fruits, but they feed their tiny, hairless dog red meat. The stunned gentleman whose room is not far from mine on the top balcony, and whom I have seen sitting with his eyes closed, holding a thin book of what look like translated *slokas,* will eat practically nothing at all. Eggs, apparently, are taboo to him, and so he can't even eat pudding.

After breakfast I went around to the Indian Airlines office to pick up a taxi that had been arranged for yesterday evening: I was to see the town in the morning and drive to Cape Comorin in the afternoon. I found, however, that my driver had no notion of what to take one to see in the town, and so I settled for the zoo and the museum, only a couple of blocks from the hotel.

The zoo was a pretty but pitiful affair, full of sad and solitary bears, tigers, snakes, etc., in excessively smelly cages. One leopard, who had been only five days in captivity, was still full of spirit, however, and snarled and pounced really mightily, when the guard annoyed him. The lion next door would answer commands like a dog. And the largest of the tigers was permitted to go down into a grassy yard and roam as though wild.

The museum had a fine collection of bronzes, undated, including two figures that seemed to me most remarkable: a very tall and thin Śiva Ardhanārīśvara,[259] and a Śiva carrying a dead *satī* on his left shoulder. I bought the only pictures the museum had of these pieces, but they are very poor.

At two, I commenced my drive to Cape Comorin, somewhat frightened by the fierceness of my heavy cold, but gradually improving in spirits as the drive proceeded. The land and village world remind me of Hawai'i and what I have seen of African photos: typical coconut and palm-thatch country. The bullock carts, however, were typically Indian, only filled now, with coconuts and coconut husks. On the left, as we drove southward, were the high mountains, at some distance.

The first, very interesting, stop was at a great palace, in the particular style of this part of the world, called Padmanābhapuram. The supervisor took me all through the long corridors and up the narrow stairs to the various chambers. An architecture of wonderful woodwork (teak and jackfruit), supplemented in certain parts by columns of stone, shaped and carved to resemble the wood. It dated from the fourteenth to seventeenth centuries.

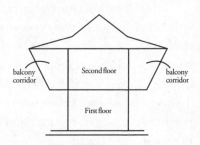

In the audience chamber the king sat with four ministers. And in a series of paintings in one of the corridors, the king was shown, weighing himself against gold (his weight in gold was then distributed to the brahmins), and going to bathe ceremonially in a huge golden jar.

The palace is immense, and part of it, now, is a museum containing some interesting examples of South Indian stone and wooden sculpture. Most unusual: a form of Kālī as the killer of children, biting off the head of a child; also, Nandi with human torso and legs, seated; and a large Kubera, looking very much like the late Javanese *yakṣas*.

My second stop was at the temple of Sucindrum, where one of the several *pandas* opened a shed to show me the vast, nine-wheeled, elaborately carved wooden car and sold me a fantastic pamphlet, *The Holy Account of Sucindrum, or the Triumph of Chastity*, containing the legend of the origin of this place.

Finally, I arrived at Cape Comorin, "the Land's End of India," had tea in the pleasant rest house, bought a few photos, and strolled down to the shore. The big thing here is the sunset. And as I walked to see it, I was greeted by a Spanish-looking couple named Lopez, he being chief police inspector of Trivandrum. This man was charming and cordial—a Catholic. More than 25% of the population in this area is Catholic.

And now, a nice theme: In the Hindu temple at Cape Comorin is an image of the Goddess Kumārī, with a diamond in her forehead that shines so brightly that it has misled ships onto the rocks. The door is now closed on her at night, for the protection of seamen. On another prominence there is an image of the Virgin Mary—two aspects of the same archetypal figure.

It occurs to me that in discussing deities one must distinguish between the archetypal and the legendary aspects. Archetypally these two Virgins are one; but their legends and historical-cultural context are totally different.

After viewing a lovely sunset from a high mound of blown and rippled sand, I bade good-bye to the Lopezes, returned home in the car, had dinner at the hotel, took two Cosavil pills, and retired.

Monday, February 21

A nice wire from Jean: "Entire trip smooth. Message makes birthday happy. Love." My cold being greatly improved, and knowing that Jean was safely home, I felt much better than yesterday and game to go on.

Last night, when I returned for dinner, I overheard a comical conversation at the next table between a rather sophisticated English homosexual gentleman and the American who will eat no eggs.

"I'm so exhausted," said the American, "from my dreams. You know, it's all there! Life! The whole thing. I wake up so exhausted!"

"Yes?" said the Englishman. "Well, that must keep you from doing all sorts of exhausting things, then, in the day."

During the course of their conversation I heard the Englishman mention the name of Gregor; so when I got up, I introduced myself and asked him to let Gregor know that I am here. Funny funny! Once again, this pattern of Chance developing my journey. Gregor and this whole crowd, I believe, are in the circle of the sage.

There is a large athletic stadium right next to the hotel. Saturday afternoon there was a track meet in progress there; this morning the R.O.T.C. of the University, together with the Police and a patch of young women in white, were having a military review there. The Occident, again, in full force.

At about 11:30 I went around to the U.S.I.S. library to meet the Otwells; only Barbara Otwell was present; and when I spoke to her about Krishna Menon, she drove me to the place where all the devotees dwell: a large mansion, called Vidyuth, in a part of town called Poojahura, with a man named Wolter Kurs in charge. Only one couple was present, however; the rest having gone to the airport to speed a parting devotee. Krishna Menon's series of talks for this season concluded last night.

Returning to the hotel, I lay down to rest. A knock: Mr. K. P. Parameswaran Tampi to see me, to whom I had written Saturday. He will call for me at five this evening and take me for a view of the beach. Will also arrange for me to see some dances.

Again I lay down. Knock. Someone downstairs to see me: Gregor, looking calm and peaceful. I may visit the ashram this evening after dinner, and he will try to arrange for me to have a talk with the sage.

After dinner I went to the hostel Vidyuth, where Sri Krishna Menon's Occidental devotees—the males dressed in Indian attire—were seated at dinner. I met them all, a group of about eight, and spent a pleasant evening chatting. My appointment with the Master is set for Thursday, 5 P.M.

The football match between Trivandrum and Russia was immensely attended. One of the spectators said to Mrs. Otwell: "Why doesn't America send a football team to India?" "Well," she said, "we play a different kind of football." "Anyhow," said the man, "You know, the game wouldn't be half as well attended as the Russian."

At the All-India Exhibition, which I visited Sunday evening, there was a large theatrical event in progress. The curtain had, on one side, a large picture of Nehru talking with Gandhi, and, on the other, one of Stalin talking with Lenin. (This, I think, is the strongest line-up so far.)

Tuesday, February 22

After breakfast, I took a taxi to Mr. Tampi's and then, with him as guide, went on a considerable tour of the town. First, with his brother in the car, we drove to the art gallery, where I was given the VIP treatment and saw a large, nicely hung collection of the usual book-illustration styles. Tampi and I drove next to the beach, while I paused, here and there, to take photographs—particularly among the fishermen, who were hauling in their nets.

Fishermen near Trivandrum

Finally, Mr. Tampi brought me to a school and orphanage, where I watched the youngsters working at hand looms, doing their lessons, and finally eating U.N. food. I was handed literature about the institution and departed at one for lunch. Everywhere, this expectation of money from the U.S.A.: would the Rockefellers be interested? And meanwhile, this love affair with China and Russia. I continue to find it repulsive. (I have been told that at the Republic Day reception, Nehru confined his attentions to the Chinese: no one else, not even the Russians, could come near him.)

After lunch I napped—and was awakened by a rap at the door: some man who wants me to give money to some sort of young men's association. I spent the better part of the afternoon on my verandah writing letters, and at about five was approached by the gentleman who eats raw vegetables, offering to loan me a little book, *Atma-darshan,* by Sri Krishna Menon. The gentleman's name is Woodland Kahler, and he is an officer in the World Vegetarian Association, visiting India, to organize a branch here. He and his wife, who is a Russian, took up vegetarianism eight years ago, and learned to eschew New York, alcohol, cigarettes, and night clubs. I recalled having heard about this couple in Bombay, from Rama Mehta.

After dinner, I was again sitting on the verandah, when the other vegetarian gentleman approached and invited me to go with him to Vidyuth for a party they were having. I spent most of the evening there talking with Arthur Gregor, who has been greatly stirred and inspired by the Indian philosophy that he has learned from Krishna Menon.

Wednesday, February 23

After lunch I slept and wrote letters. Had a lovely, absolutely lazy afternoon. The weather is hot, hot, and hot. Immediately after dinner I went to bed.

Thursday, February 24

Morning tea, breakfast, and an expedition to the Post Office, and then letters and naps until 12:30, when I went to Vidyuth for lunch.

I have been reading the second booklet of Sri Krishna Menon, *Atma-Nirvriti (Freedom and Felicity in the Self)* and I find in it, besides a good, clear statement of the Vedantic idea of the world as pure consciousness, the following well-stated formulae:

> In between thoughts and in the deep-sleep state shines that principle to which the word "I" points.... When the mind is directed to it, it changes into that, losing the characteristics of mind. This is called *samādhi.*

> I am pure happiness. All the activities of the sense-organs and the mind aim at happiness. Thus all their activities are *pūjā* done to Me.

> Since feelings rise and set in peace, their *svarūpa* is peace. Since thoughts rise and set in knowledge, their *svarūpa* is knowledge. Deep peace and pure knowledge are one and the same thing. Different names are given to it because it is looked at from different angles.

> A sage knows well that consciousness is self-luminous and that it is consciousness that illumines the entire world. He knows also that his real nature is consciousness and experience and cannot as such be known or experienced. Hence he does not desire or make any attempt to know or experience it. The sage knows from the deepest conviction that he is consciousness and that he has attained what has to be attained.[260]

Considering my own position, I think that this last paragraph just about states it; with the addition, however, that since what appears to the waking consciousness to be thought and action is actually nothing but consciousness and experience, I am willing to become as though lost in thought and action, knowing all the time that therein is consciousness and experience: *saṁsāra* and *nirvāṇa* being one and the same.

My visit to the sage of Trivandrum is to be linked in the context of this diary, with the conversations that I had with Dr. Maiti in Ahmedabad: for I am here in contact with the actual meaning and content of the *ātman-brahman* concept.[261]

And I have chosen to meet this sage, rather than another, because he *seems,* at any rate, to represent a life pattern rather closer to that of the married sages of the Upaniṣads than to that of the life-and-flesh despising monks whom I have known.

Looking forward to the meeting, I have no idea, either what to expect, or what to say; but I dare say the meeting itself will disclose its proper logic.

I went to Vidyuth for lunch, and spent the first part of the afternoon chatting with Arthur Gregor and his friends beneath a tree; then, got into a taxi with Arthur and arrived at the dwelling of Sri Krishna Menon. Two old gentlemen—one, with his full beard and white dhoti, looking much like an ancient *ṛṣi*—stood on the porch and wagged their heads in welcome, signifying that we were to proceed immediately upstairs. I went up first, and the guru, in his white dhoti and with a cloth over his right shoulder, moved back from the stair-rail to receive us. Arthur introduced me and disappeared; the guru signalled to three chairs facing his own and I chose the middle one. We sat in a large and airy room and I said that I had come to him to learn whether I was right in thinking that the monastic revulsion from life was not altogether consonant with the sense of the Upaniṣads, where it appeared that all is *brahman,* and where the way of the householder was not despised.

He replied that for some the way of *sannyāsī* was correct and for others that of the *gṛhasthī*—and that if the way of the *gṛhasthī* could be incorrect that of the *sannyāsī* could also be incorrect. As for my view of the Upanishadic teaching, it was perfectly correct. The true meaning of renunciation, he declared, was that one must renounce all thoughts and things in the contemplation of *ātman:* that is the meaning of one-pointed contemplation.

He went on to speak of the three states of waking, dream, and deep sleep—the latter not one of ignorance but of pure consciousness. In that state one "knows nothing" except "peace." The term "knows nothing" does not here mean ignorance, as some aver; it means, rather, that all else has fallen away save only that state of pure consciousness, which is peace.²⁶²

We are in our true state (*ātman*) every night in sleep, but also during the period of waking consciousness every time we are "between two thoughts."

At this point I made the sign of *namaskāra.* Twenty minutes had elapsed.

The *ātman* is never bound, the *ātman* is never released, he said; it is always free.

The way of self-identification with this *ātman* he called the "direct approach," in contrast to the "cosmic approach," which is the way of seeking *brahman* in the world.

The way of discovering *ātman* while remaining in the world, he declared, was the way of the *Gītā.*

I asked whether there were many in India today teaching this heroic way, and he answered that there were only one or two, and named a couple of names which I did not catch.

Then I thanked him for his teaching and went down the stairs to find gathered outside the company many of those who were about to go in to him for their group meeting. Arthur helped me into my shoes and walked me a way up the road; then suggested that I might join them all at the India Coffee House, and returned to his group.

I started slowly walking home, but a bit of rain came, so I took a rickshaw the rest of the way; took a bath and settled to these notes.

Sri Krishna Menon was a very gentle and eloquent teacher, of about seventy, not stingy at all with his words, and directly telling, it seemed to me, in everything that he said. It was a memorable half hour—and great luck for me, I hear, that I came to Trivandrum when I did. For his doctor has ordered him to rest, now, until June. As Mr. Kahler said to me this morning, I "got in just under the wire."

I feel (I think properly) that my India journey has been perfectly fulfilled.

During the talk in the garden, at Vidyuth, in the earlier part of the afternoon, I told of my feeling on coming to India that my own work now should be from the standpoint of the West, and we discussed, also, something of the anti-American feeling in India. In 1947, they said, America was greatly in favor. The anti-Americanism was pre-Pakistan-aid, however; pre-Korea also; probably commenced with the Chinese Communist victory in China and the debarring of Communist China from the U.N. The atom bombs on Japan also had something to do with it.

After a hot bath and a nap, I started down town, but was met at the hotel gate by Tampi, who had come to say good-bye. He brought me a couple of booklets and we had a brief talk. Then I continued down to the India Coffee Shop, where I met Arthur Gregor and a couple of the disciples of the guru, including a Jewish couple from the Argentine named Gutman—he a tall thin man with a large rudder of a nose, she a handsome, dark young woman. I thought at first that they were from New York.

The company told me that Krishna Menon had been "very happy" after his conversation with me—had said that if I were not leaving he would teach me for five days, even in spite of his doctor's orders—that I was very close to full understanding. This made me feel very good: I immediately decided, however, not to stay: it was a quick decision and I do not know whether it was a wise one, but I did not feel that I wished to press the guru beyond his doctor's orders. I think that what he gave me today will be enough for me.

After coffee, we returned to Vidyuth for dinner and then sat out on the lawn again. Presently, the gentlemen whom I had heard talking about Gregor in the hotel dining room Sunday evening arrived—John Levy—and the conversation became simply ghastly. Levy is a perfect Virgil Thompson type of pontificating gas bag—except that he knows a good deal less and consequently is even more abusive of everything and everyone but himself and his two or three ideas. His chatter, combined with Gutman's remarks, almost sufficed to ruin the day. As I left, Arthur Gregor said: "The followers! Aren't they awful?"

I returned to my hotel at about 12:30 and went directly to bed, saving my packing till tomorrow.

Friday, February 25   **Cochin**

Six months' anniversary of my departure from New York. I am debating in my mind whether to return from Cochin to Trivandrum if Krishna Menon is *really* willing to talk to me five more times. After packing I was invited down the verandah to chat with the man who is having so much trouble with his dreams, Benjamin Jerome. His foster father is a medium and he had two hours full of stories to run out to me before I finally told him I had to finish packing. Climax: a watch that he had made for him in Zürich with three extra scales indicating his biological rhythms: good and bad periods a) physically, b) emotionally, c) mentally—rhythms of 28 and 23 days. Someone for Mr. Belk, I should say![263] His principal series of experiences appears to have taken place during his visit to Brazil, where, on one occasion, Presidents Monroe and Lincoln stood at his side and dictated a speech to him.

I left my friend to finish my packing and step over to the Airlines office. Presently one of the young people from Vidyuth arrived, Wolter Kurs, a tall, thin Dutchman, who has been very sweet to me—read my *Hero* some time ago and has treated me as an honored guest. He took a snapshot and boarded the bus with me to the airport. There we found Arthur Gregor and a nice little French lady. While we sat waiting, Kurs put a garland around my neck. I was given a charming send off—and some forty minutes later came down in Cochin, to be greeted by Nissim Ezekiel's handsome, dark brother, Joseph.

Cochin is really delightful. The resort-like Malar Hotel is on Willingdon Island, around which the whole port is folded, and boats, sail boats, cargo skiffs, steamers, and naval vessels are passing to and fro all the time. Joseph, at the airport, told me that he would call for me about six; so I rode to the hotel in the bus, had lunch, admired the place, and took a nap in my large room, with its windows opening onto the port. Cargo skiffs going past all the time. Shortly after teatime, Joseph arrived, and we chatted a while about Cochin.

He and his brother Nissim are of the ben Israel Jews, who are supposed to have landed on the coast near Bombay (shipwrecked on the way to Cochin?) about 2,000 years ago. The Jews of Cochin, too, have been in India some 2,000 years. They constitute a small, inbred, diminishing group: many of the girls have to look forward to no marriage. The Cochin Jews have held to the typical Jewish life pattern of the merchant; the Jews of the north became, first, oil-pressers then agriculturalists, and when the British came many entered military service. Nissim could easily pass for a

New York Jew: Joseph, however, is too dark for that. Otherwise, he is un-Indian in appearance: Jewish wavy hair, for example.

Joseph talked about Cochin: a number of Chinese traits appear in this neighborhood which do not occur in other parts of India. Chinese sun hats on the boatmen (I have already seen a number), Chinese-type fishing nets, Chinese peppers, Chinese-style roofs. There seems to be some relationship, also, between the Jews of Cochin and those of China.

After watching the sun set like a red ball behind the roofs of the area (Cochin Fort and the Jewish quarter) just across the channel, we walked to a boat landing and took a rowboat to that part of the city (now quite dark), to visit the home of one of the leading Jews of Cochin, Sotta Koder.

A large, spacious house near the water, with a great deal of dark wood-work. One entered, and immediately faced a large staircase going up to the living rooms, a plaster swan at either side of the stairs: on the right with the neck down and stretched forward, on the left with it arched. Upstairs, we were greeted by a fat, middle-aged, absolutely Jewish woman with a Christian Indian guest (Syrian Christian). The host, Mr. Koder, entered: also fat, with a particular, relaxed and casual, Jewish charm. Everything distinctly and absolutely Jewish—we could have been in Brooklyn. We stayed for dinner—Friday night's orthodox meal: Grace was read in Hebrew (in a relaxed and mumbling, but learned style); Jewish foods and wine (grape juice because of the prohibition here) were served, with salt on chunks of bread. Finally, grace after eating, read again (at great length) from the book. Mr. Koder and Joseph put on Jewish skull-caps for the meal: here, however, not black—because black and white here mean mourning—but amusingly colorful. After the meal, Joseph sang, in sweet-tenor, from a little notebook in which Mrs. Koder had written the words of many songs: *La Paloma, Santa Lucia, Blue Danube,* etc. etc. She seemed to love to have singing going on, and kept insisting that I should add my frog's croak to the symphony. Joseph and I returned to Willingdon Island in the Koders' car, via the bridge, at about 11:30 P.M.

My conversation with Joseph included an account of my visit with Krishna Menon, whom, I learned, he regards as his guru. Again, at the Koders', this theme came up, and Mr. Koder asked me what I thought of the man. (Koder knows John Levy very well).[264] It seems there is a lot of unfavorable, as well as favorable, talk in India about Krishna Menon. He has a gold watch. He smokes English cigarettes (sent to him by John Levy). My guess is that the traditional Indian idea that a holy man has to be a *sannyāsī* is responsible for this talk; whereas the whole point of Krishna Menon's teaching is that the household can be enlightened even while living the householder's life. He pointed out to me, in our brief talk, that in the Upaniṣads we read of yogis and *sannyāsīs* going to kings to learn the truth.[265] The way of the ascetic, in fact, can be a false way, since it may stress negation, denial, world-splitting, not as a way, merely, but as a final term.

This noon at the airport, Arthur and Wolter told me some more of what Krishna Menon had said about his talk with me. He had said that he would be glad to talk with me if I came again, but that as far as my own realization was concerned it would not matter: I was already very close and would get there, presently, on my own.

When I boarded the plane I had the idea that I would return and then go to Ceylon via Madura, etc., by train; but on arriving in Cochin I found that it would be impossible to clear my papers here. I shall have to go to Madras. That cuts out Trivandrum. I shall have to pack off to Madras on Sunday, by plane, if I am to get to Ceylon within the time stipulated on my visa.

And so that half hour with Krishna Menon, yesterday, is to be the extent of my meeting with him. Somehow, it seems to me appropriate that that should be so. This whole visit has been a kind of touch-and-go affair—with each touch sufficing to fix for me a great context of ideas. The chief value of my conversation with Krishna Menon is that it assures me that my own reading of the teaching coincides with the authority of at least one Indian sage, and that, simultaneously, that sage pointed out to me a simple and basic formula of contemplation (*turīya* in deep sleep: "one's own glory" between two thoughts)[266] through which a stand in the Self might be readily attained and established. I know, furthermore, that the conversation and image of the teacher in his room of teaching will remain very clearly in my mind. I was pretty well concentrated during the entire talk.[267]

Saturday, February 26

Joseph had told me last evening that he would come to the hotel at 9:00; at 10:30 he phoned to say that he had been detained at the office and would arrive at about 11:00. (India again!) Thus I lost the morning. I made arrangements to fly tomorrow to Madras and took a few pictures of passing craft.

In the course of the conversation at Vidyuth, two nights ago, when John Levy and a Mr. Gutmann were throwing their weight around—or rather were using their guru as a club with which to batter Suzuki, and everybody else—Gutmann challenged me to name any figure in the West who might be compared to the Indian sage. I named C. G. Jung.

"But Jung does not claim," he replied, "to show you the Truth."

I have thought of this a bit, and believe that, essentially, the idea of integration amounts to one of illumination about the Self: it has to do with a realization of truth. Our Western word Truth, however, tends to refer to some sort of Object; hence it cannot be used properly in this context—and indeed it translates the Indian terms inaccurately. It is, so to say, only a figure of speech when the Indian sage speaks of revealing Truth. Even the formula, *satyam eva jayati,* is figurative; cannot be literally true if by *satya* the transcendent (the ineffable) is connoted.

Joseph arrived at about 11:00 and took me, by rowboat, across the channel to Jewtown, where we visited the old Synagogue and one of the Jewish families. On the wall of the synagogue was a list of dates:

Copper plate grant to Joseph Rabban, A.D. 379.
Jews of Cranganore in touch with China, A.D. 900.
First Synagogue, A.D. 1345
Moors vs. Cranganore Jews, A.D. 1565
Cranganore Jews flee to Jewtown, Cochin, A.D. 1567.
Build Synagogue, A.D. 1568.
Synagogue decorated with Chinese tiles and the clock tower is built, A.D. 1760.

At the time of the sixteenth-century Portuguese persecutions, the Maharaja of Cochin gave the Jews the land on which the Synagogue now stands—right next to his palace, and with a high wall, to protect them. The community has existed in orthodox style ever since.

The community consists of two groups: the "Black Jews" and the "White Jews." The White despise the Black, do not permit intermarriage, and assign to them only special places in the Synagogue.

As Joseph and I approached the Jewtown street (which is composed of houses in a Dutch 17th- and 18th-century style), we were met by a Black Jew, Mr. Salem, who invited us up to meet his father. We entered one of the houses: large upstairs rooms, walls about two and a half feet thick, European style furnishings of old and dark wood. There I met an old, dark Jew, Mr. Salem's father, who had been to Israel the year before to plead for the admission of some 4,000 Black Jews from Cochin (a very few White Jews went with them). They had sold all of their properties—synagogue properties included—to pay the fare; and great misery would be brought to them if they were refused.

The Synagogue at Cochin

The old man, after a few preliminary words with me, moved into position and launched his attack on the United States.

Why were we supporting both the Arabs and the Jews? The right to Palestine lay clearly with the Jews: God had given it to them four thousand years ago, as documented in the Bible. Did we not still read the Bible in America?

The source of all wealth is the land. America has more land per person than any nation in the world. America therefore has more money than any nation in the world—also, more science, and more traffic of bullock carts. Having a lot of money, America has to get rid of a lot of money: that is why America is spilling so much money all over the world.

Why does America not give more of its money to Israel? True, the American Jews are giving a lot of money; but why not the American Christians also? Were they not reading the Bible any more? Did they not realize that the right to Palestine belonged to the Jews?

I must confess, when the old man started, I thought him rather cute, but when he continued and I could see, not only that he was dreadfully serious, but also that he represented a point of view held by millions of his like, I began to feel a bit sick at the stomach, and I was glad when it was time to go.

We descended the stairs and were met by a White Jew, in a pink cap, who opened the Synagogue and let us in. Joseph told me later that his daughter was married to the son of the Black Jew, Mr. Salem—the youngsters had had to elope to Bombay. The synagogue looked rather Dutch (Spinoza was in my mind)[268] and cute. Lots of brass; lots of lamps; a place above and behind a grill for the women; benches around the walls (Mr. Salem, being a Black Jew, may sit on only one or two, specially allowed). I tried to take a couple of photographs. Then out we went, and after a walk up and down the one street, we returned to Mr. Salem's house for a cool drink and a chat with his wife and a shy little girl (White Jew) named Hazel. I noticed that the women wore either Western dress or saris, as they pleased. As we walked on the street we passed several clusters sitting on the thresholds of their homes (it being Saturday, the shops were closed). Many were as fair as Westerners.

The community, I was told, is fast diminishing: hardly more than a hundred now remain.[269]

At four I boarded the hotel launch for a two-hour cruise of the "backwaters": the most fascinating two hours, I think, of the entire trip. I was alone on the launch with a crew of four, who were eager to help me to good photos. Unfortunately, most of the shoreline was into the sun—and *most* unfortunately, when I reloaded I put in a cartridge made for artificial light! I could shoot myself! Anyhow, the trip was great: a world of Polynesian style fishing villages on numerous islands: lovely kids waving and screaming from the shore: a world of coconuts, rice, and fish. In many places people pounding coconut husks for copra; in others, great fish traps, and places for the spreading out and drying of prawns. In the monsoon season rice is raised in these same fish-trap areas. At the end of the first hour of the trip, the boat turned left into a lovely, palm hung canal, and stopped at a large and beautifully kept village where I disembarked, and with one of the crew, took a lovely walk. A number of charming houses with very nicely painted façades: also, a couple of new, large mansions, built by wealthy citizens. At one corner I turned into a well crowded street where baksheesh was being distributed (every Saturday) to the poor. In these villages many of the older women wear no clothing over the upper body: one has the feeling that one has come really into an earlier world. All of the village lanes are perfectly swept and clean.

In the main square (surprise) is a large, white, Spanish-Portuguese style, Catholic church. Toward the close of my walk I was followed by a cute band of six little boys, whom I photographed a couple of times, to their great pride (with the dud film). Then I was brought back to the launch and returned, in the light of the declining sun, to the hotel.

Joseph walked home with me, and declared that he would see me off tomorrow on the plane to Madras.

Sunday, February 27

A very lazy morning, breakfast, strolling about the hotel lawn, and packing. On the stroll I fell into conversation with a businessman from Bombay who—touched with the usual Indian tendency to talk—gave a long monologue on God, ethics, and his departure from Burma after the commencement of the war. An amusing story was that of his family's valuables: stored in a safe, and the safe buried in the ground. But there was a deep hollow beneath, washed out by underground water; and when the Japanese bombs dropped, the safe dropped into this and disappeared forever.

God, he told me, is our servant—just as Nehru is; and if we are good he will give us what we need, but if we are bad he will hang us. Comparably, as long as God is good, and a good servant, he can stay in office; but if he fails in his duty, we can throw him out. All said, of course, in a rather amusing, half-sophisticated manner.

Joseph arrived a bit before lunch; chatted for a while on the verandah, took his meal with me, and bade me good-bye at the bus. The stewardess on the plane was the one who had come two days ago, from Trivandrum. The flight was (and she told me, always is) rather bumpy.

MADRAS

Monday, February 28   **Madras**

This *may* be my last day in India: if I can get my permission to leave from the Commissioner of Police—and *can't* have the validity date on my Ceylonese visa extended beyond tomorrow. If I *can* do the latter, I may remain a day or two longer and visit Madura.

As I think of leaving and look back over what has happened, I feel that I have had a wonderful six months and that I am now very much at home here, though not reluctant to depart. I wish I had seen Śāntiniketan, Khajurāho, Sāñcī, Māndū, and Hampi, and should like to see Madura and Tanjore; wish that Jean and I had seen a bit of Kathakali; and regret the fumble in New Delhi that lost us our places at the Parade and the Reception on Republic Day: but otherwise, everything has been accomplished that I came to accomplish—and a bit more besides. Moreover, I have met a lot of charming people, many of whom I should like to think of as permanent friends.

The climax of the visit was my talk with Sri Krishna Menon, which settled for me a number of fundamental matters. One is my thought about the relationship of the swamis and *sannyāsīs* to Indian life and religion. I should say that one of the great needs of India is more men like Krishna Menon, who will demonstrate the dignity of secular life. I feel that the monks have the notion that their *way* is the *goal* of religion—forgetting that the goal is illumination, which few of them have achieved. Another was my problem about the real sense of the positive teaching of the *Gītā*, which the monks turn into a negative teaching. And a third was my judgment of the validity of the feeling I have had for some time that I am pretty close to understanding what the Indian scriptures are teaching.

The main difference between this teaching and the Jungian goal of integration—as I now see it—is that in the Jungian, psychological literature, one is not invited to identify the Self with the Universal: this identification is what gives to the Indian teaching its religious tone, which is precisely the tone that Jung rejects in his commentary to the *Golden Flower*.[270] I think that I may find that, whereas in Vedanta the stress of the identity experience is on the transcendent, in Zen the idea is to keep the eyes open: "There are streams and there are mountains."[271] This, certainly,

does not conflict with Krishna Menon's teaching. I told him that I felt that
one should know that in turmoil, loss, unhappiness, and passion there is
brahman, no less than in peace, victory, happiness, and repose—and he indicated assent. *Brahman* is to be found not in one term only of a dichotomy,
but beyond and within both! Clear enough! Why not hold on to it?

(Not to be forgotten is the contrast of Mr. Salem's Bible-grounded talk
with the Hinduism of Krishna Menon: historical, race-centered, aggressive, generally nasty. But here too, of course, is *brahman.*)

I suppose my second most important Indian climax was the meeting with Nehru—and here something of the contemporary historical situation came to focus. If I put together Nehru, Mrs. Pandit, and Mrs.
Hutheesingh, I think I see an elegantly cosmopolitan family undergoing in
various degrees an Asianization (enantiodromia). The most critical experiences in this crisis are that of China as Asia, and that of Hindi as Asia. The
first is dissociating India from the ideology and historical context of
Democracy, and the second is soon going to reinforce this tendency by re-
ducing the means of communication with the West. The principal motivation of the Hindi movement, I feel, is pride. "The British," said Mrs.
Hutheesingh, "never thought our English good: they always ridiculed it."
So India is going to become, more and more, an Asian, instead of modern,
cosmopolitan nation—and I think they are going to be surprised at how
far behind this leaves them pretty soon. The tables in my room wobble.
The new hotel is ill-designed. The lighting in the room is quite bad.
Copying (translation) is never as good as action out of the creative center;
and no Asian language is ever going to move into the creative center of the
industrial age.

The newspaper—*The Hindu*—this morning is full of editorials and reports of speeches attacking the United States—for its atom bombs, for its
SEATO program,[272] for its "horror comics," for its materialism. (The
same paper, meanwhile, runs a Tarzan comic.) My reaction is not very different from what it was when I first came to India and read these things. I
am not sure of what I shall or should say about India when I return to the
United States and am asked questions. One thing I know is that I do not
want to engage in any attack upon India; but another thing I know is that
I will not attempt either to mask or to defend what appears to me to be the
Indian position. I suppose the best approach would be to retain a carefully

and tentatively descriptive attitude. And I am going to be very, very chary of lending a hand to Indian causes.

India, fundamentally, has to be considered under two great categories: that of the huge majority, leading their lives in greater or lesser ignorance of the non-Indian world, and that of the leading minority, Occidentalized and in an ambivalent emotional relationship to the West.

Both groups, as far as their approach to the Occidental foreigner is concerned, can be divided in two: those whose welcoming smile is sincere, innocent, and expressive of an almost boundless hospitality, sympathy, gentleness, and warm humanity, and those whose smile is the prelude to a touch for aid.

I am sure that, actually, the great majority in both of the fundamental categories is of the first (welcoming) type; but certainly the great majority in the actual experience of the alien visitor is of the second type. Certainly the representatives of this second type run all the way from the beggar in the street and bearer in the hotel, through the merchants with their "just to look" and the journalists and professors who hope that you will be able to get things published for them in the U.S.A., to the high politicians, who, while feeling greatly superior in their spirituality to the materialism of the West, and while insulting the West in every utterance, are nevertheless hoping and asking for aid—that the Rockefellers should restore their temples, fertilize their soil, finance their visits to the U.S.A., repair their idols, send books to their libraries—and what not. It is this that makes India, veritably, *the land of waving palms* (Joseph Ezekiel's term).

I have spent the morning trying to get out of India.

1. To the Police Commissioner's Office, Foreign Registration Department at 10:00. The officer arrived at 11:30 and asked thirteen rupees for a telegram to Bombay to get me cleared.
2. To the BOAC office to get my ticket to Ceylon. Asked if I had my income tax clearance, I answered No. The clerk accompanied me to the income tax office.
3. Told that since I shall have been in India 184 days (182 days would have let me out) I have to pay *an income tax on the money I brought into India.* $1,421+$750=$2,171. Tax of 519 rupees (over a hundred dollars). "I'm going to see the U.S. Consul," I said. "I regard this as a criminal act."

4. The taximan drove me back to the hotel for lunch and charged me
    twenty rupees for the morning.

Hail to the land of waving palms. My love for India may or may not
survive this visit.

After lunch I went to see the U.S.I.S. director, Paul Sherbert, to talk
about A.N.T.A. and the Orient: first, however, I told him of this highway
robbery. He could hardly believe it, and got in touch with a chap named
Edward C. Ingraham, Jr., American Vice-Consul, who said he would see me.

When I left him, I went around to Ingraham—who was surprised at
the tax, but verified it and could give me no help. I returned to the BOAC
office and told them that I would certainly not be able to go tomorrow
(since Ingraham refused to give me a letter guaranteeing my character,
which would have permitted me to leave before the arrival of the clearing
telegram from Bombay). I returned, next, to the income tax office and
filled out my tax return: 10,313 rupees; tax 519 rupees. Then I went back to
the hotel and wrote the following letter.

Madras
February 28, 1955

Minister of Finance
Government of India
New Delhi

Dear Sir:
You will perhaps be interested in learning what good will is gained by
taxing a tourist on the funds that he brings into this country. I am an
American professor; have published four books on Indian religion,
art, and philosophy; have lectured on the spiritual culture of India for
twenty years; have looked forward eagerly to a visit to India, and have
given up a good deal to make this trip. I arrived in New Delhi,
August 30, 1954; lectured, gratis, at a number of Indian colleges and
institutions; spent as much as I could afford on Indian textiles; gave
as generously as I could to your temples and beggars; overlooked the
anti-American propaganda in the newspapers; learned to admire and
love the Indian people, as I had long admired and loved their culture—and when it came time for me to buy my ticket to depart (that
is to say, today), my way was blocked by your income tax officials, to
whom I am compelled to pay 519 rupees—not on any moneys earned

in India (for I have not received one rupee here) but out of the funds that I brought into India and spent here. After this final experience of the baksheesh motif—played *fortissimo,* now, by the government it-self—I am afraid that I am going to find it harder than it used to be, to speak and write about the Indian character with the respect it de-serves.

Hoping that you may some day be able to collect taxes from your own citizens as efficiently as you have exacted this toll from one who came as a friend, I assure you that it is going to be very difficult for me to forget you when I remember India.

Very Sincerely, etc.

I find that I am not going to be able to remain in this hotel, because it is full up after tomorrow. The desk phoned to the Victoria, where I shall go tomorrow morning. Also, I am going to have to get another Ceylonese visa. It's all simply great.

While sitting in the lounge, waiting for the desk to find a room for me, I met a nice American Negro couple, Dr. and Mrs. Cecil Marquez of New York. We talked for a while about India. He remarked, among other mat-ters, the bare feet: "there is a relationship between the wearing of shoes and health," he said. The character and depth of the poverty in India had shocked them, as it had me.

Feeling—really—like hell, I ate a late dinner and went early to bed.

Tuesday, March 1

I find myself, this morning, actually hating India and wanting to get away. The motif that struck me early, when the fortune teller caught me in New Delhi when I first arrived—"something for nothing": baksheesh, bak-sheesh—has drowned out everything else just now. I feel exactly as I would about a house in which I had been rolled. The reaction is perhaps a bit strong. But then, so is a $110 toll.

I woke up at 5:30, sat brooding for an hour and a half, had morning tea, dressed, and ate breakfast; returned to my room, packed and brooded for a while, and then paid my bill and taxied to the Victoria: a fairly crummy hotel of the upper Hindu order. I spent the rest of the morning strolling around the Mount Road area, and visited Sherbert, who invited me for lunch tomorrow and expressed helpless amazement at my plight ("I've always said," he said, "that if you can reconcile yourself to being stabbed in the back at least once by everybody who's nice to you in India, you can have a lovely time here.... They just haven't got the idea of service.") Then I left my passport at the Ceylonese High Commission, with, of course, ten rupees, and walking home through a typical Madras residential district (slum, with the kids shitting in the gutter), I entered my hotel for a lousy meal.

After lunch and a brief rest, I went around to the Police Commissioner's office and was handed my permit to leave India; went next to the Ceylon office and received my new visa; walked to the airlines office, and was told that I could pick up my ticket tomorrow for a March 3 departure; and went, finally to the U.S. Consul's office, to see if I could cash my American Express checks there for the payment of my income tax.

As I entered the building—surprise!—I was greeted by Kashi, Jason Grossman's bearer. Jason was upstairs. I found him talking to the young man who had informed me that I could not get out of the payment of this tax. Greetings—and a long talk about the tax problem.

Then I drove with Jason to a little house that someone has loaned him, for a drink. He introduced me to his hosts, and for two and a half hours, these nice people projected Jason's color photos onto the wall. I thought some of them quite fine—but began to fear for my own. I'm afraid I have not been using a wide enough aperture: 5.6 with an exposure of 1/50 or 1/25 has been Jason's norm. Mine has been more like 8 with 1/60 or 1/40.[273]

After the films finished at 9:30 P.M., Jason and I drove down Mount Road to a *Chinese* restaurant, for the best restaurant meal either of us had had in India. He wants me to join him and drive up the coast to Amarāvatī, Orissa, and Calcutta—but I feel very strongly that I am fed up with India. The Chinese meal seemed to me the promise of the future. I think it will be quite a while before I shall feel the lure of India again.

Just before dropping me at the hotel, Jason announced that he was going to have his new cholera shots tomorrow. This reminded me that my own six-month certificate is now outdated, so I shall join him tomorrow, leave my miserable hotel, and move, then, to Mr. Sherbert for my last Indian night.

Wednesday, March 2

Up at 6 A.M., shaving and packing. At 8:45 Jason called for me, and the day began.

Yesterday, in the U.S. Consul's office, studying the Indian tax manual, I noted that Kashmir was a non-taxable territory and recalled that I had been in Kashmir during the first days of my visit. I mentioned this fact to the young man in the office who was helping me, and he said he would look into the matter. When I came downstairs this morning, I was told that there had been a phone call for me last evening from the U.S. Consul's office. Our first act today, therefore, was to drive to the Consul's. We were told that the man we wanted was out and would return in about an hour. We met him, however, when we were going out the door, and he said that he had found that my days in Kashmir might be subtracted from the period of my stay. There remained a problem though; for I had absolutely no evidence of my trip.

Jason, Kashi, and I drove first to a young Australian doctor for our cholera shots, and then to the Health Office for a certification of his certification of our inoculations. Next we drove to the Income Tax bureau, and the battle began. I had two points: that I had been in Kashmir, and that uncashed travelers checks are not currency. The second point, finally, was disallowed, and the first was rejected because Kashmir had recently been brought into the taxable domain. Jason asked if it had been taxable when I had been there, and at 12:15 they found that it had not, and that if I would write out a statement, sworn to before the U.S. Consul, to the effect that I had been in Kashmir for four or five days, I would still have one or two days in which to get out of India.

We drove to see Mr. and Mrs. Sherbert for lunch. I had been invited to spend the night there, and so we brought my luggage in the car and left it—with the exception of my Indian bed-roll, which I gave to Kashi as my farewell gift. After lunch, Sherbert returned me to the Consul's office, where I wrote out my statement—hoping that it was true (five days in Kashmir, counting the day of the drive over the mountains from Pathankot). Jason drove me back to the Tax Office and at 4:15 P.M. I received my release: I have to leave India, however, by the 4th, or I shall be back under the blanket. The last problem that came up was that of $750 that had been sent to me from my New York bank in December. This was still taxable if it was a direct earning, but not if it was a remittance. I swore that it was a remittance from my savings—and was clear.

The next problem, however, was that Jason had asked for a statement from the tax people, clearly showing him when *he* would become taxable in India. The rule is fantastically complicated; for the Indian fiscal year ends on March 31, and the 182-day period must fall within any one fiscal year, to trap you. Jason arrived in October. March 31 he will not yet have been here 182 days. Therefore, he may remain for 182 days after March 31.

It was 4:45 when Jason received his letter, and we had then to dash like mad to reach the BOAC office in time for me to buy my airplane ticket to Colombo. We hit the office at 4:58. I paid with a twenty-dollar travelers check, and came out with my ticket and thirteen rupees to my name.

We drove to Jason's for a drink, then to the Chinese restaurant of last night, where I, this time, treated him. He dropped me at the Sherberts' for the night, and we bade each other good-bye and good times.

About the tax event, there is something still to be said; namely, that the group of young men, who finally managed to help me through, reminded me, not a little, of some young naval officers I met earlier in Cochin: youngsters, working India through its awkward period of transition—highly intelligent, and proud of the responsibilities. It is a fantastic situation; young law graduates holding the jobs that in any other country would be in the hands of seasoned professionals. It gives a kind of freshness and quality of impromptu to this whole affair.

I think my final image for India is going to be that of the group of boy beggars outside the Chinese restaurant. Their chief figure was an absolutely naked little kid of about seven—cute and charming, with a mop of tangled hair—who would walk alongside or in front of us saying, "No fatha, no matha, no seesta, no bratha . . . etc.," with a winning smile, and then, in the classical Indian beggar style, clap his stomach, look up at you with half-open mouth. The first night, I gave him one anna. Tonight he appeared again, as an old friend, and when I put him off, said, "Tomorrow?" I said, "Tomorrow." Another, this evening, put out his hand, and said, "Baksheesh!" I put out mine to him and said, "Baksheesh!" He looked surprised at first, and indicated that he had nothing. Then he smiled and said, "Wait," ran away and came back with two annas. When I came out of the restaurant, he appeared again. "You're the boy who gave me baksheesh?" I said. He answered yes, and I gave him two annas.

The other image that I will remember, I think, is that of the truckmen of this city, working like animals at their trucks, two in front, and one pushing with his head from behind. They are practically naked, and represent the most emphatic image of sheer physical work that I've ever seen.

And finally, the slums of this city: thousands of dirty, miserable women sitting around in the filth, playing with their babies or searching each other's heads for lice.

Thursday, March 3

The little room on the roof of the Sherbert place was delightful. After breakfast, Mr. Sherbert and I sat talking while we waited for the U.S.I.S. car to call and he told me a few things about the Maharani of Travancore, who is still "quite a gal," at about sixty.

The first wife of the Maharaja, it seems, produced only girls, so he married this one, who produced two boys and a girl. The second boy, however, is generally regarded as the son, not of the Maharaja, but of Mr. C. P. Ramaswamy Aiyar, one of the most charming and ruthless crooks in the world, is today a trustee of the Asian Institute in San Francisco, and a candidate for a position in the U.S. Foreign Service as advisor on Indian affairs.

After the Maharani had born her sons, the first wife of the Maharaja bore a son also, and a series of attempts to poison the sons of the Maharani then was initiated, which she, personally, frustrated.

With the death of the Maharaja, C. P. Ramaswamy Aiyar's influence in Travancore became enormous, and his iron suppression of the working classes is one of the major causes of the Communist tendency in that region. He and the Maharani soon began to suspect that they might have to take refuge somewhere, someday, and so they employed two men to bring up from underground a certain temple treasure, which had never been evaluated, stored it in various safe deposit vaults in Europe and America, and killed the two men who had brought it up. No one knows what the treasure was worth.

Aiyar has been writing faithfully to the U.S.I.S. directors in Washington. Senator Wiley has been taken in entirely, and it looks as if he might get a job.

We talked a bit about Sri Krishna Menon: I have talked about him also with Jason. It seems the gossip against him brings in the problem of his son, who is, apparently, a fairly unsuccessful movie director with worldly habits.

The U.S.I.S. car arrived about 8:30 and we piled in. When everyone had been delivered, I and my luggage (minus, thank God, that bed-roll) were dropped at the TWA Air Ceylon office just across the street from the U.S.I.S.

"Sir! Sir! Baksheesh!"

It was my little naked friend of the past two evenings. Just as the bus was about to leave I gave him my last piece of Indian change: a half anna— and he gave me Godspeed in his own charming style.

APPENDIX IA

HINDUISM

This essay, "Hinduism," was first printed in 1959 in *Basic Beliefs: A Simple Presentation of the Religious Philosophies of Mankind,* edited by Johnson E. Fairchild.

I imagine that when one thinks of Indian philosophy the first thought is of yoga. The great classical text of yoga is that of the sage Patanjali: the *Yoga Sūtras,* "Thread or Guiding Thread to Yoga." At the opening of this amazing work, we find the following definition—and I want to start with this, because it is a very important point: "Yoga is the intentional stopping of the spontaneous activity of the mind stuff."

Now it was the idea in ancient Oriental psychology that within the gross matter of the brain, within the grey matter, there is a very subtle substance, which is in continuous activity, taking the shapes of whatever we behold. This subtle matter is in a state of continuous activity, like the rippling of waves on a stirred pool. And when you shut your eyes, the mind stuff continues to operate that way. If you should try to make it stop, you would find the process very difficult.

Just try this some time. Take into your mind an image—somebody that you care for, some image that you would care to contemplate—and try to hold this image still in your mind. You will find that you are immediately

311

thinking of other images, associated with the first; for the mind continues spontaneously to move. Yoga is the intentional stopping of this spontaneous activity of the mind stuff. It is an intentional bringing to rest of this continuous action.

But why should one wish to do this?

A favorite simile used in Indian discussions of this subject is that of the surface of a pond with its waves in action—a wind blowing over the pond and the waves moving. If you look at the surface of a pond moving in this way you will see the many reflections—many broken forms; nothing will be perfect, nothing complete; you will have only broken images before you. But if the wind dies down and the waters become perfectly still and clear, suddenly the whole perspective shifts and you are not seeing a lot of broken images, reflecting things round about. You are looking down through the clear water to the lovely sandy bottom, and perhaps you will see fish in the water. The whole perspective changes and you behold, not a multitude of broken images, but a single, still, unmoving image.

This is the idea of yoga. The notion is that what we see when we look around, like this, are the broken images of a perfect form. And what is that form? It is the form of a divine reality, which appears to us only in broken images when our mind stuff is in action. Or, to state the case another way: we are all, as we sit here and stand here, the broken images, the broken reflections, of a single divine perfection; but all that we ever see when we look around with our mind stuff in its usual state of spontaneous activity, is the broken rainbow-reflection of this perfect image of divine light.

Let us now open our eyes, let the waters stir again, let the waves come into action—and we shall know that these flashing sights before us are reflections, broken images, of that one divine radiance, which we have experienced. And it will now be delightful to see them moving in this way; for we are no longer at a loss to know what they are. We shall have seen the source; we shall know that the source is within all of these broken reflections—including ourselves; and there will come a wonderful experience of a harmonious system: all things inflecting in various ways this one perfection. This is the realization that underlies the whole thought and sociology and action of traditional India.

Now since we are all broken reflections of that image, that image is present within us. However, it is impossible to describe it in terms of its broken reflections. How would you possibly describe its form to someone who had not seen the complete image itself? It cannot be described in terms of its fragments. The first principle of Indian thought, therefore, is that the ultimate reality is beyond description. It is something that can be experienced only by bringing the mind to a stop; and once experienced, it cannot be described to anyone in terms of the forms of this world. The truth, the ultimate truth, that is to say, is transcendent. It goes past, transcends, all speech, all images, anything that can possibly be said. But, as we have just seen, it is not only transcendent, it is also immanent, within all things. Everything in the world, therefore, is to be regarded as its manifestation.

There is an important difference here between the Indian and the Western ideas. In the Biblical tradition, God creates man, but man cannot say that he is divine in the same sense that the Creator is, whereas in Hinduism all things are incarnations of that power. There has been no "Fall." Man is not cut off from the divine. He requires only to bring the spontaneous activity of his mind stuff to a state of stillness and he will experience that divine principle within him which is the very essence of his existence. And this essence within is identical in all of us. We are, as it were, sparks from a single fire; and we are all fire. There is therefore an eternal revelation of the truth all around us, all the time, and we require only the proper focus of the eyes to experience this.

Now let me give you a couple of basic terms: the divine principle within each of us is called *ātman*. *Ātman* simply means "the self." And this "true self" is the same in all. However, each conceives of himself as being a special independent person, and this concept of oneself as an independent entity is called "ego," *aham;* also, *aham-kara,* "making the noise 'I'." "Making the noise 'I'" is what we do when we set ourselves against each other.

The name given to *ātman* when it is experienced, not only within, but also in the world, is *brahman;* and *brahman* simply means "divine power." *Brahman,* the divinity immanent in the world, and *ātman,* the divinity immanent in yourself, are the same divinity; and so the great experience in Indian thought—indeed, the fundamental illuminating principle throughout the Orient—is this realization that all of these beings that seem so various are one.

Now this realization that though we are many we are also one, is a magical realization. And what is the magic that transforms the one into the many? It is called *māyā. Māyā* means the force that builds forth form. And this *māyā* has three effects. The first one is to cut off our vision of the perfect unity of the immanent world power. This is called the "obscuring effect" of *māyā*. The second is, to project all of these broken reflections that we see around us; and this is called the "projecting effect" of *māyā*. But *māyā* holds the possibility of a third effect also; for by contemplating all of these forms with the feeling that they are one, and by going around with the thought in your mind that you are in essence one with all these beings, you may come to realize that this is true. *Māyā* thus can reveal, through the manifold, the one; and this is called the "revealing effect" of *māyā*.

I have said that it is impossible to talk about *brahman-ātman*. The goal of Indian religion, the goal of Indian philosophy, is to point people's minds toward the realization of this truth and then to let them suddenly have the experience in their own minds. The images of Indian mythology and religion that we see on the beautiful Indian temples are called, in our language, "gods." But they are not gods in the same way that the god of the Old Testament is a god. The god of the Old Testament is conceived to be the ultimate truth. There is said to be nothing beyond this god. But the Indian gods are only pointing toward truth; because it is impossible, according to the Indian view, to speak about truth or to picture truth, to personify truth. The personifications, the images, the forms, are only clues, merely guides.

And now, to give you a notion of how some of these deities are pictured:

There are three very important deities in Indian worship, and they are Viṣṇu, Śiva, and Kālī. Viṣṇu is pictured as the divine dreamer of the world dream. Viṣṇu sleeps on a great serpent, whose name is Ananta, which means "Endless." The serpent floats on the universal ocean, called the Milky Ocean. But this Milky Ocean and the Serpent and the sleeping God: these are all the same thing. They are three inflections of the same thing, and that thing can be thought of also as the subtle substance that the wind of the mind stirs into action when the universe of all these shifting forms is brought into being. Viṣṇu, the God, sleeps, and the activity of his mind stuff creates dreams, and we are all his dream: the world is Viṣṇu's dream. And just as, in your dreams, all the images that you behold and all the people who appear are really manifestations of your own dreaming power, so are we all manifestations of Viṣṇu's dreaming power. We are no more independent entities than the dream figures in our own dreams. Hence, we are all one in Viṣṇu: manifestations, inflections, of this dreaming power of Viṣṇu; broken images of himself rippling on the spontaneously active surface of his subtle mind stuff.

Moreover, this sleeping god's divine dream of the universe is pictured in Indian art as a great lotus plant growing from his navel. The idea is that the dream unfolds like a glorious flower, and that this flower is the energy—or, as the Indians say, the śakti or goddess—of the god.

I hope that some of you are recalling the counterparts of some of these images in the biblical tradition. The waters that are stirred into action when creation takes place are comparable to those of the first verse of the Bible, where it is said that the wind or breath of god blew, or brooded, over the waters. This metaphor represents the miracle of creation, bringing the world into being as a multiplicity out of the stillness of an unstirred sleep. And the bride of the divine being, coming forth in the Indian myth from the navel of a dreaming god, is drawn in the biblical myth from the rib of a dreaming man. What was originally one has become two. And how delightful it is to see such an image-reflection of an aspect of one's own being—which was not present to consciousness before, and yet was there, nevertheless! So it is with Viṣṇu's dream. The god becomes aware of his own power and is delighted by the charms of his own power, as represented in the presence derived from him: the presence of his own dream, which is the universe. Thus, the universe is the dream-bride, or dream-goddess, of God.

Another image that appears frequently in Indian art is that of the god Śiva dancing. Śiva has four arms in this manifestation, and he is dancing on a prostrate dwarf. His first right hand holds a drum; and this drum beats; and that beat is the beat of time, which sends a ripple of movement over the face of eternity. The tick of time, then, is the creating principle, and this first right hand , therefore, is the hand of creation. It is bringing forth the world-dance just by beating the drum. But on the other side of the god, one of his two left hands holds a flame: the flame of illumination, which destroys the illusion of the world. This, then, is the hand of destruction. But destruction so conceived is rather paradoxical; because what we all want, surely, is to know the truth, even though full knowledge may come only with the dissolution—or stilling—of the activity of the world. And so, whereas we have a deluding creation in the one hand, we have an illuminating destruction in this other, and between the two, flows the enigma of the universe.

The second right hand of the god Śiva is held palm outward in a posture known as *abhāya,* which means, "don't be afraid." Nothing terrible is happening. Forms are breaking, your own form is breaking, death comes; yet nothing is happening. The eternal principle, which never was born,

Śiva Naṭarāja

never will die: it is in all things: it is in you now. You are a wave on the surface of the ocean. When the wave is gone, is the water gone? Has anything
happened? Nothing has happened. It is a play, a game, a dance.

The second left hand of the god Śiva is held out before him in what is
called the elephant posture. It is a posture suggesting the forehead and
trunk of an elephant, and this is the teaching hand. For the elephant is
likened to the teacher: where the elephant has walked, all animals can follow. It is a huge animal and where it has gone ahead, breaking down the

forest, the other beasts can easily follow. This elephant or teaching hand points to the left foot, which is lifted; and that lift signifies release. Meanwhile, however, the right foot is driving down into the back of the dwarf, whose name is "Ignorance." This foot is driving souls into ignorance—that is to say, into the world, into creation, into this life that we are leading. But the other foot is lifted, yielding release.

And so here is the god Śiva's image: one foot driving souls into life and the other releasing them, in a cycle of birth-into-ignorance and return-to-truth: birth and illumination. One hand controls creation, another destruction, while a third is saying, "Don't be afraid; nothing is happening!" and a fourth, "Look at the cycle down there, and realize that your ego (*aham*) is but a wave rippling on the ocean of eternity, while your true self (*ātman*), what you really are, is the water, which endures."

A third figure commonly seen in Indian religious art is the goddess Kālī. For if you wish to personify divinity (according to Indian thought), it is no less proper to picture a mother than to picture a father. Why, indeed, should one attribute sex to a divine being who is transcendent; that is to say, beyond all attributes? If beyond description, why attribute sex? So it is optional: you may decide for yourself whether you prefer to think of the divine principle as a mother or as a father, as a dreamer, or as a dancer. Any image will do, so long as it will help you to collect the main principles of this realization and hold them in your mind.

God as the mother is pictured in a very strange way. She gives birth to beings but then eats them; and so, she is a terrifying, frightening mother, represented with a great tongue hanging out to lick up the blood of her slaughtered victims. She is a horrendous thing. And this may give you a notion of the realistic seriousness of Indian imagery. Life is not all goodness, it is also frightful. So that, if we are going to assign to the creator only the qualities of benevolence, how shall we account for these other aspects of existence? Indian thought does not trouble itself as greatly as Western with the problem of evil; because there is no evil, really. Forms come into being, forms go out of being. Of course they do; for time passes! And how do the forms go out? Some comfortably, some uncomfortably; but they all go. It is this passage and fluency of time that is the great thing: and if you realize that it is all divine, whether going or coming, there is then nothing to fear. The goddess, therefore, is depicted as a frightful consumer of all beings as well as the mother of beings. She is the sow that eats her farrow, consuming her own children. Her upper right hand is in the posture of *abhāya,* "do not fear!"; the lower is outstretched in a boon-bestowing posture; the upper left hand holds a sword and the lower left a head, which the goddess has just cut off. She is the deliverer of both life and death. Horrendous yet fascinating, she is the very image of the dual nature of life.

These deities, these supreme beings, are held before the mind as objects of contemplation because they suggest the mysteries of this created world. It hurts the dwarf to be tread upon; and the dancer himself hurts his feet, dancing. But anyone with the power of creativity, the power to live, is not afraid of life's hurt. Therefore, if our consciousness is saying *aham* all the time, saying, "I, I, I am hurt, I and my friends are hurt, I and the principles I care for are being hurt, we're not getting on, the world's going to pot!"... if we begin thinking that way, we are out of touch with the creative principle and dynamics of the world, and we are already, from the standpoint of Indian thought, dead things.

The notion of the universe, then (for I want to move on, now, from the god, down to the universe itself); the notion of the universe in Indian thought is that it is a great organism, manifesting this divine dance, or this divine dream, in a harmonious, magnificent display. And every one of us is a part of that organism. Every one of us has a role to play in it. In their sacred books the Indians commonly represent this cosmic organism as a Great Man, with each class of humanity compared to a part.

Now, in the old agrarian societies—societies of the sort fundamental to Oriental culture—there were primarily four classes of human beings: four social strata. The most important of these in India was the brahmin or priestly class, whose function it was to know the divine revelation, to know the truth and how to teach the truth, how to instruct the community and its governors in the way of truth. The brahmins are compared to the head of the Great Being; and the second class—that of the rulers, or *Kṣatriya*—to the arms and chest. It is the function of the ruling class to administer the truth that the brahmins teach, maintaining the society in the way of the cosmic order. And then we come to the merchant and land-owning class, who represent the middle of the Great Man: his trunk and viscera. These, the *vaiśya,* constitute, so to say, the backbone and guts of the social order. They are the community that we call the Middle Class. And finally, the members of the fourth class, the *śūdra,* the workers and craftsmen, are compared to the feet of the composite being.

The notion is that everybody has a fixed and proper function, just as the different organs of the body have, and that by performing his functions, each keeps the divine society in harmonious health. Suppose the moon were to say one morning, "I'd like to be the sun." Or suppose the sun one day were to think, "I'd like to get up a little later this morning." The whole universe would go out of gear. The Indian idea of the social order is that all of us are just as tightly fixed to our ways and laws of life as the sun and moon.

Furthermore, when one reads the old law books, the *Book of Manu,* for example, one sees how, in ancient India, the life rules became more and more demanding as one proceeded up the social scale. The rules for the brahmin are minute to a degree that can hardly be imagined; but the restrictions become less and less demanding as one goes down the scale to the Śūdra level. For the notion is that there is a particular morality, or virtue, appropriate to each class, in accordance with its functions in the organism of the Great Man. For example, the morality proper to the worker, the Śūdra, was simply to do as told. By doing as he was told he lost his sense of ego, and so was introduced to the great religious principle and experience of egolessness. He learned this on the simplest, crudest level. And then, it was thought, after this experience of egolessness had been assimilated on the obvious level of physical service, he would have gained a spiritual character rendering him eligible to be promoted, in his next life, to the merchant or land-owning, *Vaiśya* class. For here the duties were more severe; but, also, the honors considerably greater, so that there was a greater temptation to egoism. It is harder to be egoless, harder to learn how to be selfless, on this level of wealth and comfort than on the lower levels of obedient toil. And since, for India, the goal of life is to learn selflessness, it is important that people should be graded properly according to their capacity.

But the ruling, aristocratic, or warrior class, of course, has more temptations than even the merchant to become egocentric. The members of this class have the power to do as they will, and so here the disciplines were extremely severe. And then, finally, for the brahmin, who was worshipped as a god, the temptation to ego was prodigious, and the rules of life were almost incredibly constraining,

Now everything that is described here implies the idea of reincarnation, and this idea is fundamental to all Indian thought. It is believed that through our experiences of life, we are gradually clarified in our vision, so that we become less and less the victims of ego and its systems of hope and fear. We learn more and more how to become egoless. In our Occidental, democratic society, we do not believe that people are born into precisely the social class for which their souls are ready. We believe in a loose social structure, with equal opportunities for all. The Indian view, on the other hand, has always been that people are born into the class for which they are ready, and so the system is designed to hold them there. It is important for us to realize, however, that the Indian system of caste is not associated primarily with wealth. People even of the very lowest caste may become wealthy; and a brahmin priest in a little rural temple will almost certainly be very poor indeed. It is only on the level of the third, the *Vaiśya* caste, that life is devoted primarily to the ideology of wealth. Hence the caste organization itself is not to be understood as an organization based on money. It is based on what is regarded in India as a spiritual principle: the idea that one must learn the lesson of life first on its lowest levels, and then return in later incarnations for more and more difficult lessons, until achieving complete release from this school of rebirth.

Let me tell you a story, to indicate something about the nature of this Indian idea of the spiritual value of the performance of duty. It is taken from a very interesting Buddhist text, the *Milindapanha,* which dates back to perhaps the second century A.D., and it tells of the great Buddhist emperor Aśoka, who lived in the third century B.C., in the city of Pataliputra (which is now called Patna). The river Ganges flows past this city, and the river, according to this tale, was rising at that time with such force that it was threatening the city with a flood. The Emperor was greatly troubled, and everybody in the town was greatly troubled, and so all—the Emperor included—assembled on the bank of the river to watch the waters rise.

There is an Indian notion that if you have fulfilled your life duty to perfection, you may perform what is known as an Act of Truth. You can say (and this is magic now): "If I have performed my duty without any trace of ego, but, like the sun rising and the sun setting, have done just what I should have done, every hour of my life, then let such and such happen!" And such and such will happen. This is called an Act of Truth. For, since you are part of the organism of the universe, and perfectly so, you partake of the power of the universe. You have become a conduit of universal energy and can perform miracles.

And so now, this story tells us, when all the city had gathered along the bank of the river Ganges, the emperor Aśoka, perceiving the danger, asked: "Can no one make an Act of Truth and cause the waters of the Ganges to flow back upstream?" Apparently the Emperor himself could not do so; nor could any of the members of his court: they stood around and looked embarrassed. The brahmins hung their heads, the nobles hung their heads, and the merchants hung their heads. But way down the way there was an old prostitute, and her name was Bindumatī, and she belonged to what was regarded as the abyss of the social structure. She was the lowest of the low. And yet she said to those around her, "I have an Act of Truth."

The old woman shut her eyes and presently the Emperor noticed that the waters of the vast river were slowing down, backing up: there was a roar, and the waters of the Ganges began to flow upstream.

You may imagine the action of the people. "Who," asked the Emperor, "performed this Act of Truth?" But no one around him knew. He looked about, and no one within range of his eye gave any sign of either being or of knowing the person whose virtue had saved the city. In a little while, however, the rumor reached him, and the Emperor proceeded to Bindumatī in amazement. "You!" he exclaimed. "Wicked old sinner! Disgrace of the community! Do you mean to say that you have an Act of Truth?" "Your Majesty," she answered, "I possess an Act of Truth by means of which, if I so desired, I could turn the world of men and the worlds of the gods upside down." The Emperor requested to be told this Act of Truth, and the old prostitute replied: "Whosoever gives me money, your Majesty, whether he be a brahmin, kṣatriya, vaiśya, or śūdra, I treat him as any other. I make no distinction in his favor if he is kṣatriya; and if a śūdra, I do not despise him. Free both from fawning and from contempt, I serve the owner of the money. And this your Majesty, is the Act of Truth by which I caused the mighty Ganges to flow back upstream."

The obvious part of this remarkable tale is that any way of life whatsoever is a way to God, if followed faithfully, selflessly, in perfect humility. This woman had power as no one else in the community, because she had performed to perfection the duties of her coarse and humble role. But the second lesson of the story is that she did not rise in the social scale for having saved the city: she remained Bindumatī, serving the owner of the money.

Which indicates an important thing about Oriental thought—namely, its distinction between moral and spiritual judgment and its ultimate dedication to the latter. This is something a little difficult for us to understand, since practically all of our own religious emphasis is moral. The religious interest of the Orient, on the other hand, though moral in large measure, is finally metaphysical; and its main idea is this: that by some act, some experience, some realization, some knowledge, we should achieve an effective relationship to our essential being, which is identical with the being that creates, supports, and annihilates the world.

When one reads the *Bhagavad Gītā*, which is the most important single text of Hinduism, one comes across a very strange statement. Kṛṣṇa there declares that he is the essence of all things: of the lion, he is the power and the fury; of thieves, the thievery; and of cheats, the cheating. "I am the victory of those who conquer," he declares, "and of those who die, the death." In other words, since divinity is the essence of every being, we must not let our moral judgments obscure from us the fact that God is shining through all things, even those of which we cannot approve; yet this should not disturb us in the performance of our own duties, according to the terms of our own system of ethics. There is a very nice paradoxical principle involved here, which, though it may be difficult for us to appreciate, is fundamental to the Indian point of view.

Moreover, there are many means, or ways, by which we may learn to shift our perspective from that of the multiplicity of this world to that of the unity of all things; and all these ways are called yogas. A number of apparently contradictory teachings have therefore been developed in the great domain of Hinduism. Yoga, in the broadest sense of the word, is any technique serving to link consciousness to the ultimate truth. One type of yoga I have already mentioned: that of stopping the spontaneous activity of the mind stuff. This type of mental discipline is called *rājā yoga*, the Kingly, or Great Yoga. But there is another called *bhakti yoga*, Devotional Yoga; and this is the yoga generally recommended for those who have duties in the world, tasks to perform, and who cannot, therefore, turn away to the practice of that other, very much sterner mode of psychological training. This much simpler, much more popular, yoga of worship consists in being selflessly devoted to the divine principle made manifest in some beloved form. One may dedicate oneself, for example, to the service of some god or goddess—one of those that I have just described—or any other, for that matter. Bhakti yoga will then consist in having one's mind continually turned toward, or linked to, that chosen deity through all of one's daily tasks. But since divinity is present in *all* things, one may devote oneself equally to some living person as an incarnation or manifestation of the divine—or even to some animal or plant. In the Hindu marriage the woman is to be thus devoted to her husband. He is god for her, just as the deity of his caste or craft-guild, the deity of his particular system of duty, is God for him.

There is an illuminating story told of the deity Kṛṣṇa, who, in the form of a human child, was raised among a little company or tribe of herdsmen. One day he said to them, when he saw them preparing to worship one of the great Gods of the brahminical pantheon: "But why do you worship a deity in the sky? The support of your life is here, in your cattle. Worship these!" Whereupon, they hung garlands around the necks of their cattle and paid them worship.

This wonderful art of recognizing the divine presence in all things, as a ubiquitous presence, is one of the most striking features of Oriental life, and is particularly prominent in Hinduism. I have seen very simple people out in the country, climbing a hill, who, when they became tired and paused to rest and eat, set up a stone, poured red paint around it, and then reverently placed flowers before it. The pouring of the red paint set that stone apart. The idea was simply that those people were now going to regard it, not as a stone, but as a manifestation of the divine principle that is immanent in all things. The pouring of the red paint and placing of the flowers were typical acts of *bhakti,* Devotional Yoga: simple devices, readily available to anyone, to shift the focus of the mind from the phenomenal aspect of the object as a mere stone to its mystery of a miracle of being. And this popular form of yoga, no less than the very much sterner and more difficult discipline of Patanjali's *Yoga Sūtras,* to which I first alluded, is a technique to link consciousness to the ultimate truth: the mystery of being. The sense of the whole universe as a manifestation of the radiance of God and of yourself as likewise of that radiance, and the assurance that this is so, no matter what things may look like, round about, is the key to the wisdom of India and the Orient.

And now there is one more little story that I should like to tell, to conclude all of this with an image to remember. It is the fable of a tigress, who was pregnant and hungry, prowling about in great distress, until she came at last upon a herd of goats, whereupon she pounced. But as she sprang she gave birth to her little tiger, and this incident so injured her that she died.

The goats, of course, had scattered. But when all was still, they returned to graze and found the tiny tiger, warm and alive, beside the dead body of its mother. Being generous hearted, gentle creatures, the mother goats took the little animal to themselves and brought it up as one of their own. Learning to eat grass, which is poor fare for tigers, the foundling grew up to be a scrawny, very mild example of his species, and the members of the herd got on very well with him. None paid attention to the obvious difference in complexion, and the little tiger himself had no realization that he was the least bit different from the rest.

But then, one day, a big male tiger discovered the herd and pounced. The goats scattered, but the little tiger, now an adolescent, stood where he was. He felt no fear; he just stood there. The big one blinked and looked again. "What is this?" he roared. "What are you doing here among goats?" The little fellow, not knowing that he was not a goat, was unable to grasp the sense of the question. Embarrassed, he bleated and the other, shocked, gave him a clout on the head. Confused, the little thing began to nibble grass. "Eating grass!" the big one roared again, and the scrawny cub only bleated.

Having studied the pitiful youngster for a while, the big male took him by the nape of the neck and carried him to a pond with a quiet surface, where he sat him down. "Now look into that pond," he said. The little tiger looked, and the big one, sitting beside him, also looked into the pond. "Look at your face, mirrored there in the water," he said, "and now look at mine: this one is mine. You have the pot-face of a tiger; have you not? You are not a goat." The cub became very quiet and thoughtful, absorbing the image of himself as a tiger. Then, when the master felt he was ready, he took him again by the neck and carried him to his lair, where there were the remains of a gazelle recently killed. Forcing a large piece of this raw flesh down the gagging throat of the revolted, frightened little tiger, the one compelled him to swallow—and gave him more, until, presently, he began to feel the tingle of the warm blood going into his veins. This was a new feeling altogether, and yet one congenial to his awakening true nature. Stretching for the first time in his life in the manner of a great cat, he suddenly heard his own throat emit, to his amazement, a great tiger roar. Then said the old fellow: "Aha! Now let us hunt together in the jungle."

And the lesson of this fable? The moral?

The lesson is that we are all tigers—living among goats.

CHRONOLOGICAL CHART OF INDIAN ART

	B.C.	DRAVIDIAN PERIOD	Mohenjo-daro,
Mesopotamian Cities and Empires *(ante c. 5500–c. 1000*	c. 3000–1500	Ruins of the Indus Valley Civilization	Harappā, Chanhu-daro
Aryans enter Near East	c. 1750–1000	ARYAN SETTLEMENT OF NORTH INDIA	
Assyrian, Hittite, and Medean Empires (c. 1500–c. 550)	c. 1500–450	VEDIC PERIOD *Vedas, Brāhmaṇas, Upaniṣads*	
Achaemenid Persian Empire (550–330)	c. 500 B.C.– 550 A.D.	BUDDHISM AND THE RISE OF BUDDHIST ART EARLY HINDU AND JAINA ART Mahāvīra, 24th Tīrthaṅkara, d. c. 526 Gautama, the Buddha, c. 563–483	
	325: ALEXANDER THE GREAT ENTERS N.W. INDIA		
Seleucid Persian Empire (305–64)	c. 321–184	Maurya Dynasty Aśoka, c. 272–231	Aśoka Pillars; early stūpas
Arsacid Persian Empire (250 B.C.–226 A.D.)	c. 185–c. 73	Śuṅga and Kāṇva Dynasties	Sāñcī: Stūpa No. 2; Bhārhut reliefs; Bhājā; Bodhgayā railing
	c. 73 B.C.–II cent. A.D.	Satavahana Dynasty	Sāñcī: Stūpa No. 1; rockcut sanctuaries; Amarāvatī
	SCYTHIAN (ŚAKA INVASIONS)	I cent. B.C.–	
	YUEH-CHI (KUṢĀNA) INVASION	I cent. A.D.	
	A.D.		
Sassanian Persian Empire (226–41)	I–VII cent.	Kuṣāṇa Dynasty and successors	Mathurā, Gandhāra
	c. 320–650	Gupta and Vākāṭaka Dynasties and successors	Sārnāth, Ajaṇṭā
	WHITE HUN INVASIONS, c. 480–525		
Rise of Islam (Mohammed, d. 632) Muslim conquest of India (c. 750–1565)	c. 525–1565	MEDIEVAL INDIAN ART	
	c. 525–600	Early Kalacuri Dynasty	Elephanta, Elūrā
	c. 600–850	Pallava Dynasty	Māmallapuram
	c. 550–750	Cālukya Dynasty	Bādamī, Aihoḷe, Paṭṭadakal
	c. 750–975	Rāṣṭrakūṭa Dynasty	Elūrā
	c. 750–1250	Pāla and Sena Dynasties	Nālandā
	c. 950–1200	Candella Dynasty	Khajurāho
	c. 1076–1586	Gaṅgā Dynasty	Koṇārak, Bhuvaneśvara
	c. 850–1250	Coḷa Dynasty	Tanjore
	c. 1006–1346	Hoyśala Dynasty	Halebid, Belūr
	c. 1100–1350	Pāṇḍya Dynasty	Tiruvannāmalai
	c. 1350–1565	Rāya Dynasty	Vijayanagar
Portuguese, French, and British in India *(post* 1500)	XVI–XIX cent.	LATE STYLES	
	post 1565	Nāyak Dynasty	Madura
	XVI–XIX cent.	Rājput Dynasties	Miniatures
	1526–1857	Moghul period (Muslim)	

Note: This chart has been updated with the kind assistance of Dr. Walter Spink of the University of Michigan, who helped Campbell compile the original for The Art of Indian Asia *in 1954.*

BOOK I ENDNOTES

EDITORS' FOREWORD: BAKSHEESH & BRAHMAN

1. One of the other youths was Rajagopal, Krishnamurti's lifelong manager and companion, whom Rosalind Williams, one of the American women, would later marry. On the voyage also was Helen Knothe, the violin prodigy and international explorer, also in her early twenties, who would later become Helen Nearing. Nearing, with her husband Scott, became an internationally known authority on natural living. Together they wrote *Living the Good Life!* and many other books.
2. See *A Fire in the Mind*, p. 41–43.
3. See *A Fire in the Mind*, pp. 41 and 87–94. See also Pupul Jayakar, *Krishnamurti: A Biography*, and Jiddu Krisnamurti, *You Are the World*, and *The First and Last Freedom*.
4. See *A Fire in the Mind*, Chapters 8 and 9.
5. See *A Fire in the Mind*, pp. 426–429.

PRELUDE

Note: References to books are given in their short form for ease of reading. Full references may be found in the Bibliography.

1. Swami Nikhilananda (1895–1973) was a follower of Mahatma Gandhi and a sometime agitator for India's independence. In 1924 he gave up a career as a political journalist to join the Ramakrishna Math, the monastic order founded in 1899 by Vivekananda in commemoration of Ramakrishan, and to serve India's educational, social, and medical needs. He was appointed to the Vedanta Society in New York to replace an older swami who did not get along with his congregation.

Sought out by Heinrich Zimmer (see note 12) in 1941, Nikhilananda soon introduced him to Campbell, with enduring consequences for both men. When Nikhilananda was editing his English edition of *The Gospel of Sri Ramakrishna* and his translation of *The Upanishads,* he sought and received Campbell's assistance. "Swami . . . seduced me into editing his books for him—always keeping me, in a subtle way, pitched forward toward a vacuum, where, finally, I would discover that I had been used."

2. Campbell wrote the introduction to the *Portable Arabian Nights.*

3. Elizabeth Stieglitz Davidson (1897–1956), niece of photographer Alfred Stieglitz, married Donald Douglas Davidson, longtime member of the Vedanta Society in New York. They were among the founders of the Ramakrishna-Vivekananda Center in New York and were lifetime directors. Campbell met Nikhilananda through the Davidsons, whose daughter Peggy was Campbell's student at Sarah Lawrence College. The Davidsons' other daughter, Sue Davidson Geiger Lowe, followed her sister to Sarah Lawrence and later became Campbell's assistant. Elizabeth Davidson travelled twice to India with Nikhilananda.

    See *A Fire in the Mind,* pp. 284–285.

4. Countess Mabel Colloredo-Mansfeld (1906–1965), née Bradley, the widow of Count Colloredo-Mansfeld of Austria, entered the "inner circle" of the Ramakrishna-Vivekananda Center in New York in the late 1940s.

5. In other words, Mrs. Davidson and "the Countess."

CHAPTER 1: TRAVELS WITH SWAMI

6. "In India, the saffron robes the monks wear are the color of the garment put on a corpse. These men are dead. Are you ready to put on the garment of a corpse?" *Joseph Campbell Companion,* p. 201.

7. In reference to the Ramakrishna Center on East 94th Street in New York.

8. Built by the Mughal emperor Shah Jahan (fl. 1628–1658) after moving the capital from Agra to Delhi.

9. Campbell would often later quote this line, comparing it to the saying of Jesus in the Gnostic Gospel of Thomas: "The Kingdom of God the Father is spread upon the Earth and men do not see it." See *Occidental Mythology,* p. 368.

10. William McGuire was then Campbell's editor for *The Hero with a Thousand Faces.* He was also editor of various other Bollingen Series volumes, all of which were then being published and distributed by Pantheon Books. See William McGuire, *Bollingen: An Adventure in Collecting the Past.*

11. Humayun, Mughal emperor, reigned 1530–1556.

12. Heinrich Zimmer (1890–1943) was one of the scholars who most influenced Campbell's life and work. A friend of Thomas Mann, of Carl Gustav Jung, married to Hugo von Hofmannsthal's daughter, a great raconteur and a man of immense erudition. Campbell found in Zimmer a challenging fellow spirit. Although they knew each other for only two years, from Zimmer's arrival in New York until Zimmer's untimely death from pneumonia in 1943, Campbell became a friend, and after Zimmer's death, spent twelve years editing and completing Zimmer's work. These works include *Myths and Symbols in Indian Art and Civilization* (1946), *The King and the Corpse* (1948), *The Philosophies of India* (1951), and *The Art of Indian Asia* (1955), whose subject was the

very temples that Campbell was now visiting, and to which Campbell was giving the final polish during his Indian trip (see pp. 59, 72, 231). Zimmer himself never visited India. For Campbell's remembrance of Zimmer, see "Heinrich Zimmer (1890–1943)" in the *Partisan Review, v.* 20 (July 1943), pp. 415–416.

13. In 1953, the United States and Pakistan entered into a military aid agreement, exacerbating the Cold War in South Asia. See Robert J. McMahon, *The Cold War on the Periphery* (New York: Columbia University Press, 1994). See also p. 302 and note 272.

14. "Forty Sadhus and One Thief," or literally, "Forty Fathers and One Thief." The title is a play on *Ali Baba and the Forty Thieves.*

15. Pramod Chandra later went on to the University of Chicago and Harvard. Ananda K. Coomaraswamy (1877–1947), one of Campbell's more important sources for Indian art and scholarship. See p. 194.

16. Vijaya Lakshmi Pandit, Prime Minister Nehru's sister. See note 226.

17. *Cakra:* one of a series of nerve centers in yogic physiology, rising from the base of the spine to the crown of the head. The second is known as *svādiṣṭhāna,* and is the *cakra* of the genital area. For an explanation of the *cakra* system, see *The Mythic Image,* pp. 330–381.

18. *The Statesman.* The leading English-language daily in India, published in Calcutta.

19. The leftward-turning swastika is an ancient Indian graphical symbol suggesting well-being and conveying auspiciousness. In Mahāyāna Buddhism, it is associated with the involution of consciousness backward from the waking state into *nirvāṇa* through the practice of meditation. See "The Symbol without Meaning" in *The Flight of the Wild Gander,* figs. 12–13, p. 139.

20. *Brahman,* "universal soul" or "Absolute Reality," to be distinguished from "brahmin" (*brāhmaṇa*), the priestly caste. For a discussion of *brahman,* see Campbell's essay "Hinduism" included here as Appendix IA. For further discussion of India's devotional piety, see p. 86.

21. In Wagner's *Ring* cycle Fafnir is the greedy brother of the giant Fasolt; in *Das Rheingold* he murders Fasolt for possession of the ring, which corrupts him and transforms him into a dragon. In *Siegfried* Fafnir is slain by Siegfried, who takes his gold from him. Campbell's reference seems rather to recall Wagner's version.

22. See *Inner Reaches of Outer Space,* pp. 96–97 and figs. 16–17.

23. Avanti Varman of Kashmir founded the Utpala Dynasty c. A.D. 855 after overthrowing the Karkata Dynasty. He was especially known for his irrigation works.

24. Mokuleia: the Erdman family estate on Oahu, Hawai'i.

25. Viet Minh: Ho Chi Minh's army in Vietnam against the French.

26. Fellaheen: *Webster's* defines the word as "a peasant or agricultural laborer in Egypt, Syria, and other Arabic-speaking countries." Campbell is here using Spengler's special sense of the word to designate the population "fallout" that results from the aftermath of a collapsed and burnt-out civilization. Such peoples are no longer culturally productive but have fallen back into the sterile culture forms of their religion: "At this level all civilizations enter a stage, which lasts for centuries. . . . The whole pyramid of cultural man vanishes. It crumbles from the summit, first the world-cities, then the provincial forms and finally the land itself, whose best blood has incontinently poured into the towns: merely to bolster them up awhile. At the last only primitive blood

remains, alive, but robbed of its strongest and most promising elements. This residue is the *Fellah type.*" (*Decline of the West,* vol. 1, p. 107). See also p. 87 for more of Campbell's view of history.

27. Zimmer wrote, and Campbell edited, both of these books, *Myths and Symbols in Indian Art and Civilization,* and *The Philosophies of India.* See Bibliography.

28. Yuvaraj Karan Singh, *The Glory of Amarnāth,* p. 8. Campbell later said, "The whole idea of pilgrimage is translating into a literal, physical act the pilgrimage of moving into the center of your own heart. It's good to make a pilgrimage if, while doing so, you meditate on what you are doing and know that it's into your inward life that you are moving." *Transformations of Myth Through Time,* p. 98.

29. *Glory of Amarnāth,* p. 21.

30. *Glory of Amarnāth,* pp. 20–21.

31. Tenzing Norgay, who with Sir Edmund Hillary scaled the summit of Mt. Everest on May 29, 1953.

32. "The chief aim of Indian thought is to unveil and integrate into consciousness what has been thus resisted and hidden by the forces of life—not to explore and describe the visible world. The supreme and characteristic achievement of the Brahman mind...was its discovery of the self (*atmān*) as an independent, imperishable entity, underlying the conscious personality and bodily frame.... [T]he primary concern—in striking contrast to the interests of the modern philosophers of the West—has always been, not information, but transformation." *The Philosophies of India,* pp. 3–4.

33. Campbell attended preparatory school from 1918–1921 at the Catholic Canterbury School in New Milford, Conn.

34. "The symbolism which knows"; "the symbolism which searches"; and "the symbolism which thinks that it knows." This dichotomy (the third term being Campbell's resolution of the two) is adapted from the writings of scholar René Guénon. See also p. 175.

35. This distinction is central to Campbell's understanding of mythology. "Jung's idea of the archetypes is one of the leading theories, today, in the field of our subject. It is a development of the earlier theory of Adolf Bastian (1826–1906), who recognized in the course of his extensive travels the uniformity of what he termed 'elementary ideas' (*Elementargedanken*) of mankind. Remarking also, however, that in the various provinces of human culture these ideas are differently articulated and elaborated, he coined the term 'ethnic ideas' (*Völkergedanken*) for the actual local manifestation of the universal forms. Nowhere, he noted, are the 'elementary ideas' to be found in a pure state, abstracted from the locally conditioned 'ethnic ideas' through which they are substantialized; but rather, like the image of man himself, they are to be known only by way of the rich variety of their extremely interesting, frequently startling, yet always finally recognizable inflections in the panorama of human life." *Primitive Mythology,* p. 32. See also *Transformations of Myth Through Time,* pp. 93–94; *The Inner Reaches of Outer Space,* p. 69.

36. Sarvepalli Radhakrishnan, *Indian Philosophy.*

37. That is to say, the man looked to Campbell as he imagined his friend, the composer John Cage, might look at sixty.

38. See Zimmer, *The Philosophies of India,* plate IX.

39. In the myth, Kṛṣṇa alone can destroy the great serpent, Kāliya.

40. Campbell has made a mistake here: Aurangzeb's father was Shah Jahan, who was not blinded, although he was imprisoned by Aurangzeb in 1658. Akbar, 1542–1605, was an earlier Mughal emperor. Aurangzeb also had a son named Akbar; he led a rebellion against his father.

41. Mast Hope: a small station-town in Pike County, Penn., where the Campbell family used to spend summers.

42. Warren Hastings (1732–1818), British colonial administrator and first Governor General of Bengal. He was tried (a seven-year trial) and acquitted by the British Parliament for misdeeds in India, Edmund Burke being his main accuser. Hastings cut off the fingers and hands of the Daccan weavers as a disciplinary measure.

43. See also p. 66 for another example of an "undying banyan."

44. See *Creative Mythology*, p. 575

45. Campbell became associated with Eranos, the annual European conference on myth and symbol, from editing the posthuma of Heinrich Zimmer for the Bollingen Foundation. He later edited six volumes of the collected papers from the Eranos conferences and contributed two papers himself. "The Symbol without Meaning" was included in *Flight of the Wild Gander*, while "Myths and Rites of the Primitive Hunters and Gatherers" is available as a broadside.

46. See p. 36 for an earlier examination of this theme.

47. Surendra Nath Das Gupta wrote *A History of Indian Philosophy*, Cambridge University Press, 1922–1949.

48. The late Agehananda Bharati was author of *The Ochre Robe*, written about his years as a monk, and *The Tantric Tradition*, among other books. He later became a professor of anthropology at Syracuse University.

49. For the diffusion and practice of the Neolithic pig sacrifice and its attendant myths and rites, see *The Mythic Image*, pp. 450–481. For the Polynesian context, see "Renewal Myths and Rites of the Primitive Planters"; also *Primitive Mythology*, pp. 170–215; and *The Sacrifice* (*Atlas* II.1). See *Creative Mythology*, pp. 123–128 for its diffusion into Celtic Europe. See also below, p. 81 and note 70, for the Durgā buffalo sacrifice.

50. Jean Erdman was teaching at this time at Bard College in Annandale-on-Hudson, New York.

51. "In other words, the goal of the 'Way of Devotion' (*bhakti-māyā*) has to be transcended by the student of Vedanta. The loving union of the heart with its highest personal divinity is not enough. The sublime experience of the devotee beholding the inner vision of his God in concentrated absorption is only a prelude to the final ineffable crisis of complete illumination, beyond the spheres even of the divine form." Zimmer, *The Philosophies of India*, p. 418.

52. "The essential idea in Jainism is that the soul, what is called *jīva*, the living monad, is infected with action, which is called *karma*, which blackens and renders heavy the luminous *jīva*.... The goal of their yoga is to clean out the black, clean out action. How do they do it?... The first step, of course, is to become vegetarians. This is saying 'No' to the way life is.... The Buddha [in contrast] said no, no, no, this is reading the whole thing physically. What you must die to is, psychologically, your desires and your fears." *Transformations of Myth Through Time*, p. 109. See also Zimmer, *The Philosophies of India*, pp. 413–414.

53. See p. 56.

54. Nālandā was a celebrated Buddhist university traditionally dated from the fourth to fifth century B.C. Nāgārjuna, the famous Mādhyamika philosopher, began his studies there.

55. Ronald von Holt: one of Campbell's ranching in-laws from Hawai'i.

56. See Zimmer, *Art of Indian Asia,* plates 31–36.

57. Aurangzeb (1618–1707), the last great Mughal emperor, was a fierce promoter of Islam whose military successes were followed by political failures. See note 40.

58. See *Atlas* II.1, pp. 38–39, figs. 71–72.

59. Irma Brandeis was a friend of the Campbells' who taught first at Sarah Lawrence and then at Bard College. Campbell had arranged the connection between her and the Bollingen Foundation, which gave her a grant.

60. The Forest Lake Club in Pike County, Pennsylvania, where Campbell's family owned property and spent the summers.

61. Arjuna, the aristocratic protagonist of *The Bhāgavad Gītā.*

62. Campbell visited Central America with his family as a teenager. See *Fire in the Mind,* pp. 34–35.

63. The ideas "lifted" are from *The Philosophies of India,* pp. 169–172. See also Appendix IA, pp. 320–321, for an example of an "Act of Truth."

64. See *Oriental Mythology,* p. 211 for a fuller interpretation of the sacrifice.

65. See *Oriental Mythology,* pp. 5–6.

66. Paddy: freshly cut rice, including the stalk and husk.

67. See *Primitive Mythology,* pp. 183–190.

68. Durgā Pūjā lasts nine days, not three, and is often referred to as Nara Ratrī: "nine nights." Campbell seems to have been present for the last three days. The numbers *saptamī, ashtamī, navamī* refer to the seventh, eight, and ninth days of the waxing lunar cycle. Durgā Pūjā begins on the first day (the new moon), but according to Akos Oster, *Puja in Society,* pp. 25–26, "The major days of the Durgā festival fall on the sixth (Sasthi), seventh (Saptami), eighth (Astami), ninth (Navami), and tenth (Dasami). The Debi worship proper begins on the seventh (the sixth is the Night of Invocation). This being the major puja of the year the *tithis* [lunar calendar days] are called *maha,* or the great, so Mahasaptami, Mahastami and so on." This explains why Campbell calls the seventh day the first: it is the first day that the goddess is established and wor-shipped. After the ninth night the images (desacralized) are immersed in the river.

69. The time of the monsoon is archetypally the time of spiritual renewal. The Festival of Anthesteria, a festival of flowers, was held in the spring at Athens. There the wine of the last vintage was tasted, the theater contests were held, and the taints of the past year were purged.

70. "The supreme orthodox religious duty of man with respect to the gods and ancestors has always been to offer sacrifice. The inhabitant of the body, presiding over the works of the individual, is the one who enacts the sacred office, as well as all the other deeds of the creatures, whether present, past, or future.... Moreover, it [the Self] is not only the perpetrator of sacrifice, fundamentally it is inherent in all the utensils of the holy rite, as well as in...the 'beast of sacrifice'—the victim roped to the sacrificial post and about to be slaughtered. That one being is the offerer, the offering, and the implements

of the offering. . . . Regarded thus as the mere garbs of the one anonymity, the sacrificer and his victim, the feeder and his food, the victor and his conquest, were the same: simultaneous roles or masks of the one cosmic actor." Zimmer, *Philosophies of India,* p. 411. See also Campbell, *The Sacrifice,* pp. 75–76: "In every sacrifice of this kind, the victim is understood to be an incarnation of the god."

71. "Theodosius II summoned a council in the year 431 at Ephesus, which happened to be the city in Asia Minor that, for millenia before the Christian era, had been the chief temple site of the great Asian goddess Artemis, mother of the world and of the ever-dying resurrected God. We can reasonably assume that her lingering influence, no less than that of the virginal matriarchs of the palace, worked upon the counsels of the bishops there assembled. For it was there that the Virgin Mother was declared to be *theotokos,* the Mother of God." *Occidental Mythology,* p. 410.

72. For a comparison between Catholic liturgy and Indian temple rites, see *Creative Mythology,* pp. 167–169.

73. "[A] once powerful cult, derived from Iran, of the Mysteries of Mithra, which came to flower in the Near East during the Hellenistic age as a kind of Zoroastrian heresy, and in the Roman period was the most formidable rival of Christianity both in Asia and in Europe." *Occidental Mythology,* p. 255; see pp. 256–271 for discussion, and see fig. 23 for a portrayal of Mithra Tauroctonus (Mithra killing the Bull).

74. See *Occidental Mythology,* figs. 12, 16, 18, 27, and 28.

75. Pallava Dynasty, A.D. 600–850 in Māmallapuram. Campbell is probably referring to the image reproduced in *The Art of Indian Asia,* vol. 2, plate 284.

76. Leo Frobenius (1873–1938), a German ethnologist and explorer, originator of the cultural-historical approach to ethnology. His works were of central importance for Campbell's writings on primitive cultures and for his view of history: "I studied ecstatically some fifteen volumes of Frobenius' writings . . . and emerged with a view of history very much more relaxed and continuous than the view emphasized in [Spengler's] *Decline of the West." A Fire in the Mind,* p. 225.

77. See *Creative Mythology,* figs. 28, 58.

78. For an overview of the goddess and the bull, see *Occidental Mythology,* chapter 2, "The Consort of the Bull."

79. Henry Morton Robinson: Campbell's friend and collaborator on *A Skeleton Key to Finnegans Wake.*

80. Here again Campbell sounds a main theme; see also p. 26, where Campbell complains that he hears nothing of *brahman.*

81. See pp. 33–34 and esp. note 26 for a fuller explanation.

82. "This next phase I call the *Second Religiousness.* It appears in all Civilizations as soon as they have fully formed themselves as such and are beginning to pass, slowly and imperceptibly, into the non-historical state in which time periods cease to mean anything (so far as the Western Civilization is concerned, therefore, we are still many generations short of that point). . . . The second religiousness consists in a deep piety that fills the waking-consciousness—the piety that impressed Herodotus in the (late) Egyptians and impresses West-Europeans in China, India, and Islam. . . . It starts with Rationalism's fading out in helplessness, then the forms of the Springtime become visible, and finally the whole world of the primitive religion, which had receded before

the grand forms of the early faith, returns to the foreground, powerful, in the guise of the popular syncretism that is to be found in every culture at this phase...." Spengler, *Decline of the West,* vol. II, pp. 310–311. Also, "In the end Second Religiousness issues in the *fellah-religions." Decline of the West,* p. 314. For "*fellah-religions*" see pp. 19–20, 221, and note 26.

83. René Guénon was the author of *Introduction to the Study of the Hindu Doctrines;* Alain Danielou was the author of numerous books on Asian music, culture, and religion. (See note 257.) Ananda K. Coomaraswamy, Sinhalese scholar of Indian art, was the author of *History of Indian and Indonesian Art* and numerous other books. Campbell often consulted Coomaraswamy while editing Heinrich Zimmer's posthuma (see note 15).

84. See p. 43.

85. Eliot Elisofon, award-winning *Life* photographer, had done extensive photographing of Indian temple sculpture and art objects from European museum collections. Many of his photos fill Zimmer's *The Art of Indian Asia,* published the following year by the Bollingen Foundation.

86. "In India they are called, respectively, 'the way of the monkey' and 'the way of the kitten'; for when a kitten is in trouble it calls 'meow!' and its mother carries it to safety, but the little monkey, when carried by its mother, has to ride clinging with its own strength to her body. The type of the 'monkey' way in India is the way of the yogi; in Buddhism it is the way of Zen. Among the types in India of the 'way of the kitten carried by its savior,' the best known today and most popular is of Viṣṇu in his incarnation as Krishna...; while in Buddhism, the Savior most widely celebrated and revered is the inexhaustibly compassionate Buddha Amitabha (Amida in Japan)." *Atlas* II.I, p. 33. See also p. 166.

87. Twenty-five years earlier, at college, Campbell was a champion half-miler.

88. See Spengler, *Decline of the West,* vol. I, p. 183, for the concept of cultural entelechies, or monads, or as he calls them, *Ursymbols,* which act as a sort of cultural DNA that shapes and structures a culture from within and determines what its outlook upon the world will be.

89. See pp. 158, 219–221, for further summaries of Campbell's evolving distinctions between Orient and Occident.

90. For another view on this dichotomy, and Campbell's tentative resolution, see pp. 39–40. See also pp. 175–176 for a discussion of these ideas in terms of Campbell's vocation.

91. Māmallapuram: modern Mahabalipuram.

92. Conjeevaram: modern Kāncipuram.

93. See *Art of Indian Asia,* v. 2, plates 266–271.

94. See *Art of Indian Asia,* v. 2, plates 272–278a.

95. See *Art of Indian Asia,* v. 2, plates 294–298.

96. See *Art of Indian Asia,* v. 2, plates 286–287.

97. See *Art of Indian Asia,* v. 2, plates 284–285, 288.

98. See *Art of Indian Asia,* v. 2, plates 279–283.

99. See *Art of Indian Asia,* v. 1, pp. 275, 277 note.

100. In some reckonings, this is one of the five "element-*liṅgas*" brought by Śaṅkara from the Himalayas. See *Art of Indian Asia,* v. 1, p. 280, 281 note.

101. Rāmānuja: A Vedantist teacher of the eleventh century, of a stature comparable to that of Śaṅkara. He modulated Śaṅkara's non-dualism into a more theistic theology, *Viśiṣṭha-advaita* (monism with differentiation, or distinction). See *Philosophies of India*, pp. 458–460.

102. Vinoba Bhave: Indian ascetic and founder of Bhūdān Yajña, the land-gift movement. He was an associate of Mohandas Gandhi.

CHAPTER 2: TEMPLES AND MONUMENTS

103. "The relationship [i.e., 'Thou Art That'] is expressed by the simile of lovers, so closely embraced that there is no longer any consciousness of 'a within or without,' and by the corresponding Vaiṣṇava equation, 'each is both.'" *Coomaraswamy 2: Selected Papers, Metaphysics,* p. 22.

104. See *Art of Indian Asia,* v. 2, plates 114–115, 118–121; also v. 2, plate 213, Plate 224.

105. See *Art of Indian Asia,* plate 315; also v. 2, plate 361.

106. See *Creative Mythology,* p. 595 for a discussion of the Gothic Black Mass; see also *Creative Mythology,* pp. 165–166 for a comparison of erotic Indian temple art with the Black Mass.

107. *Basic Mythologies,* or *Basic Mythologies of Mankind,* which Campbell is here planning, would later become, in part, the four-volume *Masks of God.* "The Bollingen Foundation, having enabled Campbell to travel in the Orient, carried his fellowship well into the 1960's. With [Jack] Barrett he had followed a program that would culminate in a massive, three-volume work, *The Basic Mythologies of Mankind,* devoted to the differences between the various mythologies, whereas *Hero with a Thousand Faces* was devoted to the similarities.... [T]he *Basic Mythologies* bifurcated. Four volumes under the title *Masks of God,* presenting the mythological and religious heritage of man in a style directed to the general reader, were published by the Viking Press over the years 1959–1968." William McGuire, *Bollingen: An Adventure in Collecting the Past,* pp. 178–179. See also below, pp. 155, 177, 179, etc.

108. Sri Aurobindo (1872–1950): Seer, poet, and Indian nationalist, educated at Cambridge, later imprisoned for political activities. The founder of a new theory of gnosis in which cosmic salvation is linked to human spiritual evolution. He was founder also of an international spiritual community in Pondicherry.

109. The *yugas* are the four world ages through which we endlessly cycle, going from best to worst. They are represented by Śaṅkara as a cow standing first on four legs, then three, then two, then one. This last is called the Kālī Yuga, the current one, full of strife and evil, lasting 432,000 years. At its end a "holy" age, the Kṛta Yuga, will return. See Zimmer, *Myths and Symbols in Indian Art and Civilization,* pp. 11–19; also Campbell, "On the Mythic Shape of Things to Come—Circular and Linear" in *Horizon,* vol. 16, summer 1974, pp. 35–37.

110. "When faced with this problem of grasping the ideas of the East, the usual mistake of Western man is like that of the student in *Faust.* Misled by the Devil, he contemptuously turns his back on science, and, carried away by Eastern occultism, takes over yoga practices quite literally and becomes a pitiable imitator. (Theosophy is our best example of this mistake.) And so he abandons the one safe foundation of the Western mind and loses himself in a mist of words and ideas which never would

have originated in European brains, and which never can be profitably grafted upon them.... It is not a question of our imitating, or worse still, becoming missionaries for what is organically foreign but rather a question of building up our own Western culture, which sickens with a thousand ills. This has to be done on the spot, and by the real European as he is in his Western commonplaces, with his marriage problems, his neuroses, his social and political decisions, and his whole philosophical orientation." C. G. Jung, in "Commentary on 'The Secret of the Golden Flower'." See also p. 106, and note 88, for discussions of the dangers going in the other direction, i.e. for Indians taking from the West. See also the diagram on p. 159 for Campbell's contrast of the respective aims of the two cultures.

III.   See Sir James Frazer, *Myths of the Origin of Fire*.

112.   Gymkhana: athletic clubs established throughout India in 1861 by a Major John Trotter for British officers; later converted to various uses.

113.   Alfred Salmony (1891–1958), art historian and critic, professor of the history of Asiatic art at the Institute for Fine Arts at New York University. An authority on Chinese jade, he was the author of two monumental works: *Carved Jade of Ancient China* and *Archaic Chinese Jades*. His book *Antler and Tongue*, which stresses the relationship between the art of Europe and Asia in antiquity, came out in 1954. Salmony was educated at the universities of Bonn and Vienna, and became curator of the Cologne City Museum of Asiatic art in 1920. Salmony came to New York in 1933, fleeing the Nazis. He taught at Mills College and Vassar College before coming to NYU, and was editor of the quarterly journal *Artibus Asiae*.

114.   Enantiodromia: A word coined from the Greek by Jung to mean a situation that turns into its opposite.

115.   Nasli Heeramanek, a Parsee art dealer with whom the Campbells had become friendly in New York.

116.   Mme. Moitessier, wife of Gunvor Moitessier, who took many of the photos for *The Art of Indian Asia*.

117.   See *Art of Indian Asia*, plates 187–247.

118.   Kailāśanātha Temple, or Cave XVI. "This overpowering monument marks the victory of Brahmanism over Buddhism." *Art of Indian Asia*, vol. 1, p. 291. See also vol. 2, plates 204–226.

119.   See *Art of Indian Asia*, v. 1, pp. 185–190, v. 2, plates 142–186. "[Ajaṇṭā is] the main site safeguarding from the ravages of time fragments of an art scarcely matched in the world." *Art of Indian Asia*, p. 185.

120.   Elephanta is an island in the harbor of Bombay, of roughly the same period as the Kailāśanātha of Elūrā (later eighth century A.D.). The central figure is a threefold image of Śiva, 23 ft. high by 19 ft. across. See *Art of Indian Asia*, v. 1, pp. 297–298; v. 2., plates 253–255.

121.   For *The Art of Indian Asia*, which was due to come out shortly.

122.   Rama Mehta, an aristocratic patron of the arts from New Delhi, known to the Nikhilananda circle.

123.   Campbell met Jiddu Krishnamurti, the messiah-elect of the world Theosophical movement, on a transatlantic voyage (see Editors' Foreword, p. 5). One of the women traveling with Krishnamurti gave Campbell Edwin Arnold's book about the

life of the Buddha, *The Light of Asia.* Their friendship continued intermittently for several years. See *A Fire in the Mind,* esp. pp. 41–44 and Index notations.

124. In 1938 Jung had made the trip to India, visiting many of the same sites as Campbell. When given the opportunity in Madras, however, to visit with Ramana Maharishi, he declined, to the disappointment of Heinrich Zimmer, who had never been to India. When Zimmer died in 1943, Jung took upon himself the task of editing Zimmer's German posthuma, which consisted primarily of a single volume on Sri Ramana Maharishi, entitled *Der Weg zum Selbst: Lehre und Leben des indischen Heiligen Shri Ramana Maharishi aus Tiruvannama-lai* (1944). Jung wrote a foreword, "The Holy Men of India," in which he wrote of his visit to India and explained his refusal to visit Ramana Maharishi by saying that Maharishi was omnipresent, since Jung had actually seen him everywhere, the "true Son of Man of the land of India."

125. Four caves from the early Cālukya Period, c. A.D. 550–750. Cave III, the earliest, is dated at A.D. 578. See *Art of Indian Asia,* vol. 1, pp. 85–86, 290; v. 2, plates 124–141.

126. Cave II "shelters a magnificent rendition of Viṣṇu as the Cosmic Boar." See *Art of Indian Asia,* v. 1., p. 290, v. 2, plate 138.

127. Cave III has pillars "ornamented with magnificent human figures in the full bloom of Gupta abundance." See Coomaraswamy, *History of Indian and Indonesian Art,* p. 96.

128. "The Malegiṭṭi Śivalaya Temple...built *c.* A.D. 625, is one of the oldest structural shrines of the Dravidian type, 'the only structural temple in the style of the Māmallapuram rathas now surviving'...." See *Art of Indian Asia,* v. 1, p. 278; v. 2, plate 141.

129. The temples at Paṭṭadakal are examples of the Cālukya Period, c. A.D. 550–750. See *Art of Indian Asia,* v. 2, plates 299–308.

130. The temples at Aihoḷe are predominantly of the Cālukya Period, c. A.D. 550–750. See *Art of Indian Asia,* v. 2, plates 113, 116–123. For the Durgā temple, see v. 1, p. 84; v. 2, plates 116–120; for the shallow cave temple, see v. 2, plate 123; for the Huchimalliguḍi, see v. 2, plate 113. The Lāḍ Khān Temple is of the Gupta Period, c. A.D. 450: see v. 2, plates 114–115.

131. Belūr (a temple-city) and Haḷebīḍ (a royal residence, left unfinished, interrupted by a Muslim invasion) date from the Hoysaḷa Period, c. A.D. 1100–1310. For Belūr, see *Art of Indian Asia,* v. 2, plates 434–436. For Haḷebīḍ see v. 1, p. 264; v. 2, plates 428–433.

CHAPTER 3: THE SPACE-PLATFORM

132. Louis Horst (1884–1964), pianist, composer, and choreographer; musical director of the Denishaun Dancers (1915–1925), and the Martha Graham Dance Company (1926–1945). He was an early mentor and friend of Jean Erdman.

133. Stella Kramrisch, *The Art of India Through the Ages.*

134. Other "gurus" would include, in this context, Heinrich Zimmer (see note 12).

135. See below, Book II: Sake & Satori.

136. Probably the chapter for Sarah Lawrence President Harold Taylor's book on Sarah Lawrence College, *On Education and Freedom,* for which Campbell agreed to do a chapter.

137. The Sarabhais were a very wealthy textile family of Ahmedabad, already known to the Campbells. They were patrons also of Le Corbusier, and were associated with Gandhi. See Erik Erikson, *Gandhi's Truth.*

138. See notes 10 and 12.

139. Hervey White (d. 1944), founder of the Maverick Colony in Woodstock, New York, a more egalitarian offshoot of the utopian artists' colony, Byrdcliffe, which was founded by Ralph Radcliffe Whitehead in the early part of the twentieth century. Campbell was a friend and frequent guest at Hervey White's colony. See *A Fire in the Mind,* pp. 138–139, 219–220, 282, 314, 592.

140. Svarāj, "self-rule," coined by Gandhi during his journey by boat to South Africa.

141. See p. 104 and note 86.

142. From a Tantric psychological typology: *vīra* = hero; *paśu* = herd animal.

143. See *Oriental Mythology,* pp. 342–343.

144. "Frobenius called this new age, now upon us, the period of World Culture. Its technical determinants are to be the scientific method of research and the power-driven machine, as were agriculture and stock-breeding (*c.* 7500 B.C.) and the arts of unifying and coercive government (*c.* 3500 B.C.) of the Monumental. And the distinguishing feature of its new mankind . . . [is] of individuals, self-moved to ends proper to themselves, directed not by the constraint and noise of others, but each by his own inner voice." *Creative Mythology,* p. 575. See also *Creative Mythology,* chapter 9, esp. pp. 611–621, on the seven revolutions in man's consciousness of cosmology, from myth to science, beginning with 1492 and ending with 1900.

145. Dr. Moti Chandra: well-known art historian, originally from Benares. For his son, see note 15.

146. Bhulabhai Desai was a barrister who defended, along with Nehru, people accused of trying to subvert the British government in India. He later became India's ambassador to Switzerland. There is a road named after him in Bombay.

147. Richard McKean: a University of Chicago professor with whom Campbell studied at Columbia in the 1920s.

148. One lakh = 100,000 rupees; one anna = 1/16 rupee.

149. See p. 22 and note 9.

150. Dilip Kumar Roy first became known throughout India as a composer and singer, later as a writer and poet. In 1953 he and dancer Indira Devi undertook a world tour sponsored by the Indian government. See Dilip Kumar Roy, *Pilgrims of the Stars.*

151. See p. 160.

152. See "The Dillettante among Symbols" in *The King and the Corpse.*

153. "The orthodox sacred books (*śāstras*) of India are classed in four categories: 1. *Śruti* ('what is heard'), the Vedas and certain Upaniṣads, which are regarded as direct revelation; 2. *Smṛti* ('what is remembered'), the teachings of the ancient saints and sages, also law books (*dharmasūtras*) and works dealing with household ceremonies and minor sacrifices (*gṛhyasūtras*); 3. *Purāṇa* ('ancient; ancient lore') compendious anthologies, comparable in character to the Bible, containing cosmogonic myths, ancient legends, theological, astronomical, and nature lore; 4. *Tantra* ('loom, warp, system, ritual, doctrine,) a body of comparatively recent texts, regarded as directly revealed by Śiva to be the specific scripture of the Kālī Yuga, the fourth or present

age of the world. The Tantras are called 'The Fifth Veda,' and their rituals and concepts have actually supplanted the now quite archaic Vedic system of sacrifice as the supporting warp of Indian life." —Editor's note from *Philosophies of India,* p. 61.

For a different perspective, see Radhakrishnan's *A Sourcebook in Indian Philosophy,* pp. xvii–xxii, which divides the Indian texts into four eras: the Vedic Period (the early dating is obscure, but approximately from 2500 B.C. to 600 B.C.), during which the *śruti* texts were composed, showing primarily a demiurgic, creative spirit; the Epic Period (600 B.C. to A.D. 200), the time of the *smṛti* texts, showing a poetic spirit mixed with a great deal of philosophical and semiphilosophical material; the *Sūtra* Period (dated from the beginning of the Christian era), a time of systematic philosophical treatises; and the Scholastic Period (from the end of the *Sūtra* Period until approximately the seventeenth century and the incursion of foreign powers), which is marked by many mediocre commentaries on the *Sūtras* but also by some of India's greatest philosophers, including Śaṅkara.

154.   The reference here is to one of Campbell's favorite quotes from Goethe. "The Godhead is effective in the living and not in the dead, in the becoming and the changing, not in the become and the set-fast; and therefore, accordingly, reason (*Vernunft*) is concerned only to strive toward the divine through the becoming and the living, and the understanding (*Verstand*) only to make use of the become and set-fast." *Creative Mythology,* p. 383. Taken originally from Johann Peter Eckermann, *Gespräche mit Goethe in den letzten Jahres seines Lebens, 1823–1832* (Berlin: Deutsches Verlaghaus Bong & Co., 1916), vol. I, p. 251. Translated by Charles Francis Atkinson in Spengler's *Decline of the West,* vol. I, p. 49, note 1. The original German is: *Die Gottheit ist wirksam im Lebendigen, aber nicht im Toten; sie ist im Werdenden und sich Verwandelnden, aber nicht in Gewordnen und Erstarrten. Deshalb hat auch die Vernunft in ihrer Tendenz zum Göttlichen es nur mit dem Werdenden, Lebendigen zu tun, der Verstand mit dem Gewordenen, Erstarrten, das er es nutze.*

155.   "The goal in India, whether in Hinduism, Buddhism, or Jainism, is to purge away individuality through insistence first upon the absolute laws of caste (*dharma*), and then upon long-known, marked-out stages of the way (*mārga*) toward indifference to the winds of time (*nirvāṇa*)." *Creative Mythology,* p. 33.

156.   This "dilemma" and its solution lie at the core of Campbell's philosophical stance with regard to his material. For a full discussion, see *Creative Mythology,* "Identity and Relationship" pp. 333–348, 585. The dilemma revolves around the *Vernunft-Verstand* polarity (see above, p. 176, and note 154), which appears as a motif, in various forms and in different vocabularies, throughout this journal: as the *sadhu* as against the folk (p. 37); as *le symbolisme qui cherche* as against *le symbolisme qui sait* (pp. 39, 175); the individual as against the collective (p. 186 ff.); as the way of the monkey as against the way of the kitten (pp. 104, 166); as the pedant-scholar in contradistinction to the creative scholar (p. 152); as clinging to the past instead of creativity in the present (p. 166), and especially as *smṛti* ("what is remembered") as against *śruti* ("what is heard," i.e. the creative muse, pp. 176, 181). The table of oppositions reads thus:

Vernunft	Verstand
sadhu	folk
le symbolisme qui cherche	*le symbolisme qui sait*
innovation	tradition
forest	village
monkey	kitten
present	past
śruti	*smṛti*
yoga	*bhakti*
nirguṇa brahman	*saguṇa brahman*
individual	authority
experience	meaning
changing	set-fast
becoming	become
West	India

For other, related tables, based on East-West oppositions, see pp. 159, 220–221.

157. "We Westerners have our own heritage and are caught in its mold...as much as the Hindu are in their own.... We cannot readily dress in Indian wisdom without becoming monkeys or dilettante actors. But, in viewing India's basic attitudes and spiritual propensities, we might gain insight of two things: of the subtle and inextricable web in whose meshes the Hindu spider abides and is caught...and, thus, we might realize to a fuller extent in what self-timbered framework of ideas we abide and are caught in ourselves." Zimmer, *Artistic Form and Yoga*, p. xxiii. See also Zimmer, "On the Significance of the Indian Tantric Yoga" in *Spiritual Disciplines: Papers from the Eranos Yearbooks*, vol. 4 (Bollingen 30), pp. 19–20.

158. Some of Campbell's thoughts on Las Casas can be found in the *Atlas* II.3, pp. 310, 314, and the captions to figs. 420–421.

159. This and most other of Campbell's work on the Pacific Islands were eventually to have been included in a later volume of the *Atlas* but remain unpublished.

160. In general, these titles reflect themes elaborated on by Campbell in *Creative Mythology*.

161. The *Eranos Tagung* were a series of annual meetings held in Ascona, Switzerland, presided over by Frau Olga Froebe Kapteyn. They were attended by Jung, Zimmer, D. T. Suzuki, Mircea Eliade, and many others. The attempt was to understand culture through myth and psyche. Campbell attended in 1953, but did not lecture; he later gave two lectures, in 1957 ("The Symbol without Meaning") and 1959 ("Renewal Myths and Rites of the Primitive Hunters and Gatherers"). He eventually edited English translations of some of the papers presented there under the series title *Papers from the Eranos Yearbooks*, published by Princeton University Press. See also William McGuire, *Bollingen*.

162. *Fach*: Lit. "shelf" in German, and by extension, specialty, or area of study.

163. Verrier Elwin (1902–1964), scholar of Indian tribespeople and their religion, customs, songs, and literature.

164. See p. 176.

165. I.e., the Bombay Theatre Unit.

166. See *Oriental Mythology,* pp. 136–137.

167. See *Oriental Mythology,* pp. 13–23, "The Two Views of Ego."

168. Edward VIII of England abdicated his throne in order to marry a divorced (and hence, in the eyes of the Church of England, ineligible) woman, Wallis Simpson.

169. Rāma, after recapturing his kidnapped bride, Sītā, after many trials, refuses to take her back into his household because she has been stained by too-long contact with his enemies. See Coomaraswamy, *Myths of the Hindus and Buddhists,* pp. 28–99.

170. "...there is nothing of the fairy tale about the atmosphere of a Greek tragedy, no sense of the play of *māyā* to disengage the reality of the characters from their histories. There is no subliminal ground of repose in *Brahman* over which the passions, limitations, and catastrophes of the action play, like the fragments of a dream. The release in Greek tragedy comes, rather, at the end of a piece, in the minds of the audience, as a transformation of perspective." *Inner Reaches of Outer Space,* p. 140.

171. Parsees constitute an economic and intellectual élite in the Bombay area. Indian Parsees trace the origins of their religion directly to Persian Zoroastrian roots.

172. In Zoroastrianism, Ahura Mazda, the Lord of Light and Truth, is locked in a world struggle with Angra Mainyu, who corrupted the realm of matter by pouring darkness into the world of pure light created by Ahura Mazda. "The myth tells that there came into the world a savior to teach the way to accent the good....As a result of the action of this savior, there is now taking place a restoration. There will come a time when the crisis will occur, when all darkness will be wiped out. There will be a second coming of the savior...and darkness will be permanently eliminated, the Lord of Darkness himself eliminated. There will be nothing but light again." *Transformations of Myth Through Time,* pp. 107–108. See also *Occidental Mythology,* pp. 192–212.

173. There is no evidence that this talk was ever published.

174. *Strich darunter:* "under the wire," i.e. just in time.

175. "Pity is the feeling which arrests the mind in the presence of whatsoever is grave and constant in human sufferings and unites it with the human sufferer....Terror is the feeling which arrests the mind in the presence of whatsoever is grave and constant in human sufferings and unites it with the secret cause." James Joyce, *A Portrait of the Artist As a Young Man* (London: Jonathan Cape, 1916), pp. 232–233. See also *Creative Mythology,* pp. 94, 653–654, for this theme applied to contemporary artistic creation.

176. "It was because of superior wisdom that the Aryan invaders of India were able to defeat the native pre-Aryan populations, maintain themselves in the land, and ultimately spread their dominion over the sub-continent. The conquered races then were classified as the fourth, non-Aryan caste of the Śūdra, excluded ruthlessly from the rights and power-giving wisdom of the society of the conquerors, and forbidden to acquire even an inkling of the techniques of the Vedic religion.... We read in the early *Dharmaśāstras* that if a Śūdra chances to overhear the recitation of a Vedic hymn, he is to be punished by having his ears filled with molten lead." Zimmer, *Philosophies of India,* p. 59.

177. "Remember that old Irish question: 'Is this a private fight or can anybody get into it'?" *Hero's Journey,* p. 20.

178.   See McGuire, *Bollingen*, pp. 178–179. See also above, pp. 129, 155, 177, 179.

179.   See McGuire, *Bollingen*, pp. 140–141.

180.   Nothing came of Campbell's involvement with Coomaraswamy's papers. See the brief note in McGuire, *Bollingen*, p. 141. The comprehensive edition of Coomaraswamy was ultimately completed by Roger Lipsey.

181.   Bartholomé de las Casas is treated in the *Atlas*, II.3, pp. 310, 314, and the caption to figs. 420–421. See *Occidental Mythology*, pp. 324–325, for parallels between the Alexandrine period and our own.

182.   Appolonius of Tyana was a Neo-Pythagorean religious reformer who lived from about 4 B.C. to A.D. 80 or 90. In a third-century biography by Philostratus the Elder, he is portrayed as a godlike miracle worker who travelled the ancient world from India to Spain, absorbing knowledge and effecting miracle cures, with many parallels to the life of Christ. See Charles Eells, *Life and Times of Apollonius of Tyana*.

183.   See "The Interpretation of Symbolic Forms" in *The Binding of Proteus*, pp. 35–59, also "Indian Reflections in the Castle of the Grail" in *The Celtic Consciousness*, pp. 3–30.

184.   "Are *ignorance* and *sin*, finally, two words for the same condition? Are *enlightenment* and *redemption* two ways of pointing to the same psychological crisis?... But are not this darkened understanding, weakened will, and inclination to evil (i.e., original sin) exactly what the Buddhists mean by ignorance, fear, and desire; namely, *māyā?*" "Interpretation of Symbolic Forms," in *The Binding of Proteus*, pp. 42–43. See also *Occidental Mythology*, pp. 207–208, 466–467; *Mythic Worlds, Modern Words*, p. 277; *The Joseph Campbell Companion*, pp. 143–145.

185.   "Heaven and Hell are psychological definitions." *The Joseph Campbell Companion*, p. 159. "Purgatory and reincarnation are thus homologous." *Oriental Mythology*, pp. 308–309. Or, in one of Campbell's favorite quotes: "The Kingdom of God the Father is spread upon the earth and men do not see it." *Gospel According to Thomas*, Logion 113:114. See note 9.

186.   See "Freud, Jung, and Kundalini Yoga," a lecture delivered at Esalen Institute.

187.   The *rasas* are the nine aesthetic flavors proper to the various modes of dramatic enjoyments. According to the Gupta treatise *Daśarūpa* by Dhanaṃjaya, the nine *rasas*, classified according to the five states of dramatic enjoyment, are: 1. Cheerfulness (the erotic and the comic); 2. Exaltation (the heroic and the marvelous); 3. Agitation (the odious and the terrible); 4. Perturbation of the Mind (the furious and the pathetic); and 5. Happiness in Tranquillity (the peaceful). Number 4 corresponds to Aristotle's idea of the tragic mode. See *Inner Reaches of Outer Space*, pp. 108–112.

188.   "When one listens to Indian music, it never has a beginning or an end. You know that the music is going on all the time, and the consciousness of the musician just dips down into the music, picks it up with the instrument, and reads it again." *Mythic Worlds, Modern Words*, p. 194. Or, again: "Music, however, has a role apart; for it deals not with forms in space, but with time, sheer time. It is not like the other arts, a rendition of what Plato calls 'ideas,' but of the will itself, the world will, of which the ideas are but inflections. 'One could call the world "embodied music" as well as "embodied Will,"' Schopenhauer wrote, confirming thus the ancient theme of the music of the spheres." *Creative Mythology*, p. 83.

189. *Marg:* a Bombay journal devoted to Indian culture and the arts.

190. Jean Erdman was moving in a westerly direction on her dance tour, stopping with the writer on Asian philosophy, Alan Watts, in California.

191. Pupul Jayakar, Minister of Culture and organizer of the Festivals of India in various countries during the 1980s; biographer of Jiddu Krishnamurti and Indira Gandhi.

192. Madhuri Desai was an art collector greatly interested in Indian culture, music, dance, and fine arts. She donated her property and founded the Bhulabhai Desai Institute in Bombay.

193. Bharata Natyam, the classical dance of southern India. See Danielou, *Bharata Natyam.*

194. Heinrich Zimmer had died suddenly in 1943, leaving a widow and three boys. See note 12.

195. Le Corbusier (Charles-Édouard Jeanneret, 1887–1965), distinguished architect, built the Sarabhai villa in Ahmedabad (1951–1956); the Punjab state government building at Chandigarh (1951–1958); the Cultural Center at Ahmedabad (1951–1958); and the Villashadan, Ahmedabad (1951–1956).

196. A chowry is a whisk used in ritual devotions; often visible in temple sculpture.

197. There is no further reference in Campbell's work to a talk of this title, but a very similarly titled talk was given three years later in Japan and published as "Oriental Philosophy and Occidental Psychoanalysis."

198. See "The Impact of Science on Myths" in *Myths to Live By,* p. 20.

199. In Jung's system, the uniting symbol (i.e. a mandala, yantra, or hermaphrodite) is produced by the unconscious as an attempt at healing a psyche split by antithetical conflicts, such as thinking versus feeling, conscious *vs.* unconscious, anima/animus versus ego, etc. The symbols thus produced—through dreams, painting, writing, or some other form of active imagination—take up the incompatible value systems of the various functions and unite them harmoniously. See C. G. Jung, *Psychological Types,* definition under "symbol."

200. For Campbell's view on a collective unconscious, see *Mythic Worlds, Modern Words,* p. 193. Jung says, in *Psychological Types,* p. 485, that "[w]e can distinguish a *personal unconscious* comprising all the acquisitions of personal life, everything forgotten, re-pressed, subliminally perceived, thought, felt. But, in addition to these personal unconscious contents, there are other contents which do not originate in the personal acquisitions but in the inherited possibility of psychic functioning in general, i.e. in the inherited structure of the brain. These are the mythological associations, the motifs and images that can spring up anew anytime anywhere, independently of historical traditional or migration. I call these contents the *collective unconscious.*"

201. See note 42.

202. Śaṅkara (c. A.D. 788–850), Vedantist philosopher who expounded the Zimmer doctrine of *māyā,* the illusory nature of existence. See *The Philosophies of India,* pp. 17–19, 373, 375, 626–627.

203. See Jung, *Archetypes and the Collective Unconscious,* pp. 317, 370. Also "The Philosophical Tree" in *Alchemical Studies,* p. 253.

204. Agnes Meyer sat in on Campbell's classes at Sarah Lawrence in 1939, and later introduced him to Thomas Mann.

205. Gardiner Murphy (1895–1979). American psychologist who founded the "bio-social" approach to psychology that was influential in the 1950s. He married Lois Barclay, known for her work in child psychology. Gardiner Murphy taught at Columbia and City College of New York, and was president of the American Psychological Association. The Murphys worked together on the Indian School Project.

206. See Zimmer, "On the Significance of the Indian Tantric Yoga" in *Spiritual Disciplines,* pp. 17–18.

207. Ānanda Mayī Mā was one of the better known and revered mystics in India from the 1950s to the 1980s. She had been a school teacher in Bengal for many years when she experienced a spiritual call. She left her husband and children and lived the life of a *sannyāsin,* wandering the roads of India. She founded an ashram at Ānanda Mayī Ghat in Benares and died there in 1982. Her name means "Mother Full of Bliss," and her mere presence was said to bestow beatitude or even *samādhi,* or spiritual illumination.

208. These are the four yogas in the *Bhāgavad Gītā.* See "Confrontation of East and West" in *Myths to Live By,* pp. 97–101. 1. *Rājā yoga* is a discipline of meditation yoga that involves the "intentional stopping of the spontaneous activity of the mind stuff" (See Campbell's essay "Hinduism" in Appendix IA). 2. *Jñāna yoga* is the yoga of mental discrimination (*viveka*) between the subject of knowledge and the object of knowledge (see Campbell's essay "The Occult in Myth and Literature" in *Literature and the Occult*). 3. *Bhakti yoga* is the yoga of devotion to an object, god, person, thing, or animal, which consists in the annihilation of one's personal will in the service to that object. 4. *Karma yoga* is the yoga of action that anyone can perform; the formula is to act without desire or fear for the fruits of one's actions.

209. For a poignant evocation of those scenes, see Lex Hixon's *Great Swan: Meetings with Ramakrishna.*

210. For Campbell's interest in Huxley, see *The Flight of the Wild Gander,* pp. 152–153; for Huxley's experiments with mescaline, see Aldous Huxley, *The Doors of Perception,* and Albert Hofman, *LSD: My Problem Child* (New York: McGraw-Hill, 1980).

211. Lou Harrison, a New York composer and choreographer, friend of the Campbells'.

212. "Nietzsche's designation of music, the dance, and lyric poetry as the arts specific to the Dionysian mode…and on the other side, the side of the claims of the unique, ephemeral, induplicable moment, sentiment, or individual—the side of the principle of individuation (*principium individuationis*), Nietzsche assigned to Apollo as the lord of light and the arts of sculpture and epic poetry." *Creative Mythology,* pp. 333–334.

213. For earlier, related tables of oppositions, see pp. 158–159 and note 156.

214. For a discussion of "Fellaheen" and Spengler, see pp. 19–20 and note 26.

215. "Looked at in this way, the 'Decline of the West' comprises nothing less than the problem of *Civilization.* We have before us one of the fundamental questions of all higher history. What is Civilization, understood as the organic-logical sequel, fulfillment and finale of culture?

  "For every Culture has *its own* Civilization. In this work, for the first time, the two words, hitherto used to express an indefinite, more or less ethical, distinction, are used in a *periodic* sense, to express a strict and necessary *organic succession.* The Civilization is the inevitable *destiny* of the Culture, and in this principle we obtain the viewpoint from which the deepest and gravest problems of historical morphology become capable of solution. Civilizations are the most external and artificial states of which a species of developed community is capable. They are a conclusion, the thing-become succeeding the thing-becoming, death following life, rigidity following expansion, intellectual age and stone-built petrifying world-city following mother earth and the spiritual childhood of Doric and Gothic. They are an end, irrevocable, yet by inward necessity reached again and again." Spengler, *Decline of the West,* vol. i, p. 31.

216. Although known as the Bombay Theatre Unit, the group appears to have mounted productions in other venues as well.

217. For Khajurāho, see *The Art of Indian Asia,* v. i, pp. 134, 273–274; v. 2, plates 309–318. For Koṇārak, see v. i, pp. 10, 258, 274, 358, 362; v. 2, plates 348–375.

218. See *Oriental Mythology,* pp. 309–318.

219. For the flowering of Indian architecture during the Gupta period, see *Oriental Mythology,* pp. 326–337; for the subsequent disintegration of India, see pp. 342–343.

220. The reference here is to *The Art of Indian Asia.* See v. i, p. 123, for the symbols in question.

221. Meaning "beneath dignity."

222. Kālidāsa, Hindu dramatist, usually dated to the fifth century at the court of Candra Gupta II of Ujjain.

223. Campbell is speaking specifically of *The Art of Indian Asia,* but finishing this book also marked the end of Campbell's eleven-year involvement with Zimmer's papers, which resulted ultimately in the publication of *The Philosophies of India, Myths and Symbols in Indian Art and Civilization,* as well as *The Art of Indian Asia.*

224. A.N.T.A.: American National Theater and Academy (now defunct). John Martin was a dance critic for *The New York Times,* Walter Terry for *The Herald Tribune.* Martha Hill ran the summer dance program at Bennington, and taught dance in various schools and colleges. Jean Erdman had approached this committee of dance critics and had been turned down. With Campbell's help, nonetheless, she became the first modern dancer to tour India. Martha Graham followed several years later.

225. Ravi Shankar, son of a high-ranking Bengali, later went on to great fame in the United States; his older brother Uday was a noted dancer and choreographer who met the dancer Pavlova in Paris and became friendly with her. Ali Akbar Khan often accompanied Ravi Shankar but became known as a musician in his own right in the 1960s.

226. Jawaharlal Nehru had two sisters. One married a Bombay industrialist, Huthee Singh. This sister was known to be gracious and friendly. The other sister, Vijaya Lakhsmi (Madam) Pandit, was more political and was frequently at odds with her brother. During the most critical phase of the Indian independence movement, Mme. Pandit escaped British surveillance and addressed the U.N. General Assembly.

227. See p. 226.

228. See note 204.

229. "Society, as a fostering organ, is thus a kind of exterior 'second womb' wherein the postnatal stages of man's long gestation . . . are supported and defended." "Bios and

Mythos" in *The Flight of the Wild Gander,* and pp. 136–141. See also the 1964 essay "The Importance of Rites," collected in *Myths to Live By,* esp. pp. 45–47.

230. Nationalist Hindu organization.

231. Stella Kramrisch, *The Art of India Through the Ages.*

232. "... the myth has to deal with the cosmology of today and it's no good when it's based on a cosmology that's out of date. And that's one of our problems. I don't see any conflict between science and religion. Religion has to accept the science of today and penetrate it—to the *mystery.* The conflict is between the science of 2000 B.C. and the science of 2000 A.D." *Hero's Journey,* p. 164. See also "The Confrontation of East and West in Religion" in *Myths to Live By,* pp. 88–89.

233. See Campbell's question to Ānanda Mayī, pp. 201–202; and a discussion of the yogas as found in the *Bhāgavad Gītā,* note 208.

234. The *śunyatāvāda* school of Mahāyāna Buddhism (also known as *Mādhyamika*): a form of Buddhism based on the doctrine of the void (*śunyatā*), a positive principle from which all phenomenal existence arises. Hence it is a subtle philosophical stance to believe in "nothing." Zimmer, *Philosophies of India,* pp. 521–522.

235. See p. 213.

236. Ārya Samāj, a Hindu religious and social reform group founded by Swami Saraswati in 1875 that sought to recoup for Hinduism converts to other religions by going "back to the Vedas": condemning such practices polytheism, caste restrictions, and child marriage.

237. *Bhoodan Yajna,* p. 128.

238. *Statesman,* January 6, 1955, p. 1.

239. Mohenjo-daro, city on the Indus River in Sind in present-day Pakistan, that flourished circa 3000–1500 B.C. For the "meditating yogi," see *Myths and Symbols,* fig. 42. See also *Oriental Mythology,* p. 155, and figs. 18–19.

240. Jawaharlal Nehru (1889–1964) was the first prime minister of independent India (1947–1964). First coming to prominence through association with Gandhi's Congress Party, he committed himself to Indian independence and became head of the party in 1929. During his incumbency, Nehru sought to bring a unified India into the modern era. Internationally he espoused a policy of nonalignment.

241. Shanta Rao was originally a Bharata Natyam dancer discovered and mentored, as was Bala Saraswati (see p. 277 and note 250), by Alice Boner, a Swiss woman whom Uday Shankar (see note 225) had met in Europe, and who founded Kerala Kalamandalam, the famous school of Kathakali in Chiruthuruthi. See Danielou, *The Way to the Labyrinth,* pp. 90–91.

CHAPTER 4: DANCE TOUR WITH JEAN ERDMAN

242. A main street in Old Delhi, near the Red Fort.

243. Alexander Calder (1898–1976), originally a Scottish stonecutter, did monumental sculpture before turning to the mobiles (Marcel Duchamp's term for moving sculptures) and stabiles (Jean Arp's term, which Calder continued to use) for which he is known.

244. Mrinalini Sarabhai, dancer and teacher of traditional dance, was a cousin of Gautam and Gira Sarabhai who had traveled widely in the United States. She was a founder

of the Darpana Association of Ahmedabad, which gave instruction in dance, theater arts, and puppetry. Her daughter Malika, a little girl when the Campbells visited, later appeared in Peter Brook's film *The Mahabharata.*

245. The *Nala Upākhyana* is a subplot of the *Mahābhārata* that may represent a preexisting epic. It tells the story of Nala and Damayantī's courtship and travails, and is a common theme in miniature painting and dance.

246. See pp. 208–209.

247. See p. 160.

248. Campbell knew Arthur Gregor from New York and had met him earlier in Bombay. See p. 167.

249. Campbell and his father had traveled aboard the *Kungsholm,* in 1929. See *A Fire in the Mind,* pp. 121–126.

250. Bala Saraswati, the most important Indian dancer of modern times, brought the Bharata Natyam to the stage and to modern audiences. Jean Erdman later remembered being profoundly impressed by her mastery of Bharata Natyam, and her excellent ability to communicate to her students. Saraswati later came to New York on a tour sponsored by the Indian government.

251. A famous twelfth- or thirteenth-century bronze of Śiva dancing, wreathed in celestial flames. See Appendix IA, p. 316. Also *Myths and Symbols,* fig. 38, and *Art of Indian Asia,* vol. 2, plates 411–414.

252. See *Myths and Symbols,* Figure 41 and pp. 168–169 for a discussion of this prototype of Śiva Naṭarāja.

253. See note 202 on Śaṅkara.

254. See *Philosophies of India,* p. 1.

255. Avicenna (A.D. 980–1036) was a peripatetic Islamic scholar, philosopher, and doctor.

256. Radha Bournier was the daughter of the vice president of the Theosophical Society in Adyar, and was a student of Bharata Natyam. When Campbell met her she was a frequent companion of Danielou, and had married Danielou's lifelong friend Raymond Bournier.

257. Alain Danielou (1909–1993) was a versatile French-born artist, scholar, and author who had lived in India for twenty-five years. About a year before meeting Campbell, Danielou had moved from a long-term residence in a Benares palace to Adyar to assume the directorship of the Adyar Library. Danielou associated with many artistic and literary figures of world stature: Nehru, Tagore, and the Shankars in India, and in the West with Gide, Cocteau, Stravinsky, and many others. See also pp. 217–218, and note 83.

258. The U.S.I.S., the U.S. Information Service, a branch of the State Department dedicated to international relations.

CHAPTER 5: A GURU AND HIS DEVOTEES

259. Śiva Ardhanārīśvara, an androgynous Śiva or Śiva-Śakti/Pārvatī in one figure.

260. *Atma-Nirvriti,* pp. 18, 22, 11, 6–7, respectively.

261. See pp. 92–94, 194, 208–209, 220–221, 231, 245, 271.

262. Campbell in later years made much of this doctrine, taken from the *Māṇḍūkya Upaniṣad.* "A" = waking consciousness (*jāgrat*); "U" = dream state (*svapna*); "M" =

deep sleep (*suṣupti*) but also cosmic rapture (*turīya*). Hence "A-U-M" (or "OM") refers to all possible states of consciousness. See also pp. 177, 206, 231, and esp. below, note 266.

263. Mr. Henry Belk, a scion of the Belk family that owned a chain of department stores in the South, turned his interest to parapsychology in his later years. The concept of "biorhythms" received some credibility in the Soviet Union, Europe, Japan, and in the United States.

264. See p. 293.

265. *Bṛhadāraṇyaka Upaniṣad.* See *Oriental Mythology,* pp. 198–200.

266. "We are in our true state (*ātman*) every night in sleep, but also during the period of waking consciousness every time we are 'between two thoughts.'" *Joseph Campbell Companion,* p. 15.

   "When I was in India I met and conversed briefly with the saintly sage [Sri Krishna Menon]; and the question he gave me to consider was this: *Where are you between two thoughts?* In the *Kena Upaniṣad* we are told: 'There the eye goes not, nor the mind.... Other it is than the known. And moreover above the unknown.' For on coming back from between two thoughts, one would find that all words—which, of course, can be only of thoughts and things, names and forms—only mislead. As again declared in the Upaniṣad: 'We know not, we understand not, how It should be taught.'" In "Zen" in *Myths to Live By,* p. 129.

   "Then he gave me a little meditation, 'Where are you between two thoughts?' That is to say, you are thinking all the time, and you have an image of yourself. Well, where are you between two thoughts? Do you ever have a glimpse beyond your thinking of that which transcends anything you can think about yourself? *That's* the source field out of which all of your energies are coming." *Joseph Campbell Companion,* pp. 187–189.

267. For a general discussion of Campbell's meeting with Krishna Menon, see *Joseph Campbell Companion,* pp. 187–189; also *Power of Myth,* pt. II, "The Message of the Myth."

268. Benedict Spinoza (1632–1677), Dutch philosopher of Portuguese Jewish extraction.

269. Today there are only a handful of families left. They have no rabbi to read the Torah.

270. "Commentary on 'The Secret of the Golden Flower'" (1929), in C. G. Jung, *Alchemical Studies.*

271. See the essay "Zen" in *Myths to Live By.*

272. SEATO, Southeast Asia Treaty Organization. An organization created in Manila in 1954 by France, Australia, New Zealand, Pakistan, the Philippines, Thailand, the United Kingdom and the United States. Its explicit goal was to counteract Communist expansion in Southeast Asia.

273. Campbell's photographic ability the reader may judge from the photographs in this volume, all Campbell's own. Several entire rolls, however, were lost during this trip due to mishaps.

BOOK I BIBLIOGRAPHY

Agehananda Bharati. *The Ochre Robe*. London: George Allen and Unwin, 1961.

———. *The Tantric Tradition*. London: Rider, 1965.

Arnold, Edwin. *The Light of Asia: Or, the Great Renunciation*. London: Routledge & Kegan Paul, 1964. First published 1879.

Bhave, Vinoba. *Bhoodan Yajna*. Ahmedabad: Navajivan Publishing House, 1953.

Boethius. *The Theological Tractates and the Consolation of Philosophy*. Ed. H. F. Stewart and E. K. Rand. Loeb Classical Library. Cambridge, Mass.: Harvard University Press, 1918.

Campbell, Joseph. "Heinrich Zimmer (1890–1943)." *Partisan Review*, 20 (July 1943): 415–416.

———, and Henry Morton Robinson. *A Skeleton Key to Finnegans Wake*. New York: Harcourt, Brace and Co., 1944. New York: Penguin Books, 1977.

———. *The Hero with a Thousand Faces*. Bollingen 27. New York: Pantheon Books, 1949. 2nd ed. rev. Princeton: Princeton University Press, 1968.

———. *The Flight of the Wild Gander: Explorations in the Mythological Dimension*. New York: Viking Press, 1951. 2nd rev. ed. New York: Harper and Row, 1990. 3rd rev. ed. Novato, California: New World Library, 2002.

———, ed. *The Portable Arabian Nights*. New York: Viking Press, 1952.

———. "Hinduism." In *Basic Beliefs: The Religious Philosophies of Mankind*. Ed. Johnson E. Fairchild, 54–72. New York: Sheridan House, 1959. Subsequent ed., 39–58. New York: Hart Publishing Co., n.d.

———. "Renewal Myths and Rites of the Primitive Hunters and Gatherers." *Eranos-Jahrbücher* 28. Zürich: Rhein-Verlag, 1959. Reprint. Dallas: Spring Publications, 1989.

————. *The Masks of God.* 4 vols. New York: Viking Press, 1959–1968. Vol.1, *Primitive Mythology,* 1959. Vol. 2, *Oriental Mythology,* 1962. Vol. 3, *Occidental Mythology,* 1964. Vol. 4, *Creative Mythology,* 1968. Pb. ed. Arkana, 1991.

————. "Oriental Philosophy and Occidental Psychoanalysis." In *Proceedings of the IXth International Congress for the History of Religions, Tokyo and Kyoto, August 27–September 9, 1958,* 492–496. Tokyo: Maruzen, 1960.

————. *Myths to Live By.* New York: Viking Press, 1972. New York: Bantam Books, 1973.

————. "On the Mythic Shape of Things to Come—Circular and Linear." *Horizon* 16 (Summer 1974): 35–37.

————. *The Mythic Image.* Bollingen 100. Princeton: Princeton University Press, 1974. Pb. ed. Princeton: Princeton University Press, 1983.

————. "The Occult in Myth and Literature." In *Literature and the Occult: Essays in Comparative Literature.* Ed. Luanne Frank, 3–18. Arlington, Tex.: UTA Publications in Literature, 1977.

————. "The Interpretation of Symbolic Forms." In *The Binding of Proteus.* Ed. Marjorie W. McCune, Tucker Orbison, and Philip M. Withim. Lewisburg, Penn.: Bucknell University Press, 1980.

————. "Indian Reflections in the Castle of the Grail." In *The Celtic Consciousness.* Ed. Robert O'Driscoll. New York: George Braziller, 1982.

————. *The Inner Reaches of Outer Space: Metaphor As Myth and As Religion.* New York: Alfred van der Marck Editions, 1986. New York: HarperCollins, HarperPerennial, 1988. Novato, California: New World Library, 2002.

————. *The Hero's Journey: The World of Joseph Campbell: Joseph Campbell on His Life and Work.* Ed. Phil Cousineau. San Francisco: Harper and Row, 1990.

————. *Transformations of Myth Through Time.* New York: Harper and Row, 1990.

————. "Freud, Jung, and Kundalini Yoga." Big Sur Tapes, Big Sur, California.

————. *Historical Atlas of World Mythology.*

    Vol. 1, *The Way of the Animal Powers.* New York: Alfred van der Marck Editions, 1983. Reprint in 2 pts. Part 1, *Mythologies of the Primitive Hunters and Gatherers.* New York: Alfred van der Marck Editions, 1988. Reprint of Part 1. New York: Harper and Row Perennial Library, 1988. Part 2, *Mythologies of the Great Hunt.* New York: Alfred van der Marck Editions, 1988. Reprint of Part 2. New York: Harper and Row Perennial Library, 1988.

    Vol. 2, *The Way of the Seeded Earth.* 3 pts. Part 1, *The Sacrifice.* New York: Alfred van der Marck Editions, 1988. Reprint. Harper and Row Perennial Library, 1988. Part 2, *Mythologies of the Primitive Planters: The Northern Americas.* New York: Harper and Row Perennial Library, 1989. Part 3, *Mythologies of the Primitive Planters: The Middle and Southern Americas.* New York: Harper and Row Perennial Library, 1989.

————. *The Power of Myth.* With Bill Moyers. Ed. Betty Sue Flowers. New York: Doubleday, 1988. New York: Anchor Books, 1991.

————. *Reflections on the Art of Living: A Joseph Campbell Companion.* Ed. Diane K. Osbon. New York: HarperCollins, 1991.

————. *Mythic Worlds, Modern Words: On the Art of James Joyce.* Ed. Edmund L. Epstein. New York: HarperCollins, 1993.

―――――. *Thou Art That: Transforming Religious Metaphor.* Ed. Eugene Kenedy. Novato, Calif.: New World Library, 2002.

Coomaraswamy, Ananda K. *History of Indian and Indonesian Art.* Leipzig: Karl W. Hiersemann. Reprint. New York: Dover Books, 1985.

―――――., and Sister Nivedita (Margaret E. Noble). *Myths of the Hindus and Buddhists.* George G. Harrap and Company, 1913. Reprint. New York: Dover Publications, 1967.

―――――. *Dance of Śiva.* London: Simpkin, Marshall, Hamilton, Kent and Co., 1924. Reprint. New York: Dover Publications, 1985.

―――――. *Time and Eternity.* Ascona, Switzerland: Artibus Asiae, 1947. 2nd ed. rev. Bangalore, India: Select Books, 1989.

―――――. *Coomaraswamy 2: Selected Papers, Metaphysics.* Roger Lipsey, editor. Bollingen 89. Reprint. Princeton: Princeton University Press, 1977.

Danielou, Alain. *Introduction to the Study of Musical Scales.* London: Indra Society, 1943.

―――――. *Yoga: The Method of Reintegration.* London: C. Johnson, 1949.

―――――. *Bharata Natyam: Danse classique de l'Inde.* Berlin: Institut International d'É-tudes Comparatives de la Musique, 1970.

―――――. *Shiva and Dionysus.* New York: Inner Traditions International, 1984.

―――――. *The Way to the Labyrinth: Memories of East and West.* Translated by Marie-Claire Cournand. New York: New Directions, 1987.

de Rougemont, Denis. *Love in the Western World.* New York: Pantheon Books, 1940. 2nd ed. revised and augmented, 1956.

Dilip Kumar Roy. *Pilgrims of the Stars.* New York: Macmillan, 1973.

Eels, Charles P. *Life and Times of Apollonius of Tyana.* University Series: Language and Literature, Vol. II.1. Palo Alto, Calif.: Stanford University Publications, 1923.

Erikson, Erik. *Gandhi's Truth.* New York: W.W. Norton, 1969.

Frazer, Sir James. *Myths of the Origin of Fire.* London: Macmillan, 1930.

Frobenius, Leo. *Das Unbekannte Afrika: Aufstellung der Schicksale eines Erdteils.* Munich: Beck, 1923.

―――――. *Paideuma: Umrisse einer Kultur- und Seelenlehre.* Munich: Beck, 1923.

―――――. *Schicksalskunde im Sinne des Kulturwerdens.* Leipzig: R. Voigtlander, 1932.

―――――. *Kulturgeschichte Afrikans: Prolegomena zu einer historischen Gestaltlehre.* Zurich: Phaidon-Verlag, 1933.

Guénon, René. *Introduction to the Study of the Hindu Doctrines.* London: Luzac and Co., 1945.

Heras, Henry. *Studies in Proto-Indo-Mediterranean Culture.* Bombay, 1933. Bombay: Indian Historical Research Institute, 1953.

Hixon, Lex. *Great Swan: Meetings with Ramakrishna.* Boston: Shambhala, 1992.

Huxley, Aldous. *The Doors of Perception.* New York: Harper, 1954.

Jayakar, Pupul. *Krishnamurti: A Biography.* New York: Harper and Row, 1988.

Jung, C. G. *Archetypes and the Collective Unconscious.* Collected Works 9. Bollingen 20. Pantheon Books, 1959. 2nd ed. Princeton: Princeton University Press, 1969.

―――――. *Alchemical Studies.* Collected Works 13. Bollingen 20. Princeton: Princeton University Press, 1967.

―――――. *Mysterium Coniunctionis.* Collected Works 14. Bollingen 20. 2nd ed. Princeton: Princeton University Press, 1970.

Kramrisch, Stella. *Indian Sculpture*. Calcutta, 1933. Delhi: Motilal Banarsidass, 1981.

──────. *The Art of India Through the Ages*. London and New York: Phaidon, 1954.

Krishnamurti, Jiddu. *You Are the World*. New York: Harper and Row, 1972.

──────. *The First and Last Freedom*. New York: Harper and Row, 1972.

Larsen, Stephen and Robin. *Joseph Campbell: A Fire in the Mind*. New York: Doubleday, 1991.

Menen, Aubrey. *The Ramayana*. New York: Scribners, 1954.

Krishna Menon, called Atmananda Guru. *Atma-darshan: At the Ultimate*. Tiruvannamalai: Sri Vidya Samiti, 1946.

──────. *Atma-nirvriti: Freedom and Felicity in the Self*. Trivandrum: Vedanta Publishers, 1952.

McGuire, William. *Bollingen: An Adventure in Collecting the Past*. Princeton: Princeton University Press, 1982.

McMahon, Robert J. *The Cold War on the Periphery*. New York: Columbia University Press, 1994.

Nietzsche, Friedrich. *The Birth of Tragedy Out of the Spirit of Music*. In *Basic Writings of Nietzsche*. Edited and translated by Walter Kaufmann. New York: Modern Library, 1968.

Nikhilananda. *The Upanishads*. 4 vols. New York: Harper, 1949.

Nivedita, Sister [Margaret E. Noble]. *Notes on Some Wanderings with the Swami Vivekananda by Sister Nivedita of Ramakrishna-Vivekananda*. Calcutta: Udbodhan Office, 1922.

Ostor, Akos. *Puja in Society*. Lucknow, 1982.

Radhakrishnan, Sarvepalli, and Charles A. Moore. *A Sourcebook in Indian Philosophy*. Princeton: Princeton University Press, 1957.

Ramakrishna. *The Gospel of Sri Ramakrishna*. Trans.; introduction by Swami Nikhilananda. New York: Ramakrishna-Vivekenanda Center, 1942.

Salmony, Alfred. *Carved Jade of Ancient China*. Berkeley: Gillick Press, 1938.

──────. *Archaic Chinese Jades*. Chicago: Art Institute of Chicago, 1952.

──────. *Antler and Tongue: An Essay on Ancient Chinese Symbolism and Its Implications*. Ascona, Switzerland: Artibus Asiae Publications, 1954.

Schopenhauer, Arthur. "Transcendent Speculation upon an Apparent Intention in the Fate of the Individual." *Parerga and Paralipomena*, v. 1.

Singh, Karan. *The Glory of Amarnath*. Place and date of publication unknown.

Spengler, Oswald. *Decline of the West*. 2 vols. Translated by Charles Frances Atkinson. New York: Alfred A. Knopf, 1926–1928. One-volume edition, 1939.

Taylor, Harold. *Essays in Teaching*. New York: Harper, 1950.

──────. *On Education and Freedom*. New York: Abelard Schumann, 1954.

Wilhelm, Richard, editor and translator. *The Secret of the Golden Flower: A Chinese Book of Life*. Foreword and Commentary by C. G. Jung. Translated from the German by Cary F. Baynes. Revised ed. New York: Harcourt Brace Jovanovich, 1962.

Zimmer, Heinrich. *Der Weg zum Selbst: Lehre und Leben des indischen Heiligen Shri Ramana Maharishi aus Tiruvannamalai*. Ed. C. G. Jung. Zurich: Rascher-Verlag, 1944.

————. *Myths and Symbols in Indian Art and Civilization.* Ed. Joseph Campbell. Bollingen 6. New York: Pantheon Books, 1946. Princeton: Princeton University Press, 1972. Pb. ed., 1992.

————. *The King and the Corpse: Tales of the Soul's Conquest of Evil.* Ed. Joseph Campbell. Bollingen 11. New York: Pantheon Books, 1948. 2nd ed., 1956.

————. *The Philosophies of India.* Ed. Joseph Campbell. Bollingen 26. Princeton: Princeton University Press, 1951.

————. *The Art of Indian Asia: Its Mythology and Transformations.* Completed and edited by Joseph Campbell. Bollingen 39. Princeton: Princeton University Press, 1955. 2nd. ed., 1960. 2nd. ed., 3rd printing, with revisions, 1968. Pb. ed., 1983.

————. "On the Significance of the Indian Tantric Yoga." In *Spiritual Disciplines.* Vol. 4 of *Papers from the Eranos Yearbooks.* Ed. Joseph Campbell. Bollingen 30. Princeton: Princeton University Press, 1960.

————. *Artistic Form and Yoga in the Sacred Images of India.* Translated by Gerard Chapple and James B. Lawson. Princeton: Princeton University Press, 1984.

GLOSSARY OF INDIAN TERMS

abhināya: dramatic portrayal in dance.

advaita: "without a second." In Śaṅkara's Vedantic philosophy, the standpoint from which the world is regarded as being beyond pairs of opposites (i.e. space-time, subject-object).

ahiṁsā: "noninjury, non-killing." The injunction not to harm any living thing, a basic law of Jainism and Buddhism.

ānanda: "bliss." In Vedanta, one of the three predications of Absolute Being that is the very essence of reality, experienced in yogic *samādhi* as the rapturous root of the world of phenomenality, transcending even suffering.

apsarases: "[h]eavenly damsels [which] constitute a kind of celestial *corps de ballet* are the mistresses of those who in reward for pious and meretorious deeds during their earthly lives have been reborn among the gods." —*Art of Indian Asia.*

artha: "thing, object, substance." The first of the four aims of Indian life (see also *kāma, dharma,* and *mokṣa)* that consists in the acquisition of material possessions.

asuras: demons, titans, anti-gods, rivals of the gods.

ātman: "self." Absolute Reality, i.e. the transcendent-yet-immanent mystery that is embodied in the microcosm of the individual as the ultimate source of his consciousness. Sometimes mistranslated as "soul." See also below under "*Brahman.*"

baksheesh: alms. The pervasive begging that Campbell encountered led him to see India as caught up in a "Baksheesh Complex" that dominated its social and political life.

bhairavas: deities attending on the goddess Mahā-Kālī during the night of Kāla-Rātrī. The horrific aspect of Śiva.

bhajana: devotional song.

bhakti: "devotion." Also, *bhakti yoga,* the yoga of devotion to an object, god, person, thing, or animal, which consists in the annihilation of one's personal will in the service to that object. See note 208.

bhūmi-sparśa-mudrā: a *mudrā* (q.v.), "one of the most common in figures of the seated Buddha. The left hand rests on the lap, with upturned open palm, while the right hangs downward, the middle finger touching the earth in the so-called 'position of touching the earth'." —*Art of Indian Asia.*

brahmacarya (the stage of life), *brahmacārin* (the person): "going in Brahman." A student of sacred knowledge; refers to the first stage of life, spent in celibate study, before marriage. (See also *gṛhastha, vānaprastha,* and *sannyāsa.*)

Brahman: Absolute Reality in its macrocosmic inflection as a counter-concept to *ātman,* the "self" or microcosmic inflection; the ground of being, or ultimate mystery of which all forms are a manifestation, including the gods. (The formula that Campbell often repeats, *ātman = Brahman,* refers to the goal of transcending these apparently opposite aspects of reality.)

brahmin (*brāhmaṇa*)– priest or teacher, first of the four Indian castes. See also *kṣatriya, vaiśya,* and *śūdra.*

burqa': large, veil like covering, worn by Muslim women.

cādar: sheet or large shawl worn as a veil by women.

cakra: one of a series of nerve centers in yogic physiology, rising from the base of the spine to the crown of the head. The second is known as *svādiṣṭhāna,* and is the *cakra* of the genital area. For an explanation of the *cakra* system, see *The Mythic Image,* pp. 330–381.

caste: the social and religious divisions of people in Hindu society. They are the brahmin, or priest-teacher; *kṣatriya,* king or soldier or political or military leader; *vaiśya,* merchant, and *śūdra,* laborer.

citraśāla: painting gallery.

copra: dried sections of the meat of the coconut, used for coconut oil and many other products. A major export of south India, Sri Lanka, Indonesia, and the Philippines.

daṇḍa-śakti (see also *loka-śakti*): Vinoba Bhave's political idea, meaning "power of the stick, ruling by force."

darśana: "seeing." The experience of seeing an image in a temple, a spiritually enlightened person, etc. Also, generically, philosophy.

devadāsī: "slave girls of the god." Dancing and singing girls of temple ritual.

Devī Mahātmya: part of the *Mārkāṇḍeya Purāṇa,* "Praise Song to the Goddess." Essential text of the cult of Durgā, it includes the story of the slaying of the Buffalo Demon, a demon often depicted in sculpture.

dharma: "duty." The third of the four aims of Indian life (see also *artha, kāma,* and *mokṣa*), consisting in the performance of the various duties, rights, and privileges ascribed to each of the four castes. In Mahāyāna Buddhism, *dharma,* taken in the impersonal sense of "the way things are" or "the structure of things," means "Way" or "Path."

digambara: "clothed in space," i.e., "naked," referring to Jain ascetics. In ancient times, most of the monks went around naked, and so Alexander found them when he invaded India, calling them "gymnosophists." They are to be distinguished from the *svetambara* ("clothed in white") sect, who already in the time of the Buddha had begun to wear white garments as a concession to modesty.

dvarāpālas: door guardians in architecture.

gandharva: heavenly musician. They are the consorts of the *apsarases* (q.v.).

garbhagṛha: "womb-room." Sanctuary, inner room of a temple.

ghazal: an Urdu, Persian, and Arabic poetical form.

gopīs: "cow girls." The companions of Kṛṣṇa.

gopuras: porch towers of the later architecture of southern India.

gṛhastha (the stage of life), *gārhasthya* (the person): householder; refers to the second of the four stages of Indian life, spent in marriage and raising a family. (See also *brahmacarya,* *vānaprastha,* and *sannyāsa.*)

guṇas: "strands." In *Sāṅkhya* (the metaphysical foundations of classical yoga), the three *guṇas* are the objective attributes of *prakṛti* (nature, or matter): *tamas* is black inertia, i.e. mass; *rajas,* its opposite, is fiery, red activity, i.e. energy; while *sattva* is pure white crystalline consciousness. All matter is characterized in varying proportions by these three strands. Radhakrishnan has it thus: "*Prakṛti* is, as it were, a string of three strands: *Sattva* is potential consciousness, *rajas* is the source of activity, and *tamas* is the source of that which resists activity. They produce pleasure, pain, and indifference, respectively. All things, as products of *prakṛti,* consist of the three *guṇas* in different proportions." Radhakrishnan, *A Sourcebook in Indian Philosophy,* p. 424.

gymkhana: a Hobson-Jobson word, meaning "sports club," based on the Urdu or Hindi *geṇḍ-khāna,* "ball-house," with *geṇḍ* replaced by the English "gym." Every British-influenced city in India had a Gymkhana Club.

iṣṭadevatā: the particular god one worships. The aspect of a god one personally worships.

iti iti: "this, this." The Upanishadic phrase is *neti neti* ("not this, not this"), used to describe *Brahman.*

jīva: the individual life monad that transmigrates from life to life and is unaffected by the *guṇas.*

jīvan-mukti: "liberated in life." Enlightenment.

jñāna: "knowledge." *Jñāna yoga* is the yoga of mental discrimination between the subject of knowledge and its object. See note 208.

kāma: "eros, desire." The second of the four aims of Indian life (see also *artha,* *dharma,* and *mokṣa*), which consists in finding sensual gratification, pleasure, and love.

kīrtana: devotional song or chant.

kṣatriya: king or soldier or political or military leader, second of the four Indian castes. See also brahmin, *vaiśya,* and *śūdra.*

kumārī pūjā: worship of a little girl, during the Durgā Pūjā festival.

kuṇḍalinī yoga: form of yoga that involves the activation of *śakti* ("energy," manifested as a white serpent) in such a way that it ascends through the seven *cakras,* or centers of consciousness. Each *cakra,* when activated by the serpent, transforms the practitioner's consciousness to the aims appropriate to that particular *cakra.*

lāsya: dance in which the emotions of love are represented in gestures.

līlā: "play." The play of forms in the pouring forth of *śakti,* through the projecting power of *māyā,* into the world as a delightful presentation of separate forms. See Zimmer, *Artistic Form and Yoga,* pp. 24, 76, 86.

liṅga: phallus. Symbol of male creative and sexual energy, counterpart to *yonī* (q.v.).

loka-śakti: see also *daṇḍa-śakti.* Vinoba Bhave's political idea, meaning "worldly power" or "people power."

Mādhyamika: "Middle Way." A school of Mahāyāna Buddhism associated with Nāgārjuna (second century A.D.), wherein ultimate reality is conceived of as emptiness (*śūnyatā*) to which no thoughts, concepts, or dualisms can be predicated. All of reality, the world, its names, dreams, and forms, including the Buddha, are illusory, like a mirage. Also known as Śūnyatāvāda.

mahānavamī: "Great Ninth." Ninth day of the Durgā Pūjā.

mahāṣṭamī: "Great Eighth." Eighth day of the Durgā Pūjā.

Mahāyāna: "Greater Vehicle." A later form of Buddhism upon which most contemporary forms of Buddhism are based. Hīnayāna, "Lesser Vehicle," is an earlier form of Buddhism. In Hīnayāna the ideal is the *arhat,* or saint, who achieves *nirvāṇa* and frees himself from bondage to *karma* and renounces the world. In Mahāyāna, the ideal is the *boddhisattva,* who upon achieving release from *karma* remains in the world and dedicates himself to achieving the same release for all other sentient beings.

maithuna: image of a couple in sexual embrace.

maṇḍapa: temple porch.

mārga: path, way, trace, guidepost.

maṭha: monastery.

māyā: "illusion." Generally, the phenomenal world; the superimposition of plurality (space, time, matter) upon *Brahman,* or Absolute Reality.

mleccha: foreigner.

mokṣa: "release." The last of the four aims of Indian life (see also *artha, kāma,* and *dharma*), different from the first three, which are concerned with the relation of the individual to the world and society. *Mokṣa,* the supreme aim, is release from the world, society, and the other aims altogether.

mudrā: symbolically significant positions or poses of the hands and fingers in dance and iconography.

namaskāra: a gesture, bowing with both hands clasped together, both as homage and meaning "hello."

Nandi: Śiva's bull.

naṭarāja: an incarnation of Śiva as Lord of the Dance.

nirvāṇa: "blown out." In Buddhism, the still point of release from suffering that is found at the center of one's consciousness; it can be defined as either release from the world and its illusions (Hīnayāna Buddhism), or as release from ignorance (Mahāyāna Buddhism).

paisa: Indian monetary unit of small value.

paṇḍal: "shed." A temporary shrine put up, for instance, during a festival.

paśu: creature, animal.

piśācas: demons, as for instance those attending the goddess Mahā-Kālī during the night of Kāla-Rātrī at the Divālī festival.

prasāda: "grace." Food offered to a deity and then distributed to worshipers in its new, sacralized state.

pūjā: the basic form of modern Hindu worship, consisting of worship of a holy sanctuary, image, or person by tossing or pouring on it flowers, rice, water, oil, or milk.

Purāṇa: a class of sacred Hindu literature, it consists of volumes of poetry, fables, and myths. See note 153.

purdah: custom of veiling women in Hindu and Muslim India.

rāga: the melodic structure of Indian classical music, or of a given piece of music, e.g. *Rāga bhairava.* See note 188.

rājā: "the yoga of kings." *Rājā yoga* involves the "intentional stopping of the spontaneous activity of the mind stuff." See note 208.

rasa: an emotive essense of drama or poetry. There are variously nine or more types. See note 187.

ṛṣi: one of the seers who composed the Vedas.

sādhanā: method, technique, way of operating, spiritual practice.

sadhu: "good man." An ascetic.

sahaja: "easy, spontaneous." A Tantric coinage. "In sahaja, the adoration of young and beautiful girls was made the path of spiritual evolution and ultimate emancipation. By this adoration we must understand not merely ritual worship (the Kumārī Pūjā [q.v.]), but also 'romantic love'." —"Sahaja" in Coomaraswamy, *The Dance of Śiva.*

śakti: "energy." The energy that moves through all things, seeking to manifest itself in different forms.

samādhi: "concentration, contemplation, trance." Spiritual illumination, the absorption of individual consciousness by *Brahman.*

sāman: a verse or text of the Sāma Veda, or the Sāma Veda itself.

saṃsāra: the endless wheel of birth-death-rebirth, self-propelled by the kinetic impulses of *karma.*

sandhi: marriage, juncture.

sannyāsa (the stage), *sannyāsī* (the person): wandering ascetic; the last of the four stages of Indian life (see also *brahmacarya, gṛhastha,* and *vānaprastha*).

saptamī pūjā: ceremony during the seventh day of the Durgā Pūjā.

satī (suttee): the custom, outlawed today but still sporadically practiced, of a wife immolating herself on her husband's funeral pyre.

satya: "Truth."

satyagrāha: "holding the truth." Mahatma Gandhi's system of nonviolent civil disobedience.

satyam eva jayati: "truth indeed wins out." Upanishadic aphorism.

siddha: "perfected one." A yoga adept.

śikāra: dome or spire of northern Indian temples of the Gupta and later periods.

śloka: "meter, verse." *Śloka* meter is the epic meter.

smṛti: "what is remembered." One of the classes of sacred Hindu literature, taken as explication or furtherance of the *śruti* works. Included in it are the *Mahābhārata* (which includes the *Bhagavad Gītā*), and the *Dharmaśāstras,* treatises on ethical and social philosophy. See note 153.

śruti: "what is heard." The oldest class of sacred Hindu literature, including the Vedas and the Upaniṣads, taken as direct revelation. See note 153.

stūpa: mound, memorializing Buddha. "In its earliest known examples, at Bhārhut and Sāñcī, the form was that of a moundlike central structure surrounded by a railing with sumptuously carved gates. In the course of the subsequent centuries the *stūpa* developed variously, particularly following the spread of Buddhism throughout Asia." —*Art of Indian Asia.*

śūdra: laborer, last of the four Indian castes. See also brahmin, *kṣatriya,* and *vaiśya.*

śunyatā: "emptiness." See note 234.

suṣupti: "fully asleep."

svapna: dream.

tāla: rhythm.

tāṇḍava: dance of Śiva.

tanka: Tibetan Buddhist temple banner.

Tantra: "thread." (Thread through the palm-leaf manuscript.) One of the classes of sacred Hindu literature. See note 153.

toraṇa: one of the monumental gates of a *stūpa.*

trimūrti: "three-faced, three-imaged."

turīya: "fourth." Cosmic rapture. See note 262.

uṣṇiṣa: "the true Buddha head is bare . . . [the forehead] surmounted by a peculiar swelling, the *uṣṇiṣa,* which is one of the thirty-two traditional 'great marks' of the Buddhist superman-savior." —*Art of Indian Asia.*

vāhana: "vehicle, mount." Animals and other beings that appear beneath the feet of deities in Indian art.

vaiśya: merchant, third of the four Indian castes. See also brahmin, *kṣatriya,* and *śūdra.*

vānaprastha (the stage), *vanaprasthī* (the person)—forest dweller; the third of the four stages of Indian life spent in solitary contemplation. (See also *brahmacarya, gṛhasthya,* and *sannyāsa*).

Vedanta: "end of the Vedas." The system of monistic philosophy based on the Upaniṣads, which come at the end of the Vedas. Śaṅkara, the eighth-century Hindu philosopher, was its most famous exponent. See also *advaita.*

vidyā: knowledge of any kind.

vihāra: monastery.

vīnā: a stringed instrument related to the sitar.

vīra: "hero."

yakṣa: pre-Vedic fertility gods who serve as attendants of Śiva and Kubera (the "Goblin King").

yonī: symbol of female creative and sexual energy, counterpart to *liṅga* (q.v.).

yuga: A great world age, four of which—Krita, Tretā, Dvāpara, and Kālī—form a world cycle (Mahāyuga), and correspond to the four ages—Gold, Silver, Brass, and Iron—of the Greco-Roman tradition. At the end of a Mahāyuga there is a great world flood that reabsorbs creation back into the Absolute that it may begin again.

zamindar: large landowner.

zanāna: women's quarter in a Muslim household.

BOOK I ACKNOWLEDGMENTS

None of the work on *Baksheesh & Brahman* would have been possible without the generous and unswerving aid of Jean Erdman, who as muse to Joseph Campbell begot these diaries, and as president of the Joseph Campbell Foundation is midwife to their production. Jean was also available to help our search for detail, by reminiscing about a time, now over forty years ago, when these events unfolded.

This book would have nowhere near its present resonance and depth without the extremely valuable work of John David Ebert. His great knowledge of Campbell's work and sources and his steady flow of constructive suggestions for improvement, especially for further reading in Campbell's works, make him an important editorial contributor to this book. Arthur Moore, as well, out of interest in Campbell, and with a passion for research and detail, volunteered his time, and supplied many footnotes.

Sue Davidson Lowe, Joseph Campbell's 1945–46 research and editorial assistant, daughter of Elizabeth Davidson (a prominent figure in these pages), was extremely helpful with biographical and historical details.

Dr. Walter Spink of the University of Michigan was most helpful in updating the chronological chart of Indian art (Appendix IB).

Andrew McCord supervised and rationalized the transliteration of Sanskrit, Hindi, and Urdu words. He also marked, edited, and checked the manuscript for errors and assisted with the Glossary. Erik Rieselbach assisted with the page layout and with digitizing the photographs.

Carol Pentleton drew the illustrations and maps. Scott Taylor made fonts with Sanskrit diacriticals, relieving us of our greatest production nightmare. We'd also like to thank all the people who answered the queries posted by Antony Van Couvering on the Internet Usenet newsgroups, and most especially the generous and helpful members of the Desktop Publishing and Quark Users forums on Compuserve.

BOOK II

❧

SAKE & SATORI: JAPAN

When Joseph Campbell arrived in Colombo, Ceylon, on March 4, 1955, he was in a foul mood. He had come to India some six months before, funded by grants from the Bollingen Foundation, and driven by his own deep desire to see the country that had dominated his professional life and his dreams for so many years.

Since a chance meeting with Jiddu Krishnamurti on a transatlantic steamship in 1924, Campbell had been fascinated with the religions and philosophies of Asia, and particularly India. When his mentor, renowned Indologist Heinrich Zimmer, had died in 1943, leaving behind a huge volume of notes for uncompleted scholarly texts, Campbell had agreed with Zimmer's widow Christiane to fashion these notes into a collection of posthumous works. He had spent the next twelve years devoting most of his professional energy into these books. Indeed, he had traveled to India with the proofs for the last volume, *The Art of Indian Asia,* in his suitcase.

Campbell had arrived in India expecting to find the breath of *brahman*—the World Soul of the Hindu religion—that inspired the classical Indian art and literature that he and Zimmer had studied. What he had found instead was a society obsessed with *bhakti,* the rituals of devotion, and centered around what Campbell came to call "the Baksheesh Complex":

what he felt was a national expectation of getting something for nothing. In his journals, he said:

> The *squalor* of India is not a result of Indian *poverty* alone, but also of an indifference to dirt, the inefficiency of city officials, and an intentional spectacle of poverty presented by professional beggars: moreover, the assault that the visitor endures from the beggars gives him an exaggerated view of the seedier aspects of the Indian scene. This whole matter of Indian poverty and squalor may be summed up as a function of the *Baksheesh Complex*, which has two major forms of manifestation: that of the beggar, that of the retired pensioner. The formula for both is *Something for Nothing.*
>
> India's pretext of spiritual superiority is another consequence of the Baksheesh Complex and does not accord with the actualities of the modern international scene. India is in fact receiving all of her progressive ideals (spiritual principles) as well as machines (technological principles) from the West.[1]

Campbell had faced beggars and hucksters, pimps and fakirs, and like many Westerners before and since it had put him in a state of moral shock. He had had many wonderful, enriching experiences as well, but by the time he had finished up his tour, he was sick at heart.

The Indian government itself had dealt the final insult. As Campbell had applied for an exit visa, he had discovered that he would have to pay income tax on all the money that he had brought into the country. In Campbell's eye, this was nothing but the last, egregious, institutional form of baksheesh. As he wrote to the Indian Minister of Finance:

> I arrived in New Delhi, August 30, 1954; lectured, gratis, at a number of Indian colleges and institutions; spent as much as I could afford on Indian textiles; gave as generously as I could to your temples and beggars; overlooked the anti-American propaganda in the newspapers; learned to admire and love the Indian people, as I had long admired and loved their culture—and when it came time for me to buy my ticket to depart (that is to say, today), my way was blocked by your income tax officials, to whom I am compelled to pay 519 rupees—not on any moneys earned in India (for I have not received one rupee here) but out of the funds that I brought into India and spent here. After this final experience of the baksheesh motif—played *fortissimo,* now, by the government itself—I am afraid that I am going to find it harder than it used to be, to speak and write about the Indian character with the respect it deserves.[2]

Campbell's thoughts and feelings about the contradictions of Indian philosophy and society dominate the journals from which this volume and *Baksheesh & Brahman* are drawn as he moves from a Hindu to a Buddhist world. He was ready for a different experience than the dirt and squalor that had overwhelmed him in India, and he found it in Ceylon, Southeast

Asia, and especially Japan. Reading his daily musings, one sees a sensualist delight in the pleasures of these newfound lands. He experienced anew the joy of discovery, not only in the Buddhist temples and Shintō shrines, but also in the bath- and teahouses.

Now, by his own testimony, Campbell was a very happily married man.[3] He wrote his wife, choreographer Jean Erdman, regularly, and looked forward to his final month in Asia, when she would join him on a teaching junket. Yet he indulged in the fleshpots of Tokyo with a man-of-the-world (and almost entirely voyeuristic) verve.

From the sybaritic glee that Campbell took in immersing himself in Japanese nightclubs, baths, and theaters, he soon moved to the scholar's joy of immersing himself in this new country's language and religion. As his stay lengthened—and especially once the first copy of *The Art of Indian Asia* arrived—Campbell's physical, spiritual, and intellectual reaction to his stay in India mellowed, and he gained new perspectives on India, Japan, and his own psyche, as well as on geopolitics, a subject he had previously avoided considering.

Campbell's timing in traveling to East Asia was politically fortuitous. Nineteen fifty-five was a relative slack-water period in the Cold War: two years after the cessation of hostilities in Korea, one after the French departure from Indochina. America's post–World War II occupation of Japan was officially over (though an enormous U.S. military presence remained in the country, much to Campbell's repeatedly voiced dismay) and its involvement in Vietnam had not yet begun. Joseph McCarthy's hearings in the U.S. Senate, seeking to unearth Communists among the employees of the Department of State and the army (whom Campbell refers to somewhat sneeringly as "our Fifth Amendment boys"[4]), had ended. Yet the politics of East and West, Capitalist and Communist were very much in the air, and Campbell, a lifelong nonpartisan, found himself increasingly drawn to defend his native land.

The difficulty for Campbell was that he found the Americans working and traveling in Asia to be, for the most part, woefully uninformed, misinformed, and unconcerned about the cultures of the nations they were visiting. A classic example occurred during a dusty tour-bus ride back from the spectacular ruins of Angkor Wat. As he was to recount many times in later years, he overheard an American tourist moan to his wife, "I'd give everything I have to have had three Coca-Colas instead of all those temples."[5]

As he considered this dilemma—his love of America and what it stood for on the one hand, and the poor showing that its representatives made abroad—several initiatives shaped themselves in his mind that were to inform the rest of his career. The first was his course of lectures on world culture and religion for the Foreign Service Institute, the training program of the U.S. State Department, that he undertook soon after his return to the United States and continued well into the 1970s.

The second was the germ of the idea that was to become the series of books known as *The Masks of God*—four comprehensive volumes on comparative religion and myth aimed not only at his fellow academics but also at the broader American populace.[6] These books would engage most of his writing energy from his return home until the last volume, *Creative Mythology,* was issued in 1968.

The third initiative that he undertook after his travels in Asia was his series of popular lectures. From his homecoming until his death in 1987, Campbell embarked on an ongoing succession of lectures at colleges and churches, public venues (such as New York's Cooper Union) and private conferences, on radio and television,[7] seeking to educate the public about world myth and religion.

Indeed, it is in these journals that Campbell finally identifies his field of study: "Resolution: *Comparative mythology*... is indeed my field."[8] Amazing as it may seem to us, Campbell had always avoided defining precisely what it was that he was studying and teaching. He had studied English, biology, and medieval literature as a young man; he was on the Sarah Lawrence College English faculty. It was only now, at the age of fifty, that Campbell—the obdurate generalist—felt ready to name his specialty.

It is in these journals too that Campbell begins to realize and take into account some of his own preconceptions. In the notes that provide the first manifesto for what is to become *The Masks of God,* Campbell wrote, "As a contemporary Occidental faced with Occidental and contemporary psychological problems, I am to admit and even celebrate (in Spengler's manner) the relativity of my historical view to my own neurosis (Rorschach formula)."[9] It is in this self-aware mode that Campbell embarked on the new phase of a career that was to reshape his ideas on comparative mythology, and ours.

CHAPTER I

The Buddha Land

Ceylon,[1] Thailand, and Cambodia

Friday, March 4, 1955   **Colombo**

Up at 6:00. Morning tea and newspaper.

A few retrospective thoughts about India:

1. The Indians are great talkers. The man who will talk to you like a saint, however, about God, Soul, the Gītā, and Illumination, may well have betrayed a great many of his friends, and when you meet these friends you will certainly hear about it.

2. The Indians are great talkers. In New York I heard all the talk about the Unity of Religions. In India I found more disunity (Communalism principle) than anywhere in the modern West.

3. The Indians are great talkers. They talk of "Thou art That," and they treat human beings worse than they treat animals.

4. I cannot believe that the Brahmans in the past were less arrogant and cruel than the worst of them today. We have the evidence of the Buddhists, for example, in the fifth century B.C., and we have also the evidence of the Laws of Manu and the Institutes of Viṣṇu.

5. Swami Nikhilananda has frequently said that the altruistic principle is an insecure base for ethics, while the metaphysical is a secure one. Actually, however, the altruistic ethic of the West has yielded a society in which mutual regard is more evident than it is in India.

6. The great lesson of India is that men and women can survive under conditions that one would think impossible—and not only survive, but be charming.
7. The Indians are charming. Poverty: Charm: Eloquence: Inconsistency: Inefficiency.

After breakfast, I wrote up my diary for yesterday on a veranda overlooking the sea, then went to town to try to get organized—and the following plan developed:

I shall leave tomorrow morning by taxi for a three-day tour of the chief sites of Ceylon. I shall return Tuesday to Colombo and leave Wednesday morning for Bangkok, Siam.[2] I found that I could move into the Grand Oriental Hotel this afternoon and return to it Tuesday. Then I took a cab out to visit the museum, but found it "closed on Fridays," and to meet Dr. Paranavitana, the Commissioner of Archaeology,[3] but found him "out of station, until Tuesday." So I returned to the Galle Face Hotel for lunch, and after lunch taxied to the Grand Oriental.

Wrote a letter to Jean and after tea took a cab to the zoo, to watch an amusing elephant dance. A handsome zoo, designed, I learned from my cab driver, by a German—Hagenbeck, no doubt.[4]

At dinner, listening to a rather poor orchestra, I thought: the pleasure that the Occidental finds in the Orient is that of being an Occidental in the Orient: the tension between the two worlds is experienced (one way or another) and this is what yields the pleasure.

I went for a brief walk around the block after supper and retired early. Colombo's rickshaw boys, by the way, don't seem to have the imagination of those of Calcutta: all they can think of to offer are "Movies?" "Cold beer?"

Saturday, March 5   **Anuradhapura**

Departing from the hotel in a small taxi at 8:15, I was driven north, through Negombo and Chilaw, to Puttalam, where I arrived at 11:20 for lunch at the Rest House.

Miles and miles of coconut lands, all the way. One field of tobacco. Also, bananas, jackfruit, etc. The people, definitely, look better off than the Indian. One notes also, no turbans, few head loads, and less head wagging. The bullock carts have characteristic wattle tops.

The whole region is surprisingly Catholic: churches everywhere. One Hindu temple with a large running horse in the place of Nandi.

The people have a slightly Indonesian look. Two of the men whom I talked with in Colombo were from Indonesia. Remember the great sea trade from Sumatra too, in the ninth century. Buddhism also linked with Indonesia. From here, perhaps the influence upon Malabar and Cochin.

After a pleasant lunch in the pleasant rest house, my drive cut northeast to Anuradhapura, where I arrived about 2:00. Drive through wild forestland; good road. Huge anthills with cobra holes all along the way.

Installed in the cute little Grand Hotel, I went to see the monuments: Issurumuniyagala (my God, what they have done to this!), Sacred Bo-Tree and Brazen Palace, Ruvanweliseya Dagaba (huge: and again, what they have done to the precious images!), Thuparama Dagaba—ruins, ruins everywhere. One gets very strongly the impression of a once tremendous and magnificent center. Nice driving along well-kept roads and through country with lovely trees, grazing cattle, quiet people. Buddha images. Abhyagiri and Jetavanaramaya Dagabas. More ruins—and a lovely, huge lake, from which one sees the tremendous domes of the Ruvanweliseya and Abhyagiri—the first, restored, the second in ruins. The other *stūpas*[5] are considerably smaller.

I concluded my tour with a visit to the museum, where I found a number of fine things, and a few of particular interest:

1. Two "*garbha* stones" with twenty-five square holes, within each of which a little bronze image or symbol was contained. In the center of one, a Bodhisattva on a lotus. A number of swastikas.
2. A Vajrasattva image from the seventh century. (Definite Mahāyāna in both of these!)
3. Chinese pottery from the eighth to tenth centuries. (The China trade.)

After my trip (Hot!) I had tea on the veranda of the hotel and began a letter to Vann, summarizing my India experiences. Then people began to arrive: a German foursome: some scattered English: an American couple (seventy-ish) from New York (Mr. & Mrs. Harry Englander), who commenced conversation and with whom I had dinner. Going to Tokyo (shall meet them there). Just came from two years in Pakistan (engineering). Spoke favorably of the Pakistanis, but I could not gain much of an impression of what is going on there. When all had cleared away, I had a glass of lukewarm beer and went to bed.

Sunday, March 6   Mihintale—Polonnaruva

Off at 8:10 for Mihintale, about six miles from Anuradhapura. A lovely hill, with a great series of steps up to various *stūpas* and promontories: a hot but beautiful climb. Magnificent prospect of the land, with the great *stūpas* of Anuradhapura visible in the distance.

Then a drive to Polonnaruva. Lunch and rest at the pretty rest house, which is on an artificial lake. From 2:00 to 4:00, a view of the monuments: Old Parakrama Bahu I[6] with the "Library Dagaba" nearby; next, a great compound of ruins, including the Vata-da-ge, Thuparama, Stone Book, and Satmahal ("Seven-Storied") Prasada; further, Gal Vihara and nearby the vast area including the Ruvanweliseya, Buddha Sima Prasada, and Jetavanaramaya.

I got back to the rest house about 4:00, pretty hot & tired: tea; naps; letters—and a long evening chat with Melford, a young Englishman in the colonial service, who was three years in the Gold Coast, and is now going to England on leave after three years in Malaya. Lots of interesting news:

1. The coast of Ceylon, from Colombo to Puttalam (with all its coconut groves, thatch cottages, etc.) greatly resembles the African Gold Coast[7]—only does not seem to be so prosperous. The Gold Coast, apparently, is one of the most flourishing of the Colonies. There is a law against land being owned by non-natives, and this has prevented the development of a planter situation like that of East Africa. The natives, furthermore, are coming steadily into their own as modern citizens. They are excellent doctors and surgeons (development of the witch doctor principle); not so hot, however, as engineers.

2. Three eras of history are represented simultaneously in the native population of West Africa (this goes also, I should say, for India).
   a. Among the peasants—an archaic/medieval,

  b. among the politicians and pedagogs—the nineteenth century; and

  c. among the doctors, engineers, etc.—the twentieth century.

3. In Malaya—the Communist movement is represented, about 90 percent, by the Chinese; as follows:

  a. a basic core of Communist guerrillas, who were formerly equipped and encouraged by Great Britain

  b. a reinforcement in arms through the Japanese, who left equipment behind, for the annoyance of the British

  c. young Chinese "idealists" (Padover's term), trained in and graduated from the Chinese schools in Malaya

  d. the Chinese "rich men" of the various districts who bribe the Malayan district officers; the "rich men" themselves being threatened by the Chinese Communists, who, one way or another (families, properties, etc., in China), have them under their power

4. Victory over the Communists is being attained and may yet be won:

  a. through starvation (air-poisoning of their jungle crops; strict control of all sales of preserved foods: puncturing all tins as soon as sold, etc.),

  b. through jungle forts (paratroops into treetops, ropes to ground: clearing of forest for helicopter landings; construction of jungle forts).

5. The cost of the war is 1,000,000 Malayan dollars per day (over US $500,000). Drain on Malayan economy—but that's the idea.

6. Among the troops now being used against the Communists are Fijians (great rugby team), Gurkas, Aborigines (five kinds), and Malayan. Few Chinese enlist.

7. The Great Dilemma of democratic politics in the Orient is this: that the native regimes, which have to be supported, are inevitably corrupt (Rhee,[8] Chiang,[9] etc.). If one insists on reform, one is immediately accused of meddling in internal affairs. Meanwhile, one is preaching and teaching the very principles that condemn the crowd that one is supporting.

8. The British policy has been to induct the native peoples into the democratic system as steadily as possible, and to retire when there is no use holding on (the French, on the other hand, don't know when they're through). Example: registering voters and instruction in voting ("I always feel that I am driving the first nail into my own coffin when I do this.")

Monday, March 7   **Polonnaruva—Sigiriya—Kandy**

Off, at about 8:00, from the Polonnaruva Rest House for a visit to Sigiriya. Stiff climb. Encountered my Englishman about halfway up, at the level of the frescoes. He was troubled a bit by vertigo, but pushed on; we went through the lion's feet and scaled to the top. Amazing view. Amazing brickwork structures. Must have been a fantastic affair. Then down we went again. A company of priests at the bottom offered us coconut milk, after which we drove to the rest house for a cup of tea.

Procession in Kandy

Next, to Kandy: a very pretty little city around a charming lake (made me think, a little, of Lucerne). On the way: rubber plantations, tea, coffee, cocoa, coconut, pepper. Visited the Temple of the Tooth, the beautiful botanical gardens, and the new, handsome, still-growing university.[10]

At about 5:00, my friend and I fell into an amusing adventure. We drove in his car to see the temple elephants bathing, but were told that they had already bathed and were now in a procession of some kind. We drove to find the procession, and presently, lo! an elephant ahead. Traffic jam. We got out of the car and walking fast with our cameras, caught up to the elephant—more ahead; and both before and behind the great last elephant Kandyian dancers and drums. Behind the whole procession, a slowly walking Buddhist monk, shading his head with a palm, and walking on a long white cloth (in two pieces: picked up from behind and placed before him). We were tall and conspicuous, and were cordially invited into the enclosure into which the dancers, monk, and reliquary from atop the last elephant were gathered. "One hour of dancing," we were told. But instead, it was one hour of speeches—and we were trapped—sitting in places of honor. The elephants went back along the road; the dancers too—and there we were.

"We have fallen into a deep trap," I said.

"We can't go now," said my friend.

But toward the close of the third speech, I said, "When this one ends, let's get up and go."

We did so, and nobody seemed to mind. The most helpful of our hosts came up and talked with us. The speeches, which had been in Singhalese, had been made by police officers and lawyers, and were on the subject of the evil of crime. We had been lured into an anti-crime meeting by a troupe of elephants.

Meanwhile, of course, our driver had lost us. We started walking back to town, and then hopped a bus.

After I had bathed and rested, I came down for dinner, to find my friend (Melford) having a drink with a late-middle-aged English couple, Major & Mrs. Blake, from South America, who had just spent six weeks as guests of the state in Siam. Very nice words about Siam. I should visit, not only Bangkok and Chiang Mai, but also Korat—the Major's verdict: practically no Communism in Siam. Government corrupt? Yes! But the people are well-off and happy. A threat: the Thai of the north (South China) now do so want to join their southern brothers, who left them eight hundred years ago!!

I found Mrs. Blake very edgy and un-nice about Americans ("your people," she called them, when addressing me), and the major very strongly against the U.N. and open diplomacy. Otherwise an apparently civilized and pleasant couple.

Tuesday, March 8   Kandy—Colombo

Good-bye to my friend Melford after breakfast, and a fine drive, then, back to Colombo. Pause, on the way, at a tea factory, where I became acquainted with the secrets and the grades:

1. BOP (the best)
2. BOPF (Fannings)
3. BP
4. OP (Orange Pekoe)
5. Pekoe
6. Dust 2
7. Dust 1 (the finest grain)

Arrived at the Grand Oriental Hotel at noon, to find everything in good order: ticket ready for Bangkok, room reserved here and in Bangkok, and a letter from Jean—also, one from Arthur Gregor, and a wild affair from Ed Solomon (Sarah Lawrence),[11] who expects to arrive in India in March or April and wants quick information.

After lunch I went to the Colombo museum (excellent bronzes) and chatted with Dr. Paranavitana (Archaeological Commissioner for Ceylon) and Dr. Devendra, who is to be the editor of a Buddhist encyclopedia.[12]

They told me that Sigiriya was an imitation of Kubera's Kailasa, and that the frescoes of the *apsarases* probably ran all around the sides. On top was a garden, not a castle. The approach wound up the sides somewhat like a ziggurat.[13]

In the car, on the way back to Colombo, I meditated a bit about India and Ceylon, Hinduism and Buddhism, Religion and the modern world. One does not find in Ceylon the utterly abject castoffs that abound all over India. The wealth seems not to be so unevenly distributed. Is this the result of the Buddhist, non-caste ideology? If so—the caste system can be regarded as greatly responsible for the peculiarly Indian spectacle of squalor. The Buddhist shrines are conspicuously cleaner and more neatly kept than the Hindu. Their art is more cleanly brash. I am amazed at the strength of the Buddhist tone in the newspapers. The fundamental anti-Westernism seems to be comparable to that of India: a pride in the old-fashioned virtues: vegetarianism, nondrinking, etc. The monks seem to me to be little different from the Hindu—except that we don't seem to have any wild *sadhus* here. A more clarified, less archaic atmosphere.

One religion or another—I think—they're all out of date, and in their variety are the various hues of a sunset—Catholic *bhakti*, Hindu *bhakti*, Buddhist *bhakti*: Buddha's tooth, Christ's Cross, Śiva's *lingam*. As Jason said, the other day: "In the Madura temple, watching all those people, finally something cracked in me and I couldn't take it any longer: I sat down and laughed. People, I thought, will worship anything—absolutely anything—and so what?"[14]

Wednesday, March 9   Bangkok

A radical change of world. Up at 4:00 A.M. to catch 5:00 o'clock bus to the airport: bus late: 5:30. Standing in the somnolent lobby of the Grand Oriental Hotel, waiting. The other person leaving from the hotel was a dapper young Japanese.

Lots to do at the airport about passports, customs, and papers—then into a vast new KLM Super Constellation. Very few passengers and a dismal Dutch hostess. Only five passengers in tourist class. Breakfast rather dull. Lots of camera work by the young Japanese boys and Germans in the cabin: shooting (and I with them) the disappearance of Ceylon—and later, the arrival of Malaya: first a lovely scattering of islands; then the jungle land of the peninsula; then fields—threaded with rivers that looked, at first, like roads: houses lining the riverbanks: boats on the rivers, seen from above.

We landed at the great airport in Bangkok about 1:00 P.M. Indian time: 2:30 P.M. Bangkok time—I realized that I am now exactly halfway round the world: 2:00 P.M. here is 2:00 A.M. in New York. And lo! we have come, indeed, into the American sphere: on the airfield, American army planes; in the airport—a flock of American tourists: we are served, immediately, Pepsi-Cola. It is very hot.

A very long bus ride to the hotel; bus filled with an American tour—widows and old gentlemen from the rural parts mostly (Bennington, Vt., was on one bag): a noisy man singing "East Side, West Side" and taking up more room than he should. "Look at them horns!" anent the water buffalo. I noted *wooden houses instead of clay:* Chinese-style hats, water jars on carrying sticks, etc. Chinese-style people and clothes. And a new sensation: most of the people are vertical instead of horizontal, and although poor, do not have the look of utter squalor.

Discharged at the Metropole Hotel—which is a bit out from the center—I found myself in the sort of place that one might find, say, in a new Nevada hotel run by Chinese. The price of the room shocked me: 250 ticals air-conditioned (= $12.50) without meals (contrast the normal Indian twenty-five rupees [= $5.00] *with* meals). Not air-conditioned I would pay 130 ticals (= $6.50): that I took; but I determined to look for something cheaper elsewhere. Then I took a shower (no hot water), changed into lighter clothes, and walked along the new-looking street toward the town. Found the Trocadero Hotel and made reservations for next week. Found the World Travel Service, and made reservations for two hours tomorrow. Found the telegraph office and wired Jean for $750. Came home for dinner and after dark went for a little stroll.

My first impression: a large Chinatown. After India, it has an air of fun-in-life and prosperity. People are cleanly and neatly dressed. Lots of new buildings going up everywhere. Men and women; boys and girls in the cafés, however, mostly men. The Orient, all right; but people don't seem to be having as much trouble as the Indians with inherited habits. A relief to see people without their religion painted all over their faces. Even the Buddhist monks in their bright yellow robes (clean, for a change) seemed comparatively simple.

Furthermore, there is the electrical air here of a town on the threshold of a considerable future. Last week the great SEATO[15] meeting took place in Bangkok, and it became the capital of the alliance. In the vast new Postal and Telegraph building, there is a special window for SEATO wires.

Thursday, March 10

Up for a seven o'clock start on a launch trip, up the river and through some of the canals and smaller streams. A wonderful world of people in boats— boat restaurants, boat markets, boat transports of every kind; also, wooden homes, shops, and workshops, warehouses, etc., all along both banks, thickly packed. The navigating of the boats through the teeming, narrow channels was something marvelous: motorboats with lighters and loaded skiffs in tow. One had the sense of a happy, well-fed people, an abundance of fruits and rice (barges down to the gunwales, loaded with rice, coming down the river by the dozen). Something very different from India—even though this trip reminded me at many points of the backwaters around Cochin.

We made two stops on the launch trip. The first was at a great shed, sheltering about ten of the longest canoe-barges I have ever seen: one was over one hundred fifty feet long; the others only a little shorter. These were the royal barges and war canoes—golden prowed with dragon and Garuda figureheads, the latter having a hole, for the firing of a canon, between the spread legs of the birds. Date of the barges, said to be eighteenth century or so, made of teak. Our second stop was at the tall Dawn Temple. We climbed to about halfway up the central tower, and the Hindi woman in the party wrote "Zahria Pakistan 1955" on the inside of the top parapet.

After lunch, I went on another tour—to the royal palace and the adjacent temples: golden, pagoda, temple of the Emerald Buddha. Fabulous colors—and I ran out of color film, of course. One charming episode: an American gentleman of about seventy, from California, was standing beside me and I pointed out a frieze of Thai *apsarases*,[16] up near the ceiling. "Angels," I said. "You know," he said, with a kind look in his eyes, "there are pictures of Greek angels, Indian angels, American angels, Buddhist angels—and they're all different. I wonder which is right!"

Wired Jean twice today for money; once for my pocket, once for my fares ($750 + $600). After dinner at the Metropole Hotel, I went to my room, and wrote a set of letters to India—including Sri Krishna Menon.

Friday, March 11

No particular plan for the day. Had expected a morning tour but it didn't come through. Strolled about town, purchasing razor blades, films, etc., visiting the Chartered Bank of India, to see if my money had arrived; and then bumped into the gentleman who had asked about the angels—Mr. Farrell, of California. Joined him and his wife for a visit to the National Museum (great room of bronzes) and a large standing Buddha. By the time we were finished it was lunchtime, and when I returned to the Metropole I found that the World Travel Service had phoned. I got in touch with them immediately after lunch and was told that there would be room for me on a one day excursion that they were running to Angkor tomorrow. Did I want to go? I did. Quick changes of plan. Trip to the bank, and my first money had arrived.

After settling my travel and money affairs, I went into the Trocadero bar for a bit of air-conditioning and a cup of tea, and had been there about half an hour, when a rather fierce-looking guy came walking in and went walking around the room like a lion in a cage—sort of angry, and as though he had just been pulled out of a drunk or a beating of some kind.

He looked dimly familiar. Too loudly, he ordered ham and eggs, and, continuing his ravaged walk, suddenly stopped before me.

"Say!" he said, "Aren't you Campbell?"

"Hello there, Don," I said, gradually remembering. It was (my God!) Don Bigelow, whom Jean and I had met in Baroda—Fulbright representative of America to India.[17]

He sat down at my table, and in his hoarse voice—which he always seems to be trying to test for a better sound—began rehearsing his rough experiences: a bad BOAC[18] landing in Calcutta; a late flight; the horrible BOAC; the horrible Hindus, with whom he had lived a year: he had told them off when he was about to leave: they had asked him what he thought of India and he let them have it: a graceless, selfish, dreary people.

I too felt that there was something definitely wrong about the Hindus. One enters the country and is shocked by the squalor, the callousness of the rich, and all those other things enumerated in my early notes. Gradually, then, one gets used to the negative aspects and the positive begin to emerge. These, too, I have noted. One even begins to accept the low Indian standard as a kind of norm. But then one leaves, and even in Ceylon it is evident that life can easily be better. Here in Thailand, one is actually amazed at how bright it can be; whereas for all the American tourists here in Thailand, this place seems below par. Now that I can look back upon India, I think that what finally got me down the most was the arrogant assumption of spiritual superiority by a people in whose lives and society one can see the evidence only of a conspicuously materialistic self-interest, with a heavy sauce of *bhakti,* which is what the Hindus seem to mean by spirituality. Bigelow agreed that the spiritual arrogance was the worst of it. In Rangoon he had bumped into Santha Rama Rau and Faubian Bowers,[19] and Santha, after hearing all his complaints, had said, with perfect confidence, that, yes, but India was, after all, *the* great civilization.

It appeared that Bigelow was going to be on the trip tomorrow to Angkor. It appeared, also, that there were going to be a number of American tourists in the party. It appeared, finally, that he had met somewhere, somehow, a dismal couple who might be typical of what was coming and was going to have a drink with them at 7:00 P.M. Would I like to come? I said I would come at seven-thirty. Their name was Wallace and they were in the Trocadero Annex. The husband was about seventy and the much younger wife, somewhat desperate, was already throwing herself at Bigelow.

I returned to my own hotel, just down the street, for a bit of a nap and preparatory packing for tomorrow, then brought my smaller bag to the Trocadero, to be kept for me until my return from Angkor, and went over to the Wallace apartment in the Annex. The door was opened by a large, smiling, broad-faced, sandy blond woman of about forty-five, in a dressing gown and with her grease on her face. "My friend, Don Bigelow, told me to come," I said. "He isn't here yet," she said, still smiling, "but come in, come in. Pour yourself a drink and I'll finish dressing." I said I thought it would be better if I went over to get Don and returned in about half an hour. She consented, and I went downstairs; but instead of going to see Don immediately, I went for a brief walk, and returned to learn that Don had already gone up to the Wallace apartment. When I got there, he was sitting with a drink in his hand, while Margaret (Mrs. W.) went on with her dressing. I poured my drink and sat down. Then Mr. Wallace's quavery voice called from the bathroom for his trousers and a rather large-bellied pair was handed to him by his wife. She managed then to step into her dress and get it up over her while adroitly discarding her dressing gown and Don then opined that he had better go and change his garments too. We had decided to go to the Oasis, around the corner. (A place recommended to me by the two women I met in Darjeeling, and of which Mrs. W. had also heard a good report.) Mr. Wallace appeared: a mild, large, rather plump, oldish man; he greeted me perfunctorily (and why not?) poured himself a drink and sat down. Don went out to change and Mrs. W. went into the bathroom to finish her pruning. I was left with the old man.

"Well, of course," he said, "I'm not a professor, so I don't really understand these things; but it seems to me you can't give freedom to people until they're ready for it. Now you take the case of so-and-so, this friend of mine: he tells me that in such-and-such a place they built fine homes for the people, and what did they do? They used the bathrooms for wood and coal bins. Now, I don't know logic, of course, but it seems to me reasonable to think that people shouldn't be given things, or have things thrust upon them, till they're educated to use them." Etc. etc. One always gets it immediately from the man of money. This one has a large flat in San Francisco, a hotel room, for the moment, in Hong Kong, where he and his wife are keeping their spare luggage; this room at the Trocadero (air-conditioned), which he will keep while going to Angkor—and no idea, particularly, of why he is making the trip.

When Don returned, we finished off the drinks and walked around to the Oasis: a nightclub with a Thai band playing good Hawai'ian, American, and South American music. Two girl singers; one smoky, the other cuddly. Nice crowd—mostly Thai—and a very good dinner for about two dollars. First Mr. Wallace had to dance with his wife, so that she would be available to Don and myself. First I, then Don, then I again danced with her. "Sometimes," she said, "I feel so lonesome. . . . That's why I have to keep doing things."—Well, that was it all right: about the most dismal marriage picture I have seen. Married for money and the old man didn't die.

Saturday, March 12   Cambodia

Up at 4:00 to catch a bus at 4:45; but the bus did not arrive until 5:30. In it were an oldish man and a youngish wife: not the couple of last night, but another. This bus was an auxiliary affair: the real bus had gone on, full up, to the airport. And when we arrived, sure enough, there was a whole company of wealthy old gentlemen, petulant as babies, and forceful, variously younger wives—two, at least, with voices like men. I thought of Jung's *enantiodromia* formula:[20] here, however, it seemed to be represented with unusual force. Is this the soul of the U.S.A. that I behold?

The plane got off in due time, and I sat in the back seat with Bigelow: across from us a young anthropologist from Oregon, here on a Fulbright, to study and teach something about the teaching and study of native languages. When we got to Cambodia it appeared that neither of these Fulbright boys could speak French—or, probably, any language but English; and I could not but remember the first question that the Fulbright authorities at Columbia put to me: What about my languages? (German, French, Sanskrit, a bit of Hindi; also, Spanish and a bit of Italian, Russian, Latin and Greek.) I don't quite get it!

At the Siem Reap airport there was an extremely superior young Frenchman with a black beard, who certainly despised the arriving Americans, and though I despised his superiority, I could not but admit that he had some reason on his side. We were certainly a pitiful spectacle. It took a while to deal with the customs, and in the meantime another plane arrived on the small airfield—with a small party of French.

We were taken to the large, French-style hotel, in a bus that stalled on the way (fan-belt trouble), but finally arrived and then began, almost immediately, our tour of the sites.

First: Angkor Wat. Don and I got out ahead of the crowd; looked carefully at the mural reliefs, clockwise, to halfway round; then entered the courts and climbed the towers. Next finished the murals, clockwise, and met the crowd at the gate. Lots of color photos.

Bus back to the hotel for lunch. Off again at 3:00.

A quick drive through one of the Angkor Thom gates (to be visited tomorrow) and an arrival at Preah Khan. A wonderful adventure. I was so excited that I opened my camera before reeling back the film, and so, spoiled all of the shots of the morning. Five of us: Don Stern, the anthropologist, a young English historian from Singapore, and a young Swiss named Henri, sort of got detached from the party in the labyrinths of Preah Khan, and found, when we reached the bus, that the whole party had been sitting for fifteen or twenty minutes waiting—the atmosphere was not very good!

Our next stop was Neak Pean, which proved to be one of the prettiest symbolic compositions I've ever seen. Two serpents, tails enlaced, enfold a lotus structure, their heads, however, leaving an opening at the side opposite to their tails. Avalokiteśvara, as the Horse Cloud (Balaha), is shown carrying a great number of human souls to this entrance. They cling to his sides and hang from his tail. Within the main sanctuary of the lotus isle is a Mucalinda Buddha.[20a] The four sides of the sanctuary show the images of gods.

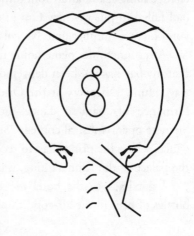

Mucalinda-Buddha sanctuary at Neak Pean

The bus guide rushed us along and we dashed next to a couple of other sanctuaries, at one of which, in my rush, I sprained my right ankle—not badly, but enough to make the ankle swell and hurt. We got back to the hotel in time for a bath and pleasant dinner, before going to bed.

I felt pretty distinctly, however, that I did not want very much to be with the main crowd again tomorrow. Two of the prize remarks:

1. We drove quickly past a ruin and the Oregon anthropologist cried, "Hey, aren't we going to look at that?" One of the men of the party leaned forward and said, "Say, you sound as though you *wanted* to see those things!" "Well," was the quiet answer, "that's what I came here to do!"
2. At the conclusion of the day, the oldest gentleman in the party said to his wife: "I'd give everything I have to have had three Coca-Colas instead of all those temples."

Sunday, March 13   **Angkor Thom**

Ankle not too bad. Aroused by the bugle practice of some kind of Boy Scout or army unit in the neighboring fields. After breakfast I managed to get the manager of the hotel to let five of us have a jeep for a quick dash out to Banteay Srei (thirty-five kilometers over a rugged road) and then a look at Angkor Thom.

The drive out was one-and-a-half hours, through roads lined by the most primitive villages I've ever seen: palm-thatch houses up on stilts; very simple people. The boys lined the roads, holding out flowers. We found a couple of small parties at Banteay Srei before us; had a fine visit to the pretty temple; then drove back to the elephant and Garuda terrace and the great heads of the Bayon. While in the latter place, it came time for me to change films again, and I found that in my hysterical moment yesterday, I had failed to put my new film in correctly, so that it had not moved beyond picture number one. No color shots, consequently, of Angkor!

After lunch, the plane home to Bangkok: arrival at about 6:00. I find that my bag has not been delivered to the Trocadero Hotel, where I am to stay. Hunt. Discovery at the Oriental. Quick change. And off to a performance of Siamese dance—actually a kind of Chinese-American, Siamese opera–musical comedy. Story: Swan maiden (Kinnara). The final dance, where the prince had to recognize his bride among her six sisters in the palace of the Kinnara king, was charming. The rest was rather dull.

I got back to the hotel too late for anything to eat; so, had three bottles of beer in the air-conditioned bar and went to bed.

Monday, March 14   **Bangkok**

Woke up feeling like hell: bad case of the runs. Went to a clinic near the hotel to see about my ankle. Nice experience of the role of the doctor in Thailand. Wired Jean about money again and picked up my travel vouchers and tickets for my trip to Chiang Mai: otherwise, a day, largely, of sitting around and recovering. Had various chats in the hotel with various members of the Angkor party, and at 5:00 P.M. set off for the station.

What a contrast with India! Clean station, clean, decently dressed people, quietness and orderliness. Had plenty of help from boys and porters who showed me to my compartment—or rather, upper berth, American style. Presently the occupant of the lower arrived: Mrs. Quentin Roosevelt— widow of the young man whom I met, with his father, Theodore Jr., at the Wallaces' in Mount Kisco, some years ago.[21] Once every three years she leaves her three little girls with their grandparents and comes to the Far East for a three-month holiday and painting spree. Across the aisle from us was a young Thai couple with a lot of luggage, on their way north. They were cute and kind, and helped us considerably with the porters and waiters.

The train, narrow guage, made in Japan, American style, was rather amusing, particularly when, at retiring time, it became apparent that there were to be no curtains to screen off the berths. Mrs. R. and I had dinner together—brought to us from the dining car; and presently, all were tucked away.

Tuesday, March 15   **Chiang Mai**

All day in the train, till 5:30 P.M. An excellent way to see the length of Thailand. Rice fields; then hilly country and second-growth forest; when low mountains began to appear, I recalled what Jean had said about this part of the world; namely, that the landscapes looked like Chinese paintings. Indeed it does.

At one junction our train was divided in two and two, sturdy, wood-burning engines pulled us through the mountains, the rest of the way; at one point, however, our little affair could hardly get its load around a bend. We stopped and then inched along, with a man out in front of the engine dusting something onto the rails to help the traction.

After our Thailand couple got off, we located a Rev. Dr. H. Gaylord Knox, of the American Presbyterian Mission, who was on his way to Chiang Mai for some kind of mission conference. He was very nice and told us a number of helpful things about the objects that we were seeing on the stations and in the hills.

The general picture on the station platforms was considerably different from that of India: fewer people, less commotion, less noise, better clothing.

The tendency is to carry things, not on the head, but on bamboo sticks, over the shoulder; however, some of the platform vendors carried their trays on their heads—with stacks of fried chicken parts, fruits of various kinds, bowls of soup, rice dinners, etc. Dr. Knox introduced us to a lovely thing called something like *yum-yum:* steamed rice packed into a joint of bamboo and baked: one strips the bamboo away, and there is a lovely, sealed packet of tasty rice.

He told us also, that if we had taken this train ride one month from today, we would be arriving drenched with water: people greet each other with splashes of water at that time (April 15, 16, 17), to bring the rains that will nourish the crops of May.

He showed us, also, the large leaves used here for roofing: they do not burn.

At the Chiang Mai station, Dr. Knox was met by two young missionaries, who packed us into their jeep truck and let us down at the distinctly odorous Chainarong Hotel. Our rooms were up on the second (i.e., top) floor hall, at the back; Mrs. R.'s no. 2; mine no. 8. I took a shower (no hot water, however, in Thailand) and a nap—feeling rather fatigued from my upset entrails and sprained ankle. When I went downstairs at about 7:30, the proprietress at the desk told me that Mrs. R. had already gone to the Chinese restaurant near the movie theater just down the street. I joined her there for a fairly good Chinese dinner, after which we took a walk around the block, looking at the closing shops. Carved wooden elephants, etc., silver bowls beaten out of Indian rupees—and black false teeth, for the betelnut chewers.

Wednesday, March 16

At 1:30 A.M. there was a powerful rap at my door: sounded like the police. "What's the matter?" I yelled; and, getting up out of a sound sleep, opened the door. There stood an American youth of moderate stature with an almost empty bottle of whiskey in his hand. "Excuse me," he said quite clearly, "but would you like to have a drink?" "For God's sake!" I said, and I slammed the door. Immediately, the knock was repeated. I opened. "Are you the rugged type?" said the youth. "No," I answered; "but I'm damned tired. I've been traveling for weeks and I want to sleep." Whereupon, the face of a young Thailander appeared beside my challenger. "Please excuse," he said. "I'm sorry. Please excuse." The two retired and I shut the door.

Precisely one hour later there was another rap at my door. "Say, what the hell *is* this?" I shouted, and I got up and opened. This time three Thai officers of some kind, in dark blue uniforms, with red bands about their caps, were in the hall, and a man who looked like one of the hotel clerks said, when he saw me, "Please excuse; so sorry." "For God's sake!" I said; and I shut the door.

One half hour later, there was the sound of a buzzer and a red light went on across the hall from me (could be seen over the top of my front wall). I heard the voice of the youth who had rapped at my door saying, "You've got a fire here. Put it out." There was a considerable noise in the hall and I got up to see what was going on. The officers in blue were in the hall; so were a number of the servants of the hotel. The young man's bed had caught fire. They were rapping at a door down the hall, across from Mrs. R.'s, out of which there presently came the proprietress in a dressing gown. I shut my door and went back to bed. When all had become quiet again, the American voice began to say loudly, "Well! Have you got another room. I want another room." A second American voice then came along the hall, with a gentle laugh. "Well, how are you feeling?" "Why, this is the kind of place," said the first voice, "that catches fire!"

I went off to sleep, in spite of the roosters that now were crowing as though a new eon were dawning, and in the morning went downstairs to learn who my countrymen were. They were, respectively, Major House and Major Britain of the U.S. Air Force.

After breakfast at the Chinese restaurant, Mrs. R. and I went in a rickshaw to the U.S. consul's compound and chatted a while with his wife, who offered to drive us tomorrow to the Leprosy Colony, directed by Dr. Buker (whose name had been given to me by the Dr. Cockran whom I met in the Air Ceylon bus going to Colombo). I returned, then, to my room to write in my diary and to nap (not feeling too well yet—and rather tired after a succession of troubled nights), while Mrs. R. went forth to meet a young Thailand lady to whom she had an introduction.

At lunchtime Mrs. R. returned to the hotel with her prey—a nice young woman, trimly dressed, Western style—and we all had lunch at the Chinese place. Her name was something like Mrs. Suchat. She let us have one of her cars for the afternoon and we were driven by her chauffeur up a lovely mountain that rises from the plain to a considerable height (reminded us both of the Colorado situation). I keep recalling what Jean said about the Chinese-painting look of the mountains in these parts. It is quite true. The curious mist that lies over all distances and the sudden type of the hills, with a peculiar vegetation composed largely of bamboo, bananas, teak, and various plants entirely unknown to the West, make for a quite distinctive impression. We stopped at the foot of a long dragon staircase that led up to a nice Buddhist temple, now being painted up freshly. A magnificent view. Mrs. R. finally settled to paint a picture of the landscape, and I wandered around with my camera, having a peaceful and pleasant time. A curious detail was a pair of white, guardian Ganeśas with four arms and very short trunks at the main entrance to the main enclosure. Lots of gold—umbrellas—a gold *stūpa*—mural of the Buddha life in a sort of Siamese-Italian-primitive style. Two nice old monks, who came down for a while to watch Mrs. R. paint. Thunder was rolling over the hills and presently drops began to fall. We returned to the car and to the hotel. Once again the Chinese restaurant and a brief walk before retiring: this time, for a sound night's sleep.

Thursday, March 17

After breakfast—again at the Chinese restaurant, which is the only safe place in town for the alien stomach—I drove with the Mrs. U.S. consul and two other ladies to the Leper Colony while Mrs. R. went in Mrs. Suchat's car to some temple that she wanted to paint. The visit to the colony was extraordinarily interesting—particularly after what I had seen of India's lepers. It is an institution dating from 1908, underwritten by the American Leprosy Mission, with about five hundred inpatients and two thousand who are being treated in various nearby towns. The idea is to give the lepers a sense of responsibility and ability to work. Some are carving little wooden elephants and carts; some are working on new buildings or in the fields. There are a number of dormitories, but most live in cottages for two, with the names of the donors painted over the doors. The men live in one area and the women in another. There are also a few families of lepers. We visited the hospital, church, and a great part of the grounds. The lepers are not even urged to become Christians and the colony does not itself provide a pastor:

but many of the lepers have become Christians and these take care of the church affairs themselves. The principal medical treatment, apparently, is by way of D.D.S. tablets, which gradually alleviate the symptoms and sort of stabilize and immunize the patient's condition. When they are ready to return to normal life they are released—but some do not want to leave.

This mission (Presbyterian sponsored, in the main) and that of the nuns on St. Thomas Mount in Madras have pretty well cured me of my anti-missionary bias—particularly since I now don't think it matters very much whether people practice one form of religion or another. Something certainly has to be said to the credit of the social orientation of the Christian tradition, which has sent these missionaries out into very difficult and dangerous areas to spread the benefits of Western science, as well as the Gospel. And I think it can be said that these benefits (those of science, that is to say) cannot be shrugged away.

Thailand is giving me a rather good picture of an Oriental nation taking on the Western benefits without too much agony of spirit—largely because these people are not troubled, as the Indians are, by a profound inferiority complex. They do not have to compensate for every benefit received by pretending to some nonexistent spiritual advantage.

After returning from the colony I took a stroll through the Chiang Mai market—which is one of the model markets of the world: the meat section is screened, to keep the flies out, and the rest is pretty and orderly, with nice-looking vendors sitting at their stands, under red parasols. The only time I heard that "Good day, sir. Please come in, just to look!" was, of course, from an Indian merchant with his textile stall. And the only beggars were three lepers sitting quietly at one of the entrances. ("Why these?" I thought, "with the colony less than twenty minutes away!")

I sent my bag to the Thai Airways office and went to the Chinese restaurant for lunch. Mrs. R. arrived just before I left and we promised to get in touch with each other in New York. Then I caught the bus—and the plane back to Bangkok.

The plane was full of military men (Thai and American) and a missionary party, which included one pleasant lady, who, when we landed, introduced me to her husband and family and drove me to my hotel.

I took a shower, ate dinner in the air-conditioned bar, went for a brief after-dinner stroll, and retired at 9:00.

Friday, March 18   **Bangkok**

I have decided not to do any more traveling in Thailand. Have a rather
nice little room at 55 ticals ($2.75), and believe that I might be able to fin-
ish up a few chores here before setting off for Japan. Spent the morning
writing up my diary and now, at exactly noon, am exactly here.

After lunch I started reading V. E. Sarachchandra's *The Sinhalese Folk
Play*,[22] which I have to review for Salmony[23]—one of my two remaining
chores (the second, a preface for Eranos volume II,[24] I hope to finish in
Hong Kong, so that I may enter Japan soul free). Also, I procured my
Japanese and Hong Kong visas for the coming trip. I have decided to add
a two-day stay in Formosa, if I can get the visa tomorrow.

For dinner I went around to the Oasis and listened to the lively
band—the two girl singers are something that one would simply not find
in India: here, however, they are quite in the groove. When I came home
I wrote a couple of letters and at eleven retired.

Saturday, March 19

Went, after breakfast, in a bicycle-rickshaw to the Chinese legation
(Nationalist Chinese) for my visa to Formosa, and spent the rest of the day
reading Sarachchandra on the folk plays of Ceylon. A very nice little book.
Had lunch at the hotel and for dinner went around to Chez Eve—which
is not as pleasant as the Oasis: a good piano, but the rest of the band is not
so hot. Wrote some more letters and retired about ten.

Sunday, March 20

A really quiet day. Finished the *Folk Play* book, wrote my review, and
mailed it off to Jean to be typed.

At lunch today, in the hotel dining room, who should walk up to
speak to me but Johnny Girshory—now grey-haired and a bit on the old
side. She is playing companion to some wealthy lady on the world tour of
the *Coronia*. The hotel is now full of those people: wealthy and old. I had
coffee at her table, and after lunch she went off to paint some river scene.
I returned to my work and finished the day. For dinner I went back to the
Oasis. To bed about ten.

Monday, March 21

A day of considerable importance, because at 5:00 P.M. I finished my Editor's Foreword to the next Eranos volume (*The Mysteries*). I worked on the piece all day. Had lunch in an American-style lunch counter that I discovered last night next to the Oasis. When I had finished the Foreword I went out to a bookstore and bought myself McGovern's *Conversational Japanese*. After my shower and before dinnertime, I studied the first chapters, and began to feel like a new man. The point is that I am now free of all commitments—first time since the Zimmer papers fell upon me thirteen years ago.[25]

Tuesday, March 22

A day of letter writing and of concluding all my travel arrangements. All meals in the hotel. Tomorrow morning I'm off for Rangoon.

And though I haven't *done* very much these past few days, in the way of seeing the sights in this nice little city, I've recovered my equilibrium and feel that the days were very well spent. Also, something of the rhythm and feeling of the life in Bangkok has soaked into me: and I can say that I like it.

The other day, as I was out walking, I passed three large Indian women, dressed in their saris and with the jewels in their noses and ears. They looked quaint—as do also the Sikhs on their motorcycles who occasionally appear in these streets. But one of the women then squatted on the curb—and I suddenly realized what a difference the prospect of an Indian and a Thailand city. Here most of the people, most of the time, are vertical and moving. I suddenly saw the streets of Calcutta and Bombay, with the people picking the lice from each other's hair, and I wondered—I wonder—whether India will ever catch up.

As for Thailand—my impression is good. It is said that the government is corrupt; but when I broached this theme to Dr. Knox, who has lived here some forty years, he did not agree. He told me, moreover, of an interesting law; namely, that if a man does not inhabit or work the land for which he has paid, he may lose it. All land belongs, legally, to the crown; and to hold a claim to it, one has to work it. The majority of the farmers in Thailand, therefore, own their land.

The literacy rate is something like 70 percent. The country is under-, not overpopulated—and food is abundant.

My impression of the press is that its international position is anti-Communist and pro-American: not at all in the between position of India.

BURMA,[26] HONG KONG, AND FORMOSA[27]

Wednesday, March 23   **Rangoon**

A considerable change of scene. Up at five. Bus to the airport. A handsome four-motor Thai Airways plane—with only three Sikh families heading home and an Englishman named Smithson, who drove me to the hotel in his station wagon.

In Bangkok they gave me a Burmese visa for three days. Actually I shall be here a little less than three full days—10:30 A.M., March 23, to 5:00 A.M. March 26; but since four dates are involved this is counted four days; hence my visa is valid only till March 25. A normal sort of Oriental situation. I have, therefore, to go to the Immigration Office for a one-day extension. I went to the Immigration Office and climbed upstairs through a fantastic crowd (Indians, mostly, but also a great many other nationalities) to the desk of the head man: a mild little, greatly wall-eyed person, who gave me a long blank to fill out, and then sent me off to get a 1.50-rupee stamp—in another building. I went to the Court Building—and again ran into an interesting crowd—this time mostly Burmese. They are a cute lot, I must say. (But we'll come to that later.) I found the tables in a long corridor where the stamps are sold and was told to come back tomorrow: stamps are "out of stock." (This means, of course, that no legal business can be effectively initiated in Rangoon, the capital of Burma, till tomorrow.) They told me to try at another place, opposite the Hong Kong Bank: I did so, but the story was the same. So I went back to the Immigration Office and my wall-eyed friend said that he would start my passport on its way, so that it would be ready in time: I could affix the stamp tomorrow.

I went next to the Strand Hotel (which is close to all of these offices) and was sitting, sort of getting my bearings, when my friend Mr. Smithson came in. We had a couple of beers together, after which he went in to get lunch and I decided that this was the kind of hotel that would have a good barber shop—so I got a haircut (first since Bombay: distinctly needed). I went next to write a couple of letters, and then, it being about 3:30 P.M., took a taxi and asked to be shown the town.

What interested me most were the long and busy dock front on the Irrawaddy River, the flower and fruit market, the immense number of movie houses, with movies from all over Europe, America, and Asia, the Shive Dagon Pagoda area, and the very colorful, somewhat chic, little people. As Smithson remarked on the drive in this morning, in Rangoon one sees women—in contrast, for example, to Calcutta—and they give a lot of color to the city. They dress very trimly here, in tight white bodices and with varicolored sarongs, tight about the hips (the men wear the same sarong). Also, they pay attention to their hair and have a number of cute ideas about hairdos (not just the pigtail of India). And finally, a number of them wear a sort of light-yellow, musklike pancake powder all over the front of the face—which adds another color and is amusing. In the sun they carry pretty, colorful parasols.

In fact, I would say that Rangoon is one of the most interesting cities, visually, that I have seen. The population is greatly mixed: Burmese, Chinese, and Indian. Hordes of the dock coolies are Indian; the hotel servants at the Strand are Indian; the people lying down in the streets are Indian; and the beggars are Indian: Also, the shopkeepers who call after you are Indian. I've come to the conclusion that for Indians begging is neither a necessity nor a habit, but a trait of character. The baksheesh formula remains the key to the whole national structure. It is the key even to the international "neutralist" position, which has the function of inviting competing handouts from both sides. It is not "balance of power" politics, as it was in England's great day, but "balance of baksheesh." In fact *bhakti* might be said to be a technique for getting baksheesh from God. (The way of the kitten; the way of the baby monkey.[28]) And while we're on the Indian theme: Smithson told me a good one about the Taj Mahal Hotel. When the architect who had designed the building saw the finished structure, he shot himself. They had built it with the front to the back.[29]

But to return to Rangoon and Burma. The main product of the south is rice, of the dry country peanuts, beans, pulses, and in the north there are mineral deposits—but nobody can work them because of the bandits. There is a good deal of graft in the business operations. The newspapers are carrying a case right now of graft in the government buying of rice.

The airfield, one immediately notes, is not very good. That in Bangkok is much better. Smithson tells me that, actually, the new Bangkok airport has drawn a good deal of the international traffic away from Rangoon. Apparently Burma and Thailand form the Continental Divide here: Burma is sticking to the Indian Orient. Neutralist, Oriental costumes. It is more picturesque, consequently—or rather, no! It is picturesque in another way—rather, it's picturesque in a more archaic way than Thailand. The two are the great rice producers also. And their people, racially, are Tai Shan.

Well, anyhow, after my drive around the city, I had tea at the Strand and then walked slowly back to the Railway Hotel. I lay down for a rest, studied my *Conversational Japanese,* had dinner, tried to wash in a sort of modified Woodstock way from a washbowl, and went to bed.

Thursday, March 24

Up at seven—and the little fat housekeeper woman invited me down the whole length of the hall to have a bath. After breakfast I sat in the lobby and read the newspaper.

Forgot, yesterday, to note that the Russians have just awarded a "Stalin Peace Prize" (created in parody of the Nobel Prize) to a little eighty-year-old Burmese writer, Thakin Kodaw Hmaing,[30] who will build a Palace of Peace and Culture with the fund that he will establish with the prize money. In his speech of acceptance the old man followed the Moscow-Nehru line in abusing the atom bomb and SEATO. Definitely, we are again in the neutralist zone; not Communist perhaps, but no less anti-American than the Communists.

At about ten I went to the stamp desks again and was told to return at noon; so I went for a nice long picture-taking walk to a small golden pagoda and along the docks. Passed, also, a community of refugee thatch huts—which fascinated me (refugees, this time, from the troubles in the north). I returned to the stamp desk at noon and was told to return at two.

Went back to my hotel for lunch and a brief rest; then returned to the stamp desk. "Another ten minutes," said the man with a smile.

It appeared that although the 1.50-rupee stamps had not come in yet, 2-rupee stamps were now available. I bought one and went to the Immigration Office. My wall-eyed man passed on my stamp to a wall-eyed boy who had an extra thumb and who sat at a desk beside a third wall-eyed man. It took a long while to get around to my passport, and when we got to it, I was told that two photos were needed. Fortunately I had some back at the hotel. Returned by rickshaw, fetched the photos, paid 10 rupees, and took my passport with the one-day extension, which it took me one day to get, to the Foreigners Registration office, where I was told that I now had to fill out a certain "D-Form" for my departure permit. I should come back tomorrow at eleven for this permit.

I went next for an interesting walk along another stretch of docks and photographed a couple of cute boat families; then returned to the Strand for tea, and went back to my own hotel for a rest and dinner. After dinner I took still another long walk through the very lively markets and streets. Rangoon certainly is an amusing place, with its cute little sidewalk restaurants filled with nice little people. In a way, the streets tonight, with all their restaurants and life, reminded me of the boulevards of Paris. And in a way, also, I think that all this is more like what I expected of India than what I found there. The main difference? A kind of chic! Which comes, perhaps, of letting the women loose.

Friday, March 25

A surprise to me is the number of Christian churches and schools (Catholic and Baptist, mostly) and Mohammedan mosques in Rangoon. One sees the Buddhist monks everywhere—as in Ceylon and Thailand—and the most prominent religious structures are the Buddhist pagodas; apparently, however, the number of Christians and Mohammedans in the city is considerable.

Today I walked from the hotel to the Dagon Pagoda, and encountered on the way a lively procession, with a tiny boy dancer in the lead, accompanied by a band of musettes and bamboo clappers. A long file of young women carrying trays of flowers on their heads came next; after which there were a couple of women dancers with their band. And finally, four boys riding ponies came along, beneath gold umbrellas. I took a lot of photos and followed the procession up to the temple. At one point they were passed by another procession coming back from the temple, and the fun was immense. When they reached the temple they simply made a U-turn and started back.

I went on into the Dagon Pagoda, where I spent about an hour and a half with a guide, and when I came out, I walked back, past the hotel, to the main section of the city, where I retrieved my passport from the Foreign Registration office, made arrangements for my air passage tomorrow to

Hong Kong and had lunch at the Strand Hotel. Then I walked back to the Railway Hotel and lay down (damn tired) for a rest.

At about 2:30 I got up and started out on another long walk; to Royal Lake—where I sat for a while under a tree among a bunch of Hindu youngsters who were swimming and generally horsing around, and then, by a long roundabout route, back to the Strand Hotel.

My final impression of Rangoon, gathered largely on this walk, is that it is the dirtiest city I've visited (Calcutta included); garbage literally dumped in the gutter to stink, in many places; dirt everywhere, for the streets, I believe, are never cleaned; many utterly squalid neighborhoods, of thatch (which frequently catch fire), or of filthy tenement alleys with open-drain gutters over which the front-room floorings may extend. The people, however, have more personal style than the Indians. Also, we have no cows in the streets, very few bullock carts—and, somehow, there is an air of people being better off than in Calcutta: very few beggars, cripples, or destitutes—and when there *are* beggars, they are usually Indians.

After my walk, I had tea at the Strand, then returned by rickshaw (tricycle with sidecar) to the Railway Hotel, to pack, shave, have dinner, and go early to bed.

Saturday, March 26 (fifty-first birthday)   Hong Kong

Up at 2:30 A.M. to catch a 3:00 A.M. airlines bus, which arrived at 4:30! Meanwhile, conversed with a nice Japanese man, Mr. Nagai, of Tokyo, and an Indian from East Africa, who were also waiting for the bus. The plane didn't take off till about 6:30. Pause in Bangkok: then, a wonderful flight to Hong Kong.

Passed over Indochina, going out to sea at a point south of Hanoi: mountains and wilderness, very few villages, no towns. I thought: "So Indochina goes Communist. What does it mean? What does it matter?"[31]

We approached Hong Kong above a thick flooring of cloud, came down through the clouds, and broke into view of the beautiful island cluster, the water being dotted with junks. Customs. Bus to the Peninsula Hotel. Arrival. Hong Kong time 5:30 P.M.

I felt ridiculous in my tropical white ducks and light shirt: Hong Kong is a large and well-dressed, temperate-zone city, and the weather is fairly cool.

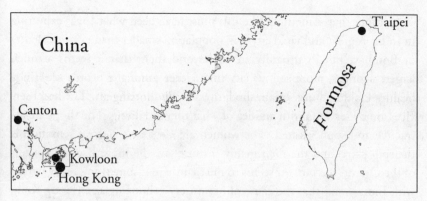

From the Peninsula Hotel, I took a rickshaw (cute little Chinese rickshaw man, loaded me and my luggage aboard and trotted away) to the Miramar Hotel, where I had reserved a room, but where no room had been reserved. They sent me on to the Shamrock Hotel, just a bit further down Nathan Ave. Nice, clean, new Chinese-run hotel. The room boy said that he would get me anything I wanted. "If a girl is required the hotel will supply one. Girls brought in from outside sometimes cause trouble." He also said that the hotel had a tailor and immediately produced one, who tried to sell me before I had even found my bearings. I told him: "Tomorrow"; and went upstairs to have a nice Chinese dinner, after which I went for a stroll along Nathan Ave. The rickshaw boys are almost as great a nuisance as they were in Calcutta. Wire to Jean, and to bed.

Sunday, March 27

Up at about eight. Breakfast upstairs: beautiful views from the top-floor restaurant. Good breakfast, too: first real orange juice since I left America.

After breakfast, I walked the length of Nathan Ave., to the Peninsula Hotel, where I booked myself for a tour of Hong Kong (discovering, to my surprise, that I am now not in Hong Kong but in Kowloon, on the mainland). Amusingly, and fortunately, my companion on this tour was a chap named Campbell—Daniel Campbell from South Carolina, an electronics engineer with Philco; has been nine years in Tokyo. A nice guy with glorious cameras. We had a wonderful day, being driven out to Aberdeen (for lunch in the floating restaurants) and back. Incredible views. Return to Kowloon about 4:30 for tea.

I think that something like this must have been what I was expecting in India. A great and vivid city—in population smaller than either Calcutta or Bombay, but in urbanity so far beyond them that it seems a much larger, stronger, more serious city than either—and the people are lively, healthy looking, busy, clean, shod, dressed, and intelligent. The hotel services are by servants with an idea of what they are doing. The shops are attractive and sophisticated. The women are elegant (the great sensation is the split skirt) and the men manly. I must say, the more I see of the rest of the Orient, the more it seems to me that there is something really wrong with India—and that the cause of her misery is not England (Hong Kong is a colony) but herself.

Campbell and I had a good talk at tea, and there were certain things he said about Japan that are valid also for India—probably for the whole Orient:

1. Americans are admired for their ingenuity—which is regarded, however, as an inferior talent. It is thought that if the Japanese were as fortunately situated as the Americans, they would be able to do much better than the Americans in the fields in which Americans excel.

2. The gadgets—not the fundamental, life-transforming factors—of the machine age are what are liked, bought, and imitated. A Japanese in a $2,000 house will have a $1,000 radio and television set, but no refrigerator. Japan has cameras but no refrigerators.

3. The front part of the home of a successful Japanese businessman will be in the Western style, and the number of the Western rooms, there for the entertainment of his Western friends and associates, will be the measure of his prestige. But his living quarters will be Japanese and without furniture; and when he returns in the evening, he puts off his Western garb and dons Japanese. The comparable situation in America would be, to have a log cabin as a residence, in which one would wear Daniel Boone's leather leggings and raccoon-skin cap.*

---

* The fact is, however, that many Americans do have this arrangement, for their weekends and holidays, in the form of a "little place" in the woods. Our National Parks are fairylands of pioneering make-believe. The problem is that of keeping in touch simultaneously with two worlds: that of the practical, rational, modern present and that of the past, from which one's systems of ethics, ideals, feeling-values, etc., were inherited. For the Westerner the dichotomy is not as great as for the Oriental, because (a) the Occidental past is generically related to the world's modern present, and (b) the stress on the reduction of the individual to the patterns of the collective archetypes has never been as strong in the West as it is in the Orient. The problem of the Westerner who wishes to hold to the two worlds of his present and his inherited past is therefore not as great as that confronted by the Oriental.

4. The appearance of law and order that one may observe in the legal codes, etc., of Japan, Campbell said, is deceptive. Actually, if you are hit by a car in the street and bring suit, you may find yourself thrown in jail for obstructing the passage of some personage who has known how and whom to bribe. The whole operation of the law is governed by the pulling of wires behind the scenes—in the grand old Oriental style. In contrast, in a colony like Hong Kong, where the final word is that of the British, we have clean streets, well-built houses, solid roads, and effective law.

After tea I returned to my hotel for a bath, a nap, and dinner, then went for an evening stroll (harried by the rickshaw boys) and went early to bed.

Monday, March 28

Up at 8:30—just in time to catch the last drop of water for my shave. (Hong Kong is suffering from an acute water shortage. Water is available only from 6:30 to 8:30 A.M., and from 6:00 to 8:00 P.M.) At 10:15 I turned up at the Peninsula Hotel for my tour—again with Campbell—of the so-called "New Territories"—inland to within a couple of miles of the Red China border. There is a railroad line (Kowloon-Canton) that carries passengers right through.

I was impressed by the fine schools that are being built in the back-country, the general state of well-being of the whole countryside: the excellent roads (certainly by far the best that I have seen in the Orient), the number of new cars (learner drivers are everywhere), the multitude of British military establishments (lots of jeeps and trucks on the roads)—and, in general, the impression of a colony optimistic about its future. A great many new and excellent factories (largely textile) are to be seen.

We had lunch at a charming Riviera-like inn by a lovely cove, and returned to the Peninsula Hotel about 4:30. Tea with Campbell, and a good-bye till Tokyo.

I arranged, next, for a night tour this evening in the company of Mr. and Mrs. Gutherie (the couple who were in the airlines truck with me on the day of the Angkor Wat adventure) and their guide, then returned to my hotel for a bit of rest.

At 7:00 P.M., off with the party to Hong Kong: (a) a touch of Chinese opera; (b) dinner at that floating restaurant in Aberdeen; (c) a night drive up over the road of views; (d) a finale in a night shot full of Chinese gentlemen and their Chinese dancing partners. Our guide got us one of his former girls, born in Saigon, sold there to a Chinese woman who brought her to Hong Kong to be a source of income, and now, at twenty-three, still at it: demure, cuddly, delicate, and ladylike; Mrs. Guthrie renamed her Tina (the girl was called simply Cissy). At about 12:50 we dashed for the last ferry—and I got to bed at 2:00 A.M.

Tuesday, March 29

Up at 8:15; breakfast in the hotel. Then, the ferry to Hong Kong, where I spent the day strolling about the wonderful streets, enjoying the sense of being in a full-fledged city again, and trying to make up my mind to buy something. Finally bought a couple of shirts at Mackintosh's. Had lunch in the Parisian Cafe (first full-fledged restaurant I have been in since leaving New York). And finally, at 2:00, rather tired, went to a movie that Campbell highly recommended: Hitchcock's *Rear Window*. The movie theater might have been in New York.

I took the ferry home at about five. Bathed and rested; then went out for dinner at a "Russian" restaurant, which was actually Chinese with a number of Russian dishes. A brief walk and to bed.

Wednesday, March 30

In the Monday morning paper there was an article by Carl T. Rowan (lecturer and observer for the U.S. State Department)[32] on the "Deep, Dangerous Chasm" that he found between India and the U.S.A. A number of points echo my own observations.

1. "I was asked about everything from sex and sin to segregation, the implication being that I should be against all three." (Better, it seems to me: divorce, drinking, and segregation.)
2. "Indians are for peace because they are spiritual and Americans for war because they are materialistic."
3. "I was not long in India before I realized that I was dealing with a national Jekyll-Hyde complex. First, I saw the friendly warmth, the generous hospitality of Indian people. This struck me more than anything except the panorama of poverty during my first few days here. But when I went out to lecture or took part in political discussions, the other side of India would emerge. The man who had poured lavish

hospitality on me as an individual would become my passionate foe as an American."

Some of the Indian explanations of their "neutralist" position that he quotes are also worth remembering.

1. "All Asia wants economic progress. It is almost as if India were racing with China to show that she can produce more relief for the miserable through Democracy than the Reds can through totalitarianism. If India fails, the Communists conquer all Asia.... In the showdown, India stands for democracy."

2. "India must have peace. We must have some years of peace at any price.... We've got problems to solve—problems we can solve only if we have peace."

3. "We are jammed up against China and Tibet. Russia is only a Blitzkrieg away through Afghanistan and the Khyber Pass. If we seem less dedicated to freedom, more soft-spoken toward our neighbors, remember that the threat of annihilation is much closer to us."

Got up this morning at 8:15, had breakfast upstairs, and strolled to the Peninsula Hotel; made a date with the Gutheries for cocktails this afternoon, and returned to my room to bring my diary up to date. Went out for lunch in what turned out to be a second-rate restaurant, and again returned to my room to write—diary and letters. Out, then, for the cocktail date and back to the hotel for a nap. Out for a fine steak dinner at the "Russian" restaurant of last night. Home to pack, and early to bed. *Finis* Hong Kong.

Some Hong Kong tidbits:

1. Slit skirts are of three degrees: (a) to the knee, (b) to mid-thigh, (c) a bit higher. When the object sits down the slit is drawn up, and when she crosses her legs, the tableau is magic.

2. Driving in the Hong Kong streets is rendered dangerous by the idea held by some Chinese that if they can manage just to miss being hit, the scare will drive away the bad spirits!

3. The women carry their babies on their backs, like papooses, in cute little slings.

4. Wooden-soled slippers on the pavement make a sort of xylophone sound; particularly charming if the shoes are small. And since no two shoes make quite the same sound, there is a delightful little music in the streets.

Thursday, March 31   T'aipei

Up at 6:30 and to the Peninsula Hotel for breakfast and to catch the Thai Airways bus. Opened conversation with a chap who had been on the last air trip I took; he turned out to be Martin Wilbur of Columbia—and we knew each other from New York and Sarah Lawrence.[33]

Interesting chat in the plane, comparing notes on India—though, like a good professor, he managed not to be the one who did most of the talking. His impression of Nehru's capitulation to the Chinese was not so strong as mine, and he seems to have let Indian hospitality blind him somewhat to the strength of the anti-American feeling.

We reached T'aipei about 1:30. From the plane one could see miles and miles of well-tended, well-cultivated fields. "Much better agriculture," said Wilbur, "than the Indian. The Indians are not good farmers." When the plane approached the airport the hostess made us all pull our blinds: war zone: not to peek! We all peeked—and saw nothing, of course, but more hills and fields.

Wilbur went to the YMCA and I to the Grand Hotel, which is a bit too far out of town. The hotel is jammed with army officers and newspaper people: all Americans. I took a little taxi drive after lunch, to view the town: the President Building, museum, movie district, university, and then Green Lake—a charming little spot some fifteen minutes out of town. When the drive was finished, I took a walk in the neighborhood of the hotel and returned for tea (no one else but me), a shower, and a spell of writing.

The scenery of Formosa is romantic in a way that would have appealed, I believe, to Rousseau. The clouds today are low on the heavily-wooded hills, and the rice fields stretch to the edges of the hills: pleasantly winding streams are numerous, with people quietly boating: an air of eighteenth-century repose in the country lies over the land, even though twentieth-century factory smoke pours up from the stacks, which are numerous. The city is by no means as potent as Hong Kong, but it is a large and strongly built industrial city, somewhat dull because of the unimaginative brick and concrete architecture, but nevertheless an impressive little city. And everywhere, in the city and in the fields, are the Free China soldiers—military jeeps and trucks fill the roads. Definitely there is an army here.

I'm rather pleased and amused by the picture of this hotel. It is situated well outside of the city proper and in a large estate of its own—somewhat as the Hotel Cecil in relationship to New Delhi. But the social tone is American, not British. And I must say, it is a very good tone. A lot of high army brass, apparently, has settled its families here: they are nice-looking, well-behaved people, with well-behaved youngsters. The dining room this evening had something of the atmosphere of a ship's dining salon: there was to be a bingo game at nine, and some of the tables were talking about it. At several of the tables were Chinese people—and at one, a cute American family with two charming young Chinese friends. My roommate (the hotel is jammed) is an eighth-grader, whose father has just been sent out here for a two-year stint. The atmosphere is that of a community that does not expect to be dislodged by the Communists very soon—or even to be troubled by their bombs. There is a great deal of road building in progress on the island and the hotel is building an annex bigger than itself.

After dinner I took a brief stroll down the hill, and went early to bed.

Friday, April 1

After breakfast, took a long walk into town, to try to find Miss Dorothy Whipple at the U.S.I.S. office,[34] whose name had been given to me by Martin Wilbur. I was given a couple of wrong-road directions, and so presently took a bicycle rickshaw and at 11:45 entered the correct office. Miss Whipple arranged for me to meet a Dr. Jao, who would guide me on a visit to the university at 3:00 P.M., and invited me, meanwhile, to accompany herself and another lady on a picnic, up on a lovely hill called Yang Ming Shan (Grassy Peak). Dr. Jao was cordial and very helpful, told me all about the college situation, showed me the excellent university museum (ethnology: the aborigines of Taiwan are extremely interesting), and finally introduced me to the president of the university, with whom I had a fine talk. From the university, we went to the Teachers College and viewed a quite good exhibition of the student paintings—Eastern and Western style, in watercolors and oils, the watercolors (as in India) being generally better than the oils.

After a shower and nap, I went to a cocktail party at a Mr. and Mrs. Cockran's, where I met a lot of the government people. Pleasant crowd. Was invited for dinner tomorrow night with a Mr. George Gurow, and Miss Whipple promised to try to arrange for something for me to do tomorrow.

Invited Miss Whipple to dinner with me at the hotel and we found there some of the people from the cocktail party. Joined them for dinner and after dinner went for drinks to their home. To bed about midnight.

The Formosan picture, as far as I can see:

The fifty years of Japanese rule were fortunate for the island:[35] good plants, factories, and buildings constructed; good roads and railways; good agricultural practices established; excellent university founded, etc. However, the native Taiwanese were at a disadvantage in their participation in the educational system and government. This situation has been corrected under the present regime.

The population is about 80 percent (or more) literate. The island is well-off as far as food and shelter is concerned. The villages are of brick and stone: the people are clean and decently dressed: beggars hardly exist.

The population consists of about eight million Taiwanese and two million mainlanders—recent arrivals, of the Kuomintang group,[36] who are the leaders in the government. The KMT are strongly anti-Communist, and believe that though they cannot reconquer the mainland, they can support, by their threat and presence, subversive movements, which are said to be increasing on the mainland. The idea of sealing off the battle and settling for an independent or U.N.-protected Formosa does not appeal to these people. In contrast, therefore, to the other "Overseas Chinese" in the Far East, those of Formosa are definitely anti-Communist and do not constitute a subversive factor.

As for the eight million Taiwanese, it is said that they too are fundamentally anti-Communist.

(In the midst of this situation, Nehru's speech yesterday denouncing the American support of the Formosans as an aggressive support of colonialism sounds ridiculous. The man, on all his cruising around Asia, should have allowed a few days for a visit to this sanctuary!)

It seemed to me, as I conversed with Jao and the president of the university, that efforts should be made to bring American students to Taiwan and Taiwanese to the U.S.A. Exchange arrangements, however, would not be practical, since the lectures here are delivered in Chinese.

Apparently, the U.S. government has caught on to the idea of giving grants to bring Chinese students from Malaya, etc., to Taiwan for a bit of democratic instead of Communistic Chinese education.

Saturday, April 2

At 8:15 A.M. I was called to the phone and heard Wilbur's voice instead of Miss Whipple's. He had left a note for me yesterday, which I had not received (while I was at the phone it was handed to me), inviting me to go with him on a trip to a mountain spot (Wu-lai), where I met a lot of the government people; a pleasant crowd. I was told we might have an opportunity to see some aboriginal dances. If I was going, I should be at the railroad station in time to catch an 8:50 A.M. bus. I made a wrong decision; that is to say, I decided, on the spur of the moment, to go with Wilbur and leave a message for Miss Whipple. Quick dressing, no breakfast, taxi—and I just made it.

We drove in a bus, up a lovely valley, with mist on the hilltops that gradually descended and turned into a light rain. Romantic, Chinese-landscape scenery. At one point, the whole crowd had to get out of the bus and walk across a swinging bridge, over which the bus then followed. At another point, we had to have our passports checked (I had forgotten mine,

but got through just the same). And finally, at the end of the line, we got out for a little walk further along—through a mountain village, along a mountain trail, amidst beautiful scenery, to a point across the chasm from a lovely waterfall. In the village there was an old woman with a vividly tattooed face—once the sign of the married woman, but during the Japanese occupation forbidden. Only the old women (with very few young exceptions) now have this mark.

Tattooed woman

Downhill from the walk along which we went we heard a steady drum beat: ♫ ♩ / ♫ ♩ / ♫ ♩ / ♫ ♩ /. The "aboriginal dance," no doubt. We would go down there on the return. A little girl overtook us as we walked, and when we arrived at the little restaurant across from the waterfall, opened her package of souvenirs of Wu-lai for us while we sipped tea. (Compare what India would have offered!) It was raining pretty steadily by now. We started back and descended to the sound of the drum. A nice little high-school girl came up with an umbrella, to cover my head, and conducted us to a little theater shelter, full of youngsters, and with a few KMT soldiers. Three girls were singing to a tom-tom, which one of them beat; and our little hostess joined the three. After a lot more singing the little girls then presented their "aboriginal dances." It was a cute affair. The dances were largely arm and hand dances with gay steps that brought the dancers around the floor in the way of Russian girl dancers. I was reminded most strongly of the Indian and Hawai'ian arm dances—a couple of hip sways occurred. The girls were distinctly Mongolian, though, not Chinese.

After this little party, we returned to the village for a decent Chinese lunch, with a drink called "Old Whisky" that had very little kick. The bus finally brought us back to town and we said good-bye to our Chinese companion, a Professor Chen.

From the YMCA, where Wilbur is staying, I phoned Miss Whipple and Mr. Gurow; then I took a bus back to my hotel, bathed, rested, and at 7:30 drove to Mr. Gurow's for a delightful and very tasty dinner. Nice crowd, good talk until about 2:00 A.M.

I found that my own tendency, in talking about India, was to lay considerable stress on the anti-Americanism that I found there. I am really wondering why we are continuing to send money to those people.

A Mr. Wang, who was at the party, brought out something of what might be called the basic Oriental view of the danger of American aid: we should not try to spread "the American way of life": the Orient should be aided to develop in its own style.

Discussing China and Japan, he said that Japan has taken over Western patterns wholesale but superficially: the Oriental style remains beside them, dissociated. The Chinese, on the other hand, have taken over fewer elements (more selectively) but have assimilated them more deeply.

He pointed out, also, that Orientals regard it as degrading when their women marry Westerners.

CHAPTER 2

THE REALM OF THE SENSES

TOKYO, JAPAN

Sunday, April 3   **Tokyo**

A day of rain. After breakfast, read the paper and packed. When it came
to paying my bill it appeared that the office, in a mix-up, had given it to
another occupant of the room who left on an early train, thus overcharg-
ing him 110 Taiwan dollars. They asked me if I could send him U.S. $5 to
his U.S. home, and they would give me the 110 Taiwan dollars. But then I
learned that I am unable to convert my Taiwan cash into any other money
on God's earth. This dished the deal—and I was left, besides, with a 175
Taiwan dollar surplus.

The airlines car didn't call for me till 12:45. Wilbur was aboard.
Approaching the airport, we saw a large military event leaving it: U.S.
Secretary of the Army Robert Stevens had just arrived in a large
Constellation, and every military man in the neighborhood above the rank
of captain had been on the receiving line. There was a lot of confusion at
the airport, but we finally got aboard—and had a fine flight to Tokyo, arriving about 8:30 P.M. Airlines bus to the (very expensive) Nikkatsu Hotel.

But, hurray for Tokyo and the Japanese. This tops Hong Kong and scores supreme for the cities of Asia visited so far. As I hoped: both are here—the past and the present; and in good form.

My hotel is an absolutely modern, absolutely clean, perfectly efficient, fine affair, with intelligent, trim hall boys and good service. The hot water is hot; the fixtures work; the room is attractive; *and*—the Japanese touch: when I entered I found the matchbox placed in a studied and pretty way against the ashtray, the desk blotter aptly placed on the desk, and the bureau drawers drawn partly out, in an ordered way.

Having settled, I went out to look for a bite to eat, moved toward the brightly lighted area leftward of the hotel, entered a little street hung with lanterns, passed a number of Chinese restaurants in search of something Japanese, and saw a sign advertising a Japanese striptease with the scholium "On Limits," i.e. OK for U.S. GIs—so in I went. A cozy nightclub atmosphere; crowds on the stairs: up I went to a little den with a mediocre band, a bit of dance space, a bit of bar with about five stools, and lots of tables for two all around the walls. Young boys with Japanese girls and lots of excess girls filled the room: young waiters and pretty waitresses (the latter in a Japanese-servant rig that was definitely cute). The hostesses all were in modest evening gowns. Obviously, there would be no food, so I ordered a whisky and soda, thinking to stay for a minute and leave, when the drink was down, to go and eat. However, a little thing came and sat beside me. "May I join you?" "Fine," I said; "so what'll you have?" A whisky and soda. Presently a tall seminude appeared in a spotlight and stalked around luxuriously to music, took off her bra, and began sitting alluringly close to a guy's arms. Then her act was over, she withdrew, and the band resumed its squawking for the dance floor. Well, it was nice to see a girl after all these weeks, but otherwise, things were very dull. My little hostess, Chiku, aged twenty-four, giggled a good deal and insisted that my arm should be around her, then asked to be kissed and finally wanted to dance. Not at all, it seemed to me, in what I had heard was the Japanese tradition: absolutely without style. I decided to wait for another nude and then go; which I did.

But the remarkable thing about this little GI joint was the age of the patrons: boys, I should say, just out of high school. One had passed out at the bar and the girls were mothering him. Nobody was over college age. And the girls, of course, were taking a lot of their money simply by ordering drinks very fast. The drinks, I can testify, were mostly ice, and the waiters usually managed to take them away before they were finished.

Chiku was very eager that I should return; for I had given her a good tip. She accompanied me downstairs, gave me the card of the house, made me give her a kiss and returned to her work. Hours: 1:00 P.M. to 1:00 A.M; my departure was at 11:00 P.M.

Monday, April 4

I went to bed last night without dinner—and woke up about four, cold and hungry. The weather had changed and was really chill. After a 9:15 breakfast in the hotel coffee shop, in the arcade basement, I found that there was a sharp wind blowing: the sort of wind that rips down the Riverside Drive side streets.[37] I had no topcoat, but decided to brave it and hunt for the American Express office. The town is full of vivid, lively people, a wonderful cocktail of East and West: women in kimonos, wearing wooden clogs, but mostly people completely at home in Western dress. One curious phenomenon: because of the soot in the air from charcoal burners, quite a few people wear a wad of cheesecloth over their mouths and nostrils—like Jains.[38]

The people at the American Express were not very good at giving me advice on how to see the town, and there was only one letter for me—from Mother. I went for a long walk around the Ginza district, then phoned my friend Campbell from Hong Kong and things began:

Lunch with Danny Campbell at the old Union Club (now Peers Club)—a club for U.S. Army personnel, with a nice-looking crowd. Met a pleasant chap named Stan Spivak who lunched with us. Danny had to go back to his office at about one, but we arranged to meet for a steam bath and steak dinner at six.

After lunch I went for another long walk and ended up at a really first-rate revue, at the Nichigeki Music Hall on the fourth floor of the Nichigeki Theater. Lots of gorgeous girls, good bands, elegant style: the girls not *quite* as naked as in Paris but a lot more active; no filth, it seemed to me—though I might have a different opinion if I had understood the comedians. One charming number toward the end brought a modern Japanese gentleman with glasses and a briefcase into collision with a sort of Kabuki-style, folk religious procession: I don't know what the point was, but it looked good. The American-style jazz and acrobatic dancing was better than good, and there were a couple of good French Apache numbers.[39] The title of the show: "The Seven Keys to Love (Not Reported by Dr. Kinsey)."

Well—it was a great pleasure to run into something like this after India. Of course, India's present ideas about "purity" and "spirituality" close them off from this sort of thing: they have no feeling for it whatsoever. As a result—their prostitutes are the filthiest whores in the world. So it goes! The rejected factor manifests itself in an inferior mode, whereas when accepted it adds a tone and sophistication to the whole picture of life.[40]

After the show, I was joined by Danny, and we proceeded to the Tokyo Onsen near Ginza: a charming affair; the N.Y.A.C. steam rooms and rubbing rooms, from now on, are to be a rank disappointment. Here a little thing in bra (Peter Pan, I think) and shorts goes to work on you for an hour. Mine's name was Otako, and she gave me the best massage of my life. Being steamed and bathed by her, also, was a pleasantly comforting and relaxing affair. Part of the delight (perhaps the greatest part of it) is the sense of being waited on completely: one is returned to the state of infancy for a gentle hour. Price ¥1,000, about $13. Definitely something that should become a sort of regular event.

Danny left the bath a little earlier than I did, to fetch a young woman who was coming up from Yokosuka navy base to have dinner with him, and I met them at 7:15 at Suehiro's (about a block from Tokyo Onsen) for one of the best steaks I've ever eaten in my life. "They massage the cows," said Danny, and I think he's right.[41] The girl, Dorothy Riggs, is quite handsome and, apparently, quite gone on my handsome bachelor friend. And the restaurant is one of the best in the world. One has to make *no* concessions to enjoy it, as one has to, even in the best restaurants in India: service, food, decor—excellent.

After dinner we drove around a bit and then went to one of Tokyo's unnumbered pinball (pachinko) emporiums. It is said that Japan's chief industries are the three Ps—Paper, Pachinko, Prostitution. After pachinko, we went to the nightclub Latin Quarter, which has an elegant band (Philippino, with an exceptionally good featured drummer) and a floor show mainly of male singers. Miss Riggs had to leave during the floor show, to catch her train back to Yokosuka. I remained and when Danny returned we proceeded to another night spot (11:00 P.M.), the Ginbasha, on Ryokan Avenue. Here we sat at a little table with a couple of hostesses, danced and watched the floor show, till closing time at about 1:30 A.M. The contrast with my club of last evening was immense. The girls—"Janie" and "Katie"—were perfectly poised little ladies: charming, decorous, handsome; without the least touch of the aggressive, but easily responsive to the patterns of conduct of their clients. Most of the people in the large nightclub were Occidentals—officers and government people. The floor show was good: a couple of remarkable contortionist dancers with a deadpan composure (identical twins, I should say) and a girl who danced with a pigeon. All very decent.

We left our ladies and took a brief drive, to view the night situation at 2:00 A.M. Those nightclub hostesses (like our own) whose customers did not come through with a bid for the night (at ¥7,000 = $20), change into street clothes and head for Fourth Street and Y Avenue, and neighborhood—where the price is down to about ¥2,000. The total take, Danny thinks, of a good Tokyo prostitute is about $400 to $500 a month. At the nightclubs we paid ¥2,000 each for the company of our little friends, and they also received a percentage on the drinks.

Tuesday, April 5

Today I went around to the Yashima Hotel, at Ginza Street and W Avenue, and arranged to move in the day after tomorrow. The Nikkatsu is much too expensive: ¥3,000 per day for room and bath. At the Yashima I shall have a room (no bath) and breakfast for ¥1,500 per day—and a good excuse (no bath) for going frequently to Tokyo Onsen. I went also to the Imperial Hotel[42] (*very, very* touristy) and arranged to go on a bus tour of Tokyo this afternoon—following which I would go to another "bath" that Danny had recommended, over in the Sumida section of town.

I lunched in the Imperial Coffee Shop and toured in the bus from 1:15 to 5:30 P.M. An excellent tour of a really wonderful city. Then I got into a taxi to go to my "bath"—and ran into one of the most awkward events of the year.

My taxi driver had a hard time locating the place, so I arrived at about 6:20. We turned into a pretty little garden area, with a cluster of Japanese wooden cottages and a row of parked American cars. Three Japanese ladies (middle-aged) in kimonos greeted my arrival with polite bows. What was it, exactly, that I would like?

"Well," I said, "I had caught a bad cold (and I certainly had: the chill of yesterday morning had been pretty bad) and should like a hot bath; steam..."

They looked at each other. "Steam?"

"Well," I said, "a good hot bath and a rest, with plenty of time to cool off."

"Fine," they said. "Will you stay all night?"

"No," I said, "just a couple of hours."

"Three hours?"

"OK," I said, "Three hours."

I was conducted through a little garden, into one of the pretty cottages, doffed my shoes, and went upstairs to a Japanese room with a low table in the center, a smaller table beside it, and a bowl of hot coals beside that. My hostess bade me sit on a little seat that faced the smaller table and place my feet under the table, under its heavy covers. It was warm as toast in there—the rest of the room was chill. My legs were resting on some kind of brazier, which contained hot coals. Tea was brought to me, and a servant began busying herself about the room and in the room adjoining. "*Gāru-san*[43] come soon," she said as she left; and she shut the door.

It dawned on me, as I peacefully sipped my cup of tea, that I had made a little mistake, and was not quite in a hot bath establishment. I was alone for about half an hour: then the panel before me slid open and *gāru-san* was there, right side to me and her head at a cordial tilt. She was in a pretty kimono, and her hair had been frizzled with the permanent waves that are fashionable now in Japan. I rose to greet her and observed a light eczema of some kind on her right cheek, which she had covered with powder.

"What is your name?" she said.

"What is yours?" I asked, and she told me (but I have forgotten).

"Mine," I said, "is Joe."

She bade me sit down again at the little table and she sat beside me, at my right hand. Then she asked me quietly what I wanted, and I told her: "A good hot bath." She nodded.

"And a massage," I added.

"A massage!?" she said, and her brow furrowed.

"Well," I said, "whatever you do here."

At this moment the panel slid open again and one of the older women knelt beside me. "Everything all right?" she said.

"Oh yes indeed," I said politely.

"And three hours?" she said.

"Three hours will be fine," I answered.

"That will be ¥4,200," she said (about $12!). The most expensive bath of my life! But I was in it—so I put the yen on the table. Everybody smiled and bowed; the lady left, and my girl and I were alone, now, for three hours.

We talked a little about Tokyo and Japan. Her English was a little hard to understand, so, to say a little took quite a while.

When a little time had elapsed, she said, "You like bath now?"

"Yes," I said, "now will be fine."

"Now?" she said.

"Yes now," I said.

She had a very serious look. She seemed to think and decide. She looked at me. "All right," she said. She got up.

"Get up," she said. I got up. "Put on kimono." She pointed to a heavy, man's kimono on a shelf. While I got out of my clothes and into the kimono, she removed her obi and top kimono. Then she helped me tie my sash and we started downstairs—narrow stairs, out into the yard, which was a pretty garden. I followed her in the moonlight to another cottage and she led me to a small, neat, Japanese room with a tiny, rectangular bath, full of hot water, flush with the floor.

"Get in!" she said. I removed my kimono and got in. She removed hers and got in too. Well—so this was different. The tub was very small indeed and the water very hot. She made it too hot and we had to get out. Then we got back in again and sat in steaming water, to our necks.

Physically, the position was extremely intimate; but there was nothing very intimate about the mood; and so we sat there, quietly splashing the water over each other's shoulders, to keep warm. "Enough?" she said, after about ten minutes. "Enough," I said. "Sit down," she said, and she pointed to a little wooden stool. I sat down and she knelt beside me and gave me a good soaping. Then she began pouring hot water over me with a little wooden bucket. When she had finished she gave me another bucketful of water for a bit of private washing then turned around to wash herself. When we had finished, she dried me, helped me back into my kimono, and conducted me again through the garden and back into the little room. It was now quite clear to me what sort of place I was in.

"What time is it now?" she said. We had used up an hour. Two hours to go.

She sat across from me—our feet and legs under the warm table, not touching. I think that by now it was as clear to her as it was to me that I had not come to get what most people came for. She looked very thoughtful for a moment, as she considered the two hours ahead. "I don't *have* to stay two hours," I said, "if you find this thing too difficult." "No," she said. "It is OK."

Then, after a brief pause, she managed to initiate the conversation. Was I married? Yes. "Papa-san?" No. We talked of Jean and the dance; marriage and children; and why she herself hadn't married. This broke the ice, and there was a lot beneath.

She was twenty-two years old; her father was "an old man" of fifty-two (when I told her that I was fifty-one, she had a hard time believing). She had to help earn money. She had a married sister with a couple of children (husband a typist) and a younger brother at school. She had been in this geisha establishment one year.

She didn't know how many girls they had in the establishment; there were two completely distinct sections, one for Japanese, one for foreigners— she was in the foreign branch: she didn't like Turks, Scandinavians, and elephants (I couldn't make out how the elephants got in here!). She liked Americans when they were gentlemen: sometimes the young ones were rough.

"My poor broken body," she said, several times. I asked for the technical details of how she protected herself from disease—and she said she went to the doctor for injections when she felt something itching: she could usually tell the next day. She didn't know how to tell if the man she was with was sick, and if he didn't use a rubber she might be infected. But she protected herself against children. "Blue eyes and red hair not so good," she said. She told me of one girl who had had ten abortions; another, eight. "Very bad, very bad," she said. And we both sat still, a while, thinking how bad. "This is very hard work," she had said several times.

"Now," I said, "I have just paid four thousand two hundred yen for three hours with you: how much of that goes to you?"

"I'm ashamed to tell you," she said. "I won't tell you."

I waited a little.

"Do the men who visit you," I said, "ever leave you money?"

"I never asked you for any money," she said.

"I know," I said; "you didn't ask me. But suppose I left something: would that be unusual?"

She changed the subject. "When people phone me at my house, I send them here. I work only here."

The talk began to lag a bit after an hour and so I thought we should have a change of scene. "Would it be possible to lie down somewhere?" I said.

She tilted her head and looked as she had looked when standing at the door. "You want to go to bed with me?" She then looked as she had looked before we started for the bath. "In there," she said. I pushed open a sliding wall and there was a vast pile of mats made up nicely as a large bed for two. She followed, after a few moments, and we got in, fully wrapped in kimonos. To let me take her sashes off, she had to sit up; then she lay down again and I could stroke her nice smooth skin.

"You Japanese women," I said, "have the smoothest skin in the world." She smiled a little. I stroked some more and she lay there, absolutely inertly.

"When people make love to you," I said, "do you ever have any feeling?"

"Feeling?" she said. "I never feel them." She had misunderstood.

"No," I said, "I mean inside: do you feel any emotion?"

She sort of laughed and shrugged it off.

After a little pause she said, "I think you are happily married."

"Yes," I said, "I think I am." So we talked some more about Jean: then about herself and of how she should get married and get out of this work. She shook her head and looked grimly desperate.

There were some sounds outside of people on the stairs. "The girl next door," she said. "She is sick. She was getting a permanent wave and something happened. Something has happened to all her hair." We listened a little, and then there was a call on the stairs.

"They want to know," she said, "if you want a taxi." Our three hours were up, and we were both, I think, very much relieved. I dressed and gave her a decent tip.

"They gave you a hard job," I said, "and you did it nicely." We bowed.

"Come on, Joe," she said, and she led me downstairs. In the garden stood a tall American gentleman, chatting easily with about six of the women of the establishment—one in full geisha regalia. My poor sparrow and I went to my waiting cab. I kissed her cheek and neck. "Good night," I said, "you were very sweet." And my driver drove me back to the Nikkatsu Hotel. 10:15 P.M. No dinner. No hunger, either. I piled into bed.

Wednesday, April 6

Booked myself this morning for the night tour of Tokyo, then went to the American Express, where I found a couple of nice letters from Jean and one from Helen McMaster; after which I went for a lovely long walk, cherry-blossom viewing, around the Imperial Palace Garden. It was a beautiful day, and there were lots of other people cherry-blossom viewing too.

Returning to the hotel at about 12:45, I found a note from my friend Danny Campbell, inviting me to lunch at noon. I phoned the Union Club but missed him.

I had a bit of lunch in the Nikkatsu Coffee Shop, then started walking to where I thought the American Embassy would be, to get my passport extended for another two years, and to try to find Jean's friend, Bryan Battey. On the way, whom do I bump into but Danny Campbell! Brief chat, and a tentative date for tomorrow noon. He is departing Saturday for the U.S.A. He directed me to the embassy, where I arranged my passport extension and met Battey. Battey drove me to the American Cultural Center, where Jean danced in January, and showed me a fine report that he had written about Jean's event for the Washington U.S.I.S. office. I left him at about 4:00 P.M., and strolled back to my hotel.

The night tour of Tokyo was great. A circuit, first, of the brightly lighted areas: the Japanese have a fabulous talent for the handling of lighted signs. An hour, next, at the Kabuki Theater, where we saw a whole Kabuki play. And finally, supper and fun for forty at a geisha house, the restaurant Mita: an excellent supplement to my experience of last evening; for this time I could see something of the proper mood and functioning of one of these establishments, and it was simply delightful.

Low table around three sides of a pleasant room; with additional area at the other end, where two samisen players[44] and two little geisha girls performed. First, two comparatively formal dances. Next, a little game (scissors-paper-stone), audience being introduced to rules of the game. Next, "How to Play Baseball"—a cute dance game to samisen music with baseball movements (pitching, batting, catching, running, "outa, safe,") and finally the scissors-paper-stone element, to see who wins—the loser sits down and someone else comes up. The girls called up the man from the visiting group—and managed, finally, to break the ice of the party completely. Finale: "Auld Lang Syne" for the whole crowd. And then the same girls—who had seemed so alien at the start— were driven to their homes in our bus, in full regalia—a wonderful idea of the mood and skills of the geisha house! They took what came and gave it a great time.

Thursday, April 7

Spent the morning dealing with money affairs, at Pan American Airways and American Express, after moving to the Yashima Hotel: nice little room, without bath: a good excuse for more baths at Tokyo Onsen. After lunch, went to the Nichigeki Theater to see a sort of Paramount Theater show. Well done, in its kind, with a rapid-fire sequence of colorful scenes: house full of kids and families: completely *à l'américain*. Trip, next, to Tokyo Onsen and then to Suehiro's for a grandiose steak dinner. Spent the evening walking in the enchantingly lighted little streets of my new neighborhood. Sent a birthday telegram to Charlie.[45]

Friday, April 8

Spent a good part of the day trying to make contact with Danny, who was likewise trying to catch me. We kept missing. At 11:00 A.M. went to the

Shimbashi Enbujo (Theater) to see the first half of the spring program of the Azuma Odori—"the celebrated geisha of Shimbashi"... the group, part of which came to New York last year. A perfectly beautiful event—went on until about 2:15. Got in touch with Battey during the afternoon and he invited me to a "modern" dance recital this evening at 6:00 P.M.—Bac Ishu's Oriental Ballet, "Human Buddha"—presented in a huge auditorium (filled), with full symphony orchestra and immense cast. Not so good: more like third-rate Balanchine[46] than like modern dance. Driven to my hotel by the Batteys: had a snack in one of these cute coffee shops that are so abundant in Tokyo, and went early to bed—today is the Buddha's birthday.

Saturday, April 9

A day somewhat cloudy, but the cherry blossoms are at their best, so I went for a huge walk: to Ueno Park, through the wonderful museum, and then to Asakusa, where I walked around admiring the wonderful little streets and great crowds and then began visiting theaters—all that weren't movies turned out to be a sort of cross between burlesque and "little theater": at least one of the short plays (three or four acts) was darned good—and it was followed immediately by a kimono striptease that was simply wonderful. One little joint, the Asakusa Strip Tease, put on a series of jobs to a jammed house that were certainly the best of the kind that I've ever seen. Finally was caught by Danny; had a drink with him and Dorothy Riggs in the Yashima bar. He leaves tonight.

Dinner with the Batteys—who very very much want Jean to be here next August and January.

Sunday, April 10

Practically all day at the Kabuki Theater—11:00 A.M. until 4:15 P.M. Never got so much theater for my money in my life. Simply great. Invited Dorothy Riggs to come with me, to take her mind off Danny's departure.

After the show, said bye-bye to Dorothy, went to Tokyo Onsen, had a grand steak dinner again at Suehiro's, took the subway up to Asakusa and strolled around again in the extraordinarily prettily lighted streets. When it started to rain I went into another theater—same sort of thing as yesterday. Left at nine and went home—again in the subway—and to bed.

Monday, April 11

A lovely sunny day—so I went again to Ueno Park, to see and photograph the blossoms. They have begun to lose their petals. The park was still full of cherry-blossom viewers. Came back to the hotel about 1:30 and took a bath and nap, to freshen up for another session of Kabuki. 4:30 to 10:15 P.M., Kabuki! (Kabuki isn't merely theater: it's a form of life!) Home, and after a hot chocolate in the little coffee shop across the street, to bed.

Tuesday, April 12

A long letter to Jean—my first since arriving in Tokyo; then, to the Maruzen bookshop, to get started on my Japanese career of study: grammars, readers, and a bit of philosophy. A wonderful bookshop, full of Japanese, English, French, and German books—and not a single Bollingen volume.47 Not a single Bollingen volume in Hong Kong either. Great job of selling the Orient!

Today, at last (first moment since my arrival in dizzying Tokyo), I feel that I can begin to settle into something like a sober stride. I think I'll spend this week and next in Tokyo, with a weekend at Kamakura, etc., to see how that might be as a place for Jean and me to stay if she decides to accept Battey's bid for her to teach here in August. Then I'd like to visit Nikko and after that transfer my center to Kyoto.

This afternoon at 2:30 I went to the Azuma Odori Theater again for part two of the program—2:30 to 5:30 P.M. Then to Suehiro's sukiyaki restaurant for a delightful dinner, served by three charming little Japanese ladies. The more I see of these wonderful women, the more apt the saying seems: for the perfect home, one should have an American house, a Chinese cook, and a Japanese wife. The husband, in such circumstances, I guess, can be anything at all.

Wednesday, April 13

Morning, by train to nearby Samezu, to get my driver's license: am to return tomorrow at two. Got back to my hotel by eleven and studied Japanese till 4:30. Next, to my Tokyo Onsen, then to Asakusa to see the big U.S.A.-type revue at the large theater. Next, a bit of burlesque across the street, and home at ten.

Thursday, April 14

To the Kanze Kaikan, Noh theater, to buy a ticket for this afternoon; then to Samezu again, to pick up my license. Noh plays from 5:00 to 10:00 P.M., then home to bed.

Friday, April 15

Studied Japanese practically all day, with a trip at noon to the American Express and at five to Tokyo Onsen. After a fine steak dinner at Suehiro's, a long stroll through the Ginza area trying to read the signs in katakana[48] (which I now have learned), and home to a bit of letter writing and bed.

I am beginning to have some ideas about Japan, India, and the modern world; but shall wait a bit before trying to put them down.

Saturday, April 16

A nice, old-fashioned, rainy day. Good day for thoughts, and a study of Japanese.

I have now seen Noh, Kabuki, Azuma's geisha troupe, two American moviehouse–style revues, one hot revue, two burlesque performances, three striptease shows, and one GI night spot; have visited two stylish nightclubs, Suehiro's elegant Japanese-style and Western-style restaurants, one geisha house, a number of little coffee shops, and my Tokyo Onsen. Have also walked through numerous miles of Tokyo's streets and parks; have dwelt in two hotels—an expensive and a moderate priced—and have visited a number of shops. Some general impressions have begun to become fixed in my mind.

1. In contrast to India: the literacy rate is over 90 percent (highest in the world), in contrast to India's 5 percent to 20 percent (perhaps the lowest): one immediately obvious correlate—a dramatically higher general intelligence. Jobs are done efficiently, intelligently, and well. But a multitude of other contrasts are evident also, and the literacy rate no doubt contributes greatly to these. As follows:

2. Whereas in India one feels that a situation of cultural catastrophe exists— the ancient civilization gone and the new not yet generally effective, with a group of bewildered amateurs now searching romantically into their own past for India and into the West for the means of social health, stalled midway between—in contrast to this, in Japan both East and West are vividly and wonderfully present, in every phase of life. That is to say, in India the

West-East tension is inadequately objectified, and so exists excessively as a spiritual or psychological tension of ideas, feelings, premonitions, and resistances, while in Japan the two worlds are brought into an actual concrete interplay, and the result is a life-enhancing integration-in-process. What I shall find when I get into the country, of course, I don't yet know. But in the city (and India has no city, in the sense that Tokyo is a city), what I find is a vivid cocktail of East and West—with its own martini flavor, which is neither gin nor vermouth: and as a martini matures and gets better in the icebox, with the passage of time, so too will this.

3. Whereas in India there is a pathological necessity to criticize and abuse the West as "materialistic," while vaunting the native "spirituality," there seems to be very little (if any) of this in Japan. India's reactionary, fundamentalist, ignorant and consequently stupid pride is perhaps her chief impediment. The machine, modern morality, and even modern dress represent a challenge to the good old "four square" gospel of the Vedas—which, of course, they do. Unable to resolve the tension of these pairs of opposites, India is at present in a condition, not merely of physical, but also of psychological, paralysis. Japan, on the other hand, jumped at the modern *means* of life with a ready will. The result is a condition of progressive spirituality that is immensely impressive.

4. This leads me to begin to believe that Japan has understood better than modern India the final import of the Indian doctrine of non-duality. The Indian psyche is locked in duality: East vs. West, Spiritual vs. Material, Hindu vs. Moslem, caste vs. outcaste, new vs. old. The Japanese, on the other hand, understand how to *rock with the waves*. The relative world is relative and the transcendent, transcendent. There is no point or position, idea or feeling in the relative world that has an absolute value; and yet *all* things are Buddha things.

5. A query, then, with respect to the contrast of Hinduism and Buddhism:
   a. It is with the Upaniṣads that India first breaks into the non-priestly sphere of a generally accessible transcendent realization: the chief teachers were not brahmins but laymen.
   b. With the Buddha (a *Nepalese;* a *kṣatriya*) this realization is freshly taught, in a definitely anti-brahminical style and with a primarily psychological inflection.
   c. Mahāyāna Buddhism, and then Zen, carried this teaching forward to its ultimate implications.
   d. With Śaṅkara's Vedanta, India lapsed into a fundamentally negative position—not greatly different, finally, from that of Jainism, which is fundamentally dualistic.
   e. India's dualism, pride of race, archaic style, etc., are perhaps as intrinsic to Hinduism as their Jewish counterparts are to Judaism. Japan's readiness for new forms is perhaps a function of her Zen.

6. In the Japanese theater I have found an excellent projection of the modern Japanese syndrome:

a. In the Noh, Kabuki, and geisha traditions the ancient pattern is maintained. New works, however, are being produced in these forms: it is possible, therefore, for the Japanese to experience the new world—or rather the continuation of their ancient world into the new—in a style appropriate to their historical past.

b. In the vast movie-theater-style revues there is an enthusiastic imitation of the American-Western style—but with an inevitable Japanese feeling for theater, decor, humor, etc: that is conditioned by the Kabuki. This reaches right down into the burlesque. One can feel distinctly the force of the native Kabuki in practically every scene. Furthermore, in every one of these shows there is at least one act or scene presenting traditional Japanese materials on the stage and in the style of the modern revue.

c. In the striptease stunts there is another very amusing sign of the dual world. The Japanese physique is distinguished by relatively short thighs: to match the long-legged ideal of the American striptease, therefore, the girls wear very high heels—and the effect is generally quite definitely OK. The Japanese woman has in reserve, however, the possibility of the low-slung effect also: and this is occasionally rendered, *by the same girls,* in the absolutely inimitable kimono striptease—where a whole new set of values and effects becomes suddenly evident.

7. The contrast of the Japanese theater—strong, healthy, and professional in style—with the Indian (which can hardly be said to exist) suggests an interesting series of thoughts.

a. India today is a nation of amateurs in *every* field—amateurs and half-baked fakers. As in all amateur events, there is a compensatory over-estimation of the value of the deed evident in all Indian spiritual, political, scientific, and aesthetic performances.

b. There is a dissociation between the Indian folk arts (Kathakali, etc.) and modern Indian experience. This is due largely to the failure of the Indians to support their own arts. The arts, supported and flourishing, assist in the process of spiritual integration. Religion, on the other hand (which is India's "strength"), resists the new and tends to impede integration.

c. The arts of the theater are associated everywhere, one way or another, with prostitution. In Japan this association is overt in the tradition of the geisha ("art person"). Prostitution is a recognized profession here, and so exists in a highly inflected, civilized, and differentiated set of manifestations. One can find what one wants or requires, on every level—and this has contributed to the grace and decorum of life. It represents and facilitates a life-furthering momentum. In India, on the other hand, where the inevitable association of the arts with prostitution led, during the nineteenth century (if not earlier), to a genteel suppression and rejection of the arts, not only prostitution, but civilization itself, has declined. Aesthetic taste is abominable. The whorehouse quarters are unspeakable. The arts are dead. And "*all life is sorrowful.*" I am sure that in the days when Indian culture may be said to have flourished (up to, say, A.D. 1200) the situation was comparable to that of present-day Japan.

And this leads me to a couple of new formulae:

8. Where the *gei-sha* ("art person") principle is repressed, civilization declines. Its fosterage leads to cultural adulthood (India today being my example of an infantile culture).

9. Where the *gei-sha* ("art person") principle is repressed, religion declines— into vulgar image worship or psalm singing.

10. The *gei-sha* ("art person") principle is at the root of the glory of Japan; its motto: "What is it you want or require? Can do! I can supply your demand in a humble, willing, likeable way."

At 12:00 noon I set off for another session of Noh, and this one beat the world's record for duration: 12:30 to 6:50 P.M.! Three plays were presented and one comic interlude. I bought a copy of P. G. O'Neill's *A Guide to No* at the theater and caught up a bit on my lesson; I find that I have seen the following:

April 14th: *Arashiyama,* by Zempō (O'Neill, p. 5), and *Fuji's Drum,* by Zeami (p. 32). April 16th: *Chikubu Shima,* by Zenchiku (p. 13); *Genji Kuyō,* by Zeami (p. 40); and *Kurama Tengu,* by Miyamasu (p. 90).

Chikubu Shima was particularly interesting to me, since it presented in essence the whole adventure of the Hero. The boat to the temple-island was marvelously rendered by means of a simple frame placed on the ground, within which the three characters settled for the voyage, hero and goddess-guide sitting; old man-dragon deity standing in the stern with a punting pole.

It is interesting to compare Noh with Kabuki. Many elements are shared: the combination of music, dance, and drama—Noh emphasizing music, however, and Kabuki drama and dance. Kabuki's dance opens out into great action at times: Noh's remains dense and intense. Noh's music is carried largely by three drums and flute with chorus; Kabuki stresses the samisen. Both theaters have approaches to the stage: Noh's however is along the back wall and Kabuki's is through the house. Noh uses no scenery or sets; Kabuki stresses surprising stage effects: Kabuki even uses trapdoors.

The modern Japanese revue, by the way, takes over the trapdoor effects: also the runway! And Kabuki takes over the house cries of the popular burlesque.

Rode home in a trolley and went then to Ten-ichi for some tempura, then to Mon (across from my hotel) for ice cream and coffee. Home at 8:45, for a bit of Japanese before bed.

CHAPTER 3

FROM SAKE TO SATORI

TOKYO AND KYOTO

Sunday, April 17   **Environs of Tokyo**

9:45 A.M. train from Tokyo Station for Yokosuka, where Dorothy Riggs met me with her car and drove me for a little tour of Yokosuka, Hayama, Zushi, and Kamakura. The day was wet and windy, but this did not destroy the scenery (reminded me a little of the Monterey Peninsula) nor did it prevent literally thousands of Japanese tourists from visiting Kamakura by bus. Saw the great Buddha figure of Kamakura;[49] visited the Tsurugaoka Hachimangū Shrine, saw the crowds going out to Enoshima, had a late lunch at a little Japanese restaurant in Yokosuka called Mikado, and took the 3:50 train back home. Evening studying Japanese. Concluded that Kamakura was *not* the place for Jean and me to set up house this August: too many people, and the swimming (in spite of the beauty of the shoreline) a bit foul.

Monday, April 18   **Tokyo**

Studied Japanese until noon, then out for a haircut and lunch at the Imperial. Back home for more Japanese, and at 4:00 P.M. started off to have

dinner with Mr. and Mrs. Wilbur, out in a little residential section of
Tokyo which it took more than an hour to reach. Cute spot though, very
Japanese. And as I came along the street I heard music, and there were five
people in Kabuki costumes doing a little dance in procession. Mrs. Wilbur
later told me that this was one of the stunts put on for advertising by the
local real estate people who are trying to advertise and build up their neighborhood.

At dinner was a young Nisei[50] from California named Laverne Senyo
Sasaki, who is studying to be a Buddhist preacher at the University of
Tokyo. There were also two ladies, one American, one Japanese, with ideas
about things that didn't quite come out—largely because my own somewhat passionate judgments of India and enthusiastic remarks about Tokyo
gave an emphatic slant to the conversation: indeed, *too* emphatic. I have
got to reform. Wilbur said—half-jokingly but wisely—that I was obviously
suffering from shock.

I believe I am, and I believe the shock can be analyzed and dissolved
as follows:

I. The sixfold shock:
   1. India's anti-Americanism, fellow-traveler style
   2. The depth and extent of India's poverty
   3. India's squalid *bhakti*
   4. The pattern of India's male-female coexistence
   5. The conceit and complacency of India's "spiritual" position
   6. The depth, extent, and importance of the Western influence in India
II. The sixfold reaction, conditioned by:
   1. My strong anti-Communist sentiments
   2. A belief that such poverty must be somebody's fault—and in this case
     not England's
   3. An ever-present contrast, in my experience, with the monuments and
     philosophies of India's past
   4. My own displeasure on finding myself in a world without women
   5. A recognition of the flimsiness of my own earlier celebration of the
     Indian superiority: a disillusionment about Coomaraswamy (the incon-
     gruity now makes me feel that I want to laugh every time I see an
     Indian)
   6. The obvious importance of this influence gives force to my whole re-ac-
     tions to the Indian anti-Westernism
III. The means of cancelling the shock:
   A. Change the order of the items:
        4. The pattern of India's male-female coexistence
        3. India's squalid *bhakti* (infantilism)

2. The depth and extent of India's poverty
6. The depth, extent, and importance of the Western influence in India
5. The complacent conceit of India's "spirituality"
1. India's anti-Americanism
B. Interpret the headings analytically.
   a. Headings 4, 3, 2, and 6 anthropologically and historically
   b. Heading 5 psychologically
   c. Heading 1 in terms of a sociological analysis, giving due recognition to the negatives on the American side

And now let me take a vow not to let myself discuss India again in terms of my personal reactions, emotions, and experiences.[51]

The force of my feelings this evening was partly caused by the contrast with India that I have felt in Japan, for instance:

4. The comparative ease with which Japan seems to be making the changeover to a modern, personalized male-female relationship
3. The beauty of Japan's shrines and temples and the ubiquitous evidence here of taste
2. The lack of any display of poverty: no sense here of people being interested primarily in baksheesh
6. A willing grasp of the Western machine as a means for heightening life
5. An attempt to adjust, psychologically, to the new age
1. An anti-Americanism based, not on a haughty reaction to American aid, but on
   a. The bombings
   b. An army of occupation
   c. An American-forced constitution
   d. The pressures of American politics and economics

Came home from the party with Sasaki, who offered to give me the introductions I shall need for Kyoto. I already have the feeling here that I had in India of my voyage developing of itself.

Tuesday, April 19

Off to the Meijiza Theater for an 11:00 A.M. to 4:20 P.M. performance of Kabuki. This time, there was no English program available, so I haven't any idea of what I saw. The first was a short two-scene piece about a child abducted by a bird who seems to turn up in scene two as an abbot visited by his bereaved and now delighted mother. The second took up the rest of the five hours: a work in many scenes, wherein a samurai slays an unpleasant woman and drops her into a well, and a woman slays a man who then gets up and lives for a moment, only to die downstairs. I could not follow this piece at all. But the fascination of the optical and musical effects was as great as ever. Kabuki seems to me to have achieved what Wagner tried to achieve—a perfect synthesis of music and theater—plus the dance.

Home for a bit of Japanese—then went downstairs to wait for a date that I thought I had made for tonight with the Batteys. Fell into conversation with a Nisei from Vancouver over here on business. Batteys didn't turn up (date is actually for tomorrow). Went across the street to Mon for a hotdog and cocoa with my new friend from Canada, returned for a half hour chat in his room, and then went to bed. During the chat I again found myself talking the wrong way about India.

Wednesday, April 20

In the morning paper, Einstein's formula for success: $A = XYZ$. A is success in life, X is work, Y is play, and Z is keeping your mouth shut. If it weren't for the fact that I seem to have a much lower resistance to silence than most people I might be able to add Z to my mixture. Meditation for the acquisition of Z:

    a. OK, nobody's talking; so what! and
    b. Formulate a question

I also find in the morning paper that what I saw yesterday were four plays, not two; as follows: *Rōbensugi no Yurai, Shinpan Utazaimon, Banchō Sarayashiki,* and *Yodogoi Shusse no Takinobori.*

Spent the greater part of the day at my Japanese; can now read both katakana and hiragana [52] scripts: am beginning, also, to catch words in people's conversations. In the mail today, I received a great load of mail forwarded from Ceylon: all of Jean's early letters, a very nice surprise.

I invited the Batteys out to dinner and discussed Jean's summer possibilities. Important: U.S.I.S. does not pick up people from scratch and set them up to a tour. Rather, it comes in with a lift for people already assured of a money-making run in the area to be visited. "They are too deeply committed to the principle of individual enterprise to do anything else." This, of course, is why the American cultural propaganda is a failure: those who have hit the bandwagon are not precisely the ones to give foreigners the idea that America is a civilized nation.

After dinner at Suehiro's, we went to a cute little coffee bar with classical music on its phonograph in the Ginza neighborhood. Home at about 11:00 P.M.

Thursday, April 21

Morning at my Japanese. Noontime went to a doctor to see about the ankle that I sprained at Angkor: it is still swollen and today developed a new set of pains. He gave me an Ace bandage and some advice. Nice guy: he thinks it will still take quite a while for this to go down, with me walking so much.

At 5:00 P.M. I went to the Noh theater again and saw *Hagoromo,* by Zeami—the play about the swan-maid–angel. I had been hoping to see this, and was delighted by the performance.

Had a snack at Mon, across the street, and retired to write letters and study. To bed about 11:00 P.M.

Friday, April 22

Morning on Japanese. Noon to American Express to find letter from Jean accepting the idea of teaching here in August. Spent the early afternoon writing letters and from 4:30 to 10:00 P.M. attended the second part of the Meijiza Kabuki. What seemed to me to be two very long works in numerous acts, and a fabulous dance-play at the conclusion. The last features two men (a samurai and a clown), a woman (chiefly partner of the samurai), and eight acrobatic, tumbler-dancers (bearing cherry-blossom branches; companions of the clown). The dance lasted about an hour.

This Kabuki group seems to go in for long pieces of a slowly moving sort, emphasizing dialogue. The pictorial aspect of the production is so good, however, that I felt no sense of tedium, even though I had no idea of what was going on. The music, also, is remarkable: largely one samisen and one singer—but with occasional flute and additional voices.

This, I think, concludes my present dose of Kabuki and Noh. I am setting my sails, now, for Kyoto: expect to leave Monday or Tuesday.

Saturday, April 23

Morning studying Japanese and catching up a bit on mail. Toward noon, a long walk to American Express through the Ginza area. Lunch—ham sandwich and coffee have become my standard Tokyo lunch: price, about sixty cents at a coffeehouse with lots of dim-light atmosphere and a good orchestra playing pleasant music.

At 1:00 P.M. the Batteys picked me up in their car and we went for a drive into the suburbs of Tokyo. Lovely countryside, and happy motoring until son David, asleep in the backseat, woke up and became the normal American child. We met another American family in the U.S. service at a finicula stop and not only the children but also the parents made a great noise and show of themselves over the heads of a large number of peacefully watching Japanese families—what the hell is it about the American family?

After the finicula ride, we drove some more and at about 7:00 P.M. stopped at a sweet little Japanese inn in Ome for dinner. But David ran loose and wild to such an extent that we were very politely asked to leave before dinner was served. Mortified departure. Dinner, finally, at the Batteys', and to bed about eleven.

New news for Jean. The Batteys think she should give a recital in Tokyo as well as teach.

Sunday, April 24

Morning, to Tsukiji Honganji Temple, to attend a Sunday morning service, held in English and Japanese, under the auspices of the International Buddhist Association. The temple architecture is based on the Occidental plan of a Protestant church: the architectural elements are from Indian Buddhist sanctuaries (largely Sāñcī and Ajaṇṭā); the shoes are not removed when one enters; there are chairs in which to sit; and both upstairs and in the basement there are offices. The temple grounds are large, enclosed by a modified imitation of the Sāñcī railings. Youngsters are playing baseball in the yard. Just outside one of the gates is a man selling goldfish, which little children carry away in cute, transparent plastic bags. There is a mild smell of fish in the air from the fish market just across the corner.

The temple interior is large and a bit chill and gloomy: the congregation for this service was small—about twenty-five people. The service began with a layman introducing the Reverend So-and-so, who, then facing the altar, read a prayer in English which we all followed in our prayer books—faith and trust in the Buddha, *dharma,* and *saṅgha,* etc. Hymns then were sung, in English and in Japanese. A sermon in Japanese was delivered by another Reverend So-and-so; one in English (on "sincerity") by my young friend, the Reverend Sasaki of Sacramento; and the service concluded with more hymns. Following the service, one was permitted to make one's "incense offering" by dropping money into a box and a pinch of incense into an incense urn.

Sasaki introduced me as a professor of comparative religion to the other two reverend gentlemen, and one of them immediately asked me whether I had any faith of my own. I replied that since I found that all the great religions were saying essentially the same thing in various ways, I was unable and unwilling to commit myself to any one, but tried to teach and understand the ultimate tenor of their various yet homologous symbolic languages. The gentleman said that he thought everyone should be committed to a single religion, and that for him Buddhism was the only one. He felt that a person with such a religion could teach comparatively better than a nonreligious scholar. I replied that I thought that such a person would inevitably favor his own religion; indeed, I declared, I have seen and heard plenty of such people from various faiths. Their position is always: "You worship God your way and I His way."

We parted cordially, and I returned to the hotel, after another stroll in the Ginza area and lunch in that dim coffeehouse.

The Tsukiji Honganji Temple is the headquarters of the Shinshū sect in Tokyo: the great center is in Kyoto. Founded in 1630, the temple has been destroyed many times by fire. The present structure dates from 1935. The image on the main altar is of Amida Buddha; and it was to Amida that the prayers of the service were addressed.*[53]

Sasaki's sermon and the whole setup suggest to me a few problems that I should like to clarify:

What is the relation of this modern, Occidental-style temple and service to the big temple in Honolulu? What is the relation of the International Buddhist Association to the sectarian situation? What is the relation of the Shinshū sect to the other orthodox Buddhist sects in Japan, and why has it furnished the platform for the I.B.A.?[54] When Sasaki and

---

* See *An Official Guide to Japan with Preparatory Explanations on Japanese Customs, Language, History, Religion, Literature, Etc.* (Tokyo: Japanese Government Railways, 1933), p. 291.

his friends speak of and pray to Amida Buddha, do they think of him as a historical character, or as purely a *Dhyāna* Buddha?[55] If as a *Dhyāna* Buddha, what do they think of the Amida legend? (Purely symbolic? or meant to be believed literally by the simpler faithful?) Sasaki spoke of the need for the individual to grasp and integrate the grace or spirit of Amida. This seems to me to contradict the fundamental Amida formula; namely, that to pronounce the name is sufficient. What is the position of the I.B.A. on such a point, and what that of the traditional sectarians?

It is possible that all of these questions are conceived from a standpoint quite alien to the thinking of a Japanese Buddhist. During the course of my conversation after the service, I had occasion to refer to the Catholic dogma of the Assumption of the Virgin as both scientifically and metaphysically untenable. (Heaven is not a *place:* a physical body has to be in a *place:* it extends in space and endures in time—no space—no body.)[56] I was told that such an image has to be taken symbolically. I replied that the Roman Catholic Church insists on the Assumption as a literal fact.

"You mean, if one were there one could have seen it?"

"Definitely. It is claimed that people were there and that people literally did see the Virgin ascend. Moreover, the body of Jesus also ascended." (And, I might have added, we are all to ascend at the moment of the Resurrection of the Dead.)

"We Buddhists," I was then told, "treat such things as symbols. The Buddha, for instance, is said to have been born from his mother's side. We don't ask ourselves whether that was a literal fact."

"Well," I said, "in the West we tend to give such themes a concrete reading—and religion then comes under the criticism of science. Young people become confused, and reasonably abandon their faith."

I spent the afternoon on my Japanese and at six went to Tokyo Onsen for my final Turkish bath and massage—Otako-san singing little geisha songs while she worked, and a new song called "Samisen Boogie-Woogie." A fine steak dinner at Suehiro's after the bath, and then a long stroll home.

Monday, April 25

Anniversary (eighth month) of my departure from New York. Shall leave for Kyoto tomorrow. Bought my third-class ticket yesterday for the 9:00 A.M. express.

Today I finally got up my nerve and purchased two new lenses for my camera (a wide-angle and a telephoto), as well as a leather bag in which to carry my photographic affairs and a universal viewfinder. I then went around the city viewing buildings and finally went to a little studio where I could try all this out in a strictly measured area. They supplied a nude model, whom I viewed happily through 135 mm, 50 mm, and 35 mm lenses—finding, however, to my distress, that the difference between the 50 and 35 was not great enough to warrant the money I had spent on the latter. I hurried back to the store (for it was now 5:00 P.M.) and swapped my wide-angle for an extra-wide-angle lens of 28 mm. This cost another four thousand yen but made me happy.

For dinner, I went tonight to Irene's Hungaria, a very nice little cellar restaurant, full of Americans. Returned home to pack and retired at peace with the world.

Tuesday, April 26   Kyoto

Nine A.M. to 4:20 P.M. Third-class: a perfectly beautiful train ride. There is no comparison possible with the trains of India! Clean crowd, very orderly and considerate, with neat packages, all nicely dressed and un-smelly, with cute little packets of things to eat. The train was swept of its clutter of tangerine skins and discarded wrappings six times during the trip.

The countryside is incredible: the farms are like gardens, perfectly kept and groomed—full of people working. The mountains and sea everywhere. Vast, busy, modern cities and charming hamlets.

Kyoto, a city of over a million, was more like Tokyo than I had expected: great and busy modern streets and buildings, but proportionately many more of the quaint little streets and temple compounds than Tokyo. As soon as I was settled in my room in the Kyoto Hotel (a small room and bath for more than I wanted to pay), I went out for a stroll, hunting for some of the restaurants that the Batteys had named for me. Had dinner at one that I found myself: the Alaska, on the top floor of a seven- or eight-storey building, with all glass walls and a fine view of the valley in which Kyoto nestles. Then strolled, enchanted again, through the multitudes of charmingly lighted little streets—all swarming with droves of schoolchildren, who are brought here in great busloads to see the ancient capital and the religious center of their country. They flood the little streets, doll shops, pachinko games, movie theaters, coffee shops, and Japanese-style inns.

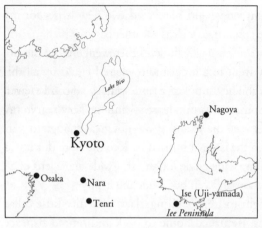

Wednesday, April 27

Up at 5:00 A.M., and write three letters before breakfast: one to Mr. Phillip Karl Eidmann,[57] in the Honganji Temple compound (Feuerring's[58] suggestion), one to Mrs. Ruth Sasaki (Alan Watts's former mother-in-law),[59] and one to Miss Ellen D. Psaty (Salmony's former student).[60] After breakfast I asked to be moved to a cheaper room, and went off for a morning's walk. Strolled from the hotel to the Sanjō-Shijō area, then across the river and up to the Yasaka Shrine, then back to Kawaramachi Street. Streetcar to the railroad station area and into the Japan Tourist Office, where I got some advice on where to study Japanese: I have a date this afternoon, 5:00 P.M., for an interview at the Japanese Language School at Nakadachiuri. Took a streetcar up to the school corner, to locate the place, then returned to the hotel for a spaghetti lunch in the grill. I moved into the new room.

After lunch, a sightseeing bus: Higashi Honganji Temple, a magnificent wooden structure, with a wonderful atmosphere, the "junior headquarters" of the Shinshū sect, the same as that of the temple I visited in Tokyo. The sect was founded by Shinran (i.e. Kenshin Daishi), A.D. 1173–1262, as a reform movement. It rejects celibacy of priesthood, vegetarianism and ascetic practices, and claims salvation by faith in Amida (*Namu Amida Butsu*[61]). It suffered many persecutions, including an eleven-year siege in the sixteenth century in Osaka.* Unlike the Tokyo temple, here the style is completely Japanese: beautiful wooden columns, mat flooring, a great sense of quiet space. It is one of the finest temple structures in Japan.

Next we visited the Imperial Palace; then paused at some shops, and

---

* *Guide to Japan,* p. 695.

finally visited the Heian Shrine and gardens. I took as many photographs as possible (black-and-white) with my new lenses.

After the tour, went to the language school and arranged to begin tomorrow: three hours a day, in a class with one other pupil, who is two weeks ahead of me. Bought the books (Naganuma's Japanese course) and went home to study. Dinner in the hotel dining room—rather dreary.

Thursday, April 28

Up at 5:30, to continue studying my new books, trying to run through as far as to lesson thirteen. Not too hard; but many new words and constructions. Eight o'clock breakfast, 8:35 streetcar; school 9:00 to 12:00—full of priests and nuns. Good teaching. I think it's going to work. Tomorrow is a holiday (the emperor's birthday),[62] and I shall be able to have a makeup session in the morning.

From one to six, I witnessed an extraordinarily interesting dramatic pantomime at the Mibu-dera Temple, the so-called Mibu-Kyōgen, which dates back to 1299. (My guide says: "It is performed from April 21 for ten days and is entirely in pantomime. There are more than thirty characters, and an orchestra of flutes, gongs, and drums. The dresses worn by the actors date in some cases from the Genroku Era (1688–1703). There are also a number of old masks in the temple.")

The temple is of the Ritsu sect, and was founded in A.D. 991. The chief image enshrined is one of Jizō-bosatsu (who appears in and is celebrated in the pantomimes), which is attributed to Jōchō, a celebrated sculptor of the eleventh century.[63]

The pantomimes are presented on a high balcony built on the south side of one of the temple structures (the Great Prayer Hall, Daibutsu-den), which faces a large pavilion where the crowd sits—a great company of little families—lots of kids—and again the miracle of five hours of excellent behavior.

A young Japanese law student named Hisashi Mita came and sat beside me and helped me to know what was going on. Six little plays were shown. (Apparently there is a repertoire of about twenty-three pieces.)

1. *Hōroku Wari.* A tale of two quarreling merchants. One, a drum seller, goes to sleep, and the second, a seller of plates, steals his drum. The judge reprimands the plate seller and the drum seller destroys his shop.

2. Tale of a priest with a wife and child. The townspeople suspect something and insist on entering to see the image.[64] The wife, wearing a mask (on top of her mask) poses as Kannon carrying a child.[65] The people depart, but return, and the priest this time, in his confusion, has put the mask on his wife upside down. The wife is driven from town and the priest, with his baby on his back, is led in ignominy through the streets with a red rope tied around his waist and passed between his legs from behind.

3. Five robbers divest voyagers of their kimonos, but presently enter an inn where a celebrated samurai does them all to death.

4. An assassin (Yogitsu?) attempts the life of the shōgun but is defeated.

5. *The Hungry Souls' Wrestling Match with the Ogres.* Three poor "hungry souls," shivering with fear, are enabled by the grace of the Bodhisattva Kṣitigarbha (Jizō-bosatsu—principal figure of the Mibu-dera Temple) to become strong enough to overcome a horde of ogres.

6. *Benkei's Ship.* Benkei is carrying Yoshitsune and Yoshitsune's wife in a vessel. A storm demon seeks to sink the craft, but Benkei rattles his beads and, after a fierce contest, the demon is overcome.

The musical accompaniment of these pantomimes remained the same throughout the afternoon: a basic rhythm marked by a gong, the secondary beats, variously, by a drum struck with two sticks, and a flute playing - - - | - - | - - - | - - | etc. all afternoon.

The characters were all masked and moved in a manner suggesting Noh, but not so slowly. No singing, and no words, however.

Gong: ♩   ♩   ♩   ♩   ♩   ♩
Drum: ♪♪♪   ♪♪   ♩   ♩   ♩   ♪♪

The balcony stage was of almost exactly the same structure as the Noh stage at the Kanze Kaikan in Tokyo. Indeed, I had the feeling, distinctly, that I was witnessing a sort of proto-Noh. I also had the feeling that I was witnessing something not very different from the religious pantomimes and morality plays of the European Middle Ages. These plays are said to have originated (circa A.D. 1170–1250) during the Kamakura period "to give the illiterated [*sic*] masses the teaching of Buddhism."[66] Noh originated about a century later: Kan'ami, circa 1333–84, and Zeami, 1363–1443.

After the performance, I had coffee with Hisashi (nicknamed Shō), and made a date with him to visit Nara on Sunday. Then to the hotel for a pleasant tempura dinner in their tempura restaurant, and an evening of work on my Japanese.

Friday, April 29

The emperor's birthday. Japanese flags all over the place. Morning from 9:00 to 11:00 at my Japanese school. After lunch, two geisha shows: the first, that of the Gion geishas at the Gion Kaburenjō Theater and the second, that of the Pontochō geishas at the Pontochō Kaburenjō Theater—the latter was the better and rather charming, though not so good as the Shimbashi geishas were, in the Azuma Odori in Tokyo. These spring geisha festivals are given every year, as advertisements of the geisha houses in the various geisha areas represented. In the programs are photos of the girls arranged according to house. Both of the little plays seen today were based on Lady Murasaki's *Tale of Genji.* The Pontochō piece, about a fox-woman and her human husband, was quite delightful. All the machinery of the Kabuki stage was used with wonderful effect.

I went to the second show with Ellen Psaty and two of her friends (one American, one Japanese) and after the performance we went (minus the Japanese lady) to Kyoto's Suehiro restaurant for a six-hundred-yen steak dinner—simply great. I told them all about my India adventures with Salmony, and left them with the promise of further events together in the future.

Before the first of the two geisha shows, I attended their "Tea Ceremonial," which was a sort of farce. A large roomful of people served a little cake and bowl of "whipped" tea, while two little geisha students sat on a high platform illustrating the act of whipping the tea. We were rushed through in lively style so that the next horde could be admitted.

Saturday, April 30

Morning and early afternoon bringing my diary up to date. It is now 3:15 P.M. Next, a letter to Jean; and the rest of the day will be spent I believe, on my Japanese.

Dinner at Prunier's: not so good: like a Midwestern restaurant and bar, with television set going full blast—in spite of a very elegant entrance and reception.

Sunday, May 1   **Nara**

A fabulous and memorable day: one of the richest of my year in the Orient. My little friend of last Thursday, Hisashi Mita, arrived at 8:10 A.M., to pick me up. There was a slight drizzle, but we set off, just the same. A fast train to Nara brought us there by 9:35, and our walk began. The weather gradually cleared.

The first phenomenon of the day was Nara's May Day parade: not very different in appearance from what I had seen before in New York— except, of course, a good deal smaller. "We have these in America too," I said. "But here," said Hisashi, "I think it is a little different. There is an anti-American side to it." "There's an anti-American side to May Day parades in America too," I said.

We talked a bit about these things during the course of the day. Among the questions that came up were:

1. American mistreatment of the negro (same theme as in India)
2. Capitalism vs. the worker (I pointed out—as I had in India—that our bricklayers get $28 per day or more: here—as in India—it is about $1.00, and $1.00 is high.)

Hisashi told me also that the students discuss in English the problem of Science vs. Religion (taking over, I suggested, a Western problem, which does not properly concern the Orient, since God is not the final term of Oriental religious thinking).

Our first stop was at the Sarusawa Pond, across which the Kōfukuji's Five-Storied Pagoda could be seen, reflected in the water. Hisashi pointed out the tree associated with the death of some legendary court lady of the past. We next walked pleasantly through the Deer Park to the Shintō Kasuga Shrine, where there was a ceremony of some kind in progress. This shrine was first constructed in A.D. 768 and has since been reconstructed many times—formerly every twenty years. All along the ways to it, and all around it, are stone lanterns, with the names of their donors inscribed on them—also, a few new lanterns of wood, with the names of department stores inscribed!* I stood a while and watched the very formal ceremonial: seven priests and two musicians—their elegant black lacquer shoes on the ground at the side of the temple area. And in another area, a sort of ve-

---

* *Guide to Japan,* pp. 724–5.

randa, were three women, sitting in absolute silence. Prayers were recited; staffs bearing paper slips (like leaves) were placed, regularly spaced, before the altar, various priests did various things, and the whole suggested in its decorum what I have seen of Noh.

Our third visit was to the Shin'yakushiji Temple (A.D. 747), which contains a large, wooden, seated image, surrounded by eleven (formerly twelve) "kings," and an eleven-faced Kannon.* And our fourth visit was to the great Tōdaiji Temple, which contains the vast Daibutsu, an image of Vairocana (Birushana-butsu), who is regarded by the Kegon sect as the spiritual body of Śākyamuni).[67] The image weighs 452 tons, is 53 feet 6 inches high, sits in the preaching *mudrā* (*seppō-in*),[68] with the right hand in the fear-not posture (*semui-in*) and the left in that granting boons (*yogan-in*). The image was com-menced in 743 and finished in 749. It is flanked by gold-covered images

Daibutsu, the Mahāvairocana Buddha, at the Tōdaiji Temple, Nara

of Kannon (Nyoirin Kannon = Cintāmaṇi Avalokiteśvara),[69] on the right, and Kokūzō (Ākāśagharba),[70] on the left.** A number of little families were sending their children through the "lucky hole" in one of the pillars of the temple, and there was a great deal of picture taking going on.

The whole temple area was decorated with banners for the Ten Thousand Lights Festival, which is to take place tonight and the two nights following. This ceremony is celebrated at this temple only once in a hun-dred years—and it is a wonderful chance that today is the day. The time is to be from 7:00 to 9:30 P.M.

---

*   *Guide to Japan,* p. 733.
** *Guide to Japan,* pp. 727–30.

Our fifth visit (last of the morning) was to the Kaidan-in. This is a large room filled with the platform of a single shrine. One can mount the platform and walk around it. The Four Kings are at the four corners, and within the central pagoda sit two small Buddha figures, that to the observer's left in the meditation posture, and the other in the posture of teaching: they are said to be Śākyamuni and Tahō Nyorai, though which is which, and who the latter is, I do not know.*

We stopped for lunch in a little outdoor restaurant, where we had tea, something called *oyako-donburi* (a bowl of rice mixed with chicken, boiled onion, and egg), and a bit of *takuan* (salt-marinated turnip slices). Then our sightseeing was resumed.

The temple bell at the Tōdaiji Temple, Nara

Our sixth visit of the day (first of the afternoon) was to the belfry, wherein there hangs one of the largest bronze bells in Japan (cast A.D. 752, broken 989, recast ca. 1239).† Visit seven was to the Sangatsu-dō, which

---

* *Guide to Japan,* p. 730.
† *Guide to Japan,* p. 731.

contains a great Kannon* and fourteen other statues, and visit eight was to the Nigatsu-dō.†

Visit nine was one of the great events of the day, namely, to the Shōsōin Treasure House—which is within a large, walled area, opened to the Japanese only once a year, but to foreign visitors by special permission. Hisashi managed to induce the very gentlemanly custodian to let us in. The area contained, as its main glory, the great and curious treasure house itself—a structure like a very large and handsome log cabin, raised on mighty stilts—of Japanese cypress and dating from the eighth century. Within this are kept many works of art and craft from the Tempyō period (A.D. 710–94), which the custodian showed me in photographs (eighteen volumes), when we had returned to the gate building. Also in this area is a smaller building in the same log-cabin style, but square, containing a complete set of the Buddhist scriptures, another large building enclosed in concrete and resembling in proportions the main treasury, and a small but beautiful wooden sanctuary. We spent about an hour and a half looking at pictures of the treasures after we had viewed the buildings: largely textiles of unique designs.

We had walked, I should say, somewhere between ten and fifteen miles and were beginning to be tired. We went to the elegant Nara Hotel for dinner, and then returned by cab to the Tōdaiji Temple for the great Ten Thousand Lights Festival (Mantō-e).[71]

The image and temple interior were extremely impressive in the dim light, illuminated by a multitude of flickering wicks placed all around the great platform. There took place a preliminary ceremony of worship, conducted by some fourteen or fifteen priests, who ascended the platform and chanted from some *sūtra*. Great offering stacks of rice cakes and oranges were very neatly arranged before the prodigious image. There were not many people present and I had a good position from which to view this event. The great Buddha could easily be experienced as the partially realized presentiment of supreme consciousness looming through the darkness beyond the comparatively bright foreground of the ceremony and the chant. The character and function of ritualistic worship as an assistance and guide to meditation was evident in an exceptionally strong way in this rite.

---

* *Guide to Japan*, p. 732.
† *Guide to Japan*, p. 731.

The vast enclosure between the temple and the great gate was illuminated by six braziers placed around the dance platform that had been built in front of the large, ancient, bronze lantern just in front of the temple entrance. Two great bronze drums, six feet in diameter, were at either side of the platform, and stage left was a pavilion in which the musicians sat: stage right was another pavilion that remained empty. The music: about five flutes, two small drums, two or three *shō*,[72] and two or three very short, reedy musettes. The costumes of the dancers and of the men who beat the big bronze drums were those of Japanese warriors of the period antedating that of the samurai.[73]

The night performance commenced at 7:00 P.M. with the sound of a deep bell, from somewhere in the distance. Then, to the music of one flute and the great drum, stage left, a single, male dancer appeared with a spear. Very slowly he ascended to the platform, and executed a stately dance. Next, to the same music, but the drum stage right, another man executed the same dance. Next to the music of flutes, *shō*, bells, and the drum stage left, four men danced. Then again, but to the drum stage right, a dance of four. The fifth dance (drum stage left) was performed by a single dancer wearing a golden animal mask and the same warrior costume. It was a long dance, one of its passages being performed in silence. Two flutes and two small drums were played. And the last dance, to the same sort of music, was performed by two dancers wearing black human masks. The evening concluded with an orchestral selection accompanied by the two great drums.

The dances consisted largely of stately turning strides, from straight to bent knees, silent stamps, great slow arm swings, knee bends with occasional spring jumps (vertical) and once or twice, genuflections to the floor.

At 9:30, we caught a cab to the station. Got to bed at about eleven.

Monday, May 2   Kyoto

A rather quiet day, after the great Nara visit of May 1. Actually, I should have gone back to Nara for the second night of the three-night festival, but I felt that I had to work hard on my Japanese, to pick up on my class; furthermore, the weather was a bit overcast and dull. Morning, nine to twelve, at the Japanese school. Lunch in a little cake shop, and all afternoon and evening on my Japanese. Dinner in Prunier's Pontochō Grill: not as bad as the other Prunier restaurant, but too expensive.

CHAPTER 4

An American Buddhist in Kyoto

Tuesday, May 3

Father Moss, my schoolmate, was to be absent today, so it was arranged that I should take my classes in the afternoon, with a young American housewife who is at lesson six. I spent the morning studying, and at one went to the school.

"Is your husband in the government service?" I asked.

"No," said the young woman, "he is with the University Field Service."*

I confessed that I knew nothing of the group, and it was explained that it was a new organization that had fourteen or fifteen men in the field making surveys and sending in reports—in Japan, India, etc.

"Your husband, then, speaks Japanese?" I said.

"Well . . . ," she parried, "a little."

So here it is again!74

At 3:00 P.M. a new phase of my visit to Japan commenced, when I went to the Nishi Honganji Temple compound to pay a visit to a young man of about thirty-three whose name had been suggested to me by Jacob Feuerring

---

* Or something like that.

in New York. I entered the compound by the Ōmiya Gate, turned to the left, and came to the back entrance of a small Japanese house. Two Japanese bowed to greet me when I said "Eidmann-san?" and I doffed my shoes to enter. I was conducted through the house and shown into a pleasant room opening onto a lovely garden where there sat on the floor, with his legs out flat beneath a low Japanese table, a paralyzed young man, who greeted me easily and bade me sit down on the cushion at his right. Then commenced a highly interesting, but rather demanding, monologue that lasted until about 7:30 P.M. It was punctuated by the visit of a tall young man, named Fillmore, who is in the army (but wearing civilian clothes) and hopes to remain in Japan to enter Tokyo University. He was just back from Tokyo, where he had been attending to the problem of his papers.

"Did anything happen May Day?" Eidmann asked.

Fillmore smiled. "No," he said. "But they expected something to happen. They were convinced that there was going to be some kind of Communist disturbance and had machine guns planted all around the camp. The colonel, on the emperor's birthday, said, 'No Communists? What are all those flags with the red ball?' They were the Japanese flags hung out for the holiday."

At about six a nice Japanese dinner was served by Eidmann's housekeeper and shared by a young Japanese who had been introduced to me as Eidmann's secretary and is a Shinshū priest. There is also a Korean houseboy, likewise a student of Shinshū.

Shortly after dinner the secretary and Eidmann staged an absolutely formal tea ceremony for my benefit, and I heard a great deal about the mysteries of tea. Whipped tea had been served to me also at the time of my arrival.

The first major event, after my arrival and the preliminaries of becoming acquainted, was a tour of the large temple compound, with Eidmann in his wheelchair being pushed by the secretary, and me walking alongside.

I learned that the Nishi Honganji Temple is one of the most important and influential Buddhist institutions in Japan.* †

---

* See *Guide to Japan,* pp. 146–47.

† Briefly summarizing the historical situation:

    A.D. 552—Buddhism enters Japan, when the King of Kudara (Paekche), in Korea, presents *sūtras* and images of Buddha to the Imperial Court of Japan. These are followed by priests and nuns, temple architects and image carvers.

Eidmann told me during the course of our tour of the temple compound that the Honganji Temple (which is the great center of the Shinshū)

A.D. 592–628—Prince Shōtoku makes Buddhism the religion of the Court, issues a code, and organizes the national administration on the basis of Buddhist teachings, builds temples and monasteries, charity hospitals, orphanages, and homes of refuge for the widowed and the aged.

A.D. 645–794—Nara period: development of "the Six Sects of the Southern Capital (Nara): Sanron, Jōjitsu, and Kusha, now extinct; and Ritsu, Hossō, and Kegon.

Many commentaries on the *sūtras* were composed. The main character of the religion is still that of the Chinese *Mahāyāna* (Daijō Bukkyō), the basic principle being faith in the Three Treasures (*ratnatraya,* i.e. the oneness of the Perfect Person (Buddha), the Truth (*Dharma*), and the Community (*Saṅgha*). This principle was demonstrated artistically in ceremonies and supported by a system of philosophy.

A.D. 794–1185—Heian period: a strong national bent is given to the imported religion, chiefly by the application of the doctrine of Honjisuijaku, according to which the Shintō deities are regarded as various manifestations of Buddhas and Bodhisattvas. The two great teachers were:

Saichō (Dengyō Daishi, 767–822), founder of Tendai; and Kūkai (Kōbō Daishi, 774–835), founder of Shingon.

The two great centers from which these doctrines then emanated were, for Tendai, Mt. Hiei, northeast of Kyoto, and for Shingon, Mt. Kōya, south of Nara.

Tendai is described as being based on "pantheistic realism," and Shingon as presenting "an esoteric philosophy" with "a complex symbolism."

A.D. 1185–1392—Kamakura period: four new sects arise for the purification of Buddhism, which has become "secularized and corrupt":

Zen, founded by Eisai (1141–1215) and Dōgen (1200–53)

Jōdo, founded by Hōnen (1133–1212)

Shinshū, founded by Shinran (1173–1262)

Hokke, founded by Nichiren (1222–82)

Jōdo and Shinshū are essentially one in doctrine, both teaching that the only way to salvation lies in absolute trust in the all-saving power of Amitābha Buddha, a doctrine which is generally styled "salvation through the absolute faith in another's power" (*tariki-hongan*). The two sects, however, have some important differences. While the Jōdo sect lays emphasis on repetition of the formula *Namu Amida-butsu,* or "Glory to Amida Buddha..." the Shinshū sect regards faith in Amida Buddha as the all sufficient and only essential thing, the repetition of the formula being considered merely an expression of a thankful heart. Another important difference is that the Shinshū sect discards the principle of celibacy of the clergy, together with all ascetic practices. Further more, the Shinshū sect is more logical in its observances. Its adherents believe in Amida Buddha alone, and although they worship before the founder's image as the revealer of the Amida doctrine, the sect has discarded all other images.

has never capitulated to the efforts of the Court to reduce Buddhism to a nationalistic, patriotic, political tool. When, during the last war, the government issued a statement that those who died in the service of their country would become, if they were Shintōists, Shintō gods, and, if Buddhists, Buddhas, the Honganji was the only Buddhist group that had the courage to publish a counterstatement to the effect that dying for Japan had nothing to do with Buddhahood: those spiritually ready to become Buddhas would become so; others, however, might go to hell. The Honganji, indeed, has always been regarded with suspicion by the government.[*]

According to Eidmann, between Nishi Honganji and Higashi Honganji there is no rivalry or contention. They are two institutions representing the same principles and sect.

During the course of our tour of the Nishi Honganji Temple I was shown two Noh theaters and a beautiful garden.

About Noh: it appears that the origins of Noh are closely associated with the Honganji (there is another Noh theater, I read, in the Higashi Honganji Temple).[†] In one of the two Noh theaters in the Nishi Honganji there is an annual performance in which representatives of all the schools of Noh participate. (The event this year will be on May 21. Eidmann will get me a ticket.) The other Noh theater in this temple is the oldest Noh theater in Japan. Only members of the temple family, royal family, etc.,

---

[*] As we read: "The new sect passed through many vicissitudes and under persecution was compelled to shift its headquarters many times. At Ishiyama, Osaka, its temple became a powerful stronghold, which successfully resisted a siege by Oda Nobunaga (1534–82), lasting for eleven years. But it was again compelled to seek a resting-place in Kii Province, and still another in Osaka. Ten years later, it became permanently settled, by favor of Toyotomi Hideyoshi, at the present site in Kyoto. In 1602 Tokugawa Ieyasu, fearing the growing power of the sect, sought to weaken it by giving a former abbot permission to found another branch of the sect. This younger branch is known as the Higashi Honganji Temple from the location of its chief temple.

"In 1617 the buildings of the Nishi Honganji were destroyed by fire, but they were soon restored, a building being added by transference from the site of Hideyoshi's famous Juraku Museum. This new building is called Hiunkaku, and is now protected as a 'National Treasure.' Again in 1636 another building was added.

"It may be noted that the Nishi Honganji Temple has 9,837 local temples, and more than six million adherents" (*Guide to Japan*, p. 695).

[†] *Guide to Japan*, p. 694.

can attend the performances here presented. Seeing these outdoor Noh theaters let me know the reason for the form of the modern Noh stage.[75]

Outdoor Noh

About gardens: the plans of the garden architect cannot be realized in one generation. They are consulted for decades; the branches of the trees are bent and trained to follow the designated forms. Every stone is considered. The temple garden that I saw was somewhat marred by the removal of one background building at the time of the war and collapse of two trees at the time of a big wind some two or three years later. But new trees have been planted and in another few decades the garden will be back in trim.

The buildings that we visited included many wonders. The two main temple halls were much like the main hall of the Higashi Honganji that I had seen on the sightseeing tour. There were also a number of court rooms of the shōgun, etc., with a "Nightingale Floor"[76] and squeaking door approaches to protect the shōgun against a sneak attack. The rooms had screenlike paintings on gold backgrounds: one charming room of sparrows, another of waves. On the outer doors were great tigers (from stuffed models) and an eagle—quite majestic. The visit, with Eidmann in his wheelchair telling the stories, gave me a strong sense of the period—and of the crucial importance of this temple in the history of Japan.

Eidmann talked of the influence of Buddhism, and particularly of the Honganji Temple, in America. It is estimated that there are about 450,000 Buddhists in the United States. There are Honganji temples in a number of American cities (including New York), and it is planned ultimately to have missions in every state. The Nisei form a kind of core, but they are by no means an overwhelming majority.

Eidmann's presence in the Honganji compound (invited by the abbot) is connected, I suspect, with the interest in America. He has just gained an M.A. from Kyoto University with a translation of some Shinshū text and is very busy on translations, articles, hymns, etc. He plans to proceed, however, after another four or five years in Japan, to Siam, then Burma, and finally India, to study the history and present state of Buddhism in the Orient.

The tea ceremonial was an extraordinarily interesting little affair, conducted with perfect and absolute decorum by Eidmann's secretary in full regalia, according to the rules of the Yabu-no-uchi school. (The other two chief schools today are the Ura-senke and the Omote-senke.) The manner of movement and posture of the tea master were very much like those of the Noh—indeed, this whole thing is closing into one great picture. Eidmann told me what I was to do when my time came to do things, and the tea master performed without a hitch, as though his guest were the mikado.

I asked Eidmann about the relationship of tea to Zen, and he was inclined to think that tea, originally, was independent of Zen, but that Zen took it over and read into it a sense that had not been there before. The prodigious decorum of tea is perhaps to be attributed as much to the aristocratic decorum of the classes that fostered it as to the spirit of ritual. Today, tea is a kind of social hobby—excellent for social climbing and with all kinds of fancy phases. One can tell immediately in what tea school a person has been trained: every detail of posture and gesture is regulated, with the very slightest differences as hallmarks. And all the implements used are variously shaped (very slightly differing) according to the school.*

---

* The history of tea in Japan is given as follows in the *Guide to Japan,* pp. 236–40:

A.D. 645–794—Nara Period. The drinking of tea was already known in Japan during the reign of the Emperor Shōmu (A.D. 729), who was said to have invited one hundred Buddhist monks to the Imperial Palace to have tea. The leaves were probably imported into Japan by the ambassadors to the Tang Court and prepared in the way then in fashion.

A.D. 794–1185—Heian Period. In 805 a priest named Saichō brought back some seeds from China, where he had stayed for studies for some years, and planted them on Mt. Hiei, near Kyoto. Many tea gardens are mentioned in literature in the succeeding centuries, as well as the delight of the aristocracy and priesthood in the beverage.

A.D. 1185–1392—Kamakura Period.

Eidmann showed me his certificate of admission to, and certificate of graduation from the tea school. He told me also that in Japan a young lady, before she can hope to get married, must have at least two of the four following certificates: tea, flower arrangement, music, sewing—or, occasionally, she can substitute for one, calligraphy.

Discussing the contemporary scene, Eidmann said, "I hate to see the United States tying its defense to Japan. It seems to me, if we want to blow up the Communist world, the best thing we could do would be to give them the J-Bomb."77 The problem: Japanese politics is run, not by or for principles and ideals, but in terms of loyalties and obligations. One votes for and supports those to whom one thinks one is obligated. When such a focal figure dies or disappears from the political scene, people turn to their

---

A.D. 1392–1573—Muromachi Period. The tea plant, a native of southern China, was known from very early times to Chinese medicine, and was highly prized for possessing the virtues of relieving fatigue, delighting the soul, strengthening the will, and repairing the eyesight. Taoists considered it an important ingredient of the elixir of immortality and Buddhists used it extensively to prevent drowsiness during their long hours of meditation. *Among the Buddhists, the southern Zen sect, which incorporated so many of the Taoist doctrines in their belief, formulated an elaborate ritual of tea.* The monks gathered before the image of Bodhidharma and drank tea out of a single bowl with the profound formality of a holy sacrament. *It was this Zen ritual which finally developed into the ceremonial tea of Japan in the 15th century.* By the 15th century, under the patronage of Yoshimasa of the Ashikaga Shōgunate, the tea ceremony had been fully constituted and made into an independent and secular performance. Tea became a means by which purity and refinement could be worshipped.

The Tea House (*suki-ya*) to accomodate not more than five persons, consists of: a service room (*mizu-ya*), where the tea utensils are washed and arranged before being brought in; a waiting room (*yoritsuki*), in which the guests wait until they receive the summons to enter the tea-room; a garden path (*roji*), which connects the yoritsuki with the tea-room; and the tea-room proper (*cha-shitsu*), which is generally nine feet square, with a special entrance for the host and another for the guests, the latter (*nijiriguchi*) being so small that they have to creep in. The room takes four and a half mats (*tatami*), the half mat filling the space in the center of the room, and at one corner of this half mat a square hearth is fitted into the floor, so as to form a brazier, on which is placed an iron kettle. By the hearth sits the host.

The utensils consist of the tea-bowl (*cha-wan*), tea-caddy (*cha-ire*), bamboo tea-whisk (*cha-sen*), bamboo spoon (*cha-shaku*), etc. The full ceremony takes about two hours. (For procedure, see *Guide*, pp. 238–40.)

next loyalty or obligation. Also, when the U.S. forced universal suffrage on Japan it opened the political machine to a multitude without any specific loyalties or obligations vis-à-vis the figures running for election. The behavior of this mass at election time is a large X quantity, subject to the most whimsical motivation. There is little chance that a pattern of consistent loyalty to any ideal or system of political ideals could be made to steady them effectively. Americans, thinking of Japanese politics in such terms as we can properly apply to our own, are completely out of touch with the hidden facts of the situation. Indeed, the Japanese themselves sometimes think that their loyalty is to the ideals of which they speak and write.

Wednesday, May 4

Studied Japanese in the morning. Class in the afternoon, one to three; then back to the hotel, to write letters and diary.

At 6:30 Ellen Psaty arrived, in a chipper mood, and we went to an elegant Japanese restaurant, named Tsuruya, for dinner. Our room opened onto a lovely garden, there was a bright three-quarter moon, and in a large banquet room at an angle to ours we could see a company of gents with the geisha girls entertaining: first, the samisen and dances; then, by magic, the whole company of gents being lured into letting down on their dignity and dancing too. There was one moment when the whole room was filled with gracefully capering Japanese gentlemen and appreciatively helpful geishas.

Ellen said: only the geishas can make them relax. They never let go at any other time. (The tension of the Japanese formality accounts, I believe, for the tendency of Japanese to weep when emotionally stirred. They weep, apparently, very easily. It requires also, I think, that there should be this ancient art of the geishas, to afford the safety valve—since the relationship to the wife is largely formal and definitely part of the public pattern.)

Ellen spoke of her researches into the life of a certain Japanese artist whose children, legitimate and illegitimate, are still alive. The principle that she had found operating here, as in everything else in Japan, is that of the *hidden motivator*. In Japanese business, in Japanese politics, in Japanese life, there is always the official front and front personage. The heads of

Japanese firms are chosen for their family connections, names, etc., and they know precisely what their role is and do not try (as do Americans elected or appointed for such reasons) to become the actual instead of apparent directors. The actual director (the politician behind the man behind the shōgun) is always deep out of sight, and must be diligently searched for to be found.

Thursday, May 5

Our seventeenth wedding anniversary. Telegram to Jean in the morning. Also, in Japan, Children's Day and a national holiday.

At 9:15 A.M. went to Eidmann's, and at 11:30 P.M., returned home: meanwhile, fourteen hours of almost continuous talk from my young master—and a long walk, with several interesting stops. We set off after an elegant Japanese lunch and went by taxi to the area of the Chion-in Temple—a prodigious institution of the Jōdo sect. This sect has six branches, and the Chion-in is the head temple of the most flourishing.* This temple is one of the largest in Japan and covers an area of about thirty acres. Some of the buildings date back to A.D. 1633–39.† We strolled past the great *sammon* (two-storied gate), paused before a stone covering a spot where a meteor fell, and paused for a delicious drink of *amazake*[78] at a little garden, and went on for a visit to a convent of Jōdo nuns, where Eidmann is to lecture in a couple of days.

The younger nuns, with their heads completely shaved and uncovered, and wearing a boyish looking type of service jumper, looked to me at first like boys: but Eidmann assured me that they were older than they seemed to be. This convent is a school, where they come to study. They may leave the order at any time they please, but seldom do; and there are about thirty at a time in this convent. In all, apparently, there are about a thousand Jōdo nuns—devoted primarily to the recitation of the *Namu Amida-butsu*. We were greeted by two older nuns—cute little darlings in sturdy black kimonos, with grey, and then white, under-kimonos (visible at the neck), who talked attentively and with typical Japanese politeness with Eidmann

---

* *Guide to Japan*, p. 148.
† *Guide to Japan*, p. 700.

and had their young nuns serve us whipped tea and cakes. When we departed they accompanied us to the road and bowed us away.

Our path took us, next, down the hill and across the river to the Pontochō, where there was a great jam of people, just getting out of the Odori. Eidmann explained the geisha institution. The Japanese never entertain in their homes. (In contrast to India.) Instead, the head of the family has a geisha house where he regularly entertains. One is introduced to such a house by a friend; one is billed by the month; and the function of the house is to take care of one's catering problems. The geishas of Kyoto are today the most honored in Japan. There are three geisha sections: Gion, Pontochō, and Shimabara.

We paused, to look at the river and take a brief rest, then went to a shop specializing in tea paraphernalia, where Eidmann made a few purchases and I was shown the different forms of the utensils of the three chief schools. We stopped for "*sofuto aisukureemu*" (soft ice cream) at a crowded restaurant where Eidmann's secretary joined us and the young man who had been pushing the wheelchair took his leave; and then we resumed our walk.

Visits to a couple of bookstores revealed the fact that a number of new Russian volumes, in Russian, as well as Russian magazines, are on display, whereas the English books for sale (except in the department store Maruzen) are largely secondhand. Problem: why the dearth of books in English? Expense? Can't be it; because in India there were lots of paperbacks, while here I haven't seen any. Eidmann tells me that Maruzen has an import monopoly of some kind. Apparently, our booksellers just haven't made a good connection here.

The remainder of the walk consisted largely of visits to little shops, with a pause at a Chinese restaurant for dinner; then a walk through the Shimabara geisha section (less high-class than the others: the geishas were actually sitting outside of their houses, at the doors), and back to the Nishi Honganji. They got me an excellent masseur to massage my right ankle and leg, which are still sore from the Angkor sprain and get a bit tied up from the pressure of the Ace bandage during a long walk (today, about six hours, not counting pauses). I returned to my hotel about 11:15 P.M.

Among the matters discussed during the day were the following:

The development of a Honganji literature and service in English.

According to Eidmann, the service now in use—which is what I experienced in Tokyo—was developed by a man named Ford who is now living in Honolulu. (Must try to meet him on my way home.) He was an Anglican clergyman before becoming a Buddhist, and modeled the service that he developed on the Anglican pattern. Eidmann is himself at work, now, trying to improve the situation—culling appropriate Buddhist hymns from the old collections, finding appropriate tunes, etc. The problem of the Honganji sponsorship of publications in English is also a serious one—which he is helping the abbot (who is a member of the great Ohtani family and a cousin of the emperor) to solve.

The Shinshū attitude toward monasticism was explained by Eidmann as a consequence of the conviction that the valid succession had been broken and that there could be no true *arhats*[79] in Japan. Under such circumstances the monastic life could not conduce to its proper end. At this point I was moved to open my eyes and exclaim, "My God!" but I refrained. Implied here is a belief in the spiritual effect of an apostolic succession; a belief that in modern Japan Buddhism cannot conduce to its proper end; and that monasticism is the supreme form of life. I must ask about this some more. At this point, it seems to me, a great chasm begins to yawn between what I should have thought was the true sense of the doctrine and the ecclesiastic interpretation of the problem of enlightenment.

Eidmann declares that *arhats* do exist in Burma; that they have been identified by examination and that monasticism is therefore validated in Burma. In Thailand too there are probably *arhats*. In Ceylon there are none.

The Hīnayāna in Burma was a twelfth- or thirteenth-century reaction against the excesses of the Tantric Mahāyāna of the centuries immediately preceding. In Ceylon, all the Mahāyāna texts were burned.

The relationship of Zen to Buddhism is not completely clear. There is a possibility that Bodhidharma was not a Buddhist at all, but a Vedantist (Bodhidharma's date, which I think was A.D. 527, is earlier, however, than the date of Śankara, I believe; for was not the latter circa A.D. 800?).[80] Furthermore, the chief development of Zen was Chinese: all of the sages whom Suzuki cites were Chinese.[81] Zen, as described by Suzuki at least, is hardly Japanese. Its closest affinities would seem to be Taoism. (Indeed Lao-tzu's *Tao-te Ching* is a fundamental text for the understanding of all so-called Buddhist philosophy in Japan.[82])

The fundamental principle of Zen would seem to be: "Do what you have to do, perfectly, and without reservations."

Paradoxically, however, there are Zen monasteries and Zen monastic disciplines. Moreover, Zen lore and life is full of what would seem to us to be superstitious practices: amulets, etc. Zen pays respect to all the Buddhas and Bodhisattvas.

Zen's relationship to tea has been noted above.[83] The relationship to painting is similar: a lay tradition is taken over and reinterpreted, and the tradition then again becomes a lay tradition serving nonreligious ends.

[T]he Zen or Contemplative sect... "seeks salvation by meditating and divine emptiness." Its doctrines may be summed up in the following injunction: "Look carefully within and there you will find the Buddha!" This sect found adherents among the powerful leaders and samurai of the Shōgun's government at Kamakura, owing to the fact that in Zen each believer must work out his own salvation by austere discipline, bodily and mental, and thus develop the measure of will-power and self-control needed by a true samurai. We see a marked development of this in Bushidō,[84] which was greatly influenced by Zen principles.*

Some rather shocking information came out about the anti-Buddhist, pro-Christian activity and propaganda of the Occupation:

Temple landholdings were confiscated, as a part of the general land reform. All of the temples except the Honganji are dependent on land rents; as a consequence, many are now in very critical financial straits. This accounts somewhat for the conspicuous decline of the other sects and prosperity of the Shinshū since the war.

It was required of every religious institution that, like the Christian churches, it should have a congregation to become legally recognized as a corporate body; and without this recognition there could be no tax exemption. Many Buddhist temples, on the other hand, do not have and never were supposed to have, congregations in the Protestant Christian sense.

MacArthur patronized a vast distribution of Bibles (one finds them, indeed, in many Japanese hotel rooms), contributing a letter over his own signature that only the Christian can be truly democratic.

---

* *Guide to Japan*, p. 146.

One can readily understand from this latter point why there is, and must inevitably be, a very strong anti-American, and even pro-Communist tendency among Buddhists. One-third of the Ceylonese clergy is Marxist, and the Southeast Asians are tending to favor Russia against the West, not so much because Russia is anti-Democratic as because Russia is anti-Christian.

One should perhaps note in this connection that the leaders whom we are supporting in the Orient are predominantly Christian: e.g. Chiang Kai-shek in China, Romulo in the Philippines, and Diem in French Indochina. What Rhee is, I don't know; but I shouldn't be surprised...[85]

Eidmann feels that the Buddhists of Asia (Ceylon, Burma, Thailand, for example) will never accept India as the leader of Asia. Here Nehru & Co. are doomed to disappointment. He feels also, however, that there is such a strong anti-Western tide that Japan, which is regarded as the most Westernized of the Asian powers, will not be accepted as the leader either. This would seem to leave China in a pretty good spot.

An interesting surprise turned up when I asked Eidmann why he was so greatly interested in Brazil and Portuguese. He replied that of the five chief Portuguese writers of the past century, two were Buddhists and wrote from Japan, namely, Antero de Quental (a poet) and Wenceslau de Morais (1854–1929, a writer of prose). He also pointed out to me that a work written in Portuguese on the subject of Indian medicine was one of the important contributions to the progress of European medicine in the sixteenth century, namely *Coloquios dos simples e drogas he cousas medicinais da India* (Goa, 1563).

We talked a bit of the Fulbright and Foundation situation and it was his opinion (as it was also Ellen Psaty's) that these grantees have cut a rather poor figure in Japan (as I should say they have in India too.) They don't seem to know anything about the material or culture and certainly nothing about the language. "The Ford people seem to be a cut above the Fulbright," was his opinion.

Finally, a motif that I forgot to record for yesterday's talk with Ellen: "The Japanese male and the American female," she said, "are the spoiled children of the world—and spoiled children aren't nice."

Friday, May 6

Awakened at 4:30 A.M. by a knock at my door—and an anniversary telegram from Jean (time problem: Japan, New York!) Back to sleep and up at 7:00 A.M. Spent the morning writing up my diary and at 12:30 went to Eidmann's again, this time to see an annual Shintō procession, which stops for breath at the Nishi Honganji gate. The procession is the passage of the fox-god Inari from his city residence to his country residence.*

---

* [See *Guide,* pp. 142–45.]

The chief shrines are in Uji and Yamada—about three hours ride from Kyoto: to be visited at some later date.

Shintō in its early stages taught the innate goodness of the human heart. *Follow the genuine impulses of your heart,* was the essence of its ethical teaching. Its pantheon of "eight million gods," with the Sun Goddess, Amaterasu-Ōmikami (Great-Heaven-Shining-Goddess) at its head (she is enshrined in the Naikū, or Inner Shrine, of the Daijingū Shrines at Uji-Yamada), embraces many nature gods and goddesses of the sea, rivers, winds, fire and mountains and many deified persons.

Under the influence of Confucianism, which came to Japan along with Buddhism in the middle of the 6th century (which marked the end of the Archaic period, and the opening of the Asuka Period: A.D. 552–645), the conception of *loyalty or filial piety* was introduced to the Japanese ethical code.

And *Buddhism* had an overwhelming influence upon Shintō after its introduction—culminating in the creation of the *Double Aspect Shintō* (*Ryōbu*). The theory is that the Buddhist pantheon in general represents the indestructible parts of the gods, while the deities in the Shintō pantheon are their partial appearances or incarnations. The real entity, or prime noumenon, is called the *Honji,* the original, and the manifestation, the *Suijaku.* In this combination every god (*Kami*) is regarded as a manifestation of a certain Buddhist deity. This state of things lasted for well nigh a thousand years.

Muromachi Period (1392–1573), Momoyama Period (1573–1615):

In the fifteenth century further progress was made in the systematization of Shintō theology. The name of Ichijō Kanera (1402–81) is prominent in this connection. Shintō, according to Kanera, teaches the existence of many deities, but metaphysically speaking they are one, because each deity is but a manifestation of the universal soul in a particular aspect of its activity and all the gods are one in spirit and entity, especially in the virtue of veracity.

Edo Period (1615–1868):

In the course of the eighteenth century Shintō entered a new path and prepared for another revival. All the earlier Shintō theorists had depended much upon either Buddhism or Confucianism in interpreting Shintō ideas; now the time became ripe for *purging the alien elements to a certain degree and restoring early Shintō by means of historical scholarship.* This was made possible by the *philological studies of the ancient records compiled in the eighth century.* The greatest of the philologists and the pioneer of "Pure Shintō" was

Appropriately, during the course of the Shintō procession that I went to the Honganji gate to see, a limousine with bride and groom, as well as parents, pulled to a stop, to wait for the street to clear. A number of little women with children on their backs spotted the bride within (a very serious little thing, dressed as a geisha) and came over to peer.

The procession was rather amusing. In the vanguard were two white and green trees carried on litters by many men: these represented the Sacred Tree of the Amaterasu myth: There followed various sorts of men in costume and finally three large, cloth-enclosed tabernacles on immense beams, carried by a great lot of rather hilarious fellows. Many had a bit more sake in them than they could handle, and I noticed as I went back by streetcar to my hotel that the path of the god was pretty well strewn with unconscious devotees.

Motoori Norinaga (1730–1801). His contention was that Shintō, when purged of all foreign accretions and influences, represented the pure, and therefore the best, inheritance of humanity from the divine ages.

Another aspect of the revival of Shintō was *the appearance of popular teachers in the first half of the nineteenth century.* Their followers today make up the so-called Shintō sects. There are two forms of Shintō:

1) *Jinsha Shintō* (Shrine Shintō), also known (up to 1945) as "National Shintō Faith," "State Shintō," and "Official Cult." The *jinsha* (shrines) belonging to this form of Shintō were maintained at the expense of the central or prefectural governments, city, town or village authorities. With the promulgation of the Religion Corporation Ordinance of December 1945, however, official support of these shrines was abolished, and all the *jinsha* are now maintained chiefly by their respective believers. As of December 1949 there were 87,802 *jinsha* belonging to this National form of Shintō.

2) Sectarian or Denominated Shintō, consisting of about 160 sects. Some of the oldest of these are Fusō-Kyō, Izumo Taisha-Kyō, Konkō-Kyō, Kurozumi-Kyō, Misogi-Kyō, Mitake-Kyō, Shintō Tai-Kyō, Shinri-Kyō, Shinshū-Kyō, Shintō Jikkō-Kyō, Shintō Shūsei-Kyō, Taisei-Kyō, and Tenri-Kyō. [I must hunt for some explanation of these.]

Worship in Shintō consists of obeisances, offerings, and prayers. Obeisance takes the form of a humble bow which lasts for a minute or two. The *offerings* presented before the altar are primarily food and drink. Formerly cloth was offered, but eventually *a symbolic offering known as gohei* or *nusa* came into use, consisting of strips of paper which represent lengths of cloth. These symbolic offerings are attached to a wand or twig of the evergreen *sakaki* tree and placed before the altar. [This is what I saw at the Shintō shrine in Nara.] The presentation of offerings regularly follows the formal *norito prayers,* which

When I arrived at Eidmann's I found a Japanese gentleman present, who was introduced to me as Professor Kasugai.[86] Eidmann made an appointment for me for tomorrow, to be shown through the great Chion-in Temple (which we merely skirted yesterday) by Professor Kasugai. The conversation, first with Kasugai and then with Eidmann alone (for Kasugai left us after we had seen the Shintō procession), made, among others, the following points:

The Buddhist iconography of India is extremely uncertain. It is even possible that there is not a single image that can be identified with absolute certainty. The Hindus, who know very little about the subject, and the Europeans, who know little more, have been very glib with their identifications; but when one compares the Japanese Buddhist iconography with that of Ajaṇṭā, etc., the sense of certainty fades. For example, at Ajaṇṭā one sees continually three figures: a Buddha seated in the center with deer below his pedestal, and with a Bodhisattva at either hand, one with a Buddha figure as his crest jewel and the other with a *stūpa*. These have been

---

appeal to the deity by virtue of vivid expression of address. *Great stress is laid on the formality of the prayers rather than their contents.* To make them impressive the words were originally the most solemn that Japanese possessed. *Norito* prayers are uttered not only in front of the shrine altar, but also within a sacred precinct, on a river bank, or in the home.

Purification is essential before worship, and is achieved by three principal methods: exorcism (*harai*), cleaning (*misogi*), and abstention (*imi*). Exorcism is performed by presenting offerings, after which the priest waves over the person to be purified the above mentioned *gohei* or *nusa* wand and pronounces a formula of purification. [This too I saw in Nara: the priest appeared for a moment before the meditating young women and waved his *gohei*.] The misogi is a cleansing rite for the removal of accidental defilement acquired by contact with unclean things, such as might be caused by death or disease. It is effected by ablutions, usually by the mere sprinkling of water and salt. Near the oratory of the shrine on the left side of the pathway, there usually stands a font at which the worshipers wash their hands before worship. *Imi,* or abstention, is a method of acquiring a positive purity by avoidance of the source of pollution. It was the duty rather of priests than of laymen to practice the necessary austerities, which consist chiefly in the observance of certain prohibitions.

Formerly Shintō priests scarcely ever performed the funeral service, the dead being given over to the care of Buddhism, but now Shintō funeral services have become quite common. On the other hand marriages until recent years were never celebrated with religious rites, whether Buddhist or Shintō. Now it is fashionable to have the wedding ceremony performed at a Shintō shrine.

identified as Gautama in the Deer Park preaching the first sermon, Avalokiteśvara, and Maitreya[87]—but such a trio does not constitute an accepted trinity. When Avalokiteśvara appears at the side of a Buddha, the Bodhisattva at the other side is Amitābha (Kannon and Amida in Japan). The whole subject has to be reviewed very carefully from this, the Japanese, end—with the Chinese caves as intermediate monuments. Nara, Honan, and Ajaṇṭā-Elūrā are about contemporary.

Rev. Phillip Eidmann and Prof. Shin'ya Kasugai

I was surprised and unsettled by this discussion, but not convinced. When asked what the symbol of Gautama flanked by the two Bodhisattvas, Maitreya and Avalokiteśvara, might symbolize, I suggested that the two great Bodhisattvas of the later Mahāyāna might be there to symbolize the content or import of the doctrine—as a kind of apologia for the Mahāyāna addition of such figures to the Theravāda teaching. My two friends were surprised and could not deny the possibility, but suggested that such an interpretation was probably too Western. The Mahāyāna, they thought, did not feel the need to justify itself. I brought up the justification implicit in the legend of Nāgārjuna and the Nāgas—but this only led us, by a little jump, to questioning how much we knew about Nāgārjuna, of whose actual writings absolutely nothing remains.[88]

I asked what the attitude of Buddhist sectarians was to the Buddhas and Bodhisattvas not included in their sectarian cult. Shinshū, for example, pays worship only to Amida. The answers were a bit confused and indecisive. It seems the problem is not much considered. In one sect, I was told (but I've forgotten which) the devotee selects his personal Bodhisattva by tossing a pellet onto a sheet of Bodhisattva names.

A couple of interesting items came out about Tibet and Japan. Apparently in the Noh dramas there occur a few words that could not be understood until they were recognized, rather recently, as Tibetan. Apparently, also, the *vajra*[89] is used in the Shingon school rites. Tantra is hush-hush in Japan. Apparently it was here, but no one will talk of it.

The Nishi Honganji is strongly unfriendly to Shintō. However, until this year, the men in the fox-god Inari's procession were allowed to slake their thirst at the Honganji gate; that, in fact, is why they stop here. This year some of the patrons of the temple pointed out the inconsistency in this custom, and, for the first time, the water was refused. Eidmann expected a bit of trouble of some kind, but nothing happened.

After the procession and before my departure Eidmann showed me something about the Japanese technique of handling Chinese in their writing—numbering the signs in a Japanese order but writing them on the page in a Chinese sequence; also, using a Chinese ideograph sequence as a single noun (somewhat in the way of a Sanskrit agglutinated term).[90]

When I got back to the hotel I found a couple of letters from Jean and another anniversary telegram, forwarded from Tokyo. Among other nice things, she tells me that *The Art of Indian Asia* has finally arrived.[91] Nice anniversary event.[92]

I went to Suehiro's for dinner and spent the evening at my diary.

Saturday, May 7

At 10:30 A.M. Professor Kasugai arrived, to take me on a wonderful visit to the Chion-in Temple.

The atmosphere in the cloister area (a handsome wooden cloister: the first in wood that I have ever seen) was closer to what I remember from the monk world of India than anything I have yet found in Japan (the nuns reminded me, rather, of New York). Kasugai and I were in that part of the temple compound at 11:15, when a group of young monks were standing in two rows, chanting *Namu Amida-butsu,* while waiting for the abbot to appear in his red robe. The abbot appeared, preceded by an older monk and followed by another who was in a robe of blue, and the younger group then followed the abbot past us to the main temple, where we later found them in a service of noonday worship which was attended by a small lay company as well. Such services take place in the morning and evening also. But I must say, as the young monks passed me one by one, they did not seem to me to be the smartest looking young men that I've seen in Japan.

The buildings of this great temple are magnificent: the *sammon* (two-storied gate), the *hondō* (main hall), the assembly hall ("hall of one thousand mats"), and the inner apartments. Kasugai and I had lunch in a lovely room of the latter area, sitting on the mat floor, Japanese style (it took me five minutes to get the blood back into my legs) with a handsome picture of Amida (Central Asian manner) hanging on the wall. We then visited the belfry (the bell was cast in 1638, the largest of its kind in Japan: 17.9 feet high, 8.9 feet in diameter, 9.5 inches thick, 74 shot tons). We ascended also to the gardens and ridges higher up, where there were graveyards and other buildings.

Everywhere I turned, everywhere we went, there were beautiful gardens—and part of the charm were the anecdotes about this stone and that, this and that lantern, that Kasugai was able to recount as we walked around. Comparable anecdotes go along with the bowls of the tea ceremony, and, no doubt, with many more of the cherished objects in Japan.

During the course of our visit to the Chion-in grounds, we came to a little Shintō shrine on the Chion-in estate. "It is bad that we have this here," said Kasugai. It is a cute little shrine, with two white fox figures sitting with lifted tails at either side of the central object on the little altar. When we turned away, there approached and passed us, on their way to the shrine, two women, apparently from the Gion geisha quarter (which is not far away). "You see," said Kasugai, "that is the type that comes here to worship the White-Tailed Fox-God."[93]

After having conducted me through the Chion-in Temple estate, Kasugai brought me to his home for a look at his library. I met his little girl and boy, and his pleasant little wife, who served us tea and cakes while we talked about books.

Kasugai has a theory that the first form of Buddhism to enter China was the Hīnayāna (Sarvastivādin, Vinaya, and Agama Śastra) via the Northern Caravan trail through the Gobi area; that the Mahāyāna (Śunyatavādin) then came through the southern route; and that a third period (Gandhavyuha and Saddharma Pundarīka) is represented by the works in Chinese Turkestan patronized by the medieval traders.

We looked at some pictures of the carvings in the Chinese cave temples at Longmen, Honan, which date from the fifth to seventh centuries A.D., and discussed a little the fact that Ajaṇṭā, Honan, and Nara are about contemporary.[94] The close connections suggest that medieval Buddhism should be studied from the standpoint of the Japanese sects, some of which continue the medieval traditions without change.

We looked at some handsome pictures of the now-destroyed (in 1949) Hōryūji frescoes. Here Amida is a prominent figure, flanked on his proper right by Mahāsthamaprapta (as Padmāpami, with a jewel as the crest jewel of his tiara: Mahāsthamaprapta is Seishi in Japan, and personified religious energy[95]) and on his proper left by Avalokiteśvara (holding a sort of boat hook in his hand, with an image of the Buddha as the crest jewel of his tiara; his Japanese name is Kannon, who personifies the quality of mercy: Kuan-yin is patroness of seamen and merchants in China: Kannon (compassion) is in all things—an Indian motif). These frescoes are dated A.D. 708, and they include a glorious, seated figure of the Bodhisattva Suryaprabha, with a lovely red lotus in his left hand. Compare all this with the Indian tendency (which I am afraid I followed too easily in *The Art of Indian Asia*) to find Avalokiteśvara wherever the lotus is held in the hand.[96]

Kasugai led me next (about 3:00 P.M.) to the Seiren-in Temple (Blue Lotus Temple), where there is a charming garden of the hill garden type. This temple is of the Tendai sect, I believe (founded by Dengyō Daishi, ca. A.D. 800), and on one of the altars we found a *vajra* and *vajra* bell,[97] which Kasugai said were characteristic of the Shingon sect (Kōbō Daishi, also ca. A.D. 800).[98]

My final event with Kasugai was a visit to the Heian Shrine and garden; after which we parted with great bows.

I spent all evening writing up my diary.

CHAPTER 5

Unimpeded

Kyoto and Nara

Sunday, May 8   **Kyoto**

A remarkable and very fruitful day. Went around to Eidmann's at 10:00
A.M., to meet and talk with Professor Takamine,[99] the leading Kegon
scholar of Japan, and left at about 9:00 P.M. Takamine left at about 1:00
P.M., but Kasugai arrived just then and remained through tea. Then
Eidmann coaxed me to stay through dinner, and finally brought in a
masseur to massage my ankle again. The conversation ran largely along the
themes of Buddhist philosophy.

Discussing Eidmann's translation of and commentary on *The Tractate
of the Golden Lion,* I opened the affair by asking the meaning of the following sentence:

"In the Perfected Mahāyāna (i.e. Kegon), everything, every speck of dust
even, can be seen as conditioned arising. Thus even in a hair there are innumerable golden lions." I asked how the second sentence followed from the first.

We were sitting on the floor, around the low table that covers
Eidmann's legs, Takamine in the place of honor, with his back to the kakemono[100] and facing Eidmann, I at Eidmann's right, and the secretary at

Eidmann's left. The secretary and I had our pens and notepaper ready for news. Takamine spoke in Japanese, the secretary—under correction from Eidmann—translated, and I put my next question.

The first question was answered with the help of an apt diagram that Eidmann gave in his paper, where he distinguished between the *ri-ji-muge* doctrine and the *ji-ji-muge* doctrine:

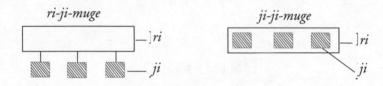

Ri-ji-muge distinguished from *ji-ji-muge*

Ri stands for Reason, Principle, Noumenon, or Absolute.

Ji stands for the particular, phenomena, the objects of the universe.

Muge means unimpeded, undivided.

Ri-ji-muge means that the Noumenon and Phenomenon, the realm of the Absolute and that of Life and Death are identical: undivided, unimpeded. In this school, however, one *thing* equals another only indirectly, i.e., only because the two things are both identical with the one transcending *ri* and not because of their own essence. The Kegon school declares that this doctrine is not that of the true immanence of the Universal Buddha.

Ji-ji-muge means, literally, "Phenomenon-Phenomenon-Undivided," or more freely, the direct identity in essence of all phenomena.

While *ri-ji-muge* causes us to seek for the Buddha in the mind, the *ji-ji-muge* concept causes us to look for the Universal Buddha in the body. Following out the former idea, the flesh is regarded as a shackle imprisoning the enquiring spirit, so that by retiring from the world one should reduce it to proper submission and thereby obtain enlightenment. With the *ji-ji-muge* school, however, illumination can be found only through perfecting the flesh by bringing out its latent potentialities, and thereby uncovering the Buddha hidden in the human heart.

I summed up the dichotomy by saying that *ri-ji-muge* is the *Way of Sitting* and *ji-ji-muge* the *Way of Moving in the World*, and both Eidmann and Takamine accepted this as OK. The two views arise from, and rationalize, these two attitudes, which might be termed the alternate bridges to a transcendent realization where the distinctions implied in the metaphysical argument disappear.[101] (Compare the reply of Ānanda Mayī to my query about renunciation and affirmation.)[102]

Takamine made the point, however, that simply moving in the world is not enough—moving in the world mechanically; for in that case one is aware only of the *ji* and *ji* as separate from each other. *In order to experience the* ji-ji-muge *two things are necessary:*

a. Compassion (*karuṇā: jihi*)
b. The Vow (of Bodhisattvahood, *praṇidhana: gan*); here we have, apparently, the main formula of Kegon

Haru, Eidmann's secretary, summed up the stages of the shift of perspective from the mechanical to the enlightened view, as follows: "Seeing a thing, one realizes, first, that 'no thing exists'; that is the negative side: simultaneously, however, the positive side must be realized, namely, that 'that is *tathatā*.'"

In sum, to use the Indian terms: we have here the way of *neti neti* and that of *iti iti*.[103] The particular point about Kegon is that it follows the way of *iti iti* with Compassion (*karuṇā: jihi*) and the Vow (*praṇidhana: gan*) as its "effective means."

According to Takamine, in Kegon, religious practice cannot be separated from life: all work and viewing is practice. In the Kegon communities there are annual short retreats; but these are not very different in purpose from the retreats for laymen in the Catholic Church. They are not the means through which enlightenment is attained. They are, rather, interludes of thought and quiet consideration.

It is to be noted that this idea of the normal life task and path as "practice" is precisely what, in Zen (as presented by Suzuki), has seemed to me to be the most important thing about Zen. We shall come to the problem of Zen in a moment.

According to Eidmann, Kegon is the fundamental doctrine of *all* truly Japanese Buddhism. All of the specifically Japanese sects may be characterized as manifestations or aspects of Kegon. Also, Japanese art developed largely out of Kegon. Jishū (the Kegon position) is the most influential, furthermore, in Japan today.

Zen, according to Takamine and Eidmann, originally had no Kegon. Its basic text was the Diamond *Sūtra* (indeed, there is a discussion as to which *sūtra* Bodhidharma handed to his disciples, the Diamond or the Lankavatāra). The doctrine of the Sixth Patriarch (Hui-neng: Enō) is based on *śunyatā*.[104]

Hui-neng's disciple's disciple's disciple (Ch'eng-ti: Chōkan) took in Kegon; from there on ... but see Suzuki's article on Kegon and Zen in his series of *Essays in Zen*.[105] (The legend now appears that Bodhidharma's *sūtra* was really the Kegon *sūtra*.)

Among the ideas taken over by Zen from Kegon is that of all work and viewing as practice.

Japanese Zen has two main streams. Sōtō Zen follows the way of *ri-ji-muge*, meditation and monastic practice; Rinzai Zen follows the Kegon way of *ji-ji-muge*. Suzuki presents, principally, his interpretation of the Rinzai.

On either path (Sōto or Rinzai) Zen stresses practice—not philosophy. While practicing, one attains satori[106]—and here philosophy is again superfluous. From the standpoint of Zen, therefore, the distinction made philosophically between *ri-ji-muge* and *ji-ji-muge* is a quibble. On the other hand, from the standpoint of Kegon it would appear that in the Sōtō the way is that of *ri-ji-muge* while in the Rinzai it is *ji-ji-muge*.

Takamine left at about this point, and presently Eidmann and I were discussing the doctrine of the multiple bodies of the Buddha.* During this phase of the day, Kasugai dropped in (all dressed up in striped trousers—looking very neat and alert; for he had just come from a ceremony confirming the status of a new Zen master), and the conversation continued. The following are the main points:

The doctrine of the Three Bodies, which has been so greatly emphasized by scholars in the West, belongs to the *Prajñāpāramitā* teachings: it evaporates (Kasugai's word) after the period of the *Prajñāpāramitā Hṛdāya Sūtra*.[107]

The *Prajñāpāramitā* teaching played no role in the philosophical

---

* See the article "Busshin," on the bodies of the Buddha, in *Hōbōgirin*—an encyclopedia of Buddhism published by the French Institute in Tokyo: only three volumes have appeared: it is written in French, but the headings are in Japanese.

thinking of Japan, except in Hossō.[108] Dengyō knew the *Prajñāpāramitā Hṛdāya Sūtra,* and wrote commentaries, but his followers of the Tendai sect used only the commentaries.

Zen is the closest of the truly Japanese sects to the three-body view of the *Prajñāpāramitā.* Shinshū (like Tibetan Buddhism) gives the Buddha seven bodies, classifying them as four with three subheadings. Tendai uses a four-body system, but in such a way that it resembles the Tibetan system of seven bodies. Nichiren is a two-body system. This is not the same, however, as that of the *Uttaratantraśastra.*[109] Shinran's two-body system is different from that of Nichiren: different also from his own four-body system. Still another two-body system is that of the Mahāsāṅghika.[110] In the *Sarvāstivādinśastra (Daibibasharon)*[111] a one-body system is offered. Systems have been built from one body (*ichi-shin*) to ten (*ji-shin*).[112]

It is a Western tendency to try to find connections and homologies between such things as these various theories of the bodies of the Buddha. In the Orient, on the other hand, such theorizing is eschewed. Best: *don't try to connect.* Nevertheless, an aid to the understanding of the Kegon conception of the infinite will be found in a study of the nineteenth-century work of Cantor on *The Infinite in Mathematics* (ca. 1880).[113] Kegon's infinite is comparable.

The Buddhism of the Yazunembutsu-shū is Kegon without the Pure Land *sūtras.* Its chief theme is "the interpenetrating name of the Buddha."

In Shinshū (Honganji) *ri* is *tariki* ("the other power") and *ji* is the individual. The two are united in "*the moment of the awakening of faith* (i.e. of realization)"; this realization being that of:

ichi soku issai	one is the same thing as everything
issai soku ichi	everything is the same thing as one

Shinshū is not *bhakti.* "The rituals of Shinshū have no meaning or aim; and that is their meaning."

Anecdote: A Christian lady saw a Buddhist praying. "What are you praying for?" "Nothing." "Whom are you praying to?" "No one." The lady moved away. The Buddhist got up and said to her: "And, Madam, there is no one praying." Compare the anecdote of Śaṅkara up a tree.[114]

Yet it can be said that Shinshū has an aim—a psychological aim. According to the *Dai-kyō (Sukhāvatī-vyuha)* the dual aim is: *anshin* (peace of mind), and *san shin ichi shin* (the realization that the three [essentials] are one); these three are: earnest thought, faith serene, and desire for *nirvāṇa*. Another and somewhat different statement of the aims will be found in the *Kan-gyo* (*Amitābha-jñāna Sūtra*), but at the time of our discussion this formula could not be recalled.

The distinguishing characteristic of the attitude of one who has attained the Awakening of Faith and lives in it is: *gratefulness to the world— to the tea, the teacup, the table, everything—which has made and makes existence and enlightenment possible.* This idea of religion as gratefulness has permeated Japan.

There do exist in the Shinshū community true *myōkōnin:* those who have attained the awakening of faith and live in it.

In Zen there are today but five recognized masters—including the one recognized in the ceremony that Kasugai had just attended. One is of the Sōtō sect; the others are Rinzai. Two are about fifty-two years old (including the one celebrated today); the others range around eighty.

The attitude of the Jōdo sect approaches that of *bhakti* (in contrast to Shinshū). There are ceremonies of a sort that resemble certain "sealing ceremonies" of the Mormons, which confirm or dedicate the individual. (I did not understand this phase of the discussion at all.) Kasugai (a member of the Jōdo sect) could not say that there were any members of the community now "living in the Buddha knowledge." "The members of the sect do not live in the Buddha knowledge; but they die in it." (I *think* I caught this correctly.)

The monks of the Jōdo sect (but not the nuns) are, for the most part, married. What the sense is of a married monk is a bit obscure: so much so, indeed, that there is no word in Japanese that can be applied to the wife of a monk. This circumstance is the result of history: Japanese laws vs. monasticism. And effort is about to be made, however, to repair the situation: young men are to be sent to Thailand, to follow the path of the true *bhikkhus.*

The difference between the Hīnayāna and the Mahāyāna was formulated by Eidmann as follows:

The aim of the Hīnayāna is to achieve egolessness through realizing that the self is egoless: the self is the Buddha; whereas, the aim of the Mahāyāna is to achieve egolessness through realizing that the universe is egoless: the Universe is the Buddha: and I am egoless by participation. The Hīnayāna can be said, therefore, to be psychological and the Mahāyāna metaphysical in stress; yet the end (egolessness) is the same.

Shinshū returns in aim to the psychological position, while preserving the vocabulary of metaphysics. See the point above about the psychological aim of Shinshū.[115] Zen remains metaphysical.

Problem of the antiquity of the Bodhisattva doctrine. The Buddha taught the prior existence of Buddhas; in one place seven, in another twenty-five, in another, many. Problem: whence did he derive this idea? Compare the *tirthankaras* of the Jains. What was the relationship of Buddha's belief about himself to the doctrines of his Jain rival Mahāvīra? Can we say, that, like reincarnation, we have here a basic Indian archetype which the teachers automatically accept and then rerender according to their diverse modes of realization?

Big jump: it is Kasugai's view that gold was not known in India before the time of Aśoka. Problem: the gold amulet of Lauriya-Nandangarh.

Another jump: the publicized Rangoon congress of Buddhists actually is two congresses:

a. A completely unimportant meeting of the World Fellowship of Buddhists, which meets regularly, every two years—with such vague aims and effects as their name would suggest; and

b. A three-year conference, now in progress, concerned with reediting the scriptures—and this one is very important.[116]

Finally we jumped to an example of Zen in the Noh drama: Beatrice Lane Suzuki, *Noh Gaku* (Wisdom of the East Series), last play, *Yuki* ("The Snow").[117]

Monday, May 9

Up at six to prepare my Japanese language lesson for today, and language class from nine to twelve. All afternoon bringing this, now very complicated, diary up to date.

I have a couple of points to make now of my own.[118]

The May 2 edition of *Time* reports on page thirty-six the inaugural lecture of Professor C. S. Lewis[119] as Professor of Medieval and Renaissance English Literature at Cambridge University, from which I lift the following:

"...whereas all history was for our ancestors divided into two periods, the pre-Christian and the Christian...for us it falls into three...the pre-Christian, the Christian, and what may reasonably be called the post-Christian....It appears to me that the second change is even more radical than the first. Christians and Pagans had much more in common with each other than either has with a post-Christian. The gap between those who worship and those who do not..." In politics, art, and religion, the old frames have been shattered.

But the biggest change of all is that born of machines. "How has it come about, that we use the highly emotive word 'stagnation,' with all its malodorous and malarial overtones, for what other ages would have called 'permanence'?...I submit that what has imposed this climate of opinion so firmly on the human mind is *a new archetypal image* [italics mine]. It is the image of old machines being superseded by new and better ones....Our assumption is *that everything is provisional and soon to be superseded* [italics again mine], *that the attainment of goods we have never yet had, rather than the defense and conservation of those we have already, is the cardinal business of life,* would most shock and bewilder [our ancestors]....I conclude that it really is the greatest change in the history of Western Man...."

This, precisely, is one of the ideas that has been most forcefully represented to me by the experiences of my voyage of this year.

The fundamental idea of Buddhism, namely, "All is without a self," would seem to me to go along very well with the idea of the discarded machines (though not, indeed, with that of striving for goods we have never yet had). There is, in fact, a good deal about both Buddhism and Hinduism that can easily appear to a Westerner (and certainly did to me, in the sweet long ago) as though it were exactly what he needed. However, the attitude of worship or piety in the Orient is totally different from anything that the post-Christian can properly use. Moreover, the Oriental doctrines are all mixed up with such problems as that represented by the Buddhist examination and confirmation of *arhats* and the Hindu proclivity to *samādhi*. It now seems to me best to leave these doctrines exactly where they are—namely, in the Orient—and to initiate the next Western step from a completely Western position. Comparisons being odious, as I have noted above,[120] let's not even use the Oriental words. Clues may be taken from the East (or from anywhere), but let's not then try to read our own reactions back into the Oriental context.

All of this implies great warnings and danger signals for me in the work ahead on my *Basic Mythologies of Mankind.*[121]

1. Beginning from the beginning, I am to follow motifs objectively and historically. Also, I am to record interpretations objectively and historically, on the basis of contemporary texts.

2. As a contemporary Occidental faced with Occidental and contemporary psychological problems, I am to admit and even celebrate (in Spengler's manner) the relativity of my historical view to my own neurosis (Rorschach formula).

3. The historical milestone represented is that of the recognition of the actual unity of human culture (the diffusion and parallelism of myths) together with the relativity of the *mores* of any given region to geographical and historical circumstance (Bastian, Sumner, Childe). The time has come for a global, rather than provincial, history of the images of thought.

4. The moral object of the book is to find for Western Man (specifically, the post-Christian Occidental) suggestions for the furtherance of his psychological opus through a transformation of unconscious into conscious symbols, a confrontation of these with the consciously accepted terms of the present period, and a dialogue of mutual criticism. This, however, is to be the minor aim, subordinated strictly to 3.

5. Make no great cross-cultural leaps, and even within a given culture, do not try to harmonize what the philosophers of that culture itself have not harmonized. Stick to the historical perspective and all will emerge of itself.

As for the problems of the young Orientals of today—Asia for the Asians: let them work them out for themselves. They will solve their problems, I think, by imitating in their own several ways our problems, and so in serving ourselves we shall serve the world.

I am finding, by the way, that my present residence and work in Japan is, somehow, helping me to assimilate the shock of India. A couple of interesting contrasts are to be noted:

1. In India, 80 percent illiterate, and the literate classes largely Anglicized, the Orient survived primarily on the folk level, in folk terms, and in a squalid condition.

2. In Japan, 90 percent literate, and this literate class fundamentally Oriental still—in spite of the miraculous grasp of the machine—one experiences the Orient in a more elegant style, in quite good form, and with its spirit still noble.

3. In India it was possible, because of the general knowledge of English, to

penetrate quickly into the Indian sphere—leaving Occidentals behind. But the penetration was into rotten wood, as it were; and it was not easy to find where the wood was still sound. In Japan, on the other hand, where very few speak English, and those few not well, one does not come quickly *into* the Japanese sphere; yet one comes immediately *against* it, and one can feel the wood. Fortunately, with Eidmann to help, I am finding some cracks that are letting me way in (the nuns, Kasugai's home, Takamine's conversation). But I can actually feel Japan as the living Orient every time I step into the street; and the Noh and Kabuki experiences were already at least as impressive as anything encountered during my first several months in India—indeed, up to the time of Ahmedabad (save for the four days in Orissa).

But halt! It is now 10:30 P.M., and I have still to prepare for tomorrow's class.

Tuesday, May 10

Up at 6:00 A.M. to resume preparations for the class. Japanese from nine to noon, then a visit to the Daimaru Department Store, to recover my light meter which I left there last week for repair; then lunch in a nearby restaurant, and back to my room, to study Japanese. At 5:00 P.M. I went to the Nishi Honganji compound for a "Mongolian" dinner (a sort of sukiyaki) and chat with Eidmann. Our range of subjects, as usual, was wide.

Gate 1

The lanterns in Japanese gardens: are they originally Japanese, or were they brought from the mainland? Such lanterns are not Chinese (and yet it seems to me that I saw two in porcelain at the Chion-in Temple). Those found in Korea may well have been brought from Japan, but in Manchuria one lone stone lantern has been found, which is a kind of enigma. Also, the torii before the Shintō shrines are probably not derived

Gate 2

from the Buddhist Sāñcī-type of gate, but an independent invention. The gate before the Chinese Buddhist temples, on the other hand, with straight uprights, is probably from India.

The cultural activities of the U.N. and UNESCO in the Orient are strongly slanted toward a propagandizing, and even enforcement, of Occidental moral values; e.g. the propaganda against polygamy. In the face of this pressure the Pakistani and Indonesian premiers are to be commended for having dared to take second wives.

There is a very strong run of Communism in the universities of Japan. This was greatly furthered by the Occupation, which expelled up to one-third of the members of the faculties as Fascists (the work of our lovely Fifth Amendment boys,[122] no doubt, whose great cause, when they themselves are called to the bench, is Academic Freedom). One university in Kyoto is completely and openly Communist today, namely Ritsumei University. The Christian Dōshisha University is very strongly Communist and is prominent in all Communist-style student agitations. There the students even participated in the election of the president of the university (a length to which our Harold's enthusiasm for student participation in the business of the college perhaps would not extend).[123] The Japanese do not have a tradition of open argument and debate, but the Communist groups are trained and geared for precisely that, and so, always win out in direct confrontations. The Japanese are using more devious methods, therefore, to combat them, and are gradually regaining ground. For example: a Communist-run committee called for an all-college meeting to be held at 1:00 P.M. The professors, to allow plenty of time for the meeting, called off all classes for that day after 9:00 A.M. Result: practically no one on hand for the meeting.

My own guess, from what Eidmann told me, is that the Communists in the universities of Japan are about where they were in those of the U.S.A. during the late thirties and early forties—perhaps even a bit ahead of that point.

America's handling of the hundreds of students now coming from Asia is, on the whole, very bad. There is no professional direction given to their studies: practically none of their advisors knows anything about the cultures from which they come; people who *do* know such things (and there *are* such people in our country: they could be found if an honest effort were made to discover them) are never consulted. Why is it that a large percentage of the intellectual leaders of the Communist movement in the Oriental countries were trained in American colleges. And why is it that those trained in Russia do not have comparable reactions against their teacher but become, in the main, ardent Communists?

We had a couple of pretty little cakes that looked like tiny money bags, made by a man who is the sole possessor of the secret formula, which has been handed down from father to eldest son. These cakes are made particularly for the Cake God, the God of Cakes, who has been brought from India. Nuns cover their eyes when they approach his shrine. He holds his consort on his lap, and he has an elephant's head—undoubtedly Ganeśa;[124] perhaps in a Tantric form. I'd like to know a bit more.

Resuming our discussion of Shinshū Buddhism, I learned:

1. That the Shinshū term for the gratitude to the world and everything in it that is coextensive with the Awakening of Faith is *hōnō kansha.*
2. That Shinshū does not regard Amida as a concrete, anthropomorphic person, or his realm as an actual place: Amida and his Realm are described as an "apparitional body and realm, which appear as a result of practice." (This is in contrast to the belief represented in the *Amitābha-jñāna Sūtra,* where it is said that one, by practice, develops an eye that really sees an actual Buddha and Buddha Realm. *I* wonder, however, whether the language of the *sūtra* may not be metaphorical, after all. In any case, Eidmann assures me that in Shinshū there is no question at all of anthropomorphic, concretistic superstition.)
3. The *practice* recommended by Shinshū is primarily that of listening to sermons and talks. The Shinshū clergy are the best lecturers in Japan. Small teaching groups are favored. One is to listen to sermons—not seeking for enlightenment, but just sitting and listening. Listening and practicing the attitude of Gratitude (*hōnō kansha*) are the Shinshū Way.
4. We can know nothing, absolutely nothing; all that can be said is but a *stepping-stone* (not a direct path, but a stepping-stone). The closest we can come to the absolute is the name and title *Namu Amida-butsu,* which arises with the instant of faith.
5. In Shinshū homes there are no images; only words—tablets usually written by the patriarch, who writes some one or two hundred every morning. The statues of Amida in the temples are an innovation of about three hundred years ago.
6. One who has attained the Awakening of Faith and lives in it is known as a *myōkōnin.*

The U.S.I.S. could do a good work by sending books to the universities of Japan—not the government universities (these already have an excessive grip on the educational situation), nor the Christian universities (for these are already pretty well taken care of), but the numerous private universities throughout the country, whose libraries are in a pitiful state. Any book would certainly be read a hundredfold.

In selecting students from Japan to educate, why choose those who will never have any influence? In Japan, family position is decisive. It is known now (with perhaps a 10 percent margin of error) who will be influential twenty years from now. The others, inevitably, will return to disappear. The democratic approach is fine, but the realistic is effective.

When I arrived Eidmann was tutoring the little son of the patriarch of the Honganji, who will himself be the patriarch—and consequently, one of the most influential men in Japan—in a few decades. I dare say Eidmann's effect will be greater than that of many of the millions now being poured into Fulbright, Ford, and Rockefeller aids—and he is working without any U.S. aid at all. Compare the situation in Ahmedabad, where the Sarabhais (like the Honganji patriarch here) are the ones who are doing the best work in bringing the most appropriate people from America to India—at least in the cultural sphere.

Wednesday, May 11

Up at 6:00 A.M. again for my Japanese. Class from 9:00 to 12:00.

The hotel is full, today, of musicians—members of the company of the NBC Symphony that is now touring Japan, to vast acclaim. I was sitting in the lounge, reading *Time* for this week, when Eidmann's friend Fillmore appeared. He was waiting for a member of the symphony orchestra. We sat and talked, and presently the member appeared: behold, George Graber, Jean's fat drummer. Greetings—and could we have dinner together tonight? Why, sure! Had I heard the symphony? I did not say that I had not come to Japan to listen to a New York orchestra, but simply: "No, I'm sorry, I missed it!"

All afternoon on my Japanese.

Graber phoned at seven, and we went, together with a young army chap named Smith, to Suehiro's, for a nice steak dinner. Home by 9:30 to catch up on the mail, and at midnight to bed.

Thursday, May 12

Due to a mix-up at the phone desk, Graber, in room 611, got my 6:00 A.M. call and I, in room 711, his 7:15 call. Breakfast with Graber and off to school. He and all the rest of the symphony are enormously impressed by Japan and the Japanese audiences and hope to return. "Apparently the audiences for American art are all outside of the United States," said he.

In class I feel that I've begun to leave my classmate a bit in the rear.

When I returned to the hotel I found a wire from Dorothy Riggs,[125] to say that she would be arriving this evening for a three-day visit to Kyoto. It's a bit wet, however: not the best weather for visits to Kyoto and Nara. I spent the afternoon on Japanese and mail. At last, I'm catching up.

I find in a little article written by Eidmann, the following classification of the Buddhist schools:

Hīnayāna
  1. Permanent *ātman* schools (*Vātsiputriyas*)
  2. "Things but no *ātman*" (*Qavastivādins*)
  3. "Void of *ātman* and past and present *dharmas*" (*Mahāsāṅghika*)
  4. "Void are *ātman* and conventional *dharmas*" (*Prajñāptivādins*)
  5. "Transcendental *dharmas* are real" (*Lokottaravādins*)
  6. "Things only words and names" (*Yahavarika*)
Mahāyāna
  7. Emptiness (*Śunatāvāda*)
  8. *Tathatā* real but not things (*Lankavatāra Sūtra* and *vādins*) (Awakening of Faith)
  9. *Tathatā* beyond description (*Vimalikirti Sūtra*)
  10. *Dharmalōka* (Kegon)

The Chinese founder of Kegon systematized the schools as follows:

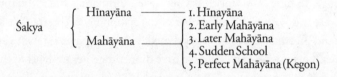

Diagram of Hīnayāna and Mahāyāna

Shinran, according to Eidmann, differentiates Hīnayāna and Mahāyāna as follows, in his *Gutoku's Notes:*[126] Mahāyāna teaches the Bodhisattva ideal (the "Great Career") and Hīnayāna the *arhat* (the "Smaller Career"). Eidmann points out, however, that the Theravādins encourage those who are suited to it to follow the Bodhisattva ideal (cf. Bhikkhu Narada Thera's *The Bodhisattva Ideal.*[127]) According to Eidmann, the real difference is that the Hīnayāna is psychological and the Mahāyāna metaphysical:

"Hīnayāna is concerned with states of mind. The *Abhidharma* of the Pāli canon[128] is almost entirely occupied with the analysis of the states of mind of man. The whole body of Pāli scriptures is chiefly concerned with the arising and destruction of states of mind, and religious emancipation is attained by realizing [that] these states of mind are without ego. The inner awakening to the emptiness and voidity of states of mind brings the individual saint to the state of *nirvāṇa*. . . .

"Mahāyāna, on the other hand, . . . concerns itself with the ultimate emptiness of the whole universe. Mahāyāna schools seek to destroy the ego by realizing [that] the whole universe is empty and void, and therefore [that] the individual ego also is devoid of any underlying eternal substance. . . .

"Zen, which is sometimes said to be psychological, on closer examination is found to be entirely metaphysical, in that it is not concerned with states of mind, but with the underlying emptiness of the universe.

"Shinshū [on the other hand], is primarily psychological. Its chief concern is with the passions and the states of mind in which *nirvāṇa* can be attained."[129]

These two ways, briefly, are those announced in the *Dṛg-dṛsya-viveka:* the subjective and the objective ways to *nirvāṇa;* and I think that they are quite well summarized in the formula, *way* of the *arhat,* and *way* of the Bodhisattva—as referring not to the activity of the Enlightened, once enlightened, but to the way proposed for the attainment of Enlightenment.

Dorothy arrived at 9:30 P.M., after having managed to get herself somewhat lost on the way from the airfield in Osaka to the Kyoto Hotel. I took her down to the Grill for dinner, then out for a walk through the shopping section southwest of the hotel.

Friday, May 13

Japanese class from nine to noon; then met Dorothy for lunch, and a sightseeing expedition to the Imperial Palace, the Heian Shrine and garden, the Chion-in Temple, the Higashi Honganji Temple, and, finally, Eidmann's dwelling in the Nishi Honganji compound. Eidmann was a very cordial host indeed; had us stay to dinner, and put on a handsome tea ceremony for Dorothy after it was over. She has been in Japan, with the army, for some nine months: had never had a Japanese meal before; had never seen a tea ceremony; had never been inside of a temple or shrine. Back to the hotel, really tired, at about eleven.

Saturday, May 14   Kyoto—Nara—Kyoto

The Five-Storied Pagoda at Nara

8:45 A.M. train to Nara. Visits to the Five-Storied Pagoda, Deer Park, Kasuga Shrine, Tōdaiji Temple and belfry; lunch at the Nara Hotel; then back to the station, after another pause at the Five-Storied Pagoda.

In Kyoto by 3:00 P.M. A bit of shopping; performance of the geisha dances at the Kamogawa Theater (my second view of this performance: viewed now from balcony front row—much better than last time: in this balcony, one removes one's shoes and sits on the floor). More shopping after the theater, then dinner at Suehiro's and—dead tired—early to bed.

Sunday, May 15

Breakfast at nine. Then out to take photographs of the Aoi Matsuri procession,* which came right past the hotel. A large tour of Americans had arrived at the hotel to see this procession, and we were such a spectacle

---

* According to a newspaper article, the Aoi Matsuri procession (Hollyhock Festival) dates back to Emperor Kimmei (509–71), when crops were seriously damaged by a spell of bad weather. A diviner declared that the deities of the Kamo Shrine had been offended, so the emperor ordered the people to appease them by offering branches of hollyhock. Thereafter the weather improved. In the Heian Period (781–1185) the festival came to be very colorfully observed at the imperial command. Due to a civil war (Ōnin no Ran) it was suspended (1467–77, the war), and it was not resumed until 1694. From 1868 to 1885 it was again suspended—then again for some of the mid- and postwar years.

taking photos from a high perch on the hotel fence, that the Japanese were busier photographing us then watching the procession.

The *kebiishi* (mounted) and four *kado-no-osa*

The procession is led by a pair of heralds; next come four police sergeants (*kado-no-osa*) in light brown; next a mounted judicial chief junior (*kebiishi*) in deep blue and a pair of fire masters (*hi-no-osa*) in pink; another *kebiishi,* of higher rank, in vermilion, with another pair of fire masters and some attendants in white bearing spears and bows; next the governor of Kyoto Prefecture in scarlet, mounted and attended; then a big flower canopy (*hanagasa*) and three coffers ornamented with sacred paper strips (*gohei*); a pair of mounted *kuratsukai,* and two racehorses, a mounted official of the Horse Affairs Board, and a lacquered court carriage drawn by an ox come next; another ox follows the cart (the *kae-ushi,* or spare ox); a pair of attendants in pink bear a stringed instrument and six court dancers follow on horseback; the mounted imperial envoy in black and a spare horse come next and seven attendants (*beijū*) on horseback, in purple; a mounted senior chamberlain bears the imperial message that is to be read at the shrine, and at the end come the great hollyhock bouquets.

The procession starts from the Imperial Palace at 9:00 or so and passes the hotel at 10:00. At 11:00 it reaches the Shimogamo Shrine, which is in the Tadasu-no-Mori, "Query Grove." The chief priest greets the procession and leads the imperial envoy into the shrine court. The officials take their seats.

The envoy reads the imperial message; the priest reads a divine message, and hands the envoy a small branch of hollyhock, which he then sticks in his crown. The *meryōtsukai* leads two horses twice around the building, the *beijū* sings a song called "Suruga-no-Uta," "Song of Suruga Province," the court dancers perform a dance called "Suruga-no-Mai," or "Dance of Suruga Province," and out on the racetrack in the grove the two horses gallop.

The procession then proceeds to the Kamigamo Shrine, where the same ceremony is repeated. At about 6:00 P.M., the procession returns to the palace.

After viewing and photographing the procession, I accompanied Dorothy to Osaka and put her on her plane bus, returning to the hotel by about three. The brief view of Osaka was quite impressive—another large and wonderful city, about thirty-five minutes by fast electric train from Kyoto.

In my room, for the rest of the day, I studied Japanese, wrote up my diary, and penned a couple of letters—feeling that I had done something to repay Dan Campbell and Dorothy for the vast introduction they had given me to Tokyo six weeks ago.

The return visits to the palace, etc. and Nara were interesting and pleasant, and from the guide at the palace I learned one new thing, namely, that the three sacred treasures of the realm are: the Jewel (= Benevolence); the Mirror (= Cleanliness); and the Sword (= Courage). One might say that these are actually the dominant virtues and ideals of the Japanese. It is evident, also, that they are symbols known also to Buddhism, with, however, a slightly different reading in that context.

Monday, May 16

Up at six, to study Japanese, and from 9:00 to 12:00 in class; then home, to study until about 3:30 P.M., when I went around to Eidmann's. Found two gents present, an oldish Mr. Mosser, who is living in the Kyoto Hotel and is touring the world with a lot of letters of commendation from American politicians, and a younger, Mr. Gold, who hopes to study in Japan when he leaves the army. After their departure, I remained for supper, which included a breaded whale cutlet that I guessed was either veal or chicken. Liked it very much—and was told that it is the cheapest and least respected meat in Japan.

A couple of points and a plan emerged from our discussion:

What has seemed to me to be a quicker adjustment here than in India to the Western style of male-female relationship is not quite what I thought it to be, yet is closer, even so, than the Indian to the West. The young men and women whom I have seen tête-à-tête in the coffee shops are not young people on the loose or on the search, but either young married people, getting away from the family for a while, or engaged people, whose engagements have been largely arranged by their families. According to Eidmann, when the family intends a marriage, the young people are allowed a first impression of each other (a sort of one-look situation), and then, after they are formally engaged, they may go out together. And the young married people, he tells me, are more numerous than I supposed: some 50 percent or so of the university students are married. Even so, the situation is closer to the Western than the Indian, where heterosexual life, either before or after marriage, hardly exists. The Japanese, retaining their own pattern, could behave in a manner resembling the American, and apparently do so: perhaps this accounts for the less emphatic moralizing resistance and more natural ease of these people in our Western forms.

It occurred to me in the light of all this that in Japan it is largely "the people," and not the aristocracy, that I am seeing in the Western mode. It is probable that the upper classes are holding more strictly to the traditional patterns. But in Europe they hold to a traditional pattern also in their marriages. This "American" pattern is actually a vulgar, popular one. But in India the "people," that is to say, those who are not of the three top castes, have hardly come into their own: they are illiterate and dwell in mud huts. The castes, like the aristocracy here and in Europe, are holding to tradition.

Eidmann pointed out that Buddhism is a religion that has been particularly favored by the merchant classes in the Orient—both in India and in the Far East. I suggested that the universalist—as opposed to vertical-traditional—character of Buddhism might be partly a cause of this circumstance; for the merchants are the ones who travel, whereas the priests and the nobles have their vested interest, so to say, in the local scene. (I think there is a good point here.) Did the universalism of Buddhism inhere in the Buddha's own teaching, or is it something that developed later. (Compare Christ and Pauline Christianity.) Is Aśoka the Universalist?

We discussed the matter of superstition and concretistic anthropomorphism in religion. How many Buddhist priests believe, when they engage, for example, in a spring rite, that their prayers or magic actually affect the weather. Catholic priests certainly think, when they pray for rain or boons, that there is an actual personal God who hears their prayers and might do something about it. Undoubtedly, this level of belief exists in Buddhism too. But when the Kegon priest dips water from a well in order to bring rain: "the all is in the atom," "the ocean is in the drop," etc. "in a single hair is an infinitude of lions"—where are we?

Eidmann feels that of the Buddhist sects, Tendai and Shingon are the most superstitious; that Zen, too, has a lot of magic and hocus-pocus; and that Jōdo's worship is very close to *bhakti*. He was willing to admit also that even in Shinshū there might well be many who, in spite of all the sermons, thought of and prayed to the Buddha as an actual person.

About my studies of Buddhism and Japanese; Eidmann made a number of fine suggestions. First, he felt I should continue at the language school, but commence study of kanji right away.[130]

He also suggested that I begin learning the *sūtras* by heart in Japanese: written in kanji, they are an excellent introduction to the chief characters in the Buddhist tradition

I had another massage for my feet and legs, which are in pretty bad shape after all this walking (Achilles' tendons; sprain still swollen; cramps from Ace bandage; all at once), and I returned home at about eleven to commence my reading with kanji:

Kanji characters = small, river, person

Tuesday, May 17

An item in this morning's paper on a meeting of the International Chamber of Commerce in Tokyo: much talk about the poverty of Asia and the need for civilization to take account of this fact if it is to prosper. The great problem: average per capita income (1949) in the world $230 per annum: in Africa $75, and in Asia $50.

OK. But the forgotten point is this: that Asia has not contributed and cannot contribute a single helpful technological or political thought to the contemporary world. All it has, apparently, are raw materials, which are of value only because they function in the context of an Occidentally invented and -furthered technology. Europe and the U.S.A. are contributing hundreds and thousands of new inventions a year (medical and agricultural included): the Orient, however? Nothing.[131]

At noon, after my Japanese class, I went downtown to have my visa extended to August 31. I had to have three pictures, so I went to a photographer and though the picture isn't great, it at least is human—which is *news* for Joe Campbell. No trouble getting the extension and—(amazement!)—no payment necessary. Then I went for a haircut and since I could not direct my barber in Japanese had to submit to what happened. I found that when a Japanese has a shave the entire face, forehead and all, is shaved. I saved my forehead, but that was all: besides, I didn't ask for the shave; it just followed the haircut before I realized what was up.

Returning home at about 3:30, worked a bit on my Japanese and diary before setting off at 6:15 for a dinner party to which Ellen Psaty invited me last week. The other guest was the new director of the U.S. Cultural Center in Kyoto, the city that is the cultural center of Japan: and he is one who knows nothing about Japanese culture (and confesses it), and very little about American. He doesn't like Japanese food or Japanese tea; he hopes that a simple, natural, American, person-to-person approach will win the hearts of the Japanese; he questions the "sincerity" of Japanese courtesy; he objects to the slowness and lack of initiative of his Japanese staff—and is generally an archetype of the wrong man in the right place.

Wednesday, May 18

Up at six; class until noon; lunch at the hotel; a bit of Japanese study, and then off to meet Ellen Psaty and her interpreter at the Municipal Modern Art Gallery, where there is a huge exhibition of Kyoto paintings. As in India, the gouaches are better than the oils. The first galleries that we visited were exclusively gouaches, and it seemed to me that they showed such similarities to each other that four-fifths of the works might have been by the same artist. Definitely, the artists were skillful and had taste. There was a consistent clarity of design and color, a firmly maintained aesthetic interest, subdued dramatic values, a predominance of nature and city sub-jects—few, but elegant (though un-"psychological") portraits: a number of really lovely realizations. I was told that this style was an intentional "mu-seum" style, for exhibitions of this kind, in the European manner, and that to see what the same artists were *really* doing I should have to go to their studios, where they were painting for *Japanese* homes and environs.

We proceeded to the oils—and here (as in the oils in India) the imita-tion of the West seemed not to have been assimilated so well: the parodies were outright, unashamed, and with no suggestion of a Japanese con-sciousness, system of values, atmosphere, or line of interest. Still worse was the sculptural exhibition, where there were nothing but studio nudes, por-trait heads, a few nonobjective organizations, and a single little piece of original effort and inspiration. I was disappointed also in the ceramics and screens, and, of course, could not understand at all the rooms of cal-ligraphy.

We were joined by one of the museum directors, who conducted us next to a small building in the Reizei-dōri area—the "oldest, smallest, and dirtiest" art studio and academy in Japan: built in the 1890s by an Italian, the site from which Occidental art spread out through Japan. The director showed us the two rooms, in one of which two young women, students, were doing charcoal sketches from plaster casts, in the good old Occidental way: the other room was full of easels bearing the pictures of a standing nude. We sat and talked for a while, then took a trolley to our several des-tinations.

I had dinner at Suehiro's and, arriving in the hotel at about 6:30, sat down in the lobby to read the *Life* article on Indian religion, in which I had had a hand last spring[132]—when along came the gentleman named Mosser, whom I had met at Eidmann's, and we chatted about travel till about eight. Then up to my room to study Japanese.

Thursday, May 19

Up at six—school till noon. Downtown then to fetch from the customs of-fice an air-mailed copy of my final Zimmer opus, *The Art of Indian Asia*. I was distinctly disappointed in the quality of the reproductions: the proofs were better, I thought—or perhaps it was simply that the margins here were too narrow, while the great two-page spreads fell apart in the gutters. Anyhow—the ordeal is far behind me and the book leaves me feeling that I'm glad I'm heading now for something of my own.[133]

I studied Japanese, and after dinner paid a visit to Eidmann. He tells me that in Japanese Buddhist meditation the aim is not trance—*samādhi*—but repose of spirit. Trance is somewhat suspect; but nevertheless in Noh, the actors often go into trance and perform in that state. Tea masters sometimes perform in trance—these trances, apparently, are one or two steps beyond the "inspired trance or state" of the performing and functioning artist or athlete in the West.

On television, these days, the sumō championship now being held in Tokyo is being shown. I've seen two sessions. Eidmann tells me that sumō originally was connected with ritual—and certainly the whole atmosphere suggests a rite. The announcements are made in a manner suggesting Noh. The wrestlers' tossing of salt and sipping of water have ritual moods. And the final swinging of the bow suggests ritual too.

Fillmore is studying calligraphy with the brush, and the effects here resemble those announced in *Zen in the Art of Archery:*[134] it is all one grand continuum.

Eidmann gave me a couple of books to help me commence my study of kanji and a nice little translation that he has made of the *Sutra of the Teachings Left by the Buddha.*[135]

Friday, May 20

Up at six. School. Studied kanji and reviewed my class lessons till about five. Sumō on TV in the hotel lobby (a couple of quite wild falls) and a tempura dinner in the hotel, then back to my Japanese. Mosser dropped into my room for a chat from about 7:00 to 8:30. To bed at 1:00 A.M.

CHAPTER 6

TEA AND FIRE

Saturday, May 21

To Eidmann's at 9:30, just in time to arrive at the start of a tea ceremony, with Yamauchi himself, the leading tea master in Japan, sitting in the place of honor, and a little old lady of eighty-six—Eidmann's teacher—in the place at the door. I was given place two, and made a mistake at the outset by crossing thither directly, instead of going around everybody's back—but no one said anything and I had a nice time watching the master and little old lady, as well as Haru (Eidmann's secretary), who made a couple of mistakes—he told me later—while conducting the affair.

We went next for a little stroll through the temple grounds—greatly crowded in honor of the festival of Shinran's birthday: the neighboring streets, too, were decorated, and many of the store and house windows contained little scenes, depicting episodes from the legend of Shinran's life. Airplanes flew low overhead scattering paper lotus petals, and the crowds were enormous.

We next returned to Eidmann's house for a pleasant lunch and then set off for the Noh theater in the temple compound—where there was a lovely crowd to see the Noh plays. We, however, took our departure after the opening few minutes of the first play, and, pausing briefly, to watch a group of college students practicing sumō, proceeded to a temple of the Shinran sect—westward of the Nishi Honganji—to see a *goma* (from Sanskrit *hōma*) festival conducted by *yamabushi* ("mountain hermits"), which turned out to be one of the really great experiences of the year.

The temple is the Fudō-dō Myō-ō-in and was originally built (it is said) in the ninth century in what then was the palace area. Kōbō Daishi is supposed to have brought to it Buddha statues from China, which, at the time of the civil wars, were buried in the ground beneath the temple, where they are supposed to be to this day. The Buddha image now worshipped in the temple is supposed to have been made by Kōbō Daishi.

The temple is closely associated with a Shintō shrine, and the two, indeed, are so closely mixed that one cannot tell where the Buddhism ends and the Shintō begins. While we were waiting for Haru to make arrangements at the temple for us to attend the ceremony, a large car pulled up and a Shintō priest stepped out in full regalia. Where he went, after entering the precincts, I do not know. Also to be seen were a couple of young Buddhist monks, wearing (which is unusual in Japan) a yellow-robe-like element over the normal black habit: suggesting the worlds of Thailand, Burma, and Ceylon.

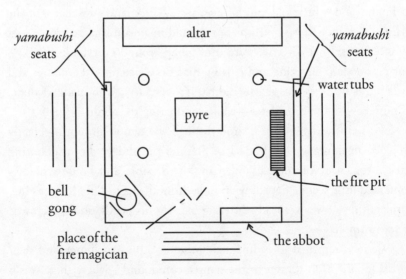

Yamabushi ceremony setup

We arrived good and early for the ceremony and were given seats on the front row benches facing the altar. There was a large, square, roped-off area before us, with a big, square pyre in the middle, covered with evergreen boughs. Beyond that was an altar, the length of one side of the area, set with offerings: cakes, oranges, etc., all neatly stacked. At each corner of the area was a large wooden tub of water with a long-handled scoop—to be used on the fire. And in the corner at our right was a large bell-gong set on a table.

The *yamabushi* arrive

At about 4:30 P.M. the *yamabushi* arrived—in their fantastic costumes. They had been on a procession through certain parts of the town. This curious order of monk-magicians is said to have appeared in the eighth century, as a protest against the governmental control of the Buddhist religion (comparable in a way, I should say, to the hermit movement in Christendom after the rule of Constantine).[136] Refusing the usual ordinations by the government, they retired to the mountains and lived as holy hermits, and, like the friars of later Europe, were responsible for spreading the religion among the common people. Buddhism in Japan before their time had been largely an aristocratic affair. Moreover, they were strongly influenced by the seventh century Tantric lore and principles (compare Zimmer's discussion of Borobudur[137]).

It is most remarkable that in the *goma* fire sacrifice that we were about to witness, elements of the Brahmanical *soma* sacrifice, as well as of the much later Tantric Buddhism of the great medieval period, were synthesized, and colored, moreover, with a tincture of Shintō. Hanging around the sacred area were strings bearing the jagged paper offerings characteristic of Shintō—not white however, but colored.

The arrival of the *yamabushi* was heralded by a blowing of conchs; they entered the area, after passing behind us, from the lower right-hand corner, and then circumambulated the pyre.

Next, they stood in two rows before the altar, and, beating time with the jingles of the staffs and batons in their right hands, chanted, ensemble, the *Prajñāpāramitā Hṛdāya Sūtra*. This finished, they went and settled on the seats prepared for them at the two sides of the area. The abbot in his robe came to our side and sat facing the altar. And another, very nice gentleman, who was a kind of second abbot, came and thanked us for being present.

In a moment, another, smaller group of *yamabushi* arrived and were ceremoniously challenged at the entrance by two *yamabushi* guardians. In a kind of Noh play dialogue they were asked a lot of test questions—imitating the procedure of more ancient days, when strangers coming to

Shooting an arrow into the air

yamabushi sacrifices and rites were actually challenged, to prove that they were not fakers and frauds. In the dialogue, the newcomers, through their leaders, were asked the meaning of the term *yamabushi* and the reason for each of the elements of the costume. The replies were given with great force—as though an actual battle were taking place; and in the end, when they had proven themselves, the new group was admitted and allowed to sit with the rest, after ceremonially circumambulating the pyre, and praying before the altar.

The next great event was performed by a little *yamabushi* who had arrived a good deal earlier than the others and while we were waiting had sat alone inside the area. Haru and another young Japanese with us had conversed with him over the ropes. He now got up, with a long bow and a sheaf of arrows, and at each of the corners pretended to shoot an arrow into the air (in the forest, he would have let it go, but here in the city, he finally released the arrows gently at his feet).

Next, another *yamabushi* got up with a sword, and, after praying before the pyre, waved it at the pyre, and then returned to his seat.

The abbot then stood before the pyre and read a *sūtra* from a piece of paper which then was tucked into the pyre. The nice gentleman who had greeted us did the same. And then the stage was ready for the great event.

It began with two *yamabushi*, bearing long, flaming faggots, one at either side of the pyre, reaching in, low, and setting the pyre aflame. It went up with a great belch of smoke, which billowed heavily to the left (our left) and completely engulfed the *yamabushi*. Since I was taking pictures, I was glad that the breeze leaned in that direction—though the air seemed, actually, quite still. Rather soon, that side of the area cleared and the smoke curved around back of the pyre and over to the right, and then, rapidly, it engulfed our part of the area: remaining, however, only for a moment, it was, presently, back where it had been at the start. It was a terrific mass of smoke, full of sparks and blazing fragments, and when it came around our way again it burned a couple of neat little holes in my blue dacron suit—which has been my chief suit throughout this journey. There was a great chant in progress that reminded me more of the noise of the Navahos than anything I've ever heard, and the general atmosphere was a bit exciting. One of the young men inside the area came over and said something to Haru, who then pointed out to me a *yamabushi* who was sitting about

The *yamabushi* making the smoke go round

eight feet off my starboard bow. "That's the one," he said, "who is making the smoke go round." I looked, and I suddenly realized what I was witnessing. The chant was filling all the air. The smoke, definitely, was circulating in the clockwise direction...

...and this *yamabushi,* with an attendant beside him, sitting on his shins, was moving his hands, pushing, conjuring, and pulling, like a cowboy turning a steer with a rope—only the rope couldn't be seen. I was so surprised I felt a sudden thump inside me, and I began taking photos of this little man, like mad. Four *yamabushi* with water scoops, meanwhile, were dipping water onto the sides of the fire—ostensibly,

Clockwise swastika

to keep the flames under control, but perhaps also to give a bit of mechanical assistance to the magic.

After a while, when the smoke diminished and the flames increased, my *yamabushi* began, ceremonially, tossing little stacks of wooden tablets into the fire, on which the votive prayers of individuals in the congregation had been inscribed. There were hundreds of these little tablets, neatly stacked between the water tubs, in rows, like cords of wood. When the magician had begun this tossing, the other *yamabushi* in the area took it up—

conjuring prayers into each packet as they held it in their hands and then giving it a toss into the flames. When all the packets had been thrown in, the pyre was pulled apart and the logs were dragged over to a pit on the right side of the area over which they were placed, as a kind of log lid. Beneath, the flaming coals and smaller wood then was shoveled, so that tongues of flame leapt up between the logs—and many of the people of the congregation, removing their getas and zōri, prepared to walk across. The nice gentleman who had welcomed us would be the first to go. The wizard was at one end of the pit conjuring a power to cure into the fire and cooling the flames; his assistant was at the other end, doing the same. And so, since I had seen, through his work on the smoke, that he was a true master of fire, I caught the fever and began to decide that I might walk across too.

I was wearing on my right ankle—the one that I had sprained at Angkor—an Ace bandage, which it took me a while to undo. This made me the last on the line, but the flames were still leaping up high between the logs—say some eight or ten inches. Two youngsters just in front of me dashed across as fast as they could, but I decided to take my time and see what it really was like to walk on a wizard's fire. My first step, with my right foot, was a bit timid, and a bit off to the side, where there were no leaping flames. But then I thought, "Well now, come on!" and seeing a nice fat flame right in front, I put my left foot down on top of it, squarely. Crackle! The hairs on the lower part of my leg were singed and a pleasant smell of singed hair went up all around me, but to my skin the flame was cool—actually cool. This gave me great courage, and I calmly completed my walk, strolling slowly and calmly right down the center of the road. Three more steps brought me to the end, and the hands of several *yama-bushi* helped me off. I went back to our seats, and the two ladies in our party were gasping with amazement at what I had done. I went out to one of the water tubs to wash my feet and get into my socks and shoes—and it was only when I was putting on my right shoe that I noticed that the swelling in my ankle had gone down. All the pain had disappeared too. Around the remains of the fire in the center of the area a lot of the little old women were standing who had gone over the fire, holding their hands out to the burning cinders and then rubbing their poor, aching backs—dear souls. It had certainly been a great and wonderful event. The courteous gentleman was greatly pleased that I had participated and invited us all to come back some day. We gathered our things, and presently strolled away.

We strolled back to the neighborhood of the Nishi Honganji Temple, where we looked again at the shop displays and then bade good-bye to the two ladies who had been with us. I was a bit high from all the excitement, and so, returned to Eidmann's for dinner and an hour's talk, before returning home.

A detail from the history of the American military Occupation of Japan: The Taishō University library was taken over by the U.S. Army (no Christian university in Japan was thus treated) and in the clearing of the rooms the card file of a Sanskrit-Japanese dictionary, on which 1,000 scholars had been working for some twenty years, were simply dumped. The Japanese hysterically sent crews to rescue what they could and many (perhaps most) of the cards were recovered: but a vast task still remains of classifying these thousands of mixed up items again. No funds are available for the work and it remains undone.

Besides dumping the cards the military gentlemen stole a number of rare and very valuable books. (This would seem to indicate, by the way, that not all of them were utterly ignorant of what they were doing.)

Sunday, May 22   Kyoto—Nara—Hōrinji—Kyoto

At 8:30 my Japanese student friend, Hisashi Mita, arrived at the hotel and we started off for Nara and Hōrinji. A magnificent day.

Stop one was at Nishinokyō, where we visited the Tōshōdaiji and Yakushiji Temples. The chief images in the first were made of japan and cloth and were large and handsome. The chief of these was of Kanshitsu. At his proper right was a Senju Kannon. The guardian to the right carried a *vajra*. Off to the left side, against another wall, was a large wooden statue of the *Ādi* Buddha with his hands in the *lingam-yoni mudrā*. We left this building (the *kondō,* or main hall) and strolled around the beautiful grounds; then entered the *kōdō,* or lecture hall, where some more fine images are preserved—among them a figure of Fudō Myō-ō—and I suddenly realized the sense of the rites in which I had participated yesterday. Fudō Myō-ō, whose name means "very still, even in fire" (according to Hisashi Mita), is a red figure sitting in a fire, with the red flames up behind him, as a kind of backing; his left eye is closed (as though gone: cf. Wotan) and his right is open.[138]

We remained an hour in this temple area and then walked to the neighboring Yakushiji Temple, where there was a lovely three-storied pagoda, and, within the main hall, three beautiful bronzes—a beautiful Kannon, and two standing Bodhisattvas, Gakkō (Moon) and Nikkō (Sun).

We returned to the station and took the train on to Tsutsui, where we changed for a bus that took us to the neighborhood of Hōrinji, which we reached about 1:00 P.M. We had a bowl of rice in a roadside restaurant and then walked on to the temple—one of the great experiences of the year. Lots of photographing: many beautiful images, including a glorious, very tall and gaunt Kannon (the so-called "Kudara Kannon," a gift from Korea in the Asuka period), and the Buddha trio illustrated in *The Art of Indian Asia*—to my shock, with the Bodhisattvas transposed—and, finally, that celebrated seated image of the world-contemplating Bodhisattva. All were beautifully exhibited, but the room of the last was usurped by a little class of students, listening to a young instructor spout such nonsense as "archaic smile," and "frontality."

Our next event was a little walk across country, to a pretty temple area called Hōryūji, where there was a charming little garden as well as some fine images, featuring Kannon. There were some *vajras* before the chief image. The temple had once been of the Shingon sect, but now is Hossō (according to the nice little lady who showed us around).

Our final walk was to the nearby Hokkiji Temple, prettily set in the country and with a small but handsome pagoda. We walked back to the road, under a slightly showery sky, past the peasants in their fields (one, a very handsome young woman wearing her makeup, but in peasant clothes), and caught the bus back to Tsutsui.

The train had trouble getting home, due to some failures in the electricity, but we arrived, finally, at seven, and, after a nice steak dinner at Suehiro's, voted it a wonderful day.

Special item: the rain was falling as we walked from Hokkiji Temple to the bus, but the sun was shining. "We call this in Japan," said Hisashi, "the marriage of the fox."

Monday, May 23   **Kyoto**

All day, Japanese. A letter from Jean, however, in which she reports on the trials and success of her production of her Saroyan play, as well as the sale of Abu (1938–1955)[139] and purchase of a new car. Had dinner at a pleasant Chinese restaurant, Hamamura, where I fell into conversation with a young American named Stoops, from California, who is working at the university and teaching. Like everyone else, he regarded the Fulbright group in Japan as a very poor lot.

Tuesday, May 24

All day, again, at Japanese. I am trying to get my hand in on kanji. The going is very tough. Went around to Eidmann's after dinner for a pleasant evening's chat. He suggested that, while in Japan, I should study tea, but somehow this didn't appeal to me very much. I think I'm just about jammed, now, as I am.

Wednesday, May 25

Another day of Japanese, and nothing but. Dinner tonight, and last evening, at a very good and reasonable restaurant called Fujiya, on the corner of Sanjō and Kawaramachi, right near the hotel.

Thursday, May 26

Still more Japanese. If this doesn't get me over the bump, I don't know what will! Dinner at another cheap restaurant, The Star, but not so good.

Friday, May 27

After my Japanese class, a long visit with Eidmann, from 2:00 to 10:30 P.M. I brought over my copy of *The Art of Indian Asia,* and we had a good deal of talk about the making of books. I am trying to stir him to write a history of Buddhism in Japan. He loaned me, some days ago, a nine-page paper on the history of Buddhism in Japan.[140]

Eidmann has mentioned also the fact that in Ceylon Buddhism is having to put up a fight to recover ground lost to the Christians during the period of British rule. Only some 2 percent of Ceylon is Christian, yet the Christians hold 50 percent of the radio time—and since most of the civil service group is Christian, they are not yielding.

One more point with respect to Japanese Buddhism—this time, in contrast to the Buddhism of Tibet. The chief period of continental influence in the Japanese tradition is that of fifth to eighth century Tantra—that of Tibet is the tenth to twelfth centuries, with its stress on the Yab-Yum motif.[141]

Going over *The Art of Indian Asia* with Eidmann and Haru, I became somewhat reconciled to the beauty of the book: which is certainly below the level of my expectations; but I had a few shocks as I went through the plates and text: a number of mistakes that I recognize—and a number of overly bold statements challenged by Eidmann and Haru.

Saturday, May 28

Japanese all morning, then with Eidmann and Haru to a delightful lecture on Nagasaki prints by the Dutch consul in Kobe, at the monthly meeting of the Kansai Asiatic Society. The prints and the lecture presented a pleasant and illuminating little view of the Dutch-Japanese interplay in the Nagasaki area from the seventeenth to the nineteenth centuries. The lecture itself was really elegant—urbane and charming; and while the gentleman talked, I had thoughts of my own about my problems when I return to New York. I want to hang on, as far as possible, to certain things that I have commenced here in Japan, and, at the same time, develop my own major work. My basic formula, worked out at the lecture, looks like this:

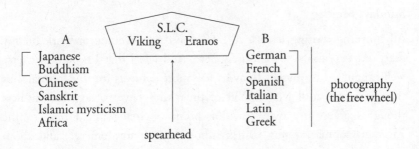

A Campbell plan for life

The approach to side A is to be through Japanese at first: Japanese language records, Vaccari's kanji, the Buddhist *sūtras* in Japanese, and modern Japanese scholarship.

The approach to side B is to be through a thoroughgoing refreshment of my European languages, commencing with German, which I now want to speak like a civilized man. Eidmann has given me some good suggestions for the refreshment of my Spanish and Latin.

My principal task at the outset, undoubtedly, will be my Sarah Lawrence class, where I shall have an opportunity to reexperience my whole experience of the present year in the light of my earlier thoughts and lectures on mythology.

My next task will be that of catching up with the Eranos series.[142] This will bring me back into the context of my *Basic Mythologies* plans.[143]

And my third problem will be, to get started as soon as possible on my first Viking contract—a book on mythology, which has already been slightly planned.[144] As soon as possible, I should begin to alternate my three-month stints on this book with those (to be commenced later) of my *Basic Mythologies*. I begin to feel, now, that I should not go to Europe next summer, but go on working diligently to get my writing and notes into gear.

Extremely important, however, is that times and plans should be arranged immediately on arrival in New York for the continuation of my Japanese, and then, as time permits, for a return to German and French, with a commencement, at some point, of Italian (for Ascona).[145]

And finally, let's see what can be done along the photography line.

Sunday, May 29

All morning writing letters. All afternoon and evening at work on my diary. At 11:15 P.M. I am precisely here. And I feel that I have now pretty well caught up to myself. I have a few more subjects for this journal, but they can wait until I have a bit of time: they have to do with my new thoughts about my own dawning point of view—in contrast to the Zimmer-Coomaraswamy matrix from which I now emerge; and about India and Japan; for I find that in Japan I have become reconciled to India—as Orient. Finally, about anti-U.S. elements in Asia, and why.

Monday, May 30

After a morning and early afternoon of Japanese, sent a letter off to Alan Watts[146] and read Eidmann's paper on the contrast of Shinshū and the *bhakti* of the Gītā. According to this little opus:

1. The Gītā distinguishes two eternal principles, ever distinct—the material body (including its psychic elements) and the immaterial soul, which is without qualities and inactive. (Problem here: Jain formula vs. Vedantic: actually, Vedanta is somewhat ambiguous, since it insists both on non-duality and on the primacy of *ātman:* perhaps another example of two-faced India wanting its "spirituality" both ways. Try to think this out.)

2. Shinshū and Theravāda Buddhism deny that man has any innate Buddha nature (*ānata*): Mahāyāna, however, though still professing *ānata,* has brought the soul in by the backdoor as "Buddha nature."

3. The Gītā teaches that the ignorant confuse body and *ātman,* imagining that it is their souls that suffer, but that the sage, distinguishing, is released.

4. Buddhist release comes in the recognition of the illusionary nature of the so-called soul substance denying both the concept of any innate Buddha nature and that of a permanent, pure, inactive soul. (I think Eidmann is here straining on a gnat. Coomaraswamy has pointed out that the *ātman* of Vedanta is not "soul"—not the soul that is denied by the Buddhist term *ānata*.)

5. The God of the Gītā is a personal God, who assumes incarnations to save the world of men. But the supreme form of God is revealed only as a rare act of grace (e.g. to Arjuna).

6. In Shinshū, the idea that God's (or Buddha's) true form can be seen is regarded as an apparitional concept. Moreover, *whatever good man does or ought to do is of purely social value; it has no bearing on his salvation.*

7. The Gītā teaches three main ways:
   a. That of knowledge (*sāṅkhya*)
   b. That of action (*yoga*)
   c. That of devotion (*bhakti*)
   It prefers the way of "indifference in action" (unselfish performance of duty), to that of knowledge and inaction.

8. The Shinshū concept of the two divisions of Buddhism is somewhat similar:
   a. The Entrance by the Holy Path (*shōdōmon*) and
   b. The Entrance by the Pure Realm (*jōdōmon*), i.e. by faith. (In Japanese Zen the concept is especially strong that somehow salvation comes by the performance of one's duty perfectly.) Shinshū insists, however, that any Buddha body seen in vision, which can be measured and depicted, is not the True Body of Buddhahood. Moreover, whereas the God of the Gītā is personal, Amida is defined in the *Topics for Discussion of Peace of Mind* (*anjin rondai*) as not a person.

9. *Karma* in the Gītā is due not to action itself, but to the desire underlying the action: acts performed without interest in their outcome have no binding

effect. In fact, it is not only wrong, but even impossible, to refrain from action: man must do his duty—which is not defined, yet accepted as a kind of categorical imperative.

10. *Karma* in Buddhism too is due not to action itself, but to the desire underlying the action. *Shinshū, however, finds no possibility of the ordinary person creating "barren* karma" (Theravāda term). Shinshū insists on the Kegon principle of conditioned arising: because man cannot free himself of his passions he suffers countless reincarnations, and he has within him no power to act unselfishly in life.

11. Devotion (*bhakti*), in the Gītā, brings man to Salvation. God is sometimes spoken of as intervening to bring his devotee to the goal; but in the main, it is through his own power that man advances in devotion.

12. In the Gītā, it is peculiarly important for man to fix his mind on God at the moment of death: indeed, the time of death is so important that the Gītā* declares that man attains salvation only if he dies at a favorable time with his mind fixed on God: waxing moon, and six months when the sun moves northward.

13. Some Buddhists, too, emphasize thinking about Buddha at the instant of death, *rinjū shōnen,* as the true cause of attainment; but Shinran rejects this theory, as well as all emphasis on auspicious times.

14. Faith in Shinshū is not the same as that of the Gītā. *Faith in Shin is an instant of perfect egolessness in which all self-confidence is surrendered.* This egolessness is not acquired by any internal power within the believer, but is *entirely due to the power of the main vow of Buddha.* (I should like to know what is meant by this last line—and whether the effective vow is the Buddha's or the devotee's.)[147]

Without quite realizing it, or knowing why, I seem to have undergone a considerable change of feeling with respect to India in the past few weeks. In the first place, with the immediate annoyances gone and some of the major shocks now taken for granted, I have begun to remember the majesty of the majestic things, the wonder of the wonderful, and the interest of the interesting. Going over *The Art of Indian Asia* the other evening with Eidmann, and seeing there the beautiful photographs of the beautiful things I had seen, I felt that all of my petty little quibbles were really petty.

Furthermore, finding in Japan much of the great Oriental past, which in India has been shattered, has given me an improved position from which

---

* Bhagavad Gītā, viii, 23–27.

to feel my way back into what once was there: what must once have in-habited those ruined shells that lie all around the land.

I don't know whether I've set this down already in my notes, but it seems to me now, that, whereas in India the upper classes have lost their Oriental character and are, for the most part, a lot of conceited fakers and confused jackanapes, in Japan it is the upper classes that have preserved their Oriental tradition; and, vice versa, in India it is the squalid illiterate lower castes that have preserved their Oriental character, whereas in Japan the lower classes—largely literate and decently groomed—are taking on the West in a big, fast, and wonderful way.

I have also new thoughts about my new thoughts, vis-à-vis the old thoughts that were inspired, largely, by Zimmer and Coomaraswamy.

A fresh approach to the Orient by way of Japan and Buddhism, on the one hand, and perhaps Persia and Islam on the other (Corbin's writings),[148] will break me decisively from the old position. My own view of India has discredited entirely, for me, Coomaraswamy's high tone about the caste system; and the mistakes of Zimmer that I had to correct while writing and that I have discovered since, have discredited for me, as a final attitude, the rather slapdash intuitivism of my dear master. I am now for a very careful, meticulous checking after all the lovely intuitions: we have got to have both, if we are going to have a book.

Tuesday, May 31

During my visit with Eidmann last Tuesday a number of interesting points emerged from the pleasantly rambling conversation, which was largely in-spired by the marvels of the *yamabushi* magician. Fillmore was present, and was interested in the matter; and when he asked how it could be ap-proached philologically, I suggested that a paper on the *philology of the words of power* would be fun: one should study the relationship of power words and divine languages (e.g. Sanskrit and Hebrew) to psychological principles. We spoke of Tantra, Kabbala, Ang, etc. Then we spoke of Purāṇic-Eddic connections, and of European witchcraft: all of these things should be approached afresh.

Eidmann declared that in Japan there were many definitely secret groups continuing some of the old mysteries: the *yamabushi* were an example. But there was also a kind of self-defense system (not sumō; not jūdō) which is taught only to elaborately and profusely recommended people of the highest character. In Tokyo an old Japanese gentleman sent two GIs who annoyed him into the moat at the Imperial Palace. The army became interested; but the old man would not teach.[149]

Eidmann mentioned also the attested miracles of the spies in ancient times: they could disappear, they could be invisible. Furthermore, on huge kites, they would ascend to look at the enemy camp (a connection here, perhaps, with the chatter in modern India about the "airplanes," etc. of "Vedic" times).[150]

Also discussed were the swordsmen (of whom there are still a few) who could pull a sword longer than their arm from its scabbard, cut off a head, and return the sword to its scabbard, so quickly that nothing of the act could be seen.

And finally, Eidmann declared that one of the reasons that the Christians were feared and suppressed in sixteenth-century Japan, was that their magicians were a particularly powerful lot.

In connection with the Purāṇic-Eddic discussion, Eidmann suggested a connection between Buddhism and the Eddas. I pointed to the Wotan-Śiva, Śiva-Buddha continuity as a possible explanation of an apparent influence; but now I think the connection (fifth to twelfth centuries A.D.!) may have been more direct. Consider the closed and the opened eye of the Fudō Myō-ō figure that I saw last week at the Tōshōdaiji Temple: the Bodhisattva "very still, even in fire."

Out of all this I drew the idea of a little work on *the actual mysteries of the Orient, which might be regarded as validation enough of the exaggerated legend of "the mysterious East."*

As for the contemporary East, some new facts and thoughts, worthy of note. In this morning's paper a letter from a troubled "foreigner," who found himself excluded from a number of eating places in Kyoto: one even exhibited a sign "Japanese Only." (In Patna I saw a sign on a hotel: "Hindus Only.") "As one who has traveled to almost all parts of the world," this letter writer writes, "nowhere before had I been so insulted or embarrassed. . . . Except in Communist-influenced areas, never before had I witnessed such an intense anti-foreign feeling. Discussing this saddening experience with other foreigners, both tourists and businessmen, I learned that almost all had en-countered the same experience in various Japanese cities."

One could speak of the anti-foreign feelings that a Japanese might en-counter in Tennessee or certain parts of California: but the point is that such feelings certainly do exist in Japan—as throughout the Orient.

An article in yesterday's paper mentioned and discussed the problem of slave girls in some of the harems of India. The problem has come to light in a number of specific cases: girls bought in childhood, forbidden to leave, tortured when reluctant, etc. Undoubtedly this phenomenon exists in India today—and if there is now an outcry against it, the cause of the out-cry is the humanitarian influence from the West.

In general the crimes of the Orient are no less spectacular than those which American journalism spreads as news from the U.S.A. out all over the world. The Oriental journalists are not so efficient: they are content to fill their papers with American boilerplate (even Occidental jokes and car-toons, that can mean nothing at all to the Oriental). Result: America's fine reputation for crime, and a sanctimonious face on your Hindu "holier-than-thou" gentleman of absolute leisure.

In Japanese, we are now just halfway through the book. The term ends July 8—and I think I'll stick it out. My first plan was to spend about six weeks at this, and then push off for more touring; but June, I am told, is a month of sheer rain—and I'm learning much here in Kyoto. Another five weeks of this sort of thing won't do me a bit of harm.

Having caught up pretty well on my letters and diary, and having doubled the track on my classmate at school by learning the kanji as well as *rōmaji*[151] texts of our lessons (the regular plan of the school is to review the whole thing in kanji next term), I am beginning to feel that I may be getting some place in this deep dig, after all.

After class today I had lunch at Fujiya, and then studied and wrote in my diary till about six. Dinner at Fujiya (which is turning out to be my great standby—lunch for ¥150 and dinner for ¥300; total, about $1.35), and then to Eidmann's, where I found a young woman missionary named Mary Jones. The talk was around religion and I learned a few things:

1. Gandhi's introduction to the Gītā was in England, through a visit to a class or lecture of Annie Besant.[152] (We hear nothing of this in India today. The Ramakrishna monks are playing up the Ramakrishna connection.)

2. About 1917 Annie Besant had practically persuaded the Congress Party to accept England's terms for a free India. Gandhi moved in against her. Result: Besant's work occluded by the great Gandhi movement: all kinds of patriotic spirituality—and an India divided.

3. The first Shinshū patriarch is Nāgārjuna[153] and the second Vasubandhu.*[154]

4. Among the Christians of Japan is a very influential group known as the Mukyōkai (no church), who meet together and read the Bible, but belong to no congregation. Among them are such influential personages as Yanaihara, president of Tokyo University;[155] also his predecessor. Eidmann claims that the direction of their thought is toward Shinshū.

5. Eidmann feels that in Zen today there are very few who represent the true Zen teachings. In the old days, in such a temple as that of Kenninji there would have been some three hundred monks, with three or four attaining satori: today there are about twenty monks: and in all of Japan there are not more than five or six *rōshi.*[156]

6. Mary Jones promised to bring me a book, at school tomorrow, about modern Christianity. I told her about the argument I had in Madras with the people who had dropped the myth of the Fall and Redemption from Christianity, and she seemed to think that the book she was going to lend me would show me what it was all about.[157]

When Miss Jones left, at about 10:00, Eidmann told me of Professor Kasugai's reaction to *The Art of Indian Asia:* he was completely knocked out. "I would never have even dreamed of dreaming of such a book appearing in a dream." He is taking it to a meeting of top Japanese scholars in Tokyo today and believes that it will totally upset all their ideas of both American scholarship and the significance of the work that has been done on India in Japan. (Eidmann claims that the Japanese underestimate American scholarship because they mistranslate the English: they read the word *passions,* and their dictionaries give them *bonnō* instead of *netsujō.*)[158]

Professor Kasugai is going to have the Chion-in Temple treasury opened and exhibited to me: The last exhibition was last year, and the next should be some fifty years hence; but this is going to happen for me because of the wonder of my book. He is simply overwhelmed.

And well, so am I—by his wonderful response.

Two letters today from Bollingen. One from Vaun,[159] asking if I would like to accept an offer for a Spanish (Mexican) translation of *The Hero;*[160] the other from Bill McGuire,[161] stating that a paper edition of

---

* See Junjirō Takakusu, *The Essentials of Buddhist Philosophy* (Honolulu: University of Hawai'i Press, 1949), p. 12 for a view of the relationship of these to the older Buddhist sects.

The Hero is about to be launched. Both announce that the publication date of *The Art of Indian Asia* was May 23: the day after my trip to Hōrinji and the day of the arrival of Jean's letter announcing our new car.

Oh yes—last Thursday a cable from Harold Taylor announced that the college yearbook for this year had been dedicated to Horace Gregory, Alistair Reid,[162] and myself (the three absentees), and would I please cable my greetings at once to the graduates? So I guess I can say that the year is over—and the pull of the next job, next year, can already be felt. Apparently, we are going to be about four thousand dollars in the hole, Jean and I: so the main job apparently again, is going to be to rake in a good bit of cash. No doubt just what is needed to pull me out of my dreams.

Wednesday, June 1

A letter from Harold Taylor today, offering me a raise for next year and asking me to give the convocation address on September 30. So the college is now really pushing in. The opening day is September 21, thirteen days after the opening of Bard[163]—which should give me time enough to get a haircut and buy a new pair of shoes.

As soon as I hit New York, I must go to work on *Eranos,* make arrangements to carry on with *Japanese,* get in touch with Volkening,[164] and start work on the Viking presentation. That, I believe, is to be my first flight of tasks.

The second flight is to be connected with the opening of *Sarah Lawrence:* preparing my course and the convocation address.

Next, I must turn to the task of oiling up either *my German or my French* (perhaps, for Jean's sake, it would be well to commence with the French), and finally some way must be found to keep the game of *photography* going. Let us schedule it, tentatively, as follows:

> September 8–20: Japanese/Eranos/Volkening: commence work on the Viking presentation and book
> September 21–30: S.L.C. convocation address and class
> October 1–10: French (or German) and photography
> December 26–March 26: Commence work on *The Basic Mythologies*

At 4:30 today, after my usual morning at the Japanese language school and early afternoon of work in my room, I headed for the Heian Shrine, to meet Hisashi Mita at the entrance and attend a wonderfully interesting presentation of Noh plays on a temporary stage erected in the court. There were about five thousand people present: a wonderful audience. Three plays and one comedy were presented. The first I had already seen in Tokyo: in fact, it was the first Noh I had ever seen, *Arashiyama*—only, this time, a fantastic episode was added of a company of monkeys enacting Noh in monkey language. The audience loved it. A comedy came next; then the lovely Noh called *Izutsu*, "The Well," and finally an astonishing piece, *Shōzon*, in which duels were enacted in a sort of Kabuki style. It was a beautiful night with a lovely moon—just a month since that magnificent evening of the Festival of Ten Thousand Lights at Nara.

Thursday, June 2

All day on Japanese—with a couple of letters, one to Jean (we are running into a money problem), one to Harold Taylor (sending in my signed contract), and one to the Batteys (about Jean's teaching this summer at the Tokyo Cultural Center).

An idea for the opening of my Viking book:

"For then only do we know God truly," wrote the great Christian theologian, Saint Thomas Aquinas, "when we know that he far surpasses anything that man may say or think of God." The great saint and theologian then, in the remainder of his work, proceeded to analyze and characterize God, until that catastrophic morning, when he was saying mass, when... etc. (get a good reference for this anecdote).[165]

"..." (Give next a comparable quote from some Pawnee or Hottentot medicine man.)[166]

(And then:) This is the sense of the whole world of myth, as it blossoms from the mind bent on the knowledge of the transcendent and the manifestation of the ineffable.

Next: Christ's life, as the typical "Life of the Hero." To be followed by Jensen's rendition of the Celebes *dema* mythos.[167] After this, the Greek Alexandrian complex, and therewith the Hebrew formula of the Hero race. Bible and Babel should then be developed.

(An idea for my classes: have a wire recorder in the room and use the lectures then as bases for either a book or a series of short articles.[168])

Two long spans: (1) The Christian theme of God's love and the myth of Hainuwele; and (2) Zen in the Art of Archery and the wall paintings at Lascaux and Pêche Merle.

An important classification: mythology as

1. *Artha* ⎫ magic (Frazer)
2. *Kāma* ⎭
3. *Dharma* ⎫ "religion" (Durkheim: Coomaraswamy)
4. *Mokṣa* ⎭
5. Entertainment
   a) Folktale
   b) Literary ornament

Classification of mythology

Two poles of interpretation: (1) Literal, concretistic (popular—exoteric—extrovert); (2) Metaphorical, symbolical (elite—esoteric—introvert).

CHAPTER 7

SURPRISES AND TRANSFORMATIONS

Friday, June 3

Two months in Japan! And how full of surprises and transformations. And three more months ahead!

I've been reading the book about Christianity that Mary Jones spoke about and handed me after Japanese class. Title: *The Christian Faith,* by Nels Ferré, abbot professor of Christian theology, Andover Newton Theological School. Going through this work here in Japan, at the close of my year in the Orient, has made very vivid to me a very important point:

1. *The traits peculiar to Christianity are not:*
   Belief in God (*Īśvarā*)
   The doctrine of the Fall (*avidyā*)
   The Incarnation (*avatāra*)
   Redemption (*mokṣa*)
   Love and selflessness as redemptive (*karuṇā*)
   Heaven-Purgatory-Hell
   Judgment (Osiris)
   Progress toward the Kingdom of God (Zarathustra)
2. The traits peculiar to Christianity are:
   a. Finality of the Personality of God (Judaism)
   b. Old Testament plus New Testament as Word of God
   c. Old Testament Fall as severing man from God to such a degree that a

special New Testament revelation was required for redemption. Also, a
vocabulary of Fall and Redemption

   d. Jesus of Nazareth as the unique revelation of God's New Testament (incarnation)

   e. B.C.-A.D. division of all time (historical rather than spiritual reading of symbols)

   f. The Church as the unique vehicle of Salvation

   g. Specific Christian inflection of traditional rites

3. Compare this (point-by-point) with the traits peculiar to Judaism analyzed by Steinberg:

   b. Old Testament as the unique Word of God

   c. This point receives less stress in Judaism than in Christianity

   d. The prophets

   e. Jew-Gentile distinction

   f. The ultimate justification of the Jewish race, who give the world its savior. The "Remnant"

   g. Specific Jewish inflection of traditional rites

Note in Ferré's account of the break with the Social Gospel that led to democracy and the Romantic that led to progressive education.[169] This honestly severs the tie-up that the Christians in Japan are trying to make between Christianity and democracy.

I must try, now, to find a good analysis of *Islam.*

At about 5:30 today I called for Ellen Psaty at her dwelling, was delightfully greeted by Obasan—who had liked my Japanese over the phone; and took her to the second evening of Noh up at the Heian Shrine. The crowd was even greater than last time. Two seats (very bad) had been saved for us by a young army couple named Poor, and we remained only through the first two plays: *Yashima* and *Hajitomi*—the latter, particularly fine, with its emergence of the Lady Yūgao from her bower. The long solo speech in *Yashima* (by Zeami) was most remarkable. Ellen tells me that in these Noh companies only the principals are professionals; the others are amateurs.

よし子

Japanese characters = "Yoshiko"

It was about 9:00 P.M. when we left—quite stiff and sore from the craning and sitting—and went for dinner to Suehiro's. Next we proceeded to a Japanese bar in the Pontochō: or Yoshiko. Two guitarists were tinkling away, the proprietress was chic and cordial, a gentleman arrived with three middle-aged geishas (these seem to me to be the most charming women in Japan!) and had a nice time on one glass of beer. In and out came other parties and finally an American couple, the girl looking a bit disgruntled and the pleasant, tall, and amusing gent having a good time testing his Japanese on the hostesses. It was a fine view of Japan's response to the Western manner of enjoying "night life." The man with his geishas went out as gaily as he came in. We had a couple of brandies and at 11:30 left.

Saturday, June 4

A wire this morning from Joe Lillard[170] suggesting that I should wire greetings to our Columbia class on its thirtieth reunion. Too late for a wire—and besides, why?

Spent the morning concluding my notes on Ferré and afternoon on my Japanese. At five I went around to Eidmann's for dinner and an evening's conversation.

Last evening at Suehiro's Ellen and I were asking each other what is so attractive to the Japanese (and Asians in general) about Communism.

My view: Asia resists the problems raised by individualism, the personal equation, etc., yet requires the machine. Communism offers a clue to a kind of Asian machine civilization.

Her view: The caste and social blockages are very strong. The paths open to graduates of Tokyo University are quite fixed; those to Kyoto grads are different; those to Doshyo[?][171] are far inferior, etc. etc. Communism promises a leveling of these barriers.

The other evening at the Gass Lump,[172] Hisashi said, rather cautiously, that the ideas of Communism had a great appeal to him. He was afraid, he said, of the "bad effects of competition." I described what seemed to me the good effects: but it's the same story as the one I encountered in India. Communism has become a kind of Asian dream.

And we agreed that the U.S.A. should not lean or hope to lean on Orientals, whose whole system of concepts and needs is so different from ours that the term "democracy" can hardly be experienced as a requirement.

Ellen spoke of several elegant young Japanese whom she has met who have studied in London, Paris, and America: they think it would be wonderful to visit India or Norway... thinking of the new Socialist style. And why are so many young of the wealthy, who live on pillows, enthusiasts for the Communist cause? Same reason, I guess, as at S.L.C.[173]—anti-Papa, plus slanted teaching.

An additional thought about the Christians: "Jung writes," says Ferré, "that the basic cure of much mental illness is religious in nature. But modern man is in search of something more than his racial, unconscious self. It is true that he must break the circle of his isolation and be reunited to the roots of his deeper self, but that self is what George Herbert Palman called the 'conjunct self.' In Royce's terms he can find it only in the 'beloved community.'"[174]

It is this proud notion that Christianity—the Christian community—is the only door through the absolute wall of "sin," that is the Christian message. Hence, a fundamental antagonism to (a) the psychological-pedagogical romanticism of such movements as that represented by Jung and progressive education, which seek to release the "image of God" that is in man as a competent force, (b) the Social Gospel of democracy, and (c) such true tolerance as that represented by the sentence in the Gītā: "By whatever path a man seek me, even so do I welcome him, for the paths men take from every side are mine."

Clearly, Christianity is opposed fundamentally and intrinsically to everything that I am working and living for: and for the modern world, I believe, with all of its faiths and traditions, Kṛṣṇa is a *much* better teacher and model than Christ.

Amen, then, to that.

The claim of Christianity to consideration as a world religion is refuted by its confining of the concept of redemption to the Christian community, which is but one community in the wide world. Kṛṣṇa's welcome is to all communities, whether of the present or of the past: with no totalitarian, imperialistic implication either; no claim or hope that Hinduism shall ultimately be the one religion of mankind.[175]

It is this universalism that may be said to constitute Hinduism's first claim to our consideration.

The second claim is its proof, through such selfless, released (i.e., redeemed) teachers as Ramakrishna, Ramanan, and Krishna Menon, that Man can be and has been released from his natural selfishness without the mediation of any messenger of Jesus Christ.

The fact that, against these claims, many modern (in fact, perhaps, most modern) Indians are besotted sectarians, superstitious, and careless of the well-being of their neighbors, is secondary. Just as Christianity has been born from the history and societies of the Mediterranean-Atlantic zone, so Hinduism from that of the Himalayas and the Vindhyas.

When I get home, instead of brooding on the inadequacies of the modern Indian transportation system, the hordes of beggars, and the conceited fakirs, I must keep my mind on this central truth; remember also, the beauty of the ancient temples; then think of the millennium of Islamic, Portuguese, French, and British wars, and be surprised that there is as much as there is of the ancient lore: indeed, it comes spouting from the mouth of everyone in the land—no matter what his actual life.

The other side is the political-economic, psychological crisis of the modern period. This I must always discuss with care and understanding—but never without remembering the force and actual threat of the anti-Americanism that I felt in every house.

My primary loyalty, now, is definitely to the West, which as I now see, is prodigiously the hope, as well as transformer, of the modern world. All other cultures are provincial—and they are facing, ten to a hundred or even five hundred years late, the tensions between the new and the old that have been—and are being—faced and resolved first in the West.

In every continent the claims of religion are being reduced: religious geography, astronomy, moral dogmatism, etc., are in full retreat before the scientific revelation; and the fundamentally religious function of "salvation/redemption/*bodhi* ('awakening')," as rendered variously in the various religions, now has to face the claims of the psychological schools, as well as the differing claims of each other. Finally, perhaps, the religion whose "myths" accord most properly with the needs recognized by psychology will be the one to survive—if any survives. And I should say, definitely that in this crisis Christianity (with its mortal sin and its one and only adequate redeemer) is out. The Gītā, as I realized very well in Ahmedabad, can not only support but can also supplement psychoanalysis, without bringing any antipathetic principle into play. Christianity cannot do this.

Christianity and Freud, by the way, have something important in common, inasmuch as for both, man's rational consciousness is absolutely sealed away from the unknown root of his soul. The Christian needs Christ's Minister and the Patient needs the Analyst. Jung, on the other hand, is more distinctly in the optimistic romantic tradition: pagan, one might say, as opposed to Judeo-Christian.

The chat tonight with Eidmann was very pleasant. Before going to see him I glanced at Henry van Straelen's "The Religion of Divine Wisdom, Japan's Most Powerful Religious Movement"[176] and learned of Tenrikyō, founded in 1838 by Miki Nakayama,[177] "in order that the true happy life and the real peace of the world might be realized and we all become brothers and sisters." "If we had mutual love among ourselves, this world of ours would be converted into a brighter and happier world," we read in one of the speeches of the present patriarch, Nakayama Shōzen. "The cause of all our troubles is our shortcomings in the love of humanity. Human beings today are driving themselves into a trap. Today we must love mankind as never before. This is our reason for introducing to the people of the world—the Religion of Heavenly Wisdom."[178]

The sect has "a few million believers, 14,200 churches with 80,000 preachers," and is constantly expanding. And I ask myself: what would Professor Ferré say of *this* religion of love? Might it not be "sufficient unto Salvation"? If not why not?

Eidmann showed me a book by Ferré, *The Sun and the Umbrella,* where it says: "Jesus never was or became God."[179] This is not an easy one to reconcile with the statements of the book by the same author that I have just read: we talked a bit about the confusion in modern Christian thinking. We discussed also the problem of *relationships between Buddhism and the early Christian tradition.* I mentioned the Vulture Peak–Mt. of Olives parallels, Peter and Ānanda, the pattern of the Sage with his followers; Eidmann mentioned the problem of the Essenes as possible Buddhists and the probable Buddhist influence on Ecclesiastes.[180]

To illustrate the difference between the Christian and the Buddhist attitude toward relics, he told the tale of *The Dog-Tooth Relic of the Buddha,* which, he declares, is a well-known and oft-repeated Buddhist tale.[181]

I brought up a query about the passage in the Acts of the Apostles in which the apostles are forbidden to go into Asia. Eidmann did not know the text: we hunted for it and found it in Acts 16:6. An explanation is still to be found.[182]

Some other matters:

Eidmann holds that plural marriage is still practiced among the Mormons; he himself was introduced to the six wives of one of the leaders of the movement. The religious idea involved? A school for altruism and a breeding of bodies for souls.

Eidmann's view of Christianity is that the two logical extremes are Unitarianism and Mormonism, the former absolutely monotheistic—and empty, and the latter polytheistic.

About marriage: *The First Commandment* in the Bible is in Genesis —to beget and multiply. All Jews must marry and have a family. And so what about Jesus? Well, read again, very carefully, the text of *The Marriage of Cana*.[183] And consider—as the Mormons do—Jesus' relationship to the sisters of Lazarus, Martha and Mary, and to all those other young women...

In modern Japan there is taking place a measurable lowering of the general IQ. Forces operating: the Shintō idea that all must think alike; government control of the universities, the exclusion of adventurous thinkers. The control is exercised via Tokyo University. Government to Tokyo University to all other universities. Faculty appointments in all Japanese universities have to be controlled from and approved by Tokyo. He told me also of a form that he has just received asking what he is now *studying*. (Compare the Council of Learned Societies form that I received at the time of the war.)

As a kind of stunt, to illustrate the capacity of the trained Japanese mind, Eidmann called Haru in, read off to him a list of twenty-five objects that we had just written out. He recalled them, perfectly—and then gave us the list again, about two hours later.

The last act of the evening was my introduction to the art of using a Chinese dictionary.

Sunday, June 5

An amusing situation has developed around *The Art of Indian Asia*. Kasugai brought the book to a scholars' dinner in Tokyo, and the waiters held the soup course in their hands for an hour and a half while the group swooned and went crazy. One man, whose son had just returned from a trip to India to make photographs, jokingly declared that he could have saved a lot of money and had good pictures if he had only seen this book first. Eidmann is stressing the fact to them that this work was produced in America through the support of Mellon money—capitalistic money. He asks them all to guess the price, and when they shoot between $150 and $300, he gives them the $19.50 and they are shattered. I think that Jean in India and this book in Japan have been the greatest blurbs for the U.S.A. that have come to the Orient without any government support this lovely year.

My thoughts are beginning to point in very strongly toward the problem of returning to New York with my present set of new feelings, plans, and studies fully functioning. One problem is going to be to assimilate the dance situation when Jean arrives. That must be worked out here. And when we hit New York the new program must be brought into play immediately.

The whole emphasis in reading is to be on Mythology and Comparative Religion. In Japanese, I must try to find simple story-texts of Japanese myths and legends, also Buddhist *sūtras;* in French or German, I must read Corbin, etc. and the Eranos volumes; at Sarah Lawrence, I must rebuild my class notes (and perhaps use a wire recorder to catch my lectures), and with Viking, I must get back into the writing swing.

As a book to follow my Viking myth volume, I am thinking more and more of the story of *Apollonius of Tyana.*[184]

And I am thinking also that, one way or another, I must manage to come back some day to Japan.[185] My visit, I feel (though it is only two-fifths done), is almost over.

All day at work on diary, letters, and Japanese.

CHAPTER 8

A Vast and Difficult Question

Monday, June 6

Some thoughts on the current U.S.-Japan situation.

The visitor to Japan distinctly has the feeling that a lot of American big wigs and little wigs are getting a lot out of what is going on here—and represent an interested force. I should like to know a lot more than I do, for example, about what goes on in and around the so-called PX.

Japanese public opinion is permeated by pacifism and antimilitarism. Much of the vote of the Socialists during the last election came from women registering a protest against rearmament. The clause renouncing arms that the Occupation wrote into the constitution is used with a telling effect by opponents of a new army. Japan is contributing no more than 2 percent of its national income to defense. Their own armed forces are not popular with the Japanese.

U.S. forces are too much in evidence throughout Japan. Many U.S. officials question whether long-term relations with Japan are not being seriously endangered in order to continue the short-term advantage of using U.S. forces in the Far East. Responsible Japanese unanimously report that the best means of improving relations would be to withdraw all American ground troops within a year or more. The navy has moved the bulk of its activities south.

The continuous display in the cities of American GIs on leave is a quite bad job, it seems to me. Conceited, complacent, bulky boys in shirt-sleeves, for the most part, on the look for girls or with girls on their arms. Eighty-five percent are said to be "shacking up." On Limits strip joints, photo joints, conspicuously and obviously for GIs; rough and ugly behavior (e.g. pimps thrown into the Ginza's river). Around all this is a vast civilian army of "carpetbaggers" and "dependents," the latter extremely unpliable and intolerant of Japanese customs: pippin housewives from Nebraska, Ohio, Michigan, etc., continually complaining about their hard lot, when they have more servants than any of their counterparts in the States. They raise their comparatively noisy children, and are generally uninterested in anything else.

学生の美術史

Japanese characters = "Art History for Students"

After dinner I visited Eidmann and commenced work with him on the reading of a little Japanese text: *Gakusei no Bijutsu-shi*. Also, spent an hour listening to the Japanese conversation records, of which I finished section one. Felt distinctly that my work on Japanese had entered a new phase. This week my original six-week enrollment in the language school ends; but I'm going to remain till the end of the term, July 8. This will leave me about twenty days in which to reach Tokyo and meet Jean: a time to travel a bit and try to put my Japanese to use.

Tuesday, June 7

All day on Japanese. Met Stoops again at dinner—this time in Fujiya, and he invited me to visit a lively bar with him over in the Gion area: set the date for next Tuesday.

A letter today from Ezekiel in Bombay, inviting me to write for the new magazine *Quest* that he is now editing. Am not going to think of writing anything, however, till I return to New York.

Wednesday, June 8

In the paper this morning: a report on the inquiry on the death of a newspaper man, Gene Symonds, murdered by a mob in Singapore last month. The reports indicate that a police car stood by, at about three hundred to two hundred yards distance, doing nothing. The mob shouted, "We want to beat up Europeans. We want to assault Europeans." The racial affinity of the majority has not been stated, but it must have been Chinese. Articles have been running recently about the prodigious Communist influence among the Chinese in Singapore: it is both ideological and patriotic. They constitute a vast portion of the population and regard China as their home.

Themes that are not sounded in the worldwide Communist-led clamor for "justice": U.N. membership for Japan; Russian imperialism in Eastern Europe (Bulgaria, Romania, Hungary, Czechoslovakia, Poland, Estonia, Lithuania, Latvia, and a chunk of Finland); Chinese imperialism in Tibet;[186] the prodigious size of the Russian army—large long before the U.S.A. reversed its disarmament efforts after the collapse of Czechoslovakia; and the propriety of India's claim to Kashmir.

At 6:00 P.M. today a student called on the phone, to whom Stoops had given my name last night at his lively Gion bar: I shall see the youth tomorrow. All sounds a bit odd to me just now.

After dinner visited Eidmann and read with him another paragraph in the *Gakusei no Bijutsu-shi*.

A nice letter from Jean today about our finances. Joe Lillard has helped her calculate, and it seems that with a loan of $1,500 from her mother, plus the $1,700 loan that I received from S.L.C., we are going to make it—just!

Thursday, June 9

These days, I am just midway in time between my departure from India (March 4) and my arrival in New York (about September 6). My chief experience at present (besides that of the wonders of Japan and the Japanese language) is that of a beautiful refreshment of all the young plans, hopes, and ambitions with which I left Germany for New York in 1929![187] I feel as though I had been given that *second chance* which people dream about—and essentially, though on a larger base, my hopes and plans are about what they were at that time. This I find most remarkable.

My plans for the return are becoming quite firm. The first problem (and the only really delicate one) will be to get going immediately on Japanese—before I lose this perilously perishable load of vocabulary and rules so recently and too rapidly acquired. That attended to, I shall—as scheduled above[188]—get going on my Eranos readings, Volkening-Viking myth book, Sarah Lawrence convocation address and classes, French or German.

For the Japanese four operations seem indicated:

a. A purchase of the record course
b. A systematic continuation of my readings (Vaccari's reader, probably, and whatever small text I may have in hand)
c. The discovery of a good teacher, to help me with free conversation and systematic reading, perhaps once a week
d. The opening of Japanese connections in New York (Honganji-Zen etc.)

And while I am voyaging between Tokyo and New York (one week in Honolulu; a couple of days in San Francisco) I must keep going on the reading: probably with the Vaccari reader.

Just now, I am *beginning* to feel that I may be catching on.

Stoops's young man arrived at 5:00 P.M. and I talked with him, over coffee, in the hotel lobby: talked at first as though his major interest were in getting to the U.S.A. after graduation; then I realized, from a couple of restrained but definite remarks, that this was the old homosexual club. Got rid of him at six, went up to my room to sit down and think a minute; then started for a good steak at Suehiro's.

On the way, a very small boy on a very small bicycle hit my right foot, coming from behind, and though the blow was slight, it was precisely at the point of my sprain. The kid fell off his bike, and I bade him Godspeed; but the ankle is a bit the worse for the shock.

As I approached Suehiro's, Stoops's young man overtook me, and I bade him good-bye again at the door of the restaurant.

After dinner, returned to my Japanese.

Friday, June 10

Time is certainly flying. A letter from Jean: she leaves next Tuesday for New Orleans, where she will give a performance, and her last class in Colorado will be July 22. She will start then for Tokyo and is now due to arrive July 25. She also has had my air ticket to New York sent on to Kyoto: I picked it up today after my morning of Japanese.

And so, the circle has been closed.

A note from Adda,[189] in praise of *The Art of Indian Asia,* which she has just received; also, one from Carl Schuster,[190] who saw a copy on the desk of John Pope[191] in the Freer Gallery in Washington, D.C.

A letter from Bill McGuire,[192] stating that plans are going ahead for paperback editions of *The Hero* and *Philosophies.*[193] New York begins to seem very much alive.

Notes from George Gurow and Martin Wong in Taiwan—inviting me back, with Jean. Unfortunately, that can't be done. Our money and time are too tight.

A good article on India by Kōji Nakamura appeared in the *Mainichi* this morning, with a number of points that help to underline some of my own ideas—which are still pretty confused:

Economically India is undoubtedly at the lowest level in the world. Per capita income, circa $50 per annum. Illiteracy 83 percent. This, certainly, has to be the starting point for any discussion of the country.

"The Four Evils" (Nehru's terms) that must be eliminated if there is to be an improvement:

1. Casteism
2. Linguism
3. Provincialism
4. Communalism

These are still everywhere and very strong.

The government stands for a welfare state based on a "socialistic pattern of society," and a neutral country in the arena of international politics. Indeed, no other formula could solve even a fraction of the gigantic problem.

Saturday, June 11

Friday, after class, Mary Jones came to the school and loaned me Ferré's *The Sun and the Umbrella,* which I glanced through, briefly, at dinner. When she gave me the book, I told her that my chief criticism of what she was giving me was that it wasn't, as she had promised, without mythology, but actually stressed the chief themes of the Christian myth, namely:

1. Sin, as something that cuts man off so radically from the divine that only a special savior can save him; and
2. Jesus of Nazareth as that unique Redeemer.

"But sin," she said; "do you mean to say that sin isn't a fact?"

"Sin isn't a fact," I said, "it's a way of interpreting facts—and implies a belief in God, God's commands, our knowledge and disobedience of God's commands, and everything else." At this point Father Moss entered the room and Mary Jones fled.

In *The Sun* [God] *and the Umbrella* [the Church's teachings, which shut God away from us instead of bringing Him close] Ferré is apparently against Christian mythologizing, and yet he accepts, as facts, 1 and 2, as above. He is in quite a tangle, however, when he tries to interpret the relationship of the human Jesus to the God who was made manifest through and in him—but then, that's a grand old Christian agony and a natural consequence of taking mythology as fact.[194]

"God was thus organically present in Jesus, fulfilling His purpose and our destiny. Here is revelation. Here is Incarnation. Here is power for the forgiveness of sin and the making of the new community in Christ. Christ is God's love come to earth. He is the Logos, the Word...."[195] There is a concession to the operation of God's will through other teachers, but the redeeming fullness, it is maintained, was only in Jesus.

The rains have come. Today is overcast and wet. This will last, I am told, for a month—which is to be the last month of my attempt to grasp my Oriental pearl—a Mikimoto pearl—my hothouse knowledge of Japanese. So, here goes!

To Eidmann's after lunch, and a very pleasant visit till 10:30 P.M. A number of important items:

In one of the U.S. Marine camps near Kyoto, the continuous ratio of venereal disease was circa 70 percent. The army gave women permits signed by commanding officers, if they would stick with one man as his steady—this as an attack on the venereal problem. If the couple was accosted by an MP the girl would have to show her permit. In general the "On Limits" dives constitute the army's solution to the sex problem. The pay of a U.S. private is higher than that of a Japanese general and most of it goes, apparently, on liquor and women. The relationship of the present deterioration of morals in the U.S.A. to the education of U.S. Army draftees abroad is a problem that would bear study.

While sanctioning and cooperating in the relationship of the GI to the prostitute, the army has done everything possible to balk marriage to a decent girl if one should be found. The girl has to be examined for disease; the couple has to be questioned by a long series of officers and during the course of this ordeal the soldier is often transferred to another post; and finally the marriage has to be sanctioned by an army chaplain—who is frequently anti-Buddhist, anti-heathen.

One U.S. Army chaplain in Japan wrote a little booklet of warnings: all Japanese women are immoral heathens; those who meet GIs are inevitably prostitutes to boot. This booklet was translated into Japanese and caused quite a stir.

The Japanese do not understand the American army man, who, on entering the army, expects to return home alive. The Japanese in the army expects to die—and this gives him a character very different from that of the civilian. (Banzai attacks in the World War, for example.) The Japanese, indeed, are afraid of restoring their own army to life and will resist all American efforts to change the constitution, to make an army legal.

The present Japanese army is unconstitutional—and with American connivance. This has created an extremely awkward and ambiguous situation. The Japanese are used, however, to "open secrets," and prefer living with a broken law to reforming a law that seems to them proper and good.

The Japanese army entered World War II expecting to lose—and had it not been for the emperor's revolution, they would have all died fighting.[196] Actually, they were practicing in the streets with bamboo sticks. How to explain such an attitude logically? Perhaps the attitude toward death of the early Christian martyrs, who actually courted death, is the nearest analogy in the West.

Near Sendai there is a mound with an inscription that is now read as identifying it as the tomb of Christ. The legend: that Jesus was not dead when removed from the Cross; healed by the medical arts of Joseph of Arimathea, he sailed to Japan in a boat and now lies here, buried.

The basic teachings of the various Buddhist sects in Japan have been summarily formulated in four-word aphorisms which proliferate from each other in each system in amplification of the lore; e.g.

即身是佛

Zen formula #1

Soku shin ze butsu
This body is Buddha

即身成佛

Shingon formula #1

Soku shin jō butsu
[That] this body [may] become Buddha

總 別 安 心

Jōdo formula #1

Sō Betsu An Jin
General [&] special peace [of] mind

Japanese characters to Zen formula and Shingon formula

Anjin, "peace of mind," in Jōdo is not synonymous with Enlightenment; and the problem implied by the terms *sō betsu,* "general and special," was one that was particularly important in the Heian period; namely: is the attainment one that is known only in a special moment, or is it maintained through the whole life. According to Jōdo, as a result of the achievement and maintenance of this Peace of Mind, one achieves Enlightenment (i.e., is projected into *nirvāṇa*) at the moment of death.

Shinshū was developed by Shinran out of Jōdo and advanced beyond it. Eidmann did not give me the number 1 Shinshū formula, but discussed two of the subordinate formulae and contrasted with them the Christian position; as follows:

> *Shinjin shōin*
> Faith awakening true cause
> [The true cause (of salvation) is the awakening of faith]

The Christian counterpart would be:

> *Kiristo shōin*
> Christ true cause
> [The true cause (of salvation) is Christ]
> *Shōki nimbo*
> Object (of) refuge, person (or) law
> [Is the object of refuge (or worship) a person or the law?]
> For Shinshū the proper object of refuge is the law
> For the Christian the object is the Christ, i.e., a person

This whole principle of formulation and presentation seemed to me extremely interesting: one that could be well employed both in analysis and in pedagogy. An excellent exercise would be that of finding comparable formulae and proliferations of formulae for the traditional (and even some of the modern) thinkers of the West. Indeed, I might ask myself some time: *What is my own basic formula?*[197] Clue One, a little statement made to Eidmann: "A myth is the imaging of a conception, or realization, of truth."

In connection with all this: a little passage then found in Ferré's *The Sun and the Umbrella:* "The Christian faith believes not that God is too holy to behold sin but that He comes to seek and to save the sinner. The Christian faith knows no absolute, either, which like an inverted rainbow dips from the eternal into finite existence only to return again to perfection; *God Himself, in coming to save us, rather, for our sake 'becomes sin';* he lives with us, among us, in us and for us."[198]

"What is this?" I asked Eidmann; giving it to him to read: "Tantra!" he said. "Exactly!" But, of course, Ferré doesn't follow this inspiration to its conclusion.

In Korea nowadays, according to Eidmann, there are two interesting phenomena: first, riots before the American embassy in Seoul, protesting against America's support of "pro-Communist Japan." Second, Korean married monks beating up the unmarried monks and nuns who have been ordered by the government to supplant the married monks in their temples. The married monks actually were established in Korea by the Japanese to break down Buddhism. Many of them are sheer thugs. For *it was an expressed intention of the Meiji to root out Buddhism.*

Ironically, since the Occupation and the new constitution, it is possible to favor Buddhism without danger to your career. (This, I think, must be balanced against the excessive Christian propaganda.)

Japan in Asia is not trusted. (The situation, probably, is comparable to that of Germany in Europe.) The Japanese actually had the idea that they could be the saviors of Asia—(and they may yet be, as the Germans may yet be the saviors of Europe). After their defeat, however, and in the face of the general anti-Japanese picture in Asia, their attitude became that of "To hell with it; let us cultivate our own garden." One great problem, however, is that they *do* need markets.

I have the feeling that we should never forget Spengler's warning about the anti-mechanical character of the Asiatic mind. They will learn to use the machine to throw off the West—but their yearning is for an Asian style of life, to which the machine is intrinsically alien. In many individual cases—chaps brought up in the Western manner—Asians *seem* to be not less at home with the machine than Occidentals (e.g. Krishnan at Bhubaneshwer). But in the character-shaping tradition itself, which is the force that affects the unconscious, an anti-mechanical principle is at work,* which in the long run and in the great mass, will probably work as Spengler warns.

And in this connection one more idea. If Nehru would come to Tokyo instead of falling in love with his brother Asians of Peking and Moscow, he would find an Asiatic nation really capable of furnishing him with the machines and technical aid that he needs. The co-prosperity sphere would really begin to come into being.

"Yes, but..." I hear, from some imaginary knower of Japan. Well, I want to hear what the but might be.

Worked with Eidmann on kanji and on the reading of a little introduction to Shinrikyō.

Sunday, June 12

I went today with Hisashi Mita to the Takarazuka Revue in Takarazuka. An excellent revue, by one of their three or four troupes; this one "The Snow Troupe," *Yuki Gumi.* First section: *Blue Hawai'i*—an amusing set of hulas, by about eighty girls, with a little plot; then, the main revue, *The*

---

* See Lily Abegg, *Ostasien denkt anders: Versuch einer Analyse des west-östlichen Gegensatzes* (Zurich: Atlantis, 1949).

Tales of the Four Flowers, and I felt again the real charm and excellence of the Japanese theater: scads of good dancers and beautiful girls; kimono and Western styles equally well done; superb stage sets and transformations; an ability to flash out and into depth (opening the stage forward, backward, and to the sides, that yielded really wonderful effects); perfect taste and lovely invention in the curtains, backdrops, scenes, and lights; a great ability to keep things moving, changing, and surprising. One of the leading ladies in a set of geisha dancers nearly knocked me out.

A couple of additional observations:

Remarkable how many of the themes culminated in suicide (compare the Kabuki: suicides and honor killings of one's own children etc.). Think now of the banzai attacks and the Pearl Harbor hara-kiri.[199] Formula: life is lived to the limit, according to a certain principle, concept, sense of the possible, or simply pragmatic plan—and when this leads to an impasse, instead of transformation (changing the lifestyle) one chooses death—which, after all, in a world where reincarnation is taken for granted, is a way of changing the style of one's dress. Contrast with this, however, the equally Japanese formula of "rock with the waves."

The first of the *Tales of the Four Flowers* was about an Ainu[200] romance (Romeo and Juliet theme of feud and suicide), where the Ainu were handled much as American Indians in, say, a revue of the Rose Marie type:[201] the forest idyll.

After the show, we strolled through the zoo and botanical garden, then took the train home: dinner at Suehiro's with Hisashi, and then a good evening of work on my Japanese.

I hope Jean can see this Takarazuka job: it will be an inspiration to her, I am sure: a city of dancers!! Four troupes of about a hundred each! Add this to the picture of the Kabuki and Noh companies! The American theater falls apart in comparison. Steady, perfect "stock" company work: A new show every month: theater, theater, theater, theater. No wonder the performances are good beyond belief. Not a ham in the whole of Japan!—except, of course, what I saw in the so-called modern dance.

A nice letter from Alan Watts, when I returned, suggesting that I look up some people in Kyoto: P. D. Perkins, at a bookstore near my hotel; a Zen priest named Sōhaku Ogata, who speaks English and who spoke to Alan's pupils at Northwestern; and a painter named Sabro Hasegawa. He also expressed amazement at *The Art of Indian Asia* and suggested that Jean and I plan to visit him at Big Sur: the latter an elegant suggestion.[202]

I have about decided to remain in Kyoto until after the Gion event July 17–18; then simply go to the Ise Peninsula for a few days, and proceed from there to Tokyo, to meet Jean.

Monday, June 13

Bad day at Japanese school: one teacher ill, and Father Moss, my classmate, managing to break down the learning tension by cracking jokes. This tendency has increased as we have gone on into the more difficult stages. I am actually beginning to wonder whether I might not do better, for the remaining three or four weeks, approaching the language some other way. We have reached lesson thirty-one—about two weeks late, and I doubt whether we shall complete the full sixty at this rate!

In the paper there has been a discussion of the question of antialien attitudes in certain Kyoto restaurants. Some "dismayed foreigner" complained May 31. The Japan Travel Bureau now replies.

The U.S. Army has classified restaurants hygienically as class A, B, or C; sending MPs around to see that no GIs are in B or C restaurants. Many army men are in civvies when on leave. Such restaurants have learned to avoid incidents by refusing service.

A number of restaurants have suffered damage to furniture from foreigners; also injury to people and the bilking of bills. GIs also may bring in their own liquor and ask for a bottle of soda; then get nasty. It is not ideology or racism that leads restaurants that have had this experience to resist foreigners.

Some restaurants are the haunts of streetwalkers: gentlemen (as distinguished from GIs, I suppose) are not welcome in such places.

Many Kyoto restaurants, especially in Gion, do not serve chance customers, whether foreign or Japanese.

Shyness, on the part of people who do not speak English, may be misinterpreted as brusqueness.

After reading this article, and after seeing what I have seen of Americans in Asia, I think it might be well, if I am to give the S.L.C. convocation address, to deal with the question of the educated American as America's only ambassador. Some further thoughts:

The idea of cultural missions—Russian and Chinese missions to India; Indian to Ceylon; The NBC Symphony in Japan; Jean in India.

In general the American citizen is being very badly served in Asia thanks to:

a. Communist ideologists and the Japanese unions
b. Businessmen and the U.S. agencies
c. Senator junkets
d. Illiteracy of the foreign staffs: two-year stints; cocktail circuit (contrast the English and the clergy)
e. Christian missionizing masquerading as democracy
f. U.S. Army wives and personnel
g. Sheer tourists

For Sarah Lawrence, I should emphasize the aspect of education through which each can serve as a human example: educating, refining, cultivating *yourself:* not learning about current ideologies only, but making yourself into a civilized character.

Moreover: solution of world's coming problems lie right here: right on this campus (S.L.C.); for the U.S.A. is the prow of the world ship right now—the individual can become self-reliant *outside* of the governmental institution.

Hisashi, yesterday, discussed a little series of incidents that have taken place on his campus, that of Kyoto University. The first took place three years ago, the second last year, and the third last week. The first occurred when the emperor arrived: a group surrounded his car and sang "The International."[203] The occasion for last year's event I failed to catch, but the students went on a strike. Last week they locked the president in his office.

There is considerable Communist sympathy among the students; the faculty, on the other hand, is very conservative. Whence the student organization and coordination Hisashi didn't know.

At dinner Hisashi said to me: you are very enthusiastic about Japan, but if you stayed here longer you would find some things you wouldn't like.

In India I had to force myself to seek the things that I could admire; here, for balance, I must recognize the "things I wouldn't like"; for example:

1. The Communist anti-Americanism—which is certainly present, but certainly not as overt (by any means) as it was in India
2. The general rudeness of men to women in the RR trains and cars: young students will sit, sprawled out over the seats, and let a woman stand with a baby on her back

3. The generally Oriental rudeness of everybody to the people with whom they are not directly in contact for the moment: pushing in ahead of the line for tickets, elbowing into and out of crowds, etc.

What else?

An apt image for my visit to India occurred to me today as I was walking to catch my trolley to school. *It was like a visit to a vast, haunted house.* The first impression was of the debris and squalor that had piled up during the centuries. Under this heading, all the bad news about poverty, disease, etc. After a while, however, the lineaments of a magnificent, ancient edifice began to be apparent beneath and behind the appalling clutter. Here, the temples, and the vestiges of ancient societies and doctrines. And, throughout, there were curious sounds and apparitions, purporting to be manifestations of the spiritual realm: but whether any of these were genuine, or all tricks, remains a matter of doubt. It is my belief, however, that one or two were real. But now comes the problem of whether anything or how much of this archaic mansion can be salvaged for contemporary living. That is a vast and difficult question, because the answer depends not only on how the supposed spirituality of the place is evaluated, but also upon our evaluation of the characteristic phenomena of the modern world.

Still another idea about India: it is a land with more people and fewer thoughts than any on earth.

A telegram, tonight, to Jean, who leaves New York tomorrow for New Orleans, Boulder, San Francisco, Honolulu, and Tokyo.

CHAPTER 9

TEMPLE TREASURES

Tuesday, June 14

My day: Japanese: letters to Bollingen and Jean: more Japanese.

Officially the "rainy season"—*tsuyu*—began Sunday, but the days have been sunny and rather warm. The heat is coming, and I'm told it can be great!

Wednesday, June 15

Some ideas for the S.L.C. address. Lay stress on:

1. The privilege and responsibility of a year of American education (compare conditions in Asiatic colleges)
2. The irony of what may be called the "barbarism" of the people that we send abroad:
   a. Experts and specialists
   b. "Halfbrights" (The Fullbright "scholars" who don't really prepare themselves adequately, nor go to the cultural depth required.)
   c. Diplomats who know nothing about either American culture or the culture of the land to which they are sent
   d. The army
   e. The missionaries
   f. The "carpetbaggers"
   g. The tourists (pink pants in Kyoto—ugh)

    h. The movies and news items
       (An idea of slaphappy spontaneous crudity as the measure of demo-
       cratic virtue—that is an international disaster)
3. Our responsibility to the Free Nations—indeed, to freedom: We *do* have
   masters who support it and represent it. Why can they not find their way
   to visibility?
4. The counterbalance to the "barbarism": NBC Orchestra, Jean
5. Responsibility of those being educated—to become civilized: not for the
   forests of Hiawatha, but for modern civilization. For instance, What is
   the matter with our children? (Asian mothers "professional," Asian fathers
   too.) The unsolved inner conflict: what is it?[204]
6. The prow of civilization, the brunt of the beating: individualism vs. the
   past—a psychological problem that *each* has to solve. Individual cultivation vs. traditional cultivation. S.L.C. at the forefront here

A serious task, and not a task of *work,* but of attitude, direction, understanding of culture.

Specialization and technology—yes, but—without culture, humanity,
civilization, it is identical with the menace that all of mankind despises:
Titanism.[205]

Discovered theme, then: *Titan or God?*

Specialization (etc.) as Titanism—known to the myths (that is to say,
the images of human evolution) of the whole world: Leprechauns, etc. who
make men's shoes, but lack mankind's culture: and here is the danger for
the U.S.A. On the other hand, there is no point in trying to play the role
of God: we just haven't what it takes for that. But we *could* be human, if
we tried a little: we have all the facilities: and, in fact, when I look at you
beautiful creatures, I know that we *are* human, and delightfully so, at least
in the feminine portion of our social anatomy. What then is the explanation of what I saw as I looked at America from Asia?

The American in Paris of the 1920s: the American in Tokyo of the
1950s.

The U.S.A. in Asia, supporting the British and the French; result:

1. Loss of prestige among the anti-Imperialists
2. No gain of prestige among the Asiatics, who still admire the British and
   the French (and these, by the way, are often identical with the first sort;
   for their idols—the British and the French—despise us, and make this
   very clear in every word that they utter)

Now add to this the picture of (a) through (g) above. Quite a fine
tableau.

Conclusion as to what is the responsibility of the American student. At home: to become civilized and to assist in the civilizing of the American. Abroad: to behave in a civilized manner.

This evening I went to Eidmann's after dinner and found Miss Margaret (Peg) McDuffy chatting with him. They had not yet had dinner. I listened to Japanese language records till they were through, then returned to the room and remained after Miss McDuffy left. Some news and the beginnings of a schedule.

I have made plans to study Japanese with a young man named Iguchi, who has been helping Fillmore. The problem is, that the work at the school has not enabled me to find a way to make Japanese work outside of the classroom. We are covering a lot of territory there, pretty fast; but I have no core of speech habits for either the actual situations of my stay in Japan, or the subjects that I care to discuss. My hope is to begin work with Iguchi as soon as Eidmann leaves for Hokkaido, and to increase my hours with him when the school closes.

Plans, also, to concentrate on a systematic learning of kanji, based on a frequency listing, as soon as school closes.

I have exactly a month, now, in which to clinch what I can of Japanese. Also, to see what I haven't yet seen of Kyoto.

Thursday, June 16

Real rain: the "rainy season" (*tsuyu*) has come for fair.

This morning at eight, right after my breakfast, Professor Kasugai arrived to invite me to the temple treasure viewing tomorrow. He brought with him a young nun, and we had tea in the lounge of the hotel. He also brought a number of photographs of *Indonesian structures with roof forms suggesting the "dragons" on the Japanese temple roofs.*

I mentioned that I had seen a number of interesting monks begging—one, a chap with *a basket over his head and a flute in his hand.* Professor Kasugai told me

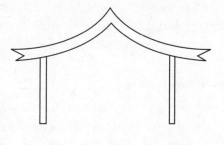

Japanese temple roofs

that this order represented a fusion of Tendai philosophy, Shingon costume (basket), and Zen symbolism (flute: the voice of nature). The leaders are called *komusō: komu* (*śunyatā*) *sō* (priest).

Kasugai and the nun left at 8:30 and I took a taxi to school: taxi home again at noon—rain and very heavy clouds.

Found something of interest in *Life,* May 30: Einstein, on a few basic matters of popular interest:

1. The mind can proceed only so far upon what it knows and can prove. There comes a point where the mind takes a leap—call it intuition or what you will—and comes out upon a higher plane of knowledge, but can never prove how it got there. All great discoveries have involved such a leap.
2. The important thing is not to stop questioning. Curiosity has its own reason for existence.
3. Try not to become a man of success but rather try to become a man of value. He is considered successful in our day who gets more out of life than he puts in. But a man of value will give more than he receives.
4. [His] belief is in the brotherhood of man and the uniqueness of the individual.

Last evening Eidmann suggested that *the three major religious developments in America*—that is to say, major native American developments—were:

> Mormonism
> American Unitarianism
> Christian Science

And I believe he is right. Perhaps one should add the Peyote cult of the American Indians, in the light of what is now happening to Aldous Huxley et al.[206]

At five today, went around to Eidmann's, to help him buy a camera and some shirts. We had a very long stroll—to my camera shop and shirt shop; had dinner at his favorite Chinese restaurant: and I returned to my room, rather tired, at ten, and went directly to bed.

Friday, June 17

Up at six, greatly refreshed. A rotten morning, however, at school. "Moss-san," Father Moss, my classmate, is now learning practically nothing and wastes more than two-thirds of our three hours with his fumbling and stalling. After class I asked the principal, Hayashi-san, if I could shift to private lessons in the afternoon. She said it was too late to do so for next week, but that something might be arranged for the week following. I am kicking myself, that I did not ask for this some three weeks back.

After class, I grabbed a chocolate bar for lunch and went up to Chion-in for Professor Kasugai's exhibition of temple treasures. He showed me, first, a huge book with the list of all the treasures, then showed me the eight choice items that he had selected for my viewing:

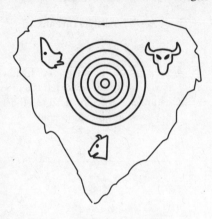

1. A Chinese kakemono map of "India" as *Iambu Dvipa* (copy ca. A.D. 1350 of earlier original) with the names of the main sites in kanji. The area included was Tibet, Afghanistan, Nepal, etc., India, and Ceylon. In the center of the Tibetan zone was a curious, mythological, snake-spiral, emanating, threefold, from three animal heads: one, a sort of hippo; one, a sort of boar; one, a sort of ox. No one knew how to interpret this.

Iambu Dvipa in the form of a heart.

2. A kakemono showing *Amida in meditation;* hands in posture in lap. Picture believed to have been brought to Japan by Kōbō Daishi (ca. A.D. 794). It is a Central Asian piece, thought to date from the second or third century A.D. (If so, probably the oldest artwork—or even object—in Japan.) The figure sits on a double-storied lotus in a white aureole, and is *clothed in a dark red (cf. Red Cap lamas).* (Kasugai thinks an original yellow robe may have turned red; but I doubt this.) At the four corners of the picture were four Sanskrit syllables on lotuses; added later, apparently, in Japan.

Amida's hands

3. A beautiful kakemono on a broad black square of silk. Descent of the Buddha Amida, on a roadway of cloud, to a meditating personage in a house. In the upper right-hand area is a city or castle in a circle; possibly the Tusita Heaven.[207] The Buddha is accompanied by Bodhisattvas and sages. In the area between the Tusita Heaven and the house (lower right)

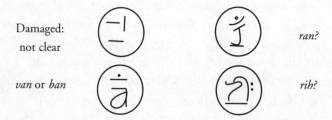

Damaged:
not clear   *ran?*

van or *ban*   *rih?*

Four Sanskrit syllables (in Sankrit)

are a number of small *arhat* figures—as though precipitated from the atmosphere. In the lower left is a mountain landscape. The natural areas are naturalistically colored, so too the Tusita circle. Amida and his entourage, however, are clothed in gold.

Buddha's descent

The work is thought to have been painted by Eshin (Genshin) (ca. A.D. 950–1000), the patriarch of Hiei, and a patriarch of Shinshū. It is possible, however, that silk of this width was not made in Japan that early—in which case, the ascription would have to be revised: ca. 1280? This panel, according to Professor Kasugai, was the left-hand member of a tryptich.

4. A kakemono showing the Buddha (Śākyamuni perhaps, or Amida) in meditation, with two standing Bodhisattvas: at his proper left,

Avalokiteśvara, with Buddha image in tiara; proper right, Mahāprasthana, with water bottle (looks like a *stūpa*) in his tiara. Date: ca. A.D. 1280? This work is a Chinese illustration of the *Smaller Sukhāvatī Vyuha* (Nanjō #200[208]), also, the *to-shwo-kwan-wu-lien-sheu-go-kin* (Nanjō #198), the Buddha robe is red.

5. An immense Chinese *kakemono* (too big to hang from the ceiling: lay half on the floor), showing a three-fold epiphany of Amida and attendant Bodhisattvas, with a red sun at the top; and multitudes of attendants and lotus pedestals. At the sides of the sun are soaring musical instruments. Among the attendants are groups playing lutes, flutes, drums, and panpipe reeds (*shō*, such as I heard at Nara?). The probable date of this glorious piece is ca. A.D. 1200–1300.

Professor Kasugai could not explain to me the threefold trinity, but suggested Buddha of the past, the present, and the future. The Bodhisattvas accompanying the three central figures are Mahāprasthana and Avalokiteśvara.

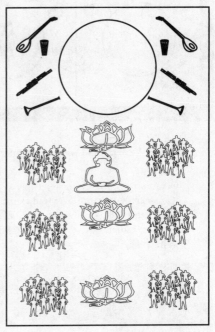

Chinese kakemono. This work is an illustration of the *Amitayur-jñana Sūtra*. The robes of the meditating figure are red.

6. A Chinese *kakemono* resembling number 5, but slightly smaller, and with a three-legged bird in the sun. No one could explain to me the three-legged bird. The date of this piece is ca. A.D. 1200–1300. Note: three-legged bird, three-fold Buddha manifestation.

7. A Chinese embroidery of ca. 500 A.D., hung as a kakemono, showing a Buddha figure in meditation with accompanying Bodhisattvas, and with a set of eighteen small scenes down the sides as borders. Again an illustration of the *Amitayur-jñana Sūtra*. The Buddha figure here has a Mongolian moustache (so too have the Buddhas in some of the other works, but I forget precisely which: I think numbers 5 and 6, but possibly also 4.). This Buddha looks very much like a Chinese Confucian sage. Whereas the tone of numbers 2, 3, 4, 5, 6 is dark, that of 7 is yellow and a kind of chartreuse-green.

Screen with conchs and *vajra* bells border

8. A vast screen, mounting as a triptych *an embroidered vestment brought from China* ca. A.D. 1200. The traditional date assigned to this work is fifth or sixth century A.D.; however, some of the elements depicted on the border suggest, rather, post-seventh or eighth century A.D.; namely—*conchs and vajra bells.*

Kasugai and a Jōdo nun exhibit screen

The central motif in each panel is an island: from the central one a Buddha emanates; from the other two, nothing emanates. That at the observer's right is a half circle: the half moon? Its opposite is a full circle: the full moon? The central island too is circular: the sun? On the central panel the *three-footed bird* is twice represented. At the lower right-hand corner of the (observer's) right-hand panel is a wonderful four-footed Chinese dragon. Other panels depict *jātaka* scenes[209]; rabbit churning butter with a watching frog, etc.

One suggestion for the three-footed bird is that there is a legend somewhere of three crows (*karasu*) in the sun.

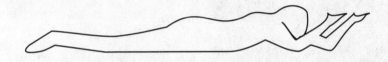

Prostrated figure

In illustration of one of the postures represented among the devotees of kakemono number 5, Professor Kasugai showed me two forms of prostration: the *turīyamaṇḍala,* with knees and hands on the floor, and the *panchamaṇḍala* (the most profound) with the head also on the floor, but, instead of the hand the elbows; *the hands being raised with palms upward to receive the feet of the Buddha.*

According to Professor Kasugai, such pictorial maṇḍalas as were exhibited in the kakemonos of this display are not actually used in modern Japanese worship. Shingon and Tendai use mandalas, but not of these types; and the other sects use none. It is possible that pictures of this type were used in Japan as illustrations and foundations for public readings of the *sūtras:* first, the *sūtra* to be read in Chinese, and next, a translation to be read.

A number of people were present at the viewing: Eidmann, Haru, a Brazilian Nisei, Mr. van Vest (a Dutch gentleman who has been some forty years in Japan), a number of young students (theological), and two Jōdo nuns (one the visitor of yesterday morning). It was a lovely afternoon, with tea, twice, on the floor of the vast room. Then we all went to Eidmann's favorite *amazake* outdoor restaurant for a sip, and finally to a little semi-Shintō shrine to some Indian snake god (*Urūgana,* messenger of

Maheśvara, symbol of women) where there was a stone *stūpa*-lantern show-ing two Buddhas in one frame and, hanging on the temple walls, two or three bunches of hair offerings, made by women for favors received.

At Chion-in Temple. The two figures at the left are Jōdo nuns. To the right is Professor Kasugai and Rev. Phillip Eidmann seated in his wheelchair.

It began to drizzle, about this time, and we strolled down the Chion hill until a taxi arrived, into which the Eidmann party and I climbed. To Eidmann's for dinner and an evening's chat. E. showed me some sixteenth- and seventeenth-century Chinese-Japanese-Sanskrit *sūtras,* with the Sanskrit furnished with kanji translations and hiragana pronunciations.

Saturday, June 18

Morning writing in my diary, to catch up with yesterday's marvels. After lunch went around to Eidmann's again for an afternoon and evening with Eidmann and Kasugai. Lots of talk: quite a number of interesting matters:

In India (Elūrā, Ajaṇṭā, etc.), the figures flanking the Buddha figure are, typically, Maitreya (*stūpa* in tiara) and Avalokiteśvara; in China and Japan, Mahāprasthana (water bottle, which looks like a *stūpa* to *me,* how-ever) and Avalokiteśvara. Is *Prajñāpāramitā* the basis for this change?[210]

We discussed the problem of the origin of the two-Buddha formula (is this what we saw yesterday at the snake-god shrine?). It is based, apparently, on the *Saddharma Puṇḍarīka*. If no examples of the formula occur in India, the problem is: why? When and where was the *Saddharma Puṇḍarīka* composed?[211]

According to Eidmann, *Buddhism is intrinsically a positive, not a negative, way.* His points are as follows:

1. The teaching of the Buddha was originally directed as much to laymen (King Bimbisāra and King Sakka, the donor of the gold-paved garden[212]) as to monks. Since, however, the tradition has come to us largely through the monks, for whom those teachings had no immediate relevance, they have disappeared. (I wonder about this.) The stress on the Four Noble Truths is largely Western: one hears little of them in the Orient. (I wonder whether this is really so.)

2. Buddhist monasticism is not negative in the same way that Hindu and Christian are. Westerners are quite happy as Hindu monks, but few have made out well as Buddhist. Their quest for escape is not served by Buddhism, which throws them on their own: they become neurotic. Consider the Buddhist nuns of yesterday afternoon in contrast with the Catholic of yesterday morning. (There is certainly a difference of some kind, but I don't know whether it can be called that of the difference between the positive and the negative approaches: from the outside, at any rate, both look like refusals.)

3. The Mahāyāna—obviously—is positive.

It seems that American (Occidental) movies and plays, when seen in the Orient, are shockingly sexy. Peg McDuffy surprised and puzzled the little Ohtone boy the other day by asking him whether the photo of a certain little girl was of his "girlfriend." He had no idea what she meant—whereas in America even the tots have their boy and girl friends (for instance in Bronxville). This led to my rehearsal of my new theme of the problem of personality-evaluation and free choice in marriage. *In Japan—as in India—at least three-quarters of the marriages are arranged by the families.* In Japan, however, the shift will not present quite as many problems as in India, because the inter-communal love problem does not exist. The culture is comparatively homogeneous.

I had some ideas for a Bollingen investment discussion:

1. The condition of education (student interest, discipline, etc.) is very low in postwar Japan, and the tendency of the Japanese is to blame this on the Occupation. The blame is misplaced (compare India and the English), and yet American influences and investments have been unfortunate enough to give some semblance of justification to the criticism.

a. American aid (Rockefeller, etc.) has gone to the big state universities (Tokyo etc.) and to the Christian universities (Dōshisha, for example), but not to the Buddhist universities. The feeling among Japanese professors (e.g. Kasugai) is that American foundations will not give money to Buddhist universities.

b. The American Culture Center in Kyoto has no books on Buddhism, and yet American scholars have done important and good work in this field—cultural ties would be greatly improved by making this evident. The Japanese themselves lack funds for the purchase of the American books in this field. In contrast to the lack of books on Buddhism, there are many in the library on Christianity: but there are fewer than 400,000 Christians in Japan. *What is the function of the Cultural Center?* To serve as an agency of cultural harmony, or to serve as an agency of the Christian missions?!

2. The Japanese scholars are *not* very good: they favor narrow specialization; they seek fields that will give them prestige among their fellows; they will not dare to argue against a theory presented by a member of their profession who holds a position of prestige—and yet, they think that they can despise American scholarship:

a. Their translations from English are very bad (based on bad dictionaries), so they really don't know what the sensitively chosen technical terms of our American scholars actually say.

Therefore, Project A: Support of careful translations of key works on the Orient into Japanese. No more Bible stuff: there are tons of that; indeed, one would think that the U.S.A. and Christianity were the same thing, to listen to what is being said and published by the Americans in Japan.

b. They are very quick to seize upon minor errors as evidence of worthless work; e.g. Professor Kasugai's glance at the American Encyclopedia donated to his university by the Occupation. He found that the dates of Aśoka given in two articles ("Buddhism" and "Asoka") differed, and concluded that the whole work was worthless. It would certainly work against such quick decisions if more American works (and good ones) were available on Buddhism and the other native subjects in which the native scholars are interested.

Therefore, Project B: Bollingen books, Harvard Oriental Library books, etc.—no more Bibles—to the Oriental universities.

c. The majority of the postwar Japanese who have studied in America are now anti-American. They lecture against, write books against, etc. Why? Compare the problem of Russians who studied in Germany in Turgenev-Tolstoy's time becoming anti-German. Dominant culture inspires negative reaction.[*]

---

[*] See Hans Kohn, *The Twentieth Century: A Mid-Way Account of the Western World* (New York: Macmillan, 1949).

Therefore, Project C: A program of selective fellowships for special ends; as follows:

The present, overly academic, stultified and stultifying condition of Japanese education is largely due to the concentration of power and authority in Tokyo University and the prestige pattern associated with the ranking universities in this system. It does no good to put more money into those universities, as the Rockefellers are doing: these funds only enforce the bad situation and align the U.S.A. with the reactionary team.

The most influential group outside of this structure is precisely the group of universities that the Americans are *not* supporting; namely, the Buddhist universities; and among these the most influential, with the most students, are the Honganji Shinshū and Jōdo. *These universities cannot begin to compete with the state systems largely because they cannot attract and hold good faculty.*

And here is the point:

I asked: "Why don't they offer higher salaries?"

Reply: "They don't have the money!"

I asked: "Why don't they *raise* the money?"

Reply: "They don't know how."

The Japanese universities are run on the fees paid by the students: they have no functioning alumni associations, no big fund-raising campaigns: but there is money in Japan, just as there is in India, and—just as in India, where enough is spent on a wedding to endow two universities—it is never donated to education. What about tapping the big department store universe?

Project C, then:

1. To bring two young men from the Nishi Honganji and two from the Jōdo sect to the U.S.A., to study school administration, fund raising, etc.; these men to be selected by the *hoshus* (patriarchs) of their order. Four young men selected in this fashion will have immense influence when they return— more than a hundred selected in the "democratic" fashion of competitive exams.

2. To set up public speech departments in the universities of these institutions, with which readings in modern problems will be included. There are thousands of students in these temple universities who are going to be the teachers and preachers to the great majority in Japan: they know nothing about the U.S.A.—and yet they are preaching against its influence today from every pulpit in Japan. Why?

We talked further about the anti-American picture, and especially the problem of Okinawa:

A survey team (Japanese) presents the following picture (from the *Mainichi* of June 17):

Many infringements of the basic human rights of islanders have occurred because of their dubious status under the American Occupation. From the legal viewpoint they are Japanese nationals, yet they are governed by the U.S. military administration. They are not protected by American laws, yet they are under American power.

U.S.A. should compensate those whose farmland has been appropriated by American forces for military use in line with land expropriation laws of Japan.

American forces employ 36,800 civilian workers of various nationalities; 80 percent are islanders who lost bond as the result of expropriation. The Japanese earn ¥25 (Okinawan yen) per hour (i.e. circa 2 cents), while Filipinos earn ¥196 and Americans ¥702.

Eidmann adds that Japan is full of Okinawans who are not permitted to return home as permanent residents, and that the Japanese know what is going on there. The disparity between American talk about democracy and illustration of the principles in action is so great that the Japanese do not trust (or respect) America—the Orient, indeed, does not trust the U.S.A.

Some additional projects for foundations:

Project D: Japanese to study the work of American philanthropic foundations.

Project E: $20,000 to two private universities for a study of the proper techniques for the teaching of kanji. (Perhaps the Keystone Co., manufacturer of the tachistoscope, will assist here.[213])

In connection with all of this: I saw the letter from Shantineketan[214] to Professor Kasugai containing a statement of the salary that he is to receive when he goes there this fall for a stint of from three to five years, bringing with him his family:

1. Three hundred rupees per month!
2. Scale 175 - 15 - 400 rupees (Whatever that means)
3. "Dearness allowance" of 30 rupees per month (Whatever that means)

We discussed for a moment a book by Charles Morris, *The Open Self*,[215] in which thirteen "ways of life" are listed and discussed; namely:

1. Apollo
2. Buddha (actually Shōdōmon [Hōnen])

3. Christianity
4. Dionysos
5. Islam
6. Prometheus-Zoroaster
7. Maitreya (actually Jōdomon)
8. Epicurean
9. Taoism
10. Stoicism
11. Meditation
12. Physical activity
13. Self as instrument of forces other than oneself

Apparently, Morris took some kind of straw vote and found that the ways preferred by Americans were numbers 2 and 7.

I had a long discussion with Eidmann (before Kasugai's arrival) of the problem of "revelation" in the religions of America. The discussion commenced with my mention of Tenrikyō (about which I have just begun to read)[216] and Ramakrishna and voodoo. Eidmann then launched into an excellent review of the "Restoration Movement" in America, from Puritan times; as follows:

The Puritans fully expected revelations in America (Zion); the revelations, however, didn't come. Roger Williams, for instance, believed church had failed, and that Christ would have to return.

1740–50: an enthusiastic movement of revelation was put down by church, which was by then a closed corporation of businessmen.

1. The Enlightenment asked: why is there no revelation today?
2. Thousands converted to Unitarianism (Harvard)[217]

1803–4: Movements for restoration of the primitive church (e.g. in Kentucky: this was a small, extreme phase, however): Disciples of Christ (Campbell)[218], Methodists of U.S.A. Then a splash of revelations claiming valid authority:

1. Mormons
2. Pentecostal movements
3. Shakers
4. Utopian movements
5. The Millerites to Mary White to the Seventh Day Adventists (the world was supposed to end in 1844: after 1844, the prophecy was reinterpreted as the beginning of a world renovation: the cleansing of the tabernacle in heaven): Battle Creek: Kelloggs products

1844–45: Spiritualism
After the Civil War: Judge Rutherford, etc., Mary Baker Eddy
1880s: New Thought Movement; Kansas City Unity
1885: Jehovah's Witnesses
World War I: Moral Rearmament Movement

All this got us talking about Restoration Movements now beginning to incorporate the World Religion theme:

The American Indian nineteenth-century "renovation" movements were probably linked to Mormonism. For the Mormons, the American Indians are descendants of several small groups of immigrants belonging to the tribes of Judah and Benjamin (*not* the ten lost tribes). Indians were initiated into Mormon rites. Were the Mormons' esoteric "garments" the model for Ghost Dance shirts? According to this movement, the Indians were again to reclaim their land. (See Dale Morgan's *Bibliography of Mormonism,* a copy of which is probably in the 42nd St. library.)[219]

Related themes: Swedenborg;[220] and the Bah'ai faith, which is a restoration movement in the Orient; and a World Religion movement in the West.[221]

Consider the World Religion theme of Ramakrishna: the Brahmo Samaj[222] influence and Unitarianism (also, German romanticism, and again Swedenborg): I think, also, that the work of such men as Bastian[223] may have had some influence here.

I have been greatly impressed by what I have read about Tenrikyō—and shall discuss this later: just now—hold the comparison of Miki,[224] Ānanda Mayī,[225] Ramakrishna, voodoo, and Pentecostalism. Nineteenth-century transformations of culture, dissolution of fixed patterns, and individual quest. See Radin on Peyote.[226]

Eidmann stresses the Jōdo Shinshū influence on Tenrikyō: idea of gratitude (Jōdo and Shinshū); idea of *kanro,* "sweet dew" (Jōdo and Shinshū from India's *amrita*).

In Mormonism, revelations now fail to come and the claim now is that inspiration is enough.

Query: Why do revelations no longer come in the traditional Western religions?

A night of pouring rain.

Sunday, June 19

Woke up last night with my first real insomnia since New York—after Eidmann's dinner of tempura. Tried to study a bit of Japanese. Back to sleep, and awake at 8:30—just in time for 9:00 o'clock breakfast and a 9:30 departure with Hisashi Mita for the puppet plays of Osaka in the Bunraku theater. A marvelous experience: 11:00 A.M. till 4:00 P.M. Five plays.

On the way, in the train I could see the Japanese rice fields happily flooded and the peasants everywhere at work in their hats and with grass rain mats on their backs, transplanting rice, blade by blade, from their first beds into fresh, more widely spaced rows; also many ploughing their rain-soaked fields with their oxen. A lovely spectacle.

Hisashi spoke a little more about the "Incident" two weeks ago at the university, and it fits into my Project B picture.[227]

The student organization had asked for a Russian-style party of good fellowship; had been denied; were angry, stormed the president and struck him: he was to leave next day (June 3 or 4) for a law conference in Greece and they were eager to rush their project through. The student who struck was a fourth-year literature student. The student organization has been dissolved, and protest scribblings (Communist-style) are now appearing on the walls: "To strike the president was bad; to dissolve the organization is worse."

Whence the inspiration to the students of the organization? Largely contacts with Japanese union organizations (the same unions as those forced on Japan by our American Occupation economic theorists—our beloved Reds of the forties). Most of the interested students are economics majors.

The big point: U.S.A. is supporting a highly conservative faculty with almost *no* student contacts. Why is Russia, instead of American democratic campus life, the only available model for these students? *Our* fault: our capitalists support the state system; our Reds advertise Russia via the unions. And so where, in all this, is the actual American ideal?

The Bunraku was full of marvels, chief among them the singer-storytellers and their samisen accompanists.

Next, the curious puppet situation, where each single puppet has three men in black to work it, and yet one's concentration goes definitely to the puppet. The leading puppeteer works the body and the right hand; the second works the left hand; and the third works the legs. The plots are Kabuki style, but I read in the program that, actually, in the eighteenth century, it was the Kabuki that borrowed from the puppet play, and not vice versa.

Quite remarkable was the competence of *all* the performers, from old Bungoro Yoshida (eighty-five years old) to the young boy who sang the boy's part in the first play. The expansion and contraction of the stage, transformations of perspective, etc., were in line with what I have come to expect of this absolutely infallible world of the Japanese theater. And the whole thing was a sheer delight.

After returning home, I went to work on my diary and my Japanese.

Monday, June 20

A pleasant, quiet day. Japanese in the morning; letters, diary, and Japanese all the rest of the day.

A slight brain wave this morning for the possible *convocation address* as follows:

"To know that you are a sparrow and not a swan; or, on the contrary, a swan and not a sparrow: to know this and to be sure of it, and to know that there is no possibility of your being otherwise—not even in your dreams—gives a great security, stability, and quality of harmony and peace to the psyche. You are not only reconciled to your place, but permanently at home there, and, since (as Lewis Mumford once wrote) 'values emerge from life at all its levels,' you are rich in life. But, on the other hand, if you are continually thinking one minute that you must be a sparrow, or then, perhaps, with a fresh inspiration, that you are possibly a lion or a whale, you will soon become so profoundly implicated in your own psychological agony that you will have little time or energy for anything else, and certainly no sense whatsoever of the bliss and wonder of being alive.

"The security, strength, majesty, and competence of man living in the rigidly stratified societies of the ancient Orient, is something that one can still see and experience in the East. . . .

"The problems of modern America, on the other hand . . . on our campus, here, they are challenged and invoked . . . *our* problem, when solved, becomes a model for the coming world. There is no question about this:

we are the growing point of humanity—humanity, at least, this side of, and halfway through, the Iron Curtain. But in our failures, conversely, we are a menace to mankind, and a danger to the human species, a really foul and disgusting example of barbarism: unformed 'primal matter.' In fact, the great question that is hanging in the balance today is precisely this: are the values of the unique, unprecedented individual which we are seeking to develop here at Sarah Lawrence, and which, I believe, are the powers that our culture itself is in principle dedicated to develop—actually the boon that we suppose them to be; or is it going to be necessary for mankind to crush them out again, as they have been crushed since the very dawn (apparently) of human society?"

The power of the ancient, nonprogressive ideal to shape men and women who are harmonious and noble, is conspicuous throughout the Orient, where the "value" of archaic man outshines even the degradation of his present cultural shipwreck: in India, in particular, one is aware of this; and this, I believe, is what constitutes the fascination of India. In a different, very vigorous and vital way one feels it also in Japan—shining through the lights and noises of the great modern cities: mingled with—but transforming and assimilating (or so, at least, it seemed to me) the miracles and gadgets of the machine age. In Japan the *cultural* life of the Orient still is unbroken—and one can see in it an elegance of style, a richness of experience, and a competence for life that (to me, at least) seem almost miraculous.

In contrast: the fumbles, amateurism, self-interests, partial systems in conflict with each other of America (e.g. the American Occupation in contrast to America's democratic talk). The result: a universal distrust of America in the Orient—on many levels, joined maddeningly with a will to imitate—for, I can tell you, the lure and promise of the individual's development (which is what we hold in promise for mankind) is a lure to which every young heart in the world spontaneously responds: it is the lure that the archaic societies were designed specifically to crush.

Theme: the danger of our educational system: the production of specialist barbarians (Titanism)—this, perhaps, is what the world most fears and the Russian peril is balanced against this. If we could convince the world that we are civilized, Communism wouldn't have a chance. (And I believe the Communists have known this for some time. One of their formulae, when their influence was strongest in our colleges in the late thirties and early forties, was to deprecate cultural subjects as "ivory tower." The political insanity of that idea is now apparent in every quarter of the civilized world.)

Tuesday, June 21

My last Japanese class with Father Moss. He looked a bit shocked and resentful when he learned that I was leaving him to flounder alone in his own swamp.

At 2:30 I went over to Eidmann's for one of the most charming afternoons of the Kyoto visit. Professor Kasugai and two of his young colleagues conducted us through the beautiful Nanzenji (Zen) Temple, with its garden of gravel and rocks, and in its beautiful hill-and-forest setting. He then took us to a delightful garden nearby, where there were little platforms for "picnic" parties—and we were served a fabulous meal of *yudōfu* by the women who prepare these bean-curd dishes for the temple. In the lovely garden with its pond and shrines and temples, six of us sitting in a circle with our bowls and chopsticks—it was like a trip into a Japanese picture.

Nanzenji Temple and garden

Returned to Eidmann's for a chat about Zen. He maintains that all the great Zen masters (e.g., all of those mentioned by Suzuki) were Chinese, and that in Japan Zen early became an instrument of the government. Its closest associations are with the spirit of Bushidō. And the beautiful gardens, for which the Zen temples are celebrated, actually are vestiges of a garden culture that was originally that of T'ang China, and was subsequently common to all the sects of Japan: plus a kind of Shintō temple-grove idea.

Ironically, Zen (government-supported) has been a Buddhism of garden retreats, whereas Honganji (against governmental control) has its great temples in the midst of the cities and (as in the Tokyo temple that I visited) is rather for modernization than for picturesque retreats. The reason, Eidmann declares, is that the Honganji is in battle for an idea, and so has advanced, so to say, into the field of life.

Eidmann is going to arrange for me, next weekend, to experience a bit of Zen meditation.

Wednesday, June 22

All morning in the hotel, at my Japanese: afternoon, from one to three, at the school. Much better! Then I went to Eidmann's, to commence a series of private conversation lessons with a young Japanese student, Iguchi-san, whom he has found for me. Monday, Eidmann will be leaving for Hokkaido, and I shall continue with Iguchi-san at his house. I begin to feel, at last, that I may crack this thing before I leave Japan.

Thursday, June 23

Morning: study in the hotel lobby and in my room: really very pleasant. About 10:15 the room quivered a little—and I had survived my first Japanese earthquake. Afternoon, one to three, Japanese school. Evening 3:30 to midnight, Japanese study in my room. Dinner at my favorite cheap restaurant, Fujiya. The ideal day!

Friday, June 24

Hotel study in the morning. Class from one to three, then to Eidmann's for my second lesson with Iguchi-san. Observable progress. Professor

ether

air

fire

water

earth

Indian five-element symbols

Kasugai and his colleagues arrived about dinnertime—and we all went out to make "rubbings" of a Mongolian stone carving in the temple compound, brought by the father of the present patriarch from his expedition to inner China. I caught a glimpse of the present patriarch (in shirt and trousers, carrying a briefcase). And heard a hawk, whose cry sounded almost like the music of a Japanese flute. Nature imitating art? After dinner, a long, pleasant, rambling chat developed, during which we viewed a great number of snapshots of a type of Japanese lantern-like *stūpa* in which the Indian five-element symbols are distinctly represented. This, apparently, is rather common in Japan after the fourteenth century—but is not found in China. What is the relation to India? One thinks also of the five buildings built by Milarepa in his initiation.[228]

I was presented with four rubbings of Buddha figures on a stone at the Imamiya Shintō Shrine in Kyoto, as well as with some photos of our earlier parties. Tuesday, at the garden, I had been presented with photos of two Japanese gardens. I promised to write to Carl Schuster[229] to learn the history of the *stūpa* form.

CHAPTER 10

At the Seventh Step

Saturday, June 25

A curious, badly broken up day. In the morning at ten, Mr. Masao Handa, the father of one of the younger teachers at the Japanese school, arrived to have me criticize his poetry and help him with a textbook on English poetry that he is composing. He remained until noon. Then, at 2:30, I went around to the meeting of the Kansai Asiatic Society to hear Ellen Psaty deliver a lecture on modern Japanese art. But I was one hour too early and so read all the copies of the *New Yorker* on the shelf until the meeting began. Mr. van Vest was presiding. I met Mr. Perkins (whom Alan Watts had written me to look up), and met again the Dutch consul, de Roos, from Kobe, who had lectured last month. After the talk, the consul and his wife drove Ellen and me to the Kyoto Hotel, where we had tea. Another Dutch couple arrived and we had more tea. Then the Dutch people left, and Ellen and I went to a cute little two-by-four bar ("Le Nid") for a drink. Cracked walnuts and drank Johnny Walker on the rocks till she had to meet a 7:45 train. Had my own dinner alone at Fujiya and returned to my room to write letters and bring my diary up to date. Somehow, even with nothing to do but study Japanese, I am managing to fall behind all the time with my mail. A system of *some* kind must be found before I return to New York, or I'm a goner.

One month from today, Jean arrives in Tokyo. Two months from the day after tomorrow we leave for Honolulu, San Francisco, and New York. Amen to a miraculous year.

Some notes on Ellen Psaty's talk, and my conversation, later, with the Dutch consul, who has been in Japan since 1921:

It seems that Europe had already received the impact of Japanese art in the late 1860s: an exhibition took place in Vienna in 1873.

Japanese interest in their own art and architecture as something of national importance began with the visit to Japan of Fenellosa,[230] circa 1878. He lectured in Kyoto in 1882, 1884, and 1886. In 1884, under his influence, an association of painting was founded. He returned to Boston after 1886.

Kakuzō Okakura[231] was Fenellosa's protégé. In 1885, he went with Fenellosa to Europe. In 1885, he and Fenellosa were responsible for the founding of the Tokyo School of Fine Arts. Okakura's interest—like that of the whole Meiji Restoration—was predominantly nationalistic: namely, that Japan should achieve rapidly what the West had achieved through the centuries in the way of skills; and this was to be achieved as a kind of national-racial triumph. Art was to be an instrument of national prestige. The tendency, therefore, was to imitate the big, the recognized, the academic, in all of the arts—instead of that aspect of the Western development that was actually closest to the Japanese sphere of taste and feeling. The whole course of Japanese modern art was thrown off the line by this insincere, unaesthetic emphasis. Moreover, what was imitated was the art of a period in the European development that is one of the lows in the whole Occidental tradition.

The art of the Orient has generally a much stronger literary emphasis than that of the (modern) West. No Western artist would feel that a picture with a poem written across it, and requiring that poem for its proper understanding, was a proper picture. But in China and Japan, the relationship between calligraphy and painting is intimate. The Japanese modern artist seems never to have broken with this feeling, and so, has never really caught the essential problem and intention of modern Western art.

By the close of the Tokugawa period Japanese art had become ossified: fixated to the imitation of a limited range of models. Western art was experienced as a refreshing change. The available teachers, however, were not good: Westerners accidentally present in Japan, who could paint or draw. In 1876 an invitation was issued to European professionals; but those who arrived were only second- or third-raters. In 1887 the Japanese who had studied abroad began to return: but their main emphasis was on the academic.

No tradition for independent individual judgment and expression has ever developed in the modern art movement in Japan. Indeed, this goes so far that the artist tries to suppress information about his life that does not fit into a fixed picture of what the artist life should be. It is almost impossible to find the material for an honest, objective study of the life and work of a modern Japanese artist.

The artist in Japan was, formerly, a craftsman with a fixed social status in a fixed social structure. The breaking of that structure has resulted in a great struggle for success, which would seem to be the primary aim of the modern artist in Japan. This leads him to do the kind of work that he feels ought to be done, to win.

The influence of the dealers (the big department stores, etc.) in creating and maintaining the careers of the artists has an immense impact—as far as the visible picture of modern Japanese art is concerned.

One sees a certain favored, relatively small number of "public" pictures that appear in many exhibitions, and are reproduced in catalogues and books. The relationship of the recognized value of these works, and their artists, to the actual condition of the modern art of Japan is impossible to estimate—for, at the opposite end of the situation we have the fact that in Japan the idea prevails that value depends on how few have seen an object or picture. People buy pictures and they disappear: no one ever sees them; no one knows where they are. The artist himself cannot tell you what has become of his work. It is impossible, therefore, for any critical, comparative estimate of the condition of modern Japanese art to be arrived at. Nor can the public form its own opinion—since the works, other than those being currently exploited by the dealers, are unavailable. And finally, to give an idea of what is behind all this: whereas an excellent traditional Japanese work of art will fetch about ¥2,000,000, the works of the top moderns sell for as much as ¥4,000,000.

Partly as a result of the emphasis of Fenellosa and Okakura on the past of Japan, there has developed no Japanese scholarship devoted to modern Japanese art. Articles on the subject appear only in magazines. And the art dealers, dealing in ancient art, do not handle the moderns. They represent two worlds. And the values of the past have not been able to leap the gap.

There are a number of Japanese words that are applied to pictures and always receive translations that do not quite fit the application. It is probable that these Japanese words, actually, are themselves based on Japanese misunderstandings of the European words by which they are now translated. Examples:

> *seishin-teki* — spiritual
> *shasei* — sketch
> *shajitsu* — realistic (actually: naturalistic)

As for "spirituality" in Japanese art: the Japanese seem to feel that any picture with a lot of space in it is "spiritual." Actually, much of what they would call "spiritual" is what in the West would be termed "sentimental."

My own bright thoughts after all of this:

"History," in the Occidental sense, can be written only in, for, and about the Occident—where at least a considerable proportion of the significant events and people are publicly known: it is a way of writing about life in the world that befits the public character of our Occidental life. No proper history of the Orient, or of anything Oriental, can be written—since the keys to all the movements, facts, and surface appearances are, as far as possible, hidden. The Orient has an intrinsic need and love for the esoteric.

The Japanese listening to Western records (e.g. in those Tokyo coffee shops where record programs are presented) is not doing the same thing as a young Westerner also listening to records. The Japanese wearing Western clothes is not as Western as he looks: the whole context of feelings, requirements, and loyalties of the spirit within the body within the clothes is non-Occidental.

Mr. de Roos supported this, as follows:

You never know an Oriental until you know his family: he has not accepted you as a friend until he has introduced you to his family.

The process of individualization in the Orient is something that is taking place very slowly—or, perhaps, not taking place at all.

Sunday, June 26

Today, what I should call a considerable crack in the glass. First, as I was about to leave the hotel, at 11:00 A.M., a phone call from Tokyo —from guess whom: Ed Solomon,[232] who will arrive for a week's stay in the Kyoto Hotel tomorrow afternoon. Second, when I arrived at Eidmann's I was told that the Zen *rōshi*, Eishū Takeda, whom we were to visit today and at whose monastery I was to get a taste of Zen meditation, would today be attending a funeral—and so the date is off. Eidmann leaves tomorrow for Hokkaido—and that's that.

I was introduced, however, to a young Japanese student who is to go with me, two weekends hence, to the Tenrikyō center for a two-day visit. His name: Kuchiba. The name of the Tenrikyō abbot: Fukaya.

After a nice lunch, I bowed my farewell and thanks and returned to my room to bring my mail, diary, and studies up to date. It is a rainy day, and a good day for work.

Miscellany:

1. *Possible subject for a book: Pope Joan*[233]
2. Name of the deity in the temple in the little Zen *yudōfu*-restaurant garden, before whose entrance two rampant boars serve as guards (one, on observer's right, with mouth open; opposite, with mouth closed): *Maricheta*. In the area near the pond was a little shrine to the "Master of the Pond"— probably a *nāga*.[234]
3. In Zen: Rinzai is a way to Enlightenment; Sōtō is not. (I don't think I understand this!)
4. In Japan, when letters are addressed to important personages, they are addressed to—
   XXXXX, to his basement; or
   XXXXX, into his wastepaper basket; or
   Abbot XXXXX, just outside the circle of his holy radiance.[235]
5. The Buddha figures that Zimmer called "*Dhyāni*" Buddhas might more properly be termed "apparitional" Buddhas. The *Dhyāni* Buddhas are eleventh- through thirteenth-century figures, proper to the Buddhism of Nepal. The figures under the bells at Borobudur would be called in Japanese *keshin* Buddhas; they represent the *Nirmānakāya;* or *hōben hōshin*, representing *Dharmakāya*.[236]

Monday, June 27

Studied Japanese all morning, left a note for Solomon at the hotel, went to Fujiya for lunch and had my classes till three. Taxi (with one of the teachers of the school whom I left at the railroad station, and with whom I found myself actually able to say a few things in Japanese) to Nishi Honganji, for my conversation lesson with Iguchi. Eidmann and Haru had left in the morning for Hokkaido—and I found Obasan learning tea from the little old lady whom I had met here before. I tried to converse a bit with them, and was on the edge of being able to say something. I feel that if I continue a bit longer, this thing will break.

After my lesson, returned at six to the hotel and found Ed in his room (two doors from mine) in his shorts. Took him out to dinner at Suehiro's, then showed him bits of the town and finished in a cute little bar (which I first visited with Ellen Psaty), where, again, I made my Japanese begin to work. We returned to the hotel at about 10:15, and I went back to work on my Japanese.

Tuesday, June 28

Ed at breakfast—and we talked till nine. Then, Japanese till dinnertime, and with Ed to dinner at Alaska (where I dined my first evening in Kyoto). Steered Ed toward the Gion geisha quarter after dinner, and returned to my Japanese.

Some notes on the conversations with Ed. I am assuming that he was sent by God, as everything else has been on this trip, and that I may think of him as standing at the opposite pole from myself, looking at the same objects. By comparing the two views I may calculate for the parallax. Actually—what I have seen white, he has seen black, with few exceptions. We both agree that the Sarabhais are great, that India is a kind of horror, and that it was nice to get to Tokyo.

Ed feels that the U.S.I.S. is doing a good job in the Orient—my feeling is precisely the opposite.

Ed feels that we should go on giving aid to the Orient: I feel that everything we send should be paid for.

Ed excuses the gaucheries of the American grantees and technical people in the Orient: I don't and I think they're a scandal. "But they're farmers!" said Ed. "Well, haven't we got any civilized city people to send out as evidence of some kind of cultural development and sophistication in our country? The Chinese and Russians send artists and we send farmers."

Ed asks why, with all the literacy in Japan, their pattern is authoritarian, not democratic, and why they behaved so militaristically in their conquered provinces. I suggest that democracy may not be the only possible term of literate ideation, and ask why the American authorities in Okinawa are militaristic, not democratic, in their government.

In a subtle way, it has been good for me to have this meeting here with Ed; for it has helped me to realize that I am still on Earth, and it has prepared me to take disparate opinions into account in my preparation for the Sarah Lawrence address.

Wednesday, June 29

News today from Tokyo. Jean's program there is shaping up. A day of Japanese—no view of Ed. I had another lesson with Iguchi from 4:00 to 6:00 P.M., and had dinner alone at the Shijō Fujiya.

Thursday, June 30

Bumped into Ed as I left my room at noon. He has spent the last two evenings at the little bar to which I introduced him and has met the president of the Kyoto Rotary Club. The latter, who was waiting downstairs with his car, announced that Gautam and Gira Sarabhai were due to arrive in Kyoto about July 17th. "All moves to one great end!" I went off to Fujiya for lunch and to my Japanese class; then returned to my room to study. Ed found me and dropped in around 5:30—and I was a little annoyed, but held together: suggested we should go to a Chinese place for dinner, so that I might return early to my work. Phone call, meanwhile, from Ellen Psaty, to ask about our tentative date for tomorrow night. Found, when I returned from dinner, that my watch (Dad's watch: "To Charles W. Campbell, from his friends in the Hosiery Business"—given to him at the farewell party in New York before his departure in 1940 for Hawai'i) had dropped from my wrist and was gone. Felt very badly. The jinx of last Sunday's turn seemed to be continuing to work. Studied Japanese till about midnight and went to bed.

Friday, July 1

Studied Japanese all morning—with a brief conference with a policeman who came to the hotel for information when I reported the loss of my watch. Saw Ed—looking a bit the worse for a hangover—about to go off on a short excursion with a couple of Japanese students. He has found a nice gang of people to help him, and so I probably shan't have to worry about him much more. Lunch at Fujiya; Japanese class; to Nishi Honganji for my conversation session with Iguchi: and there was a letter there from Tenrikyō, declaring that it would be OK for me to visit the place next weekend with my interpreter, Kuchiba. Well, that much, anyhow, is going to work out: and Mrs. Sasaki returns to Kyoto Saturday, so I may yet get a bit of the Zen world.

Fetched Ellen Psaty at 6:45 and we went first for a drink to the little bar (not the one to which I brought Ed) on the canal road. After this, we went to an excellent little restaurant at the edge of the Gion district, called Tsubosaka. Walking down the street, away from it, she showed me another restaurant, Hamasaku, which is also good. We had coffee at a coffee spot called Bel Ami, near Pontochō, then found a bar in Pontochō for a

つぼさか

Japanese characters = the restaurant name, Tsubosaka

brandy—where there was a lively crowd of Japanese, having their fun with the bar girls. We remained for about an hour, then strolled around the town some more and ended in another very nice coffee place, François, where there was a Frenchman sitting at a little table alone, behind a stack of manuscript, as though in a French café. Ellen knew him: Jean-Pierre Hauchecorne, from the Institut Franco-Japonais du Kansai. We invited him over to our table, and he talked, with a continuous, compulsive flow of loosely associated themes, till about 12:30, when we picked up and departed. Meanwhile, three young Japanese homosexuals—two with auburn hair, quite wild—entered and had their coffee at another table.

Hauchecorne's themes: "I am Zen. The great Zen saying: 'If you think you see the Buddha, do not pause; if you do not see the Buddha, pass quickly by.'" I noticed that he patted, occasionally, the handsome cut of his hair, and that his sole interest was his own character as a person who had experienced or seen many interesting things and would presently write three novels and a guide to Kyoto. He knew what the titles and contents of the novels would be and something about the style that they would have. He told of some of the startling effects he had achieved with his Zen bark (like a dog), and strung out a long tale about some interesting chap whose diary he was editing. He was a very pleasant fellow: and I guess he gave me, in the course of all this, my touch of Zen—namely, when he was saying something about the seeing or not seeing of the Buddha I suddenly realized that—well—the banality of Ed Solomon was perhaps my vision of the Buddha in Kyoto. Here, Ed had come all this way to bring me the message, so to speak, of his Buddhahood: his phone call, last Sunday, was, in a way, the cry of the Buddha-child at the seventh step:

"Hello, that Joe Campbell?"

"Yes."

"Well, this is Ed! Ed Solomon!"

"Oh, hello Ed. Where are you?"

"Tokyo!"

"Well, isn't that nice? What are you doing!"

"Coming to Kyoto! Tomorrow."

"Well, isn't that just fine? Where you going to stay?"

"Kyoto Hotel."

"Why, that's where I am."

"Yes, I know."

Actually, as I now can think of it, such a revelation of the Buddha would be the most appropriate possible for myself, whose life is to be at Sarah Lawrence and in New York—not in the Zen temples of Kyoto, which, after all, I could have chosen for my residence during these weeks here, had I been so disposed. I chose the comfort of the Kyoto Hotel. The revelation has come in the form appropriate to the recipient.

During my two hours, this afternoon, with Iguchi, we got onto the theme of the mystery of Buddhahood, and he gave me the Japanese names of some of the fundamental concepts:

Eien no shinri the permanent Truth (= *śunyatā*)

1. *Hōshin: Dharmakāya:* the "body" of *dharma:* Truth, *dharma,* itself
2. *Hōjin:* the "Rewarded" "body" of the Buddha; now in *nirvāṇa*
3. *Ōjin:* the Earthly body of the Buddha

Some theologians believe that the *hōshin* can be seen—which would bring it down (it seems to me) into the realm of ideation.

The term *aru*—existing—cannot be applied to the Buddha: the proper term for the Buddha is *sonzai suru*—(*sonzai* = being).

The *ōjin* appears in the realm of *jikan*—time. I decided that the best term to use in the translation of our word "eternity" would probably be *eien no shinri.*

Iguchi tells me also that, according to what he is being taught, the Mahāyāna is divided into two main schools: the Kūkan Gakuha ("*śunyatā*," or "idea School") of Nāgārjuna; and the Yuishiki Gakuha ("One *Vijña* School") of Vasubandhu,[237] devoted to Maitreya. I hope to hear more about all this next time.

Saturday, July 2

Up at about 7:30 (without my watch) and, after breakfast, to work on my Japanese—with a curious feeling that in concentrating on this Japanese—which I may not learn, after all—I have perhaps missed most of what I might and should have learned and experienced in Kyoto. Ed came to my table in the lounge for a ten-minute chat about his most recent night of joy, and I was pleased that he had found his crowd (actually a very nice crowd) and was not going to be on my hands. After lunch I went around to the Nishi Honganji to meet Iguchi and Fillmore, who were going to make a little tour of temples. Just when Fillmore had given up all hope of being released from the army in Japan, instead of in Minnesota, a wire came from Washington, and he is going to be able to stay.

We took a pleasant sort of picture-taking tour of the Nishi Honganji and Higashi Honganji compounds, and then went to a Zen temple, the Kōfukuji, of the Rinzai sect, supposed to date from ca. A.D. 1300. I took the trolley back to Fujiya after a brief walk through a rather poor section of the city, and studied Japanese till about ten. Sort of tired. Early to bed.

Sunday, July 3

Up at six, for the craziest day of my Japan visit. Professor Kasugai had invited me to accompany him and his students to Nara for a visit to a couple of curious and exceptionally interesting monuments. I was to meet them at 8:00 A.M. at Kyoto Station. Without my watch, I misjudged things and arrived about twenty minutes early, after stopping at Nishi Honganji, to pick up a lunch package from Eidmann's housekeeper. The party—which included Professor Kasugai's wife and kids—began appearing at about 7:55, and we caught, finally, an 8:40 train.

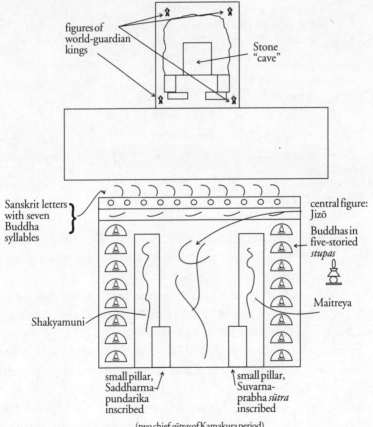

figures of world-guardian kings

Stone "cave"

Sanskrit letters with seven Buddha syllables

central figure: Jizō

Buddhas in five-storied *stupas*

Maitreya

Shakyamuni

small pillar, Saddharma-pundarika inscribed

small pillar, Suvarna-prabha *sutra* inscribed

(two chief *sutras* of Kamakura period)

The temple of Jūrin-in

The first of the monuments visited was the Jūrin-in, a neat little building constructed around a stone shrine, which had been built ca. A.D. 1200 in the form of a small cave sanctuary. The founding of the temple is attributed to Kōbō Daishi. (Kōbō Daishi is the "Mayflower" of Japan.[238])

We next went to a large earth mound, like an Indian *stūpa*, with trees and plants growing all over it and occasional stones bearing Buddha figures and inscriptions. The place is known as Zutō, or "Head," Stūpa, and is supposed to have been built on the site where the head fell off a demon slain in the air. The date is ca. A.D. 800 and the Abbot Genbō is supposed to be the founder. The *stūpa* is due south of the great Tōdaiji Temple, which can be seen from the summit.

As one walks around the *stūpa* one sees the following Buddhas. First, on the lowest tier:

> South—*Maitreya*
> West—*Amida*
> North—*Śakya*
> East—*Vaisajaya*(?)

On the next tier, seven Buddha scenes:

> Three unidentified, then
> Birth
> Enlightenment
> Meditation
> Paranirvāṇa of the Buddha

In Japan, eight scenes are common, including Descent of Elephant and three others. In the upper tier: two Buddhas, unidentified. On the summit, a small *stūpa*.

The plan, apparently, was, to have lunch at this spot; but the caretaker seemed to suggest that it would be better for us to eat elsewhere; so, after he had burned some incense for us, in honor of the Buddha, we departed, and walked about a mile and a half in the broiling sun, to the deer park, where we found the shade of a tree and ate—with the deer poking their noses into our meals.

Our next visit was to the Tōdaiji, to see what the cute children called "Daibutsu-san." We went up onto the platform and walked around, where we could see the engravings on the bronze petals of the Buddha's lotus: pictures of astronomical signs, magical continents, thirteen Buddha worlds in layers, etc.

Daibutsu-den Temple, Tōdaiji Temple, Nara

Kasugai told me that the main figures in this temple are: at the observer's left, Ākāśakośa; right Avalokiteśvara; and center, Mahāvairocana. After this visit, Mrs. Kasugai and the two children went home, and I should certainly have gone with them; for up to this point it had been a good day. Now, however, we returned to the Zutō mound and spent about three hours, dallying and then suddenly writing down the various inscriptions and taking photos. After this—when I thought we might now go home—we returned to the Jūrin-in and made some rubbings of a couple of stele in the yard.

It should be noted also that in the yard of this temple there was a *small* stūpa-*mound of earth, that looked a bit like the great Irish burial mound,* and if one peered long into the pitch-black interior a small Buddha image could be seen (so, at least, Kasugai told me; for I peered, but could not see).

Stūpa mound

It was after 6:30 when all this was finished, and I was really tired. But, after we had taken a bus to the station, Kasugai-san wanted to visit still another temple; so we boarded another bus and headed out into the country. The visit, this time, was to a small temple in a weedy lot, with a tall thirteen-stage stone pagoda at the side, and around the pagoda was a series of stones bearing the forms of Buddhas and Bodhisattvas, some with many arms. The temple was called Hannyaji, was founded A.D. 654 and rebuilt in the thirteenth century.

From the point in the road where we waited for the bus back to Kyoto, the great Tōdaiji roof and building could be seen towering far above the roofs and trees of Holy Nara.

The bus got us back to Kyoto Station about 8:40 P.M. I went to Fujiya for beer and dinner, and home directly to bed.

Monday, July 4

A very disheartening day. Rather dazed, after yesterday's heat and fatigue, I performed very badly indeed in my Japanese classes.

In my class with Iguchi, from four to six, I talked about Buddhism, and suddenly realized, what I should have known for some time, namely, that *the various sects are founded on the main tenets of the various great sūtras.* The approach to the study of Japanese Buddhism, consequently, should be through the *sūtras* here involved.

Left my class with Iguchi a little early, to rush to Mrs. Sasaki's for dinner—she having just returned to Kyoto from New York. The center of the Zen Institute of America is at 156 Waverly Place, New York City(!!!), so it is obvious what one of my early moves should be on returning home.[239]

We talked of many things, pleasantly, and had a beautiful Japanese dinner, served by her lovely girl servants, in her beautiful house, which is in the grounds of the Daikokuji Temple.

We spoke on several themes, among them the disappointment, not only of her American friends, but also of her Japanese friends, who have visited India. A sense of decline and decay.

Second, the curious generosity of Americans, which seems to be unique in world history and is universally misunderstood. This generosity is *not* a function of Christianity, which, in Europe and Asia, for instance, does not yield this pattern. The explanation may be in our frontier heritage, and in the broad margin of abundance in our rich continent.

I learned that the reason the smoke revolved around the fire at the Shingon ceremony of the *yamabushi* was—that *the fire was laid in a certain secret and complicated way.* This I believe. It suggests, however, a question that I must bring to Mrs. Sasaki when next I see her: what is the real point of the *yamabushi* making believe that a fire, which they know has a mechanical reason for its behavior, is controlled by magic?[240]

In Zen, it seems, the great road and chief exercise is *sitting in meditation; reading and study* are also strenuously practiced—in spite of all the sayings which would seem to suggest precisely the opposite. The meaning of the sayings is not that meditation and study are rejected. (The meaning would seem, rather, to be something like Spengler's rejection of the books.)[241]

All the odd goings-on of the quaint boys of the John Cage type have nothing to do with the real character of Zen.[242] (Likewise, I should think, of the dog barking of friend Hauchecorne.)

It occurred to me that Huxley's interest in the actual visions experienced after mescaline is a kind of materialistic interest in another world of things; whereas, in visionary writings, the images are not in themselves interesting, but are metaphoric of the ineffable. (There is an important point here: don't forget.)

Before I left, Mrs. Sasaki promised to have me meet a *rōshi* before my departure: so it may happen, after all.

Tuesday, July 5

No Japanese classes today (they are having exams for the upper class groups). I had a brief chat with Ed Solomon at breakfast and spent most of the remainder of the day on my Japanese—with time off for naps, however; for I'm still pretty tired after Sunday's event.

During the course of last week, I managed to complete arrangements by letter for Jean's teaching schedule in Tokyo: also, received a nice wire from Jean, stating that her Colorado recital, June 30, was a success. So this concludes, I think, all the agonies of the year.

Today was a real rainy day: a bit depressing, but a good day for work. Solomon went to Nara and Hōrinji with a social scientist from Chicago named Macmillan, whom I spoke with for a moment in the lobby of the hotel. He had spent some weeks lecturing at the University of Hawai'i, where he had been annoyed by the press as a "fellow-traveler": Aunt Louise Dillingham actually tried to have a public lecture that he was to give banned.[243] (I love the Americanism of the Dillinghams! Freedom of speech, Tom Paine, etc., seem to have nothing to do with it. It was amusing to hear this story right after reading all the Fourth of July blather in the *Mainichi* about the Rights of Man, freedom of speech, etc.)

Saw Ed again at about 9:00 P.M. (He and I tonight are the only residents on the seventh floor of the hotel.) His trip to Hōrinji and Nara had been fun, in spite of the rain. It included a couple of American social science women who have been here for some time. They visited a convent in Hōrinji and interviewed a Buddhist nun, who had been placed in the convent by her family when she was about two years old. Her life, according to Ed, was "flat": no study, no social work, just meditation. I should have loved to have heard that dialogue via interpreter, between a cluster of American social scientists of Protestant and Jewish backgrounds and a Buddhist nun.

Ed made a point, during our chat, about the inability of the Oriental students and experts to work with their hands. The Oriental tradition of scholarly study does not include anything like our *field trip* or *do it* ideas. I think that this may account for a lot of the mechanical troubles throughout the Orient. Handwork is left to ignorant laborers or to artisans whose crafts are traditional, while the new technologies are studied by men who cannot soil their hands.

Compare now the two worlds: social scientists judging the life of a Buddhist nun without themselves ever having experienced anything like meditation: Orientals judging Western life without themselves ever having worked with their hands. This might be called the polarity: *Zen meditation vs. Sarah Lawrence field trips* (or, more seriously, the lab. and the technological work).

A couple of further points from the chat with Mrs. Sasaki. The Zen people in Japan tend to contaminate their idea of the message they have to give the world with the accidents of Japanese culture. One gentleman, for instance, who wanted to see Zen spread to America, suggested erecting a Japanese Zen temple in New York, serving Japanese tea, teaching tea ceremony, etc. When Mrs. Sasaki pointed out the American resistance to bitter tea, sitting on the floor, and so on, he thought the attitude rather crude.[244]

American fellowships for Japan should be for two or three years, not one. The Fulbrights come with their families, take a couple of months to get adjusted and settled, do not know the language, and are practically ignorant of Japanese culture: by the time they begin to learn something, it is time to pack and leave.

Wednesday, July 6

Morning on Japanese; brief conversation with Ed, whose nightlife continues to yield new friends and larger visions. Le Nid (the bar), apparently, is the trapdoor to infinity. My Japanese classes today went better. I am within three lessons of the end of the course, but only one day remains: tomorrow. Friday there is going to be a little graduation ceremony—but next week I'm going to continue, as a special student, and keep at it till I start for Tokyo, on about July 21st.

A nice class this afternoon, also, with Iguchi. We have commenced reading his college text on Buddhism: *Bukkyō Gaiyō,* and I think this is going to be an excellent bridge to Japan.

佛教概要

Japanese characters = *Bukkyō Gaiyō*

At 6:00 P.M. I arrived at Mrs. Sasaki's for dinner (she had phoned this morning to invite me) and we had an excellent dinner again and a fine talk.

We discussed the point that has been on my mind ever since Calcutta and Orissa: the sacrifice of the personal factor in the Orient: archetypalization and the consequent lack of personal initiative. She declared the principle was operative here too, and that it was particularly strong among the better families. Everywhere there is a lack of what we would call personal initiative. Three extreme examples:

1. The young American instructor who assigned a paper to his class of young women and returned after the weekend holiday to find that all the papers were exactly alike. He flunked them all and was summoned before the president, who rebuked him. The girls' families had paid to have them get degrees that were required for their place in society. His notions of scholarship and student performance had nothing whatsoever to do with the reason that those young ladies had come to college. They had worked conscientiously to produce a paper for him, and had succeeded. Now, let him return and give a proper mark.

2. The professor who asked Mrs. Sasaki for a criticism of his paper on Buddhism. She thought she recognized the prose and when she mentioned

this to him, he said quite frankly, that yes, of course, it was all taken from Suzuki, but rearranged. (This is the kind of thing, by the way, that *we* frequently get from journalists, sophomores, and book reviewers—but we do not represent it as an ideal.) Consider in the light of this example, the stability of Oriental art and the pattern of the commentary in Oriental literature and philosophy.

3. The experience of Mrs. Sasaki's maid, when required to bake a cake *alone*—not with the help and advice of everybody in the household. This experience of doing something alone and making something that was *her own* was an entirely new one (and reported as a pleasurable one) for this excellent cook.

Everyone in Japan is implicated in a firmly fixed hierarchy and finds it very difficult (actually impossible) to relax and get on even terms with associates. Even the language (as I now realize) renders the crisis of a change of degree of intimacy quite considerable. The French shift from *vous* to *tu,* or the German from *Sie* to *du,* is as nothing compared to this![245] The result of this fixed external situation is a considerable context of interior tensions—which, in turn, the peculiar social institutions of Japan (geisha world, sake drinking, theater and festivals, and so on) take care of, and pretty well at that. (Mrs. Sasaki's report on the Japanese pattern of getting bingled[246] was that they relax, warm a little, and then become just silly.)

The Japanese attitude toward life, in contrast to the Indian, is definitely affirmative. (Hara-kiri, which is a social phenomenon, has nothing to do with negativism of the Indian type.)

Japanese luxury is optical, says Mrs. Sasaki (how wonderfully true!) They don't go in for great physical comfort, as we do in the West, but insist on beauty—and get it.

Japanese Buddhism is affirmative. The Epicureanism of the Zen *rōshis.* Monastery life, with tea, music, and meditation.

Japanese nuns, like the monks, are devoted primarily to meditation and worship. In some instances convents are in charge of temples. A special phenomenon (that encountered by Ed) is the tradition in the royal family and its branches of placing certain daughters in convents.

The *yamabushi* are noted for the magic of curing. The revolution of the smoke around the fire had a magical effect. One gets two layers here:

1. that of the apparent, but deceptive, influence of the priest's motions upon the fire, and
2. that of the influence of fire upon the cures that were effected.

Shinran's philosophy (Shinshū) was actually extremely profound: the popularization represented in the Amida cult is a misrepresentation—and yet it gives to the many what they want and require. The man who has been working all day in a rice field (or, one might add, broker's office) is hardly fit to follow, or to require, the teachings of the profoundest thinkers of the race.

(Enlarge, and we have the problem of modern India. The corollary, however, is that what the rice-field worker requires is hardly what the philosopher-scholar is thirsting to imbibe.)

Shinran, by the way, according to Mrs. Sasaki, had his own way with women—and this is a point not stressed by the Shinshū teachers of today. Indeed, she declares, the temples of the Heian period were hardly puritanical.

The Buddha himself was an affirmer, not a negator, of life. One has to consider the forty-nine years of his life given to teaching, after Enlightenment, and remember that his last meal but one was in a great courtesan's house. He was a teacher of kings and princes, as well as of monks and nuns.

The problem of Buddhism for the West: what is the essence of the teaching and how can it be carried without the accidental traits of Oriental life adhering to it and rendering it, not only unpalatable, but unsuitable to the Occidental mind?

Thursday, July 7

In this morning's paper, a lovely article about India's intent to enforce, gradually, a state of total prohibition—as though the country weren't already dismal enough! A still more amusing article yesterday pointed to the situation in Nepal—which is just about ripe for a Communist coup. The Indian army is ready to jump in, in that eventuality. What price "peaceful coexistence"!

Ed reported this morning that his bar life had finally hit the geisha jackpot: one of his companions, at 12:30 A.M., had invited him to a geisha session. A lovely time was had by all—"just plain good fun!" said Ed with sparkling, though somewhat baggy, eyes. He introduced me to an American woman of the somewhat dreadful social science type, who spoke of the tensions and frustrations of the Japanese, while trying to make cat's cradles with a rubber band: she spoke of suicides, bed-wetting, psychological advice, therapy, etc., and I was transported, as on the wings of dream, back to Sarah Lawrence.

My Japanese class today was not a great performance on my part, but by 10:00 P.M. this evening I had finished lesson fifty, the last in the book—just in time for my graduation day! Had a session also with Iguchi, who made a couple of good points about the distinctions between Zen, Jōdo, and Shinshū:

1. The emphasis of Zen is on meditation. The individual attains satori through his own force and effort. Moreover, the results are known and experienced in this world. The Indian counterpart is *rājā yoga*. Zen monks tend to retreat from the world.
2. The emphasis of Shinshū is on the recitation of the *nembutsu*. The individual attains the Awakening of the Faith through the power of Amida. The Awakening of Faith is experienced in this world (but is not Enlightenment?).[247]
3. Jōdo stands between the two: the stress is on *nembutsu*, but the effect is the result, partly of one's own force and effort, partly of the grace of Amida. Enlightenment is not experienced in this world, but in the Pure Land.

In contrast to Zen, in Jōdo and in Shinshū the stress and effort is toward bringing Buddhist teachings to mankind. (In Zen, perhaps, we have a large dose of Taoism: the atmosphere of old-roguism [as Lin Yu-tang calls it] is much the same.)[248]

Jōdo nuns taking tea

4. Tendai, according to Iguchi, leans in the direction of Shinshū and Jōdo, while Shingon is closer to Zen. (According to Mrs. Sasaki, Shingon is the main base of the *yamabushi*.)

Friday, July 8

The graduation exercises at 10:00 A.M. were something never to be forgotten. The graduates were, of course, all missionaries of one kind or another, four or five nuns, a couple of priests, and a company of assorted Protestants. Diplomas were distributed to applause (mine, however, postponed until I finish my further course of two weeks), after little talks had been given in English and Japanese by Miss Hibbard (principal of the school), Hayashi Sensei (the dean), and a Scandinavian chap who is the student of longest standing. Following the distribution of diplomas there took place the prize event of the day; namely, the singing of the school song. The school has no song, and so we sang *Aloha* in Hawai'ian, to the accompaniment of Miss Hibbard's zither. I nearly wept: the combination of the ridiculousness of the whole thing and the pathos of the whole missionary effort to reconstruct in alien lands—with zithers, for example, instead of cathedral organs—the accidents of their culture, hit me in a funny way, and the occasion amounted to an experience. We next went into the yard to have our pictures taken, while the Japanese kids in the large school building across the street looked on from the windows. And finally, we returned to the schoolhouse for cookies (Western and Japanese types), iced coffee, and some more singing to Miss Hibbard's zither and word games. The party ended about noon, after one of the graduating ladies sang a solo—again to the zither—with a kindly smile, but the sort of seriousness that indicates artistic effort and achievement.

Good-byes at the door of the little schoolhouse, and, after my beef sandwich, coffee, and "fruit punch" for lunch at Fujiya, I returned to the hotel for a nap. The heat is beginning to build up hard, and I'm beginning to feel the same sort of sudden fatigue that used to hit me in India.

At about 3:30 I went to Eidmann's place for my reading lesson with Iguchi, then returned to Fujiya for dinner and had another amusing experience. The waitress brought me the menu and as I took it I said what I thought was *"Konban wa"* ("Good evening"). *"Hai!"* ("Yes!") she said, and she took away the menu, wrote something on a slip of paper, and disappeared into the kitchen. I looked at the paper. Something was scribbled in katakana, and the price was written ¥170. Well, I thought, I can't go too far wrong for ¥170, so we'll just wait and see. In about ten minutes she brought me a chopped-steak platter, with spaghetti, beans, and a fried egg![249] I felt that the language school had done well to postpone the granting of my diploma. I returned to my room, to study diligently till it was time for bed.

Saturday, July 9   **Kyoto—Tenri—Kyoto**

The day opened with an amusing surprise. I was about to leave to have breakfast with Mrs. Sasaki, when there was a knock on my door: Ed Solomon. "Come," he said; "I've something to show you." He had been packing, to leave for Tokyo, when, in his suitcase, he found my watch. Mystery. How did it get there? Guess: stolen by one of the room boys, inscription on the back rendered it unmarketable (also, I had notified the Kyoto police); returned, not directly (too obvious) but via my friend.

A very nice breakfast chez Mrs. Sasaki, and a couple of interesting points emerged in the conversation:

About the Catholic Church and the Occupation—why there are so many Catholic priests and nuns now in the language school. She made several points:

The first is gossip: that when MacArthur was in the Philippines a number of the Philippine businessmen helped him to handle his money so well that he made a fortune: became a very wealthy man. The gossip goes that he promised to promote the cause of Catholicism in Japan.

The second is fact (from "reliable sources"): The U.S.A. foresaw and looked forward to a second Russo-Japanese war; but a people, to fight, must have something to fight for. People fight for two reasons: (1) their food and livelihood, and (2) their God. The Japanese had already fought one war for their food and livelihood and were not likely to engage in another right away for the same cause. Buddhism and Shintō, on the other hand, supply no real God, in the Biblical sense of the term, for which people would fight. Ergo: the Japanese must be given a God for whom to fight. The Catholic Church, as the staunchest anti-Communist force in the Western world and the best organized church outfit besides, was given the go-ahead and U.S. government aid. Project: to convert one million Japanese a year, so that in ten years there should be ten million Catholics in Japan. Result: fiasco. All the Christian sects together cannot count more than some 400,000, even after ten years of the most ambitious plans. The Catholic share, after the ten years, seems to be about 250,000. Nevertheless, the nuns and priests are continuing to push in: as witness, my cute little school.

Mrs. Sasaki told of hearing an Episcopalian bishop get the brush-off in Washington at precisely the time when the Catholic Church was receiving every possible aid. No double optics in Operation God!

Mrs. Sasaki told of hearing a sermon in St. Patrick's Cathedral, delivered before the cardinal by a very handsome young Irish priest, wherein the story was told of a nun, who would probably soon be beatified, who claimed that the Holy Trinity dwelt within her. The priest asserted that the Holy Trinity dwells within us all.

Problems: What is the function, then, of the Church? Is it that the sacraments alone open the gates to this interior trinity. Is the body of the Virgin Mary, who was assumed into Heaven, likewise in every heart?

Mrs. Sasaki suggested one explanation for the dismal failure of the Christian project in Japan; namely, that the Japanese feel that they can read the Oriental Bible at least as well as Westerners can—and they do not find in it precisely what is found by the Christian churches.

Reviewing in my mind the whole conversation, I felt that it helps me to understand the curious Religion-Business-Politics tie-up that has become so prominent in America since the war.

At about nine, Mrs. Sasaki's Japanese secretary, Takemura, arrived, and at 9:30 we went around to the Daitokuji *sōdō*, to see Oda Rōshi and view the temple. The visit to the *rōshi* was great. At the entrance to his residence, Takemura gave a short call, and immediately there was an odd call in reply, shortly after which a young monk appeared and made a deep kowtow. We bowed, and Takemura said that we had an appointment with the *rōshi*. Off went the monk, to return shortly, inviting us in. We were placed on cushions in a moderately large room, facing a kakemono, before which there was a cushion for the *rōshi*, who presently arrived and took his place: a handsome, middle-aged, Buddhist monk. We had tea. Compliments were exchanged; conversation was held, through Takemura, first, with respect to Mrs. Sasaki's New York voyage and return, then with me. On learning of my interests, the *rōshi* first spoke of Shintō and then asked me about the religions of America. I spoke first of the American Indians, then of the interest of the moderns in primitive and non-Christian traditions. He invited me to return some day and tell him more about the Indian religions, in which he was greatly interested. His own discourse on Shintō made the following points:

An earlier branch of Shintō, known as the Yamato, is rather primitive in character and stresses themes of purification. Another branch, Izumo, possibly of Korean provenance, shows similarities with Buddhism.

After the interview the *rōshi* brought us to a shrine in which a tooth—relic of the founder of the monastery—was preserved. Beautiful rooms, beautiful, black lacquer altar and steps, beautiful gardens opening into and out of the rooms at every turn. Mrs. Sasaki told me that it was this wonderful openness of the Zen temples to nature, as though there were no difference between the two worlds, which endeared her to Zen. We visited with another monk to conduct us through the meditation halls, teahouses, and the room where the acolyte faced the master. We returned to Mrs. Sasaki's for another glass of tea, and then I made off, at about noon, for the hotel.

Packed my bag, had lunch, and went to Eidmann's, to meet Kuchiba, who was to be my guide to Tenri. Fillmore was there, with a tall friend, and we had tea; then Kuchiba and I made for Kyoto Station. It turned out to be one of the great events of the year.

Mr. Fukaya, our host, met us at the station with a car and drove us directly to the Tenri main temple—a large and very handsome structure with a great, square excavation at its center, within which there is a wooden pillar—on the very spot that the mythology of Tenri regards as the origin place of mankind. When all of mankind has accepted Tenri, this pillar and the temple itself will be transformed into stone.

While we knelt on the great tatami-covered floor, worshipers came in and out, and while reciting their prayer they clapped their hands occasionally, and moved their hands in a pleasant little hand dance: the idea being that thought, word, and action should be one. Prominent among the decorative elements of the temple were the *shimenawa* and the white paper hangings of the Shintō shrines. Priests, in what seemed to me to be a modified Shintō vesture, sat behind the altar rail in immovable repose, and we saw more priests of this sort when we left the main hall of the temple and began walking through the long and spotless circumambulatories.

Inside the Tenri temple

Before we left the temple hall, a number of men with cleaning cloths arrived and began polishing all the woodwork in the great hall—and as we then walked through the long corridors, we passed a number of groups on their hands and knees, wiping the floors and singing as they moved along. These were worshipers, doing one of the standard services. It was actually an extremely touching thing to see. Mr. Fukaya said that I should point out any one of the worshipers I wished, and he would ask him why he was here. I said, "Well, how about one of the people in this group right here?" He touched a young man on the shoulder, who got up, and after a brief moment of embarrassment, told us that he had been ill about the waist and had lost his joy in life; but had come to Tenri and been cured and now was healthy and happy again. Like most of the many thousands whom I saw at Tenri, moving about in work groups, or with their friends, this was a peasant type; intelligent, however, in contrast to the Indian peasant, and wearing the standard coolie-jacket uniform of Tenri.

Our next visit was to the sanctuary where the foundress, Miki Nakayama, is supposed to be in living presence. Within the great room was another room, and within that still another—her dwelling, where she is clothed and fed and put to bed as though alive (cf. Ramakrishna, Ānanda Mayī).

Mr. Fukaya next brought us to the charming guest house, behind a bamboo fence, and with several rooms and pretty gardens, which was to be our residence for the night. Tea was served by a very nice woman servant, who presently called me to my bath. I had asked for a good hot one, and, by golly, that's what it was. I got in, quarter-inch by quarter-inch, and then soaked for about fifteen minutes, came out, dried off, and got into a nice after-bath kimono. What a luxurious affair—and, after all, so simple!

I didn't realize that Kuchiba was to use the same water, and so, pulled the plug; but we saved the situation at the last possible moment—and he was very generous and forgiving.

Feeling clean, and blithe, and wonderful, we were conducted, shortly after the bath, to the home of the patriarch—great-grandson of the foundress: we had to put on getas for the short walk—and this was quite a feeling. (Somehow, I felt much less ridiculous in this rig than I did when wearing the *dhotī* in Orissa!)[250] We entered a room where a Yale professor of sociology, named Lassway, or something like that—a man of about sixty—was asking questions through an interpreter (a splendid young man named Professor Saitō, I think), and receiving answers from a couple of Tenri people. Had Tenri ever been persecuted and how had it met the persecution? What disciplinary measures short of excommunication did it bring to bear for infractions of its rules, doctrinal and moral? At the time, the questions seemed very important, but actually, they were a bit off to the side of Tenri, and the answers, given willingly and carefully, added only one important bit of news to what I already knew about the cult. This was, that, some twenty-seven years ago, there was a man, Aijirō Ōnishi, in Yamaguchi Prefecture, who claimed that the center of the world was not at Tenri but within himself. He was excommunicated and formed a heretical group called Tenri Honmichi, "True Road Tenri."

At about 7:15, one of the men being questioned got up to attend the evening service, and I asked whether I might be present at the morning service. Answer: Yes. The service takes place at 5:00 A.M.

Dinner was at about eight, on the floor of a large and beautiful room, for a company of about twenty gentlemen and one lady—Mrs. Nakayama, the wife of the patriarch. It was a perfectly delightful evening. A troop of little Tenri girls served the sake and innumerable dishes, and while Professor Lassway, at my left hand, sat across from and conversed convivially with the patriarch, I had the good fortune to be face-to-face with the very handsome and charming Mrs. Nakayama; Kuchiba, at my right, helped me to converse.

At about nine, a company of gentlemen arrived who were introduced—curators, professors, and a monk. They remained a while and departed. They had been present—as had the patriarch—at a memorial service, held in Nara, for Professor Warner of Harvard (whom I met, two years ago, with Mrs. Coomaraswamy).[251]

The patriarch (a really cordial and even jolly host) gave us copies of his world-tour book, showed us some photos taken on the trip (one at the bedside of Professor Warner), and then invited us to a European-style room for more tea and conversation—I was a bit surprised to see how bad the decoration was of this room, after the perfect Japanese rooms and gardens everywhere else. And now Professor Lassway began a rather fine series of questions for the patriarch to answer—out of which the following points emerged as (for me, at least) the most interesting:

First, that, in contrast to Christian Science, Tenri believes that not all disease is to be cured or accounted for by mental states: it is therefore not antagonistic to the medical profession and actually has hospitals and infirmaries on its estate.

The gifts of money, made by many, are not required of the devotees, but are voluntary. For some, the "Cheerful Life" (Tenri's ideal) is best attained by renouncing property.

Third, there has as yet been no theological controversy over the point of literal vs. symbolic interpretation of the mythology. There has, however, been contention between the patriotic and non-patriotic readings—with the latter favored by the temple.

The company retired at about 11:30 P.M., and I spent my first night in a truly Japanese bed, on the floor.

CHAPTER 11

BAKSHEESH REVISITED

Sunday, July 10

Woke up every half hour, on the dot, and finally, at 4:30, got up, shaved, and was ready when Fukaya arrived to take us to the service. There were, I should say, about five thousand people in the temple. The patriarch himself—a rather different man, it seemed, in this role—conducted the prayers, which were recited in unison to the beating of a large gonglike drum. The hand movements accompanied the words. Then the company stood, and while praying, went through a quiet little dance. We moved to the hall of the foundress, and deep in the inner chamber a woman could be seen whose function it was, apparently, to serve the foundress.

Our next event was a visit to the mausoleum of the foundress, which is on a lovely height. Then we returned to the guest house for a Western-style breakfast.

Mr. Fukaya very generously answered a long string of my questions at this time, and the following main points emerged:

1. Reincarnation is taken for granted.
2. The body is a loan from God.
3. The borrower of the body was created by God, is not itself God, and yet is not distinctly different from God.

4. The moment of creation was 999,999,999 years before the moment of Miki Nakayama's revelation. This number, however, may be interpreted, simply, as meaning, a very long time ago. This is the beginning, I should say, of allegorical exegesis, to allow for scientific views.

5. Human consciousness has evolved through three great stages: (a) that of minute forms in the muddy waters, (b) that of the gaining of mental power, (c) that of reading and writing.

6. Man's consciousness is free—free to make mistakes, and does so. When man's thinking does not accord with the *michi,* or true way of God, he goes wrong and sickness, as well as other ills, result.

7. There is (or seems to be) no idea of a moment of general catastrophe in the past, like that of the Fall (or, in primitive mythologies, the discovery of fire), when mankind as a whole lost its pristine state. Mankind, as a whole, is progressing. The mistake is made by the individual.

8. The mistake is to forget that the world is one.

9. As the result of bad deeds a man may descend in the scale of progress and take birth as a plant or animal. The word "death" is used in this connection, but in no other. When such a soul returns to human birth, it is said to have "come again."

10. Some of the ills experienced in this life are the effects of earlier lives. Problem: how to break this claim of cause and effect in daily living.

11. The first thing to realize is that the body is borrowed. This realization gives happiness ("the cheerful life"). One's expression of this happiness (so achieved) is one's "daily contribution."

Mr. Fukaya says that Tenri is not opposed to, or in conflict with, other religions: one can be a Buddhist as well as a follower of Tenri. The God of Tenri is the One God—the same as the one who gave to man Buddhism and Christianity. On the other hand, the non-active, meditative lifestyle of Zen is regarded as precisely the opposite of that of Tenri (compare the Zoroastrian opposition to the yogi).

Tenri is not inclined to metaphysical speculation. There is no thought about death in its system: one does not go to any heaven or hell after death. There is little speculation about "the borrower of the body." The orientation is essentially practical, and directed to the actualization of the "cheerful life" (*yōkigurashi*) and the effective use of the "daily contribution" (*hinokishin*).

One example of the practical program is that of the work teams of one hundred young men apiece, who come to work at Tenri for ten-day periods. Their work is a form of prayer through labor—and actually, as we sat talking in the pretty guest house (which had been built, like all the other buildings in this fabulous city, by the voluntary labor of people who came here of their own free will and actually paid their own room and board while doing the work), there were the songs of the passing work teams all the time: the whole city was full of song. And one group of older men, whose voices were no good, went to work with drums and horns, whose music was no good either, but at least it could be heard and was certainly cheerful. 1,982,000 people have worked in this way at Tenri during the past year and a half. (Many, of course, are repeats.)

The great majority in this remarkable city are distinctly of the peasant type, but the clergy, professors, and intellectuals who talked with us for twenty-odd hours, were not peasant simpletons by any means. Their impression, I think on Lassway as well as on myself, was frank, intelligent, practical, and honest.

Mr. Fukaya showed me copies of the newspaper (weekly) and the magazine that he publishes. Fifty thousand copies are sent to Tenri churches; two hundred thousand to Tenri people.

I was told also of the *besseki,* or "basic instruction," and holy blessing that is given in the seminary of Tenri: it gives one the power to help people cure themselves by giving them again their intrinsic sense of proportion—clearing dust.

In Tenri there is the main temple with its immediate precincts, and then many subsidiary churches with their surrounding dormitories—the latter, looking much like fine Bronxville mansions, but à la Japanese. Tenri has about fifteen thousand churches, including some in Honolulu, Los Angeles, Seattle, and Chicago.

At about 9:30, Mr. Fukaya left us, to go to his work, and Miss Lois Uchida, a very nice young Nisei girl whose father was head of the Los Angeles Tenri church, took over. She brought us to the museum (good ethnological collection—of Peruvian textiles, especially); the library (on religion, philosophy, anthropology, and so on), where we had a brief talk with the librarian; and finally to the vast new school structure being built by voluntary labor in an elegant style, and—like all of the other buildings—sturdily and well.

A delightful lunch was served by the nice little lady in charge of our building; we took a final stroll about the grounds, for me to take a few pictures, and finally, at 4:30, a car called to drive us to Kyoto, in the company of Miss Uchida and a nice young, rather silent man.

I invited the lot to Suehiro's for dinner. Kuchiba had some other date, but the rest joined me—and, as a final fillip to a prodigious weekend, as we were about to enter the restaurant we saw the most amusing procession (Kyoto is simply nutty about processions): four groups of tiny boys; one group as samurai; one, like little peanuts on the backs of horses; one, dressed as geese—with their mothers diligently fanning them; and one (very tiny) as little Jizō with the clanking sticks of the Bodhisattva.[252]

Bade my friends good night at about 8:00 P.M. and strolled home to bed.

Monday, July 11

My first morning of special classes at the school. It went very nicely. I was invited to converse for two hours about my family, which I more or less did.

I felt a bit fatigued and feverish after lunch and slept from 12:30 till 2:30. A voyage to Eidmann's to see Iguchi was fruitless—Iguchi was absent, not well: but I got in for another session of tea. Returned home to write up my diary. Dinner at Fujiya and to bed at about 10:30.

An interesting item in the morning paper about Indian journalists interviewing Japan's new ambassador to New Delhi, Seijirō Yoshizawa. Their questions: Would Japan recognize Red China? Does Japan subscribe to the *Pancha Sīla?*

Replies: At present Japan is committed to recognize Nationalist China; but because of Japan's proximity to the Chinese mainland and the need for trade, Japan favors "some adjustment of our relations with China."

Japan is pledged to the United Nations Charter and was a party to the Bandung Declaration—both of which embody the principles of co-existence.[253]

And finally (that soul balm for India): "Japan entertains an age-old sentiment toward India as a great source of cultural heritage which has contributed to the formation of our national characteristic."

Phone call this evening from Mrs. Sasaki, inviting me to meet another *rōshi* tomorrow afternoon.

Tuesday, July 12

After my Japanese class, I went to the Kyoto branch of the Kansai Customs Office to have a blank page added to my "Foreign Exchange Record Book" and had a very amusing hour, while six young men took time off from their game of Go to discuss the problem and finally do the wrong thing. After dinner, I received a phone call, asking me to return tomorrow to have the mistake corrected.

At 1:30, I appeared at Mrs. Sasaki's for our trip to Ryōanji (with the celebrated rock-sand garden) and visit to Gōtō Rōshi at the nearby Daishu-in. Daishu-in means "Great Jewel Temple," and Ryōanji, "Dragon-Peace Temple." Gōtō Rōshi was a lovely old man of seventy-seven, clad in white: more like the Indian monks, I should say, than the comparatively formal and stately Oda Rōshi, whom I met Saturday. He is Mrs. Sasaki's Zen master, and the meeting was delightfully simple and informal. A tall, thin, young monk, who is to be the *rōshi's* successor, served us our whipped tea, and an *obasan* rolled up the shades and pattered here and there. The *roshi* talked to me about Kōbō Daishi and Dengyō Daishi, and their masters in China, and brought out a book showing the spiritual lineages of all the great Buddhist teachers from the time of Gautama to 1909. He spoke, also, briefly, of spiritualism in the religions of Japan, declaring that in Buddhism it was confined to Shingon and Tendai (or, at least, this is what I understood).

Mrs. Sasaki's secretary again acted as our interpreter, and we were accompanied also by a pleasant, rather typical, American literateur-homosexual of about fifty-seven, who prefers Noh to Kabuki and goes to all the Jūdō movies (why are they *always* the same, these guys?). He was sweet and so was everybody else. He is reading *Finnegans Wake* with the *Skeleton Key* and asked the standard question: When are we to have a key to the *Key?*[254]

After visiting the *rōshi*, we visited the rock garden, but the setting was destroyed by a lot of chaps setting up shop in the temple for an exhibition of kimonos. This led me to ask Mrs. Sasaki about the poverty of the monasteries—and there came out some more news about the Occupation.

The great land reform—to break the feudal system and turn land over to the peasants—allowed individuals (which includes the abbots of temples) to hold no more than six acres apiece. Result: the temples were deprived of both their own lands, and the support of landowners who formerly had had property and wealth from which to make donations.

(Query: Was this land reform supposed to represent the American way of life? If not what was the way, and who were the authors of the reform? Three guesses.[255] Query two: What chance would a bill restricting church properties in this way have of enactment in the U.S.A.?)

The pattern of trade unionism imposed on Japan is some twenty years ahead of that of the U.S.A., and far beyond Japan's means to support it.

The school system was completely knocked apart, and reformed idealistically, according to American ideas and again beyond Japan's means to furnish adequate support.

The big trouble: a combination of ultra–New Dealism and American provincialism, according to both of which, local conditions are not to be regarded; nor local ideals, preferences, traditions, or habits.

I returned to my room at about 6:15, for an evening of study.

Wednesday, July 13

Japanese in the morning. Another trip, at 11:00, to the customs office to have the Go players correct their mistake of yesterday, and, at 8:00 P.M., a visit from Professor Kasugai and his disciple, the Buddhist nun, to have me autograph the Zimmer volumes that I'm giving him as a present. Otherwise: a day of pleasant study—in spite of the heat, which, now that the rainy-season clouds have cleared, is hitting the middle nineties.

Thursday, July 14

A phone-call slip, this morning, from Gautam Sarabhai,[256] who is at the Miyako. I left a message that I would phone him at noon, and went off to school. Today, I finished the primer and started into the first reader, at page 125. Studied Japanese all afternoon and at 7:30 P.M., Gautam and Gira Sarabhai arrived and we went off to the Alaska for dinner. Quite a remarkable experience comparing notes on Japan with the Sarabhais. They feel and look more alien here than I do; believe—as I do—that Japan is as different from India as it is from the U.S.A. They are trying, I think, to be not too greatly impressed. Of course, as far as eating goes, they are having it a bit hard. Alaska had almost nothing that they could eat.[257] We then took a stroll through some of the cuter streets and at about 10:00 P.M. they taxied back to their hotel.

Gautam says that in the textile market, Japan has lost considerably to Indian competition, but that in the manufacture of machines they can sell to the Indian market. In Japan there are five major and nine minor export firms through which all the exporting is done. One is met and entertained by the members of these firms and does not get through to the manufacturers. The employees in the textile industry are girls, average age 17.9 years, who work for three years, eight hours a day, get room and board, plus from ¥4,000 a month to ¥7,000 (the last year), and, besides, continue their schooling. When they quit, they have a dowry and are ready for marriage. One girl can tend 4,200 spindles, which is the highest record in the world. The top in the U.S.A. is about one man to 4,000 spindles. This whole situation transforms the labor problem: it is very different from that of a country in which the work in the mill is a lifetime job.

While walking with Gautam and Gira through the streets of Kyoto, I was interested in trying to recall the picture of India: what I noted was the comparatively heavy, stoop-shouldered slouch of Gira in contrast to the springy vitality of the Japanese women: the dark languor in contrast to the flash and brilliance of these people—and, of course, all the ritualism and arrogance about food. They found seaweed difficult to like; it has, unfortunately, been the most common of the Japanese-style vegetable elements. They prefer the Western-style restaurant to the Japanese. And by a curious misfortune, I had the luck of ordering, by accident, a veal curry: my first since India.

Gautam said that Japan didn't seem anything like the rest of the Orient to him, because it is industrialized, and the rest of the Orient is agricultural. He also wondered whether the Japanese are warm friends: they seemed to him cold and formal. He was impressed by the politeness and cleanliness. (Those were the only good things he said voluntarily about Japan.) When I said I had been to Formosa, Gautam asked what I had found there: "Like being in America, I should think," he said. When I told him I was learning Japanese, he wondered what good there could be for me in learning this language. In speaking of Rangoon, he told of the dangers of brigands, only a few miles out of the city. I could feel no enthusiasm at all for any of the places in the world, outside of the borders of India. Hong

Kong is a kind of resort city. He has not yet visited Bangkok. I had a curious feeling of dullness and tediousness about Gautam and Gira this evening, whereas in Ahmedabad they had twinkled with life. Maybe it's my contrast of India with Japan that makes the difference, or maybe it's just that their pattern is that of provincials in a really alien world: self-protective and slightly piqued. The pattern is *very* strong, I feel, in Gira.

Gautam's words about *agriculture* and *industry* can be carried a long way. The agricultural, peasant ideal, for example, is expressed in the great, heavy hips of the Indian women, whereas the trim, reedy, willowy figures of the...but no! China's women are willowy too, and China is definitely agricultural; and the women of Japan were this way before the Meiji era. This idea isn't so good. Perhaps one should say, rather, that the willowy ideal of the Far East prepared its world to accept the machine age without too much psychological tension, whereas in India, where the *anima* image cannot be jammed into a bathing-beauty's bikini, there is a fundamental spiritual antagonism to the new age. Ha! A nice cocktail party thesis. Very nice indeed.

Friday, July 15

Called for Mrs. Sasaki at her home at 8:30 A.M. and then, joined by a fine young man named Walter Noak, went up Mt. Hiei, to spend a marvelously interesting day. To begin with, we spoke on several points in the taxi and on the trolley on the way to the Mt. Hiei finicula.

A nice counterpart to the Sarabhai reaction to Japan: the reaction to India of a Japanese, Mr. Tsunoda, formerly at Columbia University, as reported to me by Mrs. Sasaki. He spent ten days in the New Delhi area, and brought the following report:

On a trip to a holy mountain some two hundred miles north of New Delhi: upon arrival at the hotel he had a bath drawn and found the water very muddy. Tsunoda-san decided to let the water out of the bath and fill the tub again: he pulled the plug; the bath boy maintained that his prerogatives had been usurped, that his status had been endangered, and that the whole social structure of India had been insulted. He would supply no more water—and Tsunoda-san was openly despised by all the servants of the hotel for the period of his stay. His impression was that although in

India people talk of doing away with the caste system, they are actually doing little to change the present situation.

His car, returning, was held up at a railroad crossing for about forty-five minutes: ten or fifteen minutes before the train arrived, twenty or so while the freight train shunted and shuttled back and forth within sight, and about ten minutes after the train had moved on. Meanwhile, multitudes urinated, defecated, and did other "dirty things," all over the place, while waiting.

In his conference with Radhakrishnan,[258] he had the impression of a vain, loquacious dilettante, spouting airy platitudes and regarding these as evidence of high spirituality, while disregarding completely the actualities of the world scene.

Mrs. Sasaki spoke about the kōans of Zen. They are not odd (as the writings of Suzuki and Alan Watts would seem to suggest). Each, on the level of consciousness from which it comes, makes good sense, and receives its only possible answer in the traditional response. You have to stand on the level from which the kōan comes to appreciate its logic, however. The main road of Zen is not the kōan, but meditation; the kōan is public evidence of the level of consciousness attained.

Mr. Noak is the young man who had the experience of the students who handed in identical papers.[259] His students are studying to get the certificates of accomplishment that are prerequisite to a good marriage. In Japan (also, I think one can say, in India) a certain supersensitiveness to Western criticism leads to the maintenance of a surface (e.g. exams in college); but the true function of the elements of that surface are not what they would seem to the Western eye.

Our first visit when we reached the top of Mt. Hiei was to Jōdo-in, a small but important temple, within which is the tomb of Dengyō Daishi. The young monk in charge of this temple, and living there practically alone—with only a couple of men and boy servants to assist—is named Sōmon Horizawa. His function in the temple is to conduct all the services, utterly alone. He has been two years in the temple and is to remain there ten more—without coming down from Mt. Hiei. He is now twenty-six years old; he joined the Tendai order at the age of twenty-one, after quitting Kyoto University before receiving his degree. His day commences at

2:00 A.M., with the recitation of *sūtras* before the two shrines, which we visited—that of Dengyō Daishi and that of Amida. By 7:00 A.M. this phase
of the day's work is done and he is free for breakfast, cleaning house, and
a bit of reading. At 10:00 A.M., another spell of services, till about noon;
and then there is another two-hour spell at about 4:00 P.M. The rest of
his time is free, and the time that he spent with us today was that between 10:00 A.M. and 4:00 P.M. (I don't understand what happened to the
10:00–12:00 worship.)

Our first visit in his temple was to the main chapel. When one faces
the altar one is facing also the tomb of Dengyō Daishi, which is just outside the back wall. Sōmon slid the door open and let us look at the tomb
building—with the great tall California-like trees all around it. (Dope! I
had left my camera in the front hall!) Two trees from India flanked the
tomb; the one at our right was a sal tree, that at our left was supposed to
be (but wasn't) a banyan.

We next visited in this temple the smaller Amida chapel. Here the
paraphernalia of worship were of the Shingon type. The monk had to read
here the *Dai Hannya Sūtra,* which is stowed in a case just outside the
chapel and consists of six hundred volumes. The main image in this chapel
is a lovely standing image of Amida: it stands before a tabernacle, within
which there is another image, black, supposed to have been carved by
Dengyō Daishi himself. This image is almost never exposed. Sōmon himself has seen it only once. (Another example of Ellen Psaty's law: in Japan,
the value of a thing is estimated by the fewness of people who have seen it.)

This chapel was small and dark and silent. The wind could be heard
outside in the tall trees—and Mrs. Sasaki told me to try to imagine this
place in the winter with the young priest performing his offices in the solitude and darkness. The whole spirit of Tendon was right here: the whole
thing: the sense of solitude, darkness, and therein the Buddha's appari-
tion—a very different world from that of Zen, with its openness to the fair
garden of the world. Even the incense, said Mrs. Sasaki, has a different
smell.

After visiting the two chapels we sat in the young monk's main
room and drank orange juice. Nearby was a long calligraphic kakemono. I
asked its meaning. The young monk smiled: he couldn't read it—nobody
could: it was in a very difficult calligraphic style known as the "grass style"

(a "grass-style scroll"). Again—the sense for mystery of this curious world. I had to think of Joyce and Mallarmé. On Sōmon's desk, among many books, was one by Hakuju Ui, who, Mrs. Sasaki said, was the leading Buddhist scholar.

Sōmon got into his walking clothes and, wearing getas,[260] accompanied us on the day's excursion, as our guide. We visited first a moderately small temple with vivid red decor, called Amida-dō, then passed on to one of the most important spots in Japan, the so-called "Command Platform." This was established by Dengyō Daishi as the place for the valid ordination of monks—in rivalry with the "Command Platform" at the Kegon center in Nara, which, up to that time, had been the sole legitimate site for ordinations. After the establishment of this platform on Mt. Hiei, the capital could move from Nara to Kyoto.

Sōmon Horizawa atop Mt. Hiei

At this platform the Tendai monks are ordained to this day. Sōmon was ordained here. The ordination takes place after a long period of ritual bowing, days and nights on end with only minimal pauses for naps and nibbles, has culminated in a vision of the Buddha. Sometimes three years are required before the vision is seen: in Sōmon's case, the ordeal lasted two-and-a-half months. At the ordination itself, the candidate makes his bow before the high monks of the order, at the altar in this temple. The central Buddha of this altar is Shaka, with Miroku at his right and Monju[261] at his left. The candidate then is shaved here and takes the commandments. Sōmon said that during the course of the bowing ordeal, the neophyte sees many other visions besides that of the Buddha, music is heard, flowers fall, and the radiant Bodhisattvas of the *sūtras* appear.[262]

As Mrs. Sasaki pointed out, Zen is opposed to such visions as traps in the spheres of illusion. Zen's orientation is non-, trans-, or anti-mythological, in contrast to that of Tendai.

We moved on to a vast and impressive, red-painted temple (all of these Tendai temples, in fact, have red decor), known as, and dedicated to, Dai Nichi Nyorai, "Great Sun *Tathāgata*." This Buddha is the Absolute Buddha of the Kegon sect. We entered by a side door, and Sōmon told of a ritual in this temple where the worshiper has to get through this door quickly, just as it is being banged (slid) shut (*Symplegades* motif[263]). Within, right at the door, was a little shrine of the seven kings (Shintō motif[264]).

Our next visit was to the largest and most impressive temple of all these on Mt. Hiei, the Konpon Chūdō,[265] "Hall of the Origin of the Teaching." The decor of this large and beautiful building was freshly painted: we went into the main building and found, behind the main room, a darker, older, equally large chamber with some images in a large tabernacle; one, the so-called Yakushi Nyorai, supposed to be by Dengyō Daishi.

Time for lunch was now approaching, so we hiked off into the lovely hills and finally settled on a little height with a number of tombstones, overlooking the beautiful hills and the prodigious reach of Lake Biwa. The air was full of insect calls and of bird notes ("the Japanese nightingale") that sounded more like the bird songs of our northeastern American forests than any I've heard in Asia. It was a lovely, refreshing rest, and when it was over, we started downhill to visit Hagami Shōchō Acarya in the Mudōji Temple. This temple is dedicated to Fudō ("not moving"), the god of the *goma,* or fire ceremony;[266] and the name of the temple has almost the same meaning as the name of the god: Mudō: "immovable"; as "without" (*mu*) "moving" (*dō*); Fudō: "not" (*fu*) "moving" (*dō*). "Temple of the Immovable, Mysterious God."

The path that we followed to this temple was an extremely precipitous and tortuous one, and has an interesting function. It is part of a long route of some eight *ri* (about seventeen miles[267]) that Dengyō Daishi is supposed to have walked every night for one hundred nights. It is known as Kaihōgyō, and today is used in connection with a specific Tendai discipline. Through a period of seven years, for one hundred nights each year, the trainee walks this path, wearing the long "coiled-lotus" hat of the Tendai monks. Mrs. Sasaki walked the way one night and declares that the monks go at a fast, steady clip, without pause or alteration of speed, almost as though on air, moving like feathers in the breeze—and this in the dark. I asked whether she thought the discipline might have a value somewhat like that of *Zen in the Art of Archery,* and she answered yes. If that is so, the discipline would be that of a sort of transcendence of the ego-centralized, rational control of the body.

At the Mudōji Temple, Hagami Shōchō Acarya, who was a very pleasant and friendly man of about fifty, showed me, among other things, the "lotus-curled" hat and I took a couple of color photos. The temple is in a wonderfully romantic spot, with precipitous paths and a glorious view out over the lake.

One more bit of news about Mt. Hiei. In the sixteenth century Nobunaga destroyed the whole mountain community, to crush the power of the monks, and this was the end of the predominance of Tendai (ca. A.D. 850–1550). Hideyoshi gave permission to rebuild, and the present community dates from his time.

According to Mrs. Sasaki, the rise of the power of Zen took place in the Kamakura period, in the twelfth–fourteenth centuries. The history of Buddhism in Japan, she declares, is intimately tied up with the history of politics: the flourishing of the different sects is tied up with that of the various political teams.

An interesting point: our young monk Sōmon, apparently, feels that he is approaching an impasse in his Tendai-style of discipline and is interested in learning more about Zen. I asked, when we had said good-bye to our mountain friends and returned to the Kyoto Hotel bar for a drink, whether such a shift in discipline would amount to a radical trauma for such a monk. Walter Noak seemed to think it might. Mrs. Sasaki, however, said that in the great period the Tendai and Shingon monks had all practiced Zen: in fact, Zen had been the meditation aspect of their discipline.

We talked a bit, finally, about the Orient-Occident problem in general, and a few good points arose.

According to Mrs. Sasaki, today it is the West that is idealistic ("spiritual"), and the Orient that is grossly materialistic.

I pointed to the laughable character of much of the "democracy" and "human rights" talk of the Oriental journalists and politicians. They keep saying that the economic inequalities of the world must be corrected and love the sound of the phrase 400 million people: and yet, from those great 400 millions not a single profitable, generally useful idea has come into the modern world. The Orientals may be able to copy the machines that are supposed to, and are perhaps going to, save them, but they have not contributed one useful thought to the whole tradition. In compensation for this failure, they try to make a great thing, in India, of their "spirituality."

In Japan, according to Mrs. Sasaki, the compensation is that of the impenetrability, for Westerners, of the Oriental mind. If you say you like their food, houses, art, etc., they are delighted—but if you say you yourself actually sleep, sit, and eat on the floor, in your own home, by preference, the screen goes up and you are frozen out—because, it is *impossible* for a Westerner to do and enjoy these things. (I was amused, by the way, to find that for Gautam and Gira the Japanese style of sitting is as difficult as it is for us.)

It is a general Oriental notion that Oriental philosophy and art are impenetrable for the Westerner, and I am not inclined to contest the point. It is also true, however, that very few modern Orientals have been able to write as well on these subjects as the Occidentals. Indeed, in English, at any rate, the Indians, at least, quote from Occidentals without using quotation marks and often abuse the Occidental mind while doing so—as I learned for myself in Calcutta.[268] My own inclination, right now, is to leave the Orient, therefore, to the Orientals and point my own work toward that particular work which is perhaps the *great* work of the Occidental scholar in the field of Culture Studies, namely, the Comparative approach. This is almost completely alien to the Oriental mind, as far as I can see, and belongs to what I shall henceforth think of as the *Cartesian approach* to culture and religion.

A striking fact about the Orient is what may be termed its provincialism. Each country tries to date things by short kingly eras. It took the West to conceive of a general dating system—coordinated from the "birth of Christ," or the Augustan age of Rome. It took the West also (namely, the British) to regard the whole globe as one field, measured from Greenwich. And so, it is not remarkable that our culture has become the unique world culture of all time, and our science, philosophy, etc., the unique world science, and comparative culture field.

(Compare Nietzsche—the present age, the age of comparative competition and survival. Our age, actually, is of the formation of what is to be the common-field culture of the whole world. We have the luck to be alive and working at this wonderful moment, in this wonderful coming-into-being of the common field: and the great question for each living—as opposed to dying—culture is this: what can it contribute, what has it to contribute, to the common pool; not, what can it get by one strategem or another, from its creative neighbors. As far as I can see at present, the Orient's contribution will be in the psychological field, via the work of Western-style scholars on materials dating primarily from the fifth century B.C. to the eighth century A.D.)

Resolution: *Comparative mythology* (philology, in the German sense) is indeed my field—and the method is to be first of all *philological* (*The Basic Mythologies of Mankind*) and secondly, that of the Jungian *amplification* (example: *The King and the Corpse*[269]).

Saturday, July 16

Today and tomorrow, the great Gion Festival of Kyoto. The floats have been standing along Shijō for about a week now. Kasugai phoned to say that he would call for me at 5:00 P.M., to visit some of the floats; and when I phoned Gautam, I suggested that he and Gira join us at that time.

Worked all day until 4:45, then went to the lobby to meet my friends. Gautam and Gira were the first to appear—with a Japanese gentleman who is trying to compete with another Japanese businessman in entertaining them. The Kasugais arrived with his wife, two youngsters, Buddhist nun, and five students. We sent Gira and most of the Kasugai team off first, and while we were waiting for the car (Sarabhai's friend's car!) to return, Saitō arrived with *his* wife and child. On Shijō, at the Moon Spear float, we were met by the second Buddhist nun-friend of the Kasugais, and entered the temple building associated with the Moon Spear float. We visited the float, sat around a bit, and then went out strolling about the crowded, prettily decorated streets, saw many more floats and visited a couple of little places where children, cutely dressed, were singing hymns and lighting candles.

Japanese children beneath paper *gohei* offerings

At about seven the Sarabhais, their friend, and I bade good-bye to the rest of the company and were taken, by the friend, to Prunier's for dinner—after which we visited the beautifully lighted Yasaka Shrine, strolled around, bought a few toys, and then commenced a long quite wonderful walk (till about 11:15 P.M.) through the crowded, beautifully lighted streets of Kyoto.

Gautam and Gira now seemed to have caught on to Japan, and were liking it a lot. Our conversation covered a number of points worth recording:

Ed Solomon's visit to Ahmedabad: Lois Murphy, in her letter to the Sarabhais, had built Ed up as a rather important member of our faculty: *Director of Field Work, Sarah Lawrence College.* Gautam figured that this sounded like someone in the social science field and made appropriate plans. Ed arrived. He wasn't really interested in anything; just wanted to sit around among nice people. He said he liked adolescents, played the guitar for them, and had a nice time. Perfectly wonderful advertisement for Sarah Lawrence! Gautam thought he was a kind of joke.

I asked Gautam about India: was he pessimistic or optimistic about India's possibility of pulling out of the ditch? "What ditch?" said Gautam. "Well," I said, "according to the standards of other countries that I've visited, India's economic and health conditions would be regarded, if they were ours or theirs, as catastrophic. One of the things that one learns when one visits India is that people can go on living under these conditions. But I understand that the Indian government is trying to improve them. Do you think they are going to succeed?" And then came one of the revelations of my year's visit to the Orient. *Gautam spoke as though the conditions were actually not so bad and were pretty well under control.* The antibiotic drugs, he said, were conquering disease. Russia was going to give a steel mill: England, in competition with Russia, was going to give another steel mill, and there was even a third somewhere in the offing. Cotton quality has been improved, so there will be no need, now, to import African or American cotton. And the rice supply has been brought up to a surplus level: a great economic plan for Burma, devised by a team of Americans and based on the assumption that the export price for Burmese rice would be at a certain level, had been wrecked by India's success in growing rice (which itself had been somewhat assisted, Gautam *didn't* add, by American technical aid).

Talking with Gautam I gained (or perhaps refreshed) the impression that *the Indians do not regard their condition as being as desperate as visitors tend to:* the only point of course, though, is that other side, which one must always look for in the Indian; namely, that the baksheesh pattern was even present in Gautam's delight at the Anglo-Russian steel-mill competition—and that in India itself it is the predominant motif. Every young or old man you meet in India complains about the money he's getting; and so the conditions are *not* actually satisfactory. And one more detail: when I talked with Gautam about disease in India, I said that when I was in Calcutta they had smallpox, bubonic plague, and everything else. "All you need to protect yourself against smallpox," Gautam said, "is vaccination." "I know," I said; "but I wasn't talking about myself; I was talking about disease in India...." When tuberculosis was mentioned, Gautam said that they also had a lot of tuberculosis in Japan. *His whole pattern was defensive of the actual Indian situation.*

Gira made a good remark about Japan; namely, that whereas in most places there is a kind of hierarchy of the arts, in Japan everything—sculpture, pottery, woodwork, temples—seems to be regarded with equal seriousness and attentive respect.

While wandering about the streets, Gautam wondered why the Japanese did not keep their pretty kimono tradition instead of going over to the Western clothes. I suggested that *in Japan there is not the same patriotic antagonism to the Western style that one finds in India.* These people have accepted the machine age and made it their own. Besides, the girls are excellent seamstresses and many of them make their own clothes—they do not feel them as alien.

I do not know how to summarize the system of feelings about India that has begun to crystallize from my hours with Gautam. Perhaps if the Indians don't regard their condition as horrible, let us not regard it as horrible either—and let's withhold our baksheesh. The anti-Western feeling is definitely present, though, even in Gautam. The benefits that India is deriving automatically as a consequence of Occidental advances (anti-biotics, etc.) are simply accepted as a matter of course. In this sense, India's anti-Westernism is something very much deeper than the Japanese. Gautam, viewing the pleasant character of the Japanese crowds, had to remark that in the West, where people get drunk, there were always unpleasant episodes at festivals.

With respect to India and Pakistan, according to Gautam, no one in India regards the tension as serious any more. Nothing really serious will break between the two countries. And with respect to China: when I said that India had fallen in love with China, Gautam said that actually there was a feeling of rivalry between the two: India does not want China to get ahead of her, and yet is afraid that she is doing so.

This flashed a thought in my mind: India, China, and Russia regard themselves as the big three of Asia, fighting, perhaps, for place. Actually, the great nations of the world, today, are five: U.S.A., Britain, Russia, Germany, and Japan—in that order. The rest are beggars, or else auxiliary to one or another of the big five. Switzerland is the exception.

Sunday, July 17

Off at 8:15 to see the parade of the great floats. A field day for shutterbugs. Special license for anybody with a camera. I was at it from 8:30 till about 11:30. Iguchi found me in the multitude (minor miracle) and accompanied me to Fujiya for lunch, then to the hotel for a chat. When he left, I retired to my room for a long nap—nearly dead with heat of the sun on my head and the weight of the pavements on my feet. A wonderful day.

Gion festival procession in Kyoto

At 7:00 P.M. I went out for another stroll and at 8:15 P.M. Hisashi Mita called for me with a friend of his from the swimming team of some university and we went around the town again. The city was still very gay and there was a shrine-bearing procession that we kept bumping into: a large team of chaps in modified sumō costumes bearing the shrine (Dionysian element) and a procession of stately gentlemen coming along behind them. I thought of Lafcadio Hearn's descriptions of such processions.[270]

As we walked, Hisashi mentioned the connection of all this with the advertising campaign of the Daimaru Department Store—and, in fact, there is an important (though to me obscure) connection between the department stores and the religions (as well as secular-cultural) life of Japan. The lanterns hanging so handsomely on all the shrines generally bear advertisements for the department stores—as do the curtains in the theaters.

And something else occurred to me as we walked through the lively, pretty streets—namely, that in Japan there is a wonderful feeling for the brilliant surface of things: *the surface flash;* and this, without much thought of what in the West would be an important consideration, namely, the form-world of the sentiments. Snatches of Western tunes are thrown together in their advertising broadcasts, television shows, etc., without consideration of what we would regard as their formal relationships. Perhaps one can say that in Japan *the surface flash rides directly over* śunyatā: the in-between world (which has been the main concern of the West), *the world of the feelings and sentiments remains unexpressed*—a secret, as it were, except, of course, in the formalized plot and catastrophe patterns of the Kabuki plays, at which everybody has a good cry.

Following our walk, we returned to the hotel to view, for a minute, on television, a Western-style wrestling bout between some American and Japanese champions. How vulgar, fake, brutal, and even ridiculous they looked, in contrast to the sumō, viewed some weeks ago on the same television set. The bouts looked choreographed to me—not convincing at all—with their punching of the umpire and everything else.

Bade good-bye to Mita and returned to my room at about 10:15 for a bit of study before bedtime.

CHAPTER 12

PENELOPE RETURNS

KYOTO, YAMADA, TOKYO, AND HOKKAIDO

Monday, July 18

My last week in Kyoto. After my Japanese classes, went to the Japan Tourist Bureau to arrange for my trip from Kyoto to Tokyo via the Ise Peninsula.

Something suggestive in this morning's paper: an article on T. E. Hulme,[271] by Yoshizō Miyazaki, which caught me just at the right angle and gave me what I think is an important suggestion for the linking of my work on mythology into the field of contemporary American literary acrobatics.

According to Miyazaki, Hulme's *Speculations: Essays on Humanism and the Philosophy of Art* laid down a philosophical basis for the nature of modern poetry:

1. The central idea of the Renaissance is that Man, not God, is the measure of all things. This notion produced humanism and the sciences, then degenerated into humanism in Rousseau and the French Revolution.
2. This notion is not true in itself, because it leads us to assumptions that are false and invalid; e.g.—that man is intrinsically good; that man is a well of

possibilities. "The humanist canons are, I think, demonstrably false," declares Hulme.

3. Hulme's antihumanist thesis:
   a. We must not "introduce into human things the Perfection that properly belongs only to the divine, and confuse both human and divine things by not clearly separating them."
   b. "We are painfully aware that nothing actual can be perfect."
   c. It is therefore necessary to take up a kind of "religious attitude" and to be aware of the "futility of existence."
   d. "This realization of the tragic significance of life makes it legitimate to call all other attitudes shallow."

4. Hulme's utter pessimism: "Man is endowed with Original Sin. He is essentially bad, he can only accomplish anything of value by discipline..."

5. Hulme's anti-Romantic argument: "What are Romanticism and Classicism?" The Classical poet never forgets the limit of man; he may jump but he always returns: he never flies away into the circumambient gas. The Romantic, on the contrary, is always flying up into the eternal gasses. The Romantic poets are sloppy, furthermore; always moaning or whining about something, always craving for the infinite.

6. Hulme's ideal for poetry: It should be dry, sophisticated, and exceedingly exact in its choice of words, since poetry "is no more nor less than a mosaic of words." This is Classicism in poetry. "I want to maintain," he said, "that we are in for a classical revival."

7. Hulme's *Humanism-Romanticism, Classicism-Religion Formula:* Romanticism fails to recognize the division between the religious attitude, which postulates absolute values by which man is judged as limited and imperfect, and the humanist attitude, which regards man as fundamentally good and perfectible by his own efforts. Hulme identified humanism with romanticism and the religious attitude with classicism.

Miyazaki goes on about T. S. Eliot and the heritage of Hulme.

1. He says that Hulme's identification of humanism with romanticism and classicism with the religious attitude was taken over, refined, and elaborated by Eliot in a more orthodoxly Christian fashion.

2. Romantics, according to Eliot, are in fatal error, because they never see the hopeless imperfectibility of man and are so naive as to believe in the spontaneous secretion of human emotions. [*sic*—?!]. Emotion is not the sole subject of poetry. "There is no method except to be very intelligent."

Finally, we are told about Hulme and the American poet-critics:

1. According to these last, Hulme defined the mood and perspective of our age: Tate, Ransom, et. al. "Ours is an age of intellectual chaos and spiritual disunity." The decline of organized religion is at the bottom of the trouble, according to Tate. A system of religion is necessary because it provides standards by which man can measure his own imperfections. Man is essentially imperfect, hence humanism and romanticism are heresies.

The whole discussion seems to me sophomoric, archaic, and ridiculous—based on an identification of religion with Christian pessimism (Original Sin context) and a very sloppy use of the terms divine and absolute (see Nietzsche); furthermore, the argument that because standards are needed in poetry, organized religion is a necessity, one can hardly credit to such touted names; and finally, the tendency to regard the quandaries of our literateurs as the typical agony of our time ("intellectual chaos and spiritual disunity") is a major mistake.

Yet the connection of all this with the blather of the current book boys is obvious, and I think I should at least make a try at indicating the relationship of my studies in mythology and comparative religion to the refutation of this position. *Perhaps something of this could be touched upon in my S.L.C. address. Perhaps, also, this problem could give the touch-off to my Viking book on Mythology.* In other words, my task now is twofold:

1. Basic Mythologies: a historical study
2. Viking Mythology Volume: an amplification of the contemporary literary and aesthetic horizon

Yes, I think so!

A new thought that has come to me about the significance of Japan—in contrast to India—for the modern world:·

Gautam's first remark about Japan was that it differed from the rest of the Orient in that its economic pattern is industrial whereas that of the rest of the Orient is agricultural. Paradoxically, however, it is my feeling that the elite aspect of the Oriental spiritual heritage survives here better, certainly, than in India, and possibly better than anywhere else in the world. Here then, as nowhere else, one can study *the functioning of traditional principles in a modern, industrial society.*

Not only is India not industrialized, but her traditions survive largely on the folk level: among the upper classes largely in the dilettante style. When Gautam asked me if I was going to continue to study Sanskrit as well as Japanese, I answered yes, since the main language of India seemed to me to be Sanskrit (i.e. the main importance of India is archaic, not modern); Hindi, I said, seemed to me not very important. "It is important for *bhakti,*" said Gira. "I'm not interested in *bhakti,*" I said—and that's it! *Hindi—Bhakti—Folk—Agriculture* (by exploited peasants): second-growth India, one might say, the great elite tradition having been cracked by the Mohammedans.

In a sense comparable to India's *bhakti* are the vastly popular Japanese Buddhist Shinshū and Jōdo sects, yet, according to Eidmann, there is a difference (I have yet to discover just what it is). Zen, which is certainly an elite tradition, with a strongly secular as well as a monastic side, was developed in Japan precisely during the period of the collapse of India under Islam. Shingon and Tendai seem to me to represent a Japanese inflection of the fundamental magical and religious principles of the classical Orient. Kegon, I believe, is the gift of the Asiatic mainland.

A new thought, today, in connection with Gira's remark about the hierarchy of the arts. The idea of such a hierarchy, I believe, is Western. What she has found here is the fundamental Oriental view (artist-craftsmen) which in her own India has been lost. A nice example for my contention that what India has lost is alive in Japan.

And so now I think I am beginning to find a basis for my future discussions of my visit to India:

1. Traditional Hindu culture shattered by Islam
2. Second-growth civilization: communalism and folk-level survivals (e.g., *purdah, bhakti*); local princelings, etc.
3. England's restoration and modernization of India:
    a. Modern cities, govt., etc.
    b. Publication of Indian texts
    c. Development of a literate class capable of reading about India's past
4. *Svarāj:* Westminster-Peking polarity: U.S.A. as scapegoat and focus for baksheesh-resentment structure
5. Dead center: the quest for the past and for the future
6. In Japan: the past and the present simultaneously present (Tradition plus Industrial Society)
7. In Japan: Tradition in the patterns of the elite—Occident in the play of the folk (honky-tonk with a pretty surface flash)
8. The Orient in general concerned to maintain its self-esteem in the face of an obvious Occidental triumph:
    a. *Japan's formula: to match the West at its own game* (this is a progressive, vitalizing, refreshing motif). Symptom: Japan's easy adoption of Occidental clothing
    b. India's formula: *to fall back on an unwarranted notion of Indian "spirituality"* (a world-alienating, reactionary, and sentimental attitude). Symptom: India's sentimentalism about the sari (costume—Orient à la Occidental tourist ideology)
9. The future of the world in general is in our young people of college age— who, though in various lands and with various minor inflections and local stresses, are being taught one great system of thought: the secular thought

(scientific, cultural-historical) of the Western world. For them, as for us, the problem exists of coordinating this New World teaching with inherited ideas—and the inherited ideas (fundamentally) are those of the mythological archetypes, in their various local inflections

Some thoughts about the early lectures of my course, this fall:

Ovid: mythology in a *literary* application
Frazer: *artha-kāma:* myth as magic
Durkheim: *dharma* aspect
Freud and Jung: *"mokṣa"* aspect

What is left for religion? Does religion serve any of the above ends better than science?

Answer: Religion teaches us to view the whole range from a transcendental position (there is a contradiction in the adjective). The whole field viewed from the requirements of *mokṣa: mokṣa—dharma—kāma—artha.*

But, actually, have the religions done this? Totemism and Sectarianism bring Tension. Is Buddhism the exception?

Tuesday, July 19

After my Japanese class, went to Japan Tourist Bureau and concluded arrangements for my trip to Tokyo via Ise. At 3:00 P.M. Kasugai and the Buddhist nun came for a little good-bye exchange of presents, and at 5:00, Gautam and Gira arrived for a final chat and a promise to meet in Tokyo. At 6:30 I went for dinner to Ellen Psaty's and at 10:30 I returned to the hotel and hit the hay. The heat, these days, is a bit on the debilitating side. Some items from the day's conversations.

Gautam notices that in Japan, small industries—even "cottage" industries—are able to compete on fairly good terms with big business. Also, modern inventions are being utilized on the cottage level. A comparable situation exists in Europe (e.g. in Switzerland) but not in the U.S.A.

Why is it that the U.S. Occupation of Japan smashed the Japanese big-business trusts, while in the U.S.A. itself the comparable trusts are in a fair way to engulf the whole business situation?

Ellen spoke of the "screen exhibitions" at the time of the Gion Festival. Last Saturday, homes possessing fine screens were thrown open to public view—in half the city. Next Saturday, those in the other half of the city will be thrown open. This is an old custom of Kyoto—and many of the screens exhibited are priceless. She had quite a day, hopping around with a camera. She had received news this morning of a Rockefeller grant that will permit her to remain in Japan another year. We talked a bit of the weird matter of American grants and grantees.

Wednesday, July 20

Japanese classes in the morning. In the afternoon, visit with Iguchi and Augusto Yamazato to the Shūgakuin Detached Palace: a hot but pleasant afternoon. Dinner with Iguchi and Yamazato at Fujiya, and farewell. Home for an evening of Japanese.

Another fragment of thought for the S.L.C. convocation:

The Culture Problem is not that of Orient against Occident, but instead:

1. Frozen vs. Fluid Culture (Spengler: Civilization vs. Culture)
   a. Traditional patterns vs. experiment
   b. Religious ambience vs. free thought
   c. Acceptance of ideas vs. testing of ideas
   d. Borrowing & adaptation vs. invention
   e. Archetypology vs. individual
   f. Formality vs. informality
2. Provincial vs. Global thinking
3. Imprecision vs. Precision (cf. language contrast)
4. Periods of Creativity in Ancient "Orient," e.g.:
   a. Old Kingdom Egypt
   b. Upanishadic India
   c. Alexandrian Near East
   d. Confucian China: T'ang China
   e. Haroun's Baghdad
   f. Fujiwara Japan
5. Some dangers of the free path
   a. Titanism (ego stress, barbarity, specialization)
   b. Amateurism
   c. Group disintegration ("ivory towerism")
   d. Romanticism of "The Great Fool"

Thursday, July 21

As I walked to my trolley this morning—the next to last morning of my Japanese session—I noticed that the tiny tots of the big school on the way were not on the sidewalks this morning, coming prettily on their way to class. Apparently yesterday, July 20, was the last day of the term. The weather, moreover, is really hot: we are well into summer. Took a nap after lunch, and during the rest of the day attended to my packing and study problems.

It is a happy period of my trip that is ending, and a happier one is about to open. My large, general plan worked out rather well, I feel. It now seems to me that I got everything out of this year that I had hoped to get, and a lot more that I had not foreseen. My apprenticeship to Zimmer, Coomaraswamy, and India, certainly, is ended, and a generally fresh orientation has come of my visit to Japan. I think I've really learned enough Japanese to continue profitably with the study, and the glimpse of Japanese Buddhism has been immensely important. My program for my opening days in New York should carry me well into the work of the year—and, furthermore, I can now see no reason for accepting any outside pressure as obligatory, from now on. "Joe's Friendly Service" is closed.

A formula can be worked out for discouraging the people who ask me to do their work for them. Establish three periods a year when the "Friendly Service" is available:

One week at Christmas
One week at Easter
One week in mid-August

Accept work only with the understanding that it will be handled in the next available "service period"; and accept only as much work for each period as can be finished in five workdays of five to eight hours each. At my basic rate of $100 per day for professional side work, this amounts to a donation of about $1,500 per year to sheer friendship—and I think that's just about enough.[272]

At about 9:30 Kasugai phoned, wanting to come with Saitō, who had a gift to present—a plate of brass, lacquered, with an inlayed scene in mother-of-pearl. They came at 9:45; chat, and farewell.

Friday, July 22   Ise Peninsula

Japanese classes till eleven. Farewell greetings. Lunch at Fujiya. Vacate room at noon, and catch 1:40 train for Yamada, Ise Peninsula. Before entering upon this phase of my story, let me conclude the account of Kyoto with one more motif from the morning paper, namely, an article in the *Mainichi,* by Marquis Childs, on Nehru and Tito,[273] "Two Apostles of Coexistence."

The point that reached me was this: that what Nehru and Tito have done has been "to bring into being...a third sphere of influence made up of those who are determined to prevent a clash of the two giants. This today is a very powerful influence which has made itself felt on both sides of the Iron Curtain. By their personal diplomacy and by their stress on the necessity for independence of action, Nehru and Tito have helped to focus the hopes of many different peoples, who formerly felt themselves helplessly drawn along in the wake of one or the other of the two giants. Whether this is the way to true peace or the road to appeasement and disaster, as the critics of both leaders have often said, future events alone will tell."

Somehow this dissolved my India problem into what may be its final elements. From India's point of view: the success of the "Coexistence" position. (As noted already in my India notes.) But from America's point of view, the danger of this position, if our experience of Russia since 1945 means anything. However, with American strength and success and Russia's economic difficulties turning the tide (apparently) in favor of the West, Nehru's position may actually be functioning in everybody's favor— helping to ease the tensions, and urging Russia, as well as the West, to relent. This leaves only one big complaint against Nehru, and that is his consistently anti-American, pro–Chinese-Russian propaganda, where he is actually taking the Red side in such questions as Formosa and in accusing the West of all the aggressive moves. This, I think, plants him far enough on the pro-Red side to make American aid to India a bit paradoxical.

And so now back to Japan.

An amusing train ride, third class, among peasants and schoolkids. The former, in contrast to those of India, neat and literate: showing to each other the cellophane-wrapped bolts of cloth bought in Kyoto, and calculating their expenses in little notebooks. The ride, a bit sooty (why didn't the Japan Travel Bureau book me by the fast and cleaner electric railroad?), but the country, with its rice fields, beautiful mountains, and lovely towns, was delightful. Arrived in Yamada, 6:00 P.M. Took taxi to the nearby Seiki Ryokan Inn, Japanese style—and I was immediately and at last in Japan, thanking God for my three months of Japanese.[274]

At the door of the inn, six or eight women in kimonos: welcome, in the grand style. I was conducted to my room, passing a cute snatch of garden. Tea was served, and a young man was sent to help me make plans (in Japanese) for the big day tomorrow. Next, the hot bath—in a little bathroom: not quite as hot as that in Tenri, but hot enough—and I came out, cleaned of the dirt of the journey. More tea—and I, now, in kimono. More planning for tomorrow (the problem: how to get my luggage to Toba). Then my dinner, with a special young woman at my side (the one who had taken me to the bath), to pour my beer, cut up my meat, etc. A lovely dinner—and, connecting this in my mind with my other Japanese tatami experiences, I suddenly got the formula. During my planning of the day, I mentioned the Ise Peninsula dances, of which I had read in the guidebook. After dinner my waitress brought me a little booklet, in Japanese, about the Ise dance (*Ise ondo*), and told me to wait a minute, left the room, and presently summoned me to the cutest exhibition of the year. A chair had been placed for me in a large, gaily decorated room, and seven young ladies of the inn's staff danced the *ondo* for me, in three parts. It was a nice little folk dance, quiet, and gentle, and charming. So, here we are on the brink of the geisha world in a simple little provincial inn. It is one, very consistent Japanese pattern of pleasant living—and it certainly is pleasant. Look what I've been missing, just because I can't speak Japanese. (Without the bit that I have, this whole thing would be simply impossible!)

My hostess, after preparing the floor bed and truly beautiful mosquito net of green with red trimmings—which filled the center of the room, turning the bed into a special sort of sleeping area—sat down and chatted with me till I dismissed her at about ten.

Saturday, July 23

Woke up and got up at about 6:30. At seven, the sliding doors made their sound and my friend's voice: "*Sumimasen.*"[275] She came in with tea, and then led me off to the hot water for my shave. Ham and eggs for breakfast and at 8:40 my other friend, the young man, arrived, to help me on my sightseeing for the day. The bags would be transferred to my inn in Toba and we departed from the inn, with bows and good wishes, at about nine.

Unfortunately it was pouring rain, so the whole day had to be enacted under umbrellas. Somehow, however, it didn't much matter. The magnificent scenery was only the more romantic in the rain—and the schoolkids, of course (but now on vacation and prettily dressed—all with umbrellas), were everywhere.

The first visit was to the *gekū* ("outer shrine"), in a glorious grove of gigantic evergreens, much like the forests around San Francisco. The architecture is pre-Buddhist—and simply stunning. The shrine dates from 478 A.D., and is dedicated to the goddess Toyouke, who came down to earth by the order of Amaterasu.[276]

We took a trolley to the second shrine, the *naikū* ("inner shrine"), which is in a grove even more glorious than that of the *gekū,* and is supposed to date from 5 B.C. Besides the torii and the great shrine itself, there is a "Horse Stable" (*umaya*), with a white horse used in ceremonials—and a great dance sanctuary, where, for a contribution of ¥1,000, I saw six damsels and five musicians (big drum, small drum, reed-musette, flute, and reeds/koto),[277] perform a ritual dance before the empty shrine of Amaterasu: a priest recited a prayer to the goddess, sending my name up to her as the donor, and again, my year touched one of its climaxes.

Another trolley brought us to Futamigaura, where the two rocks, commemorating Izanagi and Izanami,[278] stand just offshore, joined by a great straw rope that is renewed every January 5.

Then a bus to Toba: a boat ride around the lovely bay (suggesting to me very strongly that of Sitka),[279] and finally a visit to the Mikimoto Pearl Island: view of the process of growing pearls, and at about 3:30 four of the girl pearl divers put on a little performance for a gallery of schoolkids and American tourists: still in the pouring rain.

My guide left me at the Toba railroad station, where he put me into a taxi and sent me to my next hotel, where I have a second floor with a balcony, overlooking the beautiful bay.

Bath and dinner—less glamourous than last night's conditions, but still rather great. I seemed to be quite alone in the inn till about 7:30, when a party of (apparently) three males arrived in the next room—and it was they, I then realized, for whom all the glamour of the establishment had been reserved. Clapping of hands initiated the singing of a series of geisha songs—and then at the other side, three young lady guests began clapping hands for a song of their own, and now (at 10:00 P.M.) the two parties seem to be beginning to get somewhat together. At any rate, the inn is in a very, very, very, lively condition. The only problem is, that I'm going to have to get up at about six, to catch a 7:15 train.

Sunday, July 24   Tokyo

Things quieted suddenly at about 10:45 P.M. Good sleep. Breakfast in my room, Japanese breakfast!—seaweed soup, rice, little dishes of things, and—two fried eggs, to be handled with chopsticks. Train at 7:15. At Nagoya the 10:00 o'clock express arrived one hour late and there was no place to sit. Stood for six-and-a-half hours in the crowded aisle. Arrival in Tokyo 5:30. Settled in Yashima Hotel again. Good steak dinner at Suehiro's, and to bed.

Monday, July 25

Cab to Haneda to meet Jean, whose plane arrived on the dot of 8:40: Jean looking fine. Cab to hotel. Lunch at Imperial, after visit to U.S. Culture Center, where Jean is to teach. 1:00 P.M. four dances by Tōhō Kabuki Company, at Takarazuka Theater: last dance used symphony orchestra in combination with samisen—rather interesting amplification of volume all of a sudden, without breaking effect. Home for a rest, then dinner at Suehiro's and stroll through Ginza with stop at a coffee shop.

Tuesday, July 26

Jean off to teach in the morning, and I have Japanese lesson at the hotel with Miss Somekawa—nice lady; good lesson. Lunch with Jean and culture center people (Irene Pines and Mr. Kobayashi) at American Club. Good conversation.

1. Buddhism-Existentialism link
2. Japanese sense of "all's well with the world": sin idea missing: sense of harmony and accord

Rest, after lunch, then to Shimbashi Enbujō to see Osaka's Bunraku theater group. Wonderful show, including an amazing exit by the Benkei puppet,[280] and a curious fox scene at the end of the last piece. Jean was pretty tired and kept falling asleep. We had dinner at the theater, and, before retiring, stopped for a cool glass of orange juice at Mon's, the coffee shop across from the hotel.

Wednesday, July 27

In the morning, to the Japan Air Lines office to meet Mr. Akira Wakasugi, who had helped Jean with her tickets when she passed through Tokyo in January. He brought us around to the Japan Travel Bureau, where Mr. Takeichi planned for us our trip next week to Hokkaido. Japan Air Lines is making a free gift to us of the air passage, round trip. Wakasugi took us to lunch—and carefully admitted, when I made the point, that it would be a good thing for international accord if the U.S. Army pulled out of Japan: their behavior has not been exactly good.

Jean and I went to the Kabuki this afternoon, where we saw two traditional and two modern plays. Some important facts became apparent:

1. Loss of musical factor in the modern plays
2. Loss of dance (movement) in the modern plays
3. Stress on dialogue (people sitting and talking)
4. Stress on problems—psychological and social
5. Realistic, rather than styled, action in the modern pieces
6. Inferior utilization of stage space in modern pieces. In general, we thought the earlier style far superior to the modern

The second piece was an amazing dance: one male and eight female (old hag) characters, in a restrained dance of senile lechery.

The last piece dealt with the problem of a doctor in the nineteenth century, trying to introduce Western methods. Very interesting sociologically, but inferior to the early Kabuki, as "theater."

Dinner at the Kabuki theater, and a coffee at Star Fire before bed.

Thursday, July 28

Jean's teaching and my Japanese lesson in the morning. Lunch at Ginza Fujiya, Japan's Schrafft's. Department store visits in the afternoon, and then a rest. Sukiyaki dinner at Suehiro's fourth floor restaurant and a visit, after dinner, to Asakusa. Coffee at Mon's, and to bed.

Friday, July 29

Shopping and purchases in the morning at Takashimaya Department Store. Rest in the afternoon (the heat is terrifically wet and sticky). Visit, at 5:00, to Shinjuku Gyōen, to get seats for the outdoor Noh plays, which commenced at 6:00 and ended at 8:30. Saw *Aoi no Ue, Yo-uchi Sōga,* and a Noh comedy. Vast crowd. Good evening. Dinner at Irene's Hungaria. Coffee at Mon's, and to bed.

Saturday, July 30

Jean's teaching and my Japanese in the morning. Lunch at Fujiya—and an early afternoon of shopping. Bumped into Gautam and Gira in one of the shops and made a date for tomorrow night. Home for a rest, and then, to the Sumida River Fireworks Festival, which was certainly the most amazing and beautiful fireworks display either of us had ever seen. Dinner, late, at Suehiro's, and home to bed.

Sunday, July 31

Lots of plans and resolutions are shaping up for the period of our return to New York. For Jean—stress on her solo programs and teaching at Bard; for me:

1. Japanese (teacher to come to apartment)
2. Henry Volkening—Viking Press Conference
3. S.L.C. convocation address
4. S.L.C. course plans
5. Eranos work
   a. finish reading
   b. work on outline
6. Commence work on Viking book
7. French—for Jean and myself (teacher to come to apartment)
8. Commence party schedule
9. Photography

My big problem, we agree, is going to be that of warding off the Joe's Friendly Service projects. Nikhilananda and Mrs. Coomaraswamy are already the major entries. Our second problem is going to be the telephone. We think that we should arrange for a telephone answering service and a secretary of some kind.

I shall take a vow not to reply to the phone, except on certain specified days at certain hours. And the answering of letters should be handled through a secretary.

The giving of parties should be a regular task, so that we capture and hold the lead in this game. Our acquaintances seem to fall into four groups:

1. Friends
2. Work connections
   a. Dance
   b. Bard
   c. Publishing
   d. S.L.C.
3. People profitable to cultivate
4. Miscellaneous (fill-ins, old shoes, etc.)

The idea is to begin as soon as feasible with some parties for the first group, and to go on then at the rate of about one event a fortnight. We must also commence an exploration of the fun possibilities of New York—to try to make it come up to Tokyo and Kyoto in interest!

Through our conversations a couple of points seem to have come out with a fresh clarity.

1. Three levels of interest:
   a. Aesthetic organization
   b. Mythological organization
   c. Zen realization (trans-mythological)
2. My leading projects
   a. Bollingen book: stress on the magical charm of the myth world: narrative emphasis
   b. Viking book: stress on the intellectual interest and problematic of the myth world: philosophical emphasis
3. Intrusive commitments, to be assimilated:
   a. Lectures—my fee $250 (this will stop them!)
   b. Book reviews—accept only from Salmony & Block
   c. Articles—do only those that grow naturally from work in hand, or that clearly further careers of Jean or myself
   d. College tasks—be careful of their number

At 11:00 A.M. to the Bunraku again—for a wonderful performance. Finished at 4:15—at about 5:30, to the Japan International House to see Gautam and Gira and to meet Mr. and Mrs. Yoshimura (he, the architect of this new building and of the Japanese house at the New York Museum of Modern Art); also present, a music critic, Yoshida (interested only in Western-style music) and an American gentleman named Greeley who works with the NHK (Japanese Broadcasting Company). Pleasant chat. Good-bye to Gautam and Gira, who leave tomorrow for home. Dinner at the International House with the Yoshimuras and the Messrs. Yoshida and Greeley. To bed at eleven, after a sip of coffee and cocoa at Mon's.

Monday, August 1   **Chitose, Hokkaido**

All morning packing; lunch at the hotel. Departure at 1:45 for Japan Airlines and the 3:30 plane to Hokkaido. Arrival at Chitose Airport: bus to Sapporo Grand Hotel, where we arrived about 8:00 P.M.

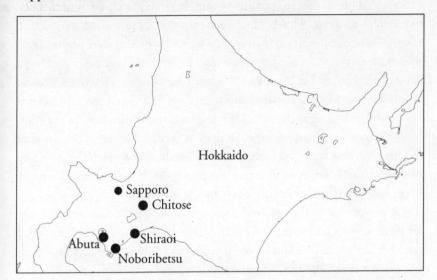

Great surprises:

1. Vast airfield and American military base at Chitose. (Our airplane landing, by the way, was the best of the year: only the squeak of the tires hitting the pavement: not even a slight jounce.)
2. Countryside not Japanese: somewhat sandy soil and scrappy vegetation, then well-forested and cultivated areas: more work horses than in Japan proper; peasants in less-pretty clothes; houses with American-style roofs or a thatch rather different from the Japanese; two or three farms with barns and silos that could have been in Indiana: grazing cattle here and there.
3. Sapporo, a large city—sort of frontier atmosphere: I thought of a combination of Alaska (Juneau) and the West: bright lights: one charming, carnival street along which we strolled after dinner.
4. Hotel, brand-new, American style, excellent food, nice little room and bath: quite a surprise.
5. Boomtown atmosphere everywhere.

Tuesday, August 2   **Shiraoi—Noboribetsu**

Up early: breakfast, and off to catch a 7:44 train. Arrived at Shiraoi at 10:30. Followed Japanese tourists to an Ainu village, where an old Ainu couple put on a lecture-demonstration in the almost utter darkness of a large Ainu house. A crowd of Japanese students and I tried to get good photos, meanwhile. After the talk of couple no. 1, Jean and I strolled to another Ainu-style house (quite new) where a second old man donned ceremonial robes and allowed me to take his picture—again, however, in semidarkness. They put a robe on Jean, who became suddenly shy about having her picture taken. We strolled, next, to the beach, where a lot of kids were playing, and then back to the main road. On the way, I found old lady no. 1 pushing a baby carriage: took her picture, and when I handed her a sixty-yen tip, she pointed to the hair on my arm and to that on hers: I put my arm against hers and the skins were the same. We laughed, and the mystery of the Ainu race's presence in Japan remained as deep as ever![281] Photographed another old man, carving bears, and then Jean and I walked to a sawmill, sat on one of the logs, and commenced eating our picnic lunch—which had been put up in very pretty little carrying boxes by the hotel.

A motorcycle pulled up, and a very pleasant, big Texan, here with the air force, got off and asked if I could change his army currency into yen. I couldn't but we invited him to join us with our sandwiches, and had a pleasant talk for about an hour. Learned about radar checks on the Russians, etc. When he left, we returned to the station and sat for two hours, waiting for our 4:05 P.M. train. Funny little railroad station, with nice people.

At 4:33, arrived at Noboribetsu and took a taxi to the Noboribetsu Grand Hotel at Noboribetsu Spa. An interesting synthesis of Occidental and Oriental elements. Japanese-style rooms: European dining room: Japanese big bath, with a pleasant mixed bathing situation, which reminded us of the Penning pool.[282] One lady took her child systematically to every pool in the big room—varieties of sulfur bath, supposed to be good for the health. After the bath, cooled off in our room, and then had dinner. Tried to locate the temple at which Eidmann is to be tomorrow, strolled a bit—but rain fell and we returned to the hotel, pretty tired after the day, and went early to bed.

Wednesday, August 3

Some good thoughts emerged at breakfast:

1. The Japanese road of approach to the divine is the aesthetic way.
2. The Japanese do not refer their morality back to the dictates of "God," but

regard the rules as social rules—extremely important social rules, for the serious breach of which hara-kiri may be the only answer. *Dharma,* that is to say, is here relative to society, which, of course, is correct.

3. It occurred to me that the Western concept of Order is now that of efficiency—mechanical—and that perhaps the Japanese concept of aesthetic order, joined to this, or playing against it, may be the main motif of the contemporary search for form: for instance in modern art.

4. The Japanese *dharma*-as-social idea seems to be related to the Chinese Confucian orientation.

After breakfast, wrote letters, then went for a walk with Jean to see if we could find Eidmann. Went up a hill road to a school at the top and came down again—paused at a temple where a young man told us that Eidmann was at the Grand Hotel. Visited a large area of sulfurous springs and boiling pits, where we took a few pictures, then returned to the hotel, only to learn that Eidmann was not there. Lunch, more letters, and at about 3:30 the phone rang: Eidmann, downstairs. Professor Fujiwara and Haru were with him. We had tea and a pleasant chat and arranged to have Eidmann and Haru with us for dinner.

At the sulphur pools near Noboribetsu

Jean and I went to the bath while Eidmann and Haru took a stroll through the town. Then they returned for dinner in our room, Japanese style, and we had an excellent talk. A few major points:

In the village of Shiraoi, which we visited yesterday, one block, or section, is wholly Ainu. In all of Hokkaido, there are probably no more than one hundred full-blooded Ainus, but twenty thousand or so who participate in the Ainu culture. All but a dozen or so speak Japanese as well as Ainu. There are a number of Ainu dialects. No thorough study has been made of the language.

The *bear sacrifice* is the principal Ainu rite. The idea is, that the gods come to the Ainu as bears, but then cannot get out of their bear incarnations, unless killed. The rite returns the god to his proper form, and the meat and skin are left behind, to the Ainu, as a gift. The Ainu keep bears as pets; the women nurse the cubs. The pets then are sacrificed. Eidmann thought the ideas absurd—but I find here the *dema* complex,[283] associated with the Animal Master (Moon Bear? Sun Bear? Totem Bear?). Is there possibly an old Stone Age connection here, comparable to that of the Eskimo-Magdalenian continuity? *I think I should use this bear myth in my Basic Mythologies.*[284]

1. In northern Hokkaido some stone circles have been discovered; also, some Paleolithic-type caves. They are regarded as late (circa A.D. 1000) and not associated with the Ainus. (Perhaps some Malekula connections?)[285]
2. According to Buddhist belief, every grain of rice in your rice bowl is a Bodhisattva; hence the Buddhist monk or priest (Haru, for instance) eats every speck of rice in his bowl. (Compare the bear sacrifice of the Ainus. I indicated the connection, and Eidmann was a bit embarrassed!)

Actually, *all religions are absolutely absurd if their symbolism is read concretely*—and the trouble with the majority of religious people is that they always read it that way.

Eidmann and Haru left at about 9:45 after preparing whipped tea for Jean; the girl prepared our room, and we hit the floor.

Thursday, August 4   Abuta

Off in a bus, after breakfast, to the station. Eidmann and Haru left at the same time for a visit to Shiraoi. We reached Abuta at 11:05 and went by bus for a beautiful ride to Lake Tōya and our next domicile, the Manseikaku Inn. Bath: lunch in room: walk through town: lovely boat ride on the beautiful lake with a young lady at the microphone announcing all the news, and twice giving us Japanese songs.

Eidmann, at the railroad station of Noboribetsu, told us the three main surprises that the Japanese experienced from his speeches:

1. That Christianity and democracy are not synonymous
2. That the money for the Christian missions is not supplied by the U.S. government
3. That missionaries are not political agents

Following our boat ride, we returned to our room for a bit of a nap, then had dinner in the room and went early to bed. Jean beginning to feel a bit queasy in her gut, after our recent Japanese meals.

One little matter of today that is worth a note; namely, the Japanese-American gentleman from Los Angeles who spoke to us in the train and then was with us for the boat ride: Mr. Mori. Twelve years a member of L.A. Rotary Club, he served as a delegate for them to conventions, including Paris, 1938. Then, when the war came, they asked him to resign. They are now asking him to rejoin: but the stab struck too deeply. Now sixty-seven and retired, he is devoting himself to the work of the Congregational Church.

Friday, August 5

Jean still a bit heavy. Spent the morning writing letters; then, at 1:30 P.M., commenced on magnificent mountain bus ride to Jōzankei: the Shikanoyū Club. Another Japanese spa—this time in a wildly mountainous area, in contrast to the beautiful lake area of yesterday.

Some things I've noted about Hokkaido: Ainus are regarded about as the Indians in the U.S.A.; farms larger than those of Japan proper, with crops like those of America—wheat, corn, beans; fields worked by horses: blacksmith shops in villages; forested areas resemble Oregon mountains: beautiful vistas, wild and rugged, with many big trees; lumbering; difficult mountain roads. Apparently, having been developed first in the Meiji period, Hokkaido, in contrast to the rest of Japan, followed Occidental models.

Saturday, August 6   Tokyo

Tenth anniversary of the Hiroshima bomb.

Went for a pleasant stroll, this morning, through the town and at 1:15 boarded an electric train for Sapporo and the conclusion of our trip. Delightful ride, and a magnificent plane back to Tokyo—5:30 to 7:40: one hour faster than the journey north. Back in our room at the Yashima Hotel by 9:15—cocoa and cake at Mon's, and early to bed.

Sunday, August 7

At 11:00 went to the Meijiza to see the Ichikawa Girls Kabuki. The girls were less strong than the men, of course,[286] but in their second piece, *Sennin Katawa,* which was a charming and amusing dance piece, they were really wonderful. I thought, also, that in the women's roles of the regular Kabuki pieces they were really better than the men. In any case, they have done a bold thing here, invading the male actors' domain, and have actually succeeded in presenting a magnificent show. The pieces: *Yoshitsune Senbon-zakura* (which I have seen already in male Kabuki), *Sennin Katawa, Keisei Awa no Naruto,* and *Kanjincho* (which I have seen in the Bunraku, and in a film of Kabuki that was shown in New York in 1953).

After the show, we went to Takashimaya Department Store, to shop a bit, and then saw, at the Nippon Seinenkan Hall, what turned out to be a children's ballet school, performing *Swan Lake.* Left after the first curtain and went to Irene's Hungaria for dinner—then to Mon's for an iced coffee, and to bed.

Monday, August 8

Dance and Japanese classes in the morning. A bit of shopping in the afternoon. Arranged air passage to and from Kyoto. At four-thirty, return to the Ichikawa Girls Kabuki (joined by Irene Pines, of the U.S.I.S.), for another wonderful show: again, the dance pieces were the best. Iced coffee at Mon's, afterwards, and to bed.

Tuesday, August 9

Dance and Japanese classes again in the morning. The weather is again pretty hot, and so, after a bit of shopping, we took it easy in our room till about five. Dinner at Suehiro's, and then to the Kabukiza, to see *The Teahouse of the August Moon.* The play is good, but the production (Itō's brother[287]) slowed the action considerably and did not do justice to the stagecraft of the Kabukiza. A wonderful satire on the stupidities of the Occupation. For me, after my four months in Japan, the charm of the Japanese phase of the play was quite delightful—excellently performed by a Japanese cast (American parts by Americans). Unfortunately at the concluding moment (reconstruction of the teahouse), the maladroit stage crew broke an important element of the set, and the curtain had to be rung down and the audience dismissed.

CHAPTER 13

CLOSING THE CIRCLE

TOKYO, HAWAI'I, CALIFORNIA, NEW YORK

Wednesday, August 10

Began calculating the job ahead in the purchasing of presents for Honolulu, San Francisco, and New York: eighty-five persons!

At one I had lunch at the hotel with the artist Sabro Hasegawa.[288] We had an excellent chat, from which the following main points emerged:

There has been in Japan a ten-year pendulation rhythm between Occidental and native movements. The defeat took place just ten years ago this month and was followed by a strong Occidentalization tendency. The reaction is due to begin (and, I dare say, will have something of a Communist tinge).

My notion that the dual life of the Japanese businessman (business suit and chairs during the day, *yukata*[289] and tatami at home) brings the Unconscious and Conscious of Japan into conscious dialogue has to be modified by the realization that for the majority this dialogue is not intentionally fostered. Hasegawa cited one friend who stated that he *had* to return to the simple life at home "because he is poor." (This, of course, would not reduce value of the dialogue.)

Hasegawa himself has felt the tension of the East-West struggle in his painting career—in the beginning he worked in oil (Western manner) but now has turned to ink and paper. Hasegawa, in his own quest for form, has found his best base and support in Tea. Tea, for Hasegawa, is intimately linked with Zen. (Contrast Eidmann, who stresses disconnection.)

Zen, according to Hasegawa, has two sides, monastic and secular. The great stress on meditation (see Mrs. Sasaki) belongs to the monastic aspect. The secular aspect operates through Tea, flower arrangement, Noh, and so on, to render life itself the field of contemplation. Hasegawa's chief masters are the founder of Sōtō, the founder of Tea, Zeami,[290] and Bashō.[291]

According to Hasegawa, the businessmen of Japan have begun to take a genuine interest in the support and development of Japanese art and culture. Hence the *department store art programs.* To be worthy of civilized patronage, the businessman must himself be civilized. This idea was derived from China, Hasegawa believes, during the thirties.

During the afternoon we shopped—heavily; and for dinner, we went to Suehiro's with Eidmann and Haru. We sparked Eidmann on the Zen-Tea theme and got the following reactions:

The founder of Tea had eight disciples: seven were Christians, one may have been a Christian, and the tea equipment went to the Yamauchi family. Moreover, the founder, compelled to commit hara-kiri, was not "calm" but greatly disturbed by the prospect. There is nothing here of Zen.

Zen temples today sell *amulets and charms:* Eidmann and Haru bought several in Hokkaido.

After dinner we took a little stroll about the Ginza, and stopped in the Shirobasha for iced coffee. Haru's amazement at the decor of the Shirobasha was a delight to see.

Thursday, August 11

Jean not feeling very well this morning. Took it easy all day. I had my Japanese lesson till noon. We had lunch at Mon's. Took a nap and did a bit of shopping in the afternoon, and for dinner joined Eidmann and Haru, first at the Shirobasha and then at an Indian restaurant. The proprietor (from Trivandrum) had learned from his Japanese wife how to be tidy. For me it was rather fun to have to enthuse again about dhal and curry. When I mentioned Indian music to the proprietor, he said that the long time that one had to wait for the singer to warm up taught patience. (Always, Jean said afterward, they have some moral handy: anything but the pleasure of experiencing art.)

We bade good-bye to Eidmann and Haru, whom we shall visit, next week, in Kyoto—and went to a "Hawai'ian Coffee House" for iced coffee, then home to bed.

Friday, August 12

Jean went off to teach her (postponed from yesterday) dance class and I wrote letters and diary all morning. A bit of shopping and resting, then cocktails at Imperial at 4:00 with a Mr. Sperry, whom Jean had met on her first visit to Tokyo. We had seen him yesterday in the Indian restaurant with an Indian couple and had made this engagement at that time. He told us now that the Indian couple were not liking Japan: the woman thought Tokyo a "man's" city—I thought, what gall: an Indian woman calling the Japanese society a man's world! Jean and I went to see the Takarazuka show at Takarazuka Theater (same show as the one I saw in Takarazuka). Then had a late supper at Peter's Restaurant and home to bed.

Saturday, August 13

Japanese and dance lessons in the morning. At about 3:00, Irene Pines called for us in her car and drove us to a curious and amusing session of *gengaku* and *bugaku* music and dance at the garden, arranged by the Asahi News and the Japanese camera business as a photo competition. Six hundred photographers—mostly Americans—politely competed for space from which to photograph the small stage. It was sort of crazy, but Jean had a chance to hear the music and to see a bit of the sort of dancing that was presented, May 1, at Tōdaiji in Nara. After the show we went for a "Mongolian-style" dinner at the delightful Genghis Khan Restaurant.

Sunday, August 14

Started our packing job in the morning. Afternoon with Sabro Hasegawa at his home. He knows Cage, Isamu, Watts,[292] and his talk about Zen and Tea had a bit of the sound of our Eighth Street friends' chitchat on the subject.[293] He served us tea, showed us his work (success just dawning in America: practically unknown in Japan), and, after a light supper with the family, we went to the station—watched the Bon dance for a while, and took the train back to Tokyo. Packing. To bed.

Monday, August 15   Kyoto

Went with Jean in the morning to her dance class at the American Culture Center and took photos of the class. After lunch, we headed for Haneda Airport. We had a lovely flight to Osaka, then by *densha*[294] to Kyoto. A taxi to Nishi Honganji—and the beginning of a large and wonderful visit.

The gate was swung open for our taxi by Eidmann's manservant and we drove directly to the door of the house. The visit commenced with a special kind of tea (*sencha*) prepared by Haru, then a viewing of some pictures (kakemono) that Eidmann had bought in Hokkaido and a general discussion of plans for the week. In the room with Eidmann when we arrived was Professor Kasugai, who would take care of our "sightseeing" till his departure Friday night.

We were put into kimonos and after dinner went out to see the Bon dance in front of the Nishi Honganji Temple. Jean, Haru, and I joined the dance for one round. We returned to the house, had a cup of some curious little sweet infusion, a bit of fruit, and at about midnight retired, after Haru conducted a little prayer service.

Tuesday, August 16

Temple gongs and roosters woke us at 5:30 A.M., and after breakfast we proceeded to one of the Nishi Honganji teahouses for a morning tea ceremony, conducted by Haru, and attended by the little tea-ceremony old lady who has taught tea to the whole Eidmann household. Next, we visited the other beautiful Nishi Honganji teahouses, the tea garden, and the temple. We saw the last part of a ceremony in the main hall, with a concluding bit of *shō* music, and then went through the palace rooms.

After lunch we paid a visit with Haru to the seventeenth-century house of Ieyasu—full of escape passages and trapdoors—and after dinner went up to the roof of the Ryūkoku University library building, to view the five fires built for the Bon ceremony on the hills surrounding Kyoto. Before retiring, we visited the Bon dance in front of the Higashi Honganji.

Wednesday, August 17

Met the Kasugai family, 9:30 A.M., at the Imperial Palace. After visiting the palace, we proceeded to an extremely interesting Tendai temple (Manshū-in), with a glorious garden representing Lake Biwa. Many important paintings were here, and the abbot told me that the founding abbot, back in the sixteenth century, (ca. A.D. 1600) had been very much interested in Christian-Buddhist parallels, liturgical and otherwise; Tantric parallels, etc. We had our *obentō* in this temple and then went on to view the glorious Shūgaku-in garden—three levels, representing the three worlds.

At four we went to Mrs. Sasaki's, to attend a beautiful tea, served by a young Zen monk, Sōhaku Kobori, in the Daikō ("Great Light") monastery, near the Daikokuji. This young man is a direct descendant of Enshū Kobori, one of the earliest tea masters, and his ceremony was conducted with considerably more ease than Haru's. After the ceremony, I had a brief discussion with the young monk on mythology.

He declared that in Zen Buddhism there was no mythology, and when I referred him to the mythological motifs associated with the birth of the Buddha, he declared that these were given spiritual interpretations by the Zen teachers. I had cited the incident of the newborn Buddha's seven steps: he paralleled it with the kōan:

"What is the origin of all the Buddhas?"

"The Eastern Mountain crosses the river."

It was a little hard for him to realize that no matter what the mode of interpretation the motif itself was still a mythological theme.

This led me to the following idea; namely, that *four levels of mythological interpretation are to be distinguished:*

1. The magical—where the symbols are employed to achieve magically-caused effects; e.g. Navaho rain rites; the Mass.
2. The concretistic—where the symbols are interpreted historically; e.g. Fall and Redemption, Christian style.
3. The mythological-psychological, where the deities, etc. are interpreted as spiritual principles; e.g. Shinshū interpretation of the Buddha (according to Eidmann).
4. The "allegorical," where the reference goes past the whole context of the symbolical to a transcendent, ineffable realization; e.g. the elite Zen interpretations of the Buddha motifs (according to Kobori).

After the tea ceremony, we had dinner with Mrs. Sasaki, and a beautiful conversation followed, which lasted till about 11:15. The main points:

A fundamental contrast between Occidental and Oriental thinking rests in the precision and intellectual consistency of the Occidental as contrasted with the multifold (or vague) and tolerant style of the East. When I (a Westerner) was through with the Church, I was through with it. In the Orient, on the other hand, Buddhists will pray to the fox-god... etc., and *rōshis* will participate in popular worship.

Such an interpretation of the Buddha as I had heard from Kobori this afternoon is hardly shared by the multitude of Japanese Buddhists. We, in reading of and studying the Orient, come in touch only with the *crème de la crème:* the multitude hold to comparatively primitive, concretistic interpretations. Mrs. Sasaki is convinced that the vast majority of the Buddhists in Japan have quite simple ideas about the Buddhas whom they worship: they literally believe that the Bodhisattvas are going to come for them when they die, to conduct them to the Paradise of Amida. (Eidmann, however, contests this view for Shinshū.) Even the actual behavior of *rōshis* is disappointing. For example, the two Zen *rōshis* whom I met on my earlier visit to Kyoto had a little affair between them in which one managed to buy a large number of lacquer boxes from the other at cost, forty each, instead of for the four thousand each, which the other expected.

"The idealists in the world today are the Americans; the Japanese, as well as the Indians, being materialists, through and through."

"Life" is not Zen but Tao: Zen is a way, a method. Zen has influenced Tea, gardens, Noh, archery practice, etc., but these are not Zen. (Contrast, here, the view of Hasegawa—see page 622.)

The Buddhist scriptures are so numerous that in the temple compounds an entire building is generally assigned to them. "*Various sūtras have been stressed at various times and by various teachers and these have furnished the bases of the various sects.*" (Eidmann's remark, while showing us the Nishi Honganji compound, July 16.)

The basic text of Kegon (Chinese: Hua-yen) is the *Avataṃsaka,* or Flower Wreath, *Sūtra.* During the Nara period, under the emperor Shōmu, this sect was the leading sect in Japan (Tōdaiji Temple). Its influence has been carried on in a number of the later Buddhist sects, and notably in Zen. Of the various themes stressed in the *Avataṃsaka Sūtra,* Zen makes a special point of that of the *Dharmadhātu* (*hokkai*), "the Universe," i.e., the Fourfold Universe as the Field of *Dharma* and Realm of Absolute Truth. This theme is developed as follows:

1. *Ji-hokkai:* the World of Things
2. *Ri-hokkai:* the Noumenal World. Śunyatā: the World of the Absolute Principle: the World of Zen: Egolessness: Unity with the Great Self
3. *Ri-ji-muge-hokkai:* the Harmonization and Unification of the *ji-hokkai* and *ri-hokkai:* the Principle of Things Without Obstruction: Phenomenal and Noumenal Worlds as identical
4. *Ji-ji-muge-hokkai:* the Realm of the Harmonious Interpenetration of All Things with Each Other, Indra's Net. The Universe as One Whole: The Eternal, Self-Recreating Play of the Absolute[295]

This is what was signified by the episode of Gautama's holding up of the flower: each existence is the totality of life.[296] (Scholium: This is the goal-thought: Consider in connection with this the conversation with Sri Krishna Menon.)

5. A fifth step or sphere is to be added, namely that of the Return to the Natural: the manifestation of our realization in our everyday life: each work, each act, is a holy world-supporting act. It is no longer necessary to think of the religious aspect. This is the state known as *mushin* (No Mind), "Having Nothing in the Mind"

One is filled with:

1. gratitude to all beings in the past, for having brought about the conditions of our enlightenment;
2. gratitude to all beings in the present, for the same reason; and
3. a sense of responsibility to all beings in the future.

(Query: How to reconcile this with the "No Mind" idea?)

After our evening with Mrs. Sasaki in her house in the Daitokuji compound, we returned to the Nishi Honganji, to find Eidmann still sitting up. We had tea, and retired at about 1:00 A.M., after discussing a bit with Eidmann some of the themes of our Sasaki evening. Result, a few more ideas:

Eidmann contested Mrs. Sasaki's statement that popular Buddhism is unilluminated. It is his belief that the followers of Shinshū really understand the Shinshū doctrine of the Buddha. An exception must perhaps be made for the cities, especially Tokyo, Kyoto, and Osaka, where the purity of the belief is contaminated by contact with the followers of other sects. Shinshū is concerned with Preaching and Lay Practice, not only with worship for the layman while the monks practice meditation. Hence, the lay community in Shinshū is well informed. The crux of Shinshū is the mystery of *the Awakening of Faith.* The object of worship in Shinshū is *myōgō.* (The term *kigō* = symbolic logic.)

As for the ontology of the Buddha: to say that the Buddha *is* or is *not* is to miss the point. The corollary: to say that the Buddha is a myth or is not a myth is equally beside the point.

Kegon is the key to Japan. It is strongest today in Shinshū. It is talked about in Zen (e.g. Suzuki).

Hōnan, the founder of Jōdo, is an object of worship in the Sōtō Zen temple in Ōjōji, Sendai.

Just as Christianity in Japan is a vehicle for the introduction of Occidental elements, so was Zen for that of Chinese. The Japanese-Chinese vocabulary from the Zen era carries a Zen tone. Zen Buddhism reenforces the Chinese influence in Japan. The term Zen in the West is associated immediately with Zen Buddhism; but in the Orient it has a broader reference—Zen = Egolessness = *muga* = *mushin* (see above , no. 5). As for *Zen in the Art of Archery:* Zen was introduced into the context of archery by Honda, a Tokugawa archer who had practiced Zen. In archery, Zen = egolessness. (Here Zen reenforces a principle that may have entered into archery already in the Paleolithic.)

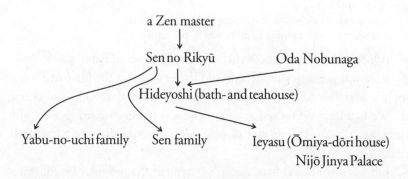

The genealogy of Tea

The idea of *mushin* in Tea: it is a kind of spontaneity (Spengler's "in Form seen") that comes *beyond* the sphere of the complicated learning of what is correct. *Note:* it is not the abandonment or loss of form (an idea that I got from my conversation with Hasegawa.) The idea of form, as it appears in Tea, permeates *all* the spheres of Japanese life (e.g. the formalities of polite conversation). Mastery (and even trance-action) consists in going *beyond.* Jean points out that in modern India, where there is no sense of this form principle, trance-ecstasy is associated with the *rejection* of society—this is a very important point. The essence of Tea (as of archery, athletics, dance, all effective action, yoga, Zen, and whatnot) is *activity and calm together:* form and ecstasis.

With Mrs. Sasaki I discussed the matter of the Zen kōans. Apparently kōans were used in China but not graded and employed in a series. The grading took place in Japan, ca. 1680, and has since become a standard and typical Zen principle. During the course of our discussion I tried to figure out the probable sort of reply to be given to the kōan announced by Kobori (see page 625), but Mrs. Sasaki laughed and said that that kind of rational cogitation was precisely the opposite to the kind of understanding that was required.

In the course of some conversations with Jean, it occurred to me that in Japan I had found examples of both:

rājā yoga—Zen meditation; and
bhakti yoga

1. Shinshū "Awakening of Faith." (Minor meditation, to calm the spirit, but with no goal of enlightenment through meditation, or symbolical understanding of the Buddha)
2. Jōdo: *Namu Amida-butsu:* Illumination at death

but that I had seen nothing of:

karma yoga, or
jñāna yoga

In conversation with Eidmann, I asked what he thought of this and he suggested as a possible example of *karma yoga* in Japan Ippen Shōnin's Jishū (thirteenth century), which, he claims, exerted a great influence on the development of Japanese culture. It now has only three or four hundred temples, and is definitely a minor sect. He pointed out, also, that in certain early Buddhist *sūtras three Bodhisattvas* are mentioned: Virgadika Bodhisattva, Śraddhadika Bodhisattva, and Panadika Bodhisattva; the path or method represented by the last, he suggested, might be likened to that of *jñāna.*

These three Bodhisattvas are sometimes represented as independent of each other, but sometimes, also, as standing in a graded series. This reminds me of the Gītā's lack of clarity about the primacy or interrelationship of the yogas. Perhaps the great answer here is that the Oriental mind (see page 630) does not, or cannot, make strict or final decisions or distinctions in matters of this kind.

Bushidō, according to Eidmann, represents not Buddhist *karma yoga,* but Shintō.

The Fujiwara term *aware* is very difficult to translate. It means "pity," but is not the word for *karunā,* which in Japanese is *jihi.*

According to Professor Kasugai, the Noh play was an expression of Zen. The voice of the Noh play is the voice of the Void. The word *Noh* means "everything."

Tendai, according to Professor Kasugai, is based on the *Saddharma Pundarīka Sūtra.* The worship of the *stūpa* is a Tendai trait, as is also the worship of Two Buddhas.

The whole question of the relationship of Zen to Tea, Noh, archery, etc., is one that I have been trying to work out, these past few days. Eidmann is most emphatic in minimizing the influence of Zen in these matters. Hasegawa, on the other hand, saw Zen everywhere in Japanese life. Professor Kasugai asserts the influence of Zen in the shaping of Noh, Tea, and gardens; Mrs. Sasaki gave what seems to me to be a quite good formulation of the relationship (see page 630). Returning now, however, to the viewpoint of Hasegawa, perhaps it would be correct to distinguish with him the points of view of the layman and the monk. Kasugai, Eidmann, and Sasaki are definitely on the monk's side of the question. If we stand on the lay side, perhaps we can say that Zen has helped us to see how the arts of Tea, archery, theater, etc., *are* ways to enlightenment—i.e., have helped *us* (if not the monks) to regard them in the manner of the *karma yogin.* Whether the Zen of the monasteries is capable of teaching intentionally what we laymen have, perhaps accidentally, been able to learn from Zen, is then beside the point.

Eidmann holds that the school of modern Zen enthusiasts, who see Zen as Life, stems from the romanticism of Kakuzō Okakura.[297] And as for the relationship of traditional Japan to the works of Japanese modern art: when Japan's true aristocrats buy modern art at all, they buy only the best (who, however, is to judge?). Modern Critics of the Yoshida type, on the other hand, spurn the traditional arts entirely. There is a full split here. They pretend to be Western (Paris, Vienna: "Tokyo is a large village," etc.), but are really not Western. *Western art is a function of Western Life*—not of the attempt of an Oriental to associate himself with the West.

In my talks with Jean I have managed to formulate some of my notions about the primary traits of the West, and their relationship to the problems of the modern Orient:

The first contribution is *the development of the interest in the uniqueness of the individual,* perhaps via the troubadour, erotic tradition and its later manifestation in marriage for love. This leads on to "Progressive Education" and Sarah Lawrence College.

The second contribution is that which I now call *the Cartesian concept of Space and Time* (B.C.–A.D., instead of dates by reigns; latitude and longitude for the whole planet). This led to:

1. The actual expansion of Occidental civilization
2. The universal application of the Scientific Method (other peoples had invented occasional engines, etc.)

And then, on the bad side

3. A totalitarian pathos and urge (Christianity, Democracy)

Then, finally, the West's third contribution: the machine.

One of the charms of Japan is the nontotalitarian character of its life: the various arts (Noh, Kabuki, etc.) survive without contaminating each other, etc.; whereas in the West we tend to have Modern vs. traditional, etc. The Indian counterpart is what Nehru calls the curse of Communalism.

The Asian penchant for Communism is perhaps to be explained as a desire to gain the material advantages offered by the machine (Contribution 3) without facing up to the spiritual-psychological problem of individualism (Contribution 1).

As an example of the nonpersonal character of Japanese life: the standard formalities of speech, which are in Japan accepted as adequate expressions of personal feeling, and to me were embarrassing to utter, as sounding insincere and merely mechanical.

Thursday, August 18   Nara

At 8:00 A.M. we met Mr. and Mrs. Kasugai at Kyoto Station for the trip to Nara. At Nara we were joined by the monk Jōkai Hiraoka (son of the archbishop of the Kegon sect, Abbot Myōkai Hiraoka, whom we also met) of the

Tōdaiji Temple. We visited the Nigatsu Temple, where a ceremony was taking place, with two monks sitting in facing chairs, at either side of the altar, exchanging words in a mock philosophical discussion (sometimes in the Honganji Temples, Eidmann later told us, such discussions are held in earnest); other monks chanted *sūtras;* we were shown the blackened ceiling—blackened by *goma* fires which, miraculously, do not ignite the building.

The Campbells and the Kasugais at Nara

We then looked at the great bell (ca. A.D. 752; forty-eight tons), and a chapel wherein the portrait image (twelfth century) of a disciple of Hōnen, and an image of Jizō into which a nail was driven, to keep it from leaving its place and walking about to shelter children.

Then we went on to the Tōdaiji Temple and the Great Buddha. Mrs. Roosevelt[298] was there with a small party of guides and journalists. We went up to the high platform and walked around the image. On to the temple with the many-armed Kannon, and finally the temple with the Four Kings and twofold Buddha shrine (see above, May 1, page 440).

After viewing the temples, we entered the reception building with the Reverend Hiraoka and had tea: he invited me to write to him for books and information and presented me with a picture book of Tōdaiji. He gave Jean and me fans, bearing rubbings from the former reception hall, which had been destroyed by the U.S. Army.

We proceeded, having said good-bye to our guide, to a hotel, for lunch, then went to the Kasuga Shrine and ran into a large practice session of the performers (dancers and musicians) who were to participate in a great festival the following day. Koto players in one room, *shō* in another, flute in a third, and musette in a fourth—each with instructor. We heard them all severally, then were treated to a brief ensemble. Also viewed the dancers (same style as that of my Ise visit).

Jean Erdman and the Kasugais at the deer park in Nara

We slowly strolled back to the station through the deer park and past the five-storied pagoda, and arrived in Kyoto about 5:00 P.M.

Jean and I went to the Kyoto Hotel, just to get to a decent Western-style toilet, and then I showed her Theater Street and the Pontochō. We returned to Eidmann at 6:20.

Eidmann bid us sit down and talk—but when 9:00 P.M. arrived and no dinner, I asked whether he knew that we had not eaten. He pretended surprise. I told him not to worry: we could go out to Fujiya. He insisted on joining us, and we all taxied to the Shijō Fujiya—where Haru and I had an amusing battle for the check.

Friday, August 19   **Kyoto**

In the morning, an amusing visit from "Cook-san" and "Mini-san"— Jean's family's old servants, who after a lifetime of service in Hawai'i, have now returned to Japan. They landed in Yokohama August 16, where they were joined by their family—two grown sons and a daughter and their children. This morning they arrived in Kyoto, after having wired us they would visit us at 9:00 A.M. Eidmann had planned to have us see Chion-in with Professor Kasugai at 10:00; but we postponed our meeting and waited around for Cook-san and Mini-san till about 9:45, when I decided to go look for them at the Nishi Honganji front office. I walked twice around the temple compound and was beginning to wonder whether they were going to show up at all, when, in my second round, I spied Cook-san standing quietly at the threshold of the front office, neatly dressed and patiently holding his hat in front of his stomach. Mini-san was standing inside, chatting with a number of people—her sons and some strangers, as well as some of the people of the office. Cook-san finally caught her attention and she greeted me very sweetly and charmingly. They both looked well and happy, and, apparently, were being very well taken care of by their families. I went back to our cottage and fetched Jean: then we brought Cook-san and Mini-san back to our rooms, while the family waited in the office.

It was a nice little visit. Cook-san had been sixty years in Hawai'i, and had a little trouble making himself comfortable on the tatami. Eidmann's boy servant, Hayashi-kun, brought us tea, and we chatted for about three-quarters of an hour about Jean's mother, Hawai'i and Japan, Mini-san's plans for living in Japan, and our own trip. At about 11:30, Eidmann appeared in the door and conversed hospitably in Japanese with the guests; and then we took our departure, returning Cook-san and Mini-san to the front office. I noticed that Cook-san had forgotten his hat and started back for it. He followed: we found it in the room. I took a few pictures of our visitors with their family and we bade them all good-bye.

When we came back to the house, Eidmann was about ready to start off with us on the day's adventure, but then Haru returned from a trip that he had made to Osaka. We all started off in a taxi for Chion-in, where we found Professor Kasugai waiting for us in the garden. The day that he had planned for us was one of the loveliest of the year. It began with a beautiful Japanese luncheon on the tatamis of the Hermitage. This was followed by a visit to Chion-in, which concluded with the presentation to me of a great book on the life and works of Hōnen. Next, at 1:30 P.M., we attended a beautiful tea ceremony at a Jōdoshū convent, where five or six nuns did the honors. At the opening and close of the ceremony the notes of a *shakuhachi* solo came from somewhere out in the garden that was faced by our big tearoom, and Jean nearly went crazy with excitement. At the close of the ceremony we viewed some kakemonos painted by an old monk, where the lines of the figures (Kannon, Amida) were composed of verses from the *sūtras*—a tour de force that in one case, at least, was quite successful. The nuns—young and old—were darling, and the whole experience was a sheer delight.

Our next event, at 3:00 P.M., was a magnificent visit to the beautiful Hōnen-in Temple, where we sipped tea and took clear, cool water from the mountain spring in the lovely garden—then attended a "*Namu Amida-butsu*" ceremony, beating "fish mouths" and chanting. [299]

At four we went to the *yudōfu* garden of the Nanzenji Temple for another of those wonderful *yudōfu* feasts. Tall, beautiful lotuses were growing in the pond. They opened the shōjis of the little garden temple for us, so that we could get out of the drizzle that had begun to fall. And when the party was over, at about 6:30, we bade Professor Kasugai farewell—and the Buddhist nun who is his disciple—and drove to town—for an evening of shopping and strolling in the streets.

Saturday, August 20

A day of shopping. In the morning, pottery and dishes; lunch in Alaska, on the top floor of the Asahi building; afternoon at Oridono's, buying silk. Jean had a wonderful time.

After a light dinner at Eidmann's, we set off with Peg McDuffy, in the car that Eidmann has just bought for her, first to see the temple of which Eidmann is to become the master, and then to join the members of the Kansai Oriental Society at a fine dance-play and drumming festival in the neighborhood of a small, Tendai-Shintō sort of temple on the outskirts of Kyoto. The performers were the members of a peasant club of actors. They began by beating in complicated rhythms small but very heavy drums, held aloft by sturdy handles; and then moved on to two to four large drums set up on the platform. Afterwards we had a little series of plays: a comic masked dance of a farmer and his wife; an episode of a samurai defeating, first a ghost, then an ape; and an episode of an acrobatic dragon, confronted and defeated by a second acrobatic dragon, who then was driven off by a samurai warrior. The audience consisted of the peasant people of the neighborhood and the members of the Kansai Oriental Society, who were given special seats and attention. I was struck by the relationship of all this to the pantomime that I had seen during my first week in Kyoto, as well as by the skill and pleasant ease of the performance.

One of the leading figures of the Kansai Society, Mr. Perkins, invited Jean and me to join him tomorrow for a visit to the geishas of the Pontochō.

Back at Eidmann's, we had *sencha,* and went to bed on our mats on the floor.

Sunday, August 21

Miscellaneous shopping in the morning, lunch at Daimaru's top-floor restaurant, and the afternoon with Mr. Perkins. We met him, a Japanese gentleman, and an army-post librarian at the Kyoto Hotel and proceeded to the Pontochō Theater building where beer was being served on the riverside veranda. Three of the geishas joined us—a young one in a full geisha wig who sat like a big cat, in complete silence, at her corner of the table, and two of the older geishas, who turned out to be two of the leading personalities of the Pontochō. Perkins talked about the traditions etc. of the Pontochō. The geishas here constitute a kind of caste, apparently, inheriting their tradition from their families. Those at our table were married to Kabuki actors (I think that this is what I was told). We drank beer and chatted, and at about 5:30 said good-bye.

Jean and I shopped, on the way home, for presents to give to Eidmann, Haru, Hayashi, Obasan and her husband, and, after dinner, made our presentations. The first was a projector, for Eidmann and Haru, the second a print-drier for Haru, and the third a fountain pen for Hayashi. All seemed perfectly delighted with the surprises—and I myself liked the Birdie projector so much that I would have bought one to bring to New York if I had been sure that the light would have worked on the New York circuit.

Monday, August 22

After breakfast, we finished our packing and then took a little final tour with Eidmann and Haru—first to the little *amazake* restaurant up near

Chion-in, then for a farewell visit with Mr. Perkins. We just caught the 12:30 train to Osaka, and took the plane, then, back to Tokyo.

Return to the Yashima Hotel: Suehiro's for dinner: and early to bed.

Tuesday, August 23   Tokyo

Jean's dance class and my Japanese lesson in the morning. Shopping for presents during the afternoon. In the evening, a nice dinner party for Jean at Irene Pines's, with lots of dancers and nice people to meet her. Chatted for a while with one Japanese who spoke German and then with another who spoke French. A pleasant, sort of international affair. Jean, I think, met some people who may be able to help her if she ever plans to dance in Japan.

Wednesday, August 24

More shopping for presents for our friends: this went on most of the day, and I began to tire of the whole project. At about 3:00 P.M. I suddenly learned that we had no reservations home on Japan Airlines—we had been on the waiting list only. This sent me scurrying to PAA,³⁰⁰ and distracted me entirely from the melancholy of having to quit Japan.

Our evening was spent with a Mr. Shibato, editor of the *Mainichi* newspapers, who was entertaining also an American magician named Furst. He took us first for a "Mongolian" dinner to the restaurant in the garden, and then to the nightclub Ginbasha, where I had gone with my friend Campbell, my first day in Tokyo.

Furst declared that both in Europe and in Asia, *the magicians of the world hope only that they can become as good as the American magicians.* Reason: the other magicians of the world have for generations been performing only the tricks handed down to them from their fathers; whereas the American magicians, who regard it as *infra dig.* (below their dignity) to go on repeating the same old tricks, are forever thinking up and performing fresh surprises. This seemed to me symbolic of the whole miracle of America's present prestige and power in the world. It requires neither wealth nor machinery to invent a new trick, but only *an attitude of mind*—and this attitude, it now seems to me, is the real key to our achievement.

Shibato, as soon as we reached the Ginbasha, called for three hostesses to take care of himself, Furst, and me, leaving Jean completely out of the picture. When the music started, however, I asked Jean to dance, and this left him with two to deal with. All the ladies were pleasant and cordial, but my girl for the evening was Jean—and this was not quite in the customary pattern of the nightlife of Japan.

Thursday, August 25

Anniversary of my departure from New York. Dance and Japanese classes in the morning. Shopping all afternoon, and at 4:30 a phone call from the manager of PAA to say (in an American businessman's comforting voice) that he had received a wire in our favor from Honolulu (we had wired for aid) and could assure us that everything possible would be done to assure our departure this weekend, either the 26th, the 27th, or the 28th.

Cocktails at the Imperial, with Jean's friend Sperry, who took us, together with two other American couples, to the Tokyo Plaza for an excellent steak dinner and then, just about at closing time, to a vast nightclub, the Nimatsu. And so we are coasting rapidly out of the atmosphere of Japanese into that of American life.

At dinner I was placed between the two young American wives, who began asking questions about Buddhism, and about whether I was a Christian. Their queries threw me back, immediately, into the worried atmosphere of young America.

"Well then, so what are you living for?"

I said I was living because my parents had begotten me and I had not yet died. As for any great single aim or hope, I had none. I might (and should) have gone on to say that I had not yet committed suicide, because I found life immensely interesting and, in the main, greatly enjoyable. (Ecstasy in the contemplation of God's tenth aspect, i.e. the world: mankind, the tenth angelic choir. Or Zen: "Have you washed the dishes.") Not one great end, but many interrelated ends constitute the rationale of my metaphysically-impelled existence.

"And so, how do you evaluate things."

I replied (here, I think, too ponderously) that "an amplification of consciousness" seemed to me to be the main sign of "evolution" and that perhaps one could evaluate his experiences and deeds in terms of their contribution to such an amplification in himself and others. (Try to bring this into relationship to my first point.)

"What happens to you when you die?"

My body decays and disappears. Eternity, however, is not to be interpreted in terms of time ("long time," "time after death," etc. etc.). It is a dimension of the present, to be known now.

Friday, August 26

Jean's last dance class and my last Japanese class in the morning. At 12:30 Jean returned to say that *passage had been booked for us today* on the six o'-clock plane PAA to Honolulu. Irene Pines joined us and helped in the packing, the shipping of packages via Takashimaya's shipping service, farewells to teachers and students, and driving to Haneda Airport.

My dear teacher, Miss Yoshiko Somekawa, returned to the hotel to see us off, and my wonderful visit to Japan was ended.

Haneda, 6:00 P.M., Flight 2, to Honolulu. In Tokyo, a drenching downpour; no visibility; up, and then up into the clear skies above.

Saturday, August 27   Wake Island

3:30 A.M. Wake Island: the pause of an hour. A bus ride to restaurant and a stroll back: big army planes and machines, machines, and machines.

Sunday, August 28   Honolulu

Recovered (dateline crossing at about 6:30 A.M.). Arrival in Honolulu, after a lovely flight, at 5:15 P.M. Mother, Alice, and Anne, Marion, Da, and Louie at the airport. Long session at the Customs. We drove to Marion's, where Jean and I are to stay, for dinner. Pleasant evening. After dinner, we went with Mother, Alice, and Anne, to spend a couple of hours with them in their cottage in Mānoa.[301]

Saturday, August 27

Up at about 9:15. After breakfast, to the Outrigger Club for a swim with Alice and Anne. Lunch at the club. More sunshine and water. The beaches full of the typical fauna. At about four, up to visit Mother in Mānoa again, and so on.

August 28 to September 3

There has been a vast increase in the population since our visit in 1949. The new dwellings and shops are, in the main, quite handsome; the new hotels, on the other hand, are vivid eyesores—suggesting Nassau, Miami, and the Riviera. Around Waikiki, a large, completely tourist population; all wearing Aloha shirts.

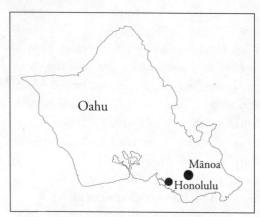

The Outrigger Club has only eight more years on its lease. The land was sold from under it to a "mainland outfit," which wants to raise its rent from $5,000 to $50,000 a year. (Not too much, actually, for the value of this site, but, apparently, too much for the Outrigger Club to pay.) They are going to try to move in with the Elks, into the wonderfully situated Elks Club, near the King's Surf—but this may not work, and all concerned are in sorrow. "This ends Waikiki," is the general word. "And the joke is, the tourists come for just what the beach boys and the surfboards mean."

On Da's birthday (August 31), Jean and I held a dinner party at Don the Beachcombers. Great disappointment. Food mediocre: music third-rate: hula, Tahitian dance, and general atmosphere, quite vapid. Alas, no more beach-boy music or first-rate dancers.

The pity of it is that Vikram Sarabhai arrived (August 31) for a one-night stay (with the Watamuls) and wanted to see a bit of Hawai'ian dance. We invited him to join us at Don the Beachcombers, and then again, the next afternoon, at the Outrigger Beach. During my brief conversation with him on the way up Tantalus, to return him to the Watamuls' place after the party, I got again a strong whiff of India's anti-American, anti-Western, pro-Chinese sentiments. The argument (not too violent) was about America's nonrecognition of China and China's continuous mistreatment of kidnapped American airmen. Just as in India, it appeared that the Chinese were doing nothing wrong and the Americans nothing right.

Wednesday August 31

At 2:30 P.M., a visit to the Bishop Museum with Jean, Alice, and Anne, under the guidance of Anne Harding and her husband, the curator of the museum, Dr. Spoer. We were shown the magnificent collection of feather cloaks (about one hundred fifty in the world; twelve in Russia, some in British Museum, Scotland, etc.; about twenty-seven here: one cloak 66 inches across—for a man over seven feet tall: Kamehameha's beautiful golden-feathered cloak: a long sort of sari-cloak for a four- or five-hundred-pound princess). Kenneth Emory joined us for a while, now grey, but otherwise looking fine. And I met again one of my old students from S.L.C., Pat Cook Peacock, whose husband is now a rancher.

The museum is in much better·form than it was before the arrival of the Spoers. René d'Harnoncourt's style of exhibiting has made a great difference.[302] Outstanding were the tapa-cloth and feather-cloak exhibits. Some ideas:

1. The crucial questions for Southeast Asian culture are
   a. Date and place of the first sea-going canoes
   b. Date and varieties of the first cultivated crops (banana, taro,—rice)
2. The Polynesian racial (blood-type) affinities, still an enigma
3. Problem of extent of America-to-Polynesia influences (Heyerdahl's new book, I saw yesterday in a bookstore)[303]

Following the museum visit, we went up to the Spoers' new and wonderful house on Makiki Heights for a drink. Then began the birthday party for Da, announced above.

Thursday, September 1

Breakfast at 8:00 with Walter Dillingham[304] and Louise, Ben and Frances present. Very pleasant and prosperous atmosphere. Louise about to set off for a day of golf, tennis, bridge, and bowling. Walter, at about eighty-one, just recovered from a major intestinal operation, looking fit, though a little older than in 1949. Ben, bulky and *sympatisch*. Walter showed us his beautiful orchids and told a few yarns of the grand old days. "Wish I could give you a piece of the old Dole property," he said to Jean, as he left for his office at about 9:30, "but I don't have any of it to give."

At noon we had lunch with Marion and Louie, and at about four we went to the beach for a chat with Vikram, who had had quite a day of sightseeing and was ready for a swim with the young Watamul. At five we went to visit Dr. and Mrs. Paul Larson and had a lively and very interesting talk. Themes:

The Alexander method of physical culture:[305] the crouched posture suggests fear to the Unconscious and actually stimulates an excessive secretion of adrenaline. Result: excessive energy expenditures and aging. Erect posture, when correct, suggests fearlessness and inspires life. Parallel: yoga and the lion roar.

India's anti-Americanism and the irony of our aid to Asia, which is being turned, by propaganda, against us.

The actual prodigious power of America—and yet our fears: fear of Russia, fear of China, etc. etc. Of the first eighteen airports in the world, all are American except London (which comes in at about nine or ten) and Paris (down around fifteen).

Dinner with Mother, Alice, and Anne, and the beginning of a new idea for Alice, namely, the writing of a book about interior decoration in Hawai'i.

Got our PAA reservations today for September 3 to San Francisco.

Friday, September 2

The chief visits today were two to Jacob Feuerring,[306] who is now staying with his new wife in a cottage not far from Noela Drive and will leave with her on the *Lurline* tomorrow for New York. His themes:

1. Buddhism in Japan is due for a very strong nationalistic trend, which has already commenced.
2. India, in the next twenty years, will recover its spiritual leadership of Asia, with a powerful universalist tendency. (This I very much doubt.)

And my themes:

1. Whenever an Indian thinks of becoming "spiritual" his first impulse is to "throw off" the world; whereas in China and Japan the elite tradition is that of the knowledge of eternity *in* time: is that not the lesson of Tea? Indeed, is that not the lesson of Civilization?
2. For the teaching of men a pedagogical schema is necessary. These schemas become the structures of the various civilizations. When the structure instead of the teaching is taken as final, however, the lesson is lost. And this is the problem of India. The Indians have become so infatuated with the schema of their civilization (e.g. that of the four *asramas* and waiting for the time of the third) that they have lost the message of their own teaching.

We visited Feuerring again after lunch and met his wife and a Chinese artist from Hong Kong named Chang, who says that there is no cultural or artistic life in Hong Kong: it is a port, a good place for shopping.

At five we drove back to pick up Marion and go to Da's for cocktails. Little Jeffie[307] was wheeled into the porch area where we were sitting; Bargie and Tad have been hoping for some kind of miracle to save him. At their church—or rather, in their community they have a very active "*praying group*," to which they credit a number of miracles: one, the recovery of Mary Lou Erdman from a lethal infection, some two months ago; another, the healing, or rather, disappearance of a brain tumor on the operating table, when the head had been opened and diagnosed as fatal... Bargie is trying, in her mind, to connect this kind of *magic, or miracle,* with the philosophical ideas that she encountered when a student—perhaps the *parapsychological* field is the one that all this leads to. I think of my *yamabushi* experience,[308] the Pueblo rain dances, and these Praying Cures, as belonging in one category.

After the cocktails, we came back to Marion's for dinner and then went to see Tad, Josephine Taylor, et al., in the Community Theater's new play, *Oh, Men! Oh, Women!* by Edward Chodorov.[309] A couple of very good points about psychoanalysis:

There are two schools: one holds the theory that the patient should be "cured" of his habits and impulses; and the other maintains that such curing is impossible and not even desirable, but rather that the patient should be helped to accept his character without fear, melancholy, and neurotic resistances. Compare Fromm's[310] distinction between returning a patient to the patterns of society, and enabling a patient to develop courageously in his own direction.

The real aims of one type of woman in marriage: a trip to Europe, a husband, a baby, and a good figure throughout her life. If husband and wife could realize that this, and not deep love, was all she wanted, things would be relatively OK.

The real aims of another type are to feel needed, loved, and not to be crushed under the spiritual or mental dominance of her husband.

In all this, there was a quite good criticism of Ibsen's *Doll's House,* as proto-psychoanalysis, and as not solving the problem of Nora's unhappiness. What is she *really* looking for "out there"? Is physical departure from the house her answer? And there is a good dig at Nora's husband, who thinks that economic security and protection is all she requires and does not realize the needs of a woman who wants to be loved, as described above. It is this insensitivity on his part that has turned the home into a Doll's House—and sent Nora outdoors to seek what she requires.

This play was handled in pretty good style, as was also a little children's production of *Jack and the Beanstalk* that we saw the day after we arrived here and in which Bargie played the part of Jack's mother. In *Jack,* I was struck (after my year in the Orient) by the character of the domestic image that emerges: the terrible father image and the rescue by magic. I thought of Samuel Butler's novels and, in contrast, of the comparable Oriental motifs. There is a problem here, to be studied. In the modern Orient, I think it is, rather, the terrible mother image that prevails: the mother-in-law vs. the young wife. Also, if one compares this contrast of Economic Titanism and "Magic" with that represented in the Chodorov play, one has a pretty clear line. Problem: Selfishness = materialism vs. Selflessness (Sympathy, Compassion) = "spiritual magic."

I was hoping to be able to chat with Alice today about her economic situation, but no opportunity came, and I shall have to try again tomorrow.[311] Actually, all seems to me to be in pretty good case up there. Alice's circle of friends, whom we met at a party in her cottage our second or third night here, is pleasant and sympathetic. (Her boss and his pretty Filipino wife; Doyle Alexander and his wife;[312] and a couple, whose daughter is Anne's best friend.) The main problem is, to get Alice's income into a higher bracket. She is trapped, as it were, by American Factor.[313]

And finally, about my *own work, as viewed from here:*

In Japan, I was in my dream boat; here, in America, I have stepped ashore. Problem: to keep lines ashore from the dream boat for unloading. How? My schedule in New York, as noted above, three hours writing; three hours outlining.[314] The rest of the day or week will be free for the land-world interests and necessities.

My writing can commence as a continuation and spontaneous expansion of these journal notes. What I now think of as *the "raindrop" approach:* a drop here, a drop there, until the whole ground is wet: a paragraph here, a paragraph there, until the whole book is drafted—after which, the material can be handled as I handled Zimmer's notes.

This journal can be continued, with increased emphasis, however, on the notation aspect and diminished attention to the daily diary.

Saturday, September 3

Last day in Hawai'i. Up to see Mother and Alice in the morning; a brief expedition to the beach at Waikiki; luncheon at Marion's with all the families (about twenty-five people!) and a pleasant run of brooding all the while. A few points to be noted before leaving:

Feuerring spoke of *two kinds of tea ceremony* in Japan—the social and the religious. In the latter no talk about the bowls etc.; more stress on the silently contemplative side.

Both Alice and Da have spoken of *the particular character of the Chinese community in Hawai'i*. Loyalty to family groups (*hui*). No participation in the Community Chest, etc., of the general community. Somewhat arrogant miserliness. Comparatively large accumulations of wealth.

In contrast, *the Japanese are eager to Americanize themselves*. Generosity, community interests, etc.

The luncheon party cleared up at about 3:00 P.M. Jean and I then went into our room to pack. At about five we were ready to push off. Da came for us, and, with Marion, Pini, and Pono,[315] we set off for the airport. Mother, Bargie, and Alice arrived in the lively, crowded airport about 6:15 and the call came for us to board the plane at 6:35. Leis and Aloha.

A jammed plane, filled with a gay company of aloha-shirted and muu-muued vacationists. Lots of noise. And we were amazed, after the rather lean and perfunctory service that PAA had accorded its "tourist" passengers on the way from Tokyo to Honolulu (where most of the "tourists" had been Filipinos), by the cordial and lavish hospitality of our steward and stewardesses. We figure that the heavy competition of the airlines had something to do with it, and that the fact that a large number of our cabin mates were obviously the members of a large tour of some kind may have helped. In any case—it was cocktails before dinner, a good meal decently served, wine, and then a large cake with ALOHA. Sleep supervened around 10:30 or 11:00.

Sunday, September 4   San Francisco

Alan Watts met us at the San Francisco Airport when we arrived, about 7:15 A.M. He looked a bit sleepy-eyed—and why not?—he had had to leave his place at Point Sur at about 3:30 A.M.! The airport was the biggest and busiest I had seen since my departure from New York: planes leaving every minute for everywhere. And the cars in the prodigious parking lot, out in front, were as amazing as anything else. The whole power of America, in contrast to Asia's world, was immediately visible.

And on the long, very beautiful drive down to Point Sur, we were easily and pleasantly returned to the feel of life in the U.S.A. First, the great machine world in and around the airport; then the great farmlands of the Santa Clara Valley; next, the holiday world of the Monterey Peninsula—the fisheries and the canneries, and all the memories I held of my year there in the early thirties;[316] then, finally, the miraculous coast—Point Lobos, Point Sur, and the golden hills. On the broad highways—six to ten lanes wide—the vast American cars seemed not too large. And the various odd rigs of the vacationers seemed not too bizarre, in the broad, traditionless land. It was most remarkable and pleasant that the countryside should have been the closest in America to that of the Ise Peninsula in Japan: and in contrast to the way I felt in Japan—here I felt that I did not really mind the lack of toriis and shrines. Shrineless America was all right too!

On the way down, we discussed Japan, Buddhism, and the U.S.A. Dorothy[317] and the three cute children greeted us when we arrived. We had a pleasant lunch on the veranda, overlooking the Pacific and then retired to our rooms for a nap. More talk at dinnertime and into the night until about 10:00, when, rather sleepy again, we all retired for a quiet, absolutely solid sleep, in the beautiful fresh air. Some of our themes:

As to whether it is proper to call the sort of *Buddhism-in-life* that Alan, Hasegawa, et al. represent, "Japanese Zen"? In Japan, Zen definitely is "sitting." Alan stated that he was sure that the Zen of Hui-neng and the fundamental Chinese texts was not "sitting," but "sitting, standing, walking, and lying." Why not use, then, I suggested, the Chinese word *ch'an?* Might be a good idea. At least, it would rub out the Japanese Zen objection that the Zen being described by Alan and his tribe is not really "Zen."

Alan made light of the kōan system. One is supposed to answer the kōans intuitively, but the field of associations that would inspire the answers must differ according to one's cultural experience. For a Westerner, the Japanese system is hardly appropriate.

Zen, properly, is undeliberated action.

Alan told of the sexual life of a Zen master: coition without movement, until, after hours, the orgasm comes for the woman of itself. *Wuwei. Sahaja.*[318]

Alan wondered whether the emphasis on personality in the Christian tradition might not be a deterioration of the all-in-each idea of Kegon-Zen.

Alan likened the Christian promise of happiness in heaven to the happy-ending formula in the fairy tale. Life itself is validated only by an uncertain future—in which one must have *faith.* Pessimism with respect to life itself: optimism only on the basis of the figment of faith.

In the plane, by the way, I found in *Time* an interesting article on the new Palestine find of *manuscripts of the Essenes.*[319] Perhaps a good point from which to start my Viking book.

Monday, September 5   **Big Sur**

A drive, in the morning, up to see Maud Oakes in her beautiful place eleven hundred feet above the coast.[320] Magnificent views. Nice chat. She is coming tonight to dinner. Also coming is a Jewish chap of the old Woodstock type, named Morgenrath, whose wife once studied at the New Dance Group. We had a picnic lunch in the woods, went for a stroll over the golden hills, paid a visit to another Woodstock-type household (chap who sells Henry Miller's books and runs a little art gallery by the road), then returned to prepare for dinner. Maud, the Morgenraths, and a fine old lady named Porter arrived, who, thinking that I was going to be Joseph Campbell the poet, brought a volume of that good gentleman's poems for me to read aloud.[321]

Lovely dinner and conversation till about 2:00 A.M. Maud left at 10:00 and Mrs. Porter at midnight—after I had read the desired poems.

The conversation was lively, but brought forth no new ideas. During the afternoon, however, Alan had told me something about *the Zen method of training for fencing*—which, after all, may be rather Bushidō than Zen. The main idea is *unfocused alertness*—a readiness to flash quickly in any direction with absolute effect.

Tuesday, September 6 (Labor Day)

Lunch at Maud's, and then good-bye. Alan drove us back to the airport, where we had a beautiful dinner. Departure at nine, United Airlines, on the last leg of my trip around the world.

The drive with Alan was magnificent. It was a beautiful day, and the coast was even more impressive than it had been two days ago, when half lost in mist. Our conversation rattled along and yielded one very good idea—namely, that the kōan test is a Japanese variant of the riddle-test motif—cf. *Eddas*, ca. A.D. ninth century.[322] Perhaps we've hit something here.

Wednesday, September 7   Idlewild Airport, New York

At 6:30—Chicago, for a brief stand-up breakfast snack in the airport. Jean, not feeling well, did not leave the plane. Arrival at Idlewild Airport, about 11:45. Bus to air terminal, New York City. Taxi home—and the round is complete.

AN OVERVIEW OF THE HISTORY
OF BUDDHISM IN JAPAN

This outline is taken from notes that Joseph Campbell took from an article by Phillip Karl Eidmann. See page 496.

A.D. 552

- Korean king at Paekche sends Buddhist scriptures and images
- Buddhist materials destroyed by Mononobe and Nakatomi clans (Japanese military)
- Soga clan (civilian leaders) favors Buddhism

ca. 585–650

- Korean king again sends scriptures, images, clergy
- Soga-Mononobe feud reopened, but Buddhism remains
- Buddhism adopted first by nobility: within a decade Emperor Yōmei himself was a Buddhist
- Prince Shōtoku (regent of Empress Suiko), a great influence: built temples; instituted a system of diocese; wrote commentaries on three scriptures
- Early monks encouraged to teach arts of road making and bridge building; monastic students included in embassies to China to study in the great monasteries

ca. 650–794 (Taika and Nara periods)

- Major period of influences from China
  - o Six schools introduced
    - **Jōjitsu** (introduced in 625—minor)
    - **Sanron** (introduced in 625—Japanese branch of the *Mādhyamika* school; introduces Nagārjuna's concept of *śunyatā*)
    - **Hossō** (introduced in 653—Japanese branch of the *Yogācāra* school)
    - **Kusha** (introduced in 658—Japanese branch of the Theravādin *Sarvastavādin* school)
    - **Kegon** (introduced in 735—Japanese branch of the Chinese Hua-yen school, based at the Tōdaiji temple in Nara)
    - **Ritsu** (introduced in 754—focused on monastic discipline [*vinaya*]; revived as part of Shingon)

ca. 794–1185 (Heian period)

- Kyoto as the permanent capital
  - o New stability and continuity in Buddhist teaching (formerly, teachers were chiefly Chinese or Korean)

- Great period of translations in China: many systems for ascribing each *sūtra* to a period of the Buddha's life, culminating in some supreme revelation just before his death
  - o **Tendai**
    - Japanese branch of Chinese *Chih-k'ai* School, at Mount T'ien-T'ai in the province of Chekiang: The Lotus *Sūtra* as the culminating doctrine.
    - Dengyō Daishi brings this teaching to Japan and continues the eclectic work by harmonizing Buddhism with Shintō; instituted a new ordination platform, and, on the grounds that the Japanese were already so pure that they did not need the monastic *vinaya* discipline, instituted a new "Bodhisattva Discipline," completely abandoning the Theravādin *Vinaya*, which had been translated earlier.
  - o **Shingon**
    - Kōbō Daishi, while in China, was initiated into the Esoteric, or *Vajrayāna*, school then fashionable there. The school virtually died in China—but continued in Tibet, and in Japan as the Shingon. Mt. Kōya became the center from which he taught his mystical rituals and doctrines.

ca. 700–1000

- Three hundred years of scholastic study and the gradual sifting of Buddhist doctrine down to the people
- Lady Murasaki Shikibu writes *The Tale of Genji* ca. 973

ca. 1000–1200

- Civil wars: weakening of six earlier Buddhist sects
- Idea of the period of the Latter Law: Emergence of new and independent Japanese Schools

1174

- Genku Hōnen establishes **Jōdo**
  - o Since the people live in the period of the Latter Law, they are incapable of rigid discipline; their only hope, therefore, is to be born into the Pure Land of the Amida Buddha and there to attain Enlightenment. The act of praising Amida is itself sufficient for rebirth into this realm.

1192

- Eisai returns from China with *Ch'an*—**Rinzai Zen**
  - o A transmission "outside of the scriptures"
  - o A transmission "from heart to heart, without words"

1223

- Dōgen founds **Sōtō Zen:**
  - o Emphasis on scholarship and research, as well as meditation
  - o Ch'an, a development of Buddhism that grew out of the effort to teach Buddhism to the untutored Chinese farmers, became, in Japanese Zen, the religion of professional militarists—it is the chief component of Bushidō

1224

- Shinran, a disciple of Hōnen, founds **Shinshū**—the most influential form of Buddhism in modern Japan: "In the egolessness of the moment of faith, the efficient cause is created for the attainment of complete enlightenment at the instant of death."

1253

- Nichiren—founder of the **Hokke** (Lotus, or Nichiren) School:
  - o. An attempt to reform Tendai, based on the Lotus *Sūtra*
  - o Opposition to Tendai eclecticism, which made the mythical Buddhas and the historical Buddha equal
  - o Lotus *Sūtra* regarded as the teaching of Śākyamuni
    - Nichiren identified himself as Viśiśtacaritra Bodhisattva, who, in the Lotus *Sūtra,* is said to be the one who, in the days of the Latter Law, would proclaim the true essence of the Buddha's teachings.

ca. 1300–1500 (Kamakura, Ashikaga, and Civil War periods)

- Very unsettled in Japan—period of the samurai movies
- Many monasteries became military camps
- Military monks fought in secular causes

1600–1867 (Tokugawa shōgunate)

- Tokugawa peace, feudalistic style
- Exacting governmental regulations affecting even Buddhist regulations: no new doctrines or sects; the focus shifts to scholarship and meditation
- Shintō revival (starting ca. 1650)
  - o   A group of scholars and politicians, led by Mabuchi, Motoori, and Hirata created a neo-orthodox doctrine, in opposition to Buddhism

1867 (Meiji Restoration)

- Admiral Perry arrives; downfall of the Tokugawa shōguns
- The principles of the neo-orthodox Shintō revival became the basis of the Meiji Restoration
- Buddhism is virtually outlawed and dissent abolished

1931–1945

- Invasion of Manchuria and Second World War
- Japanese government again outlawed Buddhism

1945–1952

- At end of war, U.S. Occupation policies unfavorable to Buddhism
  - o   "Freedom of religion" guaranteed, but nearly all temple lands were confiscated and a number of sects were thus completely impoverished
  - o   The religious corporate-body law upset twenty-five centuries of Buddhist tradition by requiring temples to be reorganized upon the congregationalist pattern of United States Protestantism.

THE NATURE WAY: SHINTŌ AND BUDDHISM IN JAPAN[1]

There is a legend telling that when the Buddha once was to give a sermon, he sat for some time in silence and then simply elevated a flower in his hand. Only one of those present understood, but he thereby was illumined. The Buddha caught his eye and smiled and a verbal sermon—the Flower Wreath *Sūtra*—then was given to the rest.[2]

The art of letting flowers deliver the message beyond words entered Japan with Buddhism itself from China, where the Indian Mahāyāna doctrine had become fused with the native Chinese doctrine of the Tao. Then in Japan, the art and Buddhism as well became fused with the native Shintō.

In Japanese art, nature is the model and unsymmetrical balance, the secret of its flight. The composition must also suggest some idea, sentiment, or wish appropriate to the occasion. For in Japanese thought, each moment of time is a total manifestation of Buddhahood and each flower itself a Buddha-thing. This principle that art can fuse nature and thought and carry us beyond both is perhaps the outstanding characteristic of Japanese civilization.

It is already evidenced in the great Shintō shrines on the beautiful peninsula of Ise. Today, every tourist learns on his first sightseeing ride that in Japan there are two types of religious sanctuaries: one is called *o-miya,* the word is translated shrine; the other *o-tera,* temple. Shrines belong to Shintō and are marked by graceful wooden gates like this, called torii. We see in the photograph on page 659 the entrance to the majestic cedar grove surrounding the grand shrine of Ise, which is devoted to the ancestral line of the imperial house. And this dynastic line, in turn, according to legend, traces itself back to the sun goddess Amaterasu. The architecture of the many buildings dates from earliest Japanese times. The structures themselves are demolished every twenty years to be rebuilt on exactly the same plan so that the wood is fresh and young, but the form more than fifteen centuries old. An important principle here is illustrated, namely that life is an expression not so much of matter as of its informing spirit.

The earliest archaeological remains in Japan date from a long, rather obscure period called *Jōmon.* The word means "cord-marked" and refers to a crude pottery that seems to have begun arising around 2500 B.C. The people of Japan at that time were probably Caucasoid, like the Ainu of today. And they certainly were hunters and fishers at that time. During the next twenty centuries, the arts of agriculture and village life arrive and the population, through a series of incursions, became gradually Mongoloid. Then, about 300 B.C., the so-called Yayoi period opened with arrivals by way of Korea, bearing a high Neolithic style of pottery like that of China 1,500 years before.

The next and final great stage of prehistoric Japan opens circa 300 A.D. with the arrival of the Kōfun or Yamato peoples, who became the nuclear force for what was to become Japanese civilization. They seem to have been of north Asiatic origin and their mythology exhibits many astounding parallels to those of the peoples of northern Europe. Moreover, they brought with them a type of mound burial that is likewise familiar to the West. The royal burials of the Yamato, however, were often of prodigious size. The level of this civilization was roughly comparable to that of pagan Europe of the same period, and as the creative spirit of modern Europe is already announced in Celtic and Germanic myth, so that of Japan becomes evident in the Shintō of this age.

Shintō is a very difficult religion to discuss, however. It rests not on theology but on a certain type of experience, as I learned in a rather amusing way at the International Congress for the History of Religions held in

Tokyo in 1958. Delegates had arrived from every nation in the world, and the Japanese committee had arranged that we should visit, under their auspices, every temple and shrine within reach. Shintō shrines are without images. To a very strange type of music, stately, very slowly moving dances are performed both by choral groups and by solo figures, the latter frequently masked. The music is of an ancient style derived from China of the T'ang period (around A.D. 618–970), when Buddhism from China was entering Japan. In the West, this was the period of Charlemagne. This music has disappeared from China, but in Japan it is used for both temple and shrine rites to summon the spirits, which indeed one can actually feel and even almost see arriving at these ceremonies.

There was a very intelligent social scientist from New York among the delegates at this conference, and after we had visited a number of the shrines and seen a number of the rites, he approached one afternoon a Shintō priest who was also a member of the conference. And my friend said to the priest, "I've been to a number of these shrines now and I've seen a number of the rites, but I don't get it. I don't get the ideology; I don't get the theology."

The priest seemed very disturbed that Shintō had disappointed his guest and he shook his head and he said, "I'm afraid we don't have ideology; we don't have theology. We dance."

It is the function of art to carry us beyond speech to experience, and that is the function also of Shintō. In a welcoming address to the members of that Congress, Prince Mikasa, the younger brother of Emperor Hirohito,[3] made the point that the evocation of a sense of awe before the wonder of being itself is the essence and the inspiration of Shintō. In illustration of this, he read to us a poem of two lines composed many centuries before by a visitor to the grand shrines of Ise, as follows:

Unknown to me what resided here,
Tears flow from a sense of unworthiness and gratitude.

It is this sense of gratitude for the wonder of the world that is the most characteristic feature of the religious mood of Japan and particularly of Shintō. This stands in direct contrast to the modern existentialist mood of shock, *nausea,* and disgust. On the popular level, this feeling of awe in nature is expressed in relation to trees, stones, water, the rising of the moon, flowers, villages, and the play of children. As we read in the Shintō text, spirits reside in all kinds of things. The basic sense of Shintō, then, is that the processes of nature cannot be evil, and since man participates in nature, his own nature partakes of this virtue.

A Shintō ceremony

To participate in the virtue, purity of heart is required. And this quality of heart is symbolized by certain tokens in the great Shintō shrines that are supposed to have been carried down from heaven by the ancestors of the royal house. The first of these is a mirror, which represents the pure heart reflecting nature and heaven without fault. The second is a keen sword symbolizing the courage to manifest virtue and the last is a jewel necklace, the ornament of benevolence.

It was into this optimistic, world-affirming context that Buddhism entered Japan, having originated in India in a period of world disillusionment and having taken root in China in one of political disaster. In Japan, the teachings of Buddha came to a young unbroken people who gave to the positive aspects of the Mahāyāna doctrine of the Jewel of *nirvāṇa* in the

Lotus of the World,[4] an extremely powerful interpretation, to a brief history of which we shall now proceed.

Buddhism entered Japan in A.D. 552 and brought with it a continental architecture with stress on the tile roof, which has become the dominant form not only of Buddhist temples but also of secular buildings and now even of Shintō shrines. The art and thought of the great continental Chinese civilization came with Buddhism to Japan and the date of this arrival, sixth to eighth centuries A.D., was exactly that of the arrival of Christianity in Germanic northern Europe. Japan is thus the young country of Asia, related to the civilization of China much as modern Europe is related to the culture of Greece and Rome.

The first phase was marked by the flowering in the eighth century A.D. of the beautiful temple city of Nara, where many of the early buildings still stand. And of these, the most important is Tōdaiji with its Hall of the Great Buddha. Within is an immense bronze Buddha, fifty-three-and-a-half feet high on a lotus ten feet high and sixty-three in circumference. The image was cast in the year 749 and weighs 452 tons. This Buddha is not the historical Buddha, Gautama Śākyamuni, but the great sun Buddha from whom historical Buddhas proceed. The Sanskrit name is Mahāvairocana, and the doctrine represented is called in Japanese *Kegon,* or "the flowering."

Let me explain. Usually, the progression of causality is reckoned as coming from past to present, in our direction, as it were. But since, according to the doctrine of the Yonder Shore, the non-dualistic *Prajñāpāramitā* doctrine,[5] "past" and "present" are not to be regarded as two separate things. The chain of causality must be reckoned also as proceeding from the future to present. Furthermore, since "here" and "there" are not to be regarded as two completely separate things, the influence of causality moves from there to here as much as it does the other way, so that all things contribute to the causality of any given situation at any moment—all things past, future, and to the sides.

Another name for this doctrine is the Doctrine of the Net of Gems, in which the world is regarded as a net of gems, each gem reflecting perfectly all the others. It is also called the Doctrine of Mutual Arising, and represents a notion of universal karma, not individually separated karmas. This is the meaning of the term the flower wreath—*Kegon.* Everything causes everything else. The doctrine works, furthermore, on all levels. In groups, for example, the leader and the group are *mutually arising.*

Now let us go on to the second stage of the history of Buddhism in Japan. In A.D. 804, two young Japanese Buddhist monks sailed to China, and when they returned, brought back some new ideas.

The younger of the two, Kōbō Daishi, returned with the doctrine known as Shingon, the True Word. The idea here is perhaps best explained by analogy with the Roman Catholic doctrine of the word "Consecration." When the priest pronounces the words *"Hoc est enim Corpus meum,"*[6] the wafer of the Mass becomes literally, according to Catholic doctrine, the body of Christ. Comparably, when the Shingon monk duly prepared pronounces certain words, a miracle of transubstantiation occurs, not in bread but within the monk himself.

The other young boy, Dengyō Daishi, then returned with the doctrine known as Tendai, the leading teaching of which is that a certain text, the Lotus *Sūtra,* is itself substantially the Buddha. There is a temple of this sect on Mt. Hiei near Kyoto where the text is revered in perpetual meditation.

Yet the heroic, effort-making deed of both of these young voyaging monks was to return with the idea that the native Shintō spirits, or *kami,* were to be regarded as manifestations on a lower life plane of the compassion of Buddhahood, so that the two traditions were now united. And today in Japan people pray in one breath to the Buddha and to the *kami.* In Japan, the main point, as I have said, is not theology, not ideology, but the sense of religious awe.

And now we come to the climax, the period of the ladies and their gallants in the fabulous court of Kyoto, the perfume of whose elegance lingers still in that town. Toward the close of the ninth century, a mad emperor in China had been responsible for a completely ghastly massacre of Buddhist monks and nuns, matched in Buddhist history only by the work of Islam in India and by what is going on right now under the Chinese in Tibet. Buddhist Japan at that time cut off connection with the mainland and from that moment onward, Japanese Buddhism developed on its own.

The first development was in the palace, in the atmosphere of Lady Murasaki's novel *The Tale of Genji.* For the art of courtly love as a knightly spiritual discipline was cultivated in Japan in the tenth century, just as it was to be celebrated in the Europe of the twelfth century. Moreover, in keeping with the Buddhist doctrine of the unity of all things in the flower wreath of mutual arising, the ladies of this love game were known as flower maidens, and their lovers cloud-gallants. In Europe the lover was to be a man endowed with a gentle heart. In Kyoto, he was one who heard the sigh of things. The technical term was *aware:* "to know the sorrow or sigh of things." Thus we hear a flower-wreath palace echo of the Prince Buddha's first noble truth: all life is sorrowful.

Torii gate at Ise

A far more serious development occurred, however, around the thirteenth century, when a series of three great reformers founded the leading Japanese Buddhist sects of the present day. The first was Hōnen, who founded the Jōdo, or Pure Land, sect, the guardian Buddha of which is the figure known as Amida in Japan, from the Sanskrit Amitābha, meaning "immeasurable light." The legend tells that Amitābha refused *nirvāṇa* for himself unless through his achievement he might bring everyone by the simplest means to *nirvāṇa*. And so indeed, anyone who so much as pronounces the name of Amitābha will find himself when he dies sitting like the Buddha on a lotus in the lotus pond of that Buddha. If he has lived and died in virtue, his lotus bud will be open. If not, it will be closed. However, the waters of the lotus pond continually murmur as they ripple, all is impermanent, all is without a self, and the radiance of the Buddha, Amida, penetrates the bud so that eventually the being inside is illumined, the bud opens, and like the rest he achieves *nirvāṇa*.

Zen garden

The second reformer, Shinran, was Hōnen's student, and he also was a devotee of Amida. Whereas Hōnen had gone so far in the affirmation of life that he had rejected celibacy for his clergy—the Jōdo priests are married, which in Buddhist practice is amazing—Shinran went even further, rejecting the specifically religious life altogether, maintaining that the ordinary tasks of life in the world when well done are adequate means to that awakening of faith which is the ultimate gift of religion. This sect is known as Shinshū, and is today the most important in Japan.

Reformer number three, then, was Eisai, the founder of Japanese Zen, which is addressed mainly to the samurai, the military caste, and so required the character of a strictly disciplined exercise, as the attitude of these monks in their meditation hall well shows.

A religion like Jōdo, which depends for salvation on the merits of the savior, is called *tariki* in Japan, which means other's strength, salvation from without. Zen, on the contrary, is of the type known as *jiriki,* one's own strength and self-reliance.

After the middle of the thirteenth century, the Japanese feudal order went pretty much to pieces. A period of baronial warfare followed in which loyalties to the overlord was a high virtue, and the ideals of Bushidō developed, the way of the warrior-caste. This really terrible period in Japanese history, which corresponds both in time and character to the fourteenth or sixteenth in the history of Europe, and is of such importance to the modern Japanese movie screen, was not brought to conclusion until 1600 when the Tokugawa shōgunate was established. All contacts with the outside world were severed at this time and cut off from the rest of the world until Admiral Perry's fleet arrived in 1854. The Japanese culture body became, so to say, completely homogenized. The aristocratic, warrior principle of honor and loyalty to one's vocation soaked down to the very simplest, humblest strata of the society. The Net of Gems, Shintō—all became fused, so to say, coming to focus in the arts that developed at this time, particularly the Zen arts of the warrior way, of painting, of arranging flowers, and of tea.

Indeed, these arts epitomize the whole heritage of the Japanese civilization—whether expressed in the language of Shintō, Bushidō, or Mahāyāna Buddhism. And so, let us now in conclusion consider some details of the method of the *chadō,* the Way of Tea.

The basic principles of the Way of Tea are expressed in the very character of the teahouse. It is a simple house in a garden. "Even a woodpecker," as the poem says, "will not harm this hermitage among summer trees. I went there and I came back. It was nothing special."

Near it you will find a little spring for the libations in the garden. All around, what meets the eye is cool and fresh, the mossy stone basin stands beside the budding branch. The entrance to the teahouse is at about the level of one's knees. It requires skill and delicacy to enter properly. Humility is taught here, the need to get rid of the mind that thinks, This is good, that is bad. Simply live without such thoughts and it is good to live. Inside, a few significant art objects are presented which one is to admire and finally, with the host as guide, comes the sipping of tea.

They spoke no word,
The visitor, the host,
*And the white chrysanthemum.*7

Finally, one regards the bowl, and the whisk that has been used for bringing the tea into the water. In form, the beauty, the simplicity. The beauty here is comparable to that of the joints of wood at the great shrine of Ise in the cedar grove, unknown to us what resideth here. For as in India, the dominant thought of Buddhism is of this world as *māyā*, illusion, a mask over the non-dual reality of *Brahman*. In Japan all things are Buddha things. All things themselves are the real. The fluid aspect of impermanence is itself the absolute state.

In the words of the great Zen master Dōgen, founder of the Sōtō sect of Zen, "Impermanence is Buddhahood.... These mountains, rivers, and earth are all the See of Buddhahood."

> The Buddha Way lies in accepting and appreciating the form as it is, the state as it is. The bloom of flowers and the fall of leaves are the state as it is and yet unwise people think that in the world of essence there should be no blossoming of flowers and no falling of leaves. Buddhahood is not something to be sought in the future, but to be realized where and as we are. The colors of the mountains, the echoes of the valleys, all, all are the form and voice of the Buddha.8

BOOK II ENDNOTES

EDITOR'S FOREWORD: SAKE & SATORI

1. See above, Book I: Baksheesh & Brahman, p. 178.
2. *Op. cit.,* pp. 304–5.
3. See p. 415.
4. See p. 473.
5. See p. 384.
6. In these journals, this series was conceived of as a single book, tentatively titled *Basic Mythologies of Mankind.*
7. This is the way in which he became most widely known, first for his series of lectures on religion that aired on New York's public television station (the transcripts of one of which provided us with appendix IIA, "The Nature Way"), and finally through his interviews with Bill Moyers, aired after his death as *The Power of Myth.*
8. See p. 595.
9. See p. 471.

CHAPTER I: THE BUDDHA LAND

1. Ceylon was to change its name to Sri Lanka in 1972.
2. Though officially known as Thailand since 1949, the country was still referred to by its older name by many Americans.
3. Professor Senerat Paranavitana was the first Singhalese Commissioner of Archeology for Ceylon, from 1940 to 1956.
4. Carl Hagenbeck was a renowned designer of zoos in the early twentieth century. He is credited with originating the modern, barless zoo.

5. A *stūpa* is a Buddhist temple mound, memorializing Buddha. "In its earliest known examples, at Bhārhut and Sāñcī, the form was that of a moundlike central structure surrounded by a railing with sumptuously carved gates. In the course of the subsequent centuries the *stūpa* developed variously, particularly following the spread of Buddhism throughout Asia." —Heinrich Zimmer, *The Art of Indian Asia,* completed and edited by Joseph Campbell (Princeton: Princeton University Press, 1983.)

6. Parakrama Bahu I "the Great" was the Singhalese king of Lanka, or Ceylon, ca. A.D. 1153–86. He ruled from Polonnaruva, reuniting his factionalized kingdom and reunifying the various Buddhist sects. The monument that Campbell is referring to is a statue reputed to be of Parakrama.

7. The Gold Coast achieved independence in 1957 as the Republic of Ghana.

8. Dr. Syngman Rhee (1875–1965) served as the president of the Republic of South Korea from 1948, through the Korean War, until his downfall in 1960.

9. Chiang Kai-shek (1887–1975) was the Chinese general and head of the anti-Communist Nationalist government, first in mainland China, then in Formosa (later known as Taiwan).

10. Campbell is referring to the University of Peradeniya.

11. Campbell meets up with Solomon in Japan, who was the director of field work at Sarah Lawrence College. See pp. 557–69.

12. D. T. Devendra, G. P. Malalasekara, et al., editors, *Encyclopedia of Buddhism* (Colombo: Government of Ceylon), volumes 1 (1963)–5.3 (1992).

13. Ziggurats were the pyramid-like temple mounds of the Sumerians and other Mesopotamian civilizations. They were built with a spiral path around the outside, and a flat top. See Joseph Campbell, *The Masks of God: Primitive Mythology* (New York: Penguin/Arkana, 1991), pp. 145–48.

14. Campbell is quoting Jason Grossman (See above, Book I: Baksheesh & Brahman).

15. The South-East Asia Treaty Organization had been established in 1954 (a few months before Campbell's voyage) for countries of Southeast Asia and part of the southwest Pacific, as a defensive alliance on the model of NATO to further a U.S. policy of containment of Communism. Its members were Australia, Britain, France, New Zealand, Pakistan, the Philippines, Thailand, and the United States. The organization was dissolved in 1977.

16. Winged female figures in classical Indian and Southeast Asian art, *apsarases* are "heavenly damsels [that] constitute a kind of celestial corps de ballet are the mistresses of those who in reward for pious and meretorious deeds during their earthly lives have been reborn among the gods." —Heinrich Zimmer, *The Art of Indian Asia.*

17. This is the "curious American" whom Campbell met after a dance performance by his wife, Jean Erdman, in Baroda, India. See above, Book I: Baksheesh & Brahman, p. 264.

18. British Overseas Airways Corporation.

19. The daughter of Indian author Dhanvanthi Rama Rau, Santha is a noted author in her own right, best known for her travel writing and for her stage and screen adaptations of E. M. Forster's *Passage to India.* Her husband, Faubian Bowers, produced volumes on Japanese theatre and poetry, and Indian dance. He also served as General MacArthur's aide-de-camp.

20. "In some people—possibly because of infant relationships—the stress goes towards

power, in which case the sexual life takes a secondary position. [...] Jung calls this person the introvert. His meaning is somewhat different from the common sense of the word. Jung defines the introvert as a power-oriented person who wants to put through his ego achievement.

"The sex-oriented person, on the other hand, turns outward. Falling in love means losing yourself in another object. This person Jung calls the extrovert. Now, he says, every individual is both, with an accent on one or the other. If you have your accent sixty percent over in the power arena, it's only going to be forty percent over in the eros area.

"Now when you run into a situation where your normal orientation doesn't function, where it isn't carrying you through, you are thrown back on the other. Then this inferior personality emerges. [...]

"Jung uses a fine word for this reversal: he calls it an *enantiodromia*. As you know (of course) from your Greek, *dromia* is 'to run': hippodrome is where the hippos (or horses) run; a dromedary is a racing camel. *Enantio* means 'in the other direction.' So, taken together, enantiodromia means running in the opposite direction, turning turtle."—Joseph Campbell, "Personal Myths," *The Joseph Campbell Audio Collection, Volume IV: Man and Myth.*

20a. Immediately following his enlightenment, the Buddha is said to have meditated at the foot of an enormous banyan tree, in the roots of which lived a serpent king, Mucalinda. The Buddha passed into a state of bliss, unaware or unconcerned with his surroundings. However, an unseasonal storm blew up. Mucalinda issued forth and, with his cobra hood, protected the Buddha from the tempest for seven days and seven nights.

21. Frances Webb Roosevelt (?–1986) was the widow of Quentin Roosevelt II. Quentin, grandson to President Theodore Roosevelt, served with his father, Theodore Jr., in the D-Day invasion of World War II. The father died of a heart attack in Normandy, a month after the landing in 1944, and the son died in an airliner crash in Hong Kong in 1948. The visit to which Campbell is referring must have taken place some time before the war.

22. Professor Veditantirige Ediriwira Sarachchandra (1915–96) was a professor of theatre and religious studies at the Ceylon University in Colombo, as well as an adapter of folk drama. V. E. Sarachchandra, *The Sinhalese Folk Play* (Colombo: Ceylon University, 1953).

23. Dr. Alfred Salmony (1890–1958) was a Hungarian-born professor of Asian art, particularly the carved stone art of China and Japan. Campbell met up with Salmony and his traveling companion, Jason Grossman, and traveled throughout India with them. He seems to have been creating a periodical for the Institute of Fine Art in New York, where he was a fellow. See above, Book I: Baksheesh & Brahman, *passim*.

24. Joseph Campbell, editor, R. F. C. Hull and Ralph Manheim, translators, *The Mysteries: Papers of the Eranos Yearbook*, volume 2 (New York: Pantheon Books/Bollingen Foundation, 1955).

25. Heinrich Zimmer (1890–1943) was one of the scholars who most influenced Campbell's life and work. A friend of Thomas Mann, of Carl Gustav Jung, married to Hugo von Hofmannsthal's daughter Christiane, a great raconteur and a man of immense erudition, Campbell found in Zimmer a challenging fellow spirit. Although they knew each other for only two years, from Zimmer's arrival in New York until

his untimely death from pneumonia in 1943, Campbell became a friend, and after his death, at the request of Zimmer's widow, spent twelve years editing and completing Zimmer's work. These works included *Myths and Symbols in Indian Art and Civilization* (1946), *The King and the Corpse* (1948), *The Philosophies of India* (1951), and *The Art of Indian Asia* (1955), which Campbell had completed while he was on the trip through India (see Book I: Baksheesh & Brahman, pp. 190, 231, 234, 325, 355, 356, 359, 360). The arrival of *The Art of Indian Asia* in Japan would serve Campbell as an excellent *carte-d'entrée* during his visit there (see pp. 515–16).

26. Burma officially changed its name to Myanmar in 1989.

27. Formosa is now known by its Chinese name, Taiwan.

28. The nineteenth century Hindu saint Sri Ramakrishna spoke of two attitudes towards God: the way of the monkey (which clings to its mother by its own strength), and the way of the kitten (which mews for its mother to carry it). See above, Book I: Baksheesh & Brahman, n. 86 (p. 334).

29. The story may be apocryphal. It is true, however, that the formal entrance of the Taj Mahal Hotel of Bombay, India, faces away from the bay on what might have been the "back" of the hotel.

30. Thakin Kodaw Hmaing (1876–1964) was an eminent Burmese author and peace activist.

31. Ho Chi Minh and his Viet Minh Army had defeated the French at Dien Bien Phu, just north of Hanoi, in May 1954. This defeat led the French to abandon Indochina. In October 1954, the Geneva Peace Accords, which spelled out the terms of the French withdrawal, created the states of Cambodia and Laos, and split Vietnam into two states—supposedly for just two years. An election in 1956 was supposed to create a unified, democratic Vietnamese state. However, in October 1955—just five months after Campbell's fly-over—Ngo Dinh Diem, the head of the South Vietnamese government, renounced the accords, fearing that their implementation favored Ho and the Communist North. The states weren't unified again until the end of the Vietnam War, in 1975.

32. Carl Thomas Rowan (1925–2000) was a widely syndicated newspaper columnist, author, biographer, television and radio commentator, and founder of the Project Excellence scholarship program. The U. S. Ambassador to Finland in 1963–64, Thomas was one of the first African-American ambassadors to a European nation.

33. Dr. C. Martin Wilbur was a professor of East Asian Studies at Columbia University.

34. The United States Information Service is a branch of the U.S. State Department concerned with public relations in foreign nations.

35. The Japanese occupied Formosa from 1895 to 1945. Not all observers agree that the Japanese rule was beneficial.

36. The Kuomintang, or KMT, are the Chinese Nationalist Party, led by Chiang Kai-shek.

CHAPTER 2: THE REALM OF THE SENSES

37. Campbell's family had an apartment on Riverside Drive in New York for several years while he was a child.

38. In fact, the Japanese wear what Westerners think of as surgical masks when they have a cold, so as not to impose on others by spreading their germs. The Jains, in practicing *ahiṃsa,* "harmlessness," mask their mouths to avoid killing airborne microorganisms and insects by inhaling them.

39. Popular in the Paris of the 1920s that Campbell had visited as a young man, Apache (pronounced "ah-PAHSH") dancing involved, at the least, a man and a woman in a sort of cross between ballroom dance and pantomime. The woman was often literally dragged and thrown as part of the dance in a semi-sadomasochistic tango, which was supposed to be an artistic depiction of domestic passion in the demimonde.

40. This would seem to be a specifically Jungian observation, though it actually comes via Campbell's work on Heinrich Zimmer's *Philosophies of India*, Bollingen Series XXVI (New York: Pantheon, 1951): "The pleasure of love...is the bliss...of Shiva and his Shakti in their eternal realization of identity; only as known in the inferior mode of egoconsciousness. The creature of passion has only to wash away his sense of ego, and then the same act that formerly was an obstruction becomes the tide that bears him to the realization of the absolute as bliss (*ānanda*)." —*Philosophies*, pp. 576–77.

41. This is what is known as Kobe beef.

42. This famous hotel was designed by Frank Lloyd Wright, built in 1922 and demolished in 1966.

43. "Gāru" is simply a Japanized version of the English word "girl."

44. A samisen is a three-stringed instrument with a long neck, played by plucking, somewhat like a banjo.

45. This is Campbell's brother, Charles Campbell Jr., one year younger than Joseph Campbell himself.

46. George Balanchine (1904–83) was one of the most influential choreographers of the twentieth century. A Russian émigré, he served as the ballet master at the New York City Ballet from 1946 until his death in 1983.

47. The Bollingen Foundation had been founded by Mary Mellon in the early 1940s to advance and preserve learning in the humanities. One of its major projects was the Bollingen Series, a collection of published works on psychology, mythology, and religion. As of 1955, Campbell had written several Bollingen books, including *The Hero with a Thousand Faces*, and had edited and contributed to many more, including the Heinrich Zimmer posthuma, *Where the Two Came to Their Father*, and the Eranos Yearbook series.

48. Katakana is a syllable-based Japanese script used especially for terms adopted from other languages.

CHAPTER 3: FROM SAKE TO SATORI

49. In the seventeenth century, a tsunami, or tidal wave, destroyed a temple building around this bronze Buddha; only the great statue remained. It has sat under the open sky ever since.

50. A Nisei is an overseas-born person of Japanese descent (usually second generation).

51. This is the third or fourth time in this journal that Campbell has undertaken to dampen his polemical tendencies, a self-acknowledged shortcoming with which he struggled throughout his life. His resolve was usually short-lived, as his true feelings continued to surface. See Robin and Steven Larsen, *A Fire in the Mind* (New York: Doubleday, 1991), pp. 507–12.

52. Hiragana is another syllable-based, Japanese cursive script form.

53. Amitābha Buddha, "The Buddha of Infinite Light" (or Amida, as he is known in Japan) is the savior-Buddha invoked in "Pure Land" sects of Buddhism such as Jōdo and Shinshū. Simply put, if one calls upon Amida, he has promised that one will gain

Sukhāvatī, "The Place of Bliss," or "The Western Paradise." Inspired by Indian masters such as Nāgārjuna (ca. A.D. 150–200), the Pure Land sects place the Lotus *Sūtra,* or *Saddharma Pundarīka,* at the center of their teaching.

54. The Shinshū sect of Buddhism was founded by Shinran in 1224 and was more aimed at the common person than the then-dominant Tendai. The I.B.A. is the International Buddhist Association.

55. A *Dhyāna* Buddha is literally a "contemplation" or abstract Buddha, as opposed to a historical figure such as Gautama Śākyamuni. The Sanskrit *dhyāna* became transliterated in Chinese as *ch'an,* thence into Japanese as Zen. This form of meditative Buddhism is reputed to have been brought into China by Bodhidharma ca. A.D. 520, and developed by Hui-neng. See pp. 466–69.

56. This is a constant refrain in Campbell's writing, an example he often used of the tendency in Western religions to take a literal rather than a metaphoric reading of myths and symbols. See Joseph Campbell, *Thou Art That: Transforming Religious Metaphor* (Novato, Calif.: New World Library, 2001), p. 20, or *The Inner Reaches of Outer Space: Metaphor as Myth and as Religion* (Novato, Calif.: New World Library, 2002), p. 5.

57. Phillip Karl Eidmann was to serve as a sort of Virgil during Campbell's stay in Japan, a guide and cultural interpreter. A Shinshū Buddhist priest, Rev. Eidmann published many articles and books on Buddhism, both in Japan and in the United States. He was paralyzed from the waist down, apparently by injuries suffered during World War II.

58. Jacob Feuerring. See pp. 642–43.

59. Ruth Fuller Sasaki (1893–1967) was a translator and author of books on Zen Buddhism, as well as a Rinzai Zen priest. Along with her husband, S. S. Sasaki, she founded the First Zen Institute of America. Her daughter, Eleanor Everett, was Alan Watts's first wife.

60. Ellen Psaty Conant was to become a leading authority on Japanese art in general and Kakuzo Okakura (see n. 231) in particular.

61. *Namu Amida-butsu* is a prayer to Amida (Amitābha). The Pure Land sects (Jōdo and Shinshū) practice a doctrine known as *nembutsu,* which holds that contemplation of the Buddha's name leads one to the Pure Land, or *nirvāṇa.* See n. 53.

62. Emperor Hirohito (1901–89) reigned from 1926, through the crises of World War II and the reemergence of Japan as an international power, until his death in 1989. This was his fifty-third birthday; he was almost exactly three years older than Campbell.

63. Statues of the Bodhisattva Jizō (Kṣitigarbha) are found everywhere in Japan. He is said to protect children, especially the dead, whose souls nestle in the sleeves of his great robe. The Mibu-Kyōgen is attended by droves of children, tended by mothers and grandparents. Jōchō (?–1057) was the most renowned sculptor of Buddhist images during the Heian period.

64. It seems almost certain that Campbell left out a sentence before this one.

65. Kannon (Chinese = Kuan-yin) is a female avatar of Avalokiteśvara, the Bodhisattva of compassion or mercy.

66. The origin of this quote is uncertain.

67. See n. 112 for more information on the Three-Body system. *Kegon* means "flower wreath" and refers to the Buddhist *sūtra* of the same name; the sect places that *sūtra* at the center of its teaching, and the Doctrine of Mutual Arising. See Appendix IIB, n. 2.

68. A *mudrā* is a ritual attitude or posture.

69. This the wish-fullfilling avatar of Avalokiteśvara.

70. Ākāśagarbha, or Kokūzō, is a Bodhisattva who embodies wisdom.

71. The Mantō-e Festival is conducted only once every hundred years. Campbell, by serendipity, was in Nara at just the right time.

72. The *shō* is an extremely sophisticated woodwind instrument that looks something like a large, upturned set of panpipes with a lacquered mouthpiece at the bottom.

73. The Yamato emperor Temmu began to create the warrior class that became the samurai ("those who serve") during the seventh century.

CHAPTER 4: AN AMERICAN BUDDHIST IN KYOTO

74. "It" is Campbell's ongoing lament, developing ever more strongly, that Americans—especially the diplomats and scholars—were lazy and presented a poor image of their country. He would seek to remedy this upon his return through his own years of service to the Foreign Service Institute and the U.S.I.S. See foreword, pp. 367–68, and Larsen, *A Fire in the Mind*, pp. 426–29, 437, 455, 472.

75. The Noh stage includes a wide platform that serves as the main playing area, with two narrower platforms that extend to either side of the audience and serve as both exit and entrance areas and secondary playing areas. The outdoor theater at the temple follow this design.

76. This floor was made of sprung wood that squeaked or "sang" as it was walked on, thus protecting the shōgun from a surprise attack.

77. There seems to have been some sentiment at this time to remove all U.S. service personnel and arm Japan with its own nuclear arsenal—hence the "J-bomb."

78. *Amazake* is sweetened sake, an alcoholic drink made from fermented rice.

79. *Arhat* is a Sanskrit word, often translated as "saint." Most often, it is used in connection with the Theravādin (or Hīnayāna) forms of Buddhism, rather than the Mahāyāna Buddhism practiced in Japan. In this context it seems to mean an advanced spiritual being who has gained enlightenment. Theravādins find the "Hīnayāna" appellation derogatory; therefore, though Campbell consistently referred to this form of Buddhism as Hīnayāna (having been introduced to Buddhism from a Mahāyāna point of view), we have tried to use the more accepted nomenclature in these notes.

80. Though there is some controversy over Śaṅkara's dates, the most accepted (circa A.D. 700–50) do indeed jibe with Campbell's suggestion; if true, this would render moot the theory that Bodhidharma, the great Indian figure of the *dhyāna* school of Buddhism that was to become Chinese *ch'an* and Japanese Zen, could have been a student of the Hindu Śaṅkara, who is the most famous exponent of the *advaita vedānta* philosophy of non-dualism, which is influential in modern Indian thought. See n. 114.

81. Daisetz Teitarō Suzuki (1870–1966) was one of the most influential early proponents of Japanese Buddhism in the West. His books and lectures had a profound impact on Alan Watts (see pp. 646–48) and Campbell himself. Among his many books were *An Introduction to Zen Buddhism*, with a foreword by C. G. Jung (New York: Philosophical Library, 1949).

82. All of the preceding is Campbell noting Eidmann's opinions. During his stay in Japan, and in the years that followed, Campbell would develop his own thoughts on these subjects, some in line with Eidmann's, and some at odds.

83. See p. 454.

84. Bushidō is the code of behavior pertaining to all traditional martial arts in Japan; it is strongly associated with the samurai.

85. For information on Chiang, see n. 9. For information on Diem, see n. 31. For information on Dr. Rhee, see n. 8; Syngman Rhee was indeed a professed Christian. The Romulo to whom Campbell is referring appears to be Carlos Peña Romulo (1899–1986), journalist and diplomat, who served as the president of the United Nations General Assembly in 1949 and ran for the presidency of the Philippines in 1953. However, it seems likely that Campbell was actually thinking of Ramon Magsaysay (1907–57), who served from 1953 until his death as president of the Philippines. He was a Christian, a strong anti-Communist, and a supporter of U.S. policy, and came to power with Romulo's support, so Campbell may have fused them in his mind.

86. Professor Shin'ya Kasugai (1917–).

87. Maitreya is the Bodhisattva of the Buddha-yet-to-come.

88. Nāgārjuna (ca. A.D. third century) was one of the great early Buddhist thinkers; none of his own writings have come down to us. Mahāyāna ("Greater Vehicle") and Hīnayāna ("Lesser Vehicle," also known as Theravāda) are the two largest branches of Buddhism. They vary in concepts of monkhood, and in the pantheon of divinely attained humans: *arhats* (Hīnayāna) and Boddhisattvas (Mahāyāna). Campbell compares these two traditions extensively throughout these journals.

89. In Indian religious art, a *vajra* is a lightning bolt representing enlightenment. This motif has corollaries in traditional art around the world.

90. In general terms, it isn't quite accurate to say the Japanese write "in a Chinese sequence"; written Japanese makes use of Chinese ideographs and two groups of simple syllabaries (hiragana and katakana), and the order of the Chinese ideographs in Japanese writing would usually differ from that in a purely Chinese sentence. Campbell seems to be referring to the reading in Japanese of pure Chinese texts. Purely Chinese writings are read by Japanese by actually translating the Chinese into Japanese while reading, with the aid of little symbols inserted into the Chinese text to clue the reader as to the order in which to read and translate the Chinese ideographs. "Writing them on the page in a Chinese sequence" seems to be Campbell's way of expressing what is simply a Japanese person writing in Chinese. The complication perhaps arises from the fact that Japanese uses Chinese ideographs to write Japanese. To give a simplistic example: writing "I am a student of Buddhism" in Japanese would contain some of the same ideographs that would be used to write the phrase in pure Chinese, but with different pronunciations in Japanese. An educated Japanese who knew no Chinese could still guess, through his knowledge of the Chinese ideographs, at the meaning of the purely Chinese sentence but likely not guess at the Chinese pronunciation, whereas a Japanese scholar trained in Chinese could do so. That same educated Japanese person could not write the purely Chinese version of "I am a student of Buddhism." Thus, the written Japanese equivalent of "I am a student of Buddhism" would resemble but not match the Chinese written version.

91. Again, this is the posthumous volume that Campbell edited from the notes of Heinrich Zimmer. See n. 25.

92. This was the seventeenth anniversary of Joseph Campbell and Jean Erdman's wedding.
93. The white *inari*, or Shintō fox-god, is related to sexuality and fertility.
94. Seiiti Miduno and Tosio Nagahiro, *A Study of the Buddhist Cave-Temples at Lung-men, Ho-nan* Tokyo: Zauho Press, 1941.
95. Actually, Seishi (also known as Daiseishi and Mahāsthamaprapta) is most commonly said to symbolize Amida's wisdom. Thus the trinity of Amitābha, Avalokiteśvara, and Mahāsthamaprapta (Amida, Kannon, and Seishi) exemplifies the idea that Amida Buddha's compassion and wisdom together bring the adherent to the Western Paradise of enlightenment.
96. The Suryaprabha Bodhisattva (known as Nikkō in Japan) is connected to light and health. Like Avalokiteśvara, Suryaprabha is often pictured holding a lotus blossom.
97. Tibetan Buddhist *vajrayāna* ceremonies combine the use of a ritual bronze *vajra* in combination with bells to symbolize spiritual awakening.
98. The Tendai Buddhist sect retains a connection to Tibetan Buddhist traditions, hence the *vajras* and the bells.

CHAPTER 5: UNIMPEDED

99. Ryosho Takamine (1898–?), scholar on Japanese Buddhism, and Kegon in particular.
100. A kakemono is a hanging scroll.
101. In his later work, Campbell often used the dichotomy between *ri-ji-muge* and *ji-ji-muge* to illustrate the world-affirming and -renunciating strains of various religions. "The Japanese call these alternatives, respectively, the *Ji Hokkai* and the *Ri Hokkai*. *Ji Hokkai* is the individual realm, *Ri Hokkai* the general. Then they say *ji-ri-muge:* individual, general, no obstruction, no difference. They are, in fact, the same.

    "Now," I continued, "when one of those light bulbs breaks, the superintendent of building doesn't come in and say, 'Well, that was my particularly favorite bulb.' He takes it out, throws it away, and puts in another one. What is important is not the vehicle, but the light.

    "And looking down at all your heads I ask myself, of what are these the vehicles? They certainly are the vehicles of consciousness; how much consciousness are they radiating? Then, I might ask any one of you, 'Which are you? Are you the vehicle—the light bulb—or are you consciousness—the light itself?'"

    "When you identify with the consciousness, with gratitude to the vehicle, you can let it go—'Death, where is thy sting?' You have identified yourself with the consciousness that is really everlasting. It is consciousness that throws up forms and takes them back again, throws up forms and takes them back again. When you realize that you are one with consciousness, you are one with all the forms that contain it. Then you can say *ji-ji-muge:* individual, individual, no obstruction, no difference. This is the ultimate mystic experience on earth." "Episode 1.2: The Spirit Land." *Mythos, Part 1: The Shaping of Our Mythic Tradition* (Los Angeles: Inner Dimension Video, 2000).
102. See Book I: Baksheesh & Brahman, pp. 215–16.
103. Sanskrit for "not this, not this!" and "it is here, it is here!" these terms express Ramakrishna's teaching that one must meditate on cleansing oneself of connection to the ego before transcending to connection with *brahman*. See *Flight of the Wild Gander*, p. 169, or *Thou Art That*, p. 26.

104. *Śunyatā* is the famous Buddhist doctrine of the emptiness or illusory nature of the world, first propounded in the *Prajñāparamitā* scriptures, including the *Prajñāpāramitā Hṛdāya*, or Heart *Sūtra*.

105. D. T. Suzuki, *Essays in Zen Buddhism* (London: Rider and Co., 1927).

106. Satori is the Japanese word meaning "sudden enlightenment." It is sometimes equated with *kenshō* ("waking up") and the Sanskrit *nirvāṇa* (which, ironically, means "blown out" like a candle; that is, emptied of self).

107. *Prajñāpāramitā* is translated variously as "the ultimate virtue that comes from wisdom" or "the wisdom of the yonder shore." In Buddhist art, *Prajñāpāramitā* is often portrayed as a female Bodhisattva: "the most spiritual feminine symbol in all the iconographies of the East...."—Zimmer, *Myths and Symbols of Indian Art and Civilization,* ed. Joseph Campbell (New York: Pantheon/Bollingen Foundation, 1946), p. 99.

108. The Hossō sect of Buddhism was one of the earliest to come to Japan, brought by the Japanese monk Dōshō ca. A.D. 664. It is related to the Chinese Fa-hsiang and Indian Yogācāra schools; it is a relatively minor sect in Japan.

109. Campbell makes note of the translation by Eugène Obermiller (1900–35) of this Tibetan Buddhist text, entitled *Uttara Tantra of Maitreya.* There are numerous editions of this translation; there is no record as to which Campbell was referring.

110. The Mahāsāṅghika were a very early Buddhist sect that pushed for the inclusion of not only members of the priestly castes, but also all classes in the practice of Buddhism. Their schism was a precursor to the establishment of what is now Mahāyāna Buddhism.

111. The Sarvastivādins were another proto-Mahāyāna Buddhist sect. The religious text to which Campbell is referring is probably the *Sarvastivādin-vinaya,* the monastic rules for the Sarvastivādin order.

112. The various sects of Buddhism view the Buddha as having various aspects. *Prajñāpāramitā*–inflected sects, such as Tibetan Vajrayāna and Zen Buddhists give the Buddha three aspects, or "bodies": the transformation or emanation body, the reward or enjoyment body, and the *dharma* or truth body. Other sects have different systems. Similarly, a typical Westerner might hold a "two-body" system of the human (mind/body) or a "three-body" system (mind/body/spirit).

113. Georg Cantor was a German mathematician of the nineteenth century who revolutionized the modern thinking about the mathematics of infinity as an acceptable but unresovable abstraction.

114. Śaṅkara, the great Hindu philosopher, taught that all the things of this world were merely *māyā,* or illusion. One day, he told a prince, "You are not actually real nor is your kingdom. It is only an illusion." The next time Śaṅkara came to teach the prince, the prince had one of his bull elephants chase Śaṅkara up a tree. "If this wild elephant is not real, why did you run from it?" Śaṅkara said, "That which you think was me was the one you thought ran up the tree. But that was not actually me."

115. See above, pp. 467–68.

116. There is no record of any major scriptural changes recommended by the Sixth Buddhist Congress of 1954–56.

117. B. L. Suzuki, *Noh Gaku,* Wisdom of the East Series (1932).

118. Apparently, Campbell here means to state his own views, rather than reporting those of Eidmann and Kasugai.

119. Clive Staples Lewis (1898–1963) was a highly regarded scholar of medieval and Renaissance literature and Christian theorist. He is best known today as the author of the Narnia series of children's books and the subject of the play and film *Shadowlands,* which dramatizes his marriage to Joy Davidman.

120. See pp. 426–27.

121. A work that was never published but did serve as the groundwork for the multi-volume *Masks of God,* which was published over the next decade.

122. Wisconsin senator Joseph McCarthy's investigations into the purported infiltration of Communists into the U.S. government—particularly into the Army and State Department—had concluded just weeks before Campbell began his journey to Asia. Though the investigations (or "witch-hunts," as they became known) ended without a single conviction, the image of career diplomats and army officers pleading their Fifth Amendment right against self-incrimination had imbedded itself into the mind of many Americans, Campbell included. He is implying that Communist-leaning U.S. administrators of the Occupation had exercised the same kind of political chicanery at Japanese universities that they complained was being practiced against their brethren in America.

123. Harold Taylor, president of Sarah Lawrence College and a personal friend of Campbell's. See *Fire in the Mind,* pp. 233, 331–32, 357, 414, 504, 545.

124. This is in fact the Indian elephant-god Ganeśa, known as Kangiten in Japan. In Tantric practice, the cakes that Ganeśa holds are said to represent the sweetness of *ātman* (the universal self) within the sordid, personal self.

125. See p. 410.

126. *Gutoku's Notes* is Shinran's brief treatise on the differences between Theravāda and Mahāyāna Buddhism.

127. This is most likely the Venerable Narada Thera's *The Life of the Buddha in His Own Words* (Colombo: Y.M.B.A, no date).

128. A major difference between Theravādin and Mahāyāna teaching that goes unstated (though implied) here is that Theravādin Buddhists concentrate on the so-called Pāli canon of *sūtras,* which they hold to be the true teachings of the Buddha, while Mahāyāna teachings include the broader "Chinese" canon, which includes many of the same writings, but also *sūtras* that are not part of the Pāli canon.

129. This seems to have been a direct quotation from Eidmann rather than from *Gutoku's Notes.*

130. Kanji are Chinese-derived ideograms that form, in addition to katakana and hiragana, the third part of Japanese script.

131. It seems evident that Campbell may have come to change this opinion.

132. This would appear to be "Hinduism," the cover article of the February 7, 1955, issue of *Life.*

133. Campbell was usually disappointed with the published form of his books, especially at first. Later he would become more reconciled to them. With the exception of *Hero with a Thousand Faces,* Campbell had devoted the previous thirteen years to Zimmer's books, rather than writing his own.

134. Eugene Herrigel, *Zen in the Art of Archery,* translated by R.F.C. Hull (New York: Pantheon, 1953, and New York: Vintage, 1971), an autobiographical and now-classic introduction to the subject of *Kyūdō,* also known as "Zen archery." *Kyūdō,* like kendō or jūdō.(-*dō* means "Way," from the Chinese *Tao*), is considered a Zen art, a form of

meditation through action. It is governed in a general way, like the other martial arts, by Bushidō.

135. Phillip Karl Eidmann, trans., *Sutra of the Teachings Left by the Buddha: Translated into Chinese by Kumarajtva in the Latter Part of the Tsin Dynasty (948–971 B.C.).* (Osaka Koyata Yamamoto, 1954).

CHAPTER 6: TEA AND FIRE

136. In the decades following the conversion of the Roman emperor Constantine (A.D. 312), the Christian church became institutionalized. Many nonconformist Christians withdrew from society, either out of protest or out of a need for ascetic retreat.

137. See Zimmer, *Art of Indian Asia,* pp. 298–312.

138. Wotan (or Odin) was the king of the Norse/Germanic pantheon. He had given up the sight in his left eye to gain the ability to see into the future with his right. See *Flight of the Wild Gander,* "Secularization of the Sacred," p. 165.

139. "Abu" was the Campbell's car from 1938 until 1955.

140. Campbell's notes from this paper form the basis for appendix IIA (see p. 649).

141. The Yab-Yum motif is the symbolic coitus of male and female deities in Tibetan iconography.

142. Throughout the mid-1950s and early 1960s, Campbell was editing the yearbooks of the Eranos conferences on psychology and religion for the Bollingen Foundation.

143. See p. 471.

144. This book, which was much in Campbell's mind during his stay in Japan, was never completed; it seems to have reappeared as the final volume of the *Masks of God* series (which was published by Viking), *Creative Mythology.*

145. Ascona, Switzerland, on the Lago Maggiore, was the site of the Eranos conferences. See n. 141.

146. Alan Watts (1915–73), author and Western interpreter of Asian culture and (in particular) Zen Buddhism, had been responsible for a few of Campbell's contacts in Japan, and the Campbells would visit Watts in Big Sur, California, upon their return to the U.S. See pp. 647–48.

147. Here the editors have omitted a rather lengthy enumeration of social and political circumstances in Asia that recapitulates earlier material.

148. Henry Corbin, Eranos participant, specialist in the Ismaili gnosis of Islam.

149. The likelihood is that the recondite martial art was aikidō, developed in the twentieth century by Morihei Ueshiba, and still not well-known to Westerners by the 1950s.

150. The "spies" are probably ninja, followers of the skill of *ninjutsu,* the Bushidō-related art invoking stealth, deception, disguise, and martial arts of unusual kinds. The ninja were feared and deadly assassins as well as spies.

151. This is Japanese transliterated into the Roman alphabet—just as the Japanese words in this work are presented.

152. Annie Besant is regarded, along with Alice Bailey, as one of the founders of the Theosophy movement, one of the first Asian-accented philosophical movements in the West.

153. See n. 88.

154. Vasubandhu (ca. fourth century A.D.) was the author of the *Discourse on the Pure Land,* a commentary on the Pure Land *Sūtra* that Shinran claimed was one of the primary

texts of Pure Land Buddhism. Thus, he, along with Nāgārjuna, was a spiritual father to the movement.

155. Dr. Tadao Yanaihara (1893–1961) was president of Tokyo University from 1951 to 1957 and was, as Campbell mentions, a prominent member of the Mukyōkai (No-Church) Christian movement.

156. *Rōshi* is a term of respect for a Zen master.

157. See pp. 509–10.

158. *Netsujō* means passion in the sense of fervor or ardor; *bonnō* refers to carnal desire.

159. Vaun Gilmore was an editorial assistant at Bollingen.

160. *The Hero with a Thousand Faces* (originally published by the Bollingen Foundation in 1949) remains Campbell's most influential (and most widely translated) academic work. In it, he examines what he calls the monomyth of the hero's journey: the universal story of the hero's departure from home, the defeat of the shadow enemy, and the return home with a boon, whether that boon is treasure or enlightenment. The Mexican edition to which Campbell refers was indeed published by Fondo de Cultura Económica in 1959 as *El héroe de las mil caras: Psicoanálisis del mito,* and remains in print at this writing.

161. See above, Book I: Baksheesh & Brahman, pp. 22, 190, n. 10 (p. 328).

162. Alistair Reid and Horace Gregory were fellow members with Campbell of the English Department at Sarah Lawrence.

163. Jean Erdman taught dance at Bard College in Annandale, New York, during 1955–56.

164. Henry Volkening of the firm Russell-Volkening was Campbell's literary agent.

165. Toward the end of his life, on December 6, 1274, St. Thomas Aquinas was visited with an "ecstasy" during the Mass. When he revived, the priest asked if Thomas was well. When the saint answered that he would not continue his writing, the priest urged him to reconsider, and St. Thomas is said to have replied, "I can do no more. Such secrets as has have been revealed to me that all I have written now appears to be of little value."

166. Campbell may have been thinking of the story of Black Elk, a Sioux medicine man who suffered a similar "shamanic crisis." See *Flight of the Wild Gander,* "Mythogenesis." This style would characterize Campbell's later comparativism—uncomfortable for many traditional theologians—that the insights of a shaman, such as the Inuit Najagneq or Black Elk, might be compared to Aquinas or St. John of the Cross. See *The Historical Atlas of World Mythology, Volume 1—The Way of the Animal Powers* (San Francisco: Harper & Row, 1983), p. 169.

167. A. E. Jensen studied the mythology of the Celebes islanders, who were primitive planters. The myth of Hainuwele described how the *dema*-divinity Hainuwele (whose name means coconut branch) was murdered. Her body was planted, and out of this grew the plants that feed the people. But a door was fashioned, so that the people no longer walk among the *dema.* This story has elements of the rebirth myths that Campbell seems to be considering for his projected book.

168. Indeed, Campbell began to record his lectures from this time on, and many of his later books (including *Myths to Live By* (New York: Viking Penguin, 1993), and *The Inner Reaches of Outer Space*) were created using this system. The Joseph Campbell Foundation has continued to create "new" volumes of Campbell's work such as *Thou Art That* and *Mythic Worlds, Modern Words* by following the same method.

CHAPTER 7: SURPRISES AND TRANSFORMATIONS

169. Nels F. S. Ferré, *The Christian Faith* (New York: Harper & Brothers, 1942), p. 211.

170. Joe Lillard was a college friend of Campbell's, and served as the Campbells' accountant.

171. The question mark is Campbell's. This is perhaps a reference to Dōshisha University, the Christian university in Kyoto.

172. It is uncertain whether this was a misspelling on the part of the Japanese proprietors of a lounge evidently known as the "Gas Lamp," Campbell's transcription of a Japanese mispronunciation, or a joke on Campbell's part on the comfort of the establishment.

173. Sarah Lawrence College, not Salt Lake City.

174. *The Christian Faith,* p. 192.

175. This realization represents a clear formulation for an attitude that was to become increasingly dominant in Campbell's later years: the Judeo-Christian complex, with its emphasis on exclusivity, was to be resisted in favor of a democracy of myths. See *The Inner Reaches of Outer Space,* or *Myths to Live By.*

176. Henry van Straelen, *The Religion of Divine Wisdom, Japan's Most Powerful Religious Movement,* Folklore Studies, vol. 13 (Tokyo: Journal of Far Eastern Folklore, 1954).

177. Miki Nakayama (1798–1887) founded the Tenrikyō sect, a monotheistic Shintō movement that believes in creation by the *Oyagami,* the "father *kami.*"

178. "Religion of Divine Wisdom," pp. 1–2.

179. Nels F. S. Ferré, *The Sun and the Umbrella* (New York: Harper & Row, 1953), p. 112.

180. The Buddhist Indian king Aśoka sent missionaries throughout Asia and the Mediterranean. Eidmann is exploring theories that these missionaries had an influence on Judeo-Christian mystic thought.

181. This tale tells of an old woman who promises her bedridden friend that she will bring back a souvenir from a pilgrimage. The woman forgets. On her way back to her village, she remembers, and, knowing her friend is too blind to know the difference, she finds a dog's tooth and presents it to her friend as a relic of the Buddha. The old woman is shocked when her friend's "relic" actually affects cures.

182. "Now when they had gone throughout Phrygia and the region of Galatia, and were forbidden of the Holy Ghost to preach the word in Asia…."

183. John 2:1–10. This famous passage recounts the miracle of Jesus turning water into wine at a wedding. At the end of the wedding "the governor of the feast called the bridegroom,/And saith unto him, Every man at the beginning doth set forth good wine; and when men have well drunk, then that which is worse: but thou hast kept the good wine until now." Campbell interprets the bridegroom—whom the governor addresses as the bringer of the wine—as being Jesus himself.

184. Apollonius of Tyana was a neo-Pythagorian mystic who was a contemporary of Jesus. Campbell never was to write on this subject.

185. This plan would be realized in the company of Mircea Eliade and other friends and colleagues at the 1958 World Congress of Religions, which took place in and around Kyoto.

CHAPTER 8: A VAST AND DIFFICULT QUESTION

186. The Chinese had invaded Tibet in 1949 and annexed it in 1951.

187. In 1929, at the end of a two-year Proudfit Fellowship that allowed him to study in France and Germany, Campbell was contemplating "a trip around the world." Because

of the onset of the Great Depression, he chose to return to the United States. See *A Fire in the Mind,* pp. 111–15.

188. See p. 516.

189. Adda Bozeman was a friend and colleague of Campbell's who taught political science at Sarah Lawrence College.

190. Carl Schuster (1904–69) was an authority on primitive art.

191. John A. Pope was an expert in Asian art and served as the director of the Freer Gallery at the Smithsonian Institution.

192. See n. 161.

193. Heinrich Zimmer, *Philosophies of India,* ed. Joseph Campbell (Princeton, N.J.: Princeton University Press/Bollingen Foundation, 1989).

194. This problem was to emerge as a central concern for Campbell, and is addressed throughout his work. It is the central issue addressed in both *The Inner Reaches of Outer Space* and *Thou Art That.*

195. *The Sun and the Umbrella,* p. 113.

196. In the days following the American bombing of Nagasaki, Emperor Hirohito broke a centuries-old tradition of the emperor remaining silent and aloof from matters of state. He spoke on radio to his people—it was the first time most of them had heard the demi-divine ruler's voice—and told them to prepare for surrender: "the unendurable must be endured." This is the "revolution" to which Campbell is referring.

197. Compare Jung asking "What is my myth?" (*Symbols of Transformation,* foreword, p. xxiv).

198. *The Sun and the Umbrella,* pp. 27–28

199. Hara-kiri is the ritual form of self-evisceration by which a samurai would commit suicide. Campbell seems to mean that the Japanese chose to attack Pearl Harbor, knowing they would lose the war (see p. 523).

200. The Ainu are a Caucasoid aboriginal tribe native to Hokkaido (the northern island of Japan) and Sakhalin Island. See pp. 615–19.

201. Rose Marie was a child radio star in the 1930s, and then a nightclub and Broadway revue performer of the 1940s and 1950s. The style of her shows was bright, broad, and brash, if occasionally sentimental. Rose Marie herself is probably best remembered as Sally Rogers, the wise-cracking writer on television's *The Dick Van Dyke Show.*

202. Campbell indeed accepted this invitation. See pp. 646–48.

203. "The International" is the Communist anthem.

CHAPTER 9: TEMPLE TREASURES

204. Campbell seems to be struggling to reconcile the constraints of traditional cultures and the naiveté of Americans abroad. Campbell admired the "professional" efficiency of the Japanese style of parenting.

205. In Greek and Roman myth, the Titans were pre-Olympian nature gods of brute force. Campbell seems to be using the term to exemplify unintelligent or one-sided fanaticism. Titanism is also defined as unreasoned rebelliousness, the knee-jerk revolt against authority.

206. The Native American Church movement grew out of the Navaho reservations of the American Southwest during the 1940s. It is a quasi-Christian cult that seeks to bring its followers visions of salvation through the ritual use of peyote, a hallucinogenic fungus. Always interested in comparing indigenous traditions, Campbell is thinking of

the peyote cult in relation to Aldous Huxley's discovery of spiritual visions from the peyote-derived hallucinogen mescaline. See Aldous Huxley, *The Doors of Perception* (New York: Harper & Row, 1954).

207. In Buddhist thought, the Tusita Heaven is where the Buddhas-to-be wait to be incarnated in this world.

208. These references are to the so-called "Nanjō Catalogue" of Chinese Buddhist texts, compiled by Bunyū Nanjō (1849–1927).

209. Presumably, scenes from the *Jātaka Tales*, a story cycle that follows the Buddha through his various animal and (finally) human incarnations.

210. It is unclear whether Campbell is referring here to the quality of *Prajñāpāramitā* itself or to the *Prajñāpāramitā Hṛdāya Sūtra*, a Mahāyāna text.

211. *Saddharma Pundarīka* is "The Lotus of the Good Law." Also known as the Lotus *Sūtra*, this Buddhist scripture is believed to have been first written down in India during the first century A.D., although it may have been composed earlier.

212. Bimbisara and Sakka were kings whom the Buddha taught.

213. A tachistoscope is a device used to flash images on a screen for a fraction of a second. It was largely used as a speed-learning tool.

214. Shantineketan is a university near Calcutta. It was founded by the Indian author Rabindranath Tagore.

215. Charles Morris, *The Open Self* (New York: Prentice Hall, 1948).

216. See n. 177.

217. The syncretic Unitarian church developed in America beginning in the Boston area throughout the eighteenth century. By the early nineteenth century, Harvard College was a hotbed of Unitarian thought.

218. Alexander Campbell (1788–1866) founded the Disciples of Christ as an attempt "to unite all Christians as one communion on a purely scriptural basis."

219. Dale L. Morgan, "A Bibliography of the Church of Jesus Christ Organized at Green Oak, Pennsylvania, July, 1862," *Western Humanities Review* 4 (Winter 1949/50): 1–28. Reprinted separately with same title (s.l.: s.n., 1950).

220. Emmanuel Swedenborg (1688–1772) was a noted Swedish scientist and spiritual philosopher. In his later writings, he spoke of the need to found a "new church" in order to create the "New Jerusalem."

221. The Bah'ai faith developed as a reform movement of Islam in the mid-nineteenth century, and has, as Campbell points out, developed as a syncretic World Religion movement in Europe and the Americas in the years since.

222. Brahmo Samaj developed as a monotheistic reform movement in India in 1828. Though it shares some philosophies with Hinduism, it supports neither the worship of idols nor the caste system.

223. Adolph Bastian (1826–1905), a German anthropologist, recognized in the cultures of the world certain recurring motifs. He termed these *Elementargedanken;* the local expressions of these motifs he termed *Völkergedanken.* Like C. G. Jung, Campbell was enormously influenced by Bastian's ideas, and referred to him frequently throughout his work.

224. Miki Nakayama, the founder of the Tenrikyō sect. See pp. 576–79.

225. See above, Book I: Baksheesh & Brahman, pp. 12, 214–17, 222–23, 271, n. 207 (p. 344).

226. Paul Radin, anthropologist, associate of Jung, and Eranos attendee, had presented papers on the Native American Church. After his death in 1959, Campbell wrote the

article, "Primitive Man as Metaphysician" in his honor; this essay appears in *Flight of the Wild Gander*. See Paul Radin, *Primitive Man as Philosopher* (New York and London: D. Appleton and Company, 1927).

227. See p. 542.

228. Jetsun Milarepa (ca. A.D. 1052–1135) was a great Tibetan Buddhist saint. His master, Marpa (Naropa), commanded him to build a house for his (Marpa's) son, if Milarepa was to receive Marpa's teaching. Whenever Milarepa had half completed the house, Marpa would say, "Who told you to build the house there?" and then had Milarepa start over again in another location. Milarepa started houses to the north, south, east, and west of the village, before Marpa finally allowed him to build in the center of the village. Then Marpa began teaching him.

229. See n. 190.

CHAPTER 10: AT THE SEVENTH STEP

230. Ernest Fenellosa was a Harvard-educated professor of philosophy at Tokyo University before becoming the curator of the Imperial Museum of Japan. He returned to Massachusetts, and promoted East Asian art and literature in the United States. His notes on Chinese poetry and Noh drama inspired Ezra Pound and William Butler Yeats.

231. Kakuzō Okakura (1862–1913), in addition to studying with Fenellosa, was the author of several influential books about Japan and East Asian culture. The most famous is *The Book of Tea* (New York: Duffield and Green, 1906).

232. Ed Solomon was the Director of Field Work for Sarah Lawrence College. Off-campus study (the field trips of which Campbell speaks elsewhere) were central to the curriculum at Sarah Lawrence, and Mr. Solomon's job seems to have been to coordinate this aspect of academic life.

233. This book was never written. Pope Joan is supposed to have served as pontiff from A.D. 853 to 855. She disguised her gender and served, first as a priest, then as a prelate, Pope John. Her deception is supposed to have been discovered when she gave birth to a child.

234. A *nāga* is a serpent-demon in the Buddhist and Hindu traditions.

235. These seem to be Japanese formulae of self-effacement.

236. *Nirmānakāya* is the transformation body of the Buddha, while *dharmakāya* is the *dharma,* or truth body. See n. 112.

237. See n. 154.

238. Kōbō Daishi, a.k.a. Kūkai, was born in the eighth century A.D.; a scholar-priest, he studied in China before founding the Shingon sect of Buddhism in Japan. Campbell seems to be saying that, just as many Americans claim to trace their ancestry back to the Mayflower, many shrines and temples have been attributed to Kōbō Daishi, whether legitimately or not.

239. One hundred fifty-six Waverly Place was less than a block away from Campbell's residence in New York City.

240. See pp. 491–93.

241. Oswald Spengler's view of history, laid out in his multivolume *Decline of the West,* suggests that history is made by the doers, rather than the thinkers.

242. John Cage, a friend of the Campbells' and noted avant-garde composer, used Zen to justify various musical techniques such as surprise and silence in his compositions.

243. The Dillinghams are Jean Erdman Campbell's maternal family. Longtime residents of Hawai'i, they were landed, wealthy, and politically conservative.

244. Subsequent observation shows that Zen has spread to America since Campbell's visit, in part through the traditional disciplines of *cha-no-yu* (Tea), the martial arts, and calligraphy.

245. Japanese includes not only different forms of address for those of higher and lower status, but also what amounts to almost different languages for men and women, including, for example, prescribed ways of communicating between a husband and wife.

246. Clearly Campbell means drunk.

247. In Pure Land sects such as Shinshū, true enlightenment is only attained in *Sukhavātī*.

248. Lin Yu-tang (1898–1977) was a Chinese author and man of letters who lived in the United States from 1936 to 1966. He described the growth of wisdom with age thus: "First the sadness and sense of defeat, then the awakening and the laughter of the old rogue-philosopher." *The Importance of Living* (New York: Reynal & Hitchcock/John Day, 1937).

249. The waitress apparently understood Campbell to say *"hambagā,"* which would be a usual way of ordering the hamburger-steak full meal! *Konban wa* is Japanese for "Good evening"; at lunchtime, *konnichi wa* ("good day") would have been more appropriate, which may have exacerbated the misunderstanding.

250. See above, Book I: Baksheesh & Brahman, pp. 99–100.

251. Doña Luisa Coomaraswamy was the widow of the Indian scholar Ananda K. Coomaraswamy. Professor Warner's identity is uncertain.

CHAPTER II: BAKSHEESH REVISITED

252. Jizō is the Boddhisattva who protects children. See p. 435 and n. 63.

253. The Bandung Declaration of 1955 asserted five principles (*pancha sīla*) that included peaceful coexistence among nations and respect for human rights. The *pancha sīla* are also the five basic precepts of a good Buddhist life: to refrain from killing, stealing, lying, wrongful sexual practice (i.e. rape), and alcohol.

254. Campbell's first major published work (coauthored with Henry Morton Robinson) was a gloss of James Joyce's notoriously opaque novel, *Finnegans Wake. A Skeleton Key to Finnegans Wake,* published in 1944, just four years after the publication of Joyce's great work, was a major boon to students, professors, and lay readers alike. Joseph Campbell and Henry Morton Robinson, *A Skeleton Key to Finnegans Wake* (New York: Harcourt Brace, 1944, and Novato, Calif.: New World Library, 2004).

255. Campbell is referring to the Keynsean social theorists who instituted the"New Deal" economics of the welfare state in the U.S. and were attempting to reproduce (or improve) that model in Japan.

256. See above, Book I: Baksheesh & Brahman, pp. 201–23, 254–62.

257. The Sarabhais were vegetarians.

258. Sarvepalli Radhakrishnan (1888–1975) was the vice president of India at the time of Campbell's visit. He later served as president. He was also a well-known Hindu philosopher. See above, Book I: Baksheesh & Brahman.

259. See p. 569.

260. Getas are thonged sandals, usually with wooden blocks to raise the wearer above the mud.

261. These three Bodhisattvas are Gautama Śākyamuni (the historical Buddha), Maitreya (the Buddha-to-come), and Mañjuśrī (a *Prajñāpāramitā* Buddha).

262. In Zen, these visitations are called *makyō,* and precede the experience of *kenshō,* or enlightenment.

263. In Greek mythology, the *Symplegades* were two floating cliffs that swung together and crushed anything going between them, until Jason's ship, the *Argo,* passed safely through them. They remained still forever after, forming the entrance to the Black Sea. Campbell often used them (and Scylla and Charybdis) as mythological illustrations of the idea of the dualistic world-of-opposites.

264. Campbell is likely referring to the Seven Gods of Luck (*Shichifukujin*) of Japanese folk mythology. (One of the seven gods—Benten—is actually a goddess, a folk variation on Kuan-yin.)

265. Konpon Chūdō actually means simply "central hall."

266. See pp. 488–93.

267. One Japanese *ri* = 2.44 miles.

268. Campbell discovered that his edition of Heinrich Zimmer's *Philosophies of India* had been plagiarized in an Indian newspaper. See above, Book I: Baksheesh & Brahman, p. 77.

269. Heinrich Zimmer, *The King and the Corpse,* ed. Joseph Campbell (Princeton, N.J.: Bollingen Foundation/Princeton University Press, 1993).

270. Lafcadio Hearn, an American writer, arrived in Japan in 1890, and stayed for the rest of his life. He was the author of *Japan: An Attempt at Interpretation* (New York: Grosset & Dunlap, 1904)—Campbell's copy was heavily annotated— and *Tokyo and Kokoro: Hints and Echoes of Japanese Inner Life* (Boston and New York: Houghton Mifflin Co., 1896).

CHAPTER 12: PENELOPE RETURNS

271. T. E. Hulme (1883–1917) was a British aesthetician, and cofounder (with Herbert Read) of the Imagist movement. Read edited Hulme's *Speculations* in 1924.

272. Campbell was unable to carry out either of these vigorous resolves. He did not renew the study of Japanese, though he retained into his later years a great deal of what he had learned in Kyoto, continuing to read and write Japanese. "Joe's Friendly Service" went on for decades as he continued to help friends and younger scholars with their projects.

273. Josip Broz Tito (1898–1980) was the president of Communist (but nonaligned) Yugoslavia from 1945 to his death.

274. To this day the Ise Peninsula remains off the tourist route, though it is a frequent destination for Japanese pilgrimages. Few signs are in *rōmaji* and fewer people speak English than in Tokyo or the Kyoto-Nara region.

275. "I am sorry (to have disturbed you)."

276. Amaterasu, the Sun Goddess, is the most important deity in the Shintō religion. It is her emblem that gives Japan its flag.

277. The koto is a long stringed instrument that lies flat on the ground.

278. In the Shintō tradition, the first wedded couple in the age of the gods (the seventh generation of deities). They gave birth to the terrestrial regions (Ōyashimaguni), mountains, rivers, seas, plants, animals, and men, and became the gods of the earth and of all things on earth. The three most important deities born to Izanagi and Izanami are Amaterasu Ōmikami (the Sun Goddess), Susanoo no Mikoto, and Tsukiyomi no Mikoto.

279. Campbell is here referring to his 1932 trip up the inland waterway to Juneau, Alaska with the biologist Ed Ricketts. (See *A Fire in the Mind,* pp. 200–9.)

280. Benkei was a warrior-priest of the twelfth century who figures in Noh, Kabuki, and Bunraku plays; this particular play is called *Kanjinchō,* and it involves the warrior Yoshitsune's attempt to escape capture by his half-brother, Yoritomo. Yoshitsune flees disguised as a porter of Benkei, his loyal retainer. At a checkpoint, Benkei's resourcefulness and profound loyalty to Yoshitsune make it possible for the company to pass through, and at the end of the play Benkei expresses his joy in a famous exit scene.

281. The Ainu—the early inhabitants of the islands of Hokkaido and Sakhalin—are a Caucasoid race with abundant body hair, not found on most other Asian ethnic groups. This has led to much speculation about their origins. Their culture is characterized by archaic rituals of bear worship that seem to date back to the Paleolithic era.

282. Tom and Elizabeth Penning had a large quarry pool behind their Woodstock, New York, home. During the 1930s and 1940s there were nude swimming parties in the pool.

283. See n. 167 and *Atlas,* vol. 2, part 1, pp. 68–69.

284. Campbell was to follow through with this resolve in both *The Masks of God* and *The Historical Atlas of World Mythology: The Way of the Animal Powers,* as well as in numerous lectures.

285. Malekula is an island in the South Pacific nation of Vanuatu. The primitive islanders created elaborate stone labyrinths, representing ritual descent into the underworld. See *Primitive Mythology,* pp. 444–551.

286. Women performing in Kabuki was an innovation. The women in this troupe were relative newcomers to the art, so Campbell was not surprised that they lacked the technical skills of their male peers, who had trained since boyhood.

287. Teiji Itō, a Japanese-born musician and friend of the Campbells, often performed in Ms. Erdman's dance and theatre productions. His brother evidently directed this production.

CHAPTER 13: CLOSING THE CIRCLE

288. Sabro Hasegawa (1906–57) was a Japanese modern artist who studied extensively in the West during the 1920s and 1930s and attempted to combine Western abstraction with Japanese traditional forms. He returned to his country to paint in 1937, but was detained during World War II for refusing to paint patriotic themes. He moved to San Francisco in 1956, became acquainted with Alan Watts, and died in 1957, just two years after meeting Campbell.

289. A *yukata* is an unlined cotton kimono used as bath/summer wear.

290. Motokiyo Zeami (1364–1443) was a playwright and one of the originators of the Noh form of theater.

291. Matsuo Bashō (1644–94) is generally considered to be the pioneer (and master) of the modern haiku. Haiku is a seventeen-syllable, three-line poem strongly associated with Zen.

292. Isamu Noguchi, a sculptor, was a contemporary and friend of Campbell's. Alan Watts, author/philosopher, and John Cage, composer, we have met before; we will meet Watts again soon.

293. The 8th Street Artists' Club was started by painter Robert Motherwell in 1948. The Campbells would become increasingly involved with the club through the next few years.

294. *Densha* is Japanese for "train."

295. See pp. 464–65.

296. See p. 653.

297. See n. 231.

298. This would appear to be Eleanor Roosevelt, President Franklin Roosevelt's widow and U.N. delegate, rather than Mrs. Quentin Roosevelt (a distant cousin) with whom Campbell had traveled in Thailand.

299. These are percussion instruments with "fish mouths" that make a gonglike sound when struck.

300. Pan-American Airways.

301. Campbell's parents had moved to Honolulu in the early 1940s. Jean was native to Hawai'i. Alice is Campbell's sister and Anne her daughter. Marion Dillingham Erdman was Jean's mother, and Da (Dorothy) and Louie (Louise) were Jean's sisters. In 1955, Mānoa was a village above Honolulu; it is now part of the city proper, and the site of the flagship campus of the University of Hawai'i.

302. René d'Harnoncourt was a former colleague of Campbell's at Sarah Lawrence. He later left Hawai'i to take a curatorial job at the Museum of Modern Art in New York City.

303. Thor Heyerdahl's *Kon-Tiki: Across the Pacific by Raft* (New York: Washington Square Press, 1995) explored the idea that trans-Pacific travel could have been achieved by early sailors. Campbell was to expound on some of these ideas in his essay "Mythogenisis," which can be found in *Flight of the Wild Gander*.

304. Jean's maternal uncle and his family.

305. F. Matthias Alexander (1869–1955), an Australian actor who wished to use his body more efficiently, developed the so-called Alexander Technique in the late nineteenth century. It is very popular among actors, dancers, musicians, and athletes. One of the trademarks of the technique is a lengthening of the neck and spine; this creates optimal relaxation and flexibility of the practitioner, but also increases their apparent stature and status.

306. Feuerring had given Campbell references to several contacts in Kyoto, most notably Phillip Eidmann. See pp. 434, 444.

307. Jeffie Fairbanks was the son of Marjory "Bargie" Erdman Fairbanks, Jean's sister. He was stricken at the age of two and a half (not long before this visit) with a form of paralysis. He lived to the age of twenty-six.

308. See pp. 488–93.

309. A Broadway hit of the previous year, and little theater staple for some years to come, *Oh, Men! Oh, Women!* was described in its publicity as "an hilarious lampoon of sex and psychiatry." The discussion of psychoanalysis that follows was clearly sparked by the play.

310. Erich Fromm (1900–80) was a psychiatrist, lecturer, and author of scholarly and popular books on psychology.

311. Alice Campbell Lenning was Campbell's younger sister, and was probably the sibling to whom he had been the closest as a young man. A sculptor, she and Campbell had

shared a cottage in Woodstock, New York, in the early years of the Depression. She had moved to Hawai'i before the beginning of World War II.

312. The Alexanders were old friends of the Campbells'. Doyle Alexander worked with Campbell's father in the hosiery business.

313. The meaning of this last sentence is obscure; we assume that Campbell's sister was working for a company called American Factor.

314. See p. 613.

315. Jean's sister Dorothy's children.

316. Campbell worked as an assistant to famed marine biologist Ed Ricketts (the real-life inspiration for the hero in John Steinbeck's novel *Cannery Row*) in 1932. See n. 279 above.

317. Alan Watts's second wife. At this writing, one of the "cute children," Mark Watts, serves as the Joseph Campbell Foundation's Media Director.

318. *Wuwei* is a Chinese Taoist term meaning "non-action" or "letting be." *Sahaja* is a Sanskrit word meaning "easy" or "spontaneous," used to describe a Tantric ritual of sexual union. See above, Book I: Baksheesh & Brahman, pp. 130, 359.

319. These are the Dead Sea Scrolls. Though the first of these scrolls had been famously discovered by a Bedouin goatherd in 1947, new excavations at Qumran had uncovered more scrolls in 1955. For Campbell's views on these manuscripts, see *Thou Art That*, pp. 47, 69–70.

320. Maud Oakes was the author and researcher of *Where the Two Came to Their Father: A Navaho War Ceremonial Given by Jeff King*, originally published in 1943, for which Campbell had written the introduction and running commentary (Princeton, N.J.: Princeton University Press/Bollingen Foundation, 1991).

321. Joseph Campbell (1879–1944) was a Northern Irish poet. His best-known work is *The Mountainy Singer* (1909; New York: AMS Press, 1981).

322. A kōan is a paradox for Zen meditation (i.e., "What is the sound of one hand clapping?"). Both the *Poetic* and *Prose Eddas* contain riddle contests—battles of wits. In one famous contest, Wotan, the Norse king of the gods, defeats a giant by asking him, "What did Wotan whisper in the ear of his son on the funeral pyre."

APPENDIX IIB: THE NATURE WAY

1. This article is drawn from an audio recording of a lecture given by Campbell in 1963 on New York's public television station, WNET, as part of a series entitled *Mask, Myth & Dream*. Originally entitled "The Way of Tea," it is listed as L80 in The Joseph Campbell Foundation audio archive.

2. This is the *Avataṃsaka Sūtra*, which is central to the Kegon and Shingon sects.

3. See n. 62.

4. This is a translation of the Tantric mantra *"Om mani padme hum."*

5. See n. 107.

6. "For this is my body." This transformative phrase from the Mass itself transformed into the stage magician's "hocus pocus."

7. This haiku is by the poet Ōshima Ryōta (1718–87).

8. This is Campbell's free translation from Dōgen's "Busshō" (Buddha Nature), a fascicle of his *Shōbōgenzō*.

GLOSSARY OF JAPANESE TERMS

Amaterasu Ōmikami: Sun Goddess, most important deity in Shintō pantheon; born of Izanagi and Izanami

amazake: sweetened alcoholic beverage made from fermented rice

Asakusa: bustling entertainment and mercantile section of central Tokyo

Azuma Odori: begun in the early twentieth century as a vehicle for showcasing the artistry of geisha, annual dance performance presented at Shimbashi Enbujō, Tokyo, in spring

Benkei: twelfth-century warrior-priest, loyal retainer to Minamoto Yoshitsune; heroism dramatized in Japanese theatre arts

Bon: Buddhist summer festival for the dead marked by special dances and a lantern-floating ceremony

bugaku: highly stylized courtly dance form introduced from China during the T'ang dynasty

Bunraku: puppet theatre with origins in the sixteenth century, characterized by stylized recitation, samisen music, and large puppets worked by three operators dressed in black

Bushidō: "Way of the Warrior," feudal-military code of chivalry

Daibutsu-den: seventeenth-century wood structure housing world's largest Buddha at Tōdaiji Temple in Nara

Dengyō Daishi (767–822): founder of Tendai sect (q.v.) of Buddhism in Japan with seat at Enryakuji Temple on Mt. Hiei near Kyoto

Enō (638–713): Hui-neng in Chinese, sixth patriarch of Zen Buddhism whose teachings emphasized "sudden enlightenment," or satori; author of the Platform *Sūtra*

Fudō Myō-ō: God of Fire, usually portrayed with a sword in his right hand and a coiled rope in his left and surrounded by flames

Gakkō: "sunlight" Bodhisattva of Yakushi Nyorai triad housed in Yakushiji Temple (q.v.) in Nara

geisha: "person of the arts," professional female entertainers trained in the traditional arts who entertain guests at teahouses, restaurants, inns, etc.; once widespread but now concentrated mainly in the Gion district of Kyoto and in Tokyo

gekū: "outer shrine," particularly of Ise Shrine near Nara

gengaku: music of traditional stringed instruments

geta: thonged wood clogs for outdoor wear

Go: board game originating in China, using round, black and white pieces and a wooden, grid-pattern playing board

gohei: white paper or cloth strips attached to a stick and offered to a deity at a Shintō shrine

goma: Buddhist fire ritual of purification with origins in ancient India

Hannyaji Temple: dating from the Asuka period (593–710), temple in Nara known for its thirteen-story stone pagoda, the tallest in Japan

hara-kiri: ritual suicide practiced by samurai involving self-disembowelment

Hiei: mountain near Kyoto, site of Enryakuji Temple, head temple of the Tendai sect (q.v.), founded by Dengyō Daishi in 788, and important spiritual and cultural center for nearly a thousand years

Higashi Honganji Temple: branch temple of Nishi Honganji Temple (q.v.) in Kyoto, built in 1602

hinokishin: selfless acts of gratitude performed daily by Tenrikyō (q.v.) followers as an expression of their joy at being alive

hiragana: set of cursive syllabic script containing forty-six symbols that comprises, with kanji (q.v.) and katakana (q.v.), the Japanese writing system

hondō: main building or hall of a Buddhist temple

Hōryūji: seventh-century temple near Nara, whose main hall, built in 680, is said to be the oldest wooden structure in the world

Inari: fox deity

Ippen Shōnin (1239–89): established in 1273 the Jishū sect of Pure Land Buddhism

Ise ondo: folk dance of Ise in which dancers beat rhythm with wooden sticks

Jishū: sect of Pure Land Buddhism established by Ippen Shōnin in 1273

Jizō-bosatsu: guardian deity of children

Jōchō (d. 1057): considered to be one of the greatest sculptors of the late Heian period, who devised a multi-block system of sculpting that allowed for larger, more varied images

Jōdo-in: temple on Mt. Hiei housing the tomb of Dengyō Daishi, founder of Enryakuji Temple, who died in 822

Jōdo Shinshū: Pure Land sect founded in 1224 by Shinran (1173–1262)

Jūrin-in Temple: temple in Nara whose main hall houses an unusual stone image of Jizō-bosatsu

Kabuki: popular theatrical art form that developed in the sixteenth and seventeenth centuries; marked by spectacular stage action, highly stylized dancing, singing, and costumes

kakemono: ornamental pictorial or calligraphic hanging scroll

Kamigamo Shrine: established in 678, one of Kyoto's oldest Shintō shrines and famous for the Aoi Festival held annually in May

kanji: Chinese ideographs used in Japanese writing

Kannon: Goddess of Mercy; Chinese Kuan-yin, Sanskrit Avalokiteśvara

Kasuga Shrine: located in Nara, the main structure was built in 768; features famous Noh stage constructed in the nineteenth century

katakana: set of angular syllabic script containing forty-six symbols that comprises, with kanji (q.v.) and hiragana (q.v.), Japanese writing system

Kenshin Daishi: *see* Shinran Shōnin

kōan: paradox for meditation used in Zen Buddhist training to discourage dependence on reason and encourage intuitive enlightenment

Kōbō Daishi (774–835): also known as Kūkai, founder of Shingon sect of Buddhism, established a monastery on Mt. Kōya in 816

Kobori Enshū (1579–1647): grand tea master and official instructor to Tokugawa shōguns

kōdō: assembly or lecture hall in a Buddhist temple

Kōfukuji Temple: established in 710, famous for its fifteenth-century five-storied pagoda, symbol of Nara

kondō: main hall of a Buddhist temple

koto: thirteen-stringed zither-like instrument with an elongated wood body; placed horizontally on the floor and plucked

Kudara Kannon: carved of camphor wood, statue of Kannon housed in a hall on the grounds of Hōryūji (q.v.), near Nara; said to be of seventh century and perhaps from the ancient Korean kingdom of Kudara

Mantō-e: Festival of Ten Thousand Lights, part of summer Bon (q.v.) ceremonies

Mibu-dera Temple: established in Kyoto in 991, setting for famous spring Mibu-Ky_gen (q.v.)

Mibu-Kyōgen: comic Buddhist pantomime originating at Mibu-dera Temple (q.v.) in Kyoto sometime in the twelfth century, portrays teachings of the Buddha; presented annually in the spring

Miroku: Japanese name for Maitreya

Monju: Japanese name for Mañjusri, Bodhisattva of wisdom and knowledge

myōkōnin: "wondrous good people," a devotee of the Shin Buddhist tradition who has reached and lives in a state of awakened faith

naikū: "inner shrine," particularly that of Ise Shrine near Nara

Namu Amida-butsu: "I take refuge in Amida Buddha," Jōdo Shinshū (q.v.) invocation expressing total faith in and reliance on Amida Buddha

Nanzenji Temple: Rinzai-sect (q.v.) Zen temple established in Kyoto in 1291

nembutsu: repeated invocation to Amitābha

Nikkō: "moonlight" Bodhisattva of Yakushi Nyorai triad housed in Yakushiji Temple (q.v.) in Nara

Nisei: "second generation," usually U.S.-born son or daughter of Japanese immigrants

Nishi Honganji Temple: Kyoto headquarters of Jōdo Shinshū (q.v.) sect, founded in late-thirteenth century by daughter of Shinran, sect's founder; noted for its ancient Noh stage and characteristic Momoyama-style architecture

Noh: theatrical art form that arose in the fourteenth century and features chorus, drums, flute, and highly stylized dance

o-bentō: box lunch

obi: broad silk sash worn with kimono

Oda Nobunaga (1534–82): military commander who united most of Japan under his rule

Omote-senke: leading school of tea ceremony founded in sixteenth century by tea master Sen no Rikyū (q.v.)

oyako-donburi: chicken and egg dish served in bowl over rice

Rinzai sect: Chinese Zen sect transmitted to Japan in the fourteenth century; emphasizes use of the kōan (q.v.) and the attainment of sudden enlightenment

rōmaji: Roman letters used in transliteration of Japanese

rōshi: "venerable master," title of respect in reference to a Zen cleric

Ryōanji: Kyoto temple founded in 1450, well-known for its rock garden

sake: alcoholic beverage made from fermented rice

samisen: three-stringed banjolike instrument played by plucking

sammon: two-storied Buddhist temple gate

-san: suffix used with personal name as a form of address

satori: experience of spiritual awakening

seishin-teki: mental, spiritual

sencha: green tea

Senju Kannon: thousand-armed Kannon

Sen no Rikyū (1522–91): tea master whose style of tea ceremony gave rise to the three great traditions of tea: Omote-senke, Ura-senke, and Mushanokōji-senke

sensei: teacher or master

shajitsu: objective, realistic

Shaka Nyorai: represents the historical Buddha, Siddhartha Gautama

shakuhachi: five-hole vertically held bamboo flutelike instrument

shasei: sketch

shimenawa: rope of twisted straw hung with strips of white paper used to mark off a sacred area

Shimogamo Shrine: built in the eighth century, one of Kyoto's oldest shrines and well-known in association with the Aoi Festival held annually in May

Shingon sect: esoteric "True Word" form of Buddhism established in Japan on Mt. Kōya by Kōbō Daishi (Kūkai) (774–835)

Shinran Shōnin (Kenshin Daishi) (1173–1263): founder in 1224 of Jōdo Shinshū

Shinshū: *see* Jōdo Shinshū

Shinyakushiji Temple: eighth-century temple in Nara whose main hall houses a statue of Yakushi Nyorai, the Buddha of Healing

shō: mouth instrument made of generally seventeen bamboo pipes and fifteen reeds set circularly in a wooden wind chamber

shōgun: feudal military ruler during twelfth to nineteenth centuries

Shōsōin Treasure House: of Tōdaiji Temple (q.v.), in Nara, constructed in the mid-eighth century, it holds thousands of precious objects dating to the seventh and eighth centuries

Shūgakuin Detached Palace: built in 1659 as imperial villa by Tokugawa shōgun, north of Kyoto

sōdō: meditation hall at a Zen temple

Sōtō sect: brought by Dōgen (1200–53) from China, Sōtō emphasizes sitting in meditation without expectation, with faith in one's intrinsic state of enlightenment

sumō: ritualized, ancient form of wrestling in which object is to force opponent out of a ring or to touch the floor of the ring with any part of the body except the bottom of the feet

Tahō Nyorai: Buddha of Abundant Treasures

Takarazuka: all-women revue troupe based in Takarazuka, near Osaka; first performance was in 1914

takuan: salt-pickled white radish eaten as a garnish

tatami: mats made of tightly woven rice straw and used as flooring in traditional Japanese-style rooms

Tendai sect: Chinese school of Buddhism centered on study of the Lotus *Sūtra;* teaching taken to Japan by Dengyō Daishi (767–822)

Tenrikyō: Shintō cult founded by Nakayama Miki (1789–1887) in 1838; based in Tenri, near Nara

Tōdaiji Temple: temple complex in Nara, built in the year 743; its best-known relic, the Daibutsu, is the world's largest gilded-bronze Buddha, housed in a wood building, the Daibutsu-den, which is the largest wooden building in the world

Tokugawa Ieyasu (1542–1616): warrior and national leader, he was founder of the Tokugawa shōgunate

torii: gateway consisting generally of two vertical pillars topped by two horizontal beams, usually painted vermilion, marking the entrance to a Shintō shrine

Tōshōdaiji Temple: built in Nara in 759 by Ganjin, Buddhist priest from T'ang-dynasty China

Toyotomi Hideyoshi (1536–98): warrior and leader who, by 1590, had become ruler of a unified Japan

Toyouke Ōmikami: Shintō goddess of agriculture

tsuyu: season of summer rains

Ura-senke: leading school of tea ceremony founded in sixteenth century by tea master Sen no Rikyū

Yabu-no-uchi: style of tea ceremony established by Yabunouchi Kenchū Jōchi (1536–1627), who advocated a return to the original principles of tea, emphasizing simplicity and aesthetics

Yakushiji Temple: built in Nara in 680; the east pagoda, dating from 730, has remained sound through the centuries

yamabushi: "mountain hermit," wandering ascetics who practiced austerities and cultivated magical powers

Yasaka Shrine: located in the Gion area of Kyoto and famous for its central part in the annual mid-July Gion Festival, its main building dates to 1654

yōkigurashi: "joyous life," basic tenet of Tenrikyō that teaches helping others leads to an actualization of a cheerful life

yudōfu: tōfu simmered in a rich seaweed-based stock and eaten with a soy dipping sauce

yukata: unlined cotton bath/summer kimono

BOOK II ACKNOWLEDGMENTS

None of the work on *Sake & Satori* would have been possible without the generous and unswerving aid of Jean Erdman Campbell, who as muse to Joseph Campbell begot these diaries, and as president of the Joseph Campbell Foundation at the time of this edition's conception in 1993, was midwife to their production. Jean was also available to help our search for detail, by reminiscing about a time, now almost fifty years ago, when these events unfolded.

Antony Van Couvering was the publishing director for the Joseph Campbell Foundation and managing editor of the Collected Works of Joseph Campbell at the time that the Asian Journals project was conceived and was centrally involved in the tasks of transcribing and editing both volumes of this series. His work is evident on every page of this work.

Robin and Stephen Larsen participated in editing these journals when it was still intended that they be published as a single volume. Their insight into these journals and into Campbell's life makes itself felt everywhere in this volume, particularly in the biographical footnotes.

John David Ebert lent his voluminous knowledge of Campbell's oeuvre to providing many of the endnotes.

Mike Ashby supervised and rationalized the transliteration of Japanese words and names and lent his knowledge of Japanese culture and customs. He also marked, edited, and checked the manuscript for errors and assembled the glossary.

Carol Pentleton drew the illustrations from Campbell's original doodles.

This book would have been impossible without the following good samaritans: Kazuaki Tanahashi (Sōtō information); Maureen Vaughn (Internet access); and James F. Vaughn, Jr. (photographic equipment).

And the associates of the Joseph Campbell Foundation shared their astonishing, eclectic breadth and depth of knowledge, answering questions of quotation attribution, Buddhist metaphysics, and Indian history through the Conversations of a Higher Order on the JCF Web site (www.jcf.org/forum/).

A JOSEPH CAMPBELL BIBLIOGRAPHY

Following are the major books authored and edited by Joseph Campbell. Each entry gives bibliographic data concerning the first edition or, if applicable, the original date of publication along with the bibliographic data for the edition published by New World Library as part of the Collected Works of Joseph Campbell. For information concerning all other editions, please refer to the Complete Works of Joseph Campbell on the Joseph Campbell Foundation website (www.jcf.org).

AUTHOR

Where the Two Came to Their Father: A Navaho War Ceremonial Given by Jeff King. Bollingen Series I. With Maud Oakes and Jeff King. Richmond, VA: Old Dominion Foundation, 1943.

A Skeleton Key to Finnegans Wake: Unlocking James Joyce's Masterwork. With Henry Morton Robinson. 1944. Second edition, Novato, CA: New World Library, 2005.*

The Hero with a Thousand Faces. Bollingen Series xvii. 1949. Third edition, Novato, CA: New World Library, 2008.*

The Masks of God, 4 vols. New York: Viking Press, 1959–1968. Vol. 1, *Primitive Mythology,* 1959. Vol. 2, *Oriental Mythology,* 1962. Vol. 3, *Occidental Mythology,* 1964. Vol. 4, *Creative Mythology,* 1968.

The Flight of the Wild Gander: Explorations in the Mythological Dimension—Selected Essays 1944–1968. 1969. Third edition, Novato, CA: New World Library, 2002.*

Myths to Live By. 1972. Ebook edition, San Anselmo, CA: Joseph Campbell Foundation, 2011.

The Mythic Image. Bollingen Series c. Princeton, NJ: Princeton University Press, 1974.

The Inner Reaches of Outer Space: Metaphor as Myth and as Religion. 1986. Reprint, Novato, CA: New World Library, 2002.*

The Historical Atlas of World Mythology:

Vol. 1, *The Way of the Animal Powers.* New York: Alfred van der Marck Editions, 1983. Reprint in 2 pts. Part 1, *Mythologies of the Primitive Hunters and Gatherers.* New York: Alfred van der Marck Editions, 1988. Part 2, *Mythologies of the Great Hunt.* New York: Alfred van der Marck Editions, 1988.

Vol. 2, *The Way of the Seeded Earth*, 3 pts. Part 1, *The Sacrifice.* New York: Alfred van der Marck Editions, 1988. Part 2, *Mythologies of the Primitive Planters: The Northern Americas.* New York: Harper & Row Perennial Library, 1989. Part 3, *Mythologies of the Primitive Planters: The Middle and Southern Americas.* New York: Harper & Row Perennial Library, 1989.

The Power of Myth with Bill Moyers. With Bill Moyers. Edited by Betty Sue Flowers. New York: Doubleday, 1988.

Transformations of Myth Through Time. New York: Harper & Row, 1990.

The Hero's Journey: Joseph Campbell on His Life and Work. Edited by Phil Cousineau. 1990. Reprint, Novato, CA: New World Library, 2003.*

Reflections on the Art of Living: A Joseph Campbell Companion. Edited by Diane K. Osbon. New York: HarperCollins, 1991.

Mythic Worlds, Modern Words: On the Art of James Joyce. Edited by Edmund L. Epstein. 1993. Second edition, Novato, CA: New World Library, 2003.*

Baksheesh & Brahman: Asian Journals—India. Edited by Robin Larsen, Stephen Larsen, and Antony Van Couvering. 1995. Second edition, Novato, CA: New World Library, 2002.* [Reissued in paperback, together with *Sake & Satori*, in 2017; see *Asian Journals* entry below.]

The Mythic Dimension: Selected Essays 1959–1987. Edited by Antony Van Couvering. 1997. Second edition, Novato, CA: New World Library, 2007.*

Thou Art That. Edited by Eugene Kennedy. Novato, CA: New World Library, 2001.*

Sake & Satori: Asian Journals—Japan. Edited by David Kudler. Novato, CA: New World Library, 2002.* [Reissued in paperback, together with *Baksheesh & Brahman,* in 2017; see *Asian Journals* entry below.]

Myths of Light. Edited by David Kudler. Novato, CA: New World Library, 2003.*

Pathways to Bliss: Mythology and Personal Transformation. Ed. David Kudler. Novato, Calif.: New World Library, 2004.*

Mythic Imagination: Collected Short Fiction. Novato, CA: New World Library, 2012.*

Goddesses: Mysteries of the Feminine Divine. Edited by Safron Rossi. Novato, CA: New World Library, 2013.*

Romance of the Grail: The Magic and Mystery of Arthurian Myth. Edited by Evans Lansing Smith. Novato, CA: New World Library, 2015.*

Asian Journals: India and Japan. Combined paperback reissue of *Baksheesh & Brahman* and *Sake & Satori.* Book I: Baksheesh & Brahman — edited by Robin Larsen, Stephen Larsen, and Antony Van Couvering; book II: Sake & Satori — edited by David Kudler. Novato, CA: New World Library, 2017.*

*   Published by New World Library as part of the Collected Works of Joseph Campbell.

EDITOR

Books edited and completed from the posthuma of Heinrich Zimmer:

Myths and Symbols in Indian Art and Civilization. Bollingen Series vi. New York: Pantheon, 1946.

The King and the Corpse. Bollingen Series xi. New York: Pantheon, 1948.

Philosophies of India. Bollingen Series xxvi. New York: Pantheon, 1951.

The Art of Indian Asia. Bollingen Series xxxix, 2 vols. New York: Pantheon, 1955.

Other books edited:

The Portable Arabian Nights. New York: Viking Press, 1951.

Papers from the Eranos Yearbooks. Bollingen Series xxx, 6 vols. Edited with

R. F. C. Hull and Olga Froebe-Kapteyn. Translated by Ralph Manheim. Princeton: Princeton University Press, 1954–1969.

Myth, Dreams and Religion: Eleven Visions of Connection. New York: E. P. Dutton, 1970.

The Portable Jung. By C. G. Jung. Translated by R. F. C. Hull. New York: Viking Press, 1971.

My Life and Lives. By Rato Khyongla Nawang Losang. New York: E. P. Dutton, 1977.

INDEX

Page references in italics indicate illustrations or material contained in their captions.

multiple bodies doctrine in, 467;
Oriental magic/religious principles
and, 604; Shinshū vs., 668n54; as spiritualistic, 585; as superstitious, 482;
temples, 462, 592, 625, 686; Tibetan
Buddhist traditions of, 671n98; Zen
vs., 590, 592
Ten-ichi restaurant (Tokyo, Japan), 424
Tenri Honmichi, 578
Tenri/Tenrikyō, 545; beliefs/practices of,
581–83, 676n177, 686, 689; Campbell's
correspondence with, 560; Campbell's
overnight in guest house of, 578–79,
581; foundress of, 514, 577, 676n177,
689; grounds of, 583–84; Jōdo/Shinshū
influences on, 546; publications of,
583; service at, 581; subsidiary
churches, 583; temple of, 576–77, 577,
583
Ten Thousand Lights Festival (Tōdaiji
Temple, Nara, Japan), 439, 441–42,
669n71, 687
Terry, Walter, 235
textile industry, 587
Thai Airways, 392, 401
Thailand: American tourists in, 380;
arhats in, 453; Buddhism in, 395;
Campbell's impressions of, 391–92;
Communism absent in, 375, 392; India
compared to, 378, 385–86, 391–92; leprosy colony in, 387, 388–89; name
change of, 663n2 (ch. 1); as SEATO
member, 348n272, 664n15; train travel
in, 385
Thakin Kodaw Hmaing, 394, 666n30
Theatre Unit. *See* Bombay Theatre Unit
Theatre Unit Bulletin, 174, 190, 196, 198,
253
Theodosius II, 333n71
Theosophical Society, 64, 65, 347n256
Theosophy, 4, 169, 180, 184–85, 188, 241,
335n110, 674n152
Thera, Bhikkhu Narada, 476
Theravāda Buddhism, 459, 476, 499, 500,
669n79, 670n88, 673n126, 673n128. *See
also* Hīnayāna Buddhism
Thomas, Gospel of, 328n9

Thomas, Saint, 108, 116, 285
Thomas Aquinas, Saint, 506, 675n165
Thompson, Virgil, 282, 293
Thorndike, Sybil, 253
Thou Art That (Campbell), 675n168,
677n194, 684n319
Three Bodies doctrine, 466–67
Thuparama (Polonnaruva, Ceylon), 372
Thuparama Dagaba (Anuradhapura,
Ceylon), 371
Tibet, 401, 460, 519, 676n186
Tibetan Buddhism, 467, 497, 671nn97–98,
672n109, 672n112, 674n141, 679n228
Tibetans, 97
tiger and goats, fable of, 323–24
Tiger Hill (Darjeeling, India), 97–98, 99
Time and Eternity (Coomaraswamy), 47
Time magazine, 157, 261, 469–70, 475, 647
Times of India, 132–33, 158, 159–60, 281
Times of India Illustrated Weekly, 269
Tīn Thal (Cave XII; Elūrā, India), 137
tirthankaras, 469
Titanism, 532, 549, 606, 644, 677n205
Tito, Josip Broz, 608, 681n273
Toba (Japan), 609, 610–11
Tōdaiji Temple (Nara, Japan): belfry at,
440, 440; Campbell visits to, 439–42,
478, 564–65; Daibutsu, *439*, 439,
564–65, *565*, 657, 685; dance perform-
ance at, 623; former reception hall
(destroyed), 632; history of, 689; as
Kegon temple, 626; monks at, 631–32;
Nigatsu-dō, 441; Sangatsu-dō, 440–41;
Shōsōin Treasure House, 441, 688; Ten
Thousand Lights Festival at, 439,
441–42
Tokugawa Ieyasu, 446n, 689
Tokugawa period, 554–55, 628, 652, 661,
687, 688
Tokyo (Japan): Asakusa district, 685;
Buddhist temple service in, 430–32;
Bunraku theater in, 611, 614;
Campbell's arrival in, 407–8, 611;
Campbell's conversations while in,
426–27, 611, 621–22; Campbell's depar-
ture from, 639; Campbell's Japanese
language studies in, 425, 611, 622, 639;

ABOUT THE AUTHOR

JOSEPH CAMPBELL was an American author and teacher best known for his work in the field of comparative mythology. He was born in New York City in 1904, and in early childhood became interested in mythology. He loved to read books about American Indian cultures and frequently visited the American Museum of Natural History in New York, where he was fascinated by the museum's collection of totem poles. Campbell was educated at Columbia University, where he specialized in medieval literature, and, after earning a master's degree, continued his studies at universities in Paris and Munich. While abroad he was influenced by the art of Pablo Picasso and Henri Matisse, the novels of James Joyce and Thomas Mann, and the psychological studies of Sigmund Freud and Carl Jung. These encounters led to Campbell's theory that all myths and epics are linked in the human psyche, and that they are cultural manifestations of the universal need to explain social, cosmological, and spiritual realities.

After a period in California, where he encountered John Steinbeck and the biologist Ed Ricketts, Campbell taught at the Canterbury School, and then, in 1934, joined the literature department at Sarah Lawrence College, a post he retained for many years. During the 1940s and '50s, he helped Swami Nikhilananda to translate the Upaniṣads and *The Gospel of Sri Ramakrishna*. He also edited works by the German scholar Heinrich Zimmer on Indian art, myths, and philosophy.

In 1944, with Henry Morton Robinson, Campbell published *A*

Skeleton Key to Finnegans Wake. His first original work, *The Hero with a Thousand Faces,* came out in 1949 and was immediately well received; in time, it became acclaimed as a classic. In this study of the "myth of the hero," Campbell asserted that there is a single pattern of heroic journey and that all cultures share this essential pattern in their various heroic myths. In his book he also outlined the basic conditions, stages, and results of the archetypal hero's journey.

Joseph Campbell died in 1987. In 1988 a series of television interviews with Bill Moyers, *The Power of Myth,* introduced Campbell's views to millions of people.

ABOUT THE
JOSEPH CAMPBELL FOUNDATION

THE JOSEPH CAMPBELL FOUNDATION (JCF) is a nonprofit corporation that continues the work of Joseph Campbell, exploring the fields of mythology and comparative religion. The Foundation is guided by three principal goals:

First, the Foundation preserves, protects, and perpetuates Campbell's pioneering work. This includes cataloging and archiving his works, developing new publications based on his works, directing the sale and distribution of his published works, protecting copyrights to his works, and increasing awareness of his works by making them available in digital formats on JCF's Web site.

Second, the Foundation promotes the study of mythology and comparative religion. This involves implementing and/or supporting diverse mythological education programs, supporting and/or sponsoring events designed to increase public awareness, donating Campbell's archived works (principally to the Joseph Campbell and Marija Gimbutas Archive and Library), and utilizing JCF's Web site as a forum for relevant cross-cultural dialogue.

Third, the Foundation helps individuals enrich their lives by participating in a series of programs, including our global, Internet-based

Associates program, our local international network of Mythological Roundtables, and our periodic Joseph Campbell related events and activities.

For more information on Joseph Campbell
and the Joseph Campbell Foundation, contact:

JOSEPH CAMPBELL FOUNDATION
www.jcf.org
136 Waverly Place, #14D
New York, NY 10014-6823
info@jcf.org